Again, Dangerous Visions

Historical Materialism Book Series

The Historical Materialism Book Series is a major publishing initiative of the radical left. The capitalist crisis of the twenty-first century has been met by a resurgence of interest in critical Marxist theory. At the same time, the publishing institutions committed to Marxism have contracted markedly since the high point of the 1970s. The Historical Materialism Book Series is dedicated to addressing this situation by making available important works of Marxist theory. The aim of the series is to publish important theoretical contributions as the basis for vigorous intellectual debate and exchange on the left.

The peer-reviewed series publishes original monographs, translated texts, and reprints of classics across the bounds of academic disciplinary agendas and across the divisions of the left. The series is particularly concerned to encourage the internationalization of Marxist debate and aims to translate significant studies from beyond the English-speaking world.

For a full list of titles in the Historical Materialism Book Series available in paperback from Haymarket Books, visit:
https://www.haymarketbooks.org/series_collections/1-historical-materialism

Again, Dangerous Visions

Essays in Cultural Materialism

Andrew Milner

Edited by
J. R. Burgmann

Haymarket Books
Chicago, IL

First published in 2018 by Brill Academic Publishers, The Netherlands
© 2018 Koninklijke Brill NV, Leiden, The Netherlands

Published in paperback in 2019 by
Haymarket Books
P.O. Box 180165
Chicago, IL 60618
773-583-7884
www.haymarketbooks.org

ISBN: 978-1-64259-039-5

Distributed to the trade in the US through Consortium Book Sales and Distribution (www.cbsd.com) and internationally through Ingram Publisher Services International (www.ingramcontent.com).

This book was published with the generous support of Lannan Foundation and Wallace Action Fund.

Special discounts are available for bulk purchases by organizations and institutions. Please call 773-583-7884 or email info@haymarketbooks.org for more information.

Cover design by Jamie Kerry and Ragina Johnson.

Printed in the United States.

10 9 8 7 6 5 4 3 2 1

Library of Congress Cataloging-in-Publication data is available.

*For Verity and Jessica,
and in memory of Andrew Keogh (1950–2017), barrister, blogger,
speculative fiction writer, Francophile and cricket buff, out for 66 hélas*

Contents

Acknowledgements XI
List of Figures and Tables XIII

Introduction
Andrew Milner and J.R. Burgmann: An Interview 1

PART 1
Sociology of Literature

1 Sociology and Literature 11

2 The 'English' Ideology: Literary Criticism in England and Australia 23

3 The Protestant Epic and the Spirit of Capitalism 44

4 *On the Beach*: Apocalyptic Hedonism and the Origins of Postmodernism 78

5 Loose Canons and Fallen Angels 93

6 Dissenting, Plebeian, but Belonging Nonetheless: Bourdieu and Williams 112

7 Deconstructing National Literature: Comparative Literature, Cultural Studies and Critical Theory 126

8 It's the *Conscience Collective*, Stupid: Philosophical Aesthetics and the Sociology of Art 140

9 Science Fiction and the Literary Field 149

10 World Systems and World Science Fiction 170

PART 2
Cultural Materialism

11 Considerations on English Marxism   187

12 Literature, History and Post-Althusserianism   222

13 The Revolutions in Favour of *Capital*   252

14 Cultural Materialism, Culturalism and Post-Culturalism: The Legacy of Raymond Williams   269

15 Cultural Studies and Cultural Hegemony: Comparing Britain and Australia   298

16 Class and Cultural Production: The Intelligentsia as a Social Class   319

17 Left Out? Marxism, the New Left and Cultural Studies   340

18 From Media Imperialism to Semioterrorism   354

PART 3
Science Fiction

19 Utopia and Science Fiction in Raymond Williams   361

20 Darker Cities: Urban Dystopia and Science Fiction Cinema   382

21 Postmodern Gothic: *Buffy*, *The X-Files* and the Clinton Presidency   403

22 Framing Catastrophe: The Problem of Ending in Dystopian Fiction   419

23 Archaeologies of the Future: Jameson's Utopia or Orwell's Dystopia?   438

24 Time Travelling: Or, How (Not) to Periodise a Genre   456

25 The Sea and Eternal Summer: An Australian Apocalypse 468

26 Ice, Fire and Flood: Science Fiction and the Anthropocene 481
   Co-authored with J.R. Burgmann, Rjurik Davidson and Susan Cousin

Conclusion: Towards 2050
Andrew Milner and J.R. Burgmann: A Dialogue 497

Bibliography 507
Index 541

Acknowledgements

Five of the chapters are previously unpublished: 'The Protestant Epic and the Spirit of Capitalism' is an expanded and amended version of a paper presented at Goldsmiths College, London, on 14 January 1985; 'Loose Canons and Fallen Angels' of a paper presented at the University of Warwick on 18 October 2000; 'Deconstructing National Literature: Comparative Literature, Cultural Studies and Critical Theory' of a paper presented at the University of Zagreb on 30 June 2007; 'The Revolutions in Favour of *Capital*' of a paper presented at the University of Technology, Sydney, on 1 October 1990; 'From Media Imperialism to Semioterrorism' of a paper presented at the Royal Melbourne Institute of Technology on 14 September 2002.

We thank the publishers for permission to reprint the remaining chapters: 'Sociology and Literature' was first published in *Meanjin*, Vol. 46, No. 3, pp. 291–300, 1987; 'The "English" Ideology: Literary Criticism in England and Australia' in *Thesis Eleven*, No. 12, pp. 110–29, 1985; '*On the Beach*: Apocalyptic Hedonism and the Origins of Postmodernism' in *Australian Studies*, Vol. 7, pp. 190–204, 1993; 'Dissenting, Plebeian, but Belonging, Nonetheless: Bourdieu and Williams' in Jeff Browitt and Brian Nelson (eds.), *Practising Theory: Pierre Bourdieu and the Field of Cultural Production* (Newark: University of Delaware Press, 2004), pp. 101–12; 'It's the *Conscience Collective*, Stupid: Philosophical Aesthetics and the Sociology of Art' in *Thesis Eleven*, No. 103, pp. 26–34, 2010; 'Science Fiction and the Literary Field' in *Science Fiction Studies*, No. 115 (Vol. 38, Part 3), pp. 393–411, 2011; 'World Systems and World Science Fiction' in *Paradoxa*, Vol. 26, pp. 15–29, 2014; 'Considerations on English Marxism' in *Labour History*, No. 41, pp. 1–28, 1981; 'Literature, History and Post-Althusserianism' in Andrew Milner and Chris Worth (eds.), *Discourse and Difference: Poststructuralism, Feminism and the Moment of History* (Melbourne: Centre for General and Comparative Literature, Monash University, 1990), pp. 141–63; 'Cultural Materialism, Culturalism and Post-Culturalism: The Legacy of Raymond Williams' in *Theory, Culture and Society*, Vol. 11, No. 1, pp. 42–71, 1994; 'Cultural Studies and Cultural Hegemony: Comparing Britain and Australia' in *Arena Journal* New Series, No. 9, pp. 133–55, 1997; 'Class and Cultural Production: The Intelligentsia as a Social Class' in *Arena Journal* New Series, No. 15, pp. 117–37, 2000; 'Left Out? Marxism, the New Left and Cultural Studies' in *Arena Journal* New Series, No. 19, pp. 85–98, 2002; 'Utopia and Science Fiction in Raymond Williams' in *Science Fiction Studies*, No. 90 (Vol. 30, Part 2), pp. 199–216, 2003; 'Darker Cities: Urban Dystopia and Science Fiction Cinema' in *International Journal of Cultural Studies*, Vol. 7, No. 3, pp. 259–79, 2004; 'Postmodern Gothic: Buffy, The

X-Files and the Clinton Presidency' in *Continuum: Journal of Media and Cultural Studies*, Vol. 19, No. 1, pp. 103–16, 2005, http://www.tandfonline.com/doi/full/10.1080/10304310520000336324; 'Framing Catastrophe: The Problem of Ending in Dystopian Fiction' in *Arena Journal* New Series, No. 25/26, pp. 333–54, 2006; 'Archaeologies of the Future: Jameson's Utopia or Orwell's Dystopia?' in *Historical Materialism*, Vol. 17, No. 4, pp. 101–19, 2009; 'Time Travelling: Or, How (Not) to Periodise a Genre' in *Foundation: The International Review of Science Fiction*, Vol. 43, No. 117, pp. 70–9, 2014; 'The Sea and Eternal Summer: An Australian Apocalypse' in Gerry Canavan and Kim Stanley Robinson (eds.), *Green Planets: Ecology and Science Fiction* (Middletown: Wesleyan University Press, 2014), pp. 115–26; 'Ice, Fire and Flood: Science Fiction and the Anthropocene' in *Thesis Eleven*, No. 131, pp. 12–27, 2015. We also thank the Australian Research Council, which generously funded the research informing the essays devoted to utopia, dystopia and science fiction.

List of Figures and Tables

Figures

1 The double location of early French science fiction within the late nineteenth-century literary field   151
2 The global science fiction field in the early twenty-first century   153

Tables

1 Contextual analysis   96
2 Textual analysis   96
3 An ideal typology of possible solutions to the problem of ending   435

Introduction
Andrew Milner and J.R. Burgmann: An Interview

JRB: You chose *Again, Dangerous Visions* as the title for this collection. Obviously this is a reference to Harlan Ellison's collection. Can I ask why you opted for this specific title?

AM: Well, one obvious reason is because many of the essays are concerned with science fiction [henceforth SF]. Ellison actually edited two collections, *Dangerous Visions* in 1967 and *Again, Dangerous Visions* in 1972. They were the key platforms for American New Wave SF. We in Britain were actually less impressed by them than were people in the States – because, of course, we already had our own New Wave, *New Worlds*, Moorcock and Ballard, and so on. But I do really like the two Ellison collections. I didn't begin writing about SF until much later, but I'd been an enthusiastic reader ever since childhood. So, yes, I was very interested in what was going on around the New Wave. I chose the second of the Ellison titles simply because many of these essays are being reprinted, that is, published again. But there were two further reasons for choosing *Dangerous Visions* itself. When I first began work as a graduate student and as an academic, I was strongly influenced by Lucien Goldmann's sociology of literature, which was essentially a sociology of the world vision. So my early work was all about visions, albeit mainly seventeenth-century ones. Also, at this time I was very actively involved as a socialist militant – I'd been in the Young Socialists[1] from 1965 until about 1973, and then in the International Socialists[2] until I moved to Melbourne in 1980 – and I thought of my academic work as running in tandem with this political activism. In short, I wanted my writing to be politically dangerous.

JRB: Why did you leave the Labour Party to join the International Socialists?

AM: In retrospect, I'm rather surprised I did. But I was by no means alone, there were literally thousands of us. The IS was still inside the Labour Party when I first encountered them during the mid-'60s – I used to sell their paper, *Rebel*, at Young Socialist meetings. I didn't leave along with them, but I did share in the

---

1 The Labour Party Young Socialists (LPYS) was the British Labour Party's youth section from 1960 until 1993, when it was relaunched as Young Labour.
2 The International Socialists (IS) was a Luxemburgist/neo-Trotskyist British socialist organisation from 1962 until 1977, when it became the Socialist Workers Party.

general sense of disillusion with the Wilson governments, which had prompted their exit. All of this now rather puzzles me. In many respects, those '60s Labour governments were astonishingly successful and astonishingly radical: they kept us out of Vietnam; they refused to recognise the racist regime in Rhodesia; they nationalised the buses, iron and steel; they legalised homosexuality and abortion; they abolished theatre censorship. The contrast with the Blair[3] governments, which achieved virtually nothing, is very striking. But the Left had expected Wilson[4] to scrap British nuclear weapons. He'd been the left-wing candidate for the leadership, the Left believed strongly in the Campaign for Nuclear Disarmament – CND – and Party Conference had voted for unilateral disarmament on two successive occasions. We felt betrayed, but with the benefit of hindsight I have to concede how much the Wilson governments actually delivered.

JRB: Considering that you've written so extensively about SF over the last dozen years, what was preventing you from doing so in the last century, as it were?

AM: Good question. I'm ashamed to say the real reason is almost certainly the appalling condescension with which academia tended – and perhaps still tends – to regard SF. It was much more respectable to write about John Milton than about John Wyndham. But as I grew older – and tenured – I was increasingly able to ignore that kind of prejudice. It's a good thing, academic tenure; which is why Thatcher got rid of it.[5]

JRB: You mentioned Goldmann. What was the appeal of his sociology of literature?

AM: First of all, you have to remember that I was trained in sociology at the London School of Economics – the LSE – both as an undergraduate and as a postgraduate. So, there's a sense in which all my work has necessarily been informed by that sociological training. And in the 1970s Lukács and Goldmann were key points of reference for sociologically-inclined literary critics, especially those who were wary of Althusserianism – as I most certainly was. Secondly, it really did seem to me a powerful way into reading Milton, both in my PhD thesis and in my first book.

---

3 Tony Blair, Labour Prime Minister of Britain, 1997–2007.
4 Harold Wilson, Labour Prime Minister of Britain, 1964–70, 1974–6.
5 Margaret Thatcher, Conservative Prime Minister of Britain, 1979–90.

INTRODUCTION 3

JRB: Why were you wary of Althusserianism?

AM: The short answer is because it's a version of structuralism and, as such, radically downplays the possibilities for human agency. The British New Left, both inside and outside the Labour Party, both inside and outside the IS, had been overwhelmingly committed to the kind of socialist humanism associated with Goldmann and Sartre in France, Williams and Thompson in Britain. But quite suddenly, with the publication in English translation of Althusser and Balibar's *Reading Capital* and Althusser's own essay on ideology, both the *New Left Review* and much of the wider academic left, including even the IS's Alex Callinicos, were converted to structuralism. It seemed to me then, and still seems to me now, to be both politically debilitating and intellectually obscurantist.

JRB: You keep referring to your student days in the '70s, which were obviously a politically active time. Do you still think of yourself as an International Socialist?

AM: Generically, I'm still an internationalist and a socialist. And, to be honest, I'm still influenced by many of the ideas of the old British IS, and some of its writers: Michael Kidron, Nigel Harris, Peter Sedgwick, David Widgery, Christopher Hitchens. But I haven't been a member since I left for Melbourne in 1980. I've no idea what I would have done if I'd stayed in Britain. Come to think of it, all the people I've just mentioned eventually left the organisation.

JRB: You've explained the title. In the process, you also referred to the titles of parts one and three. But you haven't mentioned the subtitle of the whole collection, which happens also to be the title of Part Two. What about cultural materialism, which I would argue is the single major influence on your work?

AM: You're right, it has been a major influence at least since the 1990s. The term cultural materialism comes from Raymond Williams, of course, and I've been very much influenced by his work. I first read Williams as a sixth former reading around for English Literature. But I set him aside in the turn to sociology, Goldmann and later Bourdieu. And I didn't really return to Williams's work until much later. In retrospect, however, it's clear to me both that Williams's work was essentially sociological in character, and that other writers such as Bourdieu – and even Max Weber – were themselves in the most fundamental of senses also cultural materialists. Part Two is a bit messy, since some of the essays are very explicitly about cultural materialism, others more generally about British New Left thought. So, the first in that section is not about Williams at all, but about the contradiction between socialist humanism and Althusserianism in New Left historiography. And some of the essays are also simply about socialist politics.

JRB: The three parts are ordered chronologically in relation to your academic career, but you've already said that you were a socialist before a sociologist, and an avid SF reader before either. Why did you give such primacy to academia?

AM: Well, the short answer is because it's a collection of academic essays. But it is true that biographically SF came first, socialism second, sociology third. I first encountered SF reading *Dan Dare* in the weekly *Eagle* comic, as I think did many other British boys of my generation. As for socialism, my parents were both socialists, strong supporters of the Labour Party and CND. In a sense I was born a socialist. But I had no idea what sociology was, even when I applied to study it in 1968. It was the most fashionable subject, however, and the LSE the most radical university campus, in the year I left school. Fortunately, I was quickly persuaded by sociology, especially sociological theory, not only Marx and the Marxists, but Weber too, and Durkheim.

JRB: Once again, we've time-travelled back to the 1960s and '70s. But the collection dates only from 1981, shortly after you arrived in Melbourne. Did you write much beforehand?

AM: I wrote my PhD, of course, not to mention a lot of bad poetry; I did actually publish a couple of academic articles in Britain; and I wrote for *Socialist Worker*, *Socialist Review* and *Agitator*.[6] But I didn't really become committed to academia until I moved to Monash University.

JRB: Why exactly did you choose to write your doctoral thesis on Milton?

AM: I wanted to write about something important, not *Doctor Who* or *Dan Dare*, but rather Shakespeare or Milton. And Milton appealed both because he was a revolutionary – he was in Cromwell's government – and because he was a Protestant. I was a baptised Methodist, the part of Yorkshire I come from was a centre of Methodism, and it's true that the British Labour Party's socialism

---

6 *Socialist Worker* was the weekly newspaper of the International Socialists from 1968 onwards, *Socialist Review* the group's monthly magazine from 1978, *Agitator* the magazine, by turn, of the LSE Socialist Society, the LSE IS Society and the National Organisation of IS Students (NOISS).

owes as much to Methodism as to Marx. Milton was a way into exploring the historical origins of what the British call the 'nonconformist conscience' – and also the long history of English republicanism. I still think the Restoration of the monarchy in 1660 was a world-historical catastrophe. Milton had wanted to justify the ways of God to men; I wanted to justify the ways of the seventeenth-century republic to a society besotted with monarchy. Evidently I failed, but I still have hopes for an Australian republic.

JRB: I notice that another recurring presence in the collection is Orwell. Can I ask why so many ex-IS members maintain such a fascination for him? I'm thinking of Hitchens and Sedgwick, specifically.

AM: I hadn't thought of that. The probable explanation is that, unlike the vast majority of far left groups, the IS was absolutely opposed to Stalinist totalitarianism: we thought Russia and China were both state capitalist and not in any sense socialist. And, in this double hostility to Western capitalism on the one hand, Eastern communism on the other, we adopted a position very much like Orwell's in *Homage to Catalonia*, *Animal Farm* and *Nineteen Eighty-Four*. I'm still very sympathetic to Orwell, and *Nineteen Eighty-Four* still seems to me one of the truly great works of twentieth-century SF.

JRB: On the subject of dystopias, can I suggest a connection between Australia and CND in Nevil Shute's *On the Beach*? The book is obviously important to you. Can you explain why?

AM: When I was in my immediate pre-teens and early teens, CND was clearly the most important oppositional movement in British political life. It's difficult to recapture the sense of urgency that propelled people like me and my parents into its ranks. We were terrified of nuclear annihilation. At that very impressionable age, in those very fraught circumstances, I borrowed *On the Beach* from the public library in Birstall, where I lived. The librarian tried to warn me off on the grounds that it was 'too old' for me. And she was right. It scared the living daylights out of me and it still does. And, yes, it was written in and about Melbourne, a city I'd then only heard of in the context of Test cricket. I had no idea that the places Shute names really existed. I reread the novel after moving to Melbourne – where I joined People for Nuclear Disarmament, by the way – and still found it much more impressive than literary critics tended to allow. It provides a template for politically effective dystopian writing. In strictly literary terms it's almost certainly not as good as *Nineteen Eighty-Four*, but it was much more effective politically.

JRB: You were initially appointed to a position in Sociology at Monash, but soon transferred into Comparative Literature. Why Comparative Literature rather than English?

AM: In the first place, because English wouldn't have either me personally or the sociology of literature intellectually. But, secondly, because Comparative Literature was positively welcoming. My colleagues there were an extraordinarily intellectually stimulating bunch of people. I am permanently indebted to David Roberts, Philip Thomson, Walter Veit, Marie Maclean, Kate Rigby, Kevin Hart and others for the way my work developed. And they were right: English isn't a discipline, it's a language; the discipline is literary studies. It's also worth saying that sociology itself is an essentially comparative discipline. And many of the key sociologists of literature – Robert Escarpit, Peter Bürger, Franco Moretti, for example – had actually worked in Comparative Literature programmes.

JRB: But nonetheless you've written mostly about English language authors.

AM: You mean Milton and Orwell?

JRB: And Shute.

AM: Yes, but my work on SF has also been properly comparatist. I've written about Zamyatin, Karel Čapek, Lem, Dürrenmatt, Houellebecq, the Strugatsky brothers, Schätzing.

JRB: The Monash programme was in 'Comparative Literature and Cultural Studies' and some of the essays in this collection are very positive about what you call 'immodest Cultural Studies'. The later essays, however, are much more focussed on Comparative Literature. Why this shift?

AM: The origins of Cultural Studies were in a discourse about literature and society, which became progressively extended into critical examinations of the mass media. It began as a version of what the Germans call *Kulturkritik*. This is what you find in Williams, Thompson and Hoggart in Britain, Barthes in France, Adorno and Horkheimer in Germany. This seemed to me a more promising way of studying literature than mainstream literary criticism. So I was indeed actively involved in the development of Cultural Studies in Australia. But here, as elsewhere, Cultural Studies became increasingly 'modest', as it degenerated into an often blatantly populist celebration of the banalities of postmodern

INTRODUCTION   7

life. Williams himself had become increasingly alarmed by this tendency, by the way. So it turned out that I was, after all, simply a comparative sociologist of literature.

JRB: Postmodern life might well be marred by banality; but what you call 'apocalyptic hedonism' is still with us, although now with the added threat of anthropogenic climate change.

AM: I didn't mean to suggest that postmodern life is itself necessarily banal, only that Cultural Studies tends increasingly to concentrate on its more banal aspects. But, of course, apocalyptic hedonism is still with us – that's why my later essays are so concerned with climate fiction, not least the one you and I wrote together with Rjurik and Susan.

JRB: So just how important is climate change to your current research?

AM: It's been very important both to my research and to my politics. Hence, the essays on Turner, Robinson and Schätzing; hence, the fact that I'm a fully paid-up ecosocialist member of the Greens.[7] My next book will be on *SF and Climate Change*. The threat of nuclear war hasn't gone away, but it's now massively compounded by the near inevitability of rising sea levels and desertification. And here in Australia, where we inhabit a narrow coastal plain surrounding an enormous desert, only a complete fool – like Abbott[8] – would choose to treat the matter lightly. George Turner gave us fair warning back in 1987; it's now 2015 and we've done next to nothing. True, the December 2015 UN Paris Climate Change Conference[9] produced an agreement that, at first sight, looks more promising than some of the earlier ones, like that in Copenhagen in 2009. But it's worth stressing that this was the 22nd of these conferences and that, after all those meetings and all those junkets, the problem still just gets worse. The pessimist in me thinks it's probably impossible to prevent a capitalist economy – which is what the whole world now is – from competitively accumulating capital by means of environmental despoliation. And I'll be very surprised if the petrochemical corporations don't do everything in their power to undermine the 2015 Agreement, not least by getting the Republicans to block it in the US Congress. But too much pessimism is bad for the soul. So let's conclude on a

---

7 The Greens are an Australian environmentalist political party founded in 1992. In the 2013 General Election they won 11 seats – out of 226 – in the Australian federal parliament.
8 Tony Abbott, Conservative Prime Minister of Australia, 2013–15.
9 The United Nations Climate Change Conference, Paris, 30 November–12 December 2015.

slightly more optimistic note, with Gramsci's famous borrowing from Romain Rolland for the masthead of *L'Ordine Nuovo*: 'pessimism of the intellect, optimism of the will'.

PART 1

Sociology of Literature

∴

CHAPTER 1

Sociology and Literature*

We all know what literature is: it is *writing*. Which is, of course, why disarmament groups, political parties, unions and churches set up 'literature stalls' on which to display their published *writings*. And yet this is not what is meant by that other sense of the term literature with which we are all equally familiar, that sense of 'Literature' as a 'subject' to be studied in schools and colleges. Literature in this sense quite definitely precludes the kind of ephemera which appear on disarmament stalls. What it does include, in first year English at my own university for example, is 'fiction' (Jane Austen, George Eliot, Joseph Conrad and so on), 'poetry' (T.S. Eliot, the solitary peerless example) and 'drama' (Shakespeare, Shaw, Dylan Thomas and so on). Now as a matter of fact the original fourteenth-century English sense of the word literature, as polite learning through reading, clearly anticipates each of these modern usages. As Raymond Williams tells us, from the fourteenth to the eighteenth century the word 'corresponded mainly to the modern meanings of literacy ... It meant both an ability to read and a condition of being well-read'.[1] Thus all available writing was indeed literature just as it still is on disarmament stalls, and yet, in a society in which most adults were unable to read, and in which literacy remained a mark of social privilege, what was read, 'polite learning', carried with it connotations which prefigure the modern sense of English 'Literature'. It is from the eighteenth century, Williams explains, that we can trace an 'attempted and often successful specialization of *literature* to certain kinds of writing ... understood as well-written books but ... even more clearly understood as well-written books of an *imaginative* or *creative* kind'.[2]

Williams has here caught much of the sense of what English teachers in secondary, further and higher education, both in Britain and in Australia, today tend to mean by Literature. Yet this new specialist meaning of the word remains radically incoherent. As Williams himself notes, Carlyle and Ruskin, who wrote neither novels nor poems nor plays, belong to English Literature; and, he might have added, E.E. 'Doc' Smith's 'classic Lensman series' – an imaginative creation, surely – does not. Indeed this radical incoherency is one of the more

---

* This chapter has been published previously in *Meanjin*, Vol. 46, No. 3, pp. 291–300, 1987.
1 Williams 1976b, p. 151.
2 Williams 1976b, p. 152.

striking features of the many and varied attempts to define Literature in terms of some property or another assumed to inhere in its objects of study. The most common such attempt is that to which Williams refers, in which Literature is understood as essentially a matter of imaginative creation, fundamentally fictive rather than factual in character. The implicit premise that philosophy, science or history are somehow neither imaginative nor creative is very obviously indefensible. But the central claim that Literature is fictive rather than factual remains similarly problematic, not only because Carlyle counts and Smith doesn't, but also because much that is at the very core of 'English Literature' is quite probably 'fact'.

Consider, for the moment, Milton's sonnet on his blindness:

> Cyriack, this three years' day these eyes, though clear
>   To outward view of blemish or of spot,
>   Bereft of light their seeing have forgot;
>   Nor to their idle orbs doth sight appear
> Of sun or moon or star throughout the year,
>   Of man or woman. Yet I argue not
>   Against Heav'n's hand or will, nor bate a jot
>   Of heart or hope, but still bear up and steer
> Right onward. What supports me, dost thou ask?
>   The conscience, friend, to have lost them overplied
>   In liberty's defense, my noble task,
> Of which all Europe talks from side to side.
>   This thought might lead me through the world's vain masque,
>   Content though blind, had I no better guide.

The poem is addressed to 'Cyriack', that is, to Milton's friend and former pupil, Cyriack Skinner, a real person born in 1627 who died in 1700. It was written, presumably early in 1655, some three years into Milton's blindness just as the poet claims. Obviously Milton cannot have known for sure that his eyes didn't appear disfigured, but it isn't difficult to imagine that he had been so reassured by friends or relatives. It is certainly true that he was blind and we have no reason at all to doubt the claim that his response to blindness had been essentially one of fortitude. As to the explanation that he had been sustained in this fortitude by the knowledge that his sight had been lost in the defence of liberty, we may perhaps doubt that this was so, but we cannot reasonable doubt that Milton believed it to be so. He had been appointed 'Latin secretary' to the English revolutionary government in 1649, and both *Eikonoklastes*, published in English in October 1649, and the Latin *Pro Populo Anglicano Defensio*, published in February 1651, enjoyed the status of semi-official defences of the new English republic. His sight had finally failed in 1652, sacrificed as Milton thought to his labours on behalf of the Commonwealth. If Milton might be accused of exaggerating the extent of his fame, a twentieth-century historian can still insist that 'Milton's *Defence of the People of England* enjoyed a fantastic success. Salmasius (Milton's opponent – AM) was held to be Europe's greatest scholar; Milton was unknown outside his own country. Yet by general consent David beat Goliath'.[3] Where, then, is the fiction in Milton's poem? Or that in Keats's ode *To Autumn* for that matter? Frank Hardy's *Power Without Glory* – which is sometimes Literature but more often not – may well be fiction, but its author was nonetheless prosecuted for libel, albeit unsuccessfully.

If Literature is not necessarily fictive, nor is it necessarily inherently anything else in particular. For the 'literariness' of Literature is not in fact a property of a certain type of writing, but is rather a function of the ways in which different kinds of writing are socially processed, both by writers themselves and by readers, publishers, booksellers, literary critics and so on. As Terry Eagleton argues, Literature is quite simply highly valued writing, and such valuations are socially variable. 'There is no such thing as a literary work or tradition which is valuable *in itself*, regardless of what anyone might have said or come to say about it', he writes. '"Value" is a transitive term: it means whatever is valued by certain people in specific situations, according to particular criteria and in the light of given purposes'.[4] Such valuations are not random, for as Eagleton also insists, 'there is nothing at all whimsical about such kinds of value-judgement: they have their roots in deeper structures of belief'.[5] Whatever else Literature may be it is fundamentally a *social* construct, and moreover in historical terms a comparatively recent such construct at that. In the twentieth century this process by which Literature is socially constructed typically takes place on a particular site, at a particular institutional location within the wider social formation: Literature is in fact one of a range of products manufactured by the education system. It is here in the colleges and schools that mere literature is transformed into Literature. It is here in the universities especially, and in the various academic journals sustained by the universities, that professional literary critics, who very often tend to be university academics, dispute with each other over the precise composition of the literary 'canon'. It is here in the universities and colleges that future teachers are trained, and here in the schools that new gen-

---

3   Hill 1977, p. 182.
4   Eagleton 1983, p. 11.
5   Eagleton 1983, p. 16.

erations of children are trained by those teachers, into an appreciation of this 'canon'. It is here in the university, college, and 'quality' bookshops that publishers and booksellers market certain of their products as Literature, suitable for the school or college student or the general 'educated' reader. It is to this market and to these audiences that some living writers, John Fowles for example, look even as they write. And it is here in these institutions that the general 'educated' reader is educated. At its apex this is an industry which touches only a few, those English professors and teachers who participate actively in the construction of the canon. But at its base it touches the lives of millions: in the British Isles, in North America and in Australasia 'English' is normally a core component in the school curriculum, to all intents and purposes a compulsory subject for every child.

This core subject 'English' is a subject unlike any other, for it alone of the various disciplines which make up the academic curriculum is essentially and centrally a matter of valuation. This is not to suggest, of course, that whereas Literature is concerned with values and value-judgements, all other disciplines are merely matters of value-free 'fact'. Quite the contrary, value-judgements, and especially those that are articulated to wider systems of social belief and to wider structures of social interest, are fundamentally constitutive of all knowledge in the human sciences. But whereas value-judgements and interests provide the 'fuel', as it were, by which research is powered in history, geography or political economy, the subject matter of these disciplines remains in principle analytically separable from those judgements and interests. Historians may very well study periods of which they disapprove, geographers countries which they dislike, economists movements in prices or employment levels which they find positively alarming. And this remains possible because the subject matter of history, geography or political economy has some independent existence quite apart from the motives and interests of historians, geographers and political economists. English teachers, by contrast, do not normally waste their time on books, or even types of book, which they deem not to be Literature, that is, which are not 'fine'. As Franco Moretti rather nicely puts it: 'if everyone behaved like literary critics who only study what they "like", doctors might restrict themselves to studying only healthy bodies and economists the standard of living of the well-off'.[6] It is not that Literature as an academic discipline is simply 'informed' by value-judgements, it is rather that it is positively *saturated* in values, to such an extent indeed that any attempt to eliminate those values, such as is occasionally recommended by positivistic thinkers in

---

6 Moretti 1983, p. 14.

other fields, would be to eliminate the discipline itself. For Literature is not the study of writing, nor even the study of valued writing. It is rather the study of *how* to value writing. As one historian of the discipline has commented: 'the real content of the school and college subject which goes under the name "English Literature" is not literature in the primary sense, but *criticism*'.[7]

It is as criticism that the discipline begins both to make sense of itself and to make sense for others. The case for teaching examined courses in English Literature at schools and universities isn't in fact at all self-evident. Academic disciplines are normally justified in terms of their value either as knowledge producing enterprises in which students acquire new knowledges, for example about other places, other times or the physico-chemical universe, new knowledges about things hitherto unknown to them; or alternatively as skill producing enterprises in which students acquire new practical skills, for example in medicine, engineering or accountancy. In the latter case examination procedures are conventionally justified as devices by which to exclude incompetent or inadequately trained practitioners from the profession or trade in question. In the former the rationale is rather less obvious (the harm that might be done by unleashing an inadequately trained historian into the world is by no means readily apparent), but it appears to derive in some way from the assumption that the various knowledges which students will acquire will be genuinely 'new' or unfamiliar, and that some subsequent test of acquired familiarity therefore becomes necessary as a check on the adequacy of the pedagogical process itself. A student who can 'pass' an examination is thus deemed to have attained a new skill or a new knowledge. Undoubtedly there is much that is open to question in all of this. But assuming the validity of the argument, one can still ask: what new skill or knowledge is involved in 'English'? At primary school and perhaps even at secondary school level certain basic language skills can indeed be learnt by students. And even at university or college level certain new knowledges, about the history of the English language for example, may very well be made available. However, the core of the discipline, the reading and appreciation of English literature, entails no obviously new skills nor knowledges. 'English' students are asked to do what a great many of them would do anyway, that is, to read and appreciate novels, plays and poems. Nor is this interest in reading confined to English students. A 1978 study commissioned by the Australia Council found that some 70 percent of the Australian adult population read books, spending an average of some six hours per week each on their reading.[8]

---

7 Baldick 1983, p. 4.
8 Brenac and Stevens 1978, pp. 17, 20.

By no means all of these books were 'Literature', but nonetheless more than half of those bought or borrowed by the people in this sample were in fact novels.[9] English students are examined, then, on their ability to read novels, that is, to do what nearly three quarters of the population does anyway for pleasure. It is rather as if one were asked to pass examinations in television-watching or rock concert attendance.

There is an almost self-evident absurdity about this entire process. On the one hand, we can observe universities, colleges and schools solemnly awarding certificates in 'English', on the other, millions of unlicensed readers busily working their ways through the bookshops, newsagents and libraries. In 1887 E.A. Freeman, the Regius Professor of History at Oxford, opposed the establishment of a university English school on the grounds that 'we do not want ... subjects which are merely light, elegant, interesting. As subjects for examination, we must have subjects in which it is possible to examine'.[10] English Literature, Freeman assumed, could not become an examination subject precisely because all such 'chatter about Shelley' is essentially a matter of personal taste. Even today English departments often betray a certain uneasiness about their peculiar role. 'One often hears the comment: "I just like to enjoy literature (or music, or art); you spoil it if you analyse it ..."', runs the opening sentence of the Monash University English Department's introduction to first year English, interestingly titled *Why Study English Literature?* 'Such an attitude', it continues, 'can ... be a blinkered, even a smug, response. In what other field of human endeavour could we seriously argue that the less we understand, the better? Fortunately, we don't apply this kind of logic to the physical world, or to psychology'.[11] Fortunately, we might add, not all analogies are quite so contrived. For, of course, whereas English students are asked to read books and to respond to those books, that is, to do what readers do anyway, students in the natural sciences are asked to do rather more than watch the physical world go by, and students in psychology rather more than 'think' or 'emote'. Neither the natural sciences nor psychology, nor for that matter history nor geography, are very much concerned with the matter of how to 'respond to' or of how to 'value' the phenomena with which they deal; their purposes rather are essentially explanatory. In English studies, by contrast, it is precisely this process of evaluation, of criticism, which is central to the discipline. And it is this process which distinguishes 'reading English' at university from reading books on the train. What is

---

9   Brenac and Stevens 1978, p. 26.
10 Palmer 1965, p. 99.
11 Monash University Department of English 1986, p. 1.

taught in English Literature, then, is the ability to 'discriminate', to 'evaluate', to 'criticise'. And these skills are examinable, but only on the condition that some particular criteria of literary value can be found to which both teachers and students can or at least should subscribe, and which have some greater validity than other such criteria available to the untrained reader.

In general English teachers have certainly tended to behave as if such criteria were indeed available. But the key words here are 'as if': it is not that English teachers normally argue explicitly for any given theory of aesthetics, it is rather that their teaching practices only remain intelligible if one assumes the existence of some such implicit but unstated aesthetic. Pierre Bourdieu maintains that orthodox pedagogical procedures in French secondary and higher education in the humanities tend to test not specific knowledges, but rather access to an elite culture, a culture 'which is *given* to the children of the cultivated classes – style, taste, wit – in short, those attitudes and aptitudes which seem natural in members of the cultivated classes, and naturally expected of them precisely because ... they *are* the *culture* of that class'.[12] Uldiz Ozolis has argued persuasively that Victorian HSC examiners' reports, and in particular those of English examiners, betray evidence of an 'aristocratic' ethos very similar to that identified by Bourdieu.[13] But there is rather more to it, or better something rather more specific to it, than that. Kathy MacDermott's more recent analysis of first year university examiners' comments suggests that in English studies at the University of Melbourne in the early 1970s this ethos had taken on a very distinctive form, arising from the peculiar 'discursive practice' or 'ideologeme' which was 'Leavisism'.[14] F.R. Leavis, the distinguished Cambridge literary critic, is perhaps the single most important figure in the twentieth-century history of English studies in England, and whilst much less influential in the United States, his work has enjoyed a similar pre-eminence in Australia, and for that matter throughout much of the British Commonwealth. The peculiar double-bind by which English studies insists on the absolute importance of an aesthetic that is somehow absent rather than present, is directly traceable to Leavis's own work. Thus when challenged by the philosopher René Wellek to defend his own position 'abstractly', Leavis replied that: 'My whole effort was to work in terms of concrete judgements and particular analyses: "This – doesn't it? – bears such a relation to that; this kind of thing – don't you find it so? – wears better than that"'.[15] The authentic reader responding authentically to

---

12   Bourdieu 1974, p. 39.
13   Ozolis 1981.
14   MacDermott 1983, p. 104.
15   Leavis 1976, p. 215.

the authentically literary text is in no need of any abstract theory of aesthetics because the truly literary work spontaneously elicits from the mature literary reader a properly aesthetic response.

But what if it doesn't? What if one were to reply to Leavis: 'No, I don't really think this does bear such a relation to that; no, I'm sorry but I don't find it so, I rather think that the other kind of thing wears better'? What if one were to insist with Eagleton that value is transitive, or even with Freeman that chatter about Shelley is essentially a matter of personal taste? Then, of course, the entire procedure collapses into mutual unintelligibility and perhaps even mutual recrimination. Such incidents are not entirely unfamiliar to teachers of English. For this is more or less exactly what does happen whenever first year students, invited to respond spontaneously to a literary work and strongly discouraged from reading the available literary criticism, do indeed volunteer their own spontaneous responses, only to discover from their tutors that these are not quite the types of spontaneous response for which the English Department is seeking. The cultivated theoretical inarticulacy of this Leavisite aesthetic is thus not merely one of its most distinctive features, but is also a distinctive source of anxiety for the student novitiate in English studies. It is difficult enough as it is to learn the habits of a new and unfamiliar discipline even when these are formulated explicitly; when carefully left unstated they become doubly worrisome. But it would be a mistake to imagine that Literature's problem is simply one of inarticulacy. If anything, the more explicitly argued a theory of aesthetics becomes, the more clearly indefensible it appears. For it is the very idea of aesthetics itself which is suspect. As Tony Bennett has argued, aesthetic discourse is unlike other discourses of value, such as those of sport or cuisine, insofar as it is essentially *universalising* and therefore necessarily radically *intolerant*. 'In the case of aesthetic discourse', Bennett writes, 'obliged to operate at the level of universality in order to establish the aesthetic as a distinctive mode of the subject's mental relation to reality, ... intolerance becomes absolute. Within such discourse, the subject who fails to appreciate correctly is regarded as being incompletely human rather than merely being excluded from full title to the membership of a specific valued and valuing community'.[16] To fail to appreciate Australian rules football is merely to be English or American, or to be part of those other Australian communities that have better things to do with their time on Saturday and Sunday afternoons. But for a student to fail to appreciate the moral complexity of Greek tragedy was, in the view of one Melbourne University English examiner, to raise questions 'about

---

16   Bennett 1985, p. 48.

her general fitness for humane existence'.[17] It is all nonsense, of course, for value *is* transitive; and it is dangerous nonsense insofar as its necessary intolerance remains always potentially punitive.

This is not to suggest that literature is somehow an unsuitable object for academic study. To the contrary, writing, reading and the various ancillary social practices which facilitate writing and reading are very clearly immensely important human activities. In their aggregate they represent the particular fashion by which within any given literate society what Fredric Jameson has termed 'the all informing process of *narrative* ... the central function or *instance* of the human mind'[18] comes to be socially institutionalised. Literature in this sense commands the attention of any body of scholarship worth the name. But Literature as a process of training in discrimination, that is, in effect as an induction into a particular ideologically formed valuing community, remains nonetheless quite fundamentally intellectually indefensible. Criticism of Literature must be superseded by the science of the study of literature, that is, by the systematic analysis and explanation of how writing is written, read, distributed and exchanged. Literary studies thus reformulated – as it is indeed being reformulated especially within many of the newer 'interdisciplinary' schools of humanities – becomes essentially a sociology of literature. For the production, distribution and consumption of writing are each very obviously social processes. This is not to attempt to rehabilitate that type of reductionist Marxism which Welleck and Warren disparage as dealing only 'narrowly and externally' with the relationship between 'literature and society'. It is, rather, to recognise with Wellek and Warren themselves that the relations between 'literature' and 'society' are in essence relations of interiority rather than of exteriority, that literature 'is a social institution, using as its medium language, a social creation'.[19] It is not that literature 'reflects' some other external social reality (although it may indeed sometimes do so); it is rather that literature *is* itself a social reality.[20]

---

17   MacDermott 1983, p. 177.

18   Jameson 1981, p. 13.

19   Wellek and Warren 1976, p. 94.

20   It is for this reason that arguments about the 'specificity of art' have no necessary bearing on the rival claims of aesthetics and sociology. Janet Wolff distinguishes three different senses in which the term 'specificity' is used: firstly, to refer to the institutional separation of art from other social activities; secondly, to refer to the 'relative autonomy' of artistic activity from other social practices; and thirdly, to refer to the specific characteristics of art as art. Of these only the latter concerns matters that have traditionally been deemed the business of aesthetics rather than of sociology. Wolff herself argues that even these

English studies inherits a long tradition of peculiar ambivalence in the face of sociology. It can easily find itself obliged to recognise, with Leavis himself, that 'a real literary interest is an interest in man [sic], society and civilization'[21] and is thus in a sense sociological. But it insists too, and again with Leavis, that 'no "sociology of literature" ... will yield much profit unless informed and controlled by a real and intelligent interest – a first-hand critical interest – in literature'.[22] The key term in this last sentence is, of course, 'critical'. What Leavis and many other literary critics have feared in sociology is the dead hand of a positivistic empiricism which would suppress the Literary, the critical, the aesthetic, which would subordinate Literature itself to the imperatives of what Leavis later came to term 'technologico-Benthamite' civilisation.[23] This is not simply as it is often presented a matter of Leavis's insistence on the importance of the 'internal' analysis of the text itself, as opposed to that of 'external' analyses of the text's various contexts. Much more importantly what is at stake here is the centrality of evaluation, both as applied to the text and as applied elsewhere. Leavisite practical criticism is not intended, as are some latter day structuralist criticisms, merely to explain how particular literary texts 'work': it is concerned rather to assess the literary value of such texts. And, as becomes clear for example from Leavis's criticisms of Trevelyn, such questions of value pertain as much to context as to text. The unanswered because unasked questions in Trevelyan, Leavis insists, are: 'What, as a civilization to live in and be of, did England offer at such and such a time? As we pass from now to then, what light is thrown on human possibilities – on the potentialities of civilized life?

---

questions can be answered sociologically, and that discourse theory, the philosophical anthropology of art and psychoanalytic theory are each serious contenders for the title of such a theory. But she finds each seriously lacking and concludes with little more than a vague insistence that sociology must take aesthetics seriously if it is to avoid a positivistic insistence on 'aesthetic neutrality' (Wolff 1983, chs. 5 and 6). In this she seems to me mistaken. The category of aesthetics *cannot* be separated out from the tradition of philosophical idealism to which Wolff is herself opposed. It needs to be superseded not by any quasi-positivistic notion of value-freedom, but rather by an understanding of artistic valuation as necessarily politically and socially committed, because politically and socially located, by what Eagleton has termed 'political criticism' (Eagleton 1983, pp. 194–217). Wolff's own conclusion, that 'if the debate is between sociology and aesthetics, sociology has the last word' (Wolff 1983, p. 108), is thus only half true. If the debate is between sociology and aesthetics, then sociology has not only the last word, but the first word and all of the words in between.

21   Leavis 1976, p. 200.
22   Leavis 1976, p. 198.
23   Leavis 1972a, ch. 1.

In what respects might it have been better to live then than now? What tentative conception of an ideal civilization are we prompted towards by the hints we gather from history?'.[24] These are indeed important questions and they are indeed typically suppressed in both positivistic historiography and positivistic sociology. But nonetheless, and despite Leavis, there is nothing distinctively 'literary' about the nature of a mind which might pose such questions. Nor is it at all obvious that literary texts, nor even Literary texts, constitute a peculiarly privileged source from which to draw answers to these or similar questions. By conflating value-judgements in general with aesthetic judgements in particular, by subordinating the former to the latter, and by refusing to countenance any explicit theorisation of the grounds upon which either might be justified, Leavis and with him much of literary criticism secured an entirely Pyrrhic victory in which value was preserved within the discourse that is Literature, but only at the cost, firstly, of its evacuation from the entire realm of the non-Literary, and secondly, of its persistence within Literature only at the falsely concrete level of the individual reader's response to the individual literary text.

The logic of this procedure is caught very nicely in Chris Baldick's conclusion that:

> The critical approach, which refuses to accept what is offered simply at face value, which will not rest satisfied with things as they are, was squeezed into a narrowly literary criticism; social criticism in particular was blunted to conform with the implicit norm of literary 'sensibility', and put in the service of social consensus. The title of 'criticism' was usurped by a literary discourse whose entire attitude was at heart uncritical. Criticism in its most important and most vital sense had been gutted and turned into its very opposite.[25]

Yet this need not have been so. For whatever might be said against the 'abstracted empiricism'[26] of much Anglophone sociology, there can be little doubt that in classical European social theory, both Marxist and non-Marxist, there was to be found a discourse, at once both empirical and evaluative, interested both in society and in culture, which was as absolutely preoccupied with the cultural significance of modernisation as was Leavisite criticism itself. The affinities between Leavis and Weber have on occasion been noted, as has the manner in

---

24   Leavis 1976, p. 202.
25   Baldick 1983, p. 234.
26   Mills 1970, ch. 3.

which English literary criticism has functioned in effect so as to compensate for the absence until very recently of any indigenous sociological tradition within English intellectual life.[27] What has not been stressed sufficiently, however, is the full extent to which 'English' came to be constituted as *precisely* an inferior substitute for a sociology. It is not so much that England had 'English' instead of sociology; it is rather that England had 'English' *as* a sociology. Thus Leavis's model English school would in fact address itself to exactly that set of themes and preoccupations which define the intellectual project that is classical European sociology.[28] But it is nonetheless a radically inferior sociology: amateurish and intellectually irresponsible in its manner of appropriating the work of other disciplines; theoretically inarticulate at precisely those moments of generalisation at which a proper caution would demand theoretical precision; debarred by its own insularity from the possibility of any meaningful encounter with the range and diversity of continental European sociological thinking; and as Baldick stressed, paradoxically and perversely, fundamentally uncritical. Literary criticism as we have known it is in crisis, and rightly so. But its earlier rejections both of empiricist sociology, on the one hand, and of reductionist Marxism, on the other, nonetheless retain much of their original force. Quite clearly neither can provide us with the materials by which the crisis in English studies might be resolved. For these we have to look elsewhere, to the legacy of classical European sociology, to Western sociology's own protracted crisis[29] and to the various forms of cultural theory – Western Marxism and second wave feminism, phenomenology and hermeneutics, structuralism and semiotics – the challenge of which has as much as anything else provided the occasion for the deepening crisis not merely in English, but throughout the whole of the traditional humanist academic curriculum. It is to these diverse sources that we have to look to establish the prospects for a non-empiricist sociology of literature capable of providing suitably non-Leavisite solutions to that whole set of Leavisite and neo-Leavisite problems bequeathed us by English studies.

---

27 Shuttleworth 1980; Anderson 1970.
28 Although, as an English rather than a German or French thinker, Leavis locates the central modernising experience in the seventeenth century rather than in the eighteenth and nineteenth centuries (cf. Leavis 1948, p. 54).
29 Gouldner 1971, Part III.

CHAPTER 2

The 'English' Ideology: Literary Criticism in England and Australia*

It was Henry James, of course, who observed that 'it takes a great deal of history to produce a little literature, that it needs a complex social machinery to set a writer in motion'.[1] Despite James's own peculiar status as the one authentically Anglo-American participant in the Great Tradition, it remains an observation that has proven singularly uninfluential in academic literary-critical circles both in Britain and in the United States for much of the postwar period. American New Criticism and English practical criticism converged upon a shared understanding of the social and the political as essentially 'extra-literary' and thus as matters of no real concern to the discipline of 'English'. Australian criticism, paying the customary antipodean dues to the various ANZUS pacts of the mind, generously volunteered its own assenting formalism. And these were not simply peculiarities of the English speakers: the *Werkimmanenz* of postwar West German criticism inhabited an essentially similar theoretical terrain. If Western criticism has displayed so little interest in the social machinery which sets writers in motion, it is barely remarkable that it should have been almost entirely oblivious to the ways in which that self-same machinery sets in motion criticism itself. The history that produces not only a little literature, but also a great deal of criticism, has come to constitute an important part of the repressed unconscious of contemporary liberal academia. The emergence of the New Left during the 1960s prompted a renewed interest in 'contextual' criticisms, and especially in various forms of feminist and neo-Marxist criticism. But to an extent which in retrospect might seem surprising, the New Left's main focus of attention remained 'literature' rather than 'criticism'. With the notable exception of Perry Anderson's profoundly suggestive remarks on the place of literary criticism within the English national culture,[2] the New Left's encounter with conventional academic criticism remained confined to an attempt to demonstrate the internal theoretical incoherencies and inadequacies of such criticisms, judged on their own terms either as theories of

---

* This chapter has been published previously in *Thesis Eleven*, No. 12, pp. 110–29, 1985.
1 James 1879, p. 3.
2 Anderson 1970, pp. 268–76.

literature or, more rarely, as theories of society. In itself this is undoubtedly an entirely necessary enterprise. But there is more to be said about criticism than that it is mistaken. At the very least, there are two additional questions which require some sort of answer: firstly, what type of social practice, located within what particular social institutions, is criticism?; and secondly, the question posed by Anderson, what place does criticism occupy as a particular component within a given national intellectual culture? I shall be concerned with both questions here, both as they apply to the original home of English criticism, England itself, and as they apply to Australia. Hopefully, such comparison will highlight what is specific not only to the latter, but also to the former.

1   English Criticism in England

The origins of English criticism can be located in the late seventeenth and early eighteenth centuries, in the network of London clubs and coffee houses which sustained Defoe's *Review*, Steele's *Tatler*, and Addison's *Spectator* (founded, respectively, in 1704, 1709 and 1711). The London coffee house can be seen as a direct 'functional equivalent' to the Parisian salon or the German reading circle, and like its continental equivalents it sponsored a criticism which was very much a general 'cultural' criticism rather than a technical 'literary' criticism. Whatever else this criticism may have been, it was certainly not 'academic': neither Oxford nor Cambridge taught 'English' as a university subject. Habermas's account of the changing structure of the public sphere in bourgeois society outlined originally in *The Structural Transformation of the Public Sphere*[3] provides the theoretical starting point for two very useful studies in the history of criticism, Peter Hohendahl's *The Institution of Criticism*[4] and Terry Eagleton's *The Function of Criticism*.[5] Following Habermas, both Hohendahl and Eagleton understand seventeenth- and eighteenth-century criticism as a form of discourse characteristic of the early liberal public sphere; and both identify the subsequent disintegration of that public sphere as the single most important determinant of the social history of modern criticism. Eagleton, who is concerned specifically with English criticism, stresses the essentially consensual form taken by the English variant of eighteenth-century criticism: unlike its continental counterparts it functioned so as to facilitate a fusion of aristo-

---

3   Habermas 1989.
4   Hohendahl 1982.
5   Eagleton 1984.

cratic and bourgeois – that is, Cavalier and Puritan – values. Nonetheless, early English criticism reproduces all the essential features of the early bourgeois public sphere:

> A polite, informed public opinion pits itself against the arbitrary diktats of autocracy: within the translucent space of the public sphere it is supposedly no longer social power, privilege and tradition which confer upon individuals the title to speak and judge, but the degree to which they are constituted as discoursing subjects by sharing in a consensus of universal reason.[6]

This bourgeois public sphere is progressively undermined during the nineteenth century, Eagleton argues, firstly by the expansion of the literary market and the concomitant rise of an anonymous public, and secondly by the eruption into the public sphere of social interests opposed to its rational norms, in particular the working class, radicalism, feminism, and dissent. Criticism is thus increasingly faced with the choice between, on the one hand, a general cultural humanism which becomes necessarily increasingly amateur as capitalist society develops, and on the other, an expert professionalism which can only achieve intellectual legitimacy at the price of social relevance. The eventual outcome is, of course, the institutionalisation of criticism within the universities.[7]

English had in fact been taught as a subject during the eighteenth century in both the dissenting academies and the Scottish universities (where it was intended to facilitate cultural incorporation into the Anglo-Scottish union). From the 1820s University College London offered similar such courses, and from mid-century the University of Manchester began to teach a subject recognisably akin to modern 'English'. During the late nineteenth century, chairs of English language and literature were established at Trinity College Dublin and at the Universities of Glasgow, Edinburgh, Birmingham and Newcastle.[8] Oxford and Cambridge remained stubbornly resistant, however. Chris Baldick has argued that the growth of English in higher education was determined by three main factors: the movement for working-class education; the movement for women's education; and the mid-century reorganisation of the Indian Civil Service. For both the labouring classes and the weaker sex English would provide

---

6   Eagleton 1984, p. 9.
7   Eagleton 1984, pp. 34–6, 56–7, 65.
8   Doyle 1982, pp. 21, 26–7.

a liberal education much less costly than that provided by Classics, for the Empire it would provide the means by which the natives might be educated in a civilised culture.[9] In 1906 Sir Henry Newbolt founded the English Association to promote the teaching of English; in 1917 an English paper was introduced into the public schools' common entrance examination. Of the two ancient universities it was Oxford which first appointed a 'literary' professor of English, Sir Walter Raleigh, in 1904, but the subject's future, in the face of determined hostility from both classicists and philologists, remained very uncertain. Cambridge appointed its first professor of English literature, A.W. Verrall, as late as 1911, but in general events proceeded rather more smoothly than at Oxford, and in 1917 an independent English school with a distinctly literary bias was finally established. It was the Great War which eventually enabled English studies to liberate itself from the claims of a conveniently 'Teutonic' philology: neither Raleigh nor Verrall's successor at Cambridge, Sir Arthur Quiller-Couch, were slow to identify the potentially sinister implications of too enthusiastic an interest in German culture. English Literature's contribution to postwar reconstruction, the 1921 Newbolt Report on the teaching of English, proposed to establish the study of English language and literature at the centre of a national education in national consciousness. The Newbolt Committee's vision of English Literature as the cement of national unity found enthusiastic echo at Cambridge (Quiller-Couch served as a member of the Committee), but never really gained favour at Oxford, where an older pluralist dilettantism held sway.[10] Thus it was Cambridge rather than Oxford which would witness both the initial 'revolution in English studies' and the subsequent appearance of Leavisism, a new literary-critical doctrine which would decisively shape the character of the profession of English teaching in the years after the Second World War.

It was Leavisism and the peculiar claims advanced by the Leavisites on behalf of the discipline of English which provided Anderson with one of his keys to the understanding of the structure of the English national intellectual culture. His argument is by now an old one, but one which warrants repetition nonetheless. Britain alone of the major European countries, he observes, produced neither a classical sociology nor an indigenous national Marxism. The intellectual culture thus constituted lacked any totalising conceptual system and remained indelibly marked by this absence at its very centre. Anderson adds, however, that in anthropology, the study of *other* societies, and above all in literary criticism such totalising thought did develop: 'in a culture which

---

9   Baldick 1983, pp. 61–72.
10 Baldick 1983, pp. 76–7, 80, 87–9, 93–5, 104–6.

everywhere repressed the notion of totality, and the idea of critical reason, literary criticism represented a refuge'.[11] Indeed it did, though we need to stress the full extent to which it was Cambridge rather than Oxford English which came to represent this refuge. 'It is no accident', Anderson writes, 'that in the fifties, the one serious work of socialist theory in Britain – Raymond William's *The Long Revolution* – should have emerged from literary criticism'.[12] From Cambridge literary criticism, one might perhaps add. Anderson's analysis has been supplemented and complemented by one much more recent study in the sociology of culture, Francis Mulhern's magnificent *The Moment of 'Scrutiny'*. It would be impossible to do justice here to the full complexity of Mulhern's treatment of the Leavisites. But let me draw attention to his characterisation of Leavisism as:

> a quintessentially *petit bourgeois* revolt, directed against a cultural order that it could not fundamentally alter or replace ... It was, accordingly, a *moralistic* revolt from within the given culture: bearer not of an alternative order but of the insistence that the existing order should live by its word ...[13]

Leavisism's ultimate fate, its simultaneous success and failure during the 1950s, arises precisely from its *petit bourgeois* character. In the years immediately following the 1944 Education Act the existing order finally began to live by its word. Thus, Mulhern argues, the very success of *Scrutiny*'s cultural project increasingly rendered obsolete its organised intellectual militancy, so that subsequent English criticism became dominated by a kind of tame 'Leavisism', a Leavisism increasingly shorn of both the intellectual combativity and the interdisciplinary competence that had characterised *Scrutiny* itself. The hegemony of this tame Leavisism remained effectively unchallenged until the 1970s, when the emergence of various structuralisms finally precipitated in England as elsewhere a 'crisis in English studies'.

But if postwar criticism became essentially a tame and tamed Leavisism, what then was Leavisism proper, what was Leavis's Leavisism? Here I will call attention only to what seem to me to be four especially salient features of the Leavisite system: its organicist aesthetic, its historicism, its radicalism and its nationalism. That Leavis's aesthetic represented a variant of organicism, in

---

11   Anderson 1970, p. 276.
12   Anderson 1970, p. 275.
13   Mulhern 1981, p. 322.

some significant respects structurally homologous to the organicist aesthetics of the great systems of classical idealist philosophy, has become something of an intellectual commonplace. But what must also be emphasised is the way in which for Leavis, as for Lukács, the organic properties of 'great' literature derive from the organicism of human social life itself, at least in its 'normal', 'healthy', forms. Thus the central category of Leavis's theory of value is precisely that of 'life' and great literature is that which renders a form adequate to the expression of life:

> the major novelists ... count in the same ways as the major poets, in the sense that they are significant in terms of that human awareness they promote; awareness of the possibilities of life.[14]

Leavis's historicism is most readily apparent in his theory of contemporary cultural decline as consequent upon the disintegration of the pre-industrial organic community. That process of disintegration is for Leavis and Thompson 'the most important fact of recent history'[15] and it shapes and continues to shape the entire subsequent history of English cultural life. Industrialisation causes initially a rupture between sophisticated and popular cultures; it causes the decline of popular culture and later the retreat into dream worlds on the part of nineteenth-century high culture; it causes standardisation, mass production and levelling down.[16] Here, then, is a historicism as global in its explanatory pretensions and as apocalyptic in its tone as any in the German idealist tradition. The radicalism of the Leavisite project inheres most importantly in the radical rejectionism with which Leavis responded to the claims of the already established intellectual culture. One should not perhaps accept the full text of Garry Watson's insistence that the Leavises constituted a much more serious challenge to the ruling literary culture than any mounted by subsequent Marxisms or by subsequent French structuralisms.[17] But one should at least accept Mulhern's judgement that Leavisism aspired to create 'an intellectual formation of a type virtually unknown in and deeply alien to English bourgeois culture: an "intelligentsia" in the classic sense of the term, a body of intellectuals dissociated from every established social interest'.[18] And yet for all its distinctly unEnglish intellectual sectarianism, Leavisism also came to

---

14   Leavis 1962a, p. 10.
15   Leavis and Thompson 1960, p. 87.
16   Leavis 1962a, pp. 188–92.
17   Watson 1977, p. 205.
18   Mulhern 1981, p. 326.

embody a particular form of English nationalism. As Anderson observed, 'blank prejudice and bafflement' were 'the predictable products' of Leavis's disorientation in the face of foreign literature.[19] This Leavisite nationalism is crucially evident in Leavis's theory of language, in his improbable affirmation of the non-arbitrary nature of the (English) sign. For Leavis, English is a language unlike either Latin or Greek in which 'words seem to do what they say'; hence, the famous dismissal of Milton's Latinised English as exhibiting a 'feeling *for* words rather than a capacity for feeling *through* words'.[20] One begins to understand why Martin Green saw Leavis as:

> intensely and integrally British. Not Europeanized, not of the intelligentsia, not of the upper classes, not of Bloomsbury ... Alone in all Cambridge his voice has echoes of the best things in my parents' England ...[21]

Such then was Leavisism: an organicist aesthetic built around the value of 'life' wedded to an apocalyptic historicism obsessed with the deleterious effects of industrialisation; a militantly organised *petit bourgeois* radicalism wedded to a nationalistic preoccupation with the superior virtues, if not of the contemporary English, then of their peasant ancestors and of the language bequeathed them by those ancestors.

2   English (and Australian) Criticism in Australia

English criticism has its origins in the liberal public sphere of the late seventeenth and early eighteenth centuries; the disintegration of that public sphere results in the eventual institutionalisation of a new academic criticism within the university; Leavisism, the guilty conscience of this academicism, represents, as Eagleton says, 'nothing less than an attempt to reinvent the classical public sphere, at a time when its material conditions had definitively passed';[22] the impossibility of any such project explains not only the obsessive, almost paranoid, quality of much of Leavis's own writing, but also both Leavisism's gradual decline into an increasingly inoffensive aestheticism and its ultimate demise in the face of later structuralisms as guiltless in their academicism as

---

19   Anderson 1970, p. 271.
20   Leavis 1972b, pp. 58, 53.
21   Green 1959, pp. 506–7.
22   Eagleton 1984, p. 75.

they were self-consciously 'guilty' in their choice of reading strategies. Australian literary criticism is analysable in terms of the same set of structural categories as those which Eagleton applies to England, but in Australia the temporal rhythms are quite different. What in England develops sequentially, in Australia develops simultaneously: a general cultural criticism functionally equivalent to that of the *Tatler* and the *Spectator* takes shape in the *Bulletin* and the *Boomerang*, founded respectively in 1880 and 1887, and especially from 1896 in A.G. Stephens's 'Red Page'; an academic criticism closely modelled on the English pattern is inaugurated by the appointment of E.E. Morris to the Chair of English, French, and German Language and Literature at the University of Melbourne in 1882, and more importantly that of Sir Mungo MacCallum to the Chair of Modern Literature at the University of Sydney in 1887.[23] That such a pattern of development – the virtually simultaneous constitution of a general non-academic cultural criticism and a technical academic literary criticism – should have occurred is explicable only in terms of Australia's semi-colonial status and its peculiar location in relation to the general history of nineteenth- and twentieth-century nationalisms.

That there exists some type of connection between the role of the intelligentsia and the rise of nationalism has become something of a commonplace. If it is no longer fashionable to hold German idealist philosophy responsible for the entire subsequent history of nationalism, as Elie Kedourie once argued,[24] this is so only because attention has shifted, in the work of Ernest Gellner and Tom Nairn for example,[25] away from the political implications of the content of formal, philosophical systems of thought to those of the needs and aspirations of intelligentsias, understood as particular, historically specific, social groupings. Benedict Anderson's *Imagined Communities* has considerably advanced this line of argument through its focus on the specific nexus which connects intelligentsias to the printing industries. Nations have to be understood, argues Anderson, as communities imagined in a particular way, that is, as passing through a homogeneous empty time in which simultaneity is indicated only by temporal coincidence in terms of clock and calendar. This represents a distinctly modern type of imagination, the technical preconditions for which are

---

23   On the *Bulletin* and the *Boomerang* cf. Barnes 1969, Part 2; Cantrell 1978; Lee 1976; Palmer 1963, chs. 4 and 5; Rolfe 1979; Ross 1935, chs. 3 and 4; Ward 1966, ch. 8. On academic criticism at the universities of Sydney and Melbourne cf. Blainey 1957, pp. 101, 130, 155; Heseltine 1979; Milgate 1952; Mitchell 1983; Royal Commission on the University of Melbourne 1904; Scott 1936, pp. 127–9, 175–6, 189, 209; Serle 1949, pp. 63–4, 373–4; Wykes 1974.
24   Kedourie 1960.
25   Gellner 1964; Nairn 1977.

provided by the novel and the newspaper. Thus print-capitalism is central to the rise of nationalism: it is the capitalist publishing industry, driven by the restless search for markets, which comes to assemble various vernaculars into a set of print-communities, each of which prefigures a nation. Anderson identifies four main waves of nationalism: firstly, early American nationalism in which language *per se* is irrelevant, but in which printer-journalists producing self-consciously 'provincial' as opposed to 'metropolitan' newspapers perform an absolutely central role in the development of national consciousness; secondly, European popular nationalisms centred on middle-class reading coalitions, which mobilise the popular masses in opposition to the polyvernacular dynastic state; thirdly, the official nationalism of those polyvernacular dynasties that sought through 'Russification' or 'Anglicisation' to impose a nationalism from above; and lastly, those anti-imperialist nationalisms in which an intelligentsia educated within the confines of the colonial educational system comes to imagine and later constitute the colony as a nation.[26] What is peculiar about Australia at the turn of the century is that it becomes the site upon which two rival nationalisms, an 'American' provincial nationalism on the one hand, and an Anglicising official nationalism on the other, each become operative; and that moreover they each find expression in rival forms of literary criticism situated in rival institutional locations. The *Bulletin* was the voice of Australian radical nationalism and Australian republicanism, a fierce opponent of the 'monarchic simulacrum ... supplied from a little island the size of Victoria situated on the other side of the world';[27] the academic career of Sir Mungo MacCallum by contrast represented 'his main and conscious offering to the labours of empire'.[28]

For Eagleton as for Habermas eighteenth-century literary criticism is constituted by an early bourgeois public sphere, the subsequent destruction of which is eventually assured by the very logic of capitalist development itself. In the last chapter of *The Function of Criticism*, however, Eagleton discusses the possibility of other analogous public spheres. He argues that a proletarian counter-public sphere came into existence in Germany during the Weimar Republic and, to some extent, also in Britain during the 1930s. And he suggests that the modern women's movement has succeeded in creating a counter-public sphere in which the shared fact of gender functions so as to equalise all participants in the discourse, much as did the shared attribute

---

26   Anderson 1983, pp. 30, 41, 46–7, 50–128.
27   Rolfe 1979, p. 140.
28   Milgate 1952, p. 47.

of reason for the eighteenth-century English bourgeoisie.[29] Now it is surely possible that in certain exceptional circumstances nationalism can transform nationality itself into a similarly equalising 'fact' within what is, in effect, a nationalist counter-public sphere. Indeed this is exactly what happened in late nineteenth-century Australia. The radical nationalism of this period is in Anderson's terms a nationalism of the American type, that is, one sustained centrally by the printer-journalists of the 'provincial' colonial press. That this is so is most apparent in the case of the *Bulletin* itself: the creation above all of J.F. Archibald, an Australian-born, non-university educated, journalist; its literary page the work primarily of Stephens, an Australian-born craftsman printer and journalist; it intended from its very first issue to give 'provincial matters the greatest attention' and advocated a 'consistent and distinctive AUSTRALIAN NATIONAL POLICY'.[30] *The Boomerang*, co-edited for its first three years by yet another printer-journalist, Willian Lane, and including amongst its staff at one time both Stephens and Henry Lawson, clearly occupies yet another important space within the nationalist counter-public sphere. Subsequent radical nationalist critics have no doubt constructed an essentially romanticised account of both the *Bulletin* itself and the legend of the nineties. But the point remains that from the entire history of Australian criticism only this criticism remains available for any such romanticisation. The nationalist counter-public sphere of the 1890s functioned within very clearly defined boundaries which excluded non-whites and, less clearly, women, just as the eighteenth-century English bourgeois public sphere functioned so as to exclude the non-educated classes. But within these boundaries radical nationalism was both popular and egalitarian. *Bulletin* criticism is in fact exactly an example of that type of 'cultural politics, at once broadly dispersed, instantly available and socially closed' which Eagleton observes at work in the eighteenth-century public sphere.[31] The disintegration of this Australian nationalist public sphere is partly explicable in terms similar to those which Eagleton applies to England. It is in part a consequence of the expansion of the literary market. It is in part a consequence also, not so much of the eruption into the public sphere of new social interests, as of the creation of new divisions between the social interests which already inhabited that sphere: once nation state-hood had been achieved in 1901, the division between Labor and non-Labor within Australian politics came to take on a much greater salience. But it is also a consequence in part of a third factor entirely specific to the

---

29 Eagleton 1984, pp. 112, 118.
30 Lee 1976, p. 314.
31 Eagleton 1984, p. 20.

Australian case, that is, racism. If the *Bulletin* represented the authentic voice of Australian radical nationalism in its support for republicanism and a united Australia and in its opposition to 'noble' titles, it did so too in its opposition to the 'cheap Chinaman' and the 'cheap nigger'.[32] The subsequent resubordination of Australian nationalism to British imperialism was very clearly facilitated and perhaps decisively so by the racist fears engendered by the Japanese victory in the Russo-Japanese War of 1904–5. A Labor government would soon found, not an Australian republic, but a Royal Australian Navy.

A radical nationalist criticism continues, of course, above all in the work of Vance and Nettie Palmer. But it is a criticism bereft of any available nationalist public sphere: the independent, racist, sub-imperialist state founded in 1901 precludes the possibility of any further anti-British republicanisms other than those which are self-consciously socialist or feminist. Thus radical nationalist criticism becomes increasingly parasitic on the various unsuccessful or at least only partially successful attempts to create alternative socialist or feminist counter-public spheres (as in the case of the Palmers); or else finds itself obliged to retreat into the academy, not into English departments from which it is firmly debarred by postwar Seatopolitan ideology, but into History departments, more naturally sympathetic environments perhaps for the cultivation of political archaism. Turner, Ward and Serle are the obvious examples of radical nationalist historians, though one might mischievously add McQueen.[33] In the English departments proper of the universities, Sir Mungo MacCallum

---

32 On 17 June 1893 the *Bulletin* formulated its own policies thus:
 A Republican form of Government.
 One Person one Vote.
 Complete Secularization and Freedom of State Education.
 Reform of the Criminal Code and Prison System.
 A United Australia and Protection against the World.
 Australia for the Australians – The cheap Chinaman, the cheap nigger, and the cheap European pauper to be absolutely excluded.
 A State Bank, the issue of bank-notes to be a State monopoly.
 The direct election of Ministers by Parliament, instead of Party Government or rather Government by Contradiction.
 A new Parliamentary System, – one House to be elected by constituencies as at present; the other to be chosen by the whole country voting as one Constituency.
 A Universal System of Compulsory Life Insurance.
 The entire Abolition of the Private Ownership of Land.
 The Referendum.
 The Abolition of Titles of so-called 'nobility'. (Ward 1966, pp. 224–5).
33 Turner 1968; Ward 1966; Serle 1973; McQueen 1977.

and his heirs went about their labours in the service of empire. At Sydney MacCallum held his chair for 33 years, remaining thereafter as professor emeritus, later vice chancellor and finally chancellor. He pioneered the development of extension classes and in 1923 founded and became first and only Life President of the Sydney branch of Sir Henry Newbolt's English Association. In 1921 his chair was divided into separate chairs of language and literature, occupied respectively by E.R. Holme and John le Gay Brereton. Both were Australian born, both were former students of MacCallum at Sydney, both were founder members of the Sydney branch of the English Association, both were pro-British during the Great War (Holme ardently so).[34] Brereton's successor to the Challis chair, A.J.A. Waldock, continues the pattern: Australian born and Sydney educated, he was active in extension lectures and in the English Association; although he presided over the introduction of Australian (and American) material into literature courses, both Waldock himself and his department remained preoccupied with the literature of England. Waldock's career does, however, mark the moment at which academic criticism in Australia moves from a self-consciously colonial sense of its social purpose as that of Anglicisation to a more independent sense of itself as merely another centre of humane English letters, *secundus inter pares*. Thus, whilst Holme devoted much of his efforts during the 1930s to the strident advocacy of a pro-British patriotism in the face of leftist subversion, and to the development of memorials to the young men he had urged on to their deaths in 1918, Waldock began in more properly liberal fashion to contemplate the eternal verities of the human condition. Waldock would be the Australian professor of English who would reject a rationalist reading of *Paradise Lost* on the grounds that for Milton 'it is rarely a question of finding happy compromises, comfortable and middle ways';[35] who would explain the superfluity of historical criticism in terms of 'the chief of all historical facts: that man has remained much the same';[36] who, alarmed at the prospect of a Hegelian analysis of Sophocles, would reflect thankfully that 'we are under no compulsion to apply any kind of theory to it; we are at liberty to

---

34 That Brereton, a one-time egalitarian nationalist and pro-Boer, a poet and a mate of Henry Lawson, should have supported the war tells its own sad tale of the disintegration of the nationalist counter-public sphere. Holme's position was that of an uncomplicated reactionary: in 1918 he played an important role in recruiting Sydney University undergraduates to the AIF and was duly rewarded with an honorary captaincy in the AIF's education service.

35 Waldock 1961, p. 59.

36 Waldock 1951, p. 5.

take it as it is and to forget all about patterns of tragedy'.³⁷ Australian academic criticism had come of age: here was a liberal humanism as socially irrelevant and as intellectually dilettantish as that developed and sustained by Oxford itself. As Eagleton has observed of English criticism in England, the point of such humanism is precisely to *be* marginal:

> neither decorative irrelevance nor indispensable ideology, neither structural nor superfluous, but a properly marginal presence, marking the border where ... society both encounters and exiles its own disabling absences.³⁸

On the occasion of the centenary of Sydney University's Faculty of Arts, Waldock's successor, W. Milgate, yet another Sydney educated Sydney professor of English, chose to insist virtually in the same breath on the vital importance of literature's liberal humanist vision and on the dreadful seediness of the English Department's facilities.³⁹ The pathos of a liberal humanism constituted as properly marginal presence became thus a matter for both public display and public record.

What is unusual about English studies at Sydney is neither its initial Anglicising role nor its eventual decline into liberal humanist dilettantism, but rather its solidly self-sustaining institutional identity. In this respect at least Sydney stands in marked contrast to Melbourne, where English studies suffered from both a repeatedly interrupted history and a pattern of continuing academic recruitment from Britain. Melbourne's first real professor of English, E.E. Morris, died on leave in England on 1 January 1902, and the University, at the time in the throes of a financial crisis occasioned by administrative embezzlement, seized upon the opportunity to economise by leaving the chair vacant for the next nine years. R.S. Wallace, like Morris an Oxford man, succeeded to the chair in 1911, but temporarily abandoned the department in 1916 to resume his commission with the Gordon Highlanders. Sir Archibald Strong, another Oxford graduate, though by birth if not upbringing an Australian, reluctantly accepted the post of acting head after being turned down for active service on grounds of ill health. He appears nonetheless to have devoted much of his time and energy to war work, including the production of such literary masterpieces as *Australia and the War* and *The Story of the Anzacs*. After Wallace's return

---

37   Waldock 1951, p. 35.
38   Eagleton 1984, p. 92.
39   Milgate 1952, pp. 56–8.

in 1919, Strong continued his services to the arts as chief Commonwealth film censor, before taking up the first chair of English Language and Literature at the University of Adelaide in 1922. The Melbourne pattern of recruitment from England and from amongst Oxford graduates in particular is in fact exactly reduplicated at Adelaide: of the first seven occupants of the Adelaide chair all but one were Oxford graduates (the exception, D.N. Smith, was a Cambridge man); and only one, C.J. Horne, was a graduate of an Australian university, Melbourne, though he had indeed proceeded to Oxford for further study.[40] Mistaken in the specific instance of Sydney, Archibald had, however, defined the opposition even more accurately than perhaps he himself knew when he jibed: 'I have nothing against Oxford men. Some of our best shearers' cooks are Oxford men'.[41] But when Wallace retired from the Melbourne chair in 1927 to take up the vice-chancellorship at Sydney, his successor and Waldock's approximate contemporary at Melbourne, though English, was certainly not an Oxford man: G.H. Cowling, formerly Reader in English at the University of Leeds, was both a native of the city of Leeds and a graduate from its university. This was the self-same Professor Cowling whose scepticism as to the possibilities of an Australian literature, publicly aired in the *Age*, would provoke P.R. Stephensen's famous essay on *The Foundations of Culture in Australia*.[42] Australia has no ancient churches, castles or ruins to stimulate a poetry which reflects past glories, Cowling would observe (nor actually has Leeds, but that is another matter). Stephensen's aggressively nationalist response is certainly interesting for what it has to say on the subject of English professors. But even more interesting, I suspect, is what it unwittingly reveals about the state of Australian radical nationalism. 'The Empire is in greater danger from patronizing Englishmen than from insurgent colonials', Stephensen observes.[43] Perhaps so; but an insurgent colonialism as concerned about the fate of Empire as is Stephensen's is unlikely to present any great danger to anyone. 'Literary' nationalism persisted; but the popular-democratic nationalist counter-public sphere that had once sustained the *Bulletin* had already ceased to exist. In reality it was neither English arrogance nor colonial rebellion which brought the Empire to an end. On 15 February 1942 General Perceval surrendered Singapore to the Imperial Japanese Army; anticipating events somewhat Curtin had already announced in the Melbourne *Herald* of 27 December 1941 that in future Australia would need to look to the United States rather than Britain. Soon the Labor Party would come

---

40   Duncan and Leonard 1973, p. 182.
41   Lee 1976, p. 318.
42   Stephensen 1986.
43   Stephensen 1986, p. 21.

to understand that Chifley's light shone from Capitol Hill; soon English departments would begin to read the New Criticism; soon James McAuley, Professor of English at the University of Tasmania, would begin to edit *Quadrant*.

To recapitulate: English studies at Sydney under Waldock until 1950, and at Melbourne under Cowling until 1943, remained committed to an initially Anglicising and always Anglophile liberal humanist academicism; but, whereas the Sydney department possessed a clear sense of its own independent identity and traditions, Melbourne English (as also Adelaide English) was characterised by a continuing pattern of recruitment from England, though not significantly from Cambridge. There was no inter-war revolution in English studies in Australia: these university critics went stolidly about their business of keeping Australia safe for English if not for Australian literature. Not until the 1950s was the hegemony of this traditional Anglophile liberal humanism challenged, and then by a younger generation of academics increasingly attracted towards either American New Criticism or some version or another of 'Leavisism'. In general New Criticism was much more influential at Sydney University, where it was pioneered by G.A. Wilkes, first professor of Australian Literature and later professor of English Literature; and 'Leavisism' at Melbourne, where its banner was carried by Vincent Buckley and S.L. Goldberg. In *Australian Cultural Elites* John Docker has argued that this differential intellectual evolution is best explained as a consequence of the quite different cultural traditions previously established in the two cities: on the one hand, the Melbourne tradition of a socially responsible intelligentsia, on the other, a Sydney tradition of aloofness and detachment from society.[44] There is doubtless some truth in Docker's account, though the argument is much more persuasive on Sydney than on Melbourne: it is after all not much of a tradition which begins, with the founding of *Meanjin*, in 1940. But equally important, I suspect, are the previous histories of the two universities' English departments. Docker himself notes the positive effects of the Sydney University English Department and the English Association in forming '*Southerly* writers ... so confident of their possession of English literature and the European heritage that they feel they don't have to advertise it'.[45] To this we should surely add the negative effects of the lack of any equivalent such formative influences at Melbourne. The transition from traditional liberal humanism to New Criticism was necessarily much easier to effect than that to Leavisism, even a tamed Leavisism: a new academic jargon is more easily learned than a capacity for moral 'seriousness'. Hence Leavis-

---

44   Docker 1974, ch. 7.
45   Docker 1974, p. 128.

ism's greater success at Melbourne, the department most clearly lacking in its own pre-existent self-sustaining identity. Whatever the explanation, there can be little doubt as to the extent of Sydney's resistance to Melbourne 'Leavisism'. Docker's own memoirs of a teenage Leavisite have retold with some enthusiasm the tale of Goldberg's near catastrophic four year tenure as Challis Professor: the English Department was bitterly divided between Sydney traditionalists and imported Melbourne (and English) Leavisites, to the extent that the English course was split into quite distinct A and B streams, one Leavisite and one pluralist; the split was resolved only when Goldberg returned to take up the chair at Melbourne, followed by many of his supporters, including, of course, the young John Docker.[46]

3   Critique of the Docker Programme

There is, we know, a crisis in literary studies, a crisis which provides the occasion both for Hohendahl's *The Institution of Criticism* and for Eagleton's *The Function of Criticism*. And even in Australia, where a resurgent Laborism successfully manages capital's way through the vagaries of economic crisis, even here an ingrate literary intelligentsia insists on staging a crisis of its very own. Docker's recently published *In a Critical Condition: Reading Australian Literature* is by no means an exact equivalent either to Hohendahl or to Eagleton: it is much lighter in tone, both more amused and more amusing; it is, all cultural cringes set aside, a rather less theoretically sophisticated piece of work; it suffers from a surprisingly truncated sense of the history of criticism as beginning shortly after the end of the Second World War. It is nonetheless the Australian edition of the book of the crisis and commands attention as such. Docker's central argument can be summarised thus: Australian literary criticism during the 1950s and 1960s was polarised between radical nationalism, on the one hand, which represented a distinctively Australian school of contextual criticism, and 'New Criticism and Leavisism', on the other, which together constituted a single, formalist, discursive formation; from the 1950s onwards the latter increasingly came to exercise a 'metaphysical ascendancy' over Australian literary studies, an ascendancy underpinned externally by the Cold War, and characterised internally as a critical practice by its rigorous exclusion of all possible contextual considerations; during the 1960s and 1970s, however, the ascendancy was challenged by various forms of counter-cultural utopian-

---

46   Docker 1981.

ism, Marxism, structuralism and semiology, but sought to restore itself through the appropriation of certain semiological themes, and especially through the introduction into Australia, and in particular into the Department of English at Melbourne University, of Yale deconstructionism; nonetheless, there is as yet no clear pattern of hegemony within literary studies.[47] *In a Critical Condition* is deliberately conceived as a radical intervention into precisely this uncertain state of affairs.

The radical nationalism to which Docker here refers is not that of the 1890s, but rather that of the Palmers, *Overland*, Turner, Ward and Serle, a subsequent less activist and more academic radical nationalism, but one very much based on a particular reading of the 1890s. For this radical nationalism is in fact an Australian version of historicism, and it is one which claims to detect in the 1890s the moment in which a unity between elite and popular cultures, between culture and environment, is briefly realised.[48] In Australia, it appears, the organic community lasted for about a decade. The 'New Critics' and 'Leavisites' by contrast are those who have occupied the commanding heights of the postwar critical economy: Wilkes, Goldberg, Buckley, McAuley, Leonie Kramer, H.P. Heseltine and, a more recent addition, Howard Felperin. In his second chapter Docker offers a 'bold synopsis of twentieth-century Anglo-American literary theory', in which this peculiar hybrid 'New Criticism and Leavisism' is defined in terms of its characteristic refusal of: firstly the imitative fallacy, that is, the view that literature reflects something other than literature; and secondly the intentional fallacy, that is, the view that the literary text can be understood in terms of its author's intentions.[49] Anglo-American criticism and its Australian subsidiaries are thus formalisms, and in Docker's opinion deconstructionism serves merely to reconstruct that formalism. Let us note immediately that, in terms of Leavis's own biography or the history of *Scrutiny* itself, a conflation of New Criticism and Leavisism such as that which Docker suggests is quite unwarranted. Leavis himself detected no imitative fallacy, but rather subscribed to the view that great art gave form to life. Leavis himself detected no intentional fallacy: certainly, he had stressed the importance of tradition, but authorship entailed an active engagement with such tradition. American New Criticism was perhaps 'a criticism which emphasized aesthetic form, neglected history and divorced literature from society'.[50] But Leavis himself chose

---

47 Docker 1984, pp. 83–92, 181–2, 212.
48 Docker 1984, p. 34.
49 Docker 1984, pp. 44–9.
50 Saunders 1973–4, p. 110.

neither to neglect history nor to divorce literature from society. Leavis's aesthetic is in fact radically anti-formalist: hence his preference for Lawrence, whose 'innovations and experiments are dictated by the most serious and urgent kind of interest in life', over Joyce, in whose work 'there is no organic principle ... controlling into a vital whole, the elaborate analogical structure, the extraordinary variety of technical devices'.[51] Leavis's Leavisism is a historicism, it is a radical historicism, and it is a radical nationalist historicism, a radical English nationalist historicism. It is much more akin to Australian radical nationalism than to Docker's hybrid 'New Criticism and Leavisism'. And in the very silences of his text Docker himself knows that this is so.[52]

This is not to say that Docker is necessarily mistaken about Goldberg or Buckley; only that this was not Leavis's Leavisism, and that there is surely something significant about the way in which Leavis was mistranslated from English into Australian. The fundamental weaknesses of *In a Critical Condition* are essentially twofold. In the first place, Docker's very preoccupation with the specifics of postwar Australian literary criticism, and his concomitant indifference to the history both of pre-war Australian criticism and of English criticism in England, precludes the type of comparative analysis which is actually in this case a necessary precondition to the understanding of the specific. Without an adequate understanding of English Leavisism it becomes virtually impossible to explain the significance of the way in which Leavisism was appropriated in Australia. Secondly, Docker addresses himself only to one of the three questions which we defined as central to the analysis of literary criticism, that is, to an internal analysis of the content of such criticism. He knows, of course, that postwar Australian criticism takes place as an academic practice within the institution of the academy and, indeed, he is quite acute on the subject of the particular institutional mechanisms by which the metaphysical ascendancy was both established and maintained. But Docker appears to attach no particular importance to the fact that, whatever its content, contemporary literary criticism, as distinct for example from Stephens's criticism in the *Bulletin*, remains institutionally located within higher education and not somewhere else. I shall return to this matter again. Docker is similarly uninterested in our third question, that of the place occupied by criticism within the wider intellectual culture. Thus he seems not to notice that literary studies is much more

---

51   Leavis 1962a, pp. 35–6.
52   Thus, for example, Docker notes, but attaches no significance to, Howard Jacobson's 'English nationalism and chauvinism' (Docker 1984, p. 6); thus Docker notes, but attaches no significance to, Terry Sturm's 'left-Leavisism' (Docker 1984, p. 177).

marginally located in relation to the Australian national intellectual culture than it is to the English. Leavis's Leavisism was a radical nationalist historicism occupying a central location within the English national culture. But radical nationalisms are quite simply not for export. What was exported to Australia was that version of tame and tamed Leavisism which continued in England after the demise of *Scrutiny*; and even this tame Leavisism was in fact incorporated into an American-type New Criticism as a subordinate junior partner, thus providing a fitting symbolic representation both of the postwar Anglo-American alliance and of Australia's insertion into it. It is indisputably the case that Leavis was the heir to a long tradition of English thought on the 'Culture and Society' theme. But it was nonetheless Leavisism itself which constructed English Literature as the 'displaced home of the totality' within English intellectual thought. And precisely because Leavisism was not for export to Australia, Australian academic criticism has never been able to lay claim to any equivalent such status. Australian academic criticism's critical condition arises not so much from its inability to construct a great tradition as from the fact that it is not and never has been a common pursuit.

Insofar as a totalising discourse can be located within the Australian national culture its site is certainly not literary criticism. Nor is it sociology, the normal such location according to Perry Anderson. Australian sociology is an almost entirely derivative discourse, consisting merely in a set of 'applications' of preexisting concepts and methodologies to Australian 'data', conducted so as to demonstrate this applicability rather than to discover anything in particular about Australian society. Nor is it Marxism, which as an indigenous intellectual discourse barely exists.[53] Its site is in fact the discipline of history. It is no accident, as we Marxists are wont to say, that most of the radical nationalist academics were professional historians. It is no accident that in history, unlike literature, the major chairs are occupied by professors whose main area of interest is Australia itself. It is no accident that historians are much more prominent in national political debate than are academics drawn from other disciplines. Thus Manning Clark's opposition to the Kerr Coup and Blainey's campaign against further Vietnamese migration were politically and culturally significant interventions of a type hardly ever attempted either by literary critics or by sociologists. If Australia does have an equivalent to English Leavisism, then it is almost certainly not the literary criticism of S.L. Goldberg but rather the radical nationalist school of Australian historiography. Leavis's own project

---

53   Who is the major Australian Marxist theorist? Jack Lindsay (hélas?), or perhaps, Vere Gordon Childe. Both chose to live and work in Britain.

was, of course, ultimately self-defeating: he sought to restore the organic community from within the university, an institution which he himself recognised as hostile to life. In exactly analogous fashion Australian radical nationalist historiography has sought to reconstruct the radical 1890s from within the university, an institution known neither for its radicalism nor even in Australia for its nationalism. The problem clearly is that a genuine cultural criticism of the type to which both English Leavisites and Australian radical nationalists aspired could only ever function within some wider public sphere, and that no such public sphere actually existed either in England or in Australia. Which is why Docker's *In a Critical Condition* is fatally flawed by its indifference to the matter of criticism's institutional location. Docker concludes his argument thus:

> A text has to be studied in and for itself as well as in its context ... when cultural study is centred only on the text, is formalist, it represses important aspects of literature, film, communication; and when a rigidly contextual approach makes the text disappear into a context it neglects important aspects of cultural phenomena. The two have to be combined in analysis, held in a difficult balance.[54]

Doubtless they do; but is this really all that Docker has to recommend, a new improved, more comprehensive, more balanced, academic criticism?

A socialist criticism should be no more prepared to accept this ascribed status of alternative academic theory than have been recent feminist criticisms. An armchair or professorial chair Marxism is no Marxism at all for the very reason that the point is to change it. Which means that what matters is the creation of a socialist and feminist counter-public sphere. 'The primary task of the "Marxist critic", writes Eagleton:

> is to actively participate in and help direct the cultural emancipation of the masses. The organising of writers' workshops, artists' studios and popular theatre; the transformation of the cultural and education apparatuses; the business of public design and architecture; a concern with the quality of quotidian life all the way from public discourse to domestic 'consumption'; in short, all the projects on which Lenin, Trotsky, Krupskaya, Lunacharsky and others of the Bolsheviks were intensively engaged remain, for all the differences of historical situation, the chief

---

54 Docker 1984, p. 208.

responsibilities of a revolutionary cultural theory that has refused, other than tactically and provisionally, that division of labour which gives birth to a 'Marxist literary criticism'.[55]

I frankly admit that I am not at all clear as to how exactly we should begin to set about this task; I am nonetheless certain that it is indeed what is to be done. It would have been much better had Docker said as much.

---

55 Eagleton 1981, pp. 97–8.

CHAPTER 3

The Protestant Epic and the Spirit of Capitalism

This chapter will be concerned not so much with general problems of theory or method as with the substantive analysis of a set of literary texts. But, of course, any such analysis must assume certain methodological premises and it might be as well to state these before we proceed. The method employed here derives substantially from Lucien Goldmann's now distinctly unfashionable 'genetic structuralism'.

1 Theoretical Preliminaries: The Fused Group and the Sociology of the World Vision

Despite his own self-declared distance from more conventionally 'structuralist' theoretical positions, Goldmann was himself in many respects very much a structuralist thinker. In his sociology of literature, as much as in the structural anthropology of Lévi-Strauss, Barthes's semiology of myth or Foucault's archaeology of knowledge, 'comprehension is the bringing to light of a significant structure immanent in the object studied'.[1] Goldmann's studies of Kant[2] and of Pascal and Racine[3] were as concerned to find 'the primal plan on which everything else depends'[4] as was Todorov's famous essay on Henry James. Where Goldmann parted company with mainstream structuralism, however, was in his insistence that 'structures are born from events and from the everyday behaviour of individuals and that, except for the most formal characteristics, there is no permanence in these structures'.[5] For Goldmann, then, most structuralist analysis remained incomplete insofar as it sought only to describe the structures of literature rather than to explain the processes by which these had been produced. In this insistence on the production of structures as distinct from the mere fact of their existence, Goldmann's work became at once both humanist and historicist. The central task of the literary sociologist he defined thus:

---

1 Goldmann 1967, p. 500.
2 Goldmann 1971.
3 Goldmann 1964.
4 Todorov 1973, p. 74.
5 Goldmann 1970b, p. 99.

when he replaces the work in a historical evolution which he studies as a whole, and when he relates it to the social life of the time at which it was written – which he also looks upon as a whole – ... the enquirer can bring out the work's objective meaning.[6]

Goldmann's own work is focussed simultaneously on the internal structures of the literary texts under analysis and on those wider social structures in which he aimed to discover their genesis. As in literary humanism more generally, he seeks to understand the literary work as the effect of an extratextual human agency. But where liberal humanism had discovered authoritative meaning in the intentionality of the individual author, Goldmann defined the subject of which the literary work is the object as necessarily collective or transindividual in character. For Goldmann as much as for Barthes the death of the individual author was already a theoretical *fait accompli*. But where Barthes would relocate the locus of textual meaning away from the author and toward the reader,[7] Goldmann opted to reconstitute the category of authorship at the higher level of a quasi-Durkheimian collective consciousness. Moreover, such group consciousnesses were seen as normally entailing a certain consciousness of social class. Here the Lukácsian-Marxist basis of Goldmann's work becomes readily apparent:

> Every time it was a question of finding the infrastructure of a philosophy, a literary or artistic current, ultimately we have been forced to consider, not a generation, a nation or church, not a profession or any other social grouping, but a social class and its relation to society.[8]

The crucial mediating agency between the life of a social class and the work of an individual writer is for Goldmann the 'world vision', that is, 'the whole complex of ideas, aspirations and feelings which links together the members of a social group ... and which opposes them to members of other social groups'.[9] The structures of intratextuality and intertextuality elucidated in more conventionally structuralist accounts of literature were in Goldmann's view better understood as the central informing categories of such social class world visions. Hence the general prospectus for a genetic structuralist sociology of

---

6 Goldmann 1964, p. 8.
7 Barthes 1977, p. 148.
8 Goldmann 1970b, p. 102.
9 Goldmann 1964, p. 17.

literature: to establish a series of structural homologies between the work of the individual writer, the world vision of the social group and the social situation in which the group finds itself.

As an argument in and against high structuralism, there is still surely much to be said for Goldmann's residual theoretical humanism: insofar as culture is indeed structured, then this is more plausibly the effect of human sociality than of some scientistically naturalising law of structure. The argument stands up less well, however, under more properly poststructuralist interrogation. For Goldmann social class world visions could exist on two different planes: 'that of the *real* consciousness of the group ... or that of their *coherent* expression in great works of philosophy or art'.[10] He maintained not only that all works of art do in fact coherently express such a world vision, but also that 'it is precisely because their work has such a coherence that it possesses ... literary ... worth'.[11] But if, as poststructuralism asserts, there is no fixity to textual meaning, only the infinitely plural pleasures of an 'indefinite referral of signifier to signifier',[12] possessed of determinate relation neither to linguistic signified nor to extra-linguistic referent, then there can be no deep structure of coherence immanent within the text for Goldmann's sociology to discover. The theory of the world vision thus invents that which it professes to discover: merely one more reading amongst many, it possesses no special virtue whether scientific or aesthetic. Moreover, if our current constructions of the past are as indelibly marked by their radical contemporaneity and radical indeterminacy, in short their radical textuality, as poststructuralism also asserts, then there can be no determinate extratextual history whether of social classes or of social groups to which a sociology of literature might appeal for explanatory validation: history itself is only ever creative fiction, its findings not so much constitutive of as derivative from our contemporary preoccupations.

Neither of these assertions is entirely devoid of insight: our readings of literature and of history are indeed necessarily plural and contemporary. But the second assertion is nonetheless much more suspect than the first. It is one thing to concede that we can only ever understand the past historiographically, quite another to imply that the past can have had no independent existence apart from that historiography. This proposition is simply untrue: as Fredric Jameson rightly insists, 'history is *not* a text, not a narrative', even though 'our approach to it and to the Real itself necessarily passes through its prior tex-

---

10   Goldmann 1970b, p. 130.
11   Goldmann 1964, p. 98.
12   Derrida 1978, p. 25.

tualization'.[13] Insofar as history is indeed real, then different historiographical narratives can give better or worse accounts of its reality. A history external to the literary text, although not to textuality itself, thus still remains available for any such sociology of literature as Goldmann envisaged. Poststructuralism remains on stronger ground when concerned with literature as distinct from history. There are indeed a great many readings available for any particular literary text from the hypothetical authorial original to the most recent of receptions, these readings may be more or less incoherent and certainly need not be especially coherent, and each of them is as semiotically true as any other. All of this notwithstanding, such readings are nonetheless by no means sociologically equally true. Quite the contrary, the number of available socially acceptable readings is normally neither indefinite nor indeterminate. It may well be semiotically possible to read the Christian Bible as parody; sociologically, however, it would have been extremely ill-advised to do so within the city limits of Calvin's Geneva. Goldmann's attempt to identify particular historically and socially influential readings remains perfectly legitimate, so long as these readings are understood for what they are, not the aesthetic truth of the text itself but rather the sociological truth of the history of the text's reception. Understood thus, such readings need not be especially coherent. The long history of modernist and postmodernist valorisations of the transgressive, from the Formalist espousal of defamiliarisation[14] through to Cixous's celebration of *écriture féminine*,[15] suggests how powerfully persuasive the incoherent can actually be. But in certain socio-discursive contexts, typically perhaps very different from those of our own postmodern late capitalism, an aesthetic of coherence such as Goldmann improperly seeks to universalise might well be found locally appropriate.

In this essay I intend to use something of Goldmann's sociological method to develop a reading of the literary, political and philosophical writings of John Milton, the great poet of the English bourgeois revolution. The paucity of revolutionary thought in English intellectual life suggests the interest of such a study, for Milton was above all a revolutionary, the bearer of an everyday consciousness and a literary consciousness radically alien to the distinctly unrevolutionary sensibilities of late twentieth-century England. The deep-seated incomprehension which constituted the general response to Milton's work both in the last century and for much of our own clearly derives from this

---

13   Jameson 1981, p. 35.
14   Shklovsky 1965.
15   Cixous 1981.

source. The nineteenth-century insistence on Milton as a master of poetic form whose ideas remain matters of little or no consequence[16] and the twentieth-century denigration of Milton pioneered by Eliot and Leavis[17] each alike appear as symptoms of the wider and much more general incomprehension with which a conservative national culture must view a consistently revolutionary thinker. Whatever its ultimate methodological value, Goldmann's approach seems to me especially appropriate to the analysis of a revolutionary writer such as Milton. Goldmann, we have seen, privileges the criterion of coherence both as a literary-critical value in its own right and as a characteristic feature of social class world visions. The notion seems inappropriate, we have noted, as a universalist criterion for either aesthetics or sociology. But it might well be relevant nonetheless in certain very specific, local circumstances. In the *Critique de la raison dialectique* Sartre distinguishes between the alienated series, a collective wherein the forms of interior bonding between actors are determined by the passivity of scarce matter,[18] and the fused group, in which forms of interior bonding are structured around the shared project of freedom, that is, of overcoming passivity and scarcity.[19] The fused group, we may infer, would be the type of social group most likely to subscribe to such coherent totalisations as those which interest Goldmann. Sartre's own initial example of a fused group is that presented by the storming of the Bastille, but it is clear that he intends the notion as generalisable to all modern revolutionary upsurges, most especially the Russian and the Chinese. In Cromwell and the Revolutionary Independents, the English Revolution provides us with an almost exactly analogous instance. Indeed, Sartre's account of the degeneration of the fused group toward seriality through the pledge and the terror, the organisation and the institution, seems peculiarly applicable to the fate of the English Revolution. Insofar as my genetic structuralist reading of Milton will actually work, then this suggests not so much the universal applicability of the method itself as the quite specifically fused nature of Revolutionary Independency.

2 The World Vision of Revolutionary Independency

Goldmann's sociology of literature has as one of its main aims the construction of a typology of historical social class world visions. He identifies five

---

16 Raleigh 1913.
17 Eliot 1968, pp. 9–21; Leavis 1972b, pp. 46–63.
18 Sartre 1976, pp. 262–3.
19 Sartre 1976, pp. 340–1.

main world visions which in his view have dominated human thought since the break-up of feudalism: dogmatic rationalism, sceptical empiricism, the tragic vision, dialectical idealism, and dialectical materialism.[20] Each of these he aims to situate in a particular historical context. What primarily concern me here are the two main world visions of classical bourgeois thought, the rationalist and the empiricist. In a sense both empiricism and rationalism form part of a wider world vision, that of bourgeois individualism, insofar as they each posit as their central category the isolated individual; this is as true of Locke and Hume as of Descartes and Leibniz. But where rationalism constructed a system of universal mathematics, of logical necessities, empiricism based itself much more pragmatically on the observed contingencies of the sensible world. Goldmann contrasts the growth of continental rationalism on the one hand, with that of English empiricism on the other, so much so that empiricism almost becomes the English disease. And indeed it has become something of a truism that the English national culture can be characterised by its all-pervading empiricism, by an ideological preoccupation with what is to the exclusion of consideration of alternative possibilities. Goldmann himself explains the genesis of English empiricism in terms of three main factors. Firstly, English bourgeois society was born out of a class compromise with the nobility which encouraged a much more pragmatic and less radical world vision than in France, for example, where a long class struggle kept the bourgeoisie in radical opposition to the nobility. Secondly, the consequent absence of rationalist traditions itself militated against the emergence of rationalist philosophies. Thirdly, the great British philosophers, Locke, Berkeley and Hume, wrote in a situation in which the bourgeoisie had already effectively assumed power, so that their work was predicated on the facts of bourgeois society rather than on the *a priori* necessity for its creation.[21] In its more general terms we can accept this analysis, although we might wish to add that the English class compromise between bourgeoisie and nobility occurred only on the basis of a prior transformation of the nobility into a landed bourgeoisie. Though English bourgeois ideology is characteristically pragmatic and empiricist, it is nonetheless a genuinely bourgeois ideology and not as Perry Anderson once suggested a form of ideological capitulation to the aristocracy.[22] It was utilitarianism which became the hegemonic ideology in English society and it is surely difficult to conceive of a more properly bourgeois ideology than this.

---

20   Goldmann 1964, p. 23.
21   Goldmann 1971, pp. 37–8.
22   Anderson 1970, p. 226.

We have, then, accepted the general characterisation of the English bourgeois world vision as empiricist. We should add, however, that the predominance of empiricism in English thought dates only from the Restoration in 1660 and more especially from the Glorious Revolution of 1688; and that the revolutionary crisis of the mid-seventeenth century witnessed the creation and subsequent destruction of an indigenous English rationalism. The social basis of English empiricism was to be constituted from out of the coincidence of an already established bourgeois economic power with a gradual pragmatic growth of bourgeois political power, in which the constitutional monarchy became progressively more constitutional and the House of Commons progressively more important than the House of Lords. But the mid-seventeenth-century revolutionary crisis had witnessed an alternative pattern of development. Whole sections of the bourgeoisie turned to the task of a revolutionary transformation of the English feudal state machine into a fully-fledged bourgeois republic. This conflict gave rise to a rationalist world vision which had sought to contrast the irrational present with the rational institutions, modes of behaviour, etc., to which the revolutionary bourgeoisie itself aspired. That world vision found political form in Revolutionary Independency, in the party of Milton and Cromwell, and it was only the failure of the Independent enterprise which led the English bourgeoisie to the political strategy of gradualism and the world vision of empiricism. The decades of the revolutionary crisis and its immediate aftermath witness the emergence of an indigenous English rationalism which has as its major intellectual figure the poet John Milton.[23] This rationalist world vision develops in two stages each dealing with a distinct set of problems: firstly, the period of revolutionary victory and the programme of reason triumphant; secondly, the period of reaction and the problematic of reason embattled. In each stage Milton's own work functions very much as what Goldmann would have termed the 'maximum possible consciousness' of the English revolutionary bourgeoisie.

---

23 This association between rationalism, Protestantism and the English Revolution is by no means an entirely original proposition. It is to be found in both Engels's 'Introduction' to *Socialism: Utopian and Scientific* (Engels 1970, pp. 375–93) and Weber's *The Protestant Ethic and the Spirit of Capitalism* (Weber 1930). But neither Engels nor Weber understand the full extent to which revolutionary Protestantism can be viewed as a fully-fledged rationalist world vision. Moreover, both radically overestimate, indeed misunderstand, the importance of Calvinism in the general Protestant undertaking. As we shall see, the genuinely revolutionary dynamic in Protestantism comes to fruition precisely insofar as it effected a rejection of Calvinism.

Let us attempt a brief sketch of the structure of a rationalist world vision. As we have already noted, rationalism is in the first place a form of *individualism*. For the rationalist the central datum is the discrete individual and it is the individual alone who can decide what is true or untrue. If this is so, then it follows that these rational individuals must be in the most profound sense in possession of their own freedom, for if their behaviour is in any sense determined or contingent then the centrality of the individual gives place to the centrality of some other determining agency. The rational individual must, then, be free from all forms of constraint, be they external (institutions, etc.) or internal (non-rational elements within the individual personality, i.e. the passions). This implies politically an *opposition to privilege and tradition*, ontologically a conception of the self based on a radical *dualism between reason and passion*, and ethically an *opposition to passion*. Since we are dealing with revolutionary Protestantism, that is, a specifically Christian form of rationalism, it would seem legitimate to ask where *God* stands in this system. The answer is surprising: since the discrete individual is the central datum of the system, there is logically no independent place for God whatsoever. And this is precisely what we find in revolutionary Protestantism: certainly, the existence of God is never doubted, but God is conceived as having no practical independent existence other than through the medium of the discrete individuals out of which the universe is practically composed.

Let us elaborate on each of these categories at a little more length. The central datum of the rationalist world vision, we have said, is the discrete *individual*. Revolutionary Protestantism asserted this doctrine centrally and primarily in its insistence on the individual interpretation of the Bible. For medieval Catholicism such interpretation had been the function of the church; for Luther, Calvin and Knox it was to become the prerogative of the individual. Hence the demand for an English translation of the Bible was one of the first raised by English Protestantism. But Revolutionary Independency went much further than any previous form of Protestantism in its insistence on the primacy of the individual. In the conflict within the Parliamentarian camp between the 'moderate' Presbyterians and the 'extremist' Independents, the latter argued for religious toleration and against the re-establishment of a monolithic state church, whether Anglican or Presbyterian. The theoretical basis for such tolerationism was a belief in the capacity of the individual, free from the tyranny of the state church, to distinguish truth from error.[24] On the question of tol-

---

24 'There are two things contended for in this liberty of conscience: first to instate every Christian in his right of free, yet modest, judging and accepting what he holds; secondly,

eration, the bourgeois Independents and the petty-bourgeois Levellers[25] were in full agreement: both the Independent *Heads of Proposals* and the Leveller *Agreement of the People* call for toleration of religious dissent.[26] This insistence on the individual's right to interpret the Bible might appear superficially at least more akin to a scholastic emphasis on authority (in this case Biblical authority) than to rationalism. But such an assessment ignores the practical social logic of the argument. By asserting the individual's right to interpret the Bible, Independency in fact denied the validity of all other authorities and firmly located the source of all truth, all knowledge, in the individual reason. Thus the Protestant appeal to scripture became in effect an appeal to the individual reason. As Basil Willey rightly observed:

> The 'inner light' of the Quakers ranks with the 'Reason' of the Platonists, the 'clear and distinct ideas' of Descartes, or the 'common notions' of Lord Herbert of Cherbury, as another of the inward certitudes by means of which the century was testing the legacies of antiquity and declaring its spiritual independence.[27]

Our second major rationalist category was that of *freedom*, freedom firstly from external (that is, political) constraints, and secondly from the internal constraints imposed by passion. Let us consider each in turn. That Revolutionary Independency as a political force was committed to a far-reaching attack on privilege and tradition is almost self-evident. From the initial Parliamentarian opposition to the power of the bishops and to the abuses of monarchical power, the Independents went on to launch a full-scale attack on the traditional institutions of England. They swept aside the traditionalist structure of the Parliamentarian Army and created the New Model Army which in its career structure came as near to establishing equality of opportunity as any subsequent English army; they abolished both the House of Lords and the monarchy and in the process executed a king; they broke the power of the industrial monopolies and smashed aside the constraints on improving landlordism imposed by the

---

to vindicate a necessary advantage to the truth, and this is the main end and respect of this liberty' ('The Ancient Bounds', Woodhouse 1965, p. 247).

25 The divisions within the Parliamentarian camp between the Presbyterians and the Independents were essentially within the bourgeois class, those between Independents and Levellers between classes. The Levellers were 'drawn from the lower middle class, the skilled craftsmen and the small farmers' (Brailsford 1961, p. 9).
26 Woodhouse 1965, Parts III and VIII, and Appendix D.
27 Willey 1972, p. 72.

old feudal state machinery. The Independents accepted no institution, law or tradition as valid in itself; everything was tested against the criteria of reason and justice and that which was found wanting was discarded. Indeed, one of the central features of Independency, which distinguishes it both from Presbyterianism on the right and from the Levellers on the left, is its disregard for legality. Thus, for example, when the Independents set out to bring the king to justice, they were opposed by both the Presbyterians and the Levellers for the unconstitutional manner in which they acted. The latter, Lilburne explained, 'objected against their total dissolving or breaking the House and the illegality of their intended and declared trying of the King'.[28] Independent apologists had half-heartedly attempted to argue that Charles's execution was in accord with the law. But the main drift of their argument was to sweep aside the question of legality and to concentrate on that of justice. And it fell to Milton in *Defensio pro Populo Anglicano* to provide a coherent rationale for precisely this act of illegality.[29]

In the rationalist view of the world the rational individual must be free not only from external constraints but also from the tyranny of his own passions. At the core of all rationalisms rests an ontology structured around the radical dualism between reason and passion. This is no mere contingent factor in rationalism; rather, it is a necessary component of any rationalist world vision insofar as it provides explanation for the existence of unreason. We noted that rationalism takes as its central datum the discrete individual and allows of no other factor in its interpretation of the world. It follows, then, that the existence of irrationalities (and to the bourgeois rationalist, the whole of previous human history is essentially irrational) must also be explained in terms of the faculties of the discrete individual. Hence, the category of 'passion', the principle of the anti-rational within the human individual, becomes essential to the explanatory credibility of a rationalist system. It fulfils precisely this role in the world vision of Revolutionary Independency. The Independents were characterised by a persistent soul-searching, a preoccupation with personal morality and a tendency to explain political behaviour, whether their own or that of their opponents, in purely personal terms. Thomas Collier, for example, contrasted the old political order with the new order coming into being thus: 'in respect of the person ruling, they shall be such as are acquainted with, and have an

---

28 Lilburne 1965, p. 348.
29 Milton 1848, Vol. I, pp. 1–213. All quotations from Milton's poetical works are taken from Milton 1966. *Paradise Lost* is hereinafter indicated as PL, *Paradise Regained* as PR, *Samson Agonistes* as SA.

interest in, the righteous God; that as formerly God hath many times set up wicked men to rule and govern ... so he will give it into the hands of the Saints'.[30] When the Independents accused their enemies of sin – for example, the Leveller Walwyn was accused of being a drunkard and whoremaster – this was no mere propaganda ploy. Since they themselves were in possession of reason, it had to follow that their opponents were under the sway of passion. Milton's own explanation for popular opposition to republicanism as outlined in *The Tenure of Kings and Magistrates* is thus characteristically Independent: 'being slaves within doors, no wonder that they strive so much to have the public state conformably governed to the inward vicious rules by which they govern themselves'.[31]

We noted that rationalism is in a strong sense logically *atheistic*. Now atheism would seem a very strange charge indeed to level at people such as Cromwell, Vane, Ireton, Harrison and Milton. I do not mean to suggest that they explicitly denied the existence of God. However, what they did do was to deny the independent presence of God in the world. Rather, God is present in the world only through the Elect, that is, through the medium of certain discrete individuals. Divine plans are achieved through the exercise of the rational free wills of human beings and not through any direct intervention of God in the world. I would argue that any genuine theism must maintain some separation between the human and the divine. Once God is liquidated into the reasons of particular individuals, then what remains of God? In revolutionary Protestantism this separation is abolished. In effect, Milton, Cromwell and the Independents identified themselves with God, and God with history. To quote Collier again:

> This is the great work ... that God calls for at your hands ... It is the execution of righteousness, justice and mercy, without respect of persons. It is to undo every yoke. And this being the great work in hand, and that which God calls for, and will effect, give me leave to present amongst many national grievances, some few unto you.[32]

He then proceeds to list such oppressions as denial of freedom of conscience, the use of the French language in legal proceedings, tithes and free-quartering. It is clearly not so much God as the bourgeoisie which is no respecter of per-

---

30   Collier 1965, p. 394.
31   Milton 1848, Vol. II, p. 2.
32   Collier 1965, p. 395.

sons. And only a rationalists' God could object to the use of the French language in legal proceedings. We might add that only a rationalist poet would presume to justify the ways of God to man.

Thus far we have been concerned to elucidate the structure of the Revolutionary Independent world vision as it developed in the years of triumph. But the Restoration imposed upon the former Independents a new problematic: how to explain the triumph of unreason. In Milton's later poems we find the systematic elaboration of such a response. There appear to have been two alternative though not necessarily incompatible rationalist solutions to the problem of unreason triumphant. The first is a personal individualist response which found religious expression in the quietism of the early Quakers, for example. Such notions of personal redemption and stoic resistance to the irrationalities of the world are central to that great literary monument to the Protestant conscience by an ex-soldier in Cromwell's army, Bunyan's *Pilgrim's Progress*. They are central too to Milton's later poems, but are combined there with an alternative second response to the victory of unreason, a politico-historical response which counterposes the future triumph of reason to its present defeat. I shall argue that it is this theme which becomes progressively more important in Milton's later work, so that ultimately he is obliged to work out a conception of history. The final expression of the revolutionary Protestant world vision as it appears in Milton is embodied, then, in a sense of the tension between particular defeats and the epic victory of the historical-universal. Let us turn now to a more direct account of Milton's own work.

3   Reason Triumphant

Our previous discussion of the evolution of the Revolutionary Independent world vision presents us with a relatively straightforward framework for the analysis of Milton's life-work: a schematisation concerned firstly with the works of the pre-Restoration period which express the world vision of an emergent triumphant rationalism; and secondly with the works written under the Restoration which express the world vision of reason embattled. The real shift in Milton's own view of the world comes with the Restoration and receives artistic expression in the three longer poems, *Paradise Lost*, *Paradise Regained* and *Samson Agonistes*. *Paradise Lost* was, of course, probably begun before the Restoration but was not published until 1667 and almost certainly the bulk of it was composed after 1660. Furthermore, it must have entailed a great deal of revision and so it would seem legitimate to treat it as essentially a post-Restoration work. This schematisation ignores the poems of the pre-revolutionary period, but whilst these are interesting from the standpoint of understanding Milton's individual poetic development, they do not have the same 'sociological' significance. I intend now to proceed to an examination of the way the central categories of a Protestant rationalist world vision inform and order Milton's system as it developed in the writings of the period 1640 to 1660.

In Milton's view all human beings possess *individual reason* and *free will*. This conception underlies much of his early polemic against the power of bishops and presbyters, regal tyrants and censors. In the *Areopagatica*, for example, he explicitly argues for promiscuous reading on the grounds that God has entrusted 'man ... with the gift of reason to be his own chooser'.[33] And this gift is in no sense arbitrary or accidental; rather it is of the very essence of 'man' as the son of Adam: 'when God gave him reason, he gave him freedom to chose, for reason is but choosing'.[34] As we noted, this rationalistic individualism finds expression in Protestantism primarily in the emphasis on individual scriptural interpretation. And Milton strongly adhered to this notion. In his attacks on episcopacy he asserts the right of the individual to interpret the scriptures without need of any institutional mediation.[35] As we have already noted, this appeal to scripture becomes in effect an appeal to the individual reason. Milton himself was prepared to express the logic of this position with the utmost clarity. In his unpublished and heretical *De Doctrina Christiana* he explains that: 'Under the gospel, we possess, as it were, a twofold Scripture; one external, which is the written word, and the other internal, which is the Holy Spirit, written in the hearts of believers ... that which is internal and the peculiar possession of each believer, is far superior to all'.[36] His conclusion could not be more explicit: 'everything', including Scripture itself, 'is to be finally referred to the Spirit and the unwritten word'.[37] Thus Milton's apparent fundamentalism collapses into a peculiar Miltonic *cogito*, the proud and lonely self-assertiveness of a new bourgeoisie guided only by 'that intellectual ray which God hath planted in us'.[38]

---

33 Milton 1848, Vol. II, p. 66.
34 Milton 1848, Vol. II, p. 74.
35 'The testimony of what we believe in religion must be such as the conscience may rest on to be infallible and uncorruptible, which is *only* the word of God' (Milton 1848, Vol. III, p. 139, – my emphasis).
36 Milton 1848, Vol. IV, p. 447.
37 Milton 1848, Vol. IV, p. 450.
38 Milton 1848, Vol. II, p. 387.

The earlier of Milton's pamphlets abound with a sense of the almost unlimited capacities of the individual reason: in *Apology for Smectymnuus*, for example, he maintains that matters of church government in no way 'exceed the capacity of a plain artisan'.[39] But these betray an uncharacteristically democratic tone almost certainly the product of a very specific conjuncture, that of the all-embracing Parliamentarian alliance. For the main part Milton's understanding of individual reason and free will carries no such democratic implications. Certainly he believed free will to be a universal endowment, but he most certainly did not believe in its universal exercise. For Milton we are only free when our actions are governed by reason:

> know that to be free is the same thing as to be pious, to be wise, to be temperate and just, to be frugal and abstinent, and lastly, to be magnanimous and brave: so to be the opposite of all these is the same as to be a slave ... You, therefore, who wish to remain free, either instantly be wise, or, as soon as possible, cease to be fools; if you think slavery an intolerable evil, learn obedience to reason and the government of yourselves.[40]

Milton held that in practice most people choose not to be so governed by reason and that: 'It is not agreeable to the nature of things that such persons ever should be free'.[41] In Milton's system, then, those who freely choose to subordinate their reason to their passions thereby lose their freedom. Thus the world is made up of discrete individuals each of whom possesses the capacity to exercise free will, but only some of whom actually achieve their freedom, that is, actually subordinate their passions to their reason. At the core of Milton's system we find a structure of thought essentially that of a characteristically bourgeois equality of opportunity model, in which all have the same opportunities but only some take advantage of them. This notion gives rise, as we shall see, to the Miltonic version of the theory of election.

Our second major category is that of *freedom from external constraint*. Since free rational individuals will act justly it follows that any constraints imposed upon their free action must necessarily deflect them from the path of righteousness. And so Milton is led to a profoundly libertarian conception both of social institutions in general and of three institutions in particular: the church, marriage, and the state. His conceptions of church government and of marriage

---

39   Milton 1848, Vol. III, p. 154.
40   Milton 1848, Vol. I, pp. 298–9.
41   Milton 1848, Vol. I, p. 298.

remain essentially unproblematic and need not detain us long. In each case the relevant institution is conceived as a set of rational individuals, entering into voluntary contractual relationships with each other for their own rational ends, who are thereby perfectly free to dissolve those relationships whenever they should prove unsatisfactory. Milton's hostility to the monolithic state church and to religious compulsion in general, as also his enthusiastic advocacy of divorce on demand, each derive their theoretical rationale from a specifically bourgeois structure of thought which sees in the fusion of epistemological individualism and institutional pluralism the route to both worldly and spiritual success.[42] Milton's theory of politics is based upon a somewhat analogous rejection of the feudal conception of the state as organism in favour of the notion of the state as a constructed institution. Thus any form of political government which imposes external constraints upon the exercise of individual rationality is to be rejected out of hand. 'Being therefore peculiarly God's own', writes Milton, 'and consequently things that are to be given to him, we are entirely free by nature, and cannot without the greatest sacrilege imaginable be reduced into a condition of slavery to any man, especially to a wicked, unjust, cruel tyrant'.[43]

But states do exist and they are by their very nature coercive institutions. Moreover, the Revolutionary Independents had themselves seized the government of a state. And so Milton was faced with the problem of reconciling political order with political liberty. This leads him to the version of social contract theory outlined in *The Tenure of Kings and Magistrates*.[44] Like Locke, Milton bases political legitimacy on notions of consent and trust, but unlike Locke he attaches no particular significance to the role of property. At first sight this is surprising: one might have expected a bourgeois theorist precisely to have made property pre-eminent. But where Locke would be the theorist of a class compromise between the propertied classes of England, Milton was that of a small revolutionary party which had seized power against the opposition of a probable majority of those self-same propertied classes. He could base his own theory of legitimation neither on property, which would have implied recognition of the rights of Royalists and Presbyterians, nor on simple consent, which would have meant direct concession to the democratic aspirations of the plebeian Levellers. Moreover, the problem was, in fact, extremely urgent: *The Tenure of Kings and Magistrates* was first published on 13 February 1649, just

---

42 Milton 1848, Vol. II, pp. 520–48; Milton 1848, Vol. III, pp. 169–273; Milton 1848, Vol. III, pp. 315–433.
43 Milton 1848, Vol. I, p. 63.
44 Milton 1848, Vol. II, pp. 1–47.

over two months after the purging of the Presbyterian members from Parliament, only a fortnight after the execution of the king and almost exactly three months before the crushing of the Leveller revolt at Burford. Milton's solution devolves upon the notion that political legitimacy should rest on the consent not of the propertied, still less of the masses, but rather that of the rational minority, those most fit to govern, that is, the Independents themselves.[45]

Milton's theory of the state is intimately bound up with his own particular theory of *election*. As we have seen, he believed that all humans are essentially free by nature and that they cannot properly be subjected to the tyranny of external constraint; but also that in practice many do surrender themselves up to their passions and so lose their freedom. Milton's theory of free will thus gives rise to a theory of election which becomes profoundly anti-democratic. In Calvinistic orthodoxy the ultimate salvation or damnation of each and every individual was seen as predetermined by God from the beginning of time.[46] Milton firmly rejected this notion in favour of the belief that through God's grace the option of salvation or damnation was made available to all: 'none are predestined or elected irrespectively'.[47] Thus those who stand and those who fall do so according to their own merits. Now this 'equality of opportunity' model is by no means a merely theological construct. It also has a direct political relevance. For Milton believed that the intervention of Christ and the message of the Gospel had given birth to 'Christian liberty', 'whereby WE ARE LOOSED AS IT WERE BY ENFRANCHISEMENT, THROUGH CHRIST OUR DELIVERER, FROM THE BONDAGE OF SIN AND CONSEQUENTLY FROM THE RULE OF LAW AND OF MAN'.[48] Those who freely receive Christ into themselves, that is, those who are governed by reason, thus come to constitute an elect for the purposes not only of salvation but also of worldly politics. This elect

---

45   'nothing is more agreeable to the order of nature, or more for the interest of mankind, than that the less should yield to the greater, not in numbers, but in wisdom and virtue' (Milton 1848, Vol. I, p. 265). In the *Tenure* itself Milton merely contents himself with the bald assertion that the Independent coup was indeed perfectly legal. Only in *Defensio pro Populo Anglicano* and *Defensio Secunda* does he finally come to grips with the question of legality.

46   In Prynne's words: 'God from all eternity hath, by his immutable purpose and decree, predestined unto life, not all men, not any indefinite or undetermined, but only a certain select number of particular men ... which number can neither be augmented nor diminished; others hath he eternally and perpetually reprobated unto death' (Prynne 1965, p. 232).

47   Milton 1848, Vol. IV, p. 49.

48   Milton 1848, Vol. IV, pp. 398–9.

is entitled to exercise government over sinners, for 'nature appoints that wise men should govern fools, not that wicked men should rule over good men, fools over wise men; and consequently they that take the government out of such men's hands act according to the law of nature'.[49] We should be clear that there is nothing aristocratic about this doctrine: the elect attain their position neither by hereditary right nor by predestination in the orthodox Calvinist sense of the term, but rather by merit. This Miltonic conception of election expressed theoretically the practice of the English bourgeois revolutionaries in a twofold sense. Firstly, it was based on an equality of opportunity model of human behaviour which exactly described the structure of an *ideally* functioning bourgeois society. Secondly, it provided a rationale for the Independent seizure of power, since as an elect they were both free from 'the rule of law and of man' and entitled to rule over sinners. The contempt for law and tradition characteristic of the political practice of Revolutionary Independency thus finds theoretical expression in this doctrine of election.[50]

We have identified Milton's theological beliefs as not merely non-Calvinist, but specifically anti-Calvinist. This represents something of a problem insofar as it stands in sharp contradiction to the commonplace association of Calvinism with capitalism and revolution in classical sociological theory. Weber's views on the subject are too well known to bear much repetition: the doctrine of predestination, he argued, gives rise to a doctrine of proof in which successful labour in a lay calling becomes an indispensable sign of election and which demands of its adherents 'a systematic self-control which at every moment stands before the inexorable alternative, chosen or damned'.[51] The consequent rationalisation of conduct produces an ethic essential to the 'spirit of capitalism' in which accumulation devoid of hedonism becomes an end in itself. Engels's analysis of Calvinism had run along essentially parallel lines: the doctrine of predestination 'was the religious expression of the fact that in the commercial world of competition success or failure does not depend upon a man's activity or cleverness, but upon circumstances uncontrollable by him'.[52] Both accounts seem to me mistaken. The real value of the doctrine of predes-

---

49 Milton 1848, Vol. I, p. 111.
50 Lest we should have any doubts that the elect are indeed the revolutionary bourgeoisie, Milton specifically describes the sort of men who are fit to rule both themselves and others: 'the middle sort, amongst whom the most prudent men, and most skilful in affairs, are generally found; others are most commonly diverted either by luxury and plenty, or by want and poverty, from virtue' (Milton 1848, Vol. I, p. 155).
51 Weber 1930, p. 115.
52 Engels 1970, p. 384.

tination to the early bourgeoisie had consisted in its provision of an alternative basis for legitimate authority to those of tradition and hereditary right. But an essential component of any developed bourgeois ideology is the proposition that success in society is precisely a consequence of merit, effort, hard work, etc., and that such success does indeed depend upon a man's activity or cleverness. The strength of Milton's theory of election is that it provides not just an alternative basis for legitimate authority, but one that is quite specifically meritocratic. Nor is Engels right to describe English revolutionary ideology as in general Calvinist. During the revolutionary period itself Calvinistic Presbyterianism on the Scottish model became the rallying point for the more conservative Presbyterian party, against which the Revolutionary Independents were to define themselves.[53] It was Milton's own theory of political elitism rather than any notion of predestination which most effectively legitimated the revolutionary seizure of power.

Our third major category was that of *freedom from passion*. The theme of a radical opposition between reason and passion is present in almost all of Milton's prose writings and informs each of the three longer poems. The notion underlies much of the argument, for example, in the divorce pamphlets. Milton's ideal marriage was one in which passion is subordinated to reason: 'a meet and happy conversation', he wrote, 'is the chiefest and noblest end of marriage'.[54] A marriage satisfactory only to the passions is 'therefore no marriage'[55] and should end only in divorce. Here the disposition to see sexual passion as passion *par excellence* is characteristically Puritan. But this struggle between reason and passion reappears in the more expressly political writings and there passion receives broader definition. When Milton seeks to distinguish tyranny from just government in *The Tenure of Kings and Magistrates* he does so in terms of whether the ruler is motivated by reason or by passion: a tyrant is thus one whose government is determined by 'his own brute will and pleasure'.[56] This is only one example of a much more general mode of argument: for Milton all political error, all political disaster, indeed all political opposition to the views of his own party, became explicable in terms of the triumph of pas-

---

53 The religious Independents did formally adopt the predestinarian doctrine at the Savoy Conference of 1658. But there were many amongst their number firmly opposed to it. John Goodwin, perhaps the most famous of the Independent divines, was most certainly an Arminian opponent of Calvinism (Yule 1958, p. 13). The party in Parliament included Baptists, theists and Erastians (Yule 1958, pp. 84–127).
54 Milton 1848, Vol. III, p. 187.
55 Milton 1848, Vol. III, p. 332.
56 Milton 1848, Vol. II, p. 13.

sion over reason. His verdict on Charles I that 'had his reason mastered him as it ought, and not been mastered long ago by his sense and humour ... perhaps he would have made no difficulty'[57] is thus typical. Many have been repelled by the viciousness of Milton's polemics against his opponents. But this is no mere stylistic detail, the product of a simple callousness of mind on Milton's part. Rather, it follows necessarily from the general rationalist assumption that human behaviour can only be explained in terms of factors internal to the individual human personality and from the assumption specific to the Revolutionary Independents that their own programme represented the embodiment of reason. The latter is surely unsurprising in the context of bloody civil war and revolution. Milton's ultimate explanation of the Restoration in *Paradise Lost* as an effect of the nation's decline from virtue and reason is already prefigured in the *Defensio Secunda*:

> unless that liberty which is of such a kind as arms can neither procure nor take away, which alone is the fruit of piety, of justice, of temperance, and unadulterated virtue, shall have taken deep root in your minds and hearts, there will not be one wanting who will snatch from you by treachery what you have acquired by arms.[58]

In this way all rationalisms ultimately collapse the socio-political world into the problems of individual psychology.

We turn now to what is almost certainly my most contentious point: that Milton's rationalism is logically *atheistic*. The central problem of all theologies is essentially that of establishing the correct relationship between God and humanity. However, if ever the tension between God and humankind is liquidated, then no such relationship remains possible. This, I would argue, is precisely what happens in Milton. For Milton, the deity is, above all, an impersonal 'Reason' rather than a personal God, and reason itself not so much divinely revealed as discernible to the rational inquiring mind. This particular notion of reason permits Milton's profoundly non-fundamentalist approach to the problem of scriptural interpretation.[59] It is a common criticism of *Paradise*

---

57 Milton 1848, Vol. I, p. 399.
58 Milton 1848, Vol. I, p. 295.
59 In fact Milton subjects Christianity itself to the critical light of reason. He rejects the doctrine of the trinity as offering 'violence to reason' (Milton 1848, Vol. IV, p. 86), the notion of transubstantiation as incompatible 'with reason and common sense' (Milton 1848, Vol. IV, p. 415) and the Biblical teachings on divorce as 'different and strange from the light of reason' (Milton 1848, Vol. III, p. 365).

Lost that, whereas the portrait of Satan is full-blooded and convincing, that of God never comes to life. And the reason for this is that the God of Milton's theology is equally unimpressive. His attempt at a proof for the existence of God is particularly revealing. We should note that Milton does not argue simply that we should believe, that we should obey, that God exists and that is all there is to it. Rather, he is concerned to demonstrate that God must exist in order that the truth of other necessary propositions be secured: namely, the notion of the world as orderly, of that order as essentially morally beneficent and of morality as a non-relative objective absolute.[60] The authoritative voice of religion, the imperative command to believe and to prostrate oneself in the face of the unknowable, is here entirely absent. Milton's God is a logically necessary construct, an abstraction whose function is to justify those other conceptions which are actually central to the poet's belief-system.

The emptiness of this God becomes apparent whenever Milton attempts any further analysis. As is well known, Milton's anti-trinitarianism led him to distinguish sharply between the three persons of the Christian trinity. God the Father is characterised primarily by an extreme lack of definition: 'WONDERFUL, and INCOMPREHENSIBLE',[61] he is very little else. In Milton's particular version of materialism he does admittedly play a peculiarly passive role as the stuff out of which the universe was originally made.[62] But thereafter God the Father is barely active within the universe. The Holy Spirit fares even worse at Milton's hands. The relevant chapter in *De Doctrina Christiana* contains little more than an embarrassed account of how little we know about this mysterious entity.[63] Elsewhere the Spirit performs only one significant role in Milton's system, that is as the force or power which illuminates the individual reason. The notion of God as agency within this world enters into Miltonic theology at only one point: the active role of the deity is taken by God the Son. The real significance of the Son as Christ is, however, that he is continuously incarnated into the elect, that is into real people actually present in the world: 'Believers are said TO BE INGRAFTED IN CHRIST', wrote Milton, 'when they are planted in Christ by God the Father, that is, are made partakers of Christ'.[64] Moreover, Christ's own specific intervention into the world has resulted, as we have seen, in the creation of that Christian liberty by which the elect is freed from subservience to the rule of law. The logic of the argument is that God can only be

---

60 Milton 1848, Vol. IV, pp. 14–15.
61 Milton 1848, Vol. IV, p. 29.
62 Milton 1848, Vol. IV, pp. 177–8.
63 Milton 1848, Vol. IV, pp. 150–69.
64 Milton 1848, Vol. IV, p. 342.

present in the world as an active principle through the medium of the free wills of the individual members of the elect. As another revolutionary from another century would neatly observe: 'Cromwell and his "holy" troops considered the realisation of divine commands to be the true end, but in reality the latter were merely the ideological conditions for the construction of bourgeois society'.[65]

4 Reason Embattled

Thus far we have outlined the structure of the Miltonic world vision as it developed in the years of struggle and of triumph. We turn now to the problematic of reason embattled and to a direct analysis of the three longer poems. It should be emphasised, however, that the Restoration effects a transformation not of the central categories of the rationalist world vision themselves but rather of their specific conjunctural organisation. The defeated rationalists were faced with a new problem, that of developing an adequate response to the triumph of un-reason over reason. This entailed both for Milton and for the ex-Independents as a whole a reorganisation of the central rationalist categories so as to focus their attention upon the specific problem of defeat. As I suggested earlier, two main responses were possible, the one *personal* and individualist, the other *political* and historical. Each of the last poems has as its central object the problem of defeat, either actual or potential, and each of these responses are there articulated.

In general, it is possible to observe a certain correlation between rationalist ethics, moral didacticism in art and a sustained capacity for the rational and logical organisation of artistic materials. And this particular combination is most certainly evident in Milton's longer poems. Milton's own account of the moral purpose of *Paradise Lost* is given in its opening invocation of the muse. But it should be emphasised that this introduction to *Paradise Lost* is almost equally applicable to the two later poems. Each of the three works is concerned admittedly in very different ways 'to justify the ways of God to men'.[66] The high argument broached in the opening lines of *Paradise Lost* thus reaches its final conclusion only at the end of *Samson Agonistes*. If each of the three poems is directed to the same purpose, then it should be apparent that each is premised upon the same problem, that of an apparent injustice in the ways of God. And the reasons for this are not difficult to discern. When Milton had sought to

---

65 Trotsky 1973b, p. 117.
66 *PL* I: 26.

prove the existence of God he had specifically argued from the evidence of the world as orderly and from the notion that the ordering principle in question must be morally beneficent. But with the Restoration the moral benevolence of the universal order was suddenly thrown into doubt. For Milton it became imperative to seek out a new justification and to explain the specific problem of the defeat of the godly party. It is this concrete social and political problem which poses the general moral problem that constitutes the central preoccupation of the three longer poems. Milton's capacity for logical and rational organisation in the practice of his literary art, his 'sense of structure' to use Eliot's phrase,[67] is the formal counterpart to the moral didacticism operative at the thematic level. The rational character of Milton's poetry is perhaps its most distinctive feature and has certainly been the source of much twentieth-century hostility. His epic style is indeed in a sense 'artificial',[68] but is nonetheless very far from mere 'art for art's sake'. Neither mimetic nor aestheticist, Milton's epic verse sets up a specifically literary form of deliberate artifice as a vehicle for politico-ethical critique. The parallel in our own century is with the Brechtian epic theatre rather than the Lukácsian socialist realist novel.

Generally, Milton's modern apologists have sought to reject the strictures of organicist aesthetics by pointing to the demands of the epic and tragic literary genres within which he had chosen to work. But the problem remains as to why Milton chose these particular classical models. It might prove valuable here to consider the young Lukács's suggestive remarks on the nature of the epic form in the earlier chapters of *The Theory of the Novel* and their possible relevance to an analysis of Milton's *Paradise Lost*. The classical epic, argued Lukács, 'gives form to the extensive totality of life'[69] actually present in the social reality of the 'integrated civilisations' of classical antiquity. By contrast, the novel is in Lukács's view the epic of a detotalised age in which the only conceivable totality is a postulated aim rather than a self-evident given. Significantly, however, Lukács finds in Dante's verse a notable exception to this over-all schema. Dante's epic, he argues, is 'architectural' rather than 'organic' and has as its organising principle a hierarchy of fulfilled postulates attained through a present actually experienced transcendence of reality quite different from both the postulate-free organic nature of the Homeric epic and the world of unfulfilled postulates which structures the modern novel.[70] Much of Lukács's

---

67 Eliot 1968, p. 38.
68 Eliot 1968, p. 12.
69 Lukács 1971a, p. 46.
70 Lukács 1971a, pp. 68–9.

account of Dante seems almost equally applicable to Milton's own epic: *Paradise Lost* postulates its own achieved realised transcendence of the rift between meaning and life. Such transcendence was possible even as late as the seventeenth century, we may infer, if only because the detotalisation that would eventually give birth to the novel form was in fact a product not so much of modernity *per se* as of developed capitalism. The early modern revolutionary-bourgeois idea had never been that of the thoroughly detotalised capitalist social order which would eventually emerge, but of a newly integrated society, albeit one integrated by a series of invisible hands. Nonetheless, Milton's epic is not that fully realised synthesis of the classical epic and the novel into the *epopoeia* which Lukács recognised in Dante. The Miltonic transcendence is achieved with difficulty and then only partly so: it has to be strained for, constantly asserted and reasserted. Hence, Milton's repeated interventions into his own argument so as to point the reader to the real message of the poem. This strain which runs through the whole of *Paradise Lost* attests to the peculiar poignancy of Milton's own particular historical location. For Milton's was the precise moment at which the feudal system collapsed and the new bourgeois social order came into being. The postulated transcendence was thus immanent in the new social forms but nonetheless not an idealisation of any existing social forms. Furthermore, the specific conjuncture of the Restoration colours the entire epic adventure. The postulated transcendence is strained for against all the odds, against the immediate background of colossal defeat. The achievement is astonishing; it is barely remarkable that it is flawed.

How, then, are we to read *Paradise Lost*? The poem's obvious theme is that of the Fall. In the poem itself there is a twofold fall, that of the angels and that of the first humans. But these are only case studies of a wider problem, that of the fall-in-general. Let us consider the general structural characteristics of this latter problem. As a starting point consider the nature of the beings who inhabit Milton's epic universe. All of his creatures, both people and angels, both fallen and unfallen, partake of the same essential nature. The highest common factor in this underlying affinity is *individuality of personality*. Milton's constructed epic is quite unlike the classical Homeric epic in that it permits a very real development of character and of individual personality.[71] And if both angels and

---

71 The most obvious example is Satan. The famous soliloquy at the beginning of Book IX is entirely non-epic in its deliberate revelation of the mind of Satan; it is reminiscent of Shakespeare rather than of Homer (PL IX: 99–178). But Adam, Eve, to a lesser extent the Son of God and also the leading angels and devils all provide examples of individualised and interiorised personality.

humans possess a common individuality, they are both equally honoured with the gift of rationality, they are all 'creatures rational'.[72] For in Milton's system the notion of individuality necessarily implies the notion of a corresponding rationality and free will. Thus the moral destinies of the poem's protagonists are the outcome of processes which are essentially internal and volitional rather than external and deterministic. At first sight this moral individualism might appear to stand in sharp contrast to the hierarchical nature of Milton's epic cosmos. For this world of angels and devils, of men and women, is subject to a process of very clear social stratification. But, as we noted in our discussion of the prose writings, Miltonic individualism results in a meritocratic rather than egalitarian conception of social order. Bourgeois individualism challenges not the inegalitarianism *per se* of feudalism but rather its non-meritocratic basis. And Milton's Heaven and Hell are both organised according to thoroughly bourgeois principles: the Son of God and Satan have each achieved their respective eminence 'by merit'.[73]

The world of *Paradise Lost* is, then, a world of discrete rational individuals each in possession of free will hierarchically ordered according to the principle of promotion according to merit. The only exception to this rule is to be found in the character of God. Theologically Milton's God was not so much a particular personage standing by merit at the top of the cosmological hierarchy as an abstract principle transcending that hierarchy altogether. Here we come to what is widely recognised as the poem's central weakness: even Milton's most charitable critics have found his anthropomorphic rendering of the deity profoundly unsatisfactory. In general, God's appearances are necessitated by the demand for some authoritative exposition of the poem's theology, the effect of which is to render him obsessively preoccupied with his own defence. This failure arises for the very interesting reason that the God in which Milton actually believes is not so much a person as an abstract principle. He is law, he is reason, he is the first cause and in all these respects he is necessarily impersonal. Thus lines which would seem perfectly acceptable as a summary of the workings of an abstract law become dreadfully unacceptable as the spoken words of a particular omnipotent person.[74] Why, then, did Milton so personal-

---

72 *PL* II: 498.
73 *PL* III: 309; *PL* II: 5.
74 Consider the lines in which God forbids Adam to eat from the tree of knowledge (*PL* VIII: 329–30). There God warns that if Adam does eat he will 'inevitably' die. In the mouth of a personal God these lines appear the product of an arbitrary tyranny of the most brutal and unsympathetic kind. For if God is an omnipotent person, then this inevitability follows on

ise his own impersonal God? The answer lies in the original Biblical myth itself. For whatever rationalised theology Milton might have subscribed to, the God of the Old Testament stubbornly remains a person rather than a principle, a king rather than a law. In consequence the God of *Paradise Lost* appears an unfortunate hybrid: a Biblical personage mouthing sentiments which do justice to Milton's theology, that is, to his conception of the ways of God, but which nonetheless fail to justify the person of God to men.

Thus far we have discussed the various beings that inhabit Milton's epic universe, both those who stand and those who fall. But in what does the fall itself consist? In the Biblical myth the fall is twofold: it is firstly disobedience *per se*; and secondly and more specifically the search for hidden knowledge. Milton attempts to reconstruct the myth, however, so that its central theme becomes the conflict between reason and passion. The rationalism of Milton's new reading of the Biblical myth is most clearly exemplified in the fall of the angels. The exchange between Abdiel and Satan at the beginning of Book VI is here extremely significant. In Abdiel's reply to Satan[75] is contained almost the whole of Milton's theory of politics: the doctrine that God and Nature are essentially one and that divine commands thereby conform to the laws of nature and reason; a meritocratic theory of government in which just government is seen as that of the worthy over the unworthy, servitude obedience to the tyranny of the unworthy; finally and most significantly, the recognition that the tyrant Satan is himself unfree insofar as he remains enthralled to his passions. In Milton's version the fall of the angels arises from the subordination of their reason to the dictates of the passion of pride. The fall of humankind is similarly restructured. It is neither disobedience nor, still less, the search for forbidden knowledge which precipitates this second fall, but rather a second triumph of passion over reason. Thus Raphael's final warning to Adam at the end of Book VIII contains by implication something very close to a summary of the new Miltonic theory of the fall:

> ... take heed lest passion sway
> Thy judgement to do aught which else free will
> Would not admit ...[76]

---

only as a consequence of his own arbitrary decision. But Milton intends to imply quite the contrary. The inevitability of Adam's death follows precisely from the impersonality of the laws of reason and nature rather than from any merely personal whim.

75   *PL* VI: 174–81.
76   *PL* VIII: 635–7.

In the attempt to recast this second fall Milton confronted more serious obstacles than with the angels. For, of course, the Biblical myth is here much more specific. Milton's version is clearly asserted both in Raphael's earlier warnings and in Michael's subsequent commentary, which perform the functions of, as it were, a prescript and postscript respectively to the main body of the action. The action itself, however, remains problematic. Saurat's suggestion that the fall is essentially a product of sensuality[77] undoubtedly captured the substance of Milton's intention, the form of the myth the poet would have preferred to have found in *Genesis*. But the Biblical account contains not the slightest hint that this is the case. Given Milton's commitment to the sequence of events presented there, it is barely surprising that a close reading of Book IX, in isolation from the rest of the poem, inevitably leads to the kind of exasperated bewilderment exemplified in John Peter's comment that 'God alone knows why they've fallen'.[78] But such a view is in fact disingenuous. Milton tells us over and over again that they have fallen because they have allowed their passions, specifically their sensuality, to subordinate their reasons. And the general impression of the poem from a total reading only affords impressive confirmation of his success in sustaining this impression. Against the whole weight of the initial Biblical story Milton actually manages to argue the notion that the fall of man is the product of the triumph of passion over reason.

During the angel Michael's account to Adam of the future course of human history, Milton deliberately poses the problem of the fall as a general problem with overtly political implications. The treatment of Nimrod, the world's first tyrant, is particularly telling.[79] Here we learn that those who will fail in the government of themselves will necessarily fall prey to tyrannical government from without. Milton's central conclusion is thus clear: the defeat of the godly and the triumph of unreason over reason, whether acted out in the Garden of Eden or in the England of 1660, is always determined ultimately by the moral failure of the godly themselves. This, then, is Milton's initial explanation for the problem of defeat. But the explanation is not yet a solution. In the last two books of *Paradise Lost*, however, and especially in Book XII, Milton does indeed propose a solution. For here Adam receives from Michael the double pledge of a future time when the earth will be a 'far happier place'[80] than Paradise and of a 'paradise within thee, happier far'[81] permanently and perennially available

---

77   Saurat 1924, pp. 152–5.
78   Peter 1960, p. 137.
79   *PL* XII: 82–101.
80   *PL* XII: 464.
81   *PL* XII: 587.

to the truly good. Here, then, is Milton's own initial reaction to the problem of defeat: a personal defence of reason against unreason combined with the conviction that history will ultimately secure the triumph of reason. The poem's formal conclusion is thus essentially optimistic. Yet this optimism is possible only by way of an extraordinary effort of will and of imagination on Milton's part. Its fusion of meaning and reality can be achieved only at the level of a posited abstract transcendence with no basis in experiential reality. Hence the constructed nature of the entire epic and of its last two books in particular. During the early 1640s Milton had believed in the imminent establishment of the kingdom of the saints; by the early 1660s that prospect had been relegated to the distant future.

In *Paradise Regained*, the epic synthesis attained in *Paradise Lost* collapses into a one-sided emphasis on individual salvation virtually devoid of epic significance. As the full extent of the catastrophe of the Restoration had been brought home to Milton so the imaginative basis of his posited overarching transcendental synthesis became progressively undermined. With the collapse of the poet's epic theme, so too the epic form itself is rendered similarly inaccessible. We find in *Paradise Regained* a poetic theme simply that of personal redemption and a poetic form essentially anti-epic rather than epic. *Paradise Regained* is generally much less admired than *Paradise Lost*. And the reason for this is not too difficult to discern: the quietism of its subject matter demands a literary form almost everything that *Paradise Lost* is not. The earlier poem had borrowed extensively from the main conventions of the Virgilian epic. True, the quietism of Adam and Eve's fortitude in adversity had demanded an explicit rejection of classical epic themes *per se*.[82] But Milton's double concern with universal history and individual redemption had nonetheless permitted their incorporation into the poem as subordinate *motifs*. In *Paradise Regained* this is no longer possible. Its subject is simply that of Christ's personal resistance to Satan's temptations, its central formal organising principle a purely internal movement from one state of mind to another. The poem is literally devoid of almost any action. Saurat suggested that its general mood was one of fatigue.[83] In purely technical terms this is probably not the case. But Milton's quietistic theme is an indication of a more general political fatigue in the revolutionary movement. The collapse of the Commonwealth and the subsequent persecutions of political and religious radicals had so drained English radicalism of its capacity for resistance that quietism appeared the only viable political option.

---

82   *PL* IX: 13–47.
83   Saurat 1924, p. 235.

We have emphasised the marked discontinuity between *Paradise Lost* and *Paradise Regained*. But the elements of continuity are equally significant. Milton's world is still a world of discrete rational *individuals*. Here, however, the quietistic theme demands that the poem be devoted to the characterisation of one individual, Christ himself, rather than a plurality of particular, separate individuals. Milton still adheres to the notion of *meritocracy*. Indeed there is a sense in which *Paradise Regained* is designed to demonstrate the meritocratic entitlement to the Sonship of God only asserted in *Paradise Lost*.[84] Milton remains preoccupied with the dualism between *reason* and *passion*: Christ is clearly intended as an embodiment of reason, Satan of passion. But in the treatment of the various temptations Milton also develops a distinctly new poetic theme best characterised as that of a polarisation between quietism and activism.

Let us consider Milton's handling of the temptation *motif* in a little more detail. Milton's model for the temptation sequence is the Gospel according to St. Luke. In Luke's version three particular temptations are outlined: the temptation to turn stone into bread, the temptation of the kingdoms of the world and the temptation to jump from the pinnacle of the Temple. The relative weight given to the three is interesting: the first takes up two verses, the second four verses, the third again four verses.[85] In *Paradise Regained* these relative weights are significantly altered. There, the first temptation occupies less than fifty lines of verse in Book I[86] and the third only the last 140 lines of the poem.[87] Moreover, the latter is not so much a temptation in Milton's account as the dramatic *dénouement* of all that has gone before. By contrast, the second temptation of the kingdoms of the world is so greatly expanded as to provide the subject matter for the last eighty or so lines of Book II,[88] the whole of Book III and well over a half of Book IV.[89] The second specifically political temptation provides the main subject matter for *Paradise Regained*.

Here, an underlying structural opposition between reason and passion is augmented by a sustained dialogue between Christ and Satan as to the relative merits and demerits of political activism. In part, Satan does venture an appeal to Christ's passions: wealth, power and glory if desired for their own sake would be the objects of a passionate rather than a rational striving. Satan offers these

---

84   *PR* I: 163–7.
85   *St Luke* 4: 3–4, 5–8, 9–12.
86   *PR* I: 314–56.
87   *PR* IV: 499–639.
88   *PR* II: 404–86.
89   *PR* IV: 1–393.

gifts, however, not as valuable in themselves, but as means to desirable political ends.[90] Milton is no opponent of political activism *per se*. Indeed, he is extremely careful to establish the legitimate nature of political concerns: well before Satan raises the question of politics Christ himself recalls his own youthful aspiration 'To rescue Israel from the Roman yoke'.[91] Why, then, should Christ not accept Satan's assistance in the pursuit of such perfectly moral political goals as his own entirely valid title to the government of Israel? Christ's reply to this particular temptation is extremely significant. The outcome of such matters, he argues, rests in God's hands rather than men's.[92] Here, Milton's Christ captures the patient stoicism of the Quaker-quietist response to the Restoration. But, unlike the Quakers, Milton refuses to abandon politics altogether. His rejection of the kingdoms of the world is much more conditional and much less absolute than that sustained by the followers of George Fox. For Milton, quietism is evidently a tactic rather than a strategy. As such, it is open to the objection that the political iniquity to which it counterposes itself is so immediately pressing as to demand an immediate political response. Satan raises this objection forcefully when he offers Christ, by turn, the thrones of Parthia and of imperial Rome itself. In each case Satan is particularly insistent as to the dire state of the oppressed peoples.[93] Milton's solution to the problem consists on each occasion in a discrete shift from the political to the psychological and the ethical. Neither the captive tribes nor the Romans are worthy of political liberation since they are each morally responsible for their own plight.[94] Political activism can be postponed because the political problem is not so much primary as derivative, a consequence of the more fundamental problem of internal moral collapse. The ethical preconditions for political liberation must first be established before political activism can be considered a legitimate enterprise and political quietism is thus justified wherever these preconditions are absent. There can be little doubt that Milton diagnosed such an absence not only in the body politic of the first century Roman Empire but also in that of Restoration England. The needs of the early Restoration period demanded above all in Milton's view the virtues of fortitude and resilience, faith and hope. In the myth of the second temptation, he had discerned a literary theme which would permit this ritual exorcism of his earlier political and intellectual concerns in favour of a new preoccupation with the politics of quietism.

---

90   *PR* II: 412; *PR* III: 175–6.
91   *PR* I: 217.
92   *PR* III: 188–95.
93   *PR* III: 374–80; *PR* IV: 90–102.
94   *PR* III: 3427–31; *PR* IV: 143–5.

By the time *Paradise Regained* was published along with *Samson Agonistes* in 1671 the failure of the counter-revolution to put back the clock to 1640 must have become apparent. Clarendon's impeachment in 1667 had been a portent of things to come; in the years that followed, the Restoration monarchy would stumble from crisis to crisis. It is impossible to determine the precise point at which Milton himself came to the conclusion that all was not lost. But in *Samson Agonistes* the old revolutionary returned to more overtly political concerns. Just as *Paradise Lost* is a genuine epic, so too *Samson Agonistes* is a genuine tragedy. Here, the earlier dual concern with personal morality and historical destiny reappears, but in the process it is radically transformed. Lukács's account of the evolution of classical Greek thought from epic to tragedy is relevant. The epic, he argued, had posed the question 'how can life become essential?', but as essence becomes divorced from life and located at a level beyond life, so tragedy poses the new question 'how can essence come alive?'[95] The epic unity of life and meaning achieved in *Paradise Lost*, albeit through the non-classical means of a posited transcendence, is no longer possible. Rather, *Samson Agonistes* is premised on the assumption of a rift between meaning and life, but a rift which is nonetheless bridgeable. Samson's problem is the classically tragic problem of restoring meaning to life, of actualising essence. Milton's change in form is thus determined by the shift in his overall conception of the world and the strict formal classicism of his tragedy derives from the strictly dramatic nature of his concerns. Thus, the transcendental epic synthesis of the particular and the universal attained in *Paradise Lost* is finally superseded by the new dramatic synthesis embodied in *Samson Agonistes*.

How, then, does Milton's tragedy articulate this new and later synthesis between the particular and the universal? The elements of continuity between *Paradise Lost* and *Paradise Regained* clearly persist into *Samson Agonistes*. Once again Milton is pre-eminently concerned with the characterisation of *individual personality*: Samson's own inner development provides the central focus of interest for *Samson Agonistes* just as that of Christ had for *Paradise Regained*. But in the later work the poem's protagonist is a 'world-historical individual', a concretely human embodiment of a wider socio-historical collision, rather than a merely abstract individual extracted from any wider social context. Whilst the ultimate development of Samson's individuality is in a sense immanent within his own previously defined identity, that immanence is only actualised as a consequence of a series of interactions with other human personalities. Thus, Samson's inner moral strength both determines and is

---

95   Lukács 1971a, pp. 34–6.

determined by the outcome of the major incidents in the poem. *Samson Agonistes* attests too to Milton's persistent attachment to the notion of *meritocracy*. Milton's tragedy is surely the meritocratic tragedy *par excellence*: Samson earns both his previous defeat at the hands of the Philistines and his subsequent victory over them. Again, the poem is structured around the ethical and political implications of an ontological dualism between *reason* and *passion*. Political defeat has been the direct result of a specifically sexual passion on Samson's part and, as the poem develops, he will be obliged to demonstrate a new imperviousness to the claims of such passion to himself, to his God, to the poem's other characters and so too to the reader.

Of the three longer poems *Samson Agonistes* offers most clearly and concretely a politico-historical solution to the problem of the triumph of unreason. The theme of the personal solution does not disappear, but here Samson's individual redemption is indissolubly linked to the political solution of the overthrow of the Philistines. Moreover, the action is firmly situated within the context of a concrete historical situation. *Samson Agonistes* is, as it were, an account of the fall made specific. Once more the source of the fall lies in the triumph of passion over reason and once more the decision to succumb to passion has been freely made.[96] From the very beginning Samson is fully aware of all this. Indeed, he appears at the opening of the poem in precisely that pose of repentant obedience and patient quietism which had in *Paradise Regained* appeared to Milton the only possible response to the defeat of reason. If Samson's own voice is here the voice of self-rebuke, if Samson himself is capable of an immediate justification of the ways of God, the voice of the Chorus is much less certain. Throughout the poem the Chorus functions so as to emphasise Samson's past virtue and to bewail his present fate, thus implicitly at least casting doubt on the justice of his present situation.[97] It is by no means immediately clear which of these voices can be considered more nearly that of the poet himself. In terms of the moral universe of *Paradise Regained* Samson's initial stance is clearly superior to that of the Chorus. But in *Samson Agonistes* this quietistic virtue is itself exposed to criticism. The Chorus's doubts are thus in a sense the doubts of the poem, their problem is Milton's problem and the poem's development is designed to provide its solution. This solution will entail a turn from quietism to activism. For the Milton of *Samson Agonistes* quietism and patient fortitude were no longer in themselves sufficient: Samson at the beginning of the poem is not yet truly heroic, but merely submissive to the blind

---

96   *SA*: 46–51.
97   *SA*: 667–70.

decrees of fate. In the development from *Paradise Regained* to *Samson Agonistes* the figure of the quietistic hero had been rotated in the light of Milton's vision and in the later work it displays the different and far less attractive face of fatalism.

How, then, does Milton effect this transition from quietism to activism? Dr Johnson's view that *Samson Agonistes* had a beginning and an end but no middle is well known. If Samson's state of mind at the opening of the poem, his admission of blame and acknowledgement of divine justice, were in themselves sufficient psychological preconditions for his ultimate act of heroism, then Johnson would be correct. But the middle of the poem consists precisely in the process by which Samson's personality is reconstructed so as to prepare him for the final encounter with the Philistines. That which is reconstructed is above all his martial vigour. In this respect it is the encounter with the Philistine warrior Harapha, rather than that with Dálila, which provides the poem with its key structural linkage between beginning and ending. Significantly, Harapha alone of the poem's leading characters does not appear in the original Biblical myth.[98] The dramatic function of Samson's exchange with Dálila is self-evident. If Samson betrayed reason to sexual passion in betraying the secret of his strength to Dálila, then he must now provide some firm proof of his future imperviousness. And so he does.[99] But this personal victory is no longer a sufficient answer to the problem of unreason triumphant. It still remains for the encounter with Harapha to demonstrate that Samson has reattained his own martial courage. The Christ of *Paradise Regained* could suffer and obey. But Samson must do more: Samson must act. In *Paradise Regained*, Christ had rejected the possibility of political action on the grounds that an internally unfree people deserve only an external tyranny. In *Samson Agonistes*, Samson proclaims the right and duty of the elect to resist such tyranny whatever the moral state of the people at large.[100] In the late 1660s and the early 1670s the ghosts of the Interregnum were beginning once more to walk the land.

In the poem's tragic *dénouement*, Samson's act of self-sacrifice achieves the destruction of the Philistine enemy. A subsequent commentary by the Chorus pointedly contrasts the Philistines 'only set on sport and play'[101] with the Israelite hero physically blind but nonetheless with 'inward eyes illuminated'.[102] Samson, the embodiment of reason and of an active virtue which knows no

---

98   *Judges* 13–16, esp. 16: 18–31.
99   *SA*: 932–5.
100 *SA*: 1211–17.
101 *SA*: 1679.
102 *SA*: 1689.

external tyranny, destroys the Philistine lords, whose presence here clearly symbolises that fusion of political despotism with psychological subservience to the passions which had provided perhaps the single most potent image in the whole of Milton's political thought. Thus the ageing revolutionary reasserted the possibility of political activism and indeed of political victory. Paradoxically, Milton's great tragedy is much less genuinely tragic than *Paradise Lost*: where Adam merely receives the formal promise of personal and political redemption, Samson concretely attains both. Hence, *Samson Agonistes*'s markedly optimistic conclusion, which stands in sharp contrast to the mournful tone of the last two lines of *Paradise Lost*.[103] Milton's earlier conception of history as a simple process of transition from tyranny to the free kingdom of the saints is thus finally superseded by a much more complex conception incorporating the possibilities of defeat and setback, but nonetheless retaining at its core both the major rationalist categories themselves and a conception of historical progress. In his last speech Samson's father Manoa reassures the Chorus thus:

> Come, come, no time for lamentation now
> Nor much more cause; Samson hath quit himself
> Like Samson, and heroicly hath finished
> A life heroic ...[104]

So too Milton had quit himself like Milton. He died in November 1674, three years after the publication of *Samson Agonistes* and only four before Titus Oates's denunciation of the Popish Plot. Barred from Westminster Abbey by his republicanism, he was buried in Cripplegate in the heart of old revolutionary London. Fourteen years later almost to the day the Stuart monarchy came crashing down in its own suitably ignoble ending.

The 1688 Settlement finally secured a political system which would permit the relatively unfettered development of English capitalism. Incidentally, however, this so-called 'Glorious Revolution' also ensured an apparently indefinite prolongation of the constitutional forms taken by the original class compromise of 1660. I have argued that Revolutionary Independency represented the most class-conscious sections of the mid-seventeenth-century English bourgeoisie, those most prepared to overthrow the absolutist state machine and establish a thoroughgoing bourgeois republic. During the political strug-

---

103   *SA*: 1721–4; *PL* XII: 648–9.
104   *SA*: 1708–11.

gles against Royalism and Presbyterianism, the Independents evolved into something quite close to a Sartrean fused group possessed of something equivalently close to a Goldmannesque world vision, a specifically English and Protestant version of rationalism. Subsequently, the political failure of the Independent enterprise gave rise to two modifications in that vision designed so as to cope with the problem of defeat. Each of these stages in the evolution of the Independent world vision is articulated in Milton's work. Most importantly, *Paradise Lost* and *Samson Agonistes* achieve a synthesis of personal and historical responses to the problem of defeat in which the Protestant rationalist world vision attains a peculiar coherency. There exists, then, something very much akin to what Goldmann would have termed a structural homology between the world vision of Revolutionary Independency, the social situation of the mid-seventeenth-century English bourgeoisie and the writings of John Milton. The 1688 Settlement ensured that this English rationalism was to be effectively stillborn. As the English bourgeoisie turned to gradualism, so it adopted an empiricist world vision and so too it came to renounce its own revolutionary origins. The Revolution itself, its rationalistic world vision and its great poet were all rendered progressively unassimilable to subsequent notions of England and Englishness. The combined effects of the Stuart Restoration and Glorious Revolution have thus cast a surprisingly long shadow. Jameson reminds us that the cultural past can be re-enacted only if its apparently long-dead issues are 'retold within the unity of a great collective story ... if ... they are seen as sharing a single fundamental theme ... the collective struggle to wrest a realm of Freedom from a realm of Necessity'.[105] Such has been my primary purpose in this particular retelling. But though the collective struggles of the present can indeed be brought to bear on the long-dead issues of seventeenth-century republicanism, hopefully the converse might also prove to be the case. There is still much unfinished business from the English Revolution and much still to be learnt from its poet. That too has been part of the purpose of my retelling.

---

105   Jameson 1981, p. 19.

CHAPTER 4

On the Beach: Apocalyptic Hedonism and the Origins of Postmodernism*

During 1990 and 1991 Mandarin Paperbacks released a new edition of the novels of Nevil Shute. Among the first lot of six titles was *On the Beach*,[1] the front cover of which proudly proclaimed it 'The Great Australian Novel of Our Time'. This is a judgement which finds very little echo in university English Literature departments, whether in Australia or in England. And yet there is an important sense in which it asserts little more than a commonplace: when judged by the criteria of the marketplace, *On the Beach* is indeed precisely *the* great Australian novel of our time. It was first published in 1957, by Heinemann simultaneously in Melbourne, London and Toronto,[2] and by Morrow in New York. The novel had two printings in 1957, a third in 1958 and a fourth in 1959. Subsequent reprintings followed regularly, the title remaining more or less continuously in print thereafter. The Mandarin edition was itself reprinted in 1992. In 1984 there had even been a large print edition.[3] In 1978, the UNESCO *Statistical Yearbook* would show Shute as the 133rd most translated author in the world: there had been 96 translations of his work during the period 1961–5 and 22 in 1973 alone.[4] The vast majority of these must have been of either *A Town Like Alice*[5] or *On the Beach*. Certainly, the first full-length study of Shute's work, written with the active cooperation of his family, records that *On the Beach* 'quickly became his greatest financial and critical success'.[6] The United Artists film version, a 'solid prestige job',[7] appeared in 1959. Directed by Stanley Kramer, it ran for over two hours (134 minutes!) and starred Gregory Peck as Dwight Towers, the commander of the American submarine, the *USS Scorpion*, and Ava Gardner and Fred Astaire somewhat improbably as the main

---

* This chapter has been published previously in *Australian Studies*, Vol. 7, pp. 190–204, 1993.
1 Shute 1990.
2 Shute 1957.
3 Shute 1984.
4 UNESCO 1978, p. 915.
5 Shute 1950.
6 Smith 1976, p. 133.
7 Walker 1991, p. 815.

Australian characters, Moira Davidson and John Osborne. Filming actually began near Shute's home at Langwarrin, about thirty miles south of Melbourne, and continued in or near Melbourne during the spring of 1958. At a time when the Australian cinema industry had itself fallen into near-complete decrepitude, 'the presence of a major motion picture company spending millions of dollars was a sensation generating ... massive public curiosity'.[8] The film was widely perceived as the most important thing to happen to Melbourne since the Olympic Games, and some might add that it still appears thus. In short, *On the Beach* became a major local and international cultural event, what we might today term a 'blockbuster'.

Set largely in and around Melbourne during the second year after a full-scale nuclear war, the novel's subject matter was nothing less than the slow extinction of the last affluent remains of the human race. When Shute had first broached with Heinemann the matter of a cover design, he had suggested 'a scene of the main four or five characters standing together quite cheerfully highlighted on a shadowy beach of a shadowy river – the Styx'.[9] Sophisticated critical theory has long since given up on idle speculation about authorial intentions. But were we so to indulge, we might well find in this juxtaposition between light and shade, cheerfulness and death, a concise and economical representation of what Shute himself had apparently intended as a central organising principle of the novel: *On the Beach* derives much of its power from what I will term its 'apocalyptic hedonism', that is, from the peculiar *frisson* of a textual erotics deriving from the simultaneous juxtaposition of the terrors of imminent extinction and the delights of hedonistic affluence. The novel opens with a young Australian naval officer, Peter Holmes, still sore from a day spent partly on the beach and partly sailing, drowsily recalling the Christmas barbecue of two days earlier.[10] The 'short, bewildering war ... of which no history ... ever would be written'[11] is introduced into this almost quintessentially Australian idyll at exactly the moment when Holmes and his wife, Mary, are planning to meet at their club and to go on for a swim.[12] It closes with Towers and Davidson, he aboard the *Scorpion* heading south from the Heads, she ashore near Port Lonsdale, and an analogous, though now much darker juxtaposition, that between the bottle of brandy and the Government-issue sui-

---

8   Smith 1976, p. 138.
9   Smith 1976, p. 129.
10 Shute 1990, p. 7.
11 Shute 1990, pp. 9–10.
12 Shute 1990, p. 9.

cide tablets,[13] between the 'big car' with 'plenty of petrol in the tank'[14] and the nuclear submarine. Similar motifs recur throughout: Osborne's new red Ferrari, for example, 'washed and polished with loving care',[15] and his enthusiastic pursuit of what must be the very last Australian Grand Prix; his Uncle Douglas's sturdy determination to work through the Pastoral Club's wine cellar – 'we've got over three thousand bottles of vintage port left in the cellars ... and only about six months left to go, if what you scientists say is right';[16] or the fishing trip on the Jamieson River[17] made possible by a Government decision to bring forward the trout season 'for this year only'.[18]

Asked her opinion of Melbourne, Ava Gardner is reputed to have judged it unusually well suited to a movie about the end of the world. Apocryphal or not, the remark has provoked much subsequent amusement in Sydney and equivalent umbrage in Melbourne. And yet Gardner was absolutely right: both Australia and Melbourne were indeed ideal locations for a film or a book about the end of the world. Which takes me elliptically from one blockbuster to another, to what Meaghan Morris describes as contemporary cultural theory's 'own version of cinema's blockbuster: the state-of-the-globe, state-of-the-arts, Big Speculation',[19] that is, to postmodernism. *On the Beach* was, of course, a determinedly 'popular' work, neither modernist nor postmodernist in form. But in its apocalyptic hedonism, at least, Shute's novel importantly prefigures much of what has become characteristic of contemporary postmodern sensibility. Like all blockbusters, postmodernist cultural theory derives its success in part from a capacity to appeal to as wide an audience as possible, high philosophy in the art house cinemas of the academy and middlebrow multi-screen literary criticism as much as local fleapit sociology. If not exactly meaning all things to all people, the term very obviously signifies differently within different discourses: in short, it is as polysemic a sign as they come. An apparently enduring postmodern trope, however, is that of 'being after'. '*Post*modernism', writes Ferenc Fehér, 'like many of its conceptual brethren ... understand themselves not in terms of what they are but in terms of what they come after'.[20] But after what? After modernism certainly, after modernity perhaps, and crucially

---

13 Shute 1990, p. 316.
14 Shute 1990, p. 314.
15 Shute 1990, p. 151.
16 Shute 1990, p. 102.
17 Shute 1990, pp. 273–83.
18 Shute 1990, p. 232.
19 Morris 1988, p. 242.
20 Fehér 1990, p. 87.

also after 'the War'. For the generations that would eventually attempt to theorise these many and varied postmodern conditions had grown up in a world that considered itself quite decisively 'postwar'. Here, surely, is the trope *in initio*: to quote Meaghan Morris yet again, 'the postmodern era could be said to begin in 1945, at Hiroshima and Nagasaki'.[21] The Second World War, however, unlike the First, had never been a war to end war: the defeat of the Axis had merely announced the beginnings of the Cold War, itself all too readily imaginable as the prelude to the war that would indeed finally end war, and with it all human life. Postmodernity was thus haunted from its inception by an imminent apprehension of the last days and of the end of things. And yet this was also and simultaneously a prodigiously consumerist economy of affluence, originally confined to the United States, Canada and Australia, later dispersed throughout the West. This was a culture predisposed, then, towards a much more general apocalyptic hedonism than that exhibited in Shute's novel.

Such early datings of the beginnings of 'postmodernity' as Morris's are by no means uncontroversial: the more typical focus in recent cultural theory has fallen on the supposedly more radical transformations of the late 1950s and the early 1960s, as in Fredric Jameson's *Postmodernism, or, The Cultural Logic of Late Capitalism*,[22] or even those of the 1970s and 1980s, as in the analyses of 'New Times' developed by the now defunct British journal *Marxism Today*.[23] These later datings often call attention to quite significant changes within postwar society and culture, for example the rise of the 'new social movements' or the development of new 'post-industrial' technologies. But the more fundamental shift is that registered by Morris, that to a distinctively postwar world, the more general characteristics of which continue to structure our contemporary reality. That shift is peculiarly visible in precisely the 'high cultural' social sub-sector from which the 'postmodernist' debate derives much of its vocabulary. Both modernist high culture in general and the cultural avant-garde in particular were the creations of the great cities of continental Europe – Berlin and Vienna, Moscow and St Petersburg, above all Paris[24] – and as such, they were fated to become direct casualties of the twin totalitarianisms of Nazism and Stalinism. What survived into postwar New York was an increasingly commodified imitation of avant-garde style, increasingly bereft of avant-garde social purpose. This is postmodernism in the most obvious of senses, that of the 'high' culture that survived after modernism, and it is a culture which clearly dates

---

21 Morris 1988, p. 186.
22 Jameson 1991, p. 1.
23 *Marxism Today* 1988.
24 Bradbury 1976.

from the 1940s. This is a 'postmodernism' grudgingly acknowledged by even those most hostile to the notion itself: Alex Callinicos, for example, agrees that the 'postwar stabilization of capitalism left the few still committed to avant-garde objectives beached';[25] Perry Anderson that 'the Second World War ... cut off the vitality of modernism'.[26] And as Jameson nicely observes of the latter, 'whatever Perry Anderson ... thinks of the utility of the period term – postmodernism – his paper demonstrates that ... the conditions of existence of modernism were no longer present. So we are in something else'.[27] This something else is postmodernism. Postmodernism is thus neither a specific type of art nor a specific type of cultural theory nor even a specific type of politics. It is, rather, a particular cultural space available for analysis to many different kinds of contemporary cultural theory and for intervention to many different kinds of contemporary artistic and political practice. The term is best understood, then, as denoting a 'cultural dominant', in Jameson's phrase,[28] or even, in Williams's terms, a 'structure of feeling'.[29] In this sense, Habermas's sustained polemic against the implied neo-conservatism of French poststructuralism[30] can be read as an intervention within postmodernism as much as an argument against it.

Celebratory postmodernism as a major academic event dates from the 1970s, from the first publication of Lyotard's *The Postmodern Condition*, a specifically Canadian text originally prepared for the Conseil des Universitiés of the government of Quebec.[31] For Lyotard, modernism and modernity had been characterised above all by the co-presence of science and of a series of universalising and legitimating metanarratives which ultimately derived fom the Enlightenment. These metanarrative paradigms had run aground, he argued, in the period since the Second World War:

> In contemporary society and culture – postindustrial society, postmodern culture – the ... grand narrative has lost its credibility, regardless of what mode of unification it uses, regardless of whether it is a speculative narrative or a narrative of emancipation.[32]

---

25 Callinicos 1989, p. 60.
26 Anderson 1988, p. 326.
27 Jameson 1988a, p. 359.
28 Jameson 1991, p. 4.
29 Williams 1965, pp. 64–5.
30 Habermas 1985; Habermas 1987a.
31 Lyotard 1979.
32 Lyotard 1984, p. 37.

The postmodern condition's 'incredulity towards metanarratives', whether in aesthetics or science or politics, is for Lyotard in part a consequence of the internal logic of the metanarratives themselves, which proceed from scepticism to pluralism, in part also a correlate of postindustrialism, in which knowledge itself becomes a principal form of production, thereby shifting emphasis 'from the ends of action to its means'.[33] Lyotard's slightly later 'What is Postmodernism?', first published in 1982, recapitulates much of the earlier analysis, despite its, in my view very unhelpful, retreat from the initial attempt at cultural periodisation.[34] Here, the postmodern continues to be understood as that which 'denies itself the solace of good forms, the consensus of a taste which would make it possible to share collectively the nostalgia for the unattainable; that which searches for new representations ... in order to impart a strong sense of the unpresentable'.[35] The postmodern, Lyotard tells us, will 'wage a war on totality', that 'transcendental illusion' of the nineteenth century, the full price of which has proven to be 'terror'.[36]

The term 'postmodern' was by no means an original coinage, however. To the contrary, Lyotard's initial argument is quite deliberately inserted into an already existing North American discourse: as he explained, 'the word *postmodern* ... is in current use on the American continent among sociologists and critics'.[37] One of Lyotard's North American sources was Daniel Bell, whose *The Coming of Post-Industrial Society*[38] figures in the text's very first footnote. Curiously, Lyotard makes no reference to Bell's more specific attempts at a cultural sociology of postmodernism *per se*, especially *The Cultural Contradictions of Capitalism*,[39] which had been published only three years previously, and the even more recent essay, 'Beyond Modernism, Beyond Self'.[40] For Bell, following Lionel Trilling,[41] modernism represented a radically 'adversary culture', opposed not merely to this society but to any and all conceivable societies. As the capitalist economic system had developed, he argued, it had rendered the older Puritan values progressively obsolescent, thereby unleashing an increasingly unrestrained modernism, the simultaneous product of Hobbesian indi-

---

33   Ibid.
34   Lyotard 1984a, p. 79.
35   Lyotard 1984a, p. 81.
36   Lyotard 1984a, pp. 81–2.
37   Lyotard 1984, p. xxiii.
38   Bell 1973.
39   Bell 1976.
40   Bell 1977.
41   Trilling 1967.

vidualism on the one hand, corporate capitalism on the other.[42] The 'postmodernism' of the 1960s – and this is the term Bell actually uses – finally subverts all restraints: 'It is a programme to erase all boundaries, to obliterate any distinction between the self and the external world, between man and woman, subject and object, mind and body'.[43] 'In doctrine and cultural life-style', he concludes, 'the anti-bourgeois has won ... The difficulty in the West ... is that bourgeois society – which in its emphasis on individuality and the self gave rise to modernism – is itself culturally exhausted'.[44]

By and large, Australian cultural criticism has found Lyotard's celebration of the postmodern much more interesting than Bell's indictment. But note their common origins in a specifically North American, rather than European, perception of the postmodern as at once uniquely contemporary and uniquely transgressive. Where Lyotard cries liberty and Bell finds licence, both mean transgression, in the sense of the continuous disturbance and subversion of pre-existing cultural norms. Which leads us to the proposition, firstly, that postmodernism is above all a culture of transgression; and secondly that, whatever the current fashion for French theory, this is a culture which remains peculiarly visible from a New World, extra-European vantage point. Lyotard's various accounts of the postmodern are stories told by a Frenchman it is true, but they are told in the first place to Canadians nonetheless. They are also, no doubt, in themselves grand narratives of dissolution, which bespeak a political and cultural history at once much richer and much more fraught than any endured to date by the European colonies of settlement in North America or Australasia. For Lyotard, modernity is quite specifically European, its transcendental illusion explicitly that of Hegel and Marx, its terror that of Stalin and Hitler. Doubtless, the settler colonies have had their own philosophers and their own terrors: yet theirs has been a different experience from the European, provincial in origin rather than metropolitan, often suburban rather than urban, civilising rather than cultured, terrorising rather than terrorised. This too is a postmodern condition, perhaps the paradigmatically postmodern condition which provides both Bell and Lyotard with their original empirical datum, a condition often named as 'postcolonialism',[45] but better understood, surely, as 'post-imperialism'.

---

42   Bell 1976, pp. 80–1, 84.
43   Bell 1977, p. 243.
44   Bell 1977, pp. 250–2.
45   Ashcroft et al. 1989; During 1990; Adam and Tiffin 1991.

Discounting Lyotard's later conceit that postmodernism is 'modernism ... in the nascent state',[46] we need to define postmodernism in terms of its own difference from a modernism to which it is, if not chronologically then at least logically, subsequent. High modernism can, in turn, best be characterised substantially in terms of its own antithetical relationship not only to bourgeois realism, the predecessor culture, but also to contemporary 'mass', that is, popular culture. It is only in the late nineteenth century that we can observe the more or less simultaneous emergence both of a new modernist high culture and of a new mass popular culture. The new modernism is characterised above all by its aesthetic self-consciousness, by a formalist experimentalism that recurs in painting and drama, poetry and music, the novel and sculpture; the new mass culture by the rapid development of a whole range of technically novel cultural forms each of which is in principle near universally available. Whenever we date the beginnings of modernism, whether from 1890, as does one standard academic text,[47] or from December 1910, as rather more interestingly did Virginia Woolf,[48] there can be no doubt that high modernism and mass culture are indeed contemporaneous. However we may characterise the cultural avant-garde, whether as integral to high modernism, as do Bradbury and McFarlane,[49] or as internally opposed to it, as does Peter Bürger,[50] there can be no doubt that both stand in essentially adversarial relation not only to bourgeois realism but also to mass culture.

Bürger himself argues that bourgeois art consists in a celebration in form of the liberation of art from religion, from the court, and eventually even from the bourgeoisie.[51] Modernist art thus emerges as an autonomous social 'institution', the preserve and prerogative of an increasingly autonomous intellectual class, and thereby necessarily counterposed to other non-autonomous arts. In short, both high modernism and the historical avant-garde ascribe some real redemptive function to high art. And as the historical memory of bourgeois realism recedes, it is hostility to contemporary popular culture in particular which develops into perhaps the most characteristic topos of early to mid-twentieth-century intellectual life. Which returns us to postmodernism. For, however else we might care to characterise the postmodern, there can be little doubt that postmodernist art typically attempts, or at least results from, the

---

46   Lyotard 1984a, p. 79.
47   Bradbury and McFarlane 1976.
48   Woolf 1966, p. 321.
49   Bradbury and McFarlane 1976, p. 29.
50   Bürger 1984, p. 22.
51   Bürger 1984, pp. 46–9.

collapse precisely of this antithesis between high and low, elite and popular. It is this boundary, as much as any other, that is transgressed in postmodern culture. Almost all the available theorisations of postmodernism, whether celebratory or condemnatory, whether or not themselves postmodernist, agree on the centrality of this progressive deconstruction and dissolution of what was once, in Bourdieu's phrase, 'distinction'.[52] Huyssen goes so far as to locate postmodernism quite specifically 'after the great divide' between modernism and mass culture.[53] But even for Bell, postmodernism was a kind of 'porno-pop' which 'overflows the vessels of art ... tears down the boundaries and insists that *acting out*, rather than making distinctions, is the way to gain knowledge'.[54] For Lyotard, the postmodern incredulity towards metanarratives applies not only to the metanarratives of science and politics, but also to that of art as enlightenment. For Baudrillard, postmodernity is characterised by 'the disappearance of aesthetics and higher values in kitsch and hyperreality ... the disappearance of history and the real in the televisual'.[55] For Bürger, postmodernism is initiated essentially by the failure of the historical avant-garde to subvert from within the cultural institutions of high modernism, a failure which results nonetheless in the final loss of criteria for determining the paradigmatic work of art[56] and, hence, in a loss of criteria for distinguishing between art and non-art. For Jameson, postmodernism is above all a kind of aesthetic populism, in which pastiche eclipses parody, constituted within a 'field of stylistic and discursive heterogeneity without a norm', a culture 'fascinated by this whole "degraded" landscape of schlock and kitsch, of TV series and Readers' Digest culture, of advertising and motels, of the late show and the grade-B Hollywood film, of so-called paraliterature'.[57] For Lash, postmodernist 'de-differentiation' is present in the transgression 'between literature and theory, between high and popular culture, between what is properly cultural and properly social'.[58]

Whichever account we adopt, we should note that what is being charted here is primarily an endogenous transformation, internal to elite culture itself, rather to any wider, mass or popular culture. Postmodernism proper is neither a popular culture, nor, in any sense that Leavis or even Williams might have

---

52 Bourdieu 1984.
53 Huyssen 1988.
54 Bell 1976, pp. 51–2.
55 Baudrillard 1988, p. 101.
56 Bürger 1984, p. 63.
57 Jameson 1991, pp. 17, 2.
58 Lash 1990, pp. 173–4.

understood, a common culture: it is postmodernist, but not necessarily post-popular. What postmodernism provides us with, then, is an index of the range and extent of the Western intelligentsia's own internal crisis, that is, its collective crisis of faith in its own previously proclaimed adversarial and redemptive functions. Let us be clear what is at stake here. Any society will possess some institutional arrangements for the regulation of symbolic artefacts and practices. These institutions have very often been 'cultural', in the properly 'culturalist' sense of a set of specialist, pseudo-consensual institutions for the generation of authoritative, but not in fact politically coercive, judgements of value. Such institutions are typically staffed by what Gramsci termed 'traditional' intellectuals:[59] obvious instances include the church and the academy. But their pretensions to cultural authority can also be replicated by counter-cultural intelligentsias associated with either the literary and artistic avant-garde or the revolutionary political party. It is the collapse of all such pretensions, whether traditional, avant-garde or vanguardist, which most clearly marks the moment of postmodernism.

Certain aspects of this collective crisis of faith are no doubt very specific: to the European intellectual confronted by America; to the literary intellectual confronted by the mass media; to the male intellectual confronted by the female. But their sum adds up to a Jamesonian cultural dominant, rather than to any particular literary or artistic style. Indeed, much effort to define a distinctively postmodernist style serves only so as to remind us of the latter's deeply derivative relation to high modernism. It is the general crisis of faith, rather than any particular set of cultural techniques, which is truly defining. Here Zygmunt Bauman's distinction between the role of the intellectual as legislator and that as interpreter, as also his account of the ways in which the latter function progressively displaces the former, becomes instructive.[60] As Bauman concludes:

> The postmodernity/modernity opposition focuses on the waning of certainty and objectivity grounded in the unquestioned hierarchy of values ... and on the transition to a situation characterized by a coexistence or armistice between values ... which makes the questions of objective standards impracticable and hence theoretically futile.[61]

---

59   Gramsci 1971, p. 7.
60   Bauman 1992, pp. 1–24.
61   Bauman 1992, p. 24.

The central social functions of the postwar, postmodern Western intelligentsia have, then, become primarily interpretive rather than legislative. The novelty of this situation is registered in Foucault's distinction between the 'universal' intellectual, called upon to act as 'the consciousness/conscience of us all', and the 'specific' intellectual, working 'at the precise points where their own conditions of life or work situate them'.[62] It is registered also in the only limited applicability of the Gramscian distinction between 'traditional' and 'organic' intellectuals to the cultural sociology of the postwar West. No doubt, there are still Gramscian traditional intellectuals, representative of a certain 'historical continuity',[63] at work within the clergy or the judiciary, perhaps even within academia. No doubt, there are still Gramscian organic intellectuals, integral either to the bourgeois class or to the working class, serving so as give 'their' class a certain 'homogeneity and an awareness of its own function':[64] the bourgeoisie have their economists, engineers and accountants; the proletariat its trade union officials and socialist politicians. Gramsci, however, clearly envisaged both kinds of intellectual as performing an essentially legislative or universal function, whereas in fact the dominant role of each has now become primarily interpretive and specific.

Postmodernism, Jameson argues, represents the final and full commodification of art:

> What has happened is that aesthetic production today has become integrated into commodity production generally: the frantic economic urgency of producing fresh waves of ever more novel-seeming goods ... at ever greater rates of turnover, now assigns an increasingly essential structural function and position to aesthetic innovation and experimentation.[65]

Thus understood, postmodernism is a commodity culture in a double sense: both as a set of commodified artefacts actually available for sale in the culture market, and as a set of texts the very textuality of which often affirms their own commodity status. As Jameson insists, 'the various postmodernisms ... all at least share a resonant affirmation, when not an outright celebration, of the market as such'.[66] Here, it seems to me, Jameson captures much of what it is

---

62 Foucault 1980, p. 126.
63 Gramsci 1971, p. 7.
64 Gramsci 1971, p. 5.
65 Jameson 1991, pp. 4–5.
66 Jameson 1991, p. 305.

that is truly distinctive about our contemporary culture. The more commodified that culture has become, the less plausible the intelligentsia's erstwhile pretensions to legislative cultural authority have appeared, both to themselves and to their prospective audiences. Nineteenth- and early twentieth-century conceptions of culture, whether literary-critical, anthropological or sociological, had almost invariably envisaged culture, not simply as distinct from economy and polity, but also as itself the central source of social cohesion: human society as such appeared inconceivable without culture. But it is so *now*: postmodern capitalism is held together, not by culture, understood as a normative value system, but by the market. As Jameson writes: 'ideologies in the sense of codes and discursive systems are no longer particularly determinant ... ideology ... has ceased to be functional in perpetuating and reproducing the system'.[67]

In short, postmodern intellectual culture is at once both peculiarly normless and peculiarly hedonistic. The hedonism arises very directly from out of the commodity cultures of affluence, as they impinge both on the wider society and on the intelligentsia in particular. The normlessness, however, may well have its origins elsewhere: on the one hand, in the radically internationalising nature of postwar society and culture, which progressively detached erstwhile national intelligentsias from the national cultural 'canons' of which they had hitherto been the custodians; and on the other, in a recurring apocalyptic motif within postwar culture, which must surely bear some more or less direct relation to the threat of nuclear extinction. Let me say a little more about the apocalypse. If postmodernism is indeed the cultural dominant of late capitalism, then late capitalism itself has been not only consumerist, computerised and televisual, but also, as Jameson appears to forget, hypermilitarised. Postmodernism, we must insist, has been underwritten throughout by the arms economy, the visual symbol of which – the mushroom cloud, not the missile – has become so universally culturally available as to have in effect displaced the phallus as the ultimate signifier. As such, it has signified the ultimate hurt, the ultimate refusal of desire. No matter how much it is able to consume, a civilisation permanently confronted by the prospect of its own extinction, such as ours has been, is understandably tempted by the notion that history might come to an end. That global environmental carastrophe comes increasingly to substitute for large-scale nuclear warfare in no way diminishes the power of the trope. The postmodernist effacement of history by 'the random cannibaliza-

---

67   Jameson 1991, p. 398.

tion of ... the past, the ... increasing primacy of the "neo"', which Jameson also records,[68] thus runs in counterpoint to the powerfully apocalyptic element in the postwar culture of the West.

To summarise: postmodernist intellectual culture is in its form uniquely commodified and in its content characterisable by a quite distinctive 'apocalyptic hedonism'; both form and content announce the end of the cultural authority of both traditional and counter-cultural intelligentsias. At this point, I wish to register the extent to which Australia in particular can come to exemplify the postmodern in general. For, however we may choose to define the latter, it is surely not difficult to recognise in Australian society and culture its peculiarly adequate instance. Indeed, we might well venture the hypothesis that Australian postmodernity has been the specific outcome of a history in which neither cultural nor social modernity were ever anything more than approximately realised. Thus Australia has been catapulted towards post-industrialism at a speed possible only in a society that had never fully industrialised; towards consumerism in a fashion barely imaginable in historically less affluent societies; towards an aesthetic populism unresisted by any indigenous experience of a seriously adversarial high culture; towards an integration into multinational late capitalism easily facilitated by longstanding, pre-existing patterns of economic dependence; towards a sense of 'being after', and of being post-European, entirely apposite to a colony of European settlement suddenly set adrift, in intellectually and imaginatively uncharted Asian waters, by the precipitous decline of a distant empire; towards a hypermilitarism long anticipated in the legend of ANZAC and in an unrivalled record of enthusiastic participation in brutish, imperial wars. Post-imperialism, we have said, is Australia's own distinctively postmodern condition. What intellectual reflex could be more readily understandable than to announce, as do both postmodernism and poststructuralism, the end of history to a culture which has never known that it had begun?

Let me stress in particular the ways in which the relative absence of an adversarial high culture became peculiarly overdetermining in the specifically Australian case. The post-Second World War expansion of the Australian culture industries (publishing, recording, film and TV, academia, advertising) occurred on the basis of an extraordinarily underdeveloped set of pre-existent cultural foundations: within the pre-war moral and aesthetic economy of Australia, the Greater British Imperial culture remained near-absolutely hegemonic, both normatively and institutionally, at both elite and popular levels,

---

68 Jameson 1991, p. 18.

though especially at the former. The tragi-comic failure in the 1940s of Harris and Reed's avant-gardist *Angry Penguins* remains deeply suggestive of the radically circumscribed options actually available to any indigeneously Australian high modernism. And McAuley and Stewart's exposure of Ern Malley's 'The Darkening Ecliptic' – in the Sydney *Sun* of all places – can surely be seen as in itself a wonderfully anticipatory 'postmodern' gesture. Deliberately anti-modernist in intent, the Ern Malley hoax proved all too successful. As the *Oxford Companion to Australian Literature* would later conclude: 'More important than the hoax itself was the effect that it had on the development of Australian poetry. The ... movement for modernism in Australian writing ... received a severe setback'.[69] Reversing the presumed causality but endorsing the substantive judgement nonetheless, the *Oxford History of Australian Literature* deduces that insofar as 'the hoax killed genuine experimentalism in Australia ... then it is a comment on the thinness of Australian poetic culture, and the lack of nerve in the poets themselves'.[70] The cultural resources on hand to fuel the postwar, and especially the post-Sixties, expansion were thus comparatively slight, and so much so as to demand a kind of cultural hyper-efficiency that could scarcely afford the necessary waste entailed in any rigorous policing of the elite/popular boundary.

Certain aspects of post-imperial postmodernity are as characteristic of the settler states of North America as they are of Australia: in Canada and even in the United States, intellectual high culture remained seriously dependent on Europe until well into this century; in Canada and in the United States, a relative absence of traditional status hierarchies made for a much more rapid commodification of cultural life than occurred in Europe; in Canada and in the United States, the novelty of postmodernity became peculiarly visible, the attractions of poststructuralism peculiarly telling. But neither in Canada nor in the United States are the deep historical roots of what we have been calling 'apocalyptic hedonism' so firmly entrenched as in Australia. White Australia has had a longstanding and historically by no means unrealistic sense of itself as an unusually affluent and hedonistic society: in 1950 only the United States and Canada enjoyed a higher per capita GNP. But, unlike the North American settler colonies, it has suffered from an almost equally longstanding, and perhaps less realistic, sense of itself as unusually exposed to the threat of invasion and extinction. Such threats were conceived as emanating invariably from the Asiatic north rather than from the indigeneous peoples of Australia.

---

69   Wilde et al. 1985, p. 238.
70   Smith 1981, p. 371.

As early as 1851, only three years after the first Chinese immigrants had arrived in Moreton Bay (Brisbane), Sydney and Port Phillip (Melbourne), the *Moreton Bay Courier* had declared that: 'There cannot be a shadow of doubt that the worst conjectures on this horrible subject are substantially founded. The blood thrills at the contemplation of this beautiful country being colonized by ... beings so grossly debased and wicked'.[71] White blood would continue to thrill at the fear of counter-colonisation for much of the next century. A 1907 tract *The Peril of Melbourne*, published by the Immigration League of Australia, envisaged White Australia permanently threatened by the teeming millions of Asia.[72] In 1909 C.H. Kirmess's bestselling novel *The Australian Crisis* depicted the gallant resistance of a fictional Australian 'White Guard' to a successful Japanese invasion of the Northern Territory.[73] Billy Hughes's 1920 diaries were haunted by 'fitful dreams of Japanese invasion'[74] and in retirement during the 1930s he would warn Australia, in a phrase that inspired much of postwar immigration policy, that the country must 'populate or perish', so as 'to avert national extinction'.[75] The point to note here is not so much that Australian culture was deeply racist, which was at least as true of the United States, but that this racism evolved within a very particular context – that of a relatively small colony located both at the extremes of distance from the mother country and in relative proximity to comparatively 'advanced' and populous non-European societies – which became peculiarly conducive to the genesis of dystopian collective fantasies of racial extinction. Such fantasies would find a wider audience beyond Australia only after Hiroshima. For in the coincidence of a nuclear arms race and a general economy of affluence, the whole of the West finally had Australianness thrust upon it. And it fell to Nevil Shute, bestselling popular author, British immigrant and avid enthusiast for the Australian dream, to effect the translation from a specifically Australian to a more generally Western eschatology.

---

71   Quoted in Evans 1988, p. 178.
72   Markus 1988, p. 88.
73   Kirmess 1909.
74   Evans 1988, p. 172.
75   Fitzhardinge 1979, p. 630.

CHAPTER 5

Loose Canons and Fallen Angels

Let me begin by explaining that this chapter is not an extract from my *Literature, Culture and Society*, but rather an attempt to outline the book's general argument. Its occasion is a set of worries about what I perceive to be a developing polarisation between literary studies – both English Literature and Comparative Literature – and Cultural Studies. No doubt, literary studies has often looked aghast at Cultural Studies. But in general such reaction has not amounted to much more than professorial Podsnappery. As Dickens's *Our Mutual Friend* didn't quite have it: 'We Englishmen are Very Proud of our Literature, Sir ... It was Bestowed Upon Us By Providence. No Other Country is so Favoured as This Country'. Clearly, a more substantial theoretical significance attaches to George Steiner's *No Passion Spent*, for example, to Harold Bloom's *The Western Canon*, and even to Richard Hoggart's *The Way We Live Now*.[1] Here, the literary reaction against Cultural Studies is a reaction, at once, against postmodern theoretical relativism and against the perceived intellectual triviality of much in contemporary popular culture. Steiner and Bloom both work in Comparative Literature, as distinct from English Literature; Hoggart is the figure most commonly singled out as the 'founding father' of contemporary Cultural Studies. Their concerns seem of peculiar relevance, then, to a programme in Comparative Literature and Cultural Studies such as the one in which I teach.

The clearest case is Bloom's *The Western Canon*, an impassioned defence of the idea of a literary canon, very clearly prompted by a perceived threat to literary studies from Cultural Studies. Bloom's argument rests on a very strong assumption as to the demonstrable 'reality' of literary value: the aim of literary studies, he argues, is precisely 'the search for a kind of value that transcends the particular prejudices and needs of societies at fixed points in time'.[2] A text such as *King Lear* is thus 'at the center of centers of canonical excellence', where 'the flames of invention burn away all context and grant us the possibility of what could be called primal aesthetic value, free of history and ideology'.[3] Like

---

1 Steiner 1998; Bloom 1994; Hoggart 1995.
2 Bloom 1994, p. 62.
3 Bloom 1994, p. 65.

the Leavises before him, Bloom sees Literature as in imminent danger of being 'levelled' out of existence. 'I do not believe that literary studies as such have a future', he confesses:

> The study of Western literature will ... continue, but on the modest scale of our current Classics departments. What are now called 'Departments of English' will be renamed departments of 'Cultural Studies', where *Batman* comics, Mormon theme parks, television, movies, and rock will replace Chaucer, Shakespeare, Milton, Wordsworth and Wallace Stevens.[4]

We have to choose, then, between Batman and Chaucer, between movies and Milton. Bloom knows, of course, that Cultural Studies has its eyes on Literature too, but he is just as scathing about its approaches to canonical texts: 'I sometimes wonder if a critical preference for context over text does not reflect a generation made impatient with deep reading'.[5]

There is much in contemporary Cultural Studies that would readily endorse Bloom's sense of a necessary choice to be made between literature on the one hand, popular culture on the other. From its inception, Cultural Studies has been torn between two rival conceptions of its own range and scope: on the one hand, an 'immodest' version, where the new discipline was defined in terms of a new methodology, connecting the study of the popular to that of the literary; on the other, a 'modest' version, defined in terms of its subject matter, that is, as the study of popular culture. Despite the obvious immodesty of the discipline's founding inspirational sources – whether in Williams and Hoggart, or Barthes and Eco, or Adorno and Horkheimer – its more general impulse has increasingly been to turn away from literature and towards culture, understood essentially as 'non-Literature'. In practice, Cultural Studies thus appears increasingly uninterested in literature, in the sense of acknowledged 'canonical' texts. In theory, moreover, Cultural Studies appears increasingly inclined to dispute the very validity of the category 'Literature'. An obvious instance here is Tony Bennett's *Outside Literature*, although one could easily come up with many others. In Bennett's view, aesthetic discourse is merely one discourse of value amongst many others, for example sport or cuisine. Its peculiarity pertains not to its particular object of study, as in the sense of any distinctively 'literary' texts, but only to the characteristic intolerance with

---

4 Bloom 1994, p. 519.
5 Bloom 1994, p. 65.

which it prosecutes its judgements.[6] Thus conceived, literary aesthetics is little more than an ideology of intolerance, 'really useless knowledge', as Bennett has it.[7]

Literary studies has typically defined 'Literature' as a 'canon' of writing, possessed of such high value that it takes on a qualitatively different character from mere 'fiction'. As Bloom explains: 'One breaks into the canon only by aesthetic strength, which is constituted primarily of an amalgam: mastery of figurative language, originality, cognitive power, knowledge, exuberance of diction'.[8] For Bloom, as for Eliot and the Leavises before him – or for Auerbach and Curtius in Comparative Literature – literary studies is the study of this canon. For immodest Cultural Studies, by contrast, the 'literary' is a sub-system of the 'cultural', its texts cognate with those of fiction and the audio-visual media, and analysable according to roughly similar procedures. The distinction between literature and non-literature is thus only one of degree and not of kind. Here, as in my book, I want to suggest something of the intellectual purchase of the latter approach through an exploration of the intertextual connections between a set of variously elite and popular, canonical and non-canonical texts, thematically linked around the notion of a 'fallen creation'. My four main texts are *Genesis*, *Paradise Lost*, *Frankenstein* and *Blade Runner*, a series of manuscript, print and film texts, each of which is, in turn, subjected to modes of contextual and textual analysis familiar to contemporary cultural studies. Contextually, I am interested in the mechanics of the mode of cultural production by which each text is produced; textually, in the way these myths of the fall can be variously positioned in relation to a more general history of humanism. Each text acts out its relation to this history in ways that bear the impress of the mode of cultural production which produced it. In the days of high structuralism all of this would have been represented diagrammatically almost as a matter of course. Out of nostalgia for lost certainties, not to mention fear of time's winged chariot, I represent it thus in Tables 1 and 2.

---

6   Bennett 1990, p. 165.
7   Bennett 1990, p. 143.
8   Bloom 1994, p. 29.

TABLE 1   Contextual analysis

Text	Cultural technology	Cultural form	Production	Reception
Genesis	Chirographic	Sacred text	Instituted artist	Collective (sacral)
Paradise Lost	Print	Epic	Market professional	Individual
Frankenstein	Print	Novel	Market professional	Individual
Blade Runner	Film	Science fiction	Corporate professional	Collective (social)

TABLE 2   Textual analysis

Text	Creator	Creation	Fall	Cause	Solution
Genesis	God	Serpent	Incitement	Serpent	Punishment
	God	Adam	Disobedience/forbidden knowledge	Eve	Punishment
	God/Adam	Eve	Disobedience/forbidden knowledge	Serpent	Punishment
Paradise Lost	God	Adam/Eve	Passion v. reason	Adam/Eve	Personal/history
	God	Satan	Passion v. reason	Satan	None
Frankenstein	God	Victor	Forbidden knowledge/presumption	Hubris	Nemesis
	Victor	Creature	Murder	Abandonment	Companionship
	God	Walton	Forbidden knowledge/presumption	Hubris	Social control
Blade Runner	Tyrell	Deckard	Murder	Tyrell	Love/escape
	Tyrell	Rachael	Self-knowledge	Deckard	Love/escape
	Tyrell	Batty	Murder	Slavery	Mercy

1   Genesis

I do not have the space to say very much in detail about any of these texts, but will rather emphasise a few recorded highlights from the longer argument. To begin with *Genesis*, the *Bible* is, of course, *the* central text of European high culture: at the risk of stating the obvious, there can be nothing more 'canonical' than the first book of the original canon itself. According to Judaeo-Christian-

Islamic tradition, *Genesis* was composed by the prophet Moses as early as the thirteenth century BC. Following Weber, I argue that it more plausibly dates from very much later, that it 'is an accomplishment typical of priests', probably dating from the Babylonian Exile during the sixth and fifth centuries BC.[9] As such, it seems very likely to have been collectively composed by what Williams might have termed priestly 'instituted artists';[10] and it would have been written in Hebrew, either on clay tablets or papyrus scrolls. It is thus an excellent example of what Walter Ong means by 'chirographic culture',[11] that is, a hand-written rather than an oral text, but one which nonetheless bears the clear impress of a prior oral culture.

Genesis is very obviously a pre-humanist text or, if this formulation appears too historicist, at the very least an anti-humanist text. Here, the fall is at once disobedience *per se*, but also and more specifically the search for and acquisition of forbidden knowledge, that is, knowledge of good and of evil. Adam is led to disobedience by Eve, Eve by the serpent, and all three are punished by God. The serpent is condemned to crawl 'upon thy belly' and to eat dust; Eve to 'bring forth children' in sorrow and to be ruled over by Adam; Adam to labour in sorrow and to eat bread only 'in the sweat of thy face'.[12] As many feminists have noted, Eve's punishment provides a powerful rationale for the immutability of patriarchy. But just as powerfully, Adam's preordains an equally immutable class hierarchy amongst men. The punishments God metes out to Adam and Eve thus provide both a narrative solution to the textual problem of transgression and an ideological justification for the social problem of inequality: women are doomed to be ruled over by men, and (most) men doomed to hard labour in the fields, by virtue of their own ancestral sinfulness. Moreover, the original sins of disobedience and the search for forbidden knowledge clearly enjoin upon humanity a more general commandment to obedience and ignorance. This fall and all the falls to come are very definitely humanity's own fault. The serpent has been the occasion for disobedience and it is indeed a peculiarly subtle beast of the field. But its sin is its own, for which it continues to be punished, humanity's sins humanity's, for which they too will continue to be punished. *Genesis* is thus at once both theologically authoritative and socially authoritarian. It is the last word as well as the first, not the prolegomenon to a later narrative of salvation, but rather a definitive explanation for the way

---

9   Weber 1952, p. 226.
10 Williams 1981, pp. 36–8.
11 Ong 1982, pp. 158–9.
12 *Genesis* III: 14, 16–19.

things are. As Weber concluded: 'Adam and Eve's fall is an etiological myth for death, the toil of labor, and the labor of birth, hostility to the snake and later, to all animals. This exhausts its significance'.[13]

2 *Paradise Lost*

Paradise Lost is a much later text. It was composed by an individual author, John Milton, during the late 1650s and early 1660s and finally completed in 1665. It is an epic poem, but very much a written 'art epic', intended both for mechanical reproduction through print and for sale as a literary commodity to an aggregate of individual consumers, rather than to a single patron. Milton provides us with a very early example of the writer as market professional, albeit one whose writing was sustained by a very direct dependence on the patriarchal division of domestic labour. Bloom has no doubt as to his place in the canon, nor that it is secured essentially by this great epic poem. 'There are', he observes, 'only a few works that seem even more essential to the Western Canon than *Paradise Lost*'.[14] This is rather less self-evident than Bloom allows, however: as he himself registers, there is much contemporary feminist 'resentment' against Milton;[15] and there are equally significant objections levelled by those who share Bloom's more general canonical allegiances, for example Eliot and Leavis.[16] Bloom's judgement that 'Milton's place in the canon is permanent'[17] is simply inaccurate as a description of what the actual custodians of the canon have actually done with Milton, in England if not in the United States.

Milton was one of the most prominent republican intellectuals during the revolutionary crisis of the 1640s and 1650s: as a relatively senior civil servant to Cromwell's Council of State, he had written the main semi-official justifications for republicanism and regicide; as late as 1660, when the Restoration was already imminent, he had rallied to the intellectual defence of the republic in his last published political pamphlet, *The Ready and Easy Way to Establish a Free Commonwealth*. At one level, *Paradise Lost* clearly functions as a reflection on the problems of tyranny, revolution and counter-revolution. As Bloom himself observes, Milton was 'a Protestant poet, indeed *the* Protestant poet'.[18] Bloom

---

13   Weber 1952, p. 227.
14   Bloom 1994, p. 26.
15   Bloom 1994, p. 169.
16   Eliot 1968, pp. 12, 19; Leavis 1972b, pp. 53, 60.
17   Bloom 1994, p. 169.
18   Bloom 1994, p. 171.

is much less clear, however, as to what exactly this Protestantism might have entailed. From our own late twentieth-century vantage point, it has become increasingly difficult to imagine a Protestantism that was neither intellectually obscurantist nor politically reactionary. And yet such was Milton's. In both prose and poetry, Milton's writing attests to an intellectual and political rationalism of a kind which importantly anticipated both the Enlightenment and the radical-democratic politics of the American and French Revolutions. *Paradise Lost* is thus the most obviously humanist of my four texts.

Milton's account of the poem's moral purpose is given in the opening invocation of the muse:

> That to the highth of this great argument
> I may assert Eternal Providence,
> And justify the ways of God to men.[19]

This is already very different from *Genesis*: where the Judaic text is accusatory and imperative in tone, Milton's is justificatory and apologetic. For Jewish and most later Christian and Islamic theologies, it is men, rather than God, whose ways require justification. But in Milton the polarities have been reversed: humanity questions and accuses; God must justify himself. The Restoration had unavoidably thrown into doubt the moral benevolence of the universal order. For Milton, it had thus become imperative to seek out a new justification and to explain the specific problem of the defeat of the 'godly party'. As Christopher Hill insists, all three of Milton's great poems, *Paradise Lost*, *Paradise Regained* and *Samson Agonistes*, 'deal with intensely topical problems set by the defeat of God's Cause'.[20] And it is precisely this concrete social and political problem which poses the more general moral problem *Paradise Lost* takes as its theme.

In *Paradise Lost*, unlike *Genesis*, there is a twofold fall, that of the angels and that of the first humans. As in *Genesis*, the main characters are God, the creator, and his various creations. In *Paradise Lost*, however, the creations are all either angels or humans, since the serpent is recast as Satan, the leader of the fallen angels. For Milton, both people and angels, whether fallen or unfallen, partake of the same essential nature: as Raphael tells Adam, they differ 'but in degree, of kind the same'.[21] The highest common factor in this underlying affinity is

---

19   *PL* I: 24–6.
20   Hill 1985, p. 310.
21   *PL* V: 490.

individual rationality: both angels and humans are 'creatures rational'.[22] For Milton, individuality necessarily implies both rationality and free will. Referring by turn to men and to fallen angels, God explains to the Son that:

> ... I made him just and right
> Sufficient to have stood, though free to fall.
> Such I created all th'ethereal Powers
> And spirits, both them who stood and them who failed;
> Freely they stood who stood, and fell who fell.[23]

As in *Genesis*, the moral responsibility for Adam and Eve's fall, and for all the falls to come, will rest with humankind rather than with God. But whereas in *Genesis* this provides evidence only of humanity's innate sinfulness, in *Paradise Lost* it becomes evidence for their innate capacity for rational choice. Milton attempts to reconstruct the *Genesis* myth, so that its central theme becomes that of the conflict between reason and passion. The rationalism of Milton's re-reading is at its clearest in his account of the fall of the angels, if only because here he is least tied to his Biblical sources. Witness Abdiel's indictment of Satan at the beginning of Book VI:

> Unjustly thou deprav'st it with the name
> Of servitude to serve whom God ordains,
> Or nature; God and Nature bid the same,
> When he who rules is worthiest, and excels
> Them whom he governs. This is servitude,
> To serve th'unwise, or him who hath rebelled
> Against his worthier, as thine now serve thee,
> Thyself not free, but to thyself entralled; ...[24]

The fall of the angels thus arises from the subordination of their reasons to the dictates of the passion of pride. Once established, this frame narrative allows Milton to represent the second fall, that of mankind, as a second triumph of passion over reason. In this second fall, he encountered much more serious obstacles than with the angels, since *Genesis* is very specific on the subject. Nonetheless, Milton's own version is strongly asserted both in Raphael's

---

22   *PL* II: 498.
23   *PL* III: 98–102.
24   *PL* VI: 174–81.

earlier warnings[25] and in Michael's subsequent commentary,[26] which perform the functions of prescript and postscript to the actual fall. Against much of the weight of the initial Biblical story, Milton is thus able to insist that the fall of humankind is the product of a triumph of passion over reason.

Interestingly, Milton's version renders the myth less explicitly patriarchal than in *Genesis*. For in *Paradise Lost* Adam and Eve commit essentially the same sin: they each allow their passions to overtake their reasons. Recent feminist criticism has been overwhelmingly hostile to Milton and his epic. Whatever Milton is 'to the male imagination', write Gilbert and Gubar, 'to the female imagination Milton and the inhibiting Father – the Patriarch of patriarchs – are one'.[27] That *Paradise Lost* is indeed a patriarchal text, both in general conception and in much of the detail, seems indisputable. But a great deal of this misogynism derives directly from *Genesis* and it is Milton himself who attempts to rewrite the myth in significantly less misogynist – or at least significantly more universal – a form. For Milton, the fundamental opposition runs between reason and passion, rather than between man and woman, and he is quite capable of imagining woman as reason. He had written as much in his divorce pamphlets. More to the point, *Comus* is organised around exactly the same categories as in *Paradise Lost* – reason, passion, the fall – but here it is the Lady who embodies reason, her brothers who fail at least temporarily, and Comus who is the slave to his own sensuality. Catherine Belsey concedes most of this, only to add that, 'in case this should appear to be an effect of Milton's deliberate intention ... *Samson Agonistes* offers a useful corrective'.[28] But it does no such thing. When Milton represents Dálila as sensuality, or Eve as reason seduced, how can this possibly detract from the prior representation of the Lady as reason triumphant? Quite the contrary, it suggests, rather, that these categories are much less gendered than many feminist critics have argued. No doubt, Milton was not a feminist. But he almost certainly was a bourgeois humanist, whose notions of chastity (applying to men as much as to women) and married love can be read as significantly less patriarchal than the Cavalier alternatives actually on offer at the time.

---

25 *PL* VIII: 635–7.
26 *PL* XII: 82–101.
27 Gilbert and Gubar 1984, p. 192.
28 Belsey 1988, p. 53.

3   Frankenstein

Mary Shelley's novel *Frankenstein* was begun in June 1816, completed in May 1817 and published anonymously by Lackington, Allen and Company as a 'three decker' novel in March 1818. Though critical reaction was mixed, the novel proved an immediate commercial success. A second two-volume edition appeared in 1823, by which time its authorship was already public knowledge. In 1831, Colburn and Bentley published a fully revised third edition as No. 9 in their series of 'Standard Novels'. *Frankenstein* was the product of a much more developed print-capitalism than *Paradise Lost*; its audience the enlarged literary market of the early nineteenth century; and its author, her gender not withstanding, eventually a much more successful market professional than Milton could ever have been. Until recently, *Frankenstein* had been very definitely excluded from the canon of English Literature. Neither F.R. Leavis's *The Great Tradition*, for many years the most influential account of the English novel, nor even Q.D. Leavis's attack on the corrupting effects of popular fiction, *Fiction and the Reading Public*, bother so much as to mention it. Volume 5 of *The Pelican Guide to English Literature*, an important Leavisite project in its time, judged the novel 'second-rate' and 'simple'.[29] Against much of the weight of previous canonical judgement, Bloom manages to include both Mary Shelley and her novel in his version of the Western Canon. But it is difficult not to read this as a grudging and unadmitted concession to the feminist branch of his 'School of Resentment'. Had it not been for the Hollywood cinema and feminist literary criticism, Mary Shelley would easily have been lost to contemporary historical memory.

Like *Paradise Lost*, *Frankenstein* is a reworking of the *Genesis* myth. Though God never actually appears as a character in the novel, Walton, Frankenstein and the other humans are clearly his creations and the creature's novelty consists precisely in the fact that he alone is man-made rather than God-made. From the title page on, the novel repeatedly refers both to *Genesis* and to *Paradise Lost*. Its epigraph is taken from Book X of Milton's poem, where Adam asks of God what will eventually be the monster's question to Frankenstein:

> Did I request thee, Maker, from my clay
> To mold me Man? did I solicit thee
> From darkness to promote me ...?[30]

---

29   Harding 1957, p. 45.
30   *PL* X: 743–5.

The creature is thus a new Adam and Frankenstein himself a new 'Maker'. But Frankenstein has usurped a power that properly belongs only to God. Hence, the description of his creature as 'the living monument of presumption'.[31] Like Adam and Eve in *Genesis*, Frankenstein aspires to forbidden knowledge, but, unlike Adam and Eve, he also self-consciously aspires to a truly god-like power, that of creation itself. Such presumption is what the Greeks had meant by *hubris* and its punishment what they termed *nemesis*. This, then, is the structure of Frankenstein's fall: the sin of hubris followed by the punishment of nemesis. A parallel structure informs the novel's frame narrative, that of the explorer Robert Walton. But here the fall remains a potential that is never fully realised. Where Frankenstein had laboured alone in his 'workshop of filthy creation', 'a solitary chamber, or rather cell, at the top of the house',[32] Walton's explorations require the active cooperation of an entire ship's crew. And it is they who save him from the effects of his own hubris by the exercise of a kind of collective social control. For Frankenstein himself only nemesis can 'solve' hubris; but for Walton the hubris of science can be contained – and in that sense 'solved' – if rendered socially accountable. Mary Poovey reads this as an essentially 'conservative' solution to the problem of individual ambition, Paul O'Flinn as radical, even socialistic.[33] In a sense, both are right, for such assertions of the claims of community and sociality against those of individuality and egotism have been key elements in the political rhetorics of conservatism and socialism alike.

What of the novel's core narrative, that of the monster itself? Unlike many film monsters, Shelley's daemon learns both to speak and to read: the creature's nicely canonical literary education consists in Goethe's *Sorrows of Werter*, Plutarch's *Lives* and Milton's *Paradise Lost*.[34] The effect of this autodidactic education is to suggest a clear affinity between creator and creature in their shared predilection for forbidden knowledge. But it also functions to remind us just how ungodlike Frankenstein's behaviour actually is. For he has betrayed this creation, in the first instance at least without just cause. Hence the underlying 'truth' in the creature's critique delivered when they meet on Mont Blanc:

> Remember, that I am thy creature; I ought to be thy Adam; but I am rather the fallen angel, whom thou drivest from joy for no misdeed. Every where

---

31   Shelley 1980, p. 80.
32   Shelley 1980, p. 55.
33   Poovey 1984, pp. 131–3; O'Flinn 1986, p. 202.
34   Shelley 1980, pp. 127–9.

I see bliss, from which I alone am irrevocably excluded. I was benevolent and good; misery made me a fiend. Make me happy, and I shall again be virtuous.[35]

The monster's own fall consists in the sin of murder, but the source of this sin lies, not so much with the creature himself, as with the creator who has abandoned him. Moreover, the novel gestures toward the possibility that in companionship a solution might have been available for this particular fall. An Adam without an Eve, abandoned by his God, the creature curses his creator:

> 'Hateful day when I received life!' I exclaimed in agony. 'Accursed creator! Why did you ever form a monster so hideous that even *you* turned from me in disgust? ... Satan had his companions, fellow-devils, to admire and encourage him; but I am solitary and abhorred.'[36]

If the monster's fallen condition has indeed arisen primarily from this solitariness, then the power to effect a solution clearly rests with Frankenstein. Like Adam in *Paradise Lost* (though not in *Genesis*, where the initiative is taken by God), the monster asks his creator for a mate. Frankenstein at first refuses,[37] but is eventually persuaded around by what are, by conventionally human standards, clearly reasonable arguments. Frankenstein very nearly completes this second monster, when he suddenly determines to break his word and destroy it, as it turns out in full view of the despairing creature. Frankenstein's reasons are interesting:

> one of the first results of those sympathies for which the daemon thirsted would be children, and a race of devils would be propagated upon the earth ... Had I the right ... to inflict this curse upon everlasting generations?[38]

For Shelley herself, Frankenstein's bad faith seems to require no rational justification; certainly none is given in the novel. Species-loyalty, 'speciesism' as a contemporary animal rights activist might well describe it, is sufficient in itself. This is humanism, of course, in the sense not of a generously inclusive insistence on 'our' common humanity, but that of an exclusive insistence on

---

35   Shelley 1980, p. 100.
36   Shelley 1980, p. 130.
37   Shelley 1980, p. 144.
38   Shelley 1980, p. 165.

'their' inhumanity and non-humanity, worse yet their possible 'post-humanity'. George Slusser has argued that Shelley here established what would in fact become the central problem in subsequent science fictional approaches to the 'posthuman', a problem he nicely terms 'the Frankenstein barrier': 'What is at stake with Victor Frankenstein ... is ... the sin against the second chance modern science offers humanity by remaking its fallen body and directing it toward further things to come. Victor opens the way to the future only to betray that openness'.[39]

4 *Blade Runner*

When Bloom writes of *Paradise Lost* that it 'now reads like the most powerful science fiction',[40] he is absolutely right, but right in a way that clearly threatens to subvert the notions of canonicity he claims to defend. For if there is one thing we can safely say about science fiction, it is that it most definitely is not canonical. *Frankenstein* reads even more like powerful science fiction than *Paradise Lost*. Indeed, there is a good case to be made that *Frankenstein* itself is the first real science fiction novel: it was concerned, not with ghosts, but with the possible consequences and ethical implications of a hypothetical scientific development. At one level, Frankenstein's monster is simply the first android in rebellion against his human creator. But he is by no means the last. Which takes us to *Blade Runner*, Ridley Scott's film adaptation of Philip K. Dick's novel *Do Androids Dream of Electric Sheep?* The film was first released in 1982, a second 'director's cut' in 1992. Produced for Warner Brothers by the 'Blade Runner Partnership' at a reported cost of $27 million,[41] it starred Harrison Ford as Rick Deckard, Rutger Hauer as Roy Batty, Sean Young as Rachael, and Joe Turkell as Eldon Tyrell. *Blade Runner* was a product of highly developed 'corporate professional' relations of production, a marketable commodity to be initially consumed in the cinema theatre, and subsequently recycled as video. Scott clearly regards himself as the film's author: hence, the 'director's cut'. But there is an obvious incongruity, nonetheless, in insisting on the authentic authorial voice and the authentically authorised text of a film a central theme of which is precisely the inauthenticity, or at least the indeterminacy, of identity and of memory. The very first draft for the film script was in one sense Dick's novel.

39 Slusser 1992, p. 51.
40 Bloom 1994, p. 171.
41 Kolb 1991a, p. 146n.

But thereafter a series of scripts were written and rewritten, initially by Hampton Fancher and later by David Peoples (neither of whom wrote the voice-over narration included in the 1982 version, but not in the director's cut).

Dick's novel had been concerned with what it meant to be human, with how inhuman behaviour dehumanises humans to the level of androids, and was thus predicated on an essentially humanist notion of the radical difference between humans and non-humans. *Blade Runner* is much less secure in its humanism. As Dick himself noted, Peoples's screenplay introduced an entirely new 'reciprocal motion', by which the replicants become progressively humanised as Deckard becomes progressively dehumanised. Dick insisted on reading the amendment as entirely complementary with his own preoccupations: 'this fusion of Deckard and the replicants is a *tragedy* ... This is horrifying because he is now as they are, so the theme of the novel is completely and essentially retained'.[42] Whatever Dick's own authorial intentions in *Do Androids Dream of Electric Sheep?*, this reading of *Blade Runner* remains unconvincing, if only because the film's 1982 closing sequence, where Deckard and Rachael successfully escape from Los Angeles, has been commonly read as an unambiguously happy ending. Moreover, there is one very particular condition which would entirely undermine a humanist reading of *Blade Runner*, that is, that Deckard should turn out not to be human at all, but to be yet another replicant. This view has been widely canvassed by critics and audiences alike, and apparently it is Scott's own reading.[43] Certainly, it seems to be the import of the famous 'unicorn scene', deleted from the original but reinserted into the director's cut.

Like *Genesis*, *Paradise Lost* and *Frankenstein*, *Blade Runner* is a story of the fall: each of the three main protagonists, Deckard, Rachael and Batty, either has already fallen at the outset or will fall in the course of the narrative. If Deckard is a replicant, then all three of the central characters are creations of the same creator, Dr Eldon Tyrell, head of the Tyrell Corporation. In the post-catastrophic dystopia that is the Los Angeles of November 2019, Tyrell is, in Batty's phrase, 'the God of bio-mechanics'. Neither Milton's Paradise nor yet Shelley's workshop of filthy creation, the Tyrell Corporation building is a recognisable extrapolation from the great corporate towers that cluster at the centre of most contemporary cities. And its purpose is much the same: 'Commerce is our goal here at Tyrell'. Neither a God nor even a Frankenstein, Tyrell himself is demonstrably amoral, almost banally so. Nowhere is this more apparent than in the central confrontation between Tyrell and Batty, creator and creature, the

---

42   Van Hise 1982, p. 22.
43   Kolb 1991a, p. 177n.

film's equivalent to the encounter between Frankenstein and his monster on Mont Blanc. 'I have done questionable things', Batty confesses to the man he has already described as his 'maker'. 'Also extraordinary things – revel in your times', replies Tyrell. The only ethical judgement suggested is that implied by the replicant's own comment: 'Nothing the God of bio-mechanics wouldn't let you in heaven for'. The point, of course, is that there is *nothing* that this God of bio-mechanics wouldn't let you in heaven for.

All of Tyrell's creations are in different ways much more impressive than their human creator. Where Dick had imagined his androids as inferior, Scott's relicants are much more nearly superhuman. The film's prologue informs us that: 'The NEXUS 6 *Replicants* were superior in strength and agility, and at least equal in intelligence, to the genetic engineers who created them'. And the greatest of these genetic engineers is Tyrell, who explains to Deckard that: 'More human than human is our motto'. In the confrontation with Batty, Tyrell is even more explicit: 'You were made as well as we could make you. The light that burns twice as bright, burns half as long. And you have burned so very, very brightly, Roy'. Deckard too is the best there is at his bloody trade: as Bryant tells him, 'I need you, Deck ... I need the old blade runner, I need your magic'. And, if Rachael 'is an experiment, nothing more', in Tyrell's words, then this experiment is nothing less than to produce the most convincing Nexus 6 yet. Where Tyrell is the God of Scott's 'hell-on-Earth', then, as David Desser rightly observes, Deckard, Rachael and Batty are, respectively, its Adam, Eve and Satan.[44] But since Los Angeles is precisely a hell rather than a heaven, their problem is not that of how to remain in Paradise but of how to escape it. And yet each falls, Deckard and Batty through the sin of murder, Rachael through the dawning realisation that she is replicant rather than human. Thereafter, however, each finds the way toward both personal redemption and escape.

For Batty, redemption and escape come simultaneously in the moment when he saves Deckard's life and gives up his own. Roy Batty is surely more obviously the hero of *Blade Runner* than Satan was ever that of *Paradise Lost*. Although the film's narrative movement is initially carried by Deckard, the focus shifts progressively towards Batty: he organises and directs the escaped replicants; he forces the issue of their mortality in the confrontation with Tyrell; he propels the narrative towards its climax in the film's most powerful scene, that of his own death. Unlike Satan, Batty defeats both his creator, Tyrell, and his rival creation, Deckard: it is as if Satan had not only seduced Eve and thence Adam, but successfully stormed Heaven too. And then, in the gesture

---

44   Desser 1991, pp. 54–5, 58.

that most clearly reverses Dick's intended humanism, Batty shows mercy to Deckard, to the blade runner who has shown none to the other replicants. In terms of the film's own internal morality, this gesture somehow cancels out all Batty's previous killing. His last speech reasserts the extraordinariness of his own superhuman individuality and yet also announces a final acceptance of mortality:

> I've seen things you people wouldn't believe. Attack ships on fire off the shoulders of Orion. I watched c beams glitter in the dark near the Tannhäuser Gate. All those moments will be lost in time, like tears in rain. Time to die.

Which leaves Deckard and Rachael, Scott's Adam and Eve, the monster and the bride he has not yet been cheated of. For both, redemption itself comes through love. But escape is another matter, depending very much on which of the film's two endings we use. The director's cut ends with a lift door closing on Deckard and Rachael, that is, on the ambiguous possibility of their escape from Los Angeles. The original theatre release version is much more explicit, including a subsequent sequence of their flight over what is clearly a deliberately Edenic countryside, with a voice-over explaining, not only that the rival blade runner, Gaff, has let Rachael go, but also that she is special and has no termination date.

Interestingly, Leonard Heldreth has argued that, although the first release ending 'may seem intellectually contrived and out of tone with the rest of the film, ... it's the emotional ending we want'.[45] In the most literal of senses, he is absolutely right: the studio chose this ending precisely because it was the one preferred by their pre-release sample audiences. But Heldreth himself prefers it for reasons that are explicitly humanist in ideology: 'At the end of the film', he writes, 'Deckard [is] ... no longer trying to remain a human being while he kills the very emotional responses that define his humanity ... Deckard, i.e., man, is presented as a human being who makes his escape into the new Eden with a new Eve'.[46] Deckard and Rachael are indeed a new Adam and a new Eve, escaping into a new Eden. But Rachael is certainly not a woman and, if Ridley Scott is to be believed, nor is Deckard a man: these are replicants, the first of Frankenstein's race of devils. And if this is indeed the ending 'we' want, this is so only for reasons precisely the obverse of Heldreth's, in short, because 'we', mean-

---

45 Heldreth 1991, p. 51.
46 Ibid.

ing the postmodern audiences of the late-capitalist world of the late-twentieth century, are no longer at all persuaded of our own evolutionary superiority as a species.

5 Conclusion

How well these particular analyses work is for others to judge. But whatever their strengths or weaknesses, it should be apparent that this type of analysis can in fact generate non-trivial hypotheses concerning both the texts and their institutional and discursive contexts. If this is so, then where exactly does it leave Bloom and the Western Canon? The short answer is in some difficulty, at least in the attempt to define 'Literature' as a different order of phenomenon from 'non-literature'. *Frankenstein* clearly straddles the boundaries between elite and popular cultures, Literature and non-literature, in ways that strongly suggest their impermanence. *Blade Runner* is a film of very real power, which in rather different ways also threatens to straddle these self-same boundaries. Desser has cautiously argued for its inclusion into the canon.[47] But no film has ever been admitted to the literary canon, and this is so because a canon of sacred texts can never be expanded to include even a single one of even the most interesting or exciting of profane texts. This is the point where Desser should give up on the idea of a canon altogether, the point where it becomes impossible to believe in 'primal aesthetic value', somehow adhering strongly to *Paradise Lost*, but not very much to *Frankenstein* and not at all to *Blade Runner*. For Bennett was right to insist that value is only ever produced, not by the text itself, but by the valuing community which values it. The high canonical status of *Genesis* thus denotes little more than that a great many people have believed either in Judaism or in Christianity or in Islam. And the variable valuations applied over time to *Frankenstein*, and even to *Paradise Lost*, suggest only the corollary variability of community standards. As for *Blade Runner*, its complete absence from all known versions of the canon tells us only that most science fiction fans have much better things to worry about.

But *Frankenstein* and *Blade Runner* also leave Bennett in some difficulty too, at least insofar as his argument proposes in effect to substitute institutional for textual analysis, or perhaps to subsume the latter under the former. For Bennett, 'Literature' is only an institutional arrangement for the processing of texts. In one sense, Literature is indeed what the institutions of higher and secondary

---

47 Desser 1991, p. 64.

education on the one hand, the book trade on the other, have chosen to define as such. But it is also a set of particular texts, which might still have particular textual properties. Bennett appears not to believe this and therefore seems to have no interest in literary texts, and not much even in popular cultural texts, when considered as texts. Having asserted value relativism, he seems to have no further interest in valuing. But there are at least two good reasons for persisting with the study of texts, the one literary-historical, the other contemporary. Literary history is what much of literary studies is actually about, although the habit of criticism often tends to obscure this. Once we abandon the effort to work out what is and what isn't 'great', for all times and for all places, then we can get on with the more serious business of using the literary text as a source of often quite privileged insight into a more general history of what Williams termed 'structures of feeling'. This was Williams's point in *The Long Revolution* and it still holds good.[48]

As to the contemporary reasons for persisting with texts, these are almost transparently obvious. For even if Bennett prefers to discuss institutions, most of us stubbornly prefer to discuss texts – it is what we do, after all, whenever we debate with others the film we have just seen or the book we have just read. And it would be an odd sort of expertise in Cultural Studies which required its experts to refrain from such debate. Like everybody else, these experts apply 'merely relative' values, but there is no reason to suppose that this detracts from the importance of the process. We can and we do distinguish between more or less readerly and writerly texts, more or less open and closed texts, more or less ideologically manipulative, more or less patriarchal, albeit normally as points on a continuum rather than as binary oppositions. And insofar as these distinctions are acceptable to wider valuing communities, then we can and we do engage in meaningful conversation about the value of texts, irrespective of whether or not they are Literature.

A properly immodest Cultural Studies should not aspire to substitute popular culture for literature, movies for Milton. Quite the contrary, it should study both. But it should also insist: firstly, that we take all aspects of our contemporary culture, including film and television, very seriously (for they surely take us seriously); and secondly, that there are more interesting ways to approach canonical literary texts than through acts of quasi-religious worship. In both respects, Williams's work still seems absolutely exemplary. For it was Williams more than any other individual who drafted the initial intellectual prospectus for a Cultural Studies that would include literary studies. Let me conclude by

---

48 Williams 1965, pp. 64–5.

quoting from *The Long Revolution*. 'It was certainly an error', Williams wrote, 'to suppose that values or art-works could be adequately studied without reference to the particular society within which they were expressed'.[49] His target here was Leavisite literary criticism, but the argument could today just as easily be redirected at Bloom. Williams continues: 'it is equally an error to suppose that the social explanation is determining, or that the values and works are mere by-products'.[50] His target here was Marxism, but the argument could today just as easily be redirected against many forms of postmodern relativism. He moves thence to what I take to be his central argument: 'Analysis of particular works or institutions is ... analysis of their essential kind of organization, the relationships which works or institutions embody as parts of the organization of a whole'.[51] This seems to me almost exactly right. Which is why the Western Canon will almost certainly be far safer in the hands of an immodest Cultural Studies than in those of an English Literature or Comparative Literature hell bent on turning themselves into Classics.

---

49   Williams 1965, p. 61.
50   Ibid.
51   Williams 1965, p. 63.

CHAPTER 6

Dissenting, Plebeian, but Belonging Nonetheless: Bourdieu and Williams*

> I have come here to express our support to those who have been fighting for the last three weeks against the destruction of a *civilization*, associated with the existence of public service, the civilization of republican equality of rights, rights to education, to health, culture, research, art, and, above all, work.
>
> – BOURDIEU, Speech to Striking French Railwayworkers, December 1995[1]

...

> It is here, in diversity and in respect for diversity, that new popular forces are forming and looking for some effective political articulation. It will be long and difficult in detail, but in challenging the destructive catchwords of *management, economic* and *law-and-order*, which now cover the real operations of a new and reckless stage of capitalism, the miners have, in seeking to protect their own interests, outlined a new form of the general interest.
>
> – WILLIAMS, Writing on the 1984–85 British Mineworkers Strike, *New Socialist*, March 1985[2]

∴

In his last years, Pierre Bourdieu was famously involved in radical politics. Indeed, by the late 1990s, he had become by far the most prominent academic intellectual to join in active solidarity with the new 'anti-globalisation' movement. The latter phrase is a misnomer, of course, since in its campaigns for

---

* This chapter has been published previously in Jeff Browitt and Brian Nelson (eds.), *Practising Theory: Pierre Bourdieu and the Field of Cultural Production* (Newark: University of Delaware Press, 2004), pp. 101–12.
1 Bourdieu 1998b, p. 24.
2 Williams 1989a, p. 127.

the internationalisation of human, democratic and trade union rights, this 'movement of many movements'[3] was at least as 'global' in scope as its corporate opponents. Its real target was globalisation on corporate terms, what Naomi Klein called 'the privatization of every aspect of life, and the transformation of every activity and value into a commodity'; its real aim 'a radical reclaiming of the commons'.[4] The movement tended to date its origins from 1994–5, the years of the Zapatista rising in Mexico and the public-sector strikes in France. But Bourdieu's *La Misère du monde*, first published in hardback in 1993, and in paperback in 1998, had clearly foreshadowed many of its political preoccupations. The book's combination of ethnographic interviews and sociological commentary had mounted a stunning indictment of 'economic liberalism' – what in Britain was known as 'Thatcherism'; in the United States, 'Reaganism'; in Australia, bizarrely enough, 'economic rationalism' – as setting up precisely the preconditions for 'an unprecedented development of all kinds of ordinary suffering'.[5] A bestseller in France, it became a major source of political inspiration to the new movement, both in the original and in its 1999 English translation. Bourdieu was also directly involved in militant activism: he spoke in solidarity with mass meetings of striking railway workers in 1995 and of unemployed workers in 1998;[6] he launched the 1996 petition for an 'Estates General of the Social Movement' and its May Day 2000 successor, the appeal for a pan-European Estates General; he co-founded the radical 'Raisons d'agir' group and its associated publishing house; he publicly called 'for a left Left';[7] he was a regular contributor to the radical monthly, *Le Monde diplomatique*, published in French and in English translation.

For an Anglophone observer of my generation and intellectual formation, it was difficult not to be reminded of Raymond Williams's earlier performance in this selfsame role as activist-intellectual. Williams had been a founding editor of the *New Left Review* and co-author of the 1968 *May Day Manifesto*, involved in an array of radical causes from the Vietnam Solidarity Campaign to the Campaign for Nuclear Disarmament. He was a regular contributor to *The Listener*, *The Guardian* and later the *New Socialist*. During his last years – he died in 1988 – he was Vice-President of the Socialist Environment and Resources Association in 1981; a moving spirit behind the launch of the Socialist Society in

---

3   Klein 2001, p. 81.
4   Klein 2001, p. 82.
5   Bourdieu et al. 1999, pp. 4, 181–8.
6   Bourdieu 1998b, pp. 24n, 88n.
7   Bourdieu 1998a.

1982; and active in very practical solidarity work with the Welsh NUM during the 1984–5 British coalminers' strike. His *Towards 2000*, though less immediately influential and less obviously monumental than *La Misère du monde*, had nonetheless coined the peculiarly apposite term 'Plan X' to describe the 'new politics of strategic advantage' that would be characteristic of what we have since learned to name as 'globalisation'. Even at this distance, his analysis remains startlingly prescient: 'their real politics and planning', Williams wrote, 'are ... centred on ... an acceptance of the indefinite continuation of extreme crisis and extreme danger ... there will be a long series of harshly administered checks; of deliberately organised reductions of conditions and chances; of intensively prepared emergencies of war and disorder'.[8] If Williams had been claimed by *The Times* as a British Sartre, then Bourdieu in his own later years came close to becoming a French Williams. Certainly, there is a great deal more point to this comparison than to any with Anthony Giddens, Bourdieu's counterpart in recent British Sociology, whose work has amounted to little more than a sustained apologia for the post-Thatcherism of Tony Blair's 'New Labour' Party.[9]

Moreover, there are obvious homologies between Williams's and Bourdieu's respective biographies. Both experienced what any sociologist can recognise as long-range upward social mobility: Bourdieu, the son of a peasant farmer turned postman, from Béarn, a small village in south-western France, rose to become Professor of Sociology at the Collège de France in Paris; Williams, son of a railwayman and grandson of agricultural labourers, from Pandy, a small village in eastern Wales, to become Professor of Drama at Cambridge University. Both combined a cautious wariness toward mainstream Marxism, whether orthodoxly Communist or Althusserian, with a strongly radical – and over time increasingly so – sympathy for working-class anti-capitalism. There was a certain parallelism between their respective academic efforts. Where Bourdieu's work developed in simultaneous response to and reaction against Sartrean 'subjectivism' and Lévi-Straussian 'objectivism',[10] Williams's moved in and against two respectively subjectivist and objectivist 'traditions', Leavisite literary humanism and Marxian materialism.[11] There were even points of confluence between their work: Bourdieu and his colleagues at the Centre de Sociologie Européenne had introduced writing by Williams and other British 'culturalists' – notably E.P. Thompson and Richard Hoggart – to French audiences

---

8   Williams 1983, pp. 244, 268.
9   Giddens 1994 and 1998.
10 Bourdieu 1993a, pp. 54–9.
11 Williams 1979, pp. 352–3.

through the journal *Actes de la Recherche en Science Sociales*; whilst Williams co-authored with Nicholas Garnham one of the first Anglophone introductions to *La Distinction* for the journal *Media, Culture and Society*.[12]

There are, of course, obvious differences between them: Bourdieu was always the professional sociologist, Williams a sociologically-minded literary critic, which is not quite the same thing. It is true that, by the late seventies and early eighties, the latter had come to think of his work as a 'cultural sociology', even at one point describing cultural studies as 'a branch of general sociology'.[13] But this was still primarily a text-based academic practice, a sociology more reminiscent of Lucien Goldmann than of Bourdieu. In a 1988 obituary, Garnham made something of a virtue out of the necessity that Williams 'was a man who worked, largely alone with the assistance of his wife, outside the institutional bases of communication studies ... He never received foundation or research council funding for communications research'.[14] That this might have been, at best, a cruel virtue is suggested by the results of the relatively well-funded, collaborative research undertaken by Bourdieu. The obvious instance is *La Distinction* itself, which was based on a detailed sociological survey, conducted by interview and by ethnographic observation, of the cultural preferences of over 1200 people from three different urban areas.[15] But resources of a similar magnitude are also brought to bear in *La noblesse d'État*[16] and in *La Misère du monde*. There is nothing of this order anywhere in Williams.

1   Capitalism, Class and Culture

There are nonetheless very real points of similarity between Bourdieu and Williams and these are, at once, both intellectual and political. The most obvious is a shared sense of the continuing importance of social class to the social structures of advanced capitalism. For Bourdieu, contemporary capitalist societies were above all class societies. But their dominant and dominated classes are distinguishable from each other, not simply as a matter of economics, but also and primarily as a matter of culture, or 'habitus': 'social class, understood as a system of objective determinations', he insisted, 'must be brought into relation ... with the class habitus, the system of dispositions (partially) common

---

12   Garnham and Williams 1980.
13   Williams 1981, p. 14.
14   Garnham 1988, p. 124.
15   Bourdieu 1984, p. 503.
16   Bourdieu 1996a.

to all products of the same structures'.[17] In Bourdieu, the major social classes are definable according to their 'overall volume of capital' that is, their 'set of actually usable resources and powers – economic capital, cultural capital and ... social capital'. Within each class, different class fractions can be identified, according to the 'different distributions of their total capital among the different kinds of capital'.[18] In the extended version of this model, there are 24 such 'class fractions' combined into four classes; in the more condensed, 16 fractions combined into three classes.[19] There is no equivalent attempt at classificatory complexity in Williams, but he too had insisted that even the most postmodern of advanced capitalisms are organised around 'the central systems of the industrial-capitalist mode of production' and 'its system of classes'.[20] For Williams, as for Bourdieu, this was more than merely a matter of economics: the crucial distinction between the middle and working classes, he had written early in his career, lay in 'alternative ideas of the nature of social relationship'.[21] Williams's central theoretical focus thus fell increasingly on the complex articulation between cultural tradition on the one hand, and subordinate class identity on the other, an articulation theorised primarily through the twin concepts of 'selective tradition' and 'structure of feeling'.

If Bourdieu's understanding of class was substantially 'encultured', then the obverse was also true: he saw culture as similarly 'enclassed'. 'Position in the classification struggle', he concluded, 'depends on position in the class structure'.[22] Hence, his insistence on the presence of class distinction even in the most apparently disinterested of cultural practices. Williams too would recognise such apparently disinterested categories as 'literature' and 'criticism' as forms of 'class specialization' and 'class limitation'.[23] This sense of the interestedness of apparently disinterested culture led both to a shared suspicion of the pretensions to exclusive legitimacy of bourgeois 'high culture'. As is well known, Bourdieu's general sociology had posited that 'all practices, including those purporting to be disinterested or gratuitous' can be treated as 'economic practices directed towards the maximizing of material or symbolic profit'.[24] Hence, his view of the intelligentsia as self-interested traders in cultural cap-

---

17 Bourdieu 1977b, p. 85.
18 Bourdieu 1984, p. 114.
19 Bourdieu 1984, pp. 504, 16–17.
20 Williams 1983, pp. 172–3.
21 Williams 1963, p. 311.
22 Bourdieu 1984, p. 484.
23 Williams 1977, p. 49.
24 Bourdieu 1977b, p. 183.

ital: even in the 'purely artistic', 'anti-economic economy' of 'restricted' cultural production, '*symbolic, long-term profits* ... are ultimately reconvertible into economic profits';[25] even avant-garde cultural practice remains dependent on the 'possession of substantial economic and social capital'.[26] In an analogous move, Williams came to define the literary tradition, which had been for Leavis the central repository of cultural 'truth', as necessarily 'always selective, ... related to and even governed by the interests of the class that is dominant'.[27]

In *La Distinction* Bourdieu explains legitimate bourgeois 'taste' primarily in terms of its 'aesthetic disposition' to assert the 'absolute primacy of form over function'.[28] Artistic and social 'distinction' are thus inextricably interrelated, he concludes: 'The pure gaze implies a break with the ordinary attitude towards the world which, as such, is a social break'.[29] The characteristic detachment of this 'pure gaze', he argues, is part of a more general disposition towards the 'gratuitous' and the 'disinterested', in which the 'affirmation of power over a dominated necessity' implies a claim to 'legitimate superiority over those who ... remain dominated by ordinary interests and urgencies'.[30] There is no equivalent notion in Williams, but it is clear that he saw the Leavisite distinction between minority and mass arts as radically untenable. 'There are very few absolute contrasts left between a "minority culture" and "mass communications"', he wrote, 'many minority institutions and forms have adapted, ... with enthusiasm, to modern corporate capitalist culture'.[31] Moreover, he was as suspicious as Bourdieu of avant-garde pretension: the older modernisms, which once threatened to destabilise the certainties of bourgeois life, have been transformed into a new '"post-modernist" establishment', he wrote, which 'takes human inadequacy ... as self-evident'.[32]

The corollary of this refusal to endorse legitimate bourgeois high culture is for both Bourdieu and Williams a corresponding sympathy for popular cultural aspirations. In *La Distinction* Bourdieu explains the 'popular aesthetic' as based on an affirmation of continuity between 'art and life' and on a 'deep-rooted demand for participation'.[33] This is what the aesthetic disposition deems bar-

---

25 Bourdieu 1993b, p. 54.
26 Bourdieu 1993b, p. 67.
27 Williams 1963, pp. 307–8.
28 Bourdieu 1984, pp. 28, 30.
29 Bourdieu 1984, p. 31.
30 Bourdieu 1984, pp. 55–6.
31 Williams 1983, pp. 134, 140.
32 Williams 1983, p. 141.
33 Bourdieu 1984, p. 32.

barous, Bourdieu observes. But the definition of art, he continues, and through it the art of living, is nonetheless 'an object of struggle among the classes'.[34] Citing Proudhon (and Dickens) with barely suppressed sympathy, he notes how in the popular aesthetic art 'must aim to arouse the moral sense, ... to substitute for the thing the ideal of the thing, by painting the true and not the real'.[35] Williams's reaction to the minority culture/mass civilization trope runs along parallel lines. Hence his famous insistence that: 'There are in fact no masses; there are only ways of seeing people as masses'.[36] Or, as he would later write: 'Culture is ordinary, in every society and in every mind'.[37] If the young Williams was still too Leavisite a critic to opt for 'popular culture' *per se*, he could already conclude that culture is just as 'essentially' a 'whole way of life' as a 'body of intellectual and imaginative work'.[38] This argument led directly to the defence of the 'collective democratic institution' as the central 'creative achievement' of working-class culture.[39] Less immediately, it led to a growing interest in mass communications technologies as 'the contemporary tools of the long revolution towards an educated and participatory democracy';[40] and to a stress on the fundamental commonality of all culture. 'Our real purpose', he wrote, 'should be to bring all cultural work within the same world of discourse: to see the connections between Elia and the manufactured television personality as well as the difference in value between *Lord Jim* and *Captain Condor*'.[41]

Bourdieu and Williams also shared a common assessment of the centrality of culture to the general social organisation. For Bourdieu, culture's 'symbolic power' was not some secondary effect of an economy located elsewhere, but itself fully material. So, when he cites Weber against Marx, Bourdieu insists that:

> Weber has the merit of calling attention to the producers of these particular products (religious agents, in the case that concerns him) and to their *interactions* (conflict, competition, etc.). In opposition to the Marxists, who have overlooked the existence of specialized agents of production ..., Weber reminds us that ... it does not suffice to study symbolic forms ..., or even the immanent structure of the religious message ... Weber focuses

---

34 Bourdieu 1984, p. 48.
35 Bourdieu 1984, p. 49.
36 Wiliams 1963, p. 289.
37 Wiliams 1989a, p. 4.
38 Wiliams 1963, p. 311.
39 Wiliams 1963, p. 313.
40 Wiliams 1974, p. 151.
41 Wiliams 1976, p. 147.

specifically on the producers of the religious message, on the specific interests that move them and on the strategies they use in their struggle ...[42]

This sense of culture as itself material, and of its practitioners as themselves materialists, is deeply reminiscent of Williams's own 'cultural materialism'. So Williams's critique of Marxian economic determinism proceeds in roughly analogous terms. 'From castles and palaces and churches to prisons and workhouses and schools; from weapons of war to a controlled press', he wrote: '... These are never superstructural activities. They are necessarily material production within which an apparently self-subsistent mode of production can alone be carried on'.[43] Art is not thereby necessarily diminished, but it is materially situated nonetheless. As Williams had written in *The Long Revolution*: 'The art is there, as an activity, with the production, the trading, the politics, the raising of families ... It is ... not a question of relating the art to the society, but of studying all the activities and their interrelations, without any concession of priority to any one of them we may choose to abstract'.[44]

2   Habitus and Structure of Feeling

In Bourdieu, as in Williams, the effect of such cultural materialism is to decentre the artist as 'author' – though clearly not so radically as in Barthes and Foucault – so that the central question becomes the dynamic interrelationship between social structure, individual action and cultural practice. And what applies to the artist applies also to human agents in general. At a deeper level, then, there is an interesting parallelism between Williams's and Bourdieu's notions of practice. Both attempted to theorise human sociality in terms of the strategic action of individuals within a constraining, but nonetheless not determining, context of values: the 'habitus' in Bourdieu, 'structure of feeling' in Williams. The former is almost certainly Bourdieu's key sociological concept, although he insists that its history can be traced back, through Mauss and Durkheim, to Scholastic translations of Aristotle.[45] The habitus, Bourdieu explains, is 'an acquired system of generative schemes objectively

---

42   Bourdieu 1998c, p. 57.
43   Wiliams 1977, p. 93.
44   Wiliams 1965, pp. 61–2.
45   Bourdieu 1993a, p. 86.

adjusted to the particular conditions in which it is constituted'.[46] It is simultaneously structured and structuring, materially produced and very often generation-specific.[47] Elsewhere, he draws the analogy between social life and games, likening the habitus to the 'feel' for a game and its stakes, which encompasses 'both the inclination and the capacity to play the game, to take an *interest* in the game, to be taken up, taken in by the game'.[48] The habitus, he writes:

> is a product of conditionings which tends to reproduce the objective logic of those conditionings while transforming it ... a kind of transforming machine that leads us to 'reproduce' the social conditions of our own production, but in a relatively unpredictable way ...[49]

This is clearly a much less structuralist conception than equivalent notions in Lévi-Strauss, Althusser or Foucault: its logic is one of practice, rather than of interpellation. Indeed, it can be read as giving a specifically Weberian inflexion to what is a more generally Durkheimian sociology. It is interesting to note that Bourdieu described Weber as opening the way to a 'radical materialism', capable of seeking out 'the economic determinants', even 'in areas where the ideology of "disinterestedness" prevails'.[50] This is, of course, very close to thumbnail sketch of his own long-range project.

At first sight, Williams's 'structure of feeling' appears as merely one of a family of concepts that denote the connection of text to context, roughly equivalent to 'ideology', 'world vision', 'problematic', or 'discursive formation'. Indeed, there are times when Williams employs it thus. But his repeated use of terms like 'living' and 'lived' should alert us to its peculiarly and distinctively experiential aspects. As Pickering rightly observes, the concept's real cutting edge 'lies in its application to liminal forms of experience, as a category of pre-emergence'.[51] Williams intended the concept as a near-oxymoron: 'as firm and definite as "structure" suggests, yet it operates in the most delicate and least tangible parts of our activity'.[52] 'In one sense', he wrote:

---

46 Bourdieu 1977b, p. 95.
47 Bourdieu 1977b, pp. 72, 78.
48 Bourdieu 1993a, p. 18.
49 Bourdieu 1993a, p. 87.
50 Bourdieu 1993a, p. 12.
51 Pickering 1997, p. 45.
52 Williams 1965, p. 64.

structure of feeling is the culture of a period: it is the particular living result of all the elements in the general organization. And it is in this respect that the arts of a period ... are of major importance. For here, if anywhere, this characteristic is likely to be expressed; often not consciously, but by the fact that here ... the actual living sense, the deep community that makes the communication possible, is naturally drawn upon.[53]

A structure of feeling, he makes clear, is neither universal nor class specific, though it is 'a very deep and wide possession'. Like the habitus, these structures of feeling are not the effect of formal learning and are thus normally peculiarly generational in character: 'the new generation will have its own structure of feeling', Williams observes, 'which will not appear to have come "from" anywhere'.[54] The parallel with Bourdieu should be apparent.

There are differences, of course, especially in Williams's later 'Gramscian' reformulations of the concept, which tend to render it even more explicitly experiential, as distinct from textual, but also more explicitly counter-hegemonic. In Gramsci, Williams had discovered a sustained attempt to understand culture as simultaneously both transcending class and irredeemably marked by it. Hegemony, he explained, is 'in the strongest sense a "culture", but a culture which has to be seen as the lived dominance and subordination of particular classes'.[55] An emergent culture, he argued, will require not only distinct kinds of immediate cultural practice, but also new forms or adaptations of forms. Innovation at the level of form, he continued, is thus best understood as '*pre-emergence*, active and pressing but not yet fully articulated'.[56] And it is precisely at this level that structures of feeling operate: they are 'social experiences *in solution*', he wrote, 'and it is primarily to emergent formations ... that the structure of feeling, *as solution*, relates'.[57] Structures of feeling are thus quite specifically counter-hegemonic; that is, they denote the particular elements within the more general culture that most actively anticipate subsequent mutations in the general culture itself. This is some way from Bourdieu and points to what is surely the central difference between the two theorists: their very different sense of the theoretical and practical possibilities for voluntaristic social change.

---

53   Williams 1965, pp. 64–5.
54   Williams 1965, p. 65.
55   Williams 1977, p. 110.
56   Williams 1977, p. 126.
57   Williams 1977, pp. 133–4.

3   Literary Criticism and Sociology

Although Williams and Bourdieu did indeed share a certain 'cultural materialism' in common, there were significant divergences, nonetheless, between their respective positions. These seem to be explicable, at least in part, as a consequence of 'inherited' differences between British culturalism and French structuralism. In short, Williams stood in an essentially analogous relation to the culturalist tradition as did Bourdieu to the structuralist. Where Williams insisted on the concretely experiential quality of social structure, Bourdieu's own sense of structure was much more abstract, a system of durable dispositions rather than a pattern of felt experience. Where Williams worked with a model of theory as explicitly critical, Bourdieu's work tended to affect a quasi-positivistic objectivism. Thus, although *La Distinction* was certainly 'a social critique of the judgement of taste', it was much less obviously a critique of the aesthetic disposition itself: here, the moment of critique remained concealed behind a carefully cultivated mask of scientific 'objectivity'. Even in *La Misère du monde*, clearly the most explicitly engaged of his scholarly works, Bourdieu still insisted that sociological 'science' could itself uncover 'the possibilities for action' political programmes will need to take advantage of.[58] In both respects – the experiential versus the abstract, the critical versus the positivist – these differences bear the impress of their respective disciplinary formations in (English) literary criticism and (French) sociology. But the second, at least, also denotes very different conceptions of the role of the intellectual. Where Williams conceived of the intellectual function itself as primarily critical, and of intellectuals as significantly productive of emergent sensibility, Bourdieu detected, at one level, a job like any other, at another, the dominated fraction of the dominant class, self-interested traders in cultural capital. Bourdieu's famously dismissive description of Derridean deconstruction, as 'ritual transgressions at which only traditionalists could be shocked',[59] is deeply suggestive of his more general antipathy to textual criticism, whether philosohical or literary.

The classic Anglophone statement of the case for literary criticism is Arnold's 'The Function of Criticism at the Present Time', which defined it as *'a disinterested endeavour to learn and propagate the best that is known and thought in the world'*.[60] Such criticism has a social purpose: by 'communicat-

---

58   Bourdieu et al. 1999, p. 629.
59   Bourdieu 1984, p. 495.
60   Arnold 1980, p. 265.

ing fresh knowledge, and letting his own judgement pass along with it', Arnold writes: 'the critic will generally do most good to his readers'.[61] Williams's move from literary into cultural studies was occasioned, in part, by an aversion to this exclusive stress on 'the best' in criticism of the sub-Arnoldian kind. But there was always more to Williams's own work than mere descriptive sociology: part of the point of what he 'came to say' was always, as with Arnold, to do some 'good' for his readers. And, as Williams made clear, his own objections to criticism were levelled, not at judgement *per se*, which seemed to him 'inevitable', but at the peculiar 'pseudo-impersonality' of literary-critical judgement.[62] Indeed, his generally humanist reading of the importance of social agency and social consciousness actually required non-specialist, value judgements of a more or less explicit kind. For if the long revolution was to be continued, then everyday arguments, about culture and society, politics and letters, must succeed in changing people's minds. Literature and literary criticism figured in Williams as a site for what Paul Jones has termed '"emancipatory" ideology critique', that is, the immanent analysis of the 'emancipatory promise' inherent in the utopian claims of ideologies, a promise which can turn them into a 'court of critical appeal' rather than an ideological legitimation.[63] The obvious instance of this procedure is *Culture and Society* itself. But this is precisely the move Bourdieu pointedly refuses to make, or even acknowledge, throughout the broad corpus of his sociological work.

The combination of methodological positivism, a relatively cynical reading of intellectual distinction and a relatively abstract sense of structure threatens to lead Bourdieu's sociology into a radical overestimation of the reproductive powers of the social *status quo*. This is what Garnham and Williams, in their otherwise sympathetic introduction to *La Distinction*, critiqued as the 'functionalist/determinist residue' in Bourdieu. This was mainly a matter of 'tone, nuance and attitude', they conceded, but it led him nonetheless 'to place less emphasis on the possibilities of real change and innovation than either his theory or his empirical research makes necessary'.[64] In retrospect, it becomes apparent that there was more to this residue than mere nuance and that, at the level of theory if not that of empirical research, it remained more than merely residual. The point, surely, is that, for all his acknowledged indebtedness to Weber (and Marx), Bourdieu's understanding of sociology was essentially Durkheimian: witness the positivistic rendering of the empirical as the

---

61   Arnold 1980, p. 264.
62   Williams 1979, pp. 334–6.
63   Jones 1999, pp. 43–4.
64   Garnham and Williams 1980, p. 222.

externally measurable and observable, the sense of the efficacy of collective representations, even the conception of 'sociology' as embracing what the English speakers still distinguished as 'anthropology'. Indeed, one might venture the suggestion that Bourdieu's relation to French structural anthropology – dissenting, plebeian, but belonging, nonetheless – was akin to that between the young Williams and English Literature.

All of this is much less true of *La Misère du monde* than of *La Distinction*. But, as Günter Grass observed in a 1999 ARTE television debate with Bourdieu, that kind of qualitative ethnography shares something of the 'literary' character of his own *Mein Jahrhundert*: 'I see that our work has one thing in common: we tell stories from below. We don't speak over people's heads or from the position of the victor'. Grass even mooted the possibility that he might use some of Bourdieu's 'stories' as 'raw material' for his own writing.[65] In passing, we should note that the book has indeed provided the basis for a number of plays. But this is also part of what defines its exceptionality in relation to the wider Bourdieu oeuvre. Later in the conversation, Bourdieu explains to Grass that sociologists are 'unlike other intellectuals', insofar as most of them know 'how to listen and to interpret', adding that 'this kind of work' is 'all too rare' among intellectuals, since it requires an ability 'to shed their usual egoism and narcisism'.[66] The implication – that Durkeimian or Parsonian, Habermasian or Luhmannian sociology, or even Bourdieu's own earlier work, somehow refuses to speak 'over people's heads' – is surely risible. Nonetheless, there is a certain affinity between ethnography and literature, an affinity which had registered as clearly as anywhere in the early 'culturalist' phases of British cultural studies (Hoggart's *The Uses of Literacy* is the obvious case in point). The more sociological the anthropology, however, and the more structuralist the sociology, the more likely it is to speak over people's heads, telling stories from precisely the position of the victor.

Bourdieu himself struggled to find ways of thinking the role of the intellectual which would allow for his own developing aspiration to activism. Hence, the interest in what he termed the 'corporatism of the universal', that is, the idea that intellectuals have a kind of collective self-interest in the defence of the culture sphere, which somehow translates into something close to a traditional humanist politics.[67] The problem should be obvious, however: this approach both contradicts his own earlier scepticism about the intelligentsia's preten-

---

65   Grass and Bourdieu 2002, p. 63.
66   Grass and Bourdieu 2002, p. 68.
67   Bourdieu 1989; Bourdieu 1996b, pp. 339–48.

sions to distinction and also radically understates the more general moral significance of his own political interventions. It matters, then – and perhaps more than even Garnham and Williams were willing to acknowledge – that Bourdieu's activist politics, increasingly admirable though they undoubtedly were, still seemed extrinsic to his massively 'reproductive' sociology. This should, in turn, remind us that, in Britain at least, what we now know as cultural studies had emerged from an intellectual environment barely touched by sociology. This may not be quite the burden it once seemed.

CHAPTER 7

Deconstructing National Literature: Comparative Literature, Cultural Studies and Critical Theory

I teach at Monash University in Melbourne, Australia, in a programme which combines 'Critical Theory, Comparative Literature and Cultural Studies'. By Critical Theory we mean, in part, the kind of *Kritische Theorie* associated with the Institut für Sozialforschung at the University of Frankfurt, especially Adorno and Horkheimer. But we also use the term more widely to refer to that tradition of 'critique', from Kant's *Kritik der Urteilskraft* to Sartre's *Critique de la raison dialectique*, which Anglophone 'analytical philosophy' commonly dubs 'continental philosophy'. Finally, however, we also use the term to denote the Anglophone tradition of 'literary criticism', especially as inflected through the 'culture and society tradition' Raymond Williams traced from Burke to Orwell in his *Culture and Society 1780–1950*. By Comparative Literature we mean literary studies that go beyond particular national and linguistic boundaries, to borrow Remak's definition.[1] Like most comparatists, we work alongside, both in collaboration and in competition with, an institutionally more powerful programme in the study of a 'national' literature, in our case 'English Literature', although elsewhere one could easily substitute French or German as appropriate. Despite its early appearance in New Zealand,[2] Comparative Literature is still relatively underdeveloped in Australasia: there are only three programmes, at Monash, Auckland and Sydney. The discipline has enjoyed far greater success in France, Germany and the United States – in the latter there are currently around 145 departments or programmes.[3] In Britain – and by extension in most of the former British Empire, Australia included – it was almost entirely overshadowed, both in the universities and in the schools, by 'English Literature', occasionally grudgingly expanded to include writing from other Anglophone societies.

By Cultural Studies we mean the kind of discourse about 'culture' in general, as distinct from literature in particular, which attempts to situate the latter in relation to both wider social and political contexts and other arts and media. In

---

1 Remak 1961, p. 3.
2 Posnett 1973.
3 Spivak 2003, p. 6.

part, this is what the Germans mean by the General in 'General and Comparative Literature' – *Allgemeine Literaturwissenschaft* as distinct from *Vergleichende Literaturwissenschaft* – in part, what they mean by *Kulturkritik*. But the term we use actually comes from Britain, from the margins of English Literature in the 1960s, where writers like Williams, Richard Hoggart and, later, Stuart Hall began to explore the complex and often contradictory relationships between 'high' literature and 'popular culture'. Although the term is distinctively British, it is clear that parallel intellectual concerns inform both Frankfurt School *Kritische Theorie* and Roland Barthes's rewriting of Sartrean existentialism as a semiology of demystification. The key foundational texts for Cultural Studies can thus be read as Adorno and Horkheimer's *Dialektik der Aufklärung*, first published in Europe in 1947, Barthes's *Mythologies*, published in 1957, Hoggart's *The Uses of Literacy* and Williams's *Culture and Society 1780–1950*, published in 1957 and 1958 respectively.[4] All three theoretical formations can, then, be traced to the late 1940s and the 1950s. All three also defined themselves by way of a doubled double opposition: politically, against American capitalism and Russian communism; intellectually, against traditional literary humanism and communist Marxism. Where Literary Studies, whether comparatist or national, had focussed its attention on a particular kind of culture, 'high' literature, this new Cultural Studies was concerned, at least in principle, with all kinds of textualised meaning, whether elite or popular, literary or non-literary.

1   Taking the National out of National Literature

It isn't immediately apparent that Critical Theory, Comparative Literature and Cultural Studies have very much in common, except perhaps that they are not 'English'. For, if all three have become increasingly present in English programmes since 'the crisis in English studies' of the early 1980s,[5] they were nonetheless exactly what the discipline had guarded itself against over the previous half-century or more. F.R. Leavis, the presiding genius of postwar Cambridge English literary criticism – and thereby of much Commonwealth English, for example at both Melbourne and Singapore – was famously opposed to all three. When challenged by Wellek to defend his position 'more abstractedly', Leavis famously replied that: 'My whole effort was to work in terms of concrete judge-

---

4   Adorno and Horkheimer 1947; Barthes 1957; Hoggart 1957; Williams 1958.
5   Widdowson 1982.

ments and particular analyses'.[6] At the risk of stating the obvious, this is an in principal refusal of any kind of Critical Theory. As for Comparative Literature, we need only recall Leavis's apoplectic response to the suggestion that Cambridge English students be exposed to Proust and Kafka: 'It would be a misdirection. There is nothing relevant there'.[7] And if Cultural Studies is, in part, the study of mass media institutions, forms and texts, then it seems barely compatible with Leavis's insistence that:

> the finer values are ceasing to be a matter of even conventional concern ... Everywhere below, a process of standardization, mass-production, and levelling-down goes forward, and civilization is coming to mean a solidarity achieved by the exploitation of the most readily released response.[8]

These interests were not simply excluded by English, they also threatened precisely to undermine it, perhaps even to deconstruct it: Comparative Literature would take the English out of English Literature; Cultural Studies, the exclusive preoccupation with Literature; and Critical Theory would suggest a whole series of analytical strategies – from hermeneutics to deconstruction, from psychoanalysis to feminism – by which either or both ventures might proceed.

Not being English Literature has, for comparatists, the direct corollary of not being Anglocentric, although regrettably in practice it need not also mean not being Eurocentric. Comparative Literature normally requires some training in modern (normally European) languages. At my own university we allow pass degree undergraduate students to read texts in translation, but nonetheless insist that in all research theses they be read in the original. Even in translation, however, the effect of Comparative Literature is to decentre the 'English' canon. For, as Moretti remarks:

> you become a comparatist for a very simple reason: *because you are convinced that that viewpoint is better*. It has greater explanatory power; it's conceptually more elegant; it avoids that ugly 'one-sidedness and narrow-mindedness' ... there is no other justification for the study of world literature ... but this: to be a thorn in the side, a permanent intellectual challenge to national literatures – especially the local literature.[9]

---

6 Leavis 1962b, p. 215.
7 Williams 1984b, p. 117.
8 Leavis 1938, pp. 213–14.
9 Moretti 2000, p. 68.

What intellectual point, other than nationalistic hubris, can there be in fetishising to the point of exclusivity the national literature of England (or France or Germany)? Or of the English (or French or German) speakers? English is not a discipline, it is a language: the discipline is either Literary Studies or, more broadly, Cultural Studies. And it makes as much sense, but no more, to study English (or French or German) Literature than to study English (or French or German) history, geography, politics or philosophy. These are each important regional specialisms, which belong to a generically defined discipline and, properly speaking, so too does English (or French or German) Literature. Regrettably, the long reach of cultural nationalism still tends to prevent us from seeing this.

I am not unmindful of Moretti's caution that the national literature most especially deserving of comparatist critique is the local. In Australia, however, local literature was almost entirely ignored by university English departments until as late as the 1940s and it remains a relatively minor specialism even today. The reason should be obvious: English Literature was founded in Australia as an essentially imperial enterprise and continued as such until the Second World War. E.E. Morris, the foundation Professor of English at the University of Melbourne, was an Oxford man and the first of a series of imperial patriots to occupy the position: his immediate successors were R.S. Wallace, Oxford (and the Gordon Highlanders), Sir Archibald Strong, Oxford (and the author of *Australia and the War*) and G.H. Cowling, Leeds, whose scepticism as to the possibilities of a distinctively Australian national literature were publicly aired in *The Age* newspaper in February 1935, thereby provoking one of the best-known Australian nationalist essays, P.R. Stephensen's *The Foundations of Culture in Australia*.[10] Sir Mungo MacCallum, the first Professor of English at the University of Sydney, held his chair for 33 years, remaining thereafter as professor emeritus, later vice chancellor and finally chancellor; he founded and became the first and only Life President of the local branch of Sir Henry Newbolt's 'English Association'; and, according to the Faculty's official history, his career had been a 'main and conscious offering to the labours of empire'.[11] Of the first seven occupants of the Adelaide chair of English six were Oxford graduates and one from Cambridge.[12] Of course, a British academic in Australia might well have acquired an interest in the local literature, but as a matter of fact they did not.

---

10   Stephensen 1936.
11   Milgate 1952, p. 47.
12   Duncan and Leonard 1973, p. 182.

Stephensen's essay stands in a long line of non-adacemic, Australian nationalist cultural criticism, reaching back to J.F. Archibald's *The Bulletin*, founded in 1887, and forward to Stephen Murray-Smith's *Overland*, founded in 1954. Rebranded as 'postcolonial criticism' in the last decades of the twentieth century, Australian radical nationalism finally found a place in the university English programmes. But it is a strange location nonetheless: not only because postcolonial criticism – as respresented by both Edward Said and Gayatri Spivak – had its origins in deliberately comparatist approaches; but also because Australian postcolonial criticism tends precisely to problematise the Englishness of English Literature. In itself this is unsurprising: Australia in the twenty-first century is no more a part of the British Empire than Croatia is of the Austrian. English Literature, like the constitutional monarchy, has often seemed merely part of the fading afterglow of an Empire on which the sun has finally set. One might conclude that the future therefore finally belongs to an Australian national literature. This seems improbable, however, since even its most enthusiastic advocates are hard pressed to nominate an extended canon of significant Australian writing, still less one that might seriously count as *Weltliteratur*: Harold Bloom's *The Western Canon* lists only 11 writers from Australia and New Zealand in its longer list, none in the short.[13]

Hence, the peculiar contortions in contemporary public controversy over literary education in Australia. The mainly conservative cultural commentators associated with the literary columns of Rupert Murdoch's newspaper, *The Australian*, tend to invoke Bloom's book – extensive extracts from which were published in its columns – while nonetheless arguing for either or both of the English and the Australian literary canons, without noticing that its canon had been comparatist, not national, in scope. Irrespective of national canons, however, whether imperial or postcolonial, contemporary literary taste, as indicated by the titles available in Australian bookshops, is already distinctly cosmopolitan – this is evident, for example, in the considerable enthusiasm for Latin American magic realism – and has thus long since reached escape velocity from English Literature. Indeed, if academic literary studies in Australia is to reestablish a relatively close relation to what intelligent lay readers actually choose to read, then an important long-term strategic objective for Australian universities could be to replace English Literature, or at least significantly augment it, with Comparative Literature.

---

13   Bloom 1994, p. 561.

2 Taking the Literature out of National Literature

Cultural Studies, as currently constructed, remains an unusually polysemic sign: not only is there no clear consensus about what to study, but also none about how to organise this study. The various usages seem to cluster around four main sets of meaning: as inter- or post-disciplinary; as a political intervention into the existing academic disciplines; as an entirely new discipline, defined in terms of an entirely new subject matter, that is, popular culture; and as a new discipline, defined in terms of a new theoretical paradigm. Contemporary Cultural Studies at the University of Birmingham – where the term was coined – was clearly intended by Hoggart as essentially interdisciplinary, but with literary studies its single 'most important' element.[14] A quarter of a century later this remained his view.[15] A rather different conception of Cultural Studies, that is, as a kind of political intervention, can be seen in Hall, Hoggart's immediate successor at Birmingham. For Hall, the 'seriousness' of Cultural Studies was inscribed in its 'political' aspect: 'there is something *at stake* in cultural studies', he insisted, 'in a way that ... is not exactly true of many other ... intellectual ... practices'.[16] Similarly 'political' conceptions recur throughout the Cultural Studies literature. According to Simon During, for example, this politically 'engaged form of analysis' constitutes one of the field's most obviously distinguishing features.[17]

The third conception sees Cultural Studies as an entirely new discipline defined essentially as study of popular culture. America's culture wars were substantially matters of race and ethnicity, gender and sexuality, but insofar as they also brought cultural elitism into conflict with cultural populism, they clearly touched on this issue. For cultural elitists such as Bloom, Cultural Studies threatened to substitute '*Batman* comics, Mormon theme parks, television, movies, and rock' for 'Chaucer, Shakespeare, Milton, Wordsworth and Wallace Stevens'.[18] For cultural populists such as Lawrence Grossberg, this was precisely its promise. No doubt, Cultural Studies emerged in Britain, and later in the United States, by way of a quasi-populist reaction against the elitism of older forms of literary study: both Hoggart and Williams were clearly committed to the study of popular or working-class culture. Nonetheless, neither had imagined Cultural Studies as coextensive with the study of the 'popular arts'. Thus

---

14 Hoggart 1970, p. 255.
15 Hoggart 1970, p. 173.
16 Hall 1992, p. 278.
17 During 1999, p. 2.
18 Bloom 1994, p. 519.

the more recent sense of Cultural Studies as a sociology or semiology of mass media consumption actually runs against the grain of its founding moment. It is also quite oddly misconceived since the older binary organisation of elite and popular cultures has now been increasingly superseded by a large number of cultural niche markets, each dominated by the same international media conglomerates and subject to critical commentary by the same academic and media institutions.

Francis Mulhern used the German word *Kulturkritik* to denote the elitist position in this debate, the English 'Cultural Studies' to denote the populist. There is obvious warrant for this usage. Both Williams himself and, more recently, Geoffrey Hartman have attached a crucial significance in the history of the term 'culture' to the legacy of German Romanticism, where German *Kultur* was troped against French *civilisation*, as human nature in opposition to mechanical artifice.[19] This is the legacy Mulhern acknowledges in his use of *Kulturkritik* to denote, not only the German tradition proper, but also the English tradition from Arnold to Eliot and Leavis.[20] Where this kind of *Kulturkritik* valorises high art, what Mulhern calls Cultural Studies valorises mass civilisation. But the two are by no means as antithetical as they appear, since Cultural Studies actually reproduces the same 'metacultural' discursive form as traditional *Kulturkritik*.[21] In either mode, Mulhern writes, metacultural discourse 'invents an authoritative subject, "good" culture, be it minority or popular, whose function is to mediate a symbolic metapolitical resolution of the contradictions of capitalist modernity'.[22]

There is much to be said for this argument, but Mulhern's categories are by no means as inclusive as he suggests. As he himself notes, Williams's work was an important exception, insofar as it had set out to establish a distinctive 'politics of culture'[23] in opposition to both elitist *Kulturkritik* and populist Cultural Studies. I would add, however, that, quite apart from these specifically political issues, there has always been a fourth option in play, where Cultural Studies is seen as deliberately connecting the study of the popular and the 'literary'. In this definition, it represents a shift not so much in empirical subject matter as in theoretical paradigm. This conception was important for Williams, whose 'empirical' work quite systematically transgressed the boundaries between elite and popular cultures. But it is also widely present elsewhere, for

---

19 Williams 1976a, pp. 78–80; Hartman 1997, pp. 205–7, 210.
20 Mulhern 2000, pp. xv–xvi.
21 Mulhern 2000, p. 156.
22 Mulhern 2000, p. 169.
23 Mulhern 2000, p. 72.

example in Stephen Greenblatt's description of his work on Renaissance literature as 'the new historicism in cultural studies'.[24] No doubt, all four senses of the term register important aspects of different phases in the development of Cultural Studies. But there is a cumulative logic, nonetheless, which suggests that the greater promise lies with the fourth: not in the discovery of a new subject matter, nor even in the 'deconstruction' of the disciplinary boundaries that demarcate literature from fiction, art from culture, elite from popular; but rather, in the development of new methods of analysis for both. Hence, my own half-serious 'definition' of Cultural Studies as the 'social science of the study of the production, distribution, exchange and reception of textualised meaning'.[25] If something like this is indeed what we mean by Cultural Studies, then it follows that its intellectual novelty is primarily theoretical, rather than substantive. Which will lead us back, very shortly, to the question of Critical Theory.

One last remark about Cultural Studies, however. In its original British formulation, Cultural Studies was almost as Anglocentric as English Literature. Its central intellectual achievement was to replace the notion of a single national common culture, reaching highest expression in the national literary canon, with that of a plurality of class cultures internal to the one nation. In Australia, moreover, nationalism itself was a formative influence on Cultural Studies. There, as in England, the prototypical forms of Cultural Studies had developed by way of an immanent critique of English Literature. There, however, the initial pluralisation of the concept of culture was effected by way of an appeal to nation rather than class. So Stephensen's eventual legacy extends to Australian Cultural Studies, where the most characteristic themes have been nationality, indigeneity and postcolonialism, the most characteristic approach a 'peculiarly Australian' semiotics.[26] Graeme Turner summarises the case for this kind of 'semio-nationalism' thus:

> it seems unwise to abandon ... the category of the national as if it were irredeemably tainted ... nationalism is immensely flexible. The terms in which it is currently constructed in Australia may well be established ... but they are not fixed. While nationalism has proved to be a problem ... we don't resolve this by dispensing with the category altogether; nor should we, while we can still contest it and its constitutive discourses.[27]

24 Greenblatt 1990, p. 158.
25 Milner 2002, p. 5.
26 Threadgold et al. 1986, p. 11.
27 Turner 1993, p. 154.

So what had begun as a theoretically poststructuralist argument against humanism, and with it a cosmopolitan argument against older styles of imperial cultural nationalism, would progressively acquire nationalist inflections of its own. This was often an oddly empty nationalism, however, which affirmed and asserted its Australianness, not so much out of loyalty to the particularities and peculiarities of a distinctly Australian national culture, but as a means to secure a place of its own, a niche market in fact, in the increasingly globalised business of Anglophone higher learning.

This emptiness is perhaps clearest in the case of Australian 'postcolonial theory', which often seems little more than a fashionable, that is, internationally saleable, theoretical refurbishment of older themes drawn from radical nationalist cultural criticism on the one hand, 'Commonwealth literature' on the other. If Said was absolutely right to analyse British representations of Ireland as dramatically prefiguring the subsequent history of the imperial adventure, he may nonetheless have been mistaken to treat Australia as a 'white' colony akin to Ireland and white Australians as 'an inferior race well into the twentieth century'.[28] The paradoxical effect of his argument is to obliterate rather than celebrate difference, both the difference between pre-independence and post-independence periods and that between the colonisers and the colonised. For, the colonies of European settlement are not postcolonial in any sense other than that posited by a strict periodisation between pre-independence and post-independence. In every other respect they are instances of a continuing colonisation, where the descendents of the original colonists remain dominant over the colonised indigenous peoples. Moreover, the colonies of European settlement were imagined historically as overseas extensions of Europe itself, as 'Self' rather than 'Other', 'New Britannias', in the words of W.C. Wentworth's 1823 sonnet, rather than new Irelands. The theoretical cachet and radical political glamour, which attached to writers like Said and Spivak, was thus effectively mobilised, by way of Routledge's international marketing strategies, for no better purpose than to sell Australian criticism of Australian literature to Anglo-American audiences.[29]

If such provincial nationalism is the dark underside of Australian Cultural Studies, its obverse is also apparent. In Australia, as elsewhere, the new proto-discipline has become increasingly aware of the domestic multiculturalism of its society. In the United States, Cultural Studies has already begun to address the question of popular culture in languages other than English, thus making

---

28   Said 1993, pp. xvi, 127.
29   Cf. Ashcroft et al. 1989; Ashcroft et al. 1995.

for an increasingly evident coincidence of research interests between Comparative Literature, Cultural Studies and Latino and Hispanic studies. The recent reassertion of domestic political authoritarianism, and of the othering of strangers, evident across the Western world, but perhaps especially in the Anglophone societies, has prompted a growing interest in the cultural politics of immigration and exile, asylum and internment, not only in philosophy,[30] but also in Cultural Studies. The 2006 Annual Conference of the Cultural Studies Association of Australasia, for example, was devoted to the theme of 'UnAustralia', with a keynote address from Jacques Rancière on 'What Does it Mean to be "Un"? The Thinking of Dissensus Today'.[31] Finally, we should note how the growing centrality of political and academic debates over globalisation has prompted a renewed interest in what Said described as thinking 'concretely and sympathetically, contrapuntally,' about 'the connections between things'.[32] This is as evident in the cultural geography of David Harvey[33] as in Moretti's more recent work in Comparative Literature. For these and related reasons, it is becoming clearer than ever that we will need to think of Cultural Studies as a comparative rather than merely national enterprise.

3   Theorising Comparatively

This necessarily poses the question of how to theorise comparatively. What kind of theory is best suited to a Comparative Literature understood as a sub-specialism of Comparative Cultural Studies? Clearly, it will not be the kind of literary humanism proposed in *The Western Canon*, for which Literature remains in imminent danger of being levelled out of existence by Cultural Studies and by the 'School of Resentment' represented by 'Feminists, Marxists, Lacanians, New Historicists, Deconstructionists, Semioticians'.[34] Indeed, Bloom is utterly scathing about contextual approaches to canonical texts, which he dismisses as the product of a 'generation made impatient with deep reading'.[35] His 'world canon' is, of course, an oddly Anglocentric – indeed

---

30   Agamben 2003; Badiou 1998.
31   http://www.unaustralia.com/.
32   Said 1993, p. 408.
33   Harvey 2000 and 2001.
34   Bloom 1994, pp. 519, 527.
35   Bloom 1994, p. 65.

Shakespeare-centric – restatement of Goethe's notion of *Weltliteratur*.[36] But it does, at least, manage to evade the more brutish forms of Anglocentrism very commonly associated with bardolatry. Its argument is fundamentally misconceived, nonetheless, in two fundamental premises: that there is a necessary opposition between Literature and Cultural Studies; and that there is a readily definable literary canon already established by readily available criteria of literary value.

The first seems almost the opposite of the truth, for, as the young Moretti observed of popular fiction: 'Mass literature is not the undifferentiated and meaningless expanse most critics ... say it is. It holds many surprises ... because of the light it sheds on works of a different kind'.[37] The second merely begs the question of how little we know (and of how little we know about how little we know). This too has been broached by Moretti, albeit much more recently. 'What does it mean, studying world literature?' he asks:

> I work on West European narrative between 1790 and 1830 ... Not really, I work on its canonical fraction, which is not even one per cent of published literature ... there are thirty thousand nineteenth-century British novels out there, forty, fifty, sixty thousand – no-one really knows, no-one has read them, no-one ever will. And then there are French novels, Chinese, Argentinian, American ... Reading 'more' is always a good thing, but not the solution.[38]

His solution was to move from literary criticism to social science, here represented by Wallerstein's world-systems theory.[39] But the argument had already been prefigured in Moretti's earlier work. There are, so far as I can discern, three relatively discrete phases in his work. The first includes the essays collected together in the two editions of *Segni e stili del moderno* and his study of the Bildungsroman, *Il romanzo di formazione*, all of which attempt to develop a text-based 'sociology of symbolic forms'.[40] The second opens with *Opere mondo* and runs through *Atlante del romanzo europeo* and his various 'Conjectures', all of which are underpinned theoretically by an attempt to apply world-systems theory to Comparative Literature. The third, marked to date by *Graphs, Maps, Trees*, moves beyond the specifics of this particular approach towards a wholesale

---

36 Goethe 1950, p. 895.
37 Moretti 1988, p. 15.
38 Moretti 2000, p. 55.
39 Cf. Wallerstein 2000.
40 Moretti 1988, p. 19.

and often eclectic embrace of a wide range of theories, methods and techniques drawn from the 'harder' social sciences, especially quantitative history, geography and evolutionary theory.

In retrospect, it is easy to detect the positivist drift in Moretti's thought, which carried with it, simultaneously, very real strengths and equally real weaknesses. His longstanding recognition that canonical approaches to textual criticism had necessarily defined their subject matter in advance of any kind of empirical investigation remains absolutely salutary. As he once rather nicely put it, if they 'behaved like literary critics ... doctors might restrict themselves to studying only healthy bodies'.[41] Moreover, the world-systems approach clearly has real explanatory purchase, though this is perhaps more evident in *Opere mondo* than elsewhere. But I have found it useful in explaining the genesis and evolution of the science fiction genre. The overall effect of this positivistic drift is, nonetheless, increasingly to efface textual criticism. And it is as unclear to me as to Spivak why a combination of world-systems theory, distant reading and the sociology of literary form should become *the* method of comparative literary studies, as distinct from merely one amongst many. Hence, her objection: 'Why should the ... whole world as our object of investigation be the task of every comparativist ...?'[42] Why indeed? Any fully elaborated account of cultural process must include the textual moment, as well as analysis of the conditions of its institutional production, distribution and reception. An exclusively institutional focus makes little sense, given that such institutions matter culturally only because they produce texts and these texts matter culturally only because they mean something.

More fundamentally, however, the act of textual criticism also remains important to social critique. In *The Political Unconscious*, Fredric Jameson argued for a 'double hermeneutic', which would simultaneously embrace both the negative hermeneutic of ideology-critique and the positive of a 'non-instrumental conception of culture'.[43] The negative hermeneutic, so common in Marxism, is necessary insofar as all texts are indeed ideological, the positive insofar as they are always also utopian: for Jameson, even 'the most exclusive forms of ruling-class consciousness' are in their 'very nature Utopian'.[44] As Paul Jones observed of a roughly analogous procedure in Williams, this kind of '"emancipatory" ideology critique' seeks to prosecute an immanent analysis of the 'emancipat-

---

41 Moretti 1988, p. 14.
42 Spivak 2003, p. 108n.
43 Jameson 1981, p. 286.
44 Jameson 1981, p. 289.

ory promise' inherent in the utopian claims of all ideologies, a promise which can, in turn, convert them into a 'court of critical appeal', rather than an ideological legitimation.[45] Similar procedures are clearly also of quite fundamental importance to Adorno and Marcuse.

My reference to Williams leads me, finally, to a few closing remarks on the continuing importance of his 'cultural-materialist' approach, a matter I have pursued at length elsewhere.[46] Williams coined the term 'cultural materialism' to describe the theoretical synthesis he had effected between 'left Leavisite' literary criticism and critical 'Western Marxism'. Cultural materialism, he explained, 'is a theory of culture as a (social and material) productive process and of specific practices, of "arts", as social uses of material means of production (from language as material "practical consciousness" to the specific technologies of writing and forms of writing, through to mechanical and electronic communications systems)'.[47] He sought to circumvent the false opposition between 'idealist' accounts of culture as consciousness and 'materialist' accounts of culture as 'superstructural' effect, by insisting that culture is itself both real and material: 'These are never superstructural activities. They are necessarily material production'.[48]

Williams's cultural materialism was part of a wider movement, begun in the 1960s, towards new theoretical paradigms capable of acknowledging the necessary materiality of cultural texts and institutions, a movement which provided one of the conditions of possibility for Moretti's work. For Williams himself, the key breakthrough had come with *The Long Revolution*, his first pathbreaking excursion into a seriously 'sociological' analysis of literature and culture. Let me conclude, then, by referring you to its central argument: 'The art is there', he wrote, 'as an activity, with the production, the trading, the politics, the raising of families ... Analysis of particular works or institutions is ... analysis of ... the relationships which works or institutions embody as parts of the organization of a whole'.[49] Which means that we can indeed learn from and make use of Moretti's institutional analyses, but that we must nonetheless never allow them to supersede textual criticism. The point, surely, is that these are different levels of analysis, defining different objects of study and requiring different kinds of theory and method. We will almost certainly require the whole range

---

45   Jones 1999, pp. 43–4.
46   Milner 2002.
47   Williams 1980a, p. 243.
48   Williams 1977, p. 93.
49   Williams 1965, pp. 61–3.

if we are to proceed to a Comparative Cultural Studies adequate to the increasingly globalised, but also increasingly textualised, social realities that confront us in the twenty-first century.

CHAPTER 8

It's the *Conscience Collective*, Stupid: Philosophical Aesthetics and the Sociology of Art*

It is now over fifty years since the first publication of Ernest Gellner's *Words and Things* (1959). Insofar as Gellner is remembered today, it is overwhelmingly for his writing on nationalism, commencing with *Thought and Change* in 1964, proceeding through *Nations and Nationalism* in 1983, and on to his last work on the subject, the posthumously published *Nationalism* (1997). But *Words and Things* was quite extraordinarily successful in its day. It was his first book and must be one of very few first books – perhaps, one of very few philosophy books – to have provoked a *Times* editorial and, thereafter, weeks of vigorous controversy in that newspaper's letters page, embroiling figures as distinguished as Bertrand Russell and Gilbert Ryle. Gellner had touched a very raw nerve indeed, for *Words and Things* was in fact a sustained critique of the analytic tradition in English philosophy, counting amongst its targets not only Wittgenstein and Ryle, but also J.L. Austin, A.J. Ayer, Anthony Flew, G.E. Moore and Geoffrey Warnock. 'Philosophy', Gellner wrote, had traditionally been 'the discussion of fundamentals, of the central features and problems of the universe, of life, of man, of thought, of society, of the sciences'.[1] But analytic philosophy 'has put an end to all that. It has shown ... that no proofs or justifications are required for those fundamental and intimate convictions and ideas that are central to our vision of ourselves and the world ... that no reasons are required for what we believe through linguistic habit'.[2] 'The minuteness, pedantry, lack of obvious purpose, in brief, the notorious triviality of those discussions ...', he observed, 'can only be explained in Veblenesque terms. Conspicuous Triviality is a kind of Conspicuous Waste ... Not everyone can afford it'.[3]

Gellner was not English: he was a Czech Jew, brought up in Prague, whose family had fled to England in 1939. During the Second World War he served under General Alois Liska in the 1st Czechoslovak Armoured Brigade of the British Army, which fought in the Normandy Campaign and at the Seige of

---

* This chapter has been published previously in *Thesis Eleven*, No. 103, pp. 26–34, 2010.
1 Gellner 1959, p. 247.
2 Gellner 1959, p. 251.
3 Gellner 1959, p. 246.

Dunkirk.[4] Gellner returned to Czechoslovakia with the 1st Armoured in 1945, marching in the victory parade through Prague, but fled to England a second time to escape the imminent Stalinist coup d'état. He studied Philosophy, Politics and Economics at Oxford, taught philosophy at Edinburgh and sociology at the London School of Economics (LSE), where he was appointed Professor of Philosophy in 1962. He remained at the LSE until 1984, when he became Professor of Anthropology and Fellow of King's College, Cambridge. In 1993, however, Gellner returned to Prague yet again, to become Professor of Anthropology and Sociology and Head of the Center for the Study of Nationalism at the Czech campus of the new Central European University. He died there of a heart attack on 5th November 1995.[5] I mention these biographical details because, like Gellner himself, I believe ideas to be better understood when located in their social contexts, which necessarily have a significantly biographical component. To lose one's home twice to a totalitarian dictatorship might make one very impatient of any claim that: 'Philosophy ... leaves everything as it is' ['Die Philosophie ... läßt alles wie es ist'].[6]

1   First Movement: Sociological Triumphalism

It is conventional to counterpose analytic philosophy to continental, so that one might suppose Gellner's polemic against the former to be delivered from the standpoint of the latter. And he was, in fact, kinder to Sartre, for example, than to the English linguistic philosophers.[7] But Gellner's more general judgement, made quite specifically with respect to Heidegger and Sartre, is nonetheless equally damning: 'On the fundamental issue of values', he writes:

> the two doctrines, disregarding idiosyncracies of expression and the associated meta-philosophy, are identical: both, in effect, maintain the sub-

---

4   As did Frank Knopfelmacher, the Australian social theorist, who was a lifelong correspondent of Gellner. I am grateful to Andrew Knopfelmacher for this information.

5   A far more obscure biographical datum is that Gellner taught me social philosophy when I was an undergraduate at the LSE – although I doubt very much that he ever had cause to recall this. More than any other LSE lecturer – and these included Kedourie and Popper on the Right, Miliband and Westergaard on the Left – Gellner inspired in me a notion of what it might mean to be an academic. His lectures were typically his next book in the making, and his students privileged observers of the performance of thinking.

6   Wittgenstein 1958, p. 49.

7   Gellner 1959, pp. 236, 259.

jectivity of value as an inescapable feature of the human situation. But one side maintains that, just because it is a necessary fact, it is most deeply tragic or glorious; the other, for the very same reason, ... that it must therefore be trivial, no cause for worry, or indeed that it cannot be asserted at all.[8]

Much the same might be said of Derridean deconstruction, the single most important variant of late twentieth-century continental philosophy. Indeed, much the same has been said of Derrida's *La vérité en peinture* by Pierre Bourdieu in *La Distinction*:

> It is an exemplary form of denegation – you tell (yourself) the truth but in such a way that you don't tell it – which defines the objective truth of the philosophical text in its social use; which confers on the philosophical text a social acceptability proportionate to its unreality, its gratuitousness, its sovereign indifference ... he can only philosophically tell the truth about the philosophical text and its philosophical reading, which (apart from the silence of orthodoxy) is the best way of not telling it.[9]

In short, this is a case of 'Conspicuous Triviality', as Gellner had said of the Linguistic Philosophers.

For Bourdieu, the objective alternative to the philosophical game lies in sociology. For Gellner, too, the alternative of an objectivist rather than subjectivist theory of value also lay in sociology. He was adamant that philosophical argument, properly conducted, necessarily impinges upon, and is in turn itself impinged upon by, the social sciences, especially anthropology and sociology: hence, the reference to Thorstein Veblen's *Theory of the Leisure Class* (1912). 'In fact', Gellner writes, 'Linguistic Philosophy calls for sociology. If the meaning of terms is their use and context, then those contexts and the activities therein should be investigated seriously – and *without* making the mistaken assumption that we already know enough about the world and about society to identify the actual functioning of our use of words'.[10]

The philosophical 'fundamentals' that most concerned Gellner were matters of ethics, politics and epistemology, but it is clear, nevertheless, that the argument holds for aesthetics. I want to advance a thesis of my own here. It is

---

8   Gellner 1959, p. 237.
9   Bourdieu 1984, p. 495.
10 Gellner 1959, p. 231.

tempting to see Gellner as reacting against analytic philosophy and turning to sociology because analytic philosophy is trivial. It is tempting to see Bourdieu as reacting against deconstruction and turning to sociology because deconstruction is trivial. But actually it is more likely the obverse is the case: that philosophy, whether analytic and linguistic or continental and deconstructive, had become trivial because sociology, anthropology and social science more generally were already able to provide answers to the kinds of fundamental question philosophy had once asked.

Which takes me to my title, or, at least, to the part referring to Emile Durkheim, rather than to Bill Clinton. Durkheim's last major work, *Les Formes élémentaires de la vie religieuse* (1912), has two main subjects, as he explains in his Introduction: the principal subject is an analysis of the supposedly 'simplest' religions, in practice those of indigenous Australians;[11] the secondary subject is the theory of knowledge.[12] Here, he sets up two main classes of philosophical epistemology, the empiricist, which holds that what we know is given by experience, and the 'apriorist', or what might more commonly be called the rationalist, which holds that the categories of knowledge are immanent within the human mind.

Against both, Durkheim argued that the categories were constituted by and through shared collective representations: 'A concept is not my concept,' he concludes: 'I hold it in common with other men'.[13] The 'collective consciousness', he writes – the French is 'conscience collective'[14] – 'is ... a synthesis *sui generis* of particular consciousness ...', which 'has the effect of disengaging a whole world of sentiments, ideas and images which, once born, obey laws all of their own'.[15] 'The concept of totality', he continues, 'is only the abstract form of the concept of society'.[16] And, in an extraordinary tour de force, he proceeds to argue that the concepts of space, time and cause are all similarly social in origin. I would not wish to give my unqualified support to Durkheim in this matter: there is something almost ominously idealist in his insistence that 'the collective consciousness is the highest form of the psychic life ... placed outside of and above individual and local contingencies, it sees things only in their permanent and essential aspects'.[17] Part of the argument for sociology, surely,

---

11   Durkheim 1976, pp. 1–8.
12   Durkheim 1976, pp. 9–20.
13   Durkheim 1976, p. 433.
14   Durkheim 1960, p. 605.
15   Durkheim 1976, pp. 423–4.
16   Durkheim 1976, p. 442.
17   Durkheim 1976, p. 446.

is that it acknowledges the social variability of what Durkheim here chooses to represent as permanent. But this shift from the philosophical register to the sociological – which one also finds in Marx, Weber, Simmel and others – does generate the prospectus for an empirical research programme inquiring into what exactly it is that people believe and do about politics, ethics, epistemology and aesthetics. Philosophy, by contrast, is simply incapable of generating any such project from within its own resources.[18]

2 Second Movement: Landmarks without a Landscape

The idea of a sociology of art is as old as sociology itself: Comte's *Cours de philosophie positive*, whence the name sociology derives,[19] routinely discusses the varying state of the arts in each of his three stages[20] and their likely prospects under Positivism.[21] The arts – art, music, literature, dance – are each clearly social practices, the categories we bring to their production and reception clearly aspects of the conscience collective, even if Durkheim himself had comparatively little – although not nothing – to say about them.[22] But nothing truly significant appears from sociology before the publication of Max Weber's *Die rationalen und soziologischen Grundlagen der Musik* in 1921.

Thereafter, however, it becomes comparatively easy to identify a number of key 'sociological' texts. Franco Moretti has argued that the history of the arts – and thereby also that of philosophical aesthetics – should be rewritten 'as a sociology of symbolic forms, a history of cultural conventions'.[23] The best results, he concluded, were those 'aimed at defining the internal laws and historical range of a specific genre'.[24] As instances, he cites, as perhaps most scholars would, Lukács's *Die Theorie des Romans* (1963) and *Der historische Roman* (1955), Benjamin's *Ursprung des deutschen Trauerspiels* (1928), Goldmann's *Le Dieu caché* (1955) and Adorno's *Philosophie der neuen Musik* (1949). We could add to this list Williams's *The Country and the City* (1973) – it is worth recall-

---

18 To resume the autobiographical subtext begun in my second footnote, this kind of sociological triumphalism was exactly my own position in the early 1980s, shortly after I had published my first book (Milner 1981) and moved to Melbourne.
19 Comte 1855, p. 444.
20 Comte 1855, pp. 552, 566–71, 632–3, 706–8, 755–6.
21 Comte 1855, pp. 836–8.
22 Durkheim 1976, pp. 127, 373, 380–1.
23 Moretti 1983, p. 19.
24 Moretti 1983, p. 9.

ing he had begun to style his work a 'sociology' from the late 1970s – Heller's *Immortal Comedy* (2005), Jameson's *Archaeologies of the Future* (2005) and, perhaps, Moretti's *Il romanzo di formazione* (1986). Not quite a sociology of symbolic forms, but nonetheless equally sociological in import, we must mention Benjamin's *Charles Baudelaire, Ein Lyriker im Zeitalter des Hochkapitalismus* (1969). More fundamentally, we might add in other kinds of non-reductionist sociology, especially those which locate texts within their specifically cultural-institutional contexts, Bourdieu's *La Distinction* and *Les règles de l'art* (1992) for example, but also Bürger's *Theorie der Avantgarde* (1974) and Casanova's *La république mondiale des lettres* (1999).

We can easily argue about whom to include and whom to exclude. But the most striking feature of this or any other equivalent list would be its structural character as a set of landmarks without a landscape, mountains without foothills. These are each impressive individual achievements, but with little or no sense of a continuing collective project or discipline. Which might explain why *Wikipedia* gives lengthy entries for most sub branches of sociology, but only brief 'stubs', and a handful of references for 'Sociology of art', 'Sociology of literature' and nothing at all for 'Sociology of music' (though there is an entry for 'Sociomusicology'). The contrast with the much more detailed entries for 'Sociology of deviance', 'Sociology of education', 'Sociology of the family' and 'Social stratification' is striking. This disciplinary underdevelopment persists, moreover, despite attempts by some of these landmark thinkers to institutionalise the sub-discipline: Adorno and Horkheimer through the Institut für Sozialforschung at Frankfurt; Goldmann through the Centre for the Sociology of Literature at the Free University of Brussels; Bourdieu through the Centre de Sociologie Européenne in Paris.

Philosophical aesthetics may very well be at a dead end, essentially a series of unanswered because unanswerable questions, but the sociology of art does not yet seem to provide the answers Gellner and Durkheim might have led one to expect. I am by no means sure as to why this should have been so, but I do have three alternative explanatory hypotheses, each testable, I think, even if as yet untested, which locate the source of the problem, respectively, in the nature of sociology as a discipline, in the presence of competing rival disciplines, and in the wider postmodern condition itself.

At its crudest, the first hypothesis simply postulates that 'normal' sociology is too intellectually philistine a practice to be able to accommodate the sociology of art or, indeed, any kind of philosophical sociology. This certainly was not true of the LSE Sociology Department in which Gellner taught me, nor of that at Goldsmiths College London, where I briefly taught in the very early 1980s.

But it was exactly my experience of the Sociology Section of the Department of Anthropology and Sociology at Monash: hence my own move into Comparative Literature. And it still appears true of The Australian Sociological Association, at least when viewed from a distance. I assume that Michèle Barrett, feminist sociologist of literature and former President of the British Sociological Association, no less, came to similar conclusions before moving to the School of English at Queen Mary College London. A more sophisticated version of this hypothesis might derive from Alvin Gouldner's argument that sociology has always been an 'N+1 science', 'required to finish what the other disciplines ... had ... left undone', which is indeed how it was viewed by both Saint-Simon and Comte. There are two versions of this conception, Gouldner continues:

> On the one hand, it involved focusing on intellectual leftovers, on what was not studied by other disciplines. On the other, it sometimes led sociologists to conceive of their discipline as the 'queen' of the social sciences, concerning itself with all that the others do, and more ... This ambitious claim ... was suitable to sociology only when it was still outside the university before it had to compromise with the claims of other academic disciplines.[25]

Those other disciplines necessarily include both philosophy and literary criticism. Which might well explain why the kind of sociology of literature most effectively institutionalised, both in France and the United States, was not a sociology of literature at all – since it never addressed the question of the literariness of literature – but rather a sociology of the book trade.[26]

The rival disciplines hypothesis, by contrast, is directed not at those older precursors, but rather at potential successor disciplines, especially cultural studies, media studies and communications. All of these seem to have drawn on the sociology of art for their theoretical and methodological frameworks and very often also for their personnel: obvious examples include Tony Bennett, Adrian Mellor and John Tulloch. Here, the argument would be that the sociology of art was incorporated into and then effectively cannibalised by these other disciplines, all of which tended to focus attention away from minority intellectual culture and towards popular culture. Interestingly, in Australia there is only one sociology programme west of the Victorian border, but a number of Communications programmes.

---

25 Gouldner 1971, p. 93.
26 Escarpit 1958; Escarpit 1965; Coser et al. 1985.

The third hypothesis repeats the argument of the second, whilst suggesting that this is not simply a contingent process, but rather a structural requirement of the postmodern condition. For if aesthetic populism is indeed a characteristic feature of postmodernity, as has been argued by commentators as diverse as Bauman, Jameson, Baudrillard and even, in some ways, Lyotard, then one would expect so obviously modernist a project as the sociology of art to go the way of all elitisms. On this view, the postmodernisation of the academy has meant a blend of vocationalism with cultural populism, which leaves little room for the traditional humanities themselves, still less for the sociological critique thereof. The sociology of art may thus turn out to be a perennially unfulfilled promise, a permanently uncompleted project, since sociology itself, the cutting edge discipline par excellence of the 1960s and '70s, has in effect been reduced to a form of oldspeak.[27]

3 Third Movement: Distant Reading

No doubt, there is better evidence both for and against each of the three hypotheses than the admixture of hearsay, guesswork and flawed memory gathered together here: they are testable hypotheses after all. My fear, however, is that the truth might lie with a fourth hypothesis, which is that Gellner's own argument about English analytic philosophy might actually be generalisable across the whole of the humanities and social sciences, a proposition to which he clearly did not subscribe. 'To institutionalise a subject', Gellner wrote:

> means having a steady stream of teachers and doctrine. The regularity of this supply ... is after all required by the high degree of organisation and stability of advanced educational systems. But the kind of talent and vision required for having something of interest to say about fundamental issues ... is not something that can be regulated.[28]

What if this were true of all disciplines, sociology as much as philosophy, the sociology of art as much as aesthetics? Then one might well conclude that a normalised sociology of art will require a normalised conception of art, in which both the subject and the object of study become landmarks in a land-

---

27   Autobiographically, these were the rather more sober conclusions I had reached by 1992, when I was appointed Associate Professor in Comparative Literature.
28   Gellner 1959, p. 247.

scape. I do not mean to suggest by this that all artworks are of equal value, nor that all artists are equally important, nor any other such relativist nonsense; but only that the significant acquires meaning precisely when set against the background of the less significant. Neither Lukács nor Goldmann nor Adorno seem to have entertained this proposition. But one can see Williams struggling towards it, in his by no means entirely successful attempt to substitute the category of writing for that of literature;[29] and Bourdieu in his insistence that there can be no criterion of membership in the literary field other than 'the objective fact of producing effects within it';[30] and Moretti, too, in his argument for 'distant reading' as *'a condition of knowledge'*, which permits the analyst 'to focus on units ... smaller or much larger than the text: devices, themes, tropes – or genres and systems'.[31]

This clearly suggest a much less heroic version of the sociology of art than that envisaged by Lukács, Goldmann and Adorno, so that the great artist will become a case study rather than a paradigm. It will therefore almost certainly produce a 'less innovative, much "flatter" ... repetitive, slow – boring, even' account such as Moretti predicts. But as he goes on to ask: 'are we so sure that boredom is boring?' Once confronted, Moretti continues, 'the flatness of literary conventions will appear the genuine enigma it is'.[32] Maybe, maybe not; but it's worth a shot.

---

29 Williams 1977, pp. 145–57.
30 Bourdieu 1993b, p. 42.
31 Moretti 2000, pp. 55–7.
32 Moretti 1998, p. 150.

CHAPTER 9

Science Fiction and the Literary Field*

Flaubert's only historical novel, *Salammbô*, was published in 1862, between *Madame Bovary* in 1857 and *L'Éducation sentimentale* in 1869. A bestseller in its day, it never acquired the critical acclaim accorded either of the other novels. Its publication was also roughly contemporaneous with the first of Verne's 'Voyages Extraordinaire', *Cinq semaines en ballon*, published the following year. This near-coincidence inspired Jameson to observe that 'the moment in which the historical novel as a genre ceases to be functional ... is also the moment of the emergence of science fiction (henceforth SF) ... as a form which ... registers some nascent sense of the future ... in the space on which a sense of the past had once been inscribed'.[1] For Bourdieu, by contrast, the moment of Flaubert was that of the emergence of the modern 'literary field'.[2] The genres conventionally described as 'Science Fiction and Fantasy' in the Anglophone world are commonly denoted by 'La Fantastique' in the Francophone. The latter descriptor is nicely alliterative for the purposes of my title, but unfortunately occludes the novelty of Verne's literary procedures. Which might explain why Bourdieu devoted so little attention to Verne and to science fiction more generally. This essay will attempt to rectify that omission by developing a detailed account of the locus of science fiction in the genesis and structure of the modern literary field.

1   Science Fiction and the Literary Field

For Bourdieu, 'all practices, including those purporting to be disinterested or gratuitous' can be treated as 'directed towards the maximizing of material or symbolic profit'.[3] When applied directly to literature and art, this proposition produces a model of the field of cultural production as structured externally in relation to the 'field of power'; and internally in relation to two 'principles of

---

* This chapter has been published previously in *Science Fiction Studies*, No. 115 (Vol. 38, Part 3), pp. 393–411, 2011.
1 Jameson 2005, pp. 285–6.
2 Bourdieu 1993b, pp. 161–75.
3 Bourdieu 1977b, p. 183.

hierarchization', or ways of allocating value, respectively, the 'heteronomous' and the 'autonomous'.[4] He argues that the modern literary and artistic field is a site of contestation between the heteronomous principle, which subordinates art to economy, and the autonomous, which resists such subordination. The latter is quite specific to the cultural field: 'the theory of art for art's sake ... is to the field of cultural production what the axiom "business is business" ... is to the economic field'.[5] In the short run, the two principles appear diametrically opposed: 'in the ... autonomous sector of the field of cultural production ..., the economy of practises is based ... on a systematic inversion of the principles of all ordinary economies'. In the long run, however, '*symbolic, long-term profits*' are 'ultimately reconvertible into economic profits'.[6]

Bourdieu sees human sociality as the outcome of the strategic actions of individuals operating within a context of values, which he terms 'the habitus'.[7] The literary habitus comprises a series of 'dispositions' – 'vocations', 'aspirations' and 'expectations' – schemes of perception and appreciation which reproduce 'the fundamental divisions of the field of positions – "pure art"/ "commercial art", "bohemian"/"bourgeois", "left bank"/"right bank", etc.'.[8] Bourdieu's map of the late nineteenth-century French literary field traces the specific locations of a number of key French literary formations, the Parnassians, Symbolists and Decadents, the Théâtre libre and the Naturalist novelists. It also, however, maps the locations of vaudeville, cabaret and journalism.[9] This is quite deliberate for, as Bourdieu himself explains, we only ever encounter 'historical definitions of the writer', which correspond to particular states of 'the struggle to impose the legitimate definition of the writer'. There is thus 'no other criterion of membership of a field than the objective fact of producing effects within it'.[10] I have slightly amended Bourdieu's model of the literary field so as to map on to it, in Figure 1, the double location of early French SF.

In Bourdieu's model, the principle of autonomy governs the left of the field, that of heteronomy the right, so that the most autonomous of genres, that is, the least economically profitable – poetry – is to the left, whilst the most

---

4   Bourdieu 1993b, pp. 37–8, 40–1.
5   Bourdieu 1993b, p. 62.
6   Bourdieu 1993b, pp. 39, 54.
7   Bourdieu 1977b, pp. 72–95.
8   Bourdieu 1993b, p. 64.
9   Bourdieu 1993b, p. 49.
10 Bourdieu 1993b, p. 42.

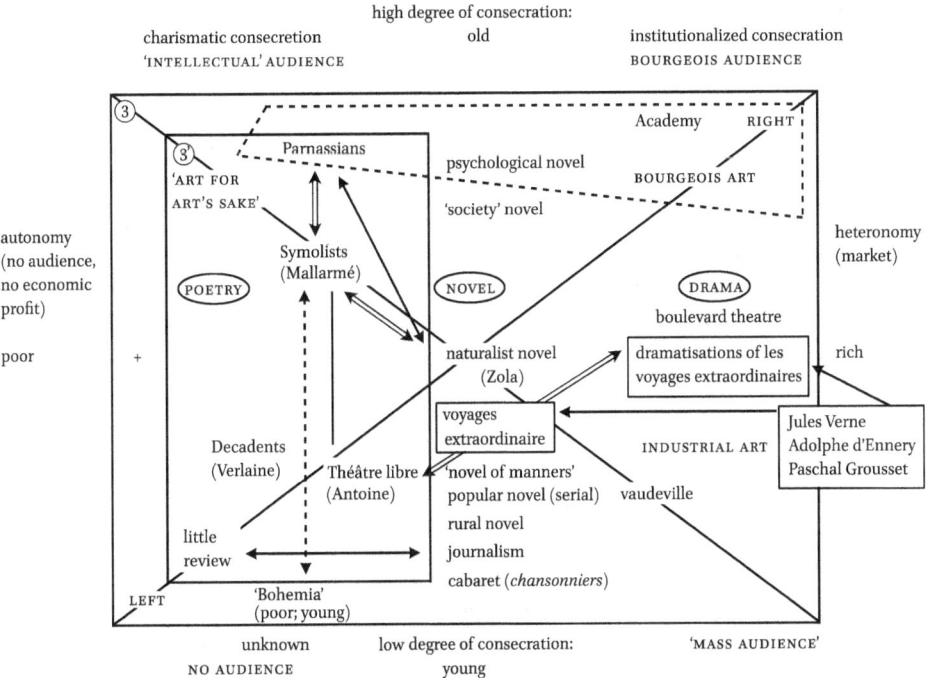

FIGURE 1   *The double location of early French science fiction within the late nineteenth-century literary field*

heteronomous, the most economically profitable – drama – is to the right, with the novel located somewhere in between. Each genre is also characterised by an internal hierarchy, which corresponds to the social hierarchy of its audiences.[11] Here, the high social status audiences – the intellectuals, the old and the bourgeois – govern the upper end of the field, whilst the low status audiences – Bohemia, the young, the masses – govern the lower. The entire field is also traversed diagonally by a left-right political spectrum. SF fits into this model at two locations: the *Voyages extraordinaires* novels written by Verne and, on three occasions, Grousset (under the pseudonym 'André Laurie'); and their dramatisation either for the Théâtre de la Porte Saint-Martin or the Théâtre du Châtelet by Verne and d'Ennery. The plays are largely forgotten, but were nonetheless hugely successful. As Margot notes of *Le Tour du monde en 80 jours*: 'After more than ten years ... barely making a living, Verne became virtually overnight a ...

---

11   Bourdieu 1993b, p. 48.

wealthy playwright'; between 1874 and 1900 the play had more than two thousand performances, featuring special effects that 'were the forerunners of ... Hollywood'.[12]

Here, we need to recall Bourdieu's reasons for locating drama at the heteronomous end of the literary field: 'drama ... secures big profits'; the theatre 'directly experiences the immediate sanction of the bourgeois public' and 'can earn the institutionalized consecration of ... official honours, as well as money'.[13] Nineteenth-century theatre was thus 'bourgeois art' *par excellence*, highly profitable both economically and symbolically. It was also ideally suited to the manufacture of special effects. Shelley's *Frankenstein* had occupied a very similar location within the English literary field. Published in novel form in 1818, its first theatrical adaptation, *Presumption, or the Fate of Frankenstein*, appeared at the English Opera House in 1823. The first French adaptation, *Le Monstre et le magicien*, was performed in 1826 at the Théâtre de la Porte Saint-Martin – the same theatre that would later stage Verne – deploying similarly spectacular special effects. Between 1823 and 1887 there were eighteen different stage adaptations of *Frankenstein* for the British or French commercial theatre.[14] This, then, was SF's original location within the field of cultural production: in the overlap between the bourgeois novel and the bourgeois theatre.

The genre's subsequent history has been one of expansion across the entire literary field. In Figure 2, I have further adapted Bourdieu's model so as to show how this process occurred. The result is by no means entirely faithful to his method: where Bourdieu maps the contours of a literary field located in a particular time and place, my procedures are more science-fictional, crossing both time and space so as to render a composite account of the genesis and structure of the SF field. They do, however, come closer to producing a diagrammatic representation of contemporary SF, considered as a globalised space for the production and reproduction of the genre's own distinctive 'selective tradition', to borrow a term from Williams.[15] The SF field is located, not in some different space from the globalised general literary field – or what Casanova calls the 'world literary space'[16] – but is rather fully within the latter. So the SF field can be visualised as a particular two-dimensional slice of the world literary field conceived as a three-dimensional space.

---

12 Margot 2005, pp. 153–4.
13 Bourdieu 1993b, pp. 47, 51.
14 Forry 1990, pp. 121–2.
15 Williams 1977, p. 115.
16 Casanova 2005, p. 4.

Science Fiction and the Literary Field

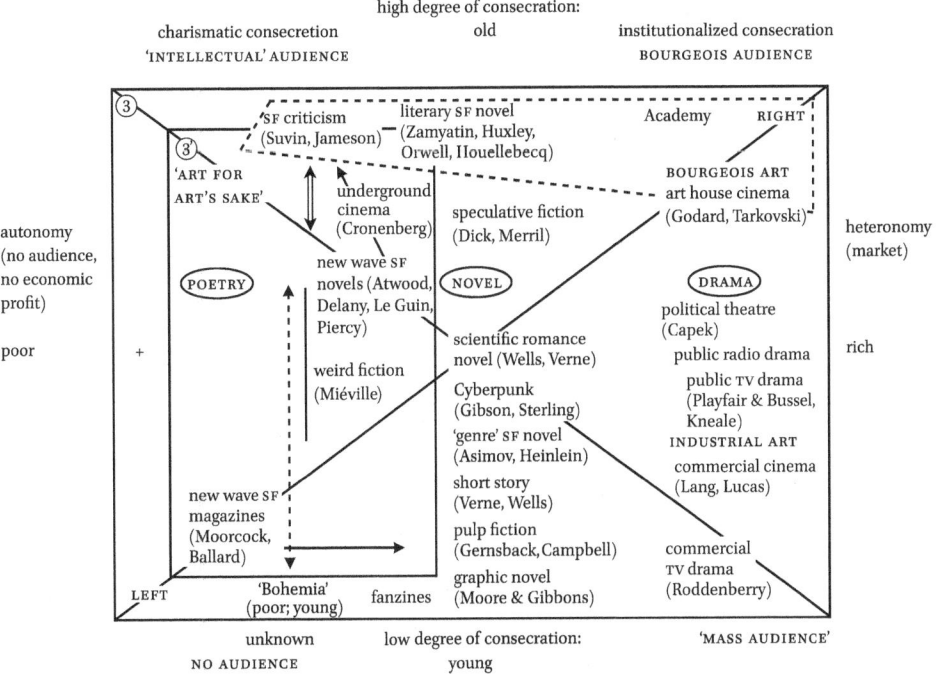

FIGURE 2 *The global science fiction field in the early twenty-first century*

2 The Genesis of the Science Fiction Field: Ideas and Effects

Unlike Bourdieu's maps, mine describes how the contemporary global field processes the legacies of its various cultural pasts. It remains, however, to explain the field's historical genesis, or, to put it in slightly different terms, to explain the historical evolution of the genre's selective tradition. The central lines of development in the SF field, from the mid-nineteenth century through to the early twenty-first, were threefold: first, the development of a range of new dramatic SF forms, from Čapek's political theatre at the bourgeois end of the field (*R.U.R.*, *Věc Makropulo*, *Bilá Nemoc*) to Rodenberry's *Star Trek* franchise at the mass end; second, the development of increasingly popular SF prose forms, most spectacularly 'pulp fiction' and the 'genre' novel; third, the development of high-cultural or avant-gardist dramatic and prose forms within the restricted economy and within institutionalised bourgeois art. The first poses a crucial theoretical question, that of the relation between what might be termed 'ideas' and 'effects'. Literary criticism tends to assume that SF is essentially an experiment with ideas. As Suvin put it: 'Significant modern SF … discusses primarily the political, psychological, and anthropological *use and effect of knowledge*'.[17] Jameson suggests much the same when he writes that 'the scientific pretensions of SF lend the Utopian genre ... epistemological gravity'.[18] No doubt, much written SF has indeed functioned thus, including even instances Jameson finds unpersuasive, such as Verne.[19] But, equally clearly, this claim cannot be made, for example, for 'Doc' Smith's 'Skylark' and 'Lensman' series.

Smith has been the butt of much academic criticism, not least Freedman's carefully understated view that: 'I do not think it can be fruitfully maintained that many very complex or interesting cognitive estrangements are produced in Doc Smith ...'.[20] If SF were indeed entirely a literature of ideas, then Smith's novels couldn't count, since a literature of uninteresting or simple ideas is oxymoronic. But this would be an absurd judgement to make of the guest of honour at the second World Science Fiction Convention in 1940. Freedman's solution is to suggest that genre is better understood as a tendency within texts rather than a totalising description of their collective essence; that the SF tendency is indeed that identified by Suvin; and that Smith's novels, much like *Star Wars* and *Star Trek*, exhibit this tendency 'only weakly and fitfully', but also exhibit a 'spectacular hypertrophy of the specifically visual dimension associated with science-fictional tales of space travel'.[21] This is, by any count, an impressive attempt to save Suvin from himself. A more economical application of Ockham's razor would conclude, however, that Smith's novels are indeed SF, but not terribly interesting or complex examples thereof.

Freedman's reference to the specifically visual aspects of SF is nonetheless suggestive. For it is clear that, no matter how interesting the ideas in *Frankenstein* and the *Voyages extraordinaires*, sheer visuality had been a crucial element in the popular appeal of *Le Monstre et le magicien* and Verne and d'Ennery's 1882 *Voyage à travers l'impossible*. This tradition of SF as visual spectacle is as old as that of SF as a literature of ideas and is crucial to the development of SF drama. Which alerts us to one of the defining features of Suvin's work, its radical indifference to drama, whether as theatre, cinema or television. This is clearly problematic, if only because one of Suvin's own canonical SF writers – Čapek – was precisely a dramatist.

---

17   Suvin 1979, p. 15.
18   Jameson 2005, p. 57.
19   Jameson 2005, pp. 63, 93.
20   Freedman 2000, p. 19.
21   Freedman 2000, pp. 19, 22.

For Suvin, Čapek was 'the most significant world SF writer between the World Wars', but the plays are nonetheless 'the weakest part' of the oeuvre.[22] Suvin is entitled to his opinion, but this is clearly not the judgement endorsed by the SF selective tradition nor reproduced in the literary field. Čapek's coinage of the word 'robot' for *R.U.R.* in 1920 marks a truly decisive – because productive – moment in the history of the genre, the invention of a radically new 'novum', to borrow a key term from Suvin's own theoretical arsenal.[23] The play's astonishing international success powerfully attests to this productivity: first performed in Czech in 1921, translations appeared in German and American English in 1922, Japanese and British English in 1923, French and Russian in 1924, Rumanian and Turkish in 1927, Italian in 1929, Bulgarian in 1931, Swedish in 1934.[24] *R.U.R.* also provided the BBC in London with the text for the first SF television programme ever broadcast, a combination of new medium and new novum immensely suggestive of the play's wider importance.

3 Genesis of the Science Fiction Field: Drama

The expansion of SF drama into the new audio-visual media – cinema, radio and television – had the character of an immanent unfolding of the specular-dramatic potential present within the genre from its very inception. What Benjamin says of Dada is thus also true of early SF: it 'attempted to create by ... literary ... means the effects which the public today seeks in film'.[25] The earliest SF film, loosely based on Verne's *De la terre à la luna* and Wells's *The First Men in the Moon*, was Méliès's *La Voyage dans la lune*, produced in 1902, less than seven years after the Lumière brothers' first film projections. The earliest SF blockbuster was Lang's *Metropolis*, nearly two years in the making and finally released in January 1927. For Méliès and Lang, as for almost all their successors, the genre's appeal was overwhelmingly in the use of special effects to achieve visual, as distinct from literary, rendition of a novum. One can trace the history of SF in popular cinema through a series of effects landmarks, from Galeen's 1928 *Alraune*, a huge success for Ama-Film and Universum Film Aktiengesellschaft in both Germany and the United States, through to Cameron's 2009 *Avatar*, the most ambitious experiment in 3D cinema to date and also the highest grossing film in Hollywood history.

---

22 Suvin 1979, pp. 280, 270.
23 Suvin 1979, p. 63.
24 Čapek 1922; Čapek 1966, pp. 117, 204–5.
25 Benjamin 1973, p. 239.

Cinematic special effects do not come cheap: *La Voyage dans la lune* had a budget of 10,000 francs, 'an unbelievable amount of money at the beginning of the twentieth century';[26] *Metropolis* cost DM 5 million and would have bankrupted UFA had it not acquired near-simultaneous distribution in Britain and the USA; Cameron's *Terminator 2* was the first American film to cost over $US 100,000,000; and, according to *Forbes* magazine in 2005, SF then accounted for 11 of the 25 most expensive films made in Hollywood.[27] A recent commentator remarks that the narrative of *La Voyage dans la lune* was merely 'a frame upon which to string a demonstration of the magical possibilities of cinema'.[28] This isn't quite true of *Metropolis*, but the architecture of the film's cityscape is, nonetheless, its central dystopian novum, a synecdoche for the wider catastrophes to have overcome its population. Much the same might be said of *Terminator 2*: the T-1000, made of a 'mimetic polyalloy' liquid metal, which can take the shape of anything it touches, *is* the film's novum.

Film theorists generally take exception to Adorno and Horkheimer's thesis that 'the culture industry has led to the predominance of the effect ... over the work itself – which once expressed an idea, but was liquidated together with the idea'.[29] But their argument seems oddly pertinent to SF cinema, for, in this particular genre, where the literary novum has, indeed, often been an 'idea', the central cinematic and dramatic device has typically been the translation of 'idea' into 'effect'. There is thus a certain necessary tension between the novum as idea and its representation as spectacle. This is only a tendency, however, towards the conceptualisation of the novum as idea in the written medium, towards its specularisation as effect in the cinematic, with each understood as points on a continuum – or, more accurately, locations within a cultural field – rather than as permanent structural properties of any particular medium. Given the sheer expense of special effects, it was virtually unavoidable that commercial SF cinema, should have been located further towards the heteronomous end of the field than the SF novel.

Radio and television are cheaper to produce than cinema and also more likely to be publicly owned and subsidised. The linked questions of ownership and subsidy have a direct bearing on the kinds of drama available in these media. As a general rule – to which there are necessarily a great many exceptions – public broadcasting's greater immunity from direct commercial

---

26 Vallorani 2005, p. 320.
27 Rose 2005.
28 Cornea 2007, p. 250.
29 Adorno and Horkheimer 1979, p. 125.

pressure has tended to make for more adventurous scripts, its relative shortage of funding for worse special effects, especially in the case of television. Commercial television thus had a distinct advantage in the manufacture of specularity. Radio dates from the early 1920s, television from the late 1930s. In Britain, the BBC began broadcasting radio in 1920, television in 1936, with a state-sanctioned monopoly, lasting until 1955 in television, 1973 in radio. Thereafter it had private competitors, but nonetheless continued to dominate the market. Most European and Commonwealth countries began with state monopolies, which were eventually opened up to private competition. In the USA, by contrast, both radio and television were organised around a system of publicly licensed but privately owned commercial stations, sustained financially by advertising and sponsorship. The first licensed American radio station was Westinghouse's KDKA (1920), the first television station NBC's W2XBS (1939). Government funded broadcasting came much later, television in 1970 and radio in 1971.

The history of SF radio is badly underesearched: neither the *The Cambridge Companion to Science Fiction* nor *The Routledge Companion to Science Fiction* contain entries and Clute and Nicholls's *Encyclopedia of Science Fiction* is uncharacteristically vague. But commercial radio seems to have broadcast SF primarily in the USA, primarily during the so-called 'Golden Age of Radio', from the mid-1930s until the early 1950s. Thereafter, drama was progressively displaced by music, news and talkback conversation. No longer significantly current, I omitted commercial radio from my map of the SF field, but its previous location is apparent: toward the mass/heteronomous corner of the field, near commercial cinema and commercial television. Much American radio SF was produced in serial form and aimed at children. But the most notorious of all commercial radio SF programmes, Welles's 1938 adaptation of *War of the Worlds*, was clearly neither. Its audience reached only about six million, but of these around 1,700,000 believed it to be 'true'.[30] The resulting panic has become the stuff of – much exaggerated – urban legend.

The BBC has played a crucial role in SF radio, especially after the decline of American commercial radio. Its best-known postwar work ranged from serials, like *Journey Into Space* (1953–5) and *The Hitchhiker's Guide to the Galaxy* (1978–80, 2004–5), through self-contained SF radio plays, especially those broadcast in the general anthology series *Saturday Night Theatre* (1943–96), to broadcast readings from SF novels. In Canada, CBC's radio anthology series, *The Vanishing Point*, ran from 1984 until 1991 and famously included versions of both

---

30   Hand 2006, p. 7.

Clarke's *Childhood's End* and Le Guin's *The Dispossessed*. German public radio also broadcast radio plays, or *Hörspiele*, some of which were generically SF: important examples included Bayerischer Rundfunk's 1955 version of Dürrenmatt's *Das Unternehmen Der Wega* and Westdeutschen Rudfunks Köln's 1969 broadcast of the Bruehl translation of Wyndham's *Die Triffids*. In France, RTF stations, especially France Inter and France Culture, produced both a string of SF radio serials and series, from *Les Tyrans sont parmi nous* (1953) through to *Renard, Maurice* (1981), and anthology series, such as *Le Théâtre de l'Étrange* (1963–74) and *La Science-Fiction* (1980–1).

The difference between the American and European patterns was replicated in television. As with radio, American television SF was originally aimed overwhelmingly at children: the earliest example is *Captain Video* (1949–56). As with radio, the BBC's earliest efforts were distinctly 'literary': its first SF television programme was the 1938 35-minute broadcast of Čapek's *R.U.R.*, adapted from the original by Playfair and Bussell, who subsequently worked together on a 90-minute version, broadcast in 1948. Barr's production of Wells's *The Time Machine* and Kneale's of Orwell's *Nineteen Eighty-Four* followed in 1949, Kneale's own *The Quatermass Experiment*, the first BBC TV serial, in 1953. All were aimed at adults, plausibly embodying Lord Reith's vision of a national broadcaster that would aim to 'inform, educate and entertain'.[31] As Cook and Wright observe: 'British TV exported to global audiences a more sceptical, perhaps even more "realistic", view of the science fiction future … manifested … by way either of ironic humour … or … something altogether more dark and despairing'.[32] All US television SF programming came from the private sector, most British from the BBC, most obviously *Doctor Who* (1963–89, 1996, 2005–), *The Hitch Hiker's Guide to the Galaxy* (1981) and *Red Dwarf* (1988–99).

In television, however, there would be no equivalent to the disappearance of drama from commercial radio. In the 1960s, American commercial television produced two important anthology series, *The Twilight Zone* (1959–64) and *The Outer Limits* (1963–5); in the decades that followed, it presided over the most successful of all SF franchises, *Star Trek* (1966–9) and its various sequels; and, in the 1990s, it produced two of the most formally innovative of late twentieth century SF television series, Straczynski's *Babylon 5* (1993–8) and Carter's *The X-Files* (1993–2002). Japanese commercial television also became a significant player in the global field, so much so that by the early twenty-first century it

---

31 De Burgh 2000, p. 199.
32 Cook and Wright 2006, p. 5.

was the major source of non-Anglophone television SF. The programmes were mainly anime and mainly produced by commercial broadcasters, such as TV Tokyo Network and Fuji TV, as distinct from NHK, the national public broadcaster. They were also initially aimed overwhelmingly at children: the earliest was Tezuka's *Tetsuwan Atomu*, first aired in Japan in 1963 and subsequently marketed internationally as *Astro Boy*.

Other public television broadcasters appear to have been less interested in the genre than the BBC. The first German public SF television series, ARD's *Raumpatrouille Orion* didn't appear until 1966, the Australian ABC's first SF series, *Vega 4*, not until 1967. In Canada, the CBC had broadcast *Space Command* as early as 1953, but this was a children's show, on the then American model. There have been subsequent experiments with television SF in all three countries, but the rising cost of special effects resulted in an increasing reliance on imported American, British or Japanese material. By the early twenty-first century the best-known SF shows from all three were commercially produced in co-production with American or British companies: *LEXX* (1997–2002), a German-Canadian co-production partly funded by the British Channel Five; *Farscape* (1999–2003), an Australian-American co-production; and a plethora of Canadian-American co-productions filmed in Canada but to all appearances American in content.

This pattern, in which 'quality' domestic public sector broadcasting was progressively displaced by imported commercial content, is peculiarly apparent in France, where SF had occupied an unusually central position in the national culture. French public television had produced a significant body of SF in the period between the foundation of RTF in 1949 and the partial privatisation of television in the 1980s. Government-run stations ran numerous adaptations of Verne, especially *L'île mystérieuse* (the first in 1963) and *Le Tour du monde en 80 jours* (the first in 1975). They broadcast telemovies, for example ORTF's 1974 version of *Frankenstein* and FR2's 1994 adaption of Andrevon's *Le Travail du furet*. And they produced a wide range of series and serials, from *Les Atomistes* (1968) through to *Bing* (1991–2). But the progressive commercialisation of French television, between 1981 and 1987, has led to a decline in domestic output and an increased reliance on imported programming.

As with cinema, an important part of the appeal of SF to radio and television producers and consumers lies in the opportunity for special effects. The tension between idea and effect seems to be resolved differently in radio and television, however, primarily because of the comparatively low-budget nature of the media. At one level, financial constraints clearly militate against both idea and effect, which is why so much radio and television is interesting as neither. But ideas can come more cheaply than their specularisation, which leads to the possibility that these media might sometimes reverse the cinematic prioritisation of effect over idea. Moreover, this is more likely to be true for public broadcasting on the one hand, and satellite and cable television on the other, both of which enjoy comparative freedom to explore smaller 'niche markets'. SF has only ever been a niche market: hence its repeated failure, children's television aside, on the three major American commercial networks from the 1950s to the 1970s, when programming was aimed overwhelmingly at 'mass' audiences.[33]

The experimental potential for radio and television SF applies at the level of form as well as content. Williams's pioneering account of broadcast drama identified three main forms: the series, the serial and the single play, often included in an anthology series.[34] All have been used in SF, but the last seems to have become less common, probably because different combinations of production and performance personnel for each episode makes it relatively high-cost. The most interesting formal innovation in late twentieth-century television SF was the development of what Reeves, Rodgers and Epstein, referring to *The X-Files*, describe as 'episodic/serial straddle', that is, the 'mini-serial within the series'.[35] Here, there are discrete episodes, but also a range of developing story lines continued from episode to episode, which allow for cumulative character development unavailable to the conventional series. This device was applied to SF by Carter in *The X-Files*, Straczynski in *Babylon 5*, O'Bannon in *Farscape* and Davies in the BBC Cymru relaunch of *Doctor Who* and in *Torchwood* (2006–9), its 'adult' spin-off.

This leaves us with a map of the heteronomous end of the SF field, where the new forms of SF drama are all market driven, but Čapek's theatre appeals to the most bourgeois audience, anime and the *Star Trek* franchise to the most massified, with public radio, public television and commercial cinema ranged in between. Clearly, these locations will not be accurate for each and every programme, but they will suffice as reasonably adequate generalisations: it must be obvious that Potter's 1996 *Cold Lazarus* could never have been produced solely by a 'free to air' network commercial television station. These comparisons are not intended invidiously. They are merely points on a map, organised horizontally, rather than positions in a hierarchy, organised vertically, but will nonetheless generate invidious comparisons within the SF field. As Bourdieu observes: 'The *boundary* of the field is a stake of struggles ... the social

---

33   Reeves, Rodgers and Epstein 1996, pp. 24–9.
34   Williams 1974b, pp. 57–61.
35   Reeves, Rodgers and Epstein 1996, pp. 33–4.

scientist's task is not to draw a dividing line between the agents involved ... but to describe ... the frontier delimiting the territory held by the competing agents'.[36]

4 Genesis of the Science Fiction Field: Prose

The most important developments in SF prose were, either directly or indirectly, effects of American 'pulp fiction'. SF short stories had been published in Europe in the nineteenth century and, indeed, both Verne and Wells experimented with the form – the best examples are collected in, respectively, *Le Docteur Ox* (1874) and *The Stolen Bacillus and Other Incidents* (1895). But European prose SF was, nonetheless, overwhelmingly a matter for the 'scientific romance', or novel. Gernsback invented neither the SF short story nor the SF pulp magazine: Aldiss is right to stress that Swedish and German SF pulps predated *Amazing Stories*.[37] But Gernsback's achievement remains: to use this magazine to open up an entirely new space in the SF field, which would be occupied by a succession of subsequent American pulps, above all, Campbell's *Astounding Science-Fiction*. For American SF enthusiasts the genre's so-called 'Golden Age' began in 1937, when Campbell was appointed editor, and continued until the early to mid-1950s, when its dominance was gradually undermined by the paperback novel.

The pulps were able to do for prose what film, radio and television had done for drama: to extend the genre towards the younger and poorer end of the heteronomous part of the literary field. Gernsback was peculiarly well placed in this, given his interests in broadcasting, as publisher of *Radio-Craft* and co-owner of station WRNY. This opening to the least consecrated end of the field was further extended in 1938 by the launch of the first SF comic book, DC's *Action Comics*, as a platform for Siegel and Shuster's Superman, quickly followed in 1939 by Marvel's the Human Torch in *Marvel Comics* and thereafter by a plethora of similar titles. For all his antipathy to Gernsback, Aldiss pays Campbell's *Astounding* its due: 'The pulps', he writes, 'were churned out for a lower middle class or working class ... entirely without privilege ... But only Campbell's heroes had the real equalizer ... Campbell gave you the future on your chipped plate'.[38]

---

36   Bourdieu 1993b, p. 42.
37   Aldiss 1986, p. 202.
38   Aldiss 1986, pp. 228–9.

As socially effective cultural institutions, both pulps and comics were American in origin, even if the first wasn't entirely so in initial invention. And both were exported internationally, with varying degrees of success. In Britain, *New Worlds* first appeared as a 'pulp' in 1946, but was relaunched in 'Digest' format in 1949 and soon transformed into the country's leading SF magazine. In France, *Fiction* (1953–90) was both the most enduring and the most important of SF magazines: as Slusser observes, it 'was the "workshop" for the French writers ... who produced ... [the SF] renaissance of the 1960s–70s'.[39] The German pulp weekly *Perry Rhodan*, published continuously since 1961, is claimed to be the longest-running of all SF series according to its publishers, Verlagsunion Pabel-Moewig. The most successful SF comic in Britain is probably *2000 AD* (1977–), in France *Métal Hurlant* (1974–87, 2002–4). More significant than either, however, for the global field were the Japanese manga, beginning in 1951 with *Tetsuwan Atomu* and including, amongst many others, *Akira* (1982–90) and *Gōsuto In Za Sheru/Kōkaku Kidōtai* (1989–91), all of which were also adapted for anime.

In the United States the pulps were largely superseded by the 'genre' novel, published initially by specialist SF publishers, like Fantasy Press, Hadley Publishing and Shasta. From the mid-1950s, large general publishers increasingly acquired or constructed their own SF lists, which were often published in both paperback and hardback. Important examples included Ace Books, which dominated SF publishing in the 1970s and 80s, Doubleday, which published Ellison's *Dangerous Visions* anthologies, and Putnam, which published Knight's *Orbit* anthologies. In Britain and France, where the pulps were institutionally less significant, SF publishing was normally conducted by general publishers. The most significant included Gollancz, Michael Joseph and Macmillan, Denoël's 'Présence du Futur', Fleuve Noir's 'Anticipation', Hachette and Gallimard's 'Le Rayon Fantastique', and Laffont's 'Ailleurs et Demain'. But, as in the US, British and French SF reached a mass market primarily through paperback publishers, such as Penguin and Pan, Livre de Poche and J'ai Lu. The German pattern was different again: neither pulps nor paperbacks, but rather something straddled in between, normally published by Pabel or Moewig or, eventually, Pabel-Moewig.

Whatever the objections to pulp fiction, Gernsback had created the space for later genre publishing, which, in turn created that for various 'New Wave' interventions. The continuity between pulp and genre is at its most apparent

---

39   Slusser 1989, p. 252.

in the USA, where novels by writers as diverse as Asimov, Blish, Heinlein and van Vogt were, in fact, 'fix-ups' of previously published magazine stories.[40] But British genre writers had also published in the pulps, Wyndham in *Wonder Stories*, for example, and Ballard in *Science Fantasy*. The latter eventually traversed virtually the entire field, moving on to the avant-garde New Wave and, thence, in turn, to the realist novel. In Figure 2, I include the genre novel, the short story, pulp fiction and the graphic novel, each with examples, toward the lower end of the prose spine of the SF field, in a descending hierarchy of legitimate consecration and an ascending hierarchy of mass popularity. Doubtless, we could readily provide alternative examples of each; we might also include a separate category for the comic book, as distinct from the graphic novel, yet further toward the lower boundary, though this would sometimes be a very fine distinction to make; we could have chosen less 'literary' examples of the short story than Verne and Wells (but also more 'literary', as in Forster); and more typical examples of the graphic novel than Moore and Gibbons's *Watchmen* (1986–7), which, as DC's most critically acclaimed title, is not so much representative as paradigmatic; and we might even describe the field as Euro-American-Japanese rather than global. But the general contours seem more or less accurate.

One outstanding problem remains, that of where to locate the various New Wave movements, which arise intermittently, in antipathetic reaction to the predominant formations within the SF field. I included five of these in Figure 2: the loose and not entirely satisfactory linkage of Merril's notion of 'speculative fiction' to Dick's novels; a relatively uncontentious identification of cyberpunk with Gibson and Sterling (although one could give non-American examples, such as Dantec in France and Oshii in Japan); an equally uncontentious linkage of Moorcock and Ballard through the British New Wave; a defensible, but more precarious, identification of the American New Wave with countercultural political radicalisms of one kind or another (which underestimates the role of writers like Ellison and Spinrad); and 'Weird Fiction', which could better be exemplified by Lovecraft than Miéville, except that the latter deliberately situates his own work in relation to the SF field. I located three of these within the restricted economy and will postpone their discussion for the moment. Speculative fiction and cyberpunk fall within the extended economy, however, even though they developed at least in part in response to the logic of the restricted economy. But both escaped that logic, one in the direction of 'literary'

---

40   Clute and Nicholls 1993, p. 432; Van Vogt 1973, pp. 85, 135.

SF – what else can it mean for Jameson to describe Dick as the 'Shakespeare of Science Fiction'?[41] – the other towards the mass market. Hence, their respective locations.

5 Genesis of the Science Fiction Field: The Restricted Economy and Institutionalised Bourgeois Art

Turning, finally, to our third region, there are two distinct, but overlapping, parts of the SF field to be addressed: the restricted economy and institutionalised bourgeois art. We should note, in passing, that academic SF criticism lies at the upper end of the restricted field, consecrated 'charismatically' by intellectual rather than bourgeois audiences. It clearly commands little attention beyond the academic intelligentsia: neither Suvin nor Jameson has been shortlisted for a Hugo, not even in the non-fiction categories. More importantly, the restricted field also poses the question of the avant-garde, often deemed anachronistic in much commentary on postmodernism, which tends to insist, with Bürger, that 'art has passed beyond the historical avant-garde movements'.[42] Thus Jameson: 'we are beyond the avant-gardes ... the collaborative ... eschews the organization of a movement or a school, ignores the vocation of style, and omits the trappings of the manifesto or program'.[43] There is some truth in this, but it seems oddly inapplicable to SF. If avant-gardism is closely identified with high modernism, either as integral[44] or internally opposed to it,[45] then by definition there can be no avant-gardes in so unmodernist a field as SF. But SF history is nonetheless replete with intellectual formations the organisation, vocation and trappings of which bear close resemblance to those of the historical avant-garde. An obvious example – especially interesting given its close proximity to the pulp milieu – is provided by the New York 'Futurians'.

Organisationally, the Futurians were as much a 'school' or 'movement' as Futurism itself. The vexed relationship between Campbell and Futurianism has been explored elsewhere.[46] Suffice it to note here that avant-gardist styles of organisation, vocation and trapping were clearly present in American SF, even at this most apparently mass-commercial of moments. The Futurians actively

---

41 Jameson 2005, p. 345.
42 Bürger 1984, p. 94.
43 Jameson 1991, p. 167.
44 Poggioli 1968, p. 15.
45 Bürger 1984, p. 22.
46 Milner and Savage 2008, pp. 36–43.

published their own alternative pulp magazines.[47] These were barely viable commercially, typically avant-gardist products of a restricted rather than extended economy: Wollheim brought out only four issues of *Stirring Science Stories*, only three of *Cosmic Stories*. Often little more than fanzines, these magazines were located well within the restricted economy, but nonetheless at positions proximate to the more commercially successful pulps. Many individual authors later achieved success within the extended economy, but Futurianism itself remained irreparably a product of the restricted economy.

Much the same can be said of the British and American New Waves of the 1960s and '70s, cyberpunk in the 1980s and the New Weird in the early twenty-first century. The British New Wave cohered around *New Worlds* during Moorcock's term as editor (1964–71) and found quintessential expression in Ballard's *The Atrocity Exhibition* (1970). Moorcock's opening editorial, programmatically entitled 'A New Literature for the Space Age', approvingly cited Burroughs's argument that, if 'writers are to describe the advanced techniques of the Space Age, they must invent writing techniques equally as advanced'.[48] Twenty-five issues later, Moorcock would insist, equally programmatically, that Ballard had become 'the first clear voice of a movement destined to consolidate the literary ideas ... of the 20th century, forming them into ... a new instrument for dealing with the world of the future contained ... in the world of the present'.[49] For Moorcock, the '*New Worlds* group' was clearly a 'Movement'[50] with its own style and programme. It was also very obviously autonomous rather than heteronomous. Funded by the British Arts Council, but blacklisted by W.H. Smith, the leading British bookseller, the magazine's financial arrangements were typical of a restricted economy: 'precarious ... but this helped direct it in adventurous directions'.[51] The American New Wave was in part a spin-off from the British: Spinrad, Disch, Ellison, Farmer, Zoline had all been published in *New Worlds*. But Ellison's 1967 *Dangerous Visions* anthology announced the repatriation of the American New Wave. Here, too, we find a similarly avant-gardist tone: 'What you hold in your hands is more than a book ...', Ellison wrote, 'it is a revolution ... It was intended to shake things up. It was conceived out of a need for new horizons, new forms, new styles, new challenges in the literature of our times'.[52] In the US, however, where there had been no direct counterpart to *New*

---

47   Ashley 2000, pp. 149, 159–62.
48   Moorcock 1964, p. 2.
49   Moorcock 1966, p. 2.
50   Greenland 1983, p. 205.
51   Luckhurst 2005, p. 145.
52   Ellison 2002, p. xxxiii.

Worlds, New Wave writing would be published in mainstream SF magazines, anthologies or novels. Historically a few years later and geographically closer to the epicentre of 'new social movement' radicalism, the American New Wave was directly exposed to the impact of both feminist and Afro-American identity politics. It would thus become simultaneously more commercially successful, more politicised and less avant-gardist than the British: Le Guin's two Hugos, for *The Left Hand of Darkness* in 1970 and *The Dispossessed* in 1975, are nicely symptomatic. Both feminist SF (here represented by Le Guin and Piercy, though one could easily add Russ, Ermshwiller and Butler) and Afrofuturist SF (here Delany, but also Butler once again, Moseley and others) are thus best understood as direct products of the New Wave, rather than as distinct successor formations akin to cyberpunk. Delany and Ermswhiller were published in *Dangerous Visions*, Le Guin and Russ in *Again, Dangerous Visions* and Butler was to have been included in the unpublished *Last Dangerous Visions*. I located this formation within the restricted economy since it is clear that some writers – Russ and Delany – vigorously resisted the claims of the extended economy, but also towards its outer edge since others – Atwood and Le Guin – achieved a kind of commercial success which pointed toward institutionalised consecration by the intelligentsia, if not the bourgeoisie.

Cyberpunk also espoused, rather than eschewed, the organisation of a movement: Shiner even described it thus;[53] it actively embraced the vocation of style – 'they are in love with style', Sterling wrote, favouring a 'crammed' prose, with 'rapid, dizzying bursts of novel information, sensory overload that submerges the reader';[54] and it too had its manifestos and programmes – what else is the 'Preface' to *Mirrorshades*? Cyberpunk quickly became a commercial success, which is why I have located it close to scientific romance at the centre of the SF field, but its origins were in the restricted economy nonetheless. To quote Sterling again: 'Before ... the labels, cyberpunk was simply ... a loose generational nexus of ambitious young writers, who swapped letters, manuscripts, ideas, glowing praise, and blistering criticism'.[55]

Weird Fiction is less obviously an SF avant-garde than either New Wave because it is less obviously SF: Lovecraft would never have considered his writing thus. But it is clear that his work has been an important influence on others who might: Houellebecq (1991), Miéville[56] and the New Weird more generally. The latter's avant-gardist aspirations are as evident as those of earlier New

---

53   Shiner 1992, p. 25.
54   Sterling 1986, pp. viii, xii–xiii.
55   Sterling 1986, p. ix.
56   Gordon 2003, p. 358.

Waves. Witness the characteristically programmatic introduction and overall programmatic structure of the VanderMeers' *New Weird* anthology (2008). And Miéville, at least, is happy to locate Weird Fiction in relation to the SF selective tradition. The first and last volumes of his Bas-Lag trilogy won Clarke Awards for the 'best science fiction novel' published in the United Kingdom. 'Weird Fiction', Miéville has written, is 'the bad conscience of the Gernsback/Campbell sf paradigm, ... rebuke to ... theorizing that takes that paradigm's implicit self-conception as its starting point'.[57] Both literary avant-gardist and political vanguardist – and thus doubly consigned to the restricted economy – Miéville has also determinedly prosecuted his case for the Weird in the most improbably Marxist of circumstances.[58] This is in itself reminiscent of earlier encounters between avant-garde and vanguard formations, such as Mayakovsky's attempts to negotiate a passage between Futurism and Bolshevism. Interestingly, he too wrote SF.

The first of our SF avant-gardes, Futurianism, was originally a 'fan' formation, its core membership recruited from the Brooklyn Science Fiction League, the local branch of Gernsback's fan-based Science Fiction League. Which serves to remind us of one of the genre's most distinctive features, its unusually strong set of identifications between audiences, writers and texts. The much maligned 'Trekkies' still provide the paradigmatic instance here: their 'Save *Star Trek*' campaign famously generated over 114,667 letters of protest to NBC.[59] At the risk of oversimplification, we can state that SF studies has in general tended to move away from a quasi-Adornian understanding of fandom, as manipulation by the culture industry, towards Jenkins's view of fans as 'consumers who also produce',[60] 'textual poachers', in the words of his famous borrowing from de Certeau.[61] The 'filker' and 'slash fiction' writer thus become instances of what de Certeau meant by the *braconnier*. On Adornian readings of fandom, the phenomenon belongs to the mass audience region of the heteronomous end of the SF field. But on Jenkins's reading, it belongs in the restricted field as art for art's sake, or SF for SF's sake. The fans' efforts are thus a labour of love as utopian as that of any avant-garde, aimed only at symbolic profit before a limited audience of peers, or like-minded 'experts'. As Penley observed of K/S slash fiction, these 'amateur women writers' wrote their own 'sexual and social utopias' using

---

57 Miéville 2009a, p. 510.
58 Miéville and Bould 2002.
59 Tulloch and Jenkins 1995, p. 9.
60 Jenkins 1992, p. 208.
61 De Certeau 1984, p. 174.

materials to hand from *Star Trek*.[62] I have therefore located the most strictly fannish of fan behaviours very close to the Bohemian border of the restricted economy, but close also to the graphic novel in the extended economy.

One further avant-garde position remains within the SF field, that of underground cinema, represented in Figure 2 by Cronenberg. No matter how we define underground, whether as subversive, oppositional, independent, experimental, countercultural or merely 'cult', his substantial body of SF cinema, from *Scanners* (1981) to *eXistenZ* (1999), is close to paradigmatic. But in the mid-1960s Godard's *Alphaville* (1965) and Truffaut's *Fahrenheit 451* (1966) seemed equally so. The first New Wave was, after all, the French *nouvelle vague* and Godard and Truffaut, both protégés of Bazin, both writers for *Cahiers du cinéma*, were its leading *auteurs*. Tarkovsky's two SF films, *Solyaris* (1972) and *Stalker* (1979), might also be considered underground, though this notion is not easily transferable to late-Soviet Russia. In retrospect, however, for Tarkovsky as for Godard, the claim to underground status is belied by the sheer scale of their eventual success with institutionalised (Western) bourgeois audiences: Tarkovsky won the Grand Prix Spécial du Jury at the Cannes Film Festival for *Solyaris* and the Prix du Jury OEcuménique for *Stalker*; Godard the Goldener Bär at the Berlin International Film Festival for *Alphaville*. Hence, my decision to identify both as 'art house' rather than 'underground'. But this is a fine distinction, which probably works better synchronically than diachronically.

This takes us to the single most important component of institutionalised bourgeois art, 'literary' SF. The category barely exists for 'high Literature', which treats such texts as ' "not really SF" or as somehow "transcending the genre" '.[63] But it clearly does exist for SF: witness the meticulous fashion in which both Clute and Nicholls and Lofficier and Lofficier distinguish between, but also incorporate, both 'genre' and 'mainstream' writers.[64] 'Literary' SF is best understood as that fraction of the SF field currently incorporated into contemporary versions of the literary canon. It includes France's *L'île des pingouins*, Zamyatin's *Mi*, Čapek's *R.U.R.* and *Válka s mloky*, Huxley's *Brave New World*, Orwell's *Nineteen Eighty-Four*, Lem's *Solaris*, the Strugatsky brothers' *Piknik na obochine* and Houellebecq's *Les Particules élémentaires*. Indeed, all the many SF texts included in the longer version of Bloom's *The Western Canon* belong here.[65] They do so, however, not necessarily because of any distinctively literary 'merit',

---

62 Penley 1997, p. 145.
63 Bould 2009, p. 1.
64 Clute and Nicholls 1993, pp. 483–4, 768–70; Lofficier and Lofficier 2000, p. 349.
65 Bloom 1994, pp. 542–65.

as Bloom himself would argue, but because they have been canonised as 'literary' by educational and publishing institutions and, as a result, relocated away from the bookshop shelves marked 'Science Fiction and Fantasy'.

But this removal has little effect within the SF field, where intertextual and other references to canonical writing proceed essentially uninterrupted. Which is why the SF texts included in Bloom's canon still rate entries in Clute and Nicholls. This is not to suggest that individual SF writers are indifferent to 'literary' recognition: some clearly attempt to gain entry into the canonical field by way of either the SF restricted field or institutionalised bourgeois SF. Dick and Ballard clearly aspired to this, though only the latter with real success. Interestingly, Houellebecq, perverse as ever, seems to have moved in the opposite direction from avant-garde poet to SF novelist. The eventual price of such perversity might well be exclusion from the canonical field, given that literary gatekeepers seem far more reluctant to countenance relatively free movement between canonical and SF fields than their counterparts within SF.

6 Conclusion

These reflections lead me to postulate, by way of conclusion, two axioms. The first is that SF is a subfield of the general literary field, with a structure homologous to that of the wider field, which simultaneously constructs and is constructed by, produces and reproduces, the SF selective tradition. The second is that the boundary between the SF field and the canonical 'literary' field takes a form loosely analogous to that of a membrane – that is, a selective barrier, impermeable to many but by no means all elements – located in the overlap between the SF restricted field and institutionalised bourgeois SF. From the canonical side, this impermeability tends to allow SF to enter the canon, but not to return to SF; from the SF side, movement is normally permitted in both directions.

CHAPTER 10

World Systems and World Science Fiction*

World systems theory is an approach to modern economic history developed by Immanuel Wallerstein in his massive four-volume *The Modern World System* and helpfully summarised in *World-Systems Analysis: An Introduction*. Its enduring concern has been with how modern capitalism has functioned as a world system, comprising a 'core', 'periphery' and 'semi-periphery', defined in relation to three main variables, the degree of profitability, the degree of monopolisation and the degree of state patronage. Core-like processes tend to constitute the bulk of the production in comparatively few states, Wallerstein argues, peripheral in a much larger number, semi-peripheral in an intermediate zone containing a near-even mix of core-like and peripheral production.[1] This, in outline, is the model Franco Moretti has sought to apply to Comparative Literature, and which I would argue can, in turn, be applied to science fiction (henceforth SF).

At one level, Moretti merely re-mobilises Goethe's notion of *Weltliteratur*, an idea long familiar to Comparative Literature, whilst also reminding us that it was taken up by two of capitalism's most unrelenting critics, Karl Marx and Friedrich Engels. World-systems theory first appeared in Moretti as a means to understand a relatively small number of exceptional texts, beginning with Goethe's *Faust* and concluding with Gabriel García Márquez's *Cien años de soledad*. These, Moretti argued, were 'world' texts, whose geographical frame of reference is no longer the nation-state'. They were each also products of the system's semi-periphery, sites of 'combined development', where 'historically non-homogeneous social and symbolic forms, often originating in quite disparate places, coexist in a confined space'.[2] The argument resurfaced in more explicitly quantitative and sociological guise in Moretti's map of how, in the nineteenth century, an Anglo-French cultural core pre-empted the development of other national literatures, whilst simultaneously opening up positive possibilities for innovation in the periphery.[3]

Moretti subsequently expanded on the analysis to advance an ambitious map of how Comparative Literature might be refigured as a discipline. He

---

* This chapter has been published previously in *Paradoxa*, Vol. 26, pp. 15–29, 2014.
1 Wallerstein 2004, p. 28.
2 Moretti 1996, p. 50.
3 Moretti 1998, pp. 195–7.

argued that the study of *Weltliteratur* could no longer be conceived simply as national literature writ large, 'literature, bigger', but should rather be reorganised around entirely different categories and conceptual problems. It 'is not an object', he continued, 'it's a *problem*, and a problem that asks for a new critical method'. The model he proposes, directly adapted from Wallerstein, is that of a world literary system, simultaneously '*one*, and *unequal*: with a core, and a periphery ... bound together in a relationship of growing inequality'.[4]

If this is how the system functions, then the appropriate mode of analysis becomes 'distant reading', Moretti concludes, where distance '*is a condition of knowledge*', permitting the analyst 'to focus on units ... much smaller or much larger than the text: devices, themes, tropes – or genres and systems'.[5] The result is a history of the modern novel understood as a 'system *of variations*', in which pressure from the Anglo-French core tends towards uniformity, whilst variable local realities in the periphery and semiperiphery tend towards difference. Tendency and counter-tendency thus produce a series of localised structural 'compromises', between foreign plot, local characters and local narrative voice, in which the 'one-and-unequal literary system' becomes embedded in the form itself.[6]

1   World Systems Theory and Science Fiction

In *Distant Reading*, Moretti doesn't so much apply world systems theory as invoke it.[7] For there is no equivalent here to Wallerstein's own detailed account of the interconnections between profitabilty, monopolisation and patronage, only the borrowed vocabulary of core, semi-periphery and periphery. The nearest Moretti comes to this kind of detail is in the earlier *Atlas of the European Novel 1800–1900*, which uses the number of titles published and the volume of translations recorded in national bibliographies as key empirical indicators. So he shows how more than half of all nineteenth-century European novels were originally published in either London or Paris.[8] French novelists were more successful in translation in the Catholic South and British in the Protestant North, but the whole continent nonetheless read Walter Scott, Edward Bulwer-Lytton

---

4 Moretti 2013, p. 46.
5 Moretti 1996, pp. 48–9.
6 Moretti 1996, pp. 57–9.
7 I owe this formulation to Stephen Shapiro of the Department of English and Comparative Literary Studies at the University of Warwick.
8 Moretti 1998, p. 186.

and Charles Dickens, Alexandre Dumas, Eugene Sue and Victor Hugo.[9] He also shows how France finally out-competed Britain, 'making Paris ... the Hollywood of the nineteenth century'. By mid-century, translations of French novels into Italian outnumbered British by a ratio of eight to one, and even those into Danish were running roughly even.[10]

The number of titles and volume of translations need not correlate with profitability, monopolisation and state patronage, but in the long run they are very likely to do so, and in the case of nineteenth-century British and French publishing almost certainly did. Allowing for the peculiarities of state capitalist publishing in Russia and China, where state patronage often radically outweighed profitability, much the same could be said of twentieth-century publishing. During the second half of the century, the six major book national publishing industries were located in Britain and America, Germany and France, Russia and China: in the 1960s only these produced over 20,000 book titles per annum.[11] By 1996 the annual book output of those six states had reached 107,263 titles in the United Kingdom, 100,951 titles in China (1994 figure), 75,515 titles in Germany, 68,175 titles in the United States, 36,237 in Russia and 34,766 in France (1995 figure).[12] Neither Moretti's analyses of the nineteenth century nor UNESCO's aggregate data for the later decades of the twentieth identify SF titles as distinct from book titles in general. We do, however, have figures for some national industries of general 'literary' texts, which include popular fiction, although none for SF in particular. So, for example, out of the over 107,000 books published in the United Kingdom in 1996, 21,686 were literary; out of over 71,500 in Germany, 9,622; out of over 34,750 in France in 1995, 10,545.[13] The interesting point to note here is the much greater proportional commitment to 'literary' publishing in France.

The methodological problems entailed by any attempt to identify specifically science-fictional sub-sets of these aggregate figures are considerable, not least those posed by changes over time in definition and nomenclature, and by the institutionalised effects of policing the boundaries between 'genre fiction' and the 'literary canon'.[14] But even if those were solved, the scale of data collection required would be well beyond the scope of an essay like this. My method here will thus be much the same as Moretti's own, not so much an application

---

9   Moretti 1998, pp. 178–9.
10 Moretti 1998, p. 184.
11 Laurenson and Swingewood 1972, p. 140.
12 UNESCO 1999, IV-82–3-86–88–9.
13 UNESCO 1999, IV-86, 87, 89.
14 Milner 2012, pp. 22–40.

of Wallerstein as an invocation, centred on the core-periphery model, and taking as its base data a combination of aggregate book publishing figures with translation details, especially from and into English and French, and a distant reading of the history of the genre, derived in part from my own earlier close readings, in part from secondary accounts, most especially those provided in the third on-line third edition of the *Encyclopedia of Science Fiction*. The latter is, as Fredric Jameson rightly observed of the hardcopy second edition, a 'superb' resource:[15] it can confidently be assumed to be my source wherever I fail to provide any other reference.

What is true for the novel in general is in my view also true for SF. Conceived in England and France, at the core of the nineteenth century world literary system (Mary Shelley and, above all, Jules Verne and H.G. Wells), it continued in both countries throughout the twentieth century and into the twenty-first (through Aldous Huxley, George Orwell, C.S. Lewis, John Wyndham, Fred Hoyle, Arthur C. Clarke, Michael Moorcock, J.G. Ballard, Iain M. Banks, Ken Macleod and China Miéville in Britain, J.-H. Rosny aîné, Anatole France, Maurice Renard, Jacques Spitz, Pierre Boulle, Robert Merle, Daniel Walther, Serge Brussolo, G.-J. Arnaud, Maurice Dantec, Jean-Marc Ligny and Michel Houellebecq in France). The United States has a fitful presence in the early tradition, essentially through Edgar Allan Poe and Edward Bellamy, but each of these is arguably more significant for their impact on the Anglo-French core, through Verne and William Morris respectively, than on America itself.

Verne and Wells are clearly crucial. In 1990, the last year in which the *UNESCO Statistical Yearbook* published figures for the most frequently translated authors, Verne was the fourth most translated author in the world, Wells the 68th.[16] In 2013, UNESCO's online *Index Translationum* had Verne in second place, with 4,751 new translations recorded between 1979 and 2013. The University of Illinois holds translations of Wells's work in 19 different European languages, including 53 titles in French, 47 in Spanish and 32 in German.[17] First published in England in 1895, *The Time Machine* was translated into French and Brazilian Portuguese as early as 1899, into Hungarian in 1900, Russian in 1901, Italian in 1902, German in 1904 and Czech in 1905; *War of the Worlds*, published in England in 1898, was translated into Dutch, Hungarian and Norwegian in 1899, into French in 1900, German and Italian in 1901, Spanish in 1902 and Czech in 1903.[18]

---

15   Jameson 2005, p. 111.
16   UNESCO 1990, 7–110; 7–111.
17   Parrinder 2005, p. 2.
18   Parrinder and Barnaby 2005, pp. xxiii–xxv.

It is central to Moretti's application of Wallerstein's model that semiperipheral status is itself conducive to new cultural possibilities – in short, that a 'new space ... gives rise to a new form'[19] – a process with no direct equivalent in the original world-systems model of the global political economy. For Moretti, as not for Wallerstein, the distinction between periphery and semiperiphery amounts to that between simple cultural reception and imitation on the one hand, creative cultural innovation on the other. This is why Moretti sees the literary system's semiperiphery as variable and changing from case to case. The semiperipheral SF societies are therefore those that can be seen, retrospectively, as having substantially contributed to the global SF 'field', in Pierre Bourdieu's sense of the term,[20] and to the evolving global SF 'selective tradition', in Raymond Williams's sense.[21] The periphery, by contrast, comprises those cultures that have received texts from and to some extent imitated the core, but did not independently contribute to the development of the global selective tradition.

The semiperipheral SF cultures are thus: the Weimar Republic (Otto Willi Gail, Thea von Harbou and Fritz Lang, Otfrid von Hanstein) and early Soviet Russia (Alexander Belyaev, Alexander Bogdanov, Mikhail Bulgakov, Vladimir Mayakovsky, Andrei Platonov, Alexei Tolstoy, Yevgeny Zamyatin); inter-war Czechoslovakia (Karel Čapek, J.M. Troska); Communist Poland (Konrad Fialkowski, Stanisław Lem, Adam Wisniewski-Snerg) and late-Communist Russia (Genrikh Altov, Dmitri Bilenkin, Kir Bulychev, Mikhail Emtsev, Eremey Parnov, Arkady and Boris Strugatsky, Alexei Tarkovsky); inter-war North America (the genre's expansion into a whole range of new mass media, which we might well describe as 'the Gernsback moment'); post-Second World War Japan; and, arguably, also post-Cold War Russia and Germany.[22]

The periphery, by contrast, includes both late nineteenth-century Japan and early twentieth-century Poland. Verne's *Le Tour du monde en 80 jours* was translated into Japanese as early as 1879, six more of his *Voyages extraordinaires* in the early 1880s. These prompted a series of Japanese imitations, the best known of which is probably Oshikawa Shunrō's *Kaitei gunkan*, a reworking of *Vingt mille lieues sous les mers*. Wells's *The Time Machine* and *The War of the Worlds*

---

19   Moretti 1998, p. 197.
20   Bourdieu 1993b, pp. 37–41.
21   Williams 1977, pp. 115–16.
22   Here, one might well add in Italy and Argentina, if one accepted that Primo Levi, Italo Calvino and Jorge Luis Borges were SF writers. No doubt, there is a good case to be made to that effect on formal grounds, but the international reputations of all three rest on claims to 'literariness' quite distinct from those conventionally associated with SF as a genre.

were translated into Polish in 1899, prompting a series of Polish imitations, so that the earliest 'Polish writers of science fiction ... worked more or less consciously under Wells's spell'.[23] Good examples include Jerzy Żulawski's lunar trilogy (1901–10), Antoni Słonimski's sole SF novel, *Torpeda Czasu* (1924) and Bruno Winawer's *Doktor Przybram* (1924). Again, however, these do not acquire any lasting international significance, that is, they do not enter into the global SF selective tradition.

2   Structural Compromises

Setting aside the American and Japanese cases for the moment, we can begin by asking what kind of 'structural compromises' occurred in the European semi-periphery. The most influential instance of Weimar SF is clearly *Metropolis* (1926), directed by Lang and scripted by von Harbou, the latter of whom also wrote the novelisation. Both had admired Wells's *The Sleeper Awakes* and they used it as a source for both the film and novel versions of *Metropolis*. Apparently, Wells disliked their film, in part precisely for this reason.[24] The clearest debt to Wells is in the architecture of the dystopian cityscape, which functions as a synecdoche for the wider catastrophe that has overcome its population. As in Wells, that catastrophe is a massively exploitative class structure, vertically stratified between the darkest proletarian depths where the workers live and the city of light inhabited by the privileged classes.

This vertical social stratification – which would become a standard trope in SF cinema – had no equivalent in reality, where cities still tended to be stratified horizontally, but it is nonetheless exactly how Wells's future city functions in *The Sleeper Awakes*. The film's crowds and riots similarly echo Wells's story. And the eventual solution, in which the heroine, Maria, inspires Freder to unite capital and labour, Fredersen and Grot, is as Fabian as anything Wells could have imagined. What finally excites our admiration in the film is not, however, its ideas, which are rarely better than trite by comparison with *The Sleeper Awakes*, but rather the spectacular visual effects used to create the city. It is in this respect that it most creatively reworks the legacies of the Anglo-French core: *Metropolis* provided the template for all the SF cityscapes to come, from William Cameron Menzies's *Things to Come* and Ridley Scott's *Blade Runner* to Alex Proyas's *Dark City* and Luc Besson's *The Fifth Element/Le Cinquième Élément*.

---

23   Juszczyk 2005, p. 126.
24   Schenkel 2005, pp. 96–9.

A similar pattern can be observed in early Soviet Russia. By 1917, Verne and Wells were the most popular of all foreign authors published in Russian translation. Alexei Tolstoy's *Aelita* (1924) is indebted to both, whilst Bulgakov draws on more specifically Wellsian motifs in *Rokovye yaitsa* (1925), *Sobach'e serdtse* (1925) and *Master i Margarita* (1929–39). The key figure, however, is Zamyatin, who published Russian translations of *The Time Machine*, *The War in the Air* and *The Sleeper Awakes* in 1919–20 and wrote introductory commentaries to each of these and to the 12-volume edition of Wells's collected works published in 1924–6.[25] The latter is full of breathless admiration: Wells, Zamyatin insisted, is 'one of the greatest, most weighty and most interesting English writers' and 'the most contemporary of contemporary writers'.[26] Yet Zamyatin's *Mi* was nonetheless predicated on a powerful critique of exactly the kind of scientific positivism Wells enjoyed. The 'dystopian turn' commonly associated with Huxley and Orwell, and with mid-twentieth-century Anglo-American SF more generally, is actually effected in Russia much earlier. This turn, which had far reaching consequences for the shape of late twentieth century SF, provides an unusually telling example of a structural compromise between the then dominant Anglo-French utopian positivism and local Russian characters and voice.

Verne had been translated into Czech as early as the 1870s, Wells not until *The Island of Doctor Moreau* in 1901, but thereafter the latter was to prove the more decisive influence. Čapek visited Wells during his tours of Britain. Wells, in turn, repeatedly visited Czechoslovakia, often on Čapek's invitation, and they maintained regular contact until the latter's death in December 1938. Nonetheless, Čapek's own work tended to poke fun at much that Wells most believed in, from science to socialism. Čapek's last great novel, *Válka s mloky* satirises utopians like Wells by name. *R.U.R.* parodies the kinds of progressive feminism Wells admired, and the religiosity underpinning Čapek's critique of both capitalist robotics and robotic communism stands diametrically opposed to Wells's own atheistic scientism. The play's robot is, without doubt, one of the most significant innovations in the whole of inter-war SF and it too thus seems to be the effect of a structural compromise between Anglo-French core plotlines and local Czech characters and voice.

Polish SF came to international prominence later than Czech, in the context of an imposed postwar Communism. Both Wells and SF had then received an official seal of approval, and thereby became significant presences in the general culture. The key figure was Lem. Like Wells, Lem was scientifically trained;

---

25   Cockrell 2005, pp. 74–87.
26   Zamyatin 1997, pp. 268, 274.

like Wells, he was a would-be polymath; like Wells, he was clearly a child of the Enlightenment rather than Romanticism; and, like Wells, he experimented with both utopia and SF. Yet, where Wells retained a persistent optimism about the potentialities of scientific knowledge, an enduring focus in Lem, learnt from science itself, is that of the finite limits of what science can know. The paradigmatic case is *Solaris* (1961), where all the efforts of the state-of-the-art Solaris Station, and of the science of solaristics more generally, including the characteristically positivist decision to bombard the planet with X-rays, fail to discover anything of significance about the conscious planetary intelligence they attempt to understand and contact.

The equivalent figures in late Communist Russia were Arkady and Boris Strugatsky, both of whom clearly shared an abiding fascination with Wells's *The War of the Worlds*. The obvious example is their *Vtoroe nashestvie marsian* (1968), which is written in the form of a sequel to Wells's novel. But here, too, we encounter the kind of structural compromise Moretti predicts. Unlike Wells, and very much like Lem, the Strugatsky brothers do not imagine the alien other as ultimately known or knowable. The analogy that famously gives *Piknik na obochine* (1972) its title, that of the abandoned alien artefacts as debris from a roadside picnic, bespeaks a version of the alien, not so much as hostile, but as simply indifferent to our very existence.

3   New Cores: North America and Japan

Hugo Gernsback famously coined the term 'scientifiction' to describe the genre and traced its origins back retrospectively to Verne and Wells (and also Poe). But this new American 'pulp' SF was overwhelmingly an escapist response to the Great Depression rather than an easy celebration of scientific triumphalism: hence, the quasi-Marxian character of Asimov's early Futurianism. The 'Golden Age' of American SF is the product of a moment when the United States still remained an essentially semiperipheral literary economy. As late as 1996, the United Kingdom annual output of books amounted to 107,263 titles, the US to only 68,175.[27] This provides the answer to Moretti's question as to why, in comparably 'peripheral' circumstances, the US failed to produce a paradigm shift akin to that of Latin American magic realism.[28] It did; and it was SF.

---

27   UNESCO 1999, IV-82–89.
28   Moretti 1998, p. 196n.

Between the 1930s and the 1950s the US very rapidly became near-hegemonic within the genre (Gernsback, J.W. Campbell, Isaac Asimov, Robert Heinlein, 'the pulps' more generally), a situation which continued through the New Wave (Philip K. Dick, Harlan Ellison, Norman Spinrad, James Tiptree, Jr., Roger Zelazny), feminism (Usula K. Le Guin, Joanna Russ, Marge Piercy), Afrofuturism (Samuel R. Delany, Octavia Butler), cyberpunk (William Gibson, Bruce Sterling) and the new humanisms of writers like Kim Stanley Robinson and Paolo Bacigalupi. Moreover, North American hegemony extended from print to film (James Whale, Stanley Kubrick, George Lucas, Stephen Spielberg, Ridley Scott, James Cameron, Tim Burton and Paul Verhoeven all worked in Hollywood, even though some were of European extraction) and television (Gene Roddenberry, J. Michael Straczynski, Chris Carter and Joss Whedon).

The structural compromise between the then dominant forms of Anglo-French scientific romance and more local North American registers is performed with wonderful precision in the Gernsback moment. His opening editorial for *Amazing Stories* promised its American readers the best that European SF could offer, that is, Verne and Wells – a promise it would keep – but also two American writers, Poe and Bellamy, who would not have been accorded equivalent status in Europe.[29] The magazine itself, Gernsback's associated interests in broadcasting and his assiduous efforts to cultivate a fan base all suggest the mechanisms by which an essentially European literary genre would be reconstituted as American and relocated in and around the audio-visual mass media.

This Americanised SF was exported into Japan during the immediate post-Second World War period, in part as a result of the American military occupation. The genre's new Japanese semiperiphery responded to its new (Anglo-)American core much as America had responded to European SF, that is, by productively reworking inherited forms in ways that register local Japanese peculiarities. The key Japanese SF writers – Kōbō Abe, Shinichi Hoshi, Sakyo Komatsu, Haruki Murakami – all achieve this kind of structural compromise. The cruel evolutionism of Abe's 1959 *Dai yon kan pyōki* – often claimed as the foundational text of postwar Japanese SF – can be read as reworking Clarke's *Childhood's End*, just as Murakami's *Sekai noowari to hādo-boirudo wandārando* (1985) can be read as playing on Gibson's 'Johnny Mnemonic'.

But the decisive breakthrough comes in the way Japanese writers, directors and animators appropriated the products of the American audio-visual media. Thematically, this is spectacularly evident in Inoshiro Honda's *Gojira* (1954) – and the fourteen movies which followed between it and Kohji Hashimoto's

---

29   Gernsback 1926, p. 3.

remake, *Gojira 1985* – which rework the conventions of the American monster movie, through the prism of the distinctively Japanese experience of American nuclear attack, thinly disguised as nuclear testing. Formally and technically, however, the crucial innovations are the synthesis of American comic book SF with an older Japanese 'manga' tradition – the term dates from 1814 – to produce contemporary manga SF; and the synthesis of American animation with manga to produce anime.

Osamu Tezuka's 1949 reworking of Lang's *Metropolis* is perhaps the earliest example of SF manga, his 1951 *Tetsuwan Atomu* certainly the best known, albeit as *Astro Boy*. Tezuka adapted *Tetsuwan Atomu* for television anime in 1963, in an interesting early example of the now common process by which manga, television anime and feature film anime are produced in combination. Many of these have met with international acclaim, for example Katsuhiro Otomo's *Akira* (1988), Mamoru Oshii's *Gōsuto In Za Sheru/Kōkaku Kidōtai* (1995) and Hideaki Anno's *Shin Seiki Evangerion* (1997). Japanese SF has, then, moved from the genre's periphery to its semiperiphery and, in some respects, now threatens to rival American SF at the core.

4 Post-Cold War Russia and Germany[30]

I deliberately avoided any discussion of post-Cold War SF in either Russia or Germany when I canvassed this 'world systems' model in my *Locating Science Fiction*.[31] SF in both countries was disrupted by totalitarianism – National Socialism in Germany, high Stalinism in Russia – but recovered thereafter, both during and after the Cold War. In late-Communist Russia, as in Eastern Europe more generally, the genre had enjoyed official tolerance, within certain well defined political limits, and also benefitted from relatively easy available translations between different Eastern European languages and from these into English or French. Russian (and Ukrainian) SF had thus increasingly taken on the character of an alternative 'core'. In Germany, SF had been refashioned during the Cold War period, in the DDR as periphery to the putative new Russian core, in the Bundesrepublik as periphery to the Anglo-American core, but later

---

30 This part of the argument is indebted to colleagues in both the European Utopian Studies Society and the World Science Fiction Society (Burianyk et al.; Layh; Stricker et al.) but, above all, to the students in the Sommersemester 2013 Tutorium on Critical Theory, Utopian Studies and Science Fiction I taught at the Freie Universität Berlin.

31 Milner 2012, pp. 162–77.

as itself a developing semiperiphery. Russia and Germany followed rather different trajectories after the end of the Cold War and, although both are still significant centers of SF production and consumption, the precise extent to which they might be considered semiperiphy or core is still unclear.

Post-Cold War Russian SF built on the late-Communist legacy, but with a new openness to the West, especially to fantasy as distinct from SF. It also, however, suffered from a relative loss of access to neighbouring Eastern European cultures, whether as centres of production or consumption. Russian SF's relationship to the world system was thus increasingly dependent on mediation through the American core. At the 'literary' extreme, Vladimir Sorokin's *Lyod* trilogy (2002–5) both revisited the earlier Russian preoccupation with alien invasion and borrowed the form of the trilogy from American SF. It also revisited a specifically Russian phenomenon, albeit one which has also fascinated Western SF, the 1908 Tunguska Event, investing it with the peculiarly occult/fantastic significance of the sinister Brotherhood, which expands its influence through Tsarist, Bolshevik, Stalinist, Nazi-occupied and, eventually, global-capitalist Russia. Such mysticism would have been much less acceptable in late Communist SF. At the 'popular' extreme, Dimitri Glukhovsky's *Metro* novels (2005–9) borrowed the Western SF topos of nuclear apocalypse, but injected it into the very Russian context of the Moscow Metro. These have also been hugely popular in adaptation to the distinctly Western forms of the computer game and the sequel franchise. Both extremes thus seem to provide interesting examples of the kind of structural compromise Moretti found characteristic of semiperipheral cultural production.

SF in the Bundesrepublik initially owed far more to imported American influences than to the legacy of Weimar. The new German pulps that appeared in the 1950s, such as *Galaxis-Magazin* and *Terra SF*, made extensive use of translations from American texts. Even the famous *Perry Rhodan*, launched in 1961 as a vehicle for original German production, nonetheless often masqueraded as American, through devices such as Anglo-American authorial pseudonyms or character names. In the last two decades of the Cold War, however, West German SF acquired an increasingly semiperipheral character, evident in the expansion of Lichtenberg Verlag's SF list during the 1970s and Heyne Verlag's SF and Fantasy list during the 1980s. These were each much more 'literary' in form than the earlier pulps: Lichtenberg's list was entitled SF 'für Kenner', literally for those in the know. The annual World Science Fiction Convention was first held in Germany in 1970; the first Deutscher Science Fiction Preis was awarded in 1985; and in 1990 Heyne's SF editor, Wolfgang Jeschke, was Guest of Honour at the 1990 World Convention. Thereafter, however, the genre seems to have suffered a series of setbacks, pointedly signalled by the coincidence of Jeschke's retirement in 2002 and Heyne's acquisition by Random House the following year.[32] The excess of translations from American into German over those from German into other languages seemed to expand progressively. This should not be read as evidence of any weakness in German publishing per se: as we've seen, Germany housed one of the six leading national book publishing industries. The problem seems rather to lie in how German literary culture, from the book trade through to the academy, tends to make a very sharp distinction between 'Literatur' proper and 'Trivialliteratur', firmly consigning SF to the latter.

The obvious exception to this last observation – and itself a striking instance of creative structural compromise – is the special significance for recent German SF of what might be termed 'ecofiction'. 'Cli-Fi', as Daniel Bloom dubbed it,[33] has, of course, been important in recent American SF: witness Robinson's 'Science in the Capital trilogy' or Bacigalupi's *The Windup Girl*. But it seems even more important in Germany. Die Grünen were, of course, the world's first organised Green Party and are still amongst the most electorally successful, currently holding 63 seats out of 630 in the Bundestag. So it is perhaps unsurprising that climate change has been a more pressing issue for German SF than for American or British. But ecofiction texts also very often enjoy the advantage of being marketed as serious literature rather than mere SF.

German Cli-Fi texts cover almost the whole range of political response to the threat of anthropogenic climate change: from Juli Zeh's *Corpus Delicti* (2009), which deals critically with the possibilities of ecodictatorship; through Ilija Torjanow's *Eistau* (2011), quite literally an elegy for melting ice; to Nele Neuhaus's *Wer Wind sät* (2011) and Sven Böttcher's *Prophezeiung* (2011), which evince climate scepticism akin, respectively, to that in Michael Crichton's *State of Fear* and Ian McEwan's *Solar*. Frank Schätzing's *Der Schwarm* (2004) has been by far the most influential text, however, both domestically and internationally. It was the bestselling novel in Germany for most of 2004 and went on to win the 2005 Deutscher Science Fiction Preis for best novel. It has subsequently been translated into twenty languages, including English and French, and the film rights sold to Hollywood. Almost Lovelockian in its ecopolitics – Schätzing's 'yrr' are in effect Gaia surrogates – the novel is also heavily indebted to American SF cinema and TV. The 2006 Science Fiction Preis went to Jeschke's *Das Cusanus-*

---

32 Fitzgerald 2012, p. 299. This isn't simply the instance of American cultural imperialism it might at first appear, given that Random House had itself been acquired by Bertelsmann, one of the largest German publishers, in July 1998 (Fitzgerald 2012, p. 284). Heyne's increasing preference for translations of American SF into German, rather than of German SF into other languages, was thus essentially a matter of profitability rather than patriotism.

33 Merchant 2013.

Spiel (2005), a time travel novel, but one which nonetheless powerfully evoked the likely possible effects of climate change. Like *Der Schwarm*, *Das Cusanus-Spiel* has been widely translated, including into English and French.

Environmentalism is also a recurring motif in the work of Dirk C. Fleck, who twice won the Deutscher Science Fiction Preis for best novel: in 1994 for his 'ecodystopia', GO! *Die Ökodiktatur* (1993); and in 2009 for *Das Tahiti-Projekt* (2008), an experiment in fictive postcolonial ecopolitics. *MAEVA!*, the 2011 sequel to *Das Tahiti-Project*, explored the radical-democratic alternatives to ecodictatorship, through the fictional Tahitian ex-President Maeva's 'United Regions of the Pacific' and, later, the 'United Regions of the Planet'. This did not actually win the 2012 Preis, but was nonetheless one of the year's more distinctive German SF novels, not least for its explicitly utopian content. Unlike Schätzing and Jeschke, Fleck's ecofictions are as yet untranslated into English and French, which, by Moretti's definition, suggests they are still not 'world texts'. But they have attracted international attention – including an invitation to speak in Cuba – and an English translation of *Das Tahiti-Projekt* is reportedly in progress.[34]

5   Coda

This leaves us with two outstanding theoretical problems. The first, that posed by the international success of Sorokin and Glukhovsky, Schätzing and Jeschke, not to mention the Glukhovsky game adaptations, is whether these are perhaps evidence of emergent new cores or merely instances of the kind of intermittent core production characteristic of semiperipheral literary economies. As yet, we cannot know for, in sociological analysis as in philosophy, the owl of Minerva tends to fly at dusk. The second, more obviously political in character, is that of Eurocentrism or occidentalism. Both Moretti and Wallerstein have been so accused.[35] Moretti's own response is simply that: 'Theories will never abolish inequality: they can only hope to explain it'.[36] Clearly, however, a parallel accusation can be levelled at my argument here. In self-defence, I can only comment that, writing from Australia as I do, in what is very definitely a peripheral SF culture, I have no vested interest in valorising the global system's cultural core. I could add that Australian SF has been unjustly neglected by the global SF select-

---

34   Ellis 2010.
35   Kristal 2002; Spivak 2003, p. 108n; Dussel 1998.
36   Moretti 2013, p. 113.

ive tradition, a neglect I have even attempted to redress on occasion in my own work. But what such neglect means, in Moretti's terms, is only that Australia remains at the periphery of the global SF system. I can, of course, make a case for changing this state of affairs, but as yet only unsuccessfully. Which surely makes the world-systems approach all the more persuasive.

PART 2

Cultural Materialism

CHAPTER 11

Considerations on English Marxism*

Edward Thompson and Perry Anderson are undoubtedly Britain's two most distinguished socialist historians. They also share the rather rare distinction of each having served on the editorial committee of the *New Left Review*, probably the most influential English-language Marxist journal in the world today. And there perhaps the similarities end. For in the years that have passed since Anderson's 'New New Left' succeeded Thompson's 'Old New Left' (Sedgwick, 1976) to the editorship of the *Review* the two have been divided by a whole series of differences, some personal, some political, some historiographical and each compounding the others so that what may have begun as a difference of opinion has evolved into a clash of worldviews. In 1978 Thompson published his *The Poverty of Theory* the title essay of which, though substantially focused on a critique of the Althusserian theoretical project, actually had as its prime political target Anderson and the present editorial committee of the *New Left Review*.[1] After two years of studied silence (constituting perhaps a 'significant absence'?) on the part of the *Review*'s Parisian mentor himself, Anderson has replied to Thompson in his recently published *Arguments Within English Marxism*.[2] This exchange between Thompson and Anderson can be seen at one level as the latest episode in a prolonged personal feud and at another as the last in a series of 'in-house' seminars for professional historians on the nature and purpose of historical research. But it also poses questions as to the relationship between Marxist theory and socialist politics that must be of significance not only to the British Left but also to the Left in general. And, given the influence that a certain form of Althusserianism has exercised over both the Australian Left and Australian intellectual life in recent years, it has a peculiar relevance to this country. Hence the need to draw up some sort of 'balance sheet' on Thompson's and Anderson's respective contributions, a need that this essay is intended in part to meet.

---

* This chapter has been published previously in *Labour History*, No. 41, pp. 1–28, 1981.
1 Thompson 1978a, p. 405.
2 Anderson 1980.

1   The Poverty of Theory: Thompson's Critique of Althusser

The key political 'experience' (and I use the term advisedly) in Edward Thompson's life, the great event that has given it meaning and purpose, is almost certainly not the Second World War as Anderson has suggested,[3] but rather the Hungarian Revolution of 1956 and the crisis it occasioned within the Western Communist Parties. Thompson's breach with the British Communist Party during 1956 involved not only a detailed protest against Party policy, but also the formulation of a theoretical critique of the very nature of Stalinist Marxism. For Thompson (as for many others both in Britain and elsewhere) Stalinism had come to represent a peculiar perversion of Marxism characterised, firstly, by a theoretical economic determinism and, secondly, by a theoretical and practical anti-humanism. And the two were linked: it was the deterministic denial of the role of human agency in history that permitted Stalinism theoretically to reject the need for a socialist morality, and practically to prosecute the most monstrous barbarisms in the name of 'socialism'. To this Thompson and the nascent New Left counterposed their own 'socialist humanism', an alternative Marxism that emphasised precisely the role of consciousness and human action in social change, and the consequent importance of culture, values, morality, to the struggle for socialism. This theoretical perspective has informed the whole of Thompson's subsequent career both as a political activist and a professional historian. Whatever may have become of his one-time collaborators (and their fates have been many and varied), Thompson has indeed, as he himself claims, paid in full his dues to '1956'.[4]

There can be little reasonable doubt – and certainly Thompson has none – that the optimistic expectations of the mid-fifties New Left have been largely unfulfilled in the realm of practical politics. But in Thompson's view certain theoretical gains had indeed been secured in Britain for socialist humanism and for the type of socialist history that it permits; secured, that is, until suddenly attacked 'from the rear' by Althusser[5] and by Anderson's *New Left Review* in its role as an import agency into Britain of 'every product, however banal, of the Althusserian *fabrik*'.[6] The result, according to Thompson, has been the emergence in Britain of a new Althusserian '*lumpen intelligentsia*';[7] of 'barrels of enclosed Marxisms which stand, row upon row, in the corridors of Polytech-

---

3   Anderson 1980, p. 142.
4   Thompson 1978a, p. 384.
5   Thompson 1978a, p. 194.
6   Thompson 1978a, p. 405.
7   Thompson 1978a, p. 195.

nics and Universities';[8] of a generation of elitist socialist intellectuals with less experience of practical struggle than any hitherto;[9] of a generation, moreover, which though deluded into thinking itself 'post-Stalinist' is in fact theoretically complicit in a 'resurgent Stalinism'.[10] Thus Thompson sees the seventies. And hence the urgent necessity for the theoretical broadside directed at Althusserianism by Thompson in *The Poverty of Theory*.

In what, then, does Thompson's critique of Althusserianism consist? There are two distinct theoretical components within this critique, the one epistemological and concerned with the status of theory, the other historiographical and concerned with the status of human agency in history, and each of these is in turn connected to a political critique of Althusserian Stalinism. Neither the epistemological critique nor the historiographical critique is especially novel. But both combine previously rehearsed anti-Althusserian arguments with an unprecedented display of intellectual seriousness, polemical verve and scholarly wit. The structure of each of the two arguments is fundamentally the same. The 'core' of the Althusserian position is in each case identified as an opposition to a particular bourgeois ideology that has supposedly infected Marxism: thus Althusserian epistemology is essentially anti-empiricist (and anti-historicist) and Althusserian historiography essentially anti-humanist. In each case Thompson argues persuasively that Althusser has so expanded the meaning of his respective categories that perfectly legitimate procedures proper to Marxism itself become assimilated into bourgeois ideological conceptions. Thus Althusser confuses reference to empirical controls, on the one hand, with empiricism as ideology, on the other, so that he is unable to comprehend either the dialogue between social being and consciousness that constitutes experience within the real processes of history, or the dialogue between theory and evidence that constitutes knowledge within the discipline of historical research.[11] Similarly, Althusser confuses a general humanist stress on the importance of human agency in history with the specifically bourgeois notion of history as the product of the agency of an aggregate of individual wills.[12] The result in this case is Althusser's expulsion of human agency from history and a consequent conception of historical process as fate.[13]

---

8   Thompson 1978a, p. 383.
9   Thompson 1978a, pp. 376–7.
10 Thompson 1978a, p. 320.
11 Thompson 1978a, pp. 224–5.
12 Thompson 1978a, pp. 278–80.
13 Thompson 1978a, p. 281.

Thompson then probes each of these Althusserian positions for their own theoretical underpinnings, and in each case identifies those underpinnings as exhibiting a marked affinity with the conventional anti-Marxism of conservative academia. Thus, argues Thompson, Althusser's epistemological critique of empiricism and historicism actually inhabits a similar theoretical terrain to that of Karl Popper. Both insist on a radical rupture between thought and the real, but whereas Popper is content to assert the ultimate unknowability of the real except perhaps in the form of discrete 'facts', Althusser seeks instead to reduce the real to thought.[14] Such an epistemology, which sees knowledge production as occurring entirely within thought, is, of course, an example of '*exactly* what has commonly been designated, in the Marxist tradition, as idealism'.[15] Similarly, Althusser's historiographical critique of humanism substitutes a vocabulary of stasis for the classical Marxist vocabulary of process in just such a way as does functionalist sociology.[16] Thus Althusser's notion of history as a 'process without a subject' and of human beings as merely the 'supports' of 'functions' within the 'structure' runs exactly parallel to Talcott Parsons's structural-functionalism.[17] An idealist epistemology and a determinist 'science' of history, such then is Althusserianism; 'as always with Althusser', writes Thompson, 'we are offered an ideological penny, greasy with bourgeois use, and told it is Marxist gold'.[18]

What, then, are the implications for political practice of this Althusserian theatre of the absurd? At one level, Thompson insists, Althusserianism is deeply implicated in the elitist and anti-political practices of the bourgeois academy within which it had its origins. Althusserian epistemological idealism can be seen to derive in part from a peculiar academic model of cognition, and from the philosophical/mathematical model in particular;[19] and Althusserian historiographical determinism is at many points, as for example in its treatments of historical time, peculiarly compatible with reputable academic procedures.[20] But all of this is of secondary importance. The distinguishing feature of Althusserianism with respect to political practice is for Thompson its intimate relationship to Stalinism. Indeed Thompson goes further: Althusserianism *is* Stalinism 'given its true, rigorous and totally coherent theoretical

---

14   Thompson 1978a, pp. 212–15.
15   Thompson 1978a, p. 205.
16   Thompson 1978a, pp. 265–71.
17   Thompson 1978a, pp. 335–40.
18   Thompson 1978a, p. 340.
19   Thompson 1978a, pp. 199–202.
20   Thompson 1978a, p. 286.

expression'.²¹ Stalinism as an ideological mode of thought and as a political practice displayed precisely that idealistic imperviousness to empirical discourse and that anti-humanist, and inhuman, treatment of people as mere bearers of structures which constitute the two central features of the Althusserian theoretical edifice. Hence Thompson's final call to arms and his marvellously polemical conclusion that the socialist and labour movement 'can have no business with theoretical practice except to expose it and drive it out'.²² It is difficult to disagree with any of this. Thompson has cast himself in the role of tragic hero and he has played out his part to the full. Surrounded on all sides by a resurgent Stalinism, isolated, embattled, but unbowed, Britain's most distinguished socialist historian has stepped forth alone on to the field of battle and torn down the pillars of the temple of theoretical practice upon the heads of the Althusserian Philistines. And, as the aesthetics of catharsis demand, the tragedy finally resolves itself into a tone of reconciliation and muted hope: 'I may now, with a better conscience, return to my proper work and to my garden. I will watch how things grow'.²³

2 The Poverty of Theory: The Limits of Thompson

But Thompson did not return to his garden. On the contrary, he has apparently flung himself with enthusiasm into the recent British campaign against the Cruise missiles. Which poses immediately the question of Thompson's own politics and of the nature of his alternative to Althusserianism. At one level the answer is obvious: Thompson's epistemology is materialist, his historiography non-determinist, his politics anti-Stalinist. But what type of materialism? What type of non-determinism? What type of anti-Stalinism? Let us consider each in turn.

To Althusser's thoroughly idealistic notion of a self-enclosed and self-confirming theory, Thompson quite properly counterposes the notion of dialogue between theory and evidence. But what is the nature of this dialogue? Thompson is insistent on two points: firstly, that historical evidence has a determinate objectivity, an independent existence quite apart from any significance the historian may accord it;²⁴ and secondly, that there is a common 'historical logic' defined in terms of both theoretical and evidential procedures to which both

---

21 Thompson 1978a, p. 333.
22 Thompson 1978a, p. 381.
23 Thompson 1978a, p. 384.
24 Thompson 1978a, pp. 231–5.

Marxist and non-Marxist history must submit.[25] Clearly the latter proposition follows on from the former. Now at one level Thompson is obviously right: the past is past and (setting aside for the moment Dr. Who and his Tardis) what has happened cannot be changed by the significance we in the present attach to it. Thompson forgets, however, that historical knowledge is not the same thing as 'the past'; rather, it is always a reconstitution of the past, conducted in the present and for the purposes of the present. Which is why the late Lucien Goldmann's insistence that 'historical reality changes from epoch to epoch with modifications in the hierarchy of values',[26] which Thompson finds so disturbing,[27] is in fact entirely legitimate. Thompson is, of course, no positivist. He doesn't for a moment question the propriety of our passing evaluative and subjective judgements on the past. But he is nonetheless insistent both that such judgements are radically distinct from the process of historical research itself, and that they do not in any way call into question the objective determinacy of historical evidence.[28]

Note that Thompson sees such judgements of value as essentially 'subjective', that is, individual. If historical research were indeed a simple confrontation between the individual researcher and an external objective reality, then this separation between fact and value would be entirely appropriate. But it is not. As Goldmann himself, rehearsing with approval the arguments of the young Lukács, once put it:

> what characterises historical action is precisely the fact that it is not carried out by isolated individuals, but by groups who *simultaneously know and constitute history*. Therefore neither the group nor the individual who is part of it can consider social and historical life from the outside in an objective fashion. The knowledge of historical and social life is *not science but consciousness* although *it must obviously strive towards the attainment of a rigour and precision comparable to those achieved in an objective fashion by the natural sciences*. Any separation of judgements of fact and judgements of value, and, similarly, any separation of theory and practice is impossible in the process of understanding history; the very affirmation of such a separation will have an ideological and distorting effect.[29]

---

25 Thompson 1978a, pp. 236–7.
26 Goldmann 1969, p. 43.
27 Thompson 1978a, p. 212.
28 Thompson 1978a, p. 233.
29 Goldmann 1972, p. 18.

Precisely. And it is surely just such a distorting effect which persuades Thompson that Marxist history should submit itself to the banalities of the 'reality rule' proposed by the ferociously anti-Marxist historian, J.H. Hexter.[30] In truth there can be no such common court of appeal. There is socialist history and there is liberal history, and each does indeed conduct its own dialogue between theory and evidence; but they are constituted for different purposes, by different individuals, linked by membership or affiliation to different social classes; and the history they constitute is different and cannot, therefore, be subsumed under any common historical logic.

Thompson's anti-determinism is similarly problematic. In general terms his emphasis on 'history as unmastered human practice', as opposed to 'history as process without a subject',[31] is not only unobjectionable in itself, but also serves as a necessary and long-overdue corrective to the Althusserian nonsense of the past 15 years. Indeed Thompson's suggestion that Engels's famous discussion of the 'parallelogram of forces' can provide a useful starting point for any understanding of the role of agency in human history, but that Engels's formulation needs to be modified so as to substitute class 'wills' for individual wills,[32] seems entirely helpful. The problem is, as Thompson says, to understand how at the same time, we make history and history makes itself.[33] But this perfectly proper stress on human practice leads Thompson in some very peculiar directions. In the first place, it leads him to an original but unfortunately not at all helpful reading of Marx's work. For years academic Marxism has worried itself over the supposed opposition between the critical philosophical anthropology of the younger Marx and the scientific political economy of the older Marx. Thompson proposes to reorganise the board upon which this game will be played in future. He argues in fact for the theoretical primacy of Marx's 'historical' work of the mid- to late 1840s, especially *The German Ideology*, *The Poverty of Philosophy* and the *Communist Manifesto*,[34] and represents the later works of political economy, *Capital* and especially the *Grundrisse*, as a theoretical detour in which Marx, setting out to overthrow the structuralism of bourgeois political economy, became partly entrapped by that self-same structure. The result was 'not the overthrow of "Political Economy", but *another* "Political Economy"'.[35] Thus we find the implication that there are not two but three Marxes, the youth-

---

30 Thompson 1978a, p. 387.
31 Thompson 1978a, p. 295.
32 Thompson 1978a, pp. 278–9.
33 Thompson 1978a, p. 279.
34 Thompson 1978a, pp. 251, 354.
35 Thompson 1978a, p. 252.

ful philosopher, the historical materialist of the middle period and the later political economist.[36] The problem with all such classificatory schema is, of course, that they destroy the fundamental unity of Marx's thought. There is in fact no need to counterpose either the earlier philosophical anthropology and the later political economy or each of these and the middle historical writings. The earlier theory of alienation, the later theoretical account of the laws of motion of the capitalist mode of production and the middle 'historical' writings – which as Thompson quite rightly says take as their central theoretical project the production of a 'unitary knowledge of society'[37] – are each important component elements within the theoretical legacy of the Marxist tradition. Their relationship to each other is essentially one of complementarity rather than of contradiction.

What exactly is the purpose of Thompson's new reading of Marx? The answer, quite simply, is to assert the importance of the category of 'experience' to historical materialism. Thompson argues that there is a real theoretical silence in Marx, a failure to explain the precise 'genetics' by which the correspondence between mode of production and real historical process is effected.[38] The missing term is that of experience:

> Men and women ... return as subjects, within this term ... as persons experiencing their determinate productive situations and relationships, as needs and interests and as antagonisms, and then 'handling' this experience within their *consciousness* and their *culture* ... in the most complex ... ways, and then ... acting upon their determinate situation in their turn.[39]

It is this category of 'experience' that has permitted Marxist historians to explore those systems which structure familial and social life, systems that the Marx of *Capital* rigorously excluded from analysis:

> kinship, custom, the invisible rules of social regulation, hegemony and deference, symbolic forms of domination and of resistance, religious faith and millenarial impulses, manners, laws, institutions and ideologies.[40]

---

36 To be fair, Thompson, always more interested in matters of substance than in classificatory schema, refuses to spell this out. But Anderson is not so reticent (Anderson 1980, pp. 61–2).
37 Thompson 1978a, p. 257.
38 Thompson 1978a, p. 356.
39 Ibid.
40 Thompson 1978a, p. 362.

Thompson is here addressing himself to one of the central problems in Marxist theory, that of the relationship between, to use two overworked and often unhelpful terms, the economic 'base' and the various 'superstructures'. As is well known, the 'orthodox' Marxism of the Second International, as represented in the work of Kautskty in particular, conceived this relationship in terms of a simple economic determinism in which the economic base mechanically determined the superstructures. An alternative tradition, that of the 'Hegelian' Marxism of the immediate post-First World War period, the Marxism of Korsch, Gramsci and the young Lukács, posed the question quite differently. Here the key category became not that of base/superstructure, but rather that of totality. As Lukács argued in *History and Class Consciousness*:

> *The primacy of the category of totality is the bearer of the principle of revolution in science* ... It was Marx who transformed the Hegelian method into ... the 'algebra of revolution'. It was not enough, however, to give it a materialist twist. The revolutionary principle in Hegel's dialectic was able to come to the surface less because of that than because of the validity of the method itself, viz. the concept of totality, the subordination of every part to the whole unity of history and thought.[41]

Thompson's almost complete indifference to this Hegelian Marxist tradition is in many respects distinctly odd. For, of course, Thompson's Marxism shares many common themes with Hegelian Marxism: the stress on consciousness and agency, the rejection of economic determinism, the insistence on the impossibility of assimilating Marxist method to that of the natural sciences, the emphasis on the historicity of Marxist categories, above all perhaps the notion of Marxism as unitary knowledge of society. And, although Thompson does not seem to appreciate this, Althusserian theoretical practice in fact developed as a reaction against precisely this Hegelian Marxist tradition, rather than against that tradition of English Marxist history which he himself represents.

But Thompson's position is not that of Hegelian Marxism. Despite the repeated references to historical materialism as a system of 'unitary knowledge', Thompson's Marxism is not essentially 'totalistic'. It is rather a theory of multi-causality, a theory which stresses the separate and distinct causal potencies of both the economic and the cultural. In itself Thompson's argument concerning the evidential significance of the experience is both helpful and instructive. But the cumulative weight of Thompson's repeated insistence on the active

---

41   Lukács 1971b, pp. 27–8.

energising role of moral beliefs serves so as to suggest that material and cultural factors in practice exercise a separate and equivalent determining force. There is, as Perry Anderson quite rightly observes, a 'creeping culturalism'[42] at work here. Indeed at one point in the argument, Thompson announces in terms thoroughly reminiscent of the functionalist sociology of which he is elsewhere so critical: 'Ends are chosen by our culture, which affords us, at the same time, our own medium of choosing and of influencing that choice'.[43] The limitations of Thompson's critique of functionalism suddenly become apparent: he has much to say, and all of it entirely apposite, on the subject of functionalism's structuralism of stasis, but not a word on that of its other most obviously distinguishing feature, its culturalism, its stress on the determining effectivity of the normative order.

There is a fine irony in all of this. For, of course, Althusser is not an economic determinist. On the contrary, Althusser himself proposes precisely a theory of multi-causal determinism, a theory in which each of the levels in the social formation is seen as having its own 'specific effectivity', a theory which is only rendered (formally) compatible with the Marxist tradition by its insistence that in the last instance the economy determines which of these levels will be dominant. Thus Anderson is quite right to reject Thompson's attempted indictment of Althusser on the charge of economic determinism, and quite right too to suggest the existence of certain affinities between the two positions.[44] But where Anderson detects a common strength, there is in reality merely a common weakness. Precisely because both Althusser and Thompson reject both the Second International positivist tradition and the Hegelian Marxist tradition, they each end up in the last instance, as it were, advocating a multi-causalism that is simply non-Marxist. Thompson's multi-causalism is the superior of the two because it resolutely refuses to see the social totality as 'determined' in its entirety, because it insists on the potency of human agency. But neither his multi-causalism nor that of Althusser can be seen as in any sense proper to Marxism.

Which leads us to Thompson's critique of Stalinism. Thompson's characterisation of Stalinist Marxism in terms of its deterministic anti-humanism, and his concomitant insistence on the intimate connection between an anti-humanist theory and an inhuman political practice, is both powerful and suggestive. And his situation of the origins of Althusserianism, as theory, in

---

42 Anderson 1980, p. 82.
43 Thompson 1978a, p. 372.
44 Anderson 1980, pp. 67–8.

relation to the political reaction within the Communist Parties against both the liberalising tendencies within the USSR associated with Kruschevism, and the post-1956 socialist humanist opposition in the West, is undoubtedly correct. Althusserianism came into the world in the early 1960s as a theoretical accomplice to Maoism, and the Maoism that developed within the Communist Parties at that time was in all its essential features simply a revivified and recharged form of Stalinism. But the subsequent history of theoretical practice has proven rather different. At one level Thompson is perfectly aware of this. With considerable acumen, he traces out the correlation between the rise of theoretical practice and the growth of an elitist, anti-political 'Marxist' intelligentsia within Britain's Universities and Polytechnics.[45] But there is a second and in fact more important level to which Thompson pays no attention, that of Althusserianism's relationship to the developing Eurocommunist tendency within the Communist Parties. Althusserianism may well have *begun* as theorised Stalinism. But, as Thompson would be quick to remind us, we must always be wary of an over-static conceptualisation which ignores the logic of process. And Althusserianism has *become* a theoretical expression of the political practice of Eurocommunism. Thus the Althusserian emphasis on the 'complexity' of the social formation, and on the relative autonomy of the superstructures, has fused with a peculiar reading of Gramsci to produce a theoretical Eurocommunism which stresses, above all, both the necessary complexity of the transition to socialism (and hence its necessary gradualism) and the particular importance of 'counter-hegemonic' ideological struggle to the whole process of transition.

Now this is, to coin a phrase, *exactly* what has commonly been designated in the Marxist tradition as reformism.[46] The debate between revolutionaries and reformists is an old one in the socialist movement, but not one that has found much echo of late on the Australian Left (presumably because no strategy for

---

45   Thompson can be very funny indeed when discussing this phenomenon. See especially his wickedly 'Althusserian' account of the works canteen meeting (Thompson 1978a, p. 335).

46   By reformist I mean not any variety of social-democratic or liberal politics such as are propounded by most ALP parliamentarians, but rather the properly socialist view of socialism as attainable through the progressive introduction of a series of cumulative reforms whose ultimate effect will be the elimination of capitalism. Its alternative within the socialist tradition is revolutionism, which insists on the necessity for the overthrow of the capitalist state and for a decisive revolutionary 'break', a rupture between the old capitalist and the new socialist societies. For an account of the influence of revolutionary and reformist ideas on the pre-Communist left in Australia see Burgmann 1980. On the Communist Party see Gollan 1975.

socialism, be it revolutionary or reformist, seems particularly likely to succeed at least for the forseeable future in Australia). It is, however, an important debate, perhaps the single most important within socialist politics. And it is so, firstly, because it provides us with the relevant criteria with which to assess the behaviour of socialists in those countries and in those circumstances in which a successful transition to socialism does appear feasible (for example, Chile under Allende, Portugal shortly after the fall of the dictatorship); and secondly, because it permits Australian socialists to determine in advance, insofar as that is possible, those strategies that would prove most effective were Australia itself to be confronted with similar such circumstances. As Anderson quite rightly observers, neither the reformist nor the revolutionary position 'is free from certain central problems, whose common root is the absence of any successful transition ... at all in the advanced capitalist countries to date'.[47] Only once, in Russia in 1917, has a working class revolution ever achieved success;[48] many more such revolutions have been ruthlessly suppressed, often amidst appalling bloodshed (for example, the Paris Commune, the Hungarian and German revolutions immediately after the Great War) the repetition of which no civilised mind can contemplate with equanimity. Moreover, the ultimate fate of that one successful revolution is not such that any non-Stalinist could possibly wish for its replication elsewhere. On the other hand, there is not one single example of a successful gradualist transition to socialism to which reformists might point in support of their case; and on those few occasions when such a strategy has been attempted (Spain in 1936, Chile in 1970) the outcome has been a bloodbath equally as horrifying, if not more so, as any that have occurred as a result of failed revolutions. There is, then, much wisdom in Anderson's observation that 'all strategic conceptions of the transition to socialism inherently contain arguments of a *probabilistic* type'.[49] But this cautionary rider not withstanding, the example of that one (temporarily) successful working class revolution remains compelling. As Anderson himself concludes, on the ground not of speculation on an unknowable future, but of examination of a known past, the 'evidence points to the greater cogency and realism of the tradition of Lenin and Trotsky',[50] that is, of the revolutionary tradition.

Now Thompson is peculiarly silent on this matter of Althusser's support for the neo-reformist politics of Eurocommunism. And for one very obvious

---

47 Anderson 1980, p. 196.
48 Whatever else may be said of the Chinese, Cuban and Vietnamese revolutions, they were certainly not *working class* revolutions.
49 Anderson 1980, p. 197.
50 Ibid.

reason: his own politics are imbued with a parallel reformism. Thompson is, though, no orthodox Eurocommunist. His experience of the 1956 crisis appears to have deposited as its legacy within his consciousness an enduring loathing for the Communist Party of Great Britain and all its works. But Thompson's objections to Eurocommunism rest not on any opposition to reformism *per se*, but rather on a simple disbelief in the capacities of formerly Stalinist parties wholeheartedly to commit themselves to a 'democratic' road to socialism. And when Thompson is prepared temporarily to suspend that disbelief, the fundamental affinity between his politics and those of Eurocommunism becomes apparent:

> There *is* movement. There is even genuine self-questioning, real discussion, dialogue. It moves at different paces, here and there. With Italian Communism ... it has moved in interesting ways. It has even moved in France ... I think that ... the outcome of Communist participation in governments of the Left might be one which opened new and more democratic socialist possibilities.[51]

In other words, Thompson adheres to an almost identical position to that of Althusser on the key questions of strategy and tactics with which the Left is faced. Hence presumably Thompson's membership of the British Labour Party. And hence too his utterly dismissive approach to almost the entire revolutionary socialist tradition. Revolutionary socialism does not figure largely amongst Thompson's pre-occupations in *The Poverty of Theory*. There are a few cursory references to revolutionary 'pharisees'[52] and the 'religious cast of thought'[53] of 'self-enclosed sects'.[54] There is a distinctly odd dismissal of Trotskyism on the peculiar grounds of Peter Fryer's support for epistemological reflection theory in 1957.[55] And that is about all. Now Thompson has every right to pick and choose both his opponents and his allies. But this failure even to confront

---

51 Thompson 1978a, pp. 330–1.
52 Thompson 1978a, p. ii.
53 Thompson 1978a, p. 375.
54 Thompson 1978a, p. 397.
55 Peter Fryer was the Hungarian correspondent of the British Communist Party's *Daily Worker* at the time of the 1956 Hungarian Revolution. He resigned from the Communist Party and subsequently became a Trotskyist. Thompson's dismissal is odd, firstly, because Fryer was a new recruit to Trotskyism and might therefore have been expected to retain some old Stalinist habits; and odd, secondly, because Trotsky himself actually rejects reflection theory in his *Literature and Revolution* (Trotsky 1960).

the issue of revolution versus reform with any appropriate seriousness does seem to indicate a very real point of weakness within his overall argument, and one moreover that undermines the intellectual credibility of his account of the evolution of Marxist thought.

Thompson's version of the history of Marxism runs as follows: in the decades preceding the Great War, the gradual but steady growth of the socialist movement permitted the emergence of an essentially 'evolutionist' Marxism, an evolutionism temporarily checked by the rupture of the October Revolution, but subsequently refurbished in utopian form by the promise of the future development of 'socialism' in Russia; from 1936 to 1946, however, the dynamics of the anti-fascist struggle gave rise to a second Marxism essentially 'voluntarist' in form, which came to stress the role of human agency and choice; and finally, the Cold War stasis of the postwar period encouraged yet a third type of Marxism, that which spoke the language of structuralism and disallowed the logic of process.[56] It should be obvious that Thompson's own preference is for the voluntaristic Marxism of the period 1936–46. But there is one rather important problem with this account: as history, it is quite simply inaccurate. Thompson's understanding of pre-1936 socialist thought exhibits an analytical carelessness that one simply would not expect from so distinguished a socialist historian. It ignores the existence of non-evolutionist currents within Second International and Two-and-a-Half International reformism (most obviously the neo-Kantianism of writers such as Vorlander and the Austro-Marxism of Max Adler); it ignores the voluntarism of the Comintern's ultra-left 'Third Period'; and more importantly it ignores the voluntarism of the two most obviously revolutionary traditions within Marxism, that of the revolutionary opposition within the pre-1914 International (Lenin, Luxemburg and Trotsky) and that of early Hegelian Marxism (Korsch, Gramsci and the young Lukács).

The glowing portrayal of the voluntaristic Marxism of the years of anti-fascist struggle is little better. That decade, writes Thompson:

> was a decade of heroes, and there were Guevaras in every street and in every wood. The vocabulary of Marxism became infiltrated from a new direction: that of authentic liberalism (the choices of the autonomous individual) and perhaps also of Romanticism (the rebellion of spirit against the rules of fact). Poetry, rather than natural science or sociology, was welcomed as a cousin.[57]

---

56   Thompson 1978a, pp. 263–5.
57   Thompson 1978a, p. 264.

It is difficult to understand how any British historian can seriously suggest that 1930s Marxism displayed a preference for poetry as opposed to natural science. For, of course, the 1930s was precisely the period in which the British Communist Party acquired an unusual degree of influence in natural scientific circles, and in which conversely natural scientific ideas acquired an unusual degree of influence in Communist circles.[58] But this is a minor point of interest mainly to the professional historian of ideas. More significant is Thompson's almost perverse misrepresentation of the nature of Communist politics during this period. On Thompson's account it all sounds to have been very wonderful indeed. But wasn't this precisely the period of the Moscow Trials, when an entire generation of Old Bolsheviks were liquidated by Stalinist terror to the accompanying applause of foreign Communists? Wasn't this precisely the period of the Spanish Civil War, during which the Russian Government (and also its agents within the Western Communist Parties), in the words of George Orwell, did 'all in their power to crush the Spanish revolutionary movements, defend private property and hand power to the middle class as against the working class'?[59] Wasn't this decade of uninterrupted anti-fascist struggle interrupted precisely by the Nazi-Societ Pact of 1939–41, which the vast majority of Western Communists dutifully and shamelessly defended? Wasn't this in fact precisely the period of high Stalinism? One is tempted to doubt either the sincerity of Thompson's anti-Stalinism or alternatively the strength of his skills as a historian. But neither surely can be faulted. The fault lies elsewhere, in that peculiar myopia which Thompson exhibits in the face both of the vicious reality of pre-1956 Stalinism and of the various traditions of left-wing anti-Stalinist criticism which developed prior to that year (the most notable of which was revolutionary Trotskyism).

At one point in his argument Thompson directs a considerable amount of entirely justifiable scorn at Althusser's belated pretensions to anti-Stalinism. '*So where was Althusser in 1956?*' he asks.[60] A fair question; and Thompson is too honest a writer not to detect the obvious corollary, an equally fair question, 'where was Thompson before 1956?' Certainly Thompson anticipates the question, but his answer that 1956 was somehow different – because in '1956 it was, at length, officially "revealed" that Stalinism had, for decades, been swatting down men like flies'[61] – cannot be accepted as at all adequate. It is

---

58   Samuel 1980, pp. 78–81.
59   Orwell 1966, p. 242.
60   Thompson 1978a, p. 324.
61   Thompson 1978a.

difficult to believe that this offcial admission of guilt can have been so salient a consideration in the deliberations of as independently minded a thinker as Thompson. And even if it were so, then surely *now* Thompson can attempt an honest reappraisal of the pre-1956 period. But the blindness remains: 1936–46 is still the 'decade of heroes' and there remains only silence as to the merits of those earlier left-wing anti-Stalinisms. The most obvious silence is that directed towards Trotsky and Trotskyism. But there is another perhaps less obvious but in many respects even more remarkable silence, that directed towards George Orwell, a writer much of whose political career was characterised by an honourable and principled socialist anti-Stalinism, a man who in the late 1930s at least was very definitely, to borrow a phrase of Thompson's, a socialist internationalist speaking in an English tongue. Perhaps the Prophet Outcast in Mexico was too distant a voice for Thompson to hear. But Orwell, a much less distant voice for a British writer, must surely command some belated respect on Thompson's part.[62]

Which brings us finally to Thompson's account of postwar Marxism and to his version of the history of the last fifteen years, with which it is intimately connected. Postwar Marxism, argues Thompson, is essentially a structuralism, and in Britain in the late sixties and the seventies it has spawned the heresy against reason which is theoretical practice. Now Thompson's judgements on both Althusserianism in general and the English Althusserian intelligentsia in particular might well be perfectly acceptable. But there has been more to the history of the socialist movement in the sixties and seventies than this peculiar renaissance of medieval scholasticsm in Marxist guise. The socialist humanism of Thompson's own mid-fifties New Left, the rediscovered Hegelian Marxism of Gramsci, Korsch and Lukács, the existentialist Marxism of Jean-Paul Sartre, the revolutionary Marxism of Lenin, stripped of the Stalinist crust which had encased it for decades, and of Luxemburg and Trotsky, all these were thrown into the scales against both Stalinism and Althusserianism during these last twenty years which Thompson has found so barren. On the most charitable estimate Thompson's account can only be adjudged both partial and distorting. His account of the contemporary British Left is incidentally similarly distorted. Thompson writes as if Althusserianism had swept all before it and

---

62 Thompson's brief discussion of Orwell in the 'Outside the Whale' essay republished in *The Poverty of Theory*, though perfectly fair insofar as it goes, deals with Orwell at the point of his politico-intellectual collapse into pessimism, and concentrates on the subsequent uses which Western Cold War ideology has made of Orwell's work. So far as I am aware Thompson has written nothing more extensive.

established a near-total hegemony over British socialist politics. But even the casual observer can see that this has not in fact been the case. Theoretical practice has been merely one amongst many intellectual currents whose (transient) influence has been confined almost entirely within the narrow circles of academia. Much more significant surely has been the growth since 1969 of a new British revolutionary left, self-consciously anti-Stalinist in politics, and normally distinctly anti-Althusserian in its theoretical preoccupations. In reality Thompson is nothing like as alone in his opposition to Althusserianism as he appears to believe, though one doubts he will take much comfort in that thought.

To sum up: Thompson's epistemology is marred by his belief that a single 'historical logic' can somehow straddle class boundaries and therefore act as a neutral arbiter between liberal and socialist history; his historiography by a culturalism that radically overestimates not the potency of values (for in this respect he is entirely correct) but their autonomy, and that leads him ironically to a multi-causalism somewhat similar to Althusser's; and his politics by an uncritical reformism, again ironically similar to Althusser's own, that leads him to a radical underestimation of the revolutionary socialist tradition, and hence to an essentially unsatisfactory account of the history of Marxist thought. In each of these respects the positions that Thompson advances in *The Poverty of Theory* demonstrate a certain common tendency to subvert the centrality of the concept of class to Marxist theory. Thus a neutral historical logic is only possible if the professional historian is seen to stand in some sense outside the wider class structure; a separate autonomous effectivity can only be attributed to the normative order if it too is seen as functioning in some sense outside the class structure; and a reformist political strategy is only possible if the state in turn is seen as possessing a more than relative autonomy from the wider class structure. But these are only *tendencies* at work within Thompson's overall theoretical framework. And the central achievement of the essay remains. Here is a masterly statement of the case for a Marxism that is both humanist and activist, a Marxism that affords due respect to the role of consciousness and agency, a Marxism that believes with Marx that the point, however, is to change it. Here is a Marxism that exposes theoretical practice for the sterile obscurantism which it is, a Marxism that knows Stalinism for the theoretical and practical abomination which it is, a Marxism that restores to socialism what must always be its central project, the struggle for human liberation. 'Stalinism', writes Thompson,

> was not one 'error', not even two 'errors', which may be identified, 'corrected', and Theory thus reformed. Stalinism was not absent-minded about crimes: it *bred* crimes ... Its very breath stank (and still stinks) of inhu-

manity, because it has found a way of regarding people as the bearers of structures ... and history as a process without a subject. It is not an admirable theory, flawed by errors; it is a heresy against reason.[63]

This is not the whole truth about Stalinism (which is not merely an ideology, but also a social order, a system of *class* domination) nor about Althusserianism (which appears able to accomodate itself to reformism as well as to Stalinism). But it is as good a place to begin as any.

3   Arguments within English Marxism: In Defence of Althusserianism

The Marxism that Perry Anderson and the 'New New Left' introduced into British intellectual life represented a radical departure from the common preoccupations and concerns of the 'Old New Left'. The reconstructed *New Left Review* adopted as its central theoretical project the translation and importation into Britian of a selectively 'weighted' version of the tradition of 'Western Marxism' that had developed in France, Germany and Italy during the inter-war and postwar periods. This interest in continental Marxism can be seen to represent at one level a simple disengagement from the analysis of British history and society, and from the practicalities of British politics, that had concerned the Old New Left. But such an interpretation of Anderson's *New Left Review* captures a part only of the truth. The New New Left did in fact develop an analysis of British history, society and politics, and their concern with the Western Marxist tradition arose precisely out of this analysis. In a series of intellectually extremely ambitious essays, Anderson and his colleagues, and in particular Tom Nairn, propounded a distinctly original account of British history. In their view the seventeenth-century English bourgeois revolution remained essentially uncompleted, its central political legacy a class compromise between the aristocracy and the bourgeoisie rather than a fully-formed bourgeois polity, its central ideological legacy a deeply conservative combination of traditionalism and empiricism. Out of this class compromise, they argued, there arose in England a peculiarly archaic state form, a peculiarly supine bourgeoisie, a peculiarly subordinate proletariat, and a peculiarly philistine intelligentsia capable of producing neither an indigenous Marxism nor even an indigenous classical sociology.[64] These alleged English peculiarities have, of course, been the object

---

63 Thompson 1978a, p. 323.
64 Anderson 1964; Anderson 1970; Nairn 1964a; Nairn 1964b; Nairn 1964c.

of much theoretical contention.⁶⁵ But those debates, important though they are, need not detain us here. For our purposes the main point to note is this: that Anderson, Nairn and their collaborators saw the importation into Britain of Western Marxism as a device by which to break this politico-intellectual logjam they had detected. Sustained exposure to continental Marxist ideas would, they hoped, make possible the emergence of a new English Marxist intelligentsia, and this in turn would permit the construction of a new socialist politics.

We have suggested that the version of the Western Marxist tradition with which the *New Left Review* sought to guide the English intelligentsia was in fact selectively 'weighted'. This observation requires some elaboration since Anderson in *Arguments Within English Marxism* explicitly denies the charge that the *Review* had adopted an essentially Althusserian stance: 'rather than insisting on Marxism as a single "doctrine"', the journal 'has emphasized the plurality and diversity of schools of thought within 20th century Marxism, and has purposively published criticisms of all of them'.⁶⁶ And again:

> NLR set out from the mid-sixties onwards to introduce the major intellectual systems of continental socialism in the post-classical epoch into the culture of the British Left. Successive translations were made of the works of Lukács, Korsch, Gramsci, Adorno, Della Volpe, Colletti, Goldmann, Sartre, Althusser, Timpanaro and other thinkers ... The review also criticized, calmly and systematically, every one of the theoretical schools within 'Western Marxism'.⁶⁷

Now it is undoubtedly the case that the *New Left Review* and its associated publishing house, New Left Books, did indeed devote resources to the (more or less) critical appraisal of each of these schools. Thus Thompson's allegation that 'from France or about France, they have *issued nothing else*'⁶⁸ other than the products of the Althusserian school, is not *literally* true. But the *New Left Review* editorial committee did nonetheless, and perhaps inevitably, exercise a real discrimination in the way in which it allocated those resources.⁶⁹

---

65 Cf. Thompson 1965.
66 Anderson 1980, p. 133.
67 Anderson 1980, p. 149.
68 Thompson 1978a, p. 405.
69 A brief exercise in crude empiricism serves to demonstrate the point. Taking the various thinkers that Anderson himself names we find that, since early 1967 when Althusser's presence first graced its columns, the *New Left Review* has published six pieces, articles by, commentaries upon or interviews with Lukács (in Nos. 60, 68, 70, 84, 91 and 110), *one*

Thus, though Thompson's charge does not in fact represent the literal truth, it is nonetheless the case that for much of the late sixties and the seventies the *Review*'s theoretical interests and sympathies were defined primarily in relation to Althusserian theoretical practice. Sufficiently so at least for the North American 'Hegelian Marxist' journal *Telos* to refer in 1976 to the *Review*'s 'inability to come to terms with its own culture, opting instead for the most sterile version of post-Althusserian word games'.[70] Now the *New Left Review* has every right to distribute its theoretical favours as it pleases (and equally Thompson has every right to subject that distribution to a ruthlessly 'unforgiving' critique). But Anderson's denial of the presence of any Althusserian sympathies on the part of the *Review* is at best disingenuous, at worst dishonest.

It is precisely the *Review*'s Althusserianism that occasioned Thompson's attack on Althusser in *The Poverty of Theory*. How, then, does Anderson reply to the central charges that Thompson's prosecution lays against theoretical practice? We suggested earlier that there were three distinct components in Thompson's indictment: a critique of Althusserian epistemological idealism, a critique of Althusserian historiographical determinism, and finally a critique of Althusserian Stalinism. It might be as well to consider in turn Anderson's responses to each of these charges. Let us note immediately that, whatever position Anderson and the *New Left Review* may have adopted in the past, he is no longer prepared to confer anything remotely resembling unqualified assent upon the Althusserian theoretical problematic. Anderson readily concedes Thompson's point that Althusserian epistemology is essentially idealist[71] and proceeds, moreover, to a surprisingly fulsome endorsement of the latter's notion of historical inquiry as a dialogue between theory and evidence.[72]

(a short interview his widow) on Korsch (in No. 76), four on Gramsci (Nos. 51, 65, 100 and 112), five on Adorno (Nos. 46, 47, 81, 87–88 and 121), three on Della Volpe (Nos. 59, 113–14 and 117), five on Colletti (Nos. 56, 61, 65, 86 and 93), three on Goldmann (Nos. 56, 67 and 92), five on Sartre (Nos. 41, 48, 58, 97 and 100), *eight* on Althusser (Nos. 41, 55, 64, 71, 101–2, 104 and 109) and four on Timpanaro (Nos. 85, 91, 94 and 118). Moreover, Anderson's list is itself a little deceptive since it makes no mention of other Althusserian contributors to its pages, for example the late Nicos Poulantzas, whose work was brought to the attention of *New Left Review* readers on *seven* occasions during the same period (in Nos. 43, 58, 78, 82, 95, 109 and 119). The same pattern appears in NLB's publishing schedule. And this is to say nothing of the manifestly Althusserian tenor of many of the various articles and book written by members of the *Review*'s editorial committee.

70 Toronto *Telos* group 1976, p. 258.
71 Anderson 1980, p. 6.
72 Anderson 1980, pp. 6–7.

Indeed he goes so far as to observe that 'Thompson's ... affirmation of the irreducible, independent reality of historical evidence, and of the various ways in which it can be interrogated, is in general a model of good sense'.[73] But there Anderson and Thompson part company. Anderson rejects both Hexter's reality rule, in particular, and Thompson's notion of a distinct historical logic, in general.[74] As an alternative he proposes a quasi-positivist conception of history as a science, one which owes much to both Popper and Lakatos,[75] and which even makes use of that hackneyed positivist cliché, the supposed parallelism between history and meteorology.[76] Anderson's objections are directed not at Thompson's insistence that liberal and socialist history can be subsumed under a common historical logic, but rather at Thompson's perfectly proper recognition that historical and social knowledge and natural science cannot be assimilated to each other under the rubric of a common scientific method. Here, then, is the authentic voice of a fairly orthodox positivism. Thus, when Anderson denies the similarities between Popperian and Althusserian epistemologies that Thompson had identified in *The Poverty of Theory*, he does so in order to salvage the theoretical integrity not of Althusser's theoretical practice, but of Popper's philosophy of science.[77] From one scientism to another, such is the theoretical journey that Anderson has chosen to travel in response to Thompson's critique of Althusserianism. Apparently theory, like history, repeats itself, the first time as tragedy, the second as farce.

Just as Anderson accepts much of Thompson's critique of Althusserian epistemology, so too he admits the weaknesses of Althusserian historiographical determinism. But Thompson's 'voluntarism' is in Anderson's view equally suspect:

> the two antagonistic formulae of a 'natural-human process without a subject' and 'ever-baffled, ever-resurgent agents of an unmastered practice' are both claims of an essentially apodictic and speculative character – eternal axioms that in no way help us to trace the actual, variable roles of different types of deliberate venture, personal or collective, in history.[78]

---

73   Anderson 1980, p. 8.
74   Anderson 1980, pp. 8–13.
75   Anderson 1980, pp. 11–12.
76   Anderson 1980, p. 10.
77   Anderson 1980, p. 7.
78   Anderson 1980, p. 21.

Anderson is here concerned above all to emphasise the variable incidence of potent human agency. Defining agency as conscious goal-directed activity,[79] he distinguishes three levels at which such agency may be operative, that of purely private goals, that of public goals which operate within existing social relations, and that of collective projects which seek to transform social relations, and argues that Thompson's failure to distinguish between these three levels leads to a corresponding failure to appreciate both the rarity and the comparative modernity of the latter type of agency.[80] 'A *historical*, as opposed to an axiomatic, approach to the problem would', he writes, 'seek to trace the *curve* of such enterprises, which has risen sharply ... in the last two centuries'.[81] There is in itself nothing objectionable in this insistence on 'the millenial negations of self-determination in the kingdom of necessity',[82] nor in the corresponding affirmation of the uniqueness of socialism as a social order which will permit '*real popular self-determination for the first time in history*'.[83] But Anderson is mistaken to assume that his remarks here necessarily contradict the Thompsonian formula of 'ever-baffled, ever-resurgent agents of an unmastered practice'. On the contrary, the two are entirely compatible. 'Men make their own history', wrote Marx, 'but ... they do not make it under circumstance chosen by themselves'.[84] Now due weight has to be attached to both halves of this formulation of Marx. Men (people, actually) have always made history, but the extent to which they are able to influence the circumstances in which they do so is nonetheless historically variable. Thus the uniqueness of socialism consists not in the fact of people finally making history, but rather in that of their finally being able to exercise a qualitatively different degree of choice as to the circumstances in which they will do so. Or, to translate the problem into Thompsonian terms, in the attainment of a type of agency which is no longer baffled and a type of practice which is no longer unmastered. Anderson therefore detects an entirely false symmetry between Althusserian and Thompsonian positions. For, whereas Althusser's formulation is indeed apodictic and speculative in its insistence that history is *always* a process without a subject, Thompson's by contrast permits a recognition of the variable incidence, not of agency *per se*, but of different *types* of agency (more of less baffled, more or less unmastered). The critical remarks that Anderson directs at Thompson would be pertinent to

---

79   Anderson 1980, p. 19.
80   Anderson 1980, pp. 19–21.
81   Anderson 1980, p. 21.
82   Anderson 1980, p. 58.
83   Anderson 1980, p. 22.
84   Marx 1970a, p. 96.

a super-voluntarism which supposed human history to consist in its entirety of the intended consequences of successful human projects. But, since this is not Thompson's view, Anderson's arguments can only be deemed irrelevant to the point at issue.

Anderson is, however, quite right to suggest that in practice Thompson's voluntarism tends to lead to an overemphasis on the autonomous potency of values, to a 'creeping culturalism'. And Anderson's observations as to both the 'disconcerting lack of objective coordinates'[85] in *The Making of the English Working Class* and the problematic nature of the concept of 'class struggle without classes' employed in Thompson's essay on 'Eighteenth-Century English Society'[86] are both original and instructive. But these theoretical weaknesses have their origins neither in Thompson's stress on agency nor in that on experience as Anderson would have us believe, but rather in that analytically distinct, multi-causalism to which we drew attention earlier. Anderson in fact inflates the importance of these weaknesses on Thompson's part and he does so with a particular theoretical purpose: by exaggerating the necessary voluntarism of Thompson's position he seeks to disarm any possible opposition to his own, which now appears to encompass not so much the multi-causal determinism of Althusserian theoretical practice as a much more traditional economic determinism. This becomes apparent especially in Anderson's discussion of the 'problem of order'. Anderson here takes issue with that correction to Engels's 'parallelogram of forces', substituting class wills for individual wills, which Thompson proposed in *The Poverty of Theory*. Thompson has defined class so as to make it dependent on the sum of individual wills, Anderson argues, and this must necessarily lead him to an infinite regress towards Engels's own position.[87] Let us note in passing that, whatever else may be the case, there is certainly no 'regression towards infinity' in Engels's formulation. Mistaken Engels may be, but he is no theoretical 'buck passer'; rather the buck very definitely stops, as it does in orthodox methodological individualism, with the concrete individual. More importantly, Anderson misconstrues Thompson's theoretical stance. When Thompson argues that 'the process of class formation is a process of self-making, although under conditions which are "given"',[88] he is *not* defining class wills as a simple aggregate of individual wills. In fact he quite correctly identifies the dual nature of class consciousness as at one and the same time

---

85 Anderson 1980, p. 33.
86 Anderson 1980, pp. 40–3; Thompson 1978a.
87 Anderson 1980, pp. 50–1.
88 Thompson 1978a, p. 299.

both a product of individual wills ('self-making') and a product of the common objective class position that structures those individual wills ('conditions which are given'). The inner logic of this duality is comprehensible in terms neither of individualistic subjectivism nor holistic determinism. For it is in its very nature essentially complex, and this complexity remains accessible only to an equivalently complex logic, a logic which much of Thompson's work displays, a logic which has a long tradition in socialist thought, a logic for which Marxism even has a term: that term is 'dialectics'.

By assimilating Thompson's position to that of Engels, Anderson is able however to prepare the ground for the introduction into the argument of his own economic determinism. 'The problem of *social order*', he writes,

> is irresoluble so long as the answer to it is sought at the level of intention (or valuation), however complex or entangled the skein of volition, however class-defined the struggle of wills, however alienated the final resultant from all the imputed actors. It is, and must be, the dominant *mode of production* that confers fundamental unity on a social formation, allocating the objective positions to the classes within it, and distributing the agents within each class.[89]

In general terms no Marxist could reasonably object to this stress on the importance of the mode of production (although one might object both to the language of determinism in which Anderson couches the proposition, and to that preoccupation with 'the problem of order' which Anderson takes over from functionalist sociology – for, of course, historical process is actually much more disorderly than such neo-Hobbesian formulations suggest). But a mode of production is both a determinate set of forces of production and a determinate set of relations of production, and relations of production are at once both constitutive of and constituted by social classes, which are in turn both constitutive of and constituted by real, concrete individuals. Thus any invocation of the mode of production that is more than mere ritual poses immediately the necessity for analysis at the level of intention and valuation (as also at other levels). To take an obvious example, the overthrow of the Allende government cannot be rendered fully intelligible without some analysis of the intentions and valuations of different groupings (and individuals) within the Chilean ruling class and the Chilian military, within the Chilean left, within the Christian Democracy and the petty bourgeoisie, within the local and international man-

---

[89] Anderson 1980, p. 55.

agements of the relevant multinational corporations, within the leaderships of the American military, political and intelligence establishments, and so on.

The example we have chosen is significant, for it is in the examination of exactly such political struggles – revolutions, counter-revolutions, coups, electoral confrontations, strikes – that the explanation of intentionality becomes especially important. And it is precisely such phenomena which constitute the specially privileged objects of study for Marxist theory: Marxism is not in its essence a contemplative social science, but rather a theoretical guide to political action. Anderson comes close to recognising this when he writes that:

> Thompson's passionate sense of the potential of human agency to shape collective conditions of life ... is much closer to the political temper of Marx and Engels themselves in their own time ... Strangely, of two unbalanced sets of generalizations, Althusser's inclines better towards history, Thompson's better towards politics.[90]

We have already suggested the grounds upon which this might be adjudged an over-generous assessment of Althusser's contribution to Marxism. But, even assuming its adequacy, the judgement on Thompson remains perverse. If Thompson's position does indeed incline better towards politics, if in other words it is stronger on Marxism's own preferred terrain, that of political practice, then any supposed symmetry between it and that of Althusser must be false. For, as we had cause to remark earlier, the point, however, is to change it.

Anderson's response to Thompson's critique of Althusserian Stalinism is similarly inadequate. He argues, firstly, that Althusser's politics were essentially Maoist rather than Stalinist,[91] whilst conceding both that Althusserian anti-Stalinism is much less principled and passionate than Thompson's and that this is one of the necessary costs of any anti-Stalinism based on Maoism.[92] The niceties of this theoretical distinction between Stalinism and Maoism have plagued the *New Left Review* throughout much of its history. Admittedly, in the late 1960s and the early 1970s much Western European 'Maoism' did exhibit, in a peculiar confused fashion, a certain 'anti-Stalinism'. This is much less true, however, of the Maoism of the early 1960s towards which Althusser himself had gravitated. This earlier Maoism represented little more than a rallying point for those elements of 'unreconstructed Stalinism' that had proven radically

---

90 Anderson 1980, p. 58.
91 Anderson 1980, p. 107.
92 Anderson 1980, p. 116.

unamenable to the 'liberalising' tendencies within the European Communist Parties. And if one situates Althusser's initial theoretical interventions in relation to this particular form of Maoism, then one is bound to conclude, with Thompson, that Althusserianism is indeed a Stalinism. Anderson's second argument runs thus:

> There is no intrinsic relation between a causal determinism and a callous amoralism ... Spinoza ... was known in his own life-time as the noblest and gentlest of men, and was canonized by his successors as the 'saint of philosophers' ... There is no reason to suppose ... that this (i.e. Althusser's – A.M.) ethical outlook would be especially different.[93]

But Anderson here attempts an entirely illegitimate conflation of two quite distinct levels of analysis, that appropriate to the contingencies of individual moral practice, and that to the political import of transindividual theoretical-ideological constructs. What matters here is not the personal moral behaviour of any particular determinist philosopher, but rather the implications for political morality of a determinist world vision. And Anderson's list of '*an impressively wide range of works dealing with the real world, both past and present*'[94] that theoretical practice has generated, provides no real answer to Thompson's indictment of Althusserianism on politico-moral grounds. It may well be true that Guy Bois's *Crisis of Feudalism* 'is a landmark of medieval scholarship';[95] but this tells us nothing about the possible relationships which might exist between theoretical determinism, on the one hand, and political amoralism, on the other. We may very well concede that there is no necessary logical relationship between the two. There can, however, be no doubt that high Stalinism brought them into a peculiarly close intimate relationship; and it would seem plausible at least to suggest that a theoretical anti-humanism would normally provide a less effective guarantee against political immorality than would its humanist antithesis.

---

93 Anderson 1980, p. 125.
94 Anderson 1980, p. 126.
95 Ibid.

4 Anderson's Counter-Critique

Anderson's response to Thompson's critique of Althusserianism can, then, be seen to proceed at three levels: firstly, he accepts much of that critique and in particular many of its more significant elements; secondly, he develops a series of criticisms from a broadly positivist standpoint of Thompson's own alternative, some important, but most rather less so, and attempts to represent that alternative as prone to theoretical errors opposite to those characteristic of theoretical practice; and thirdly, through the device of this posited symmetry between Althusserian and Thompsonian positions, he seeks to distance himself and the *New Left Review* from both Althusser and Althusserianism. This 'distancing' process is central to Anderson's *Arguments Within English Marxism*. For it is in fact one of the key themes running through the book that Thompson has simply misunderstood the issues which divide him from Anderson's *New Left Review*. The point at issue was never Althusserianism, argues Anderson; rather, if anything, it was Trotskyism. The Trotskyist tradition, he explains, 'became in time a central and unevadable pole of political reference within NLR', and it was this which became one of the most 'substantial real differences of all between Thompson and ourselves'.[96] From the mid-1960s onwards:

> NLR never lost sight of the centrality of Trotsky's heritage ... This engagement with the thought of Trotsky was ... by no means confined to the *New Left Review*. In different ways, and with diverse interpretations, it has been a very general phenomenon among the younger generation of socialist militants in the past decade – far more so than the Althusserianism which preoccupies Thompson.[97]

Anderson is almost certainly correct in his assessment of the relative influence of Althusser and Trotsky on the British left during the late 1960s and the 1970s. But his claim that the *New Left Review*'s own development has run parallel to that of the wider British Left should be regarded with some suspicion.

We have already pointed to the considerable attraction that Althusserianism exercised for the *New Left Review*. We should now perhaps also note that this 'centrality of Trotsky's heritage' to the *New Left Review* has never been quite as visible in its pages as Anderson's remarks might here lead one to sup-

---

96 Anderson 1980, pp. 152–3.
97 Anderson 1980, p. 155.

pose. Certainly it was insufficiently so for Thompson, a normally perceptive reader, even to register its presence. And for this reason: whereas the *New Left Review* devoted considerable attention to the Western Marxist tradition, it has exhibited no equivalent interest in either Trotsky's own work (the *Review* has never actually published anything by Trotsky) or the development of Trotskyist and neo-Trotskyist politics in Britain. This relative indifference to the post-1968 British revolutionary left is, moreover, almost certainly no mere contingent phenomon. On the contrary, the *New Left Review*'s sustained theoretical encounter with Western Marxism, and the analyses both of the nature of British society and of the appropriate socialist strategies for changing that society upon which that encounter was predicated, all combined so as to militate against any similarly sustained engagement with the revolutionary Marxist tradition.

Trotskyism is, then, a rather less central and a rather more evadable pole of reference within NLR than Anderson would have us believe. Nonetheless, this interest in Trotskyism and in classical revolutionary Marxism on the part of both the *Review* and its editor is undoubtedly genuine. In a remarkable earlier essay, *Considerations on Western Marxism*, Anderson himself has expressed a distinct preference for the Trotskyist tradition over that of Western Marxism.[98] And in *Arguments Within English Marxism* Anderson returns to this theme, although here the distribution of preferences is rather less weighted in favour of Trotskyism. Here too the resort to Trotskyism serves a very specific ulterior theoretical purpose, as a device by which to counter and turn back upon itself Thompson's critique of Althusserian Stalinism. We have already pointed to the inadequacies of Anderson's defence of Althusser himself against the charge of Stalinism. But at the point at which the theoretical legacy of Trotsky is introduced into the debate, when Anderson turns from a defence of Althusser to a counter-critique of Thompson, the argument becomes at once both more genuinely problematic and more properly innovative. There appear to be five main elements within this counter-critique: a critique of Thompson's reformism, of his assessment of the significance of '1956', of his account of Stalinism, of his version of the history of Marxist theory, and finally of the nature of his internationalism. This counter-critique, which occupies much of the second half of the book, is important for what it tells us both about Thompson and about Anderson, and it thus warrants a fairly detailed theoretical scrutiny.

---

98   Anderson 1976.

Anderson's critique of Thompson's reformism is from our point of view almost entirely uncontentious. Positioning himself securely on the terrrain of the classical revolutionary Marxism of Lenin, Trotsky, Luxemburg and Gramsci,[99] Anderson very ably demonstrates both the reformist underpinnings of much of Thompson's writing and the crucial theoretical weaknesses to which such reformism is susceptible. Indeed Anderson's commentary on Thompson's *William Morris*,[100] which combines a timely and generous acceptance of Thompson's case for the importance of utopianism to socialist thought[101] with a robust critique of Thompson's failure to appreciate the revolutionary and explicitly anti-reformist nature of Morris's political credentials,[102] almost certainly represents the high point of his argument. The second and third components within Anderson's counter-critique need not detain us long either. In each case Anderson counterposes a fairly orthodoxly Trotskyist position to that of Thompson. Thus he rejects Thompson's view of 1956 socialist humanism as an especially privileged 'total critique' of Stalinism, and insists quite rightly on the theoretically and chronologically prior claims of Trotskyist anti-Stalinism.[103] Similarly, he points to the limitations of socialist humanism as an exclusively moral critique of Stalinism, and argues, again quite rightly, for that type of analysis of the social forces and historical conditions productive of Stalinism which Trotskyism itself pioneered.[104] There is little to object to in any of this. But we should note the oddly 'Stalinist' (although that is not at all the the right word – perhaps 'Deutscherist' would be better) coloration of parts of Anderson's argument. Socialist humanism may not have represented a total critique of Stalinism. But it was at least sufficiently critical to avoid judgements such as Anderson's that the 'Cuban Revolution of '59' was 'more important and hopeful for the future' than 'the East European turmoil of '56'.[105] The socialist humanist critique of Stalinism may well have suffered from its exclusive attention to moral questions. But a greater moral sensitivity would have prohibited such callousnesses as those implied in Anderson's cosily comfortable reassurance that 'by and large the socialist revolutions since October have benefited from the change in the world balance of forces it set in motion: the costs of social transformation, in political brutality and irrationality, have been proportion-

---

99 Anderson 1980, p. 195.
100 Thompson 1977.
101 Anderson 1980, p. 160.
102 Anderson 1980, p. 185.
103 Anderson 1980, pp. 116–17.
104 Anderson 1980, pp. 119–20.
105 Anderson 1980, p. 151.

ately less'.[106] One cannot help but be reminded here of an earlier, equally smug, and equally patronising, critical endorsement of Stalinism, that of Sidney and Beatrice Webb.[107]

This oddly ambivalent stance in relation to Stalinism on Anderson's part is probably both cause and consequence of his recent accommodation to Trotskyism. It is well known that Trotsky himself regarded Russia as a 'degenerated workers' state', a social formation in which an essentially socialist economic system remained shackled by a tyrannical and totalitarian state structure. The theoretical and political tensions generated by this analysis were bequeathed to subsequent Trotskyisms as one of the least satisfactory elements in Trotsky's intellectual legacy. The result has been that Trotskyism has regularly and repeatedly divided between those who would place the stress on the first term in Trotsky's phrase, thus emphasising the awful degeneracy of Stalinism, and those who would place it on the second, thus highlighting the socialist character of the so-called 'communist' states (this view is perfectly exemplified in the work of the late Isaac Deutscher). Clearly, the version of Trotskyism that Anderson has embraced is very definitely of the latter type. It is this 'Deutscherist' Trotskyism that permits the *New Left Review* to position itself with equanimity in that particular political space which exists between the 'left-wing' of Eurocommunism and the 'right-wing' of the Trotskyist Fourth International. It also presumably underlies much of Anderson's transparent unease at the vehemence of Thompson's own anti-Stalinism.

Anderson's objections to Thompson's account of the history of Marxism also derive much of their theoretical inspiration from the Trotskyist tradition. His argument at this point develops in very similar fashion to our own. Anderson points to the anti-evolutionism of Lenin, Trotsky and Luxemburg, and to the voluntarism of Gramsci and Lukács, and of the Comintern's Third Period.[108] But he goes further, and dissents from Thompson's description both of the postwar period itself as one of political stasis, and of its Marxism as a structuralism which reduplicated that stasis at the level of theory. We have already suggested that Thompson's account is both partial and distorting insofar as it attempts to effect an illegitimate equation of Althusserianism with postwar Marxism in its entirety. Nonetheless, there is much truth in Thompson's overall characterisation of the nature of the Cold War period, as also in his attempt to situate structuralist Marxism in relation to the wider political imperatives of

---

106   Anderson 1980, p. 121.
107   Webb and Webb 1937.
108   Anderson 1980, p. 101.

the period. Anderson, however, perceives the postwar world quite differently. The years since 1946, he observes, have witnessed the Chinese Revolution and 'the victory of the socialist movement in the most populous nation on earth – a decisive hinge of world history'; the Cuban Revolution, 'the first successful break in capitalism in the Western hemisphere'; the Vietnamese Revolution, 'the greatest feat of sustained revolutionary "will" in the 20th century'; and also major working class struggles in both France and Britain.[109] In Anderson's view structuralism cannot be 'the ideology of a time ... becalmed', as Thompson imagines it, quite simply because the postwar period has been rather a time 'of gathering turbulence'.[110] Now at one level Anderson is entirely correct: the great anti-imperialist struggles in China, Cuba and Vietnam were certainly 'turbulent'; and the heightened level of class struggle in Western Europe since the mid- to late 1960s does, again, indicate the presence of gathering turbulence. But nonetheless Anderson's analysis is here quite clearly insufficiently discriminating in its sense both of time and place.

The years since the Second World War have indeed witnessed an almost continuous process of decolonisation and 'retreat from empire' throughout the 'Third World', a process at times effected through relatively peaceful means, at others through anti-imperialist struggles such as those which occurred in China, Cuba and Vietnam, and also, for example, in Kenya, Algeria, Mozambique, Angola and Zimbabwe. But this process was greatly facilitated by the existence of a global arms economy that functioned so as to sever the connection between capitalist prosperity and imperialist expansion.[111] Now precisely this very severance meant also the relative immunity of the heartlands of advanced capitalism to those destabilising effects that a conventional Leninist account of imperialism might have led one to expect such successful anti-imperialist struggles to produce. Thus the postwar boom *was* peculiarly conducive to political stasis in Europe and North America (and also in Australia), just as Thompson suggests. Since the mid-1960s this relative stability has been undermined. But Thompson's account of the generally prevalent conditions prior to that time in the industrial centres of both eastern and Western blocs remains essentially valid. Anderson's failure to distinguish, historically between the earlier and the later periods, and geographically between the industrialised centre of the world system and its comparatively unindustrialised periphery, leads to an unwarranted dismissal of Thompson's explan-

---

109   Anderson 1980, p. 102.
110   Anderson 1980, p. 103.
111   Kidron 1974, ch. 6.

ation for the emergence of structuralist Marxism. But this failure on Anderson's part is no mere accident. On the contrary, it too arises out of his view of the eastern bloc countries as 'workers' states'. At one point Anderson observes that:

> the Vietnamese Revolution does not rate a mention in Thompson's account of the past two decades. One can only conclude that it is omitted because it does not conform to his idea of what a socialist revolution should look like.[112]

It is indeed remiss of Thompson to ignore such a momentous anti-imperialist struggle as that which developed in Indochina. But, whilst orthodox Trotskyist metaphysics may be capable of transforming that struggle into a 'socialist revolution', it cannot appear as such to those who retain the classical Marxist conception of socialism as the self-emancipation of the working class, as does Thompson, for all his reformism.[113]

Anderson's critical examination of the nature of Thompson's internationalism is similarly indebted to the Trotskyist tradition. In the course of previous polemical encounters the 'New New Left' has had occasion to level the charge of nationalism against Thompson.[114] In *Arguments Within English Marxism* Anderson has wisely chosen to withdraw the allegation.[115] He proceeds to argue, however, that Thompson's internationalism and that of the *New Left Review* are nonetheless very different in kind: whereas Thompson's was a product of a political experience characterised by 'a unique fusion of *international* and *national* causes on the Left'[116] (the Second World War, '1956'), the *Review*'s developed in quite different circumstances that 'required frontal rejec-

---

112 Anderson 1980, p. 102.
113 'if we look towards any future described as "socialist", there is no error more disabling and actively dangerous to the practice of any human freedom than the notion that there is some "socialist" mode of production (as public ownership or State ownership of the means of production) within which some "socialist" relations of production are *given*, which will afford a categorical guarantee that some immanent socialist society ... will *unfold itself* ... This is wholly untrue: every choice and every institution is still to be made, and to suppose otherwise is to fall into an error as astonishing in its mystical crudity as Althusser's notion that under Stalin the "socialist *infrastructure*" was able "to develop without essential damage"' (Thompson 1978a, pp. 353–4). Precisely.
114 Nairn 1977, pp. 303–4.
115 Anderson 1980, p. 141.
116 Anderson 1980, p. 142.

tion of national mystifications'[117] (the Cold War, anti-British colonial revolts), and came to exhibit as as result a 'fierce hatred' of English nationalism. Apparently it was precisely this political experience, and in particular the international movement in solidarity with the Vietnamese Revolution, that attracted Anderson towards the politics of the Fourth International:

> It is no accident that in America the most consistent, as in England and France the most pioneering, impulse within the broader movement against the War in Vietnam came from sections of the Fourth International. For the tradition founded by Trotsky ... has always incarnated the most intransigent refusal to compromise with national sentiments within the ranks of the labour movement in the developed world.[118]

Now this judgement should not be accepted at its face value. For in reality militant internationalism has rarely, if ever, been the exclusive property of the Fourth International and its followers, and it was certainly not such during the period of the Vietnam War. Which poses the question: what quality peculiar to the Fourth International's internationalism is it, then, that Anderson finds so attractive?

At one level the answer is obvious: in Anderson's view, Mao and Ho (and presumably also Pol Pot) are socialist revolutionaries ('deformed' and 'degenerate' though their revolutions may be) and this is, of course, precisely the Trotskyist view. But at a second level the answer is both less obvious and rather more interesting. It has become something of a commonplace in much recent commentary to contrast the sensitivity to national peculiarities displayed by Gramsci with the 'abstract internationalism' of Trotsky.[119] Stated in such bald terms this opposition cannot be sustained in the face of any serious theoretical and historical interrogation. On the contrary, much of Trotsky's work exhibits precisely a sensitive appreciation of the particularities and peculiarities of Russian national development (for example, the theory of permanent revolution, the history of the Russian Revolution and the analysis of the origins of Russian Stalinism). In the period between the revolutions of 1905 and 1917 it was Lenin rather than Trotsky whose prognoses sought to confine the Russian revolutionary movement within the 'abstract internationalism' of Second International orthodoxy. Nonetheless there is such an element in Trotsky's work, and

---

117 Anderson 1980, p. 148.
118 Anderson 1980, p. 152.
119 Merrington 1968, p. 149.

it is one that becomes progressively more important the greater the distance between Trotsky himself and Russian developments. It achieves its culmination in the *Transitional Programme*[120] the founding document of the Fourth International, a document that consistently operates at a hair-raising level of abstraction and generality. The point to make here is not that *Transitional Programme* was almost entirely mistaken in virtually all of its predictions (which it was), but that theory constructed in such abstract fashion could not possibly have proven otherwise. We are now hopefully in a position to offer some more precise assessment of the nature of Anderson's internationalism. What attracted Anderson to the Fourth International, we may plausibly infer, was not its internationalism *per se*, but rather the characteristically 'abstract' nature of that internationalism. And it is presumably the lack of such abstractness, and not any supposed nationalism, that the *New Left Review* has always found so objectionable in Thompson's work. For, as Thompson himself cheerfully admits, his socialism has been that of 'a socialist internationalist speaking in an English tongue'.[121]

A brief exercise in recapitulation now seems in order. Anderson and the *New Left Review* sought to break through the conservative *impasse* in British society (the origins of which they bizarrely traced back to the failures of the seventeenth century English bourgeois revolution) by the importation into Britain of Western Marxist Theory (with a capital 'T'). This importation displayed a certain catholicity (initially the *Review*'s preferred Western Marxist was in fact Sartre) but tended ultimately to crystallise around a distinct editorial sympathy for Althusserian theoretical practice. Subsequently, however, Anderson became both much more aware of the inherent limitations of Western Marxism and much more susceptible to the claims of the Trotskyist tradition. At first sight, then, the history of Anderson's *New Left Review* might appear to be characterised above all by a series of radical discontinuities (between existentialism and theoretical practice, between Althusserianism and Trotskyism). But, as any longstanding *New Left Review* reader can confirm, its evolution actually displays remarkably little evidence of theoretical caesura. This is so partly because the *Review*'s catholicity has indeed been genuine: shifts in editorial emphasis there have been, but its columns have remained open to opposed perspectives. But more importantly there is also a very real element of continuity in its history, a single thread to which Anderson has carefully clung as he journeyed through the labyrinth of Western Marxism to the feet of the Trotskyist minotaur. That

---

120 Trotsky 1973a.
121 Thompson 1978a, p. iv.

thread is best characterised in terms of a persistent tendency towards 'theoreticism', a persistent preference for grand theory over anything that might smack of vulgar (or even not so vulgar) empiricism.

At each decisive stage in its evolution the *New Left Review* has opted, within the available range of choice, for the more abstractly theoretical alternative over the more concretely political, for formal intellectual elegance over empirical richness. Thus the appeal for the *Review* of Sartre's existentialism consisted in its often elaborately impenetrable intellectual sophistication rather than in its powerful invocation of the imperatives of politico-moral practice. Althusserian theoretical practice represented the *reductio ad absurdum* of this tendency. And even the more recent flirtation with the politics of the Fourth International exhibits a similar pattern. The growth of the new revolutionary left in Britain, we may surmise, has impelled the *New Left Review*'s intellectual mandarinate towards a new respect for the theoretical legacy of classical revolutionary Marxism (for, whatever the theoretical practitioners may care to believe, theory does not function within a historical vacuum). But, when confronted with this new set of theoretical options, the *Review* has characteristically decided in favour of Ernest Mandel's 'Maginot Marxism', as lifeless a scholasticism and as sterile a formalism as revolutionary socialism has proven capable of.[122] That, however, cannot and should not be our last word on either Anderson himself or the *New Left Review*. Formalist and scholastic Anderson's politics may be, but they are nonetheless formally *revolutionary*. Anderson's argument for the theoretical superiority of revolutionary over reformist socialism is both cogent and convincing. It is an argument that is rarely heard on the Australian Left, and still more rarely heard presented with such intelligence, such proper caution and such moral seriousness. It is an argument that represents a considerable advance at the level of theory on both the cosy reformism of the Old New Left and the earlier almost apolitical obscurantism of Anderson's own New New Left. It is formally an advance too (and these are not easy words to write) on the reformism of Edward Thompson.

---

122 The phrase 'Maginot Marxism' is Michael Kidron's. Kidron's description of Mandel's work warrants repetition: 'It is useless to look for independent or critical thinking in Mandel. Nowhere ... is there a sense of fresh exploration or the feel that capitalism is posing old problems in new ways, and that the explanations need to be worked afresh out of the loose body of analysis written in the marxist tradition. On the contrary, doctrine is first, its use secondary' (Kidron 1974, p. 88).

CHAPTER 12

Literature, History and Post-Althusserianism*

Neither Marxism nor the discipline of history currently enjoys much of a reputation for predictive accuracy. It comes as something of a surprise, then, to recall the hostages to fortune given by Edward Thompson – both a Marxist and a historian and thus doubly at risk one might have imagined – in the 'Afternote' to his 1978 *The Poverty of Theory*. 'I will not predict Althusser's future evolution ...', he wrote: 'What I will predict is that all the high and rigorous theory will collapse, for a decade, into a shambles, and that the tenacious posthumous Stalinism of the French Communist intelligentsia will vanish in a year or two amidst cries of *sauve qui peut!*'.[1] Rarely are historical predictions so rapidly confirmed. By early 1979, when Colin MacCabe (who would acquire both public notoriety and a chair in English studies for his part as the infamous 'Cambridge structuralist') took sabbatical leave in Paris, 'the intellectual and political atmosphere was poisonous'.[2] MacCabe continued: 'Many of the intellectuals who had profoundly influenced me as a student had effectively defected to the right, demonstrating how much of their leftism had simply been a response to Parisian fashion rather than a genuine commitment to the ideas and practices of '68'.[3] Ten years on, at the end of Thompson's decade, French Marxism continued a shambles and the intellectual and political atmosphere of Paris remained poisonous.

1 French Connections

In France itself the demise of Althusserianism and the so-called 'crisis of Marxism' it engendered were only particular moments within a more general passage from structuralism to poststructuralism. Althusserian Marxism suffered from structuralism's auto-deconstruction as surely as it had earlier profited

---

* This chapter has been published previously in Andrew Milner and Chris Worth (eds.), *Discourse and Difference: Poststructuralism, Feminism and the Moment of History* (Melbourne: Centre for General and Comparative Literature, Monash University, 1990), pp. 141–63.
1 Thompson 1978a, p. 406.
2 MacCabe 1985, p. 16.
3 Ibid.

from the intellectual prestige that attached to high structuralism. For Althusser's achievement was not to 'refound' Marxism, still less to re-establish the original bases upon which Marx's own Marxism had been founded (though both claims have been canvassed). It was, rather, to reformulate Marxism in a quite different discursive register, so as to render it both accessible and amenable to the surrounding structuralist intellectual culture. Althusserianism thus represented an accommodation on the part of French Marxism to the then dominant structuralist motifs in the national intellectual life, an accommodation previously resisted in different ways by both Sartre and Goldmann. The position which Althusserianism eventually came to occupy within the Anglophone radical intellectual sub-culture was, however, very different indeed. Whilst French Althusserianism was essentially a product of the early to mid-1960s a subsequent delay in translation postponed its importation into the English-speaking world until the period after 1968. British Althusserianism was, then, a phenomenon of the early to mid-1970s, that is, of a period when whole sections of the Anglophone intelligentsia moved sharply to the left. Far from constituting an accommodation to an already existing structuralism, it thus entailed rather a defiantly radical rejection of a previously dominant liberal humanism. Both the British *New Left Review*, which sponsored the main translations into English of the Althusserian corpus, and *Intervention*, which championed the Althusserian cause in the antipodes, affected a leftist 'revolutionism' quite alien to earlier 'new lefts'. This contrast between French and English Althusserianism is nowhere more apparent than in the arena of literary theory. For whilst Macherey's *Pour une théorie de la production littéraire*[4] shared much common ground with that central high structuralist text first published in the same year, Roland Barthes' *Critique et vérité*,[5] Terry Eagleton's *Criticism and Ideology*,[6] published ten years later, mounted a sustained assault not only on Leavisite critical orthodoxy but also on the major form of oppositional critical practice currently available in England, that of the 'culturalist' Marxism of Raymond Williams. For much of the English and Australian radical intelligentsia Althusserianism provided an introduction both to Marxism and to structuralism and one moreover which strongly endorsed the pretensions to political and theoretical radicalism of the latter. It did so, however, at a time when French structuralism itself and with it Althusserianism were already collapsing into poststructuralism. Hence the irony by which Derrida

---

4 Macherey 1966.
5 Barthes 1966.
6 Eagleton 1976.

chose to announce structuralism's theoretical deconstitution at an academic conference designed precisely to celebrate its introduction into Anglophone intellectual life.[7]

The American reception of structuralism was in any case significantly different from the British. Althusserianism itself only ever established a relatively minor and marginalised constituency within the American radical intelligentsia. Indeed, the tribute rendered up to Paris by Anglo-Australian radicalisms was typically delivered to the *Bundesrepublik* and to Frankfurt in particular by their North American counterparts. The Frankfurt School in both its native German and its emigré American manifestations, together with Lukács's heirs in the Budapest School, were able to provide the American New Left with a Western Marxist alternative to the theoretical vulgarities of Stalinised Communism functionally equivalent in many respects to Anglo-Australian Althusserianism. *Telos* and *New German Critique* thus developed as a North American counterpoint, at once both historicist and humanist, to the *New Left Review*'s astringent structuralism. Again the contrasts are illustrated most effectively within radical literary theory. If Eagleton's *Criticism and Ideology* marked a temporary (as we can now see it) predominance of Anglo-Althusserianism, then Fredric Jameson's *Marxism and Form*,[8] published five years earlier, had marked a similar though less temporary local predominance for American Hegelian Marxism. Initially ignored by the New Left, structuralism itself secured entry into American intellectual life through the liberal academy rather than through its radical opponents: the publication of Jonathan Culler's *Structuralist Poetics* in 1975 denoted the moment at which an appropriately depoliticised version of structuralist theory bearing a more than passing resemblance to earlier North American native formalisms, both New Critical and Fryean, first acquired a large audience within the American literary intelligentsia.[9]

In France the passage to poststructuralism typically led in one of three main directions: towards deconstruction in its late Barthesian and in its Derridean forms; towards Lacanian psychoanalysis; or towards the Foucauldian concern with the nexus between institutionalised knowledge and institutionalised power. A fourth possible direction is that suggested by Bourdieu's sociology of culture, but it remains open to question whether this particular enterprise can properly be regarded as specifically poststructuralist. Whatever their respective theoretical merits and demerits, there can be little doubt that the

---

7   Derrida 1970.
8   Jameson 1971.
9   Culler 1975.

Foucauldian, Lacanian and deconstructive departures from structuralism have each borne the dual impress of, firstly, the initial political disillusionments of the immediate post-1968 period, and secondly, and latterly, an emergent anti-Communism within the French intelligentsia. This is not, of course, to suggest that an anti-Communist is necessarily *un chien*. It is simply to note the general shape of a political culture in which, for example, Foucault could announce both the 'end of politics' and the necessity for NATO;[10] in which *Tel Quel* could devote an entire issue to the celebration of the American way of life;[11] in which André Glucksmann could emerge as the chief propagandist of the *nouvelle philosophie*; and in which Régis Debray could seriously aspire to make the Pacific safe for French nuclear weaponry.[12] The ten years after 1974 witnessed the translation into English of a series of key poststructuralist texts. As with Althusserianism, subsequent Anglophone receptions of French poststructuralism clearly bore the impress of this delay in translation. But whereas the earlier delay had assured a marked disjuncture between French and Anglophone responses, this latter brought the two into a paradoxical synchrony. By the latter half of the 1970s, when French post-Marxist poststructuralisms were first becoming widely available in English, the political centre of gravity had already begun to shift to the right throughout the English-speaking world. The products of French disillusion in the late 1960s and early 1970s thus found their moment of consumption in the Anglophone disillusions of a decade later.

But as with structuralism so too with poststructuralism, its British and North American receptions differed significantly. In Britain the intellectual establishment and the literary establishment in particular continued in its implacable hostility to 'structuralism' (which came to signify not only structuralism proper but also the various poststructuralist successor doctrines and indeed all manner of exotically alien 'isms'). Hence the so-called 'structuralist controversy' at Cambridge, which finally claimed MacCabe as its victim late in 1981 and also astonishingly resulted in the English Faculty's decision to remove its two most distinguished members, Frank Kermode and Raymond Williams, from its appointments committee. Neither Kermode nor Williams were in any sense 'structuralists'. But both had attempted to engage in some sort of encounter with contemporary French theory and both thereby earned the ire of mainstream English 'thought'.[13] Hence too the corresponding and continuing iden-

---

10   Foucault 1977a, p. 160.
11   Kristeva 1977, pp. 3–19.
12   Cf. Frankel and Roberts 1983, pp. 154–61.
13   MacCabe 1985, pp. 17–31; Williams 1984a, Part 4.

tification between structuralist theory and radical politics, which secured both the temporary creation of an indigenous English left-wing 'poststructuralism', most obviously represented in the work of Hindess and Hirst,[14] and the construction of a disproportionately leftist audience for the subsequent importations of French poststructuralism proper. That audience centred – or better, perhaps, increasingly decentred – around such alternative cultural institutions as *Screen*, the Birmingham Centre for Contemporary Cultural Studies and *Theory, Culture and Society*, though certainly disillusioned and dispirited by the political reversals of the late 1970s and even more so those of the early 1980s, nonetheless abjured the kind of wholesale conversion to anti-Marxism evident in the *nouvelle philosophie*. Much more characteristic of the British intellectual left was that type of gradual accommodation to a rightward moving political culture, entailing a partial appropriation of certain poststructuralist themes, which could be observed in the intellectual milieu surrounding the increasingly mistitled *Marxism Today*.[15] As significant, however, were the various leftist responses to poststructuralism associated with the *New Left Review*: on the one hand, Eagleton's sustained and determinedly 'ultraleft' attempt to read French poststructuralism against its own grain;[16] on the other, Anderson's combination of a scathing denunciation of French structuralisms and poststructuralisms with a distinctly positive reassessment of Habermas.[17]

In North America, where the academy is committed in principle neither to a necessary opposition to theory nor to a belief in the inferiority of all things foreign, structuralist controversies were of a very different order to those at Cambridge. The institutionally dominant North American response to poststructuralism was that represented by the Yale School's singular appropriation both of Derrida himself (who taught for some years in the Department of Comparative Literature) and of Derridean deconstruction. In this reading, which acquired both the shape of a collective enterprise and the apparent stamp of Derrida's own approval with the publication in 1979 of *Deconstruction and Criticism*,[18] deconstruction became yet another depoliticised literary formalism. Partly by way of reaction against the Yale school much American radical criticism acquired a distinctly Foucauldian cast. Both Frank Lentricchia's *After*

14 Cf. Macdonnell 1986, ch. 4.
15 Cf. Laclau and Mouffe 1985.
16 Eagleton 1981 ad 1986.
17 Anderson 1983.
18 Hartman 1979.

the New Criticism[19] and Edward Said's *The World, the Text and the Critic*[20] quite deliberately invoked Foucault against Derrida. Yet there was an irony here: whatever the 'ultimate' political implications of Foucauldian and Derridean poststructuralisms (and whatever 'metaphysical' meanings may attach to the term 'ultimate'), Derrida himself had deliberately chosen to exempt Marxism from deconstructive critique and deliberately refused to join in the 'anti-Marxist concert' of the post-68 period.[21] Hence the possibility for a politically radical version of Derridean deconstruction such as that attempted by both Gayatri Spivak and Michael Ryan.[22] The paradigmatic North American Marxist response to poststructuralism remained, however, Jameson's *The Political Unconscious*,[23] a magisterially Hegelian attempted *Aufhebung* of both structuralism and its poststructuralist progeny. Whatever the eventual judgement on North American academic Marxism, Jameson's work is clearly the most intellectually distinguished example of the genre to date.

2   A New Orthodoxy

In Australia we too have had our Althusserianisms, our structuralisms and our poststructuralisms. Here, though, cultural criticism remained polarised between these various Francophile theoreticisms on the one hand, and radical nationalism on the other. Docker's *In a Critical Condition* provided perhaps the clearest instance of a radical nationalist intervention into both the poststructuralist 'crisis of Marxism' and the 'crisis in English studies' with which it had often been coterminous, in the English-speaking world at least. For Docker literary poststructuralism represented yet one more resource available to the Australian academic literary establishment for mobilisation against those proper concerns with contextual analysis and with the specifics of the Australian experience that were central to an earlier non-academic radical nationalist criticism. 'The deconstructionists', he wrote, 'are attempting to regain dominance for formalist criticism by returning to the common source of New Criticism (and Leavisism) in late 19th-century symbolist, and early 20th-century modernist, literature and theories of language'.[24] Poststructuralism was, then, very little

---

19   Lentricchia 1980.
20   Said 1984.
21   Fraser 1984, p. 133.
22   Spivak 1987; Ryan 1982.
23   Jameson 1981.
24   Docker 1984, p. 183.

more than a recharged New Criticism and its local exponents, like the New Critics and Leavisites before, merely the 'colonial servants of an overseas cultural dominance'.[25] Docker quite rightly registered an affinity between earlier New Critical and later poststructuralist formalisms, an affinity much more apparent let it be said in the American than in the Australian context. He registered also the very real danger that poststructuralism might become a new orthodoxy in the Australian academy, that 'Marxists and so-called post-Marxists (will) become attracted to this kind of semiology, so that a new formalist orthodoxy will embrace right and left, and hence be so heterogeneous as not to appear an orthodoxy at all'.[26] Docker's fears remain grounded, however, on little more than a strong sense of the efficacy of 'intellectual imperialism': he was preoccupied with the simple fact of poststructuralism's status as imported cultural doctrine. What he failed to register was the significance of the way in which poststructuralism had been imported into Australia; or, which is another way of saying the same thing, of the way in which the internal structure of the Australian intellectual culture had been overdetermined by the manner of its own insertion into the larger circuits of Anglo-American cultural production, distribution and exchange.

Let us state the case baldly. The existence of a common English language on the one hand, and the bipolar organisation of the Anglophone cultural industries around the United States and Britain (or, at least, London) on the other, together render both Australian society in general and the Australian intelligentsia in particular peculiarly exposed both to British and to American cultural themes, trends and motifs (and much more so exposed than is either 'metropolitan' centre to the other). Hence the indebtedness of an earlier generation of Australian academic literary studies both to Anglo-Leavisism and to American New Criticism. What this meant more recently was the simultaneous Australian award to French poststructuralism of a mantle of academic legitimacy deriving from the Yale School, and of theoretical and political radicalism deriving from the British intellectual left's protracted encounter with Althusserianism and with what it had interpreted, perhaps wrongly, as post-Althusserianism. French poststructuralism thus secured for itself the endorsement in Australia of both Howard Felperin and John Frow. It was as unlikely a combination as one can imagine and thus very possibly one which pointed to the likely shape of Docker's new orthodoxy embracing both left and right.

---

25   Docker 1984, p. 218.
26   Docker 1984, p. 210.

Felperin's *Beyond Deconstruction* and Frow's *Marxism and Literary History* were published within twelve months of each other.[27] Each took as its starting point the current crisis in criticism; unlike Docker neither was intended as a purely local polemic, but rather both aspired to the status of an intervention within a wider international, or at least Anglo-American, critical discourse; each remained centrally preoccupied with structuralism, poststructuralism and structuralist Marxism (though Felperin did pay the University of Melbourne's Department of English the backhanded compliment of a brief dismissal of Leavisism in his first chapter, just as Frow, in an almost identical textual move, used his introductory chapter to lay the ghost of Lukácsian Marxism); neither seemed at all interested in recent feminist literary theory, ritual obeissances on Frow's part aside; and both opted decisively for a poststructuralist theory of reading that was at once both formalist and elitist. Frow himself seemed very clear as to the political status of his work: 'The theoretical framework and intent of the book is a nondogmatic and nonorthodox Marxism', he assures us, '... My argument is Marxist above all in its commitment to the concept of class and class struggle and to considering the intrication of power in symbolic systems'.[28] By contrast Felperin promised only a 'sceptical or pragmatic ... interpretive practice that thinks, in the terms available to it, what it is doing with the texts it takes up, even as it goes on taking them up'.[29]

Nondogmatic though Frow's Marxism proclaimed itself to be, *Marxism and Literary History* nonetheless opens with a blanket dismissal of all non-structuralist Marxisms, whether 'humanist or culturalist or dogmatic', as 'intellectually moribund and politically sterile',[30] which the unsympathetic reader might be forgiven for interpreting as itself perilously close to the dogmatic. Not that the assertion remains entirely unsupported by ancillary argument. But the fairly conventional account which follows of Lukács's various sins both of omission and commission seems far too slight to bear the weight of what is by implication a wholesale rejection of the work of Adorno and Horkheimer, Sartre and Goldmann, Williams and Thompson, Trotsky and Plekhanov. Non-Althusserian Marxism thus summarily dispatched, Frow is able to concentrate his attentions almost exclusively on theoretical practice in both its French and English variants. To a surprising extent indeed both Frow and Felperin devote their respective second chapters to what is in effect one and the same brief moment in the history of Marxist literary theory, that of Eagleton's translation of Macherey

---

27 Felperin 1985; Frow 1986.
28 Frow 1986, pp. vii–viii.
29 Felperin 1985, p. 2.
30 Frow 1986, p. 5.

into an English idiom. For both Althusserianism in particular stands in for Marxism in general, and for both Althusserianism's fundamental weakness is its scientism. Thus Felperin:

> The privileging of history as the means of explaining – scientifically no less – a now deprivileged literature turns out to be itself wholly problematic. The very historiography that is supposed to confer explanatory power is ... beset by the same difficulty as the literature it was supposed to explain, namely its mode of existence in the form of texts, the meaning of which remains open to interpretation.[31]

Frow in turn advances an almost identical argument:

> What happens here ... is the re-establishment of a hierarchy in which one level ... is located outside of discourse, as its source and its ultimate referent ... The gestural appeal to the 'materiality' of history, and its definition as 'the real' in opposition to the 'less real' of ideology, are indicative of the theological function the concept plays ... The absolute existence of the referent outside any semiotic framework is the tautological guarantee of a truth which transcends ideology.[32]

One is tempted to the observation that only a literary theorist or perhaps a philosopher could accuse Althusserianism thus of an excessive reliance on history. For it was central to Thompson's polemic against Althusser (and in this respect at least Thompson can be considered representative of the historians' profession) that theoretical practice entailed precisely a radical indifference to history as real object. For the moment, however, let us follow Frow's argument a little further. Both Felperin and Frow note the theoretical complicity between Althusserian Marxism and non-Marxist structuralisms. But where this provides Felperin only with occasion to readdress his anti-positivism from Eagleton to Barthes and with cause for evident satisfaction at the latter's collapse into poststructuralism, it prompts Frow rather to a consideration of what he terms the 'poststructuralist moment' in Marxist literary theory. By this Frow means essentially Jameson's *The Political Unconscious* and Eagleton's *Walter Benjamin*. This is, of course, a rather odd pairing of texts which share little other than a common recognition of the 'fact' of poststructuralism. Nor does Frow deal with

---

31   Felperin 1985, p. 69.
32   Frow 1986, pp. 27–8.

them at all similarly. He finds Eagleton guilty of an 'overpoliticization of textual analysis' and of a 'rejection of the possibility of a dispersed, plural, decentred politics', which in 'the England of the eighties ... is close to Benjamin's messianism'.[33] Whatever the weaknesses of Eagleton's alleged messianism, this sudden gestural appeal on Frow's part to the materiality of history and to a referent outside any semiotic framework ('the England of the eighties') seems oddly inconsistent with the entire preceding argument. Against Jameson by contrast Frow firstly repeats a criticism of Eagleton's that *The Political Unconscious* fails to come to terms with the more radical aspects of the Althusserian challenge to historicism, and secondly dismisses the Jamesonian view of history as 'a case of having one's referent and eating it'.[34] It is difficult to see this as adding up to anything more than an insistence that Jameson remains an unreconstructed historicist, a less than profound observation of a text the opening words of which are 'Always historicize!'.[35] The point of Frow's pairing of Jameson and Eagleton nonetheless now becomes clear: it allows him to persist in the almost transparently false claim that non-structuralist Marxism remains 'intellectually moribund'. By assimilating Jameson to a supposed 'poststructuralist moment' in Marxism rather than to the Hegelian Marxist variant of historicism, Frow is able simultaneously both to postpone indefinitely any adequate theoretical encounter with historicist Marxism and also to judge Jameson's 'poststructuralism' a failure (because it has not even properly worked through Althusserianism!).

All hitherto existing Marxisms and structuralisms finally disposed of, both Felperin and Frow proceed to elaborate their own respective poststructuralisms. For Felperin this is, of course, a version of Yale deconstruction, but one which resists, or so it claims, the temptations of its own prospective academic institutionalisation. For Frow it derives in part from Bakhtin, Pêcheux and M.A.K. Halliday, but in the main from Foucault. Frow's central Foucauldian thesis is that: 'The decisive criterion of analysis can ... no longer be the relation between discourse and a reality which is external to it ... Instead, the relevant criterion is that of the relations between discourse and power, the intrications of power in discourse'.[36] He continues:

> The political force of the concept of ideology must be retained. But if the ideological is not to be ontologized, it should be regarded as a *state* of dis-

---

33   Frow 1986, p. 49.
34   Frow 1986, p. 38.
35   Jameson 1981, p. 9.
36   Frow 1986, p. 57.

course or of semiotic systems in relation to the class struggle. Rather than being thought through an opposition to theory ... it would be thought as a differential relation to power.[37]

Frow's resistance to the notion of a dichotomous opposition between (true) theory and (false) ideology is wholly unobjectionable. But that opposition is nonetheless very much a problem of Althusserianism's own making: the science/ideology distinction, as indeed the binary opposition itself, is a characteristically structuralist trope with which historicist and humanist Marxisms have only rarely been burdened. Furthermore, Frow provides us with no good theoretical reason as to why notions of 'power' and of 'class struggle' should be exempted from his own previous injunction against the appeal to an extra-semiotic referent. And such reasons are necessary: power, let alone class struggle, is no more obviously intra-discursive and no less obviously 'real' than 'mode of production' or any other of the discarded concepts of structuralist Marxism. Indeed Frow treats of power as if it were the true referent of discourse. Doubtless discourse is powerful and power discursive. But a recognition that this is so sits uneasily beside Frow's polemic against those such as Perry Anderson and Terry Lovell who would persist in identifying 'the real' as a source of both epistemological and political authority.[38]

Frow's position is, then, an instance of Foucauldian poststructuralism. Now it is a commonplace that Althusserianism in particular and high structuralism in general afforded a radically depleted, if not an entirely attenuated, role both to the human subject and to human subjectivity. This structuralist decentring of the subject clearly persists into poststructuralism; and it equally clearly leads much more readily to an understanding of discourse as socially integrative and of ideology as dominant than it does to the counter-understanding of discourse as socially disruptive and of ideology as counter-hegemonic. Insofar as it was Frow's intention to supplement Foucault's notion of the 'discursive formation' with that of 'genres of discourse', which function at the level of the particular speech situation, and to represent the two together as governing the realm of the utterance, which as *parole* is understood in Saussurean linguistics as essentially non-systemic,[39] then this clearly gestures towards a linguistic determinism even more powerful, and by implication even more socially integrative, than is conventional even in structuralist theory. But it is social disrup-

---

37   Frow 1986, p. 61.
38   Frow 1986, p. 58.
39   Frow 1986, pp. 66–72.

tion which provides political radicalism, whether Marxist or feminist, with its own *sine qua non*. Thus Frow is obliged to open up some space for resistance, as opposed to complicity, within what is nonetheless a generally Foucauldian account of discourse. His solution, though strangely reminiscent of American functionalist accounts of individual 'action', remains distinctly novel. For Frow: 'The crucially important factor here is the discontinuity between discursive positions and the actual social position of a speaker'.[40] At first sight this seems very peculiar indeed: much of contemporary socio-linguistics (the obvious examples are Bourdieu and Bernstein) has been concerned to demonstrate precisely the continuity between discursive and social positions. But Frow insists upon discontinuity so as to ensure that 'the possibility of disruption of discursive authority, and the integration of this disruption into general political struggle ... can be thought in terms which do not rely upon the postulation of a realm of freedom external to discourse'.[41] Just as American functionalist sociology subsumed individual human action, in which it claimed to believe, under a set of mutually complementing social structures that effectively diffused both actors and actions, the better so as to secure the social order which really did command its loyalties; so Frow locates a space for human action, in which he claims not to believe, in the non-correspondence between mutually contradictory socio-discursive structures, the better so as to subvert theoretically the social order which does not command his loyalty. What this demonstrates, apart from the intellectual agility of both social and literary theorists, is, I suspect, the fundamental necessity of a theory of the human subject and of human agency and the corresponding embarrassment occasioned by the absence of such a theory for any viable politically radical intellectual practice.

By comparison with either Lukácsian theories of consciousness or Sartrean theories of praxis, this understanding of disruption as the product of necessarily contingent discontinuities between discursive and social positions seems able to generate at best a peculiarly enfeebled account of the dynamics both of cultural production and of political resistance, let alone those of social revolution. Frow, however, attaches considerable significance to this departure from Foucault: the possibility of disruption is the 'crucial question for a theory of ideology'.[42] Moreover, there is an important sense in which this image of discontinuity within systematicity provides him with the key, if not to all *Mythologies*, then at least to the literary history of modernity. For, in his account of

---

40   Frow 1986, p. 73.
41   Frow 1986, p. 81.
42   Ibid.

the literary discursive formation, as also in that of the historical dynamics of literary evolution, Frow very obviously subscribes to what he terms 'a general modernist paradigm',[43] in which experimentation is valorised over and against but also therefore in relation to convention. Thus for Frow the literary discursive formation is constituted centrally around those processes of automatisation and defamiliarisation first analysed by Russian Formalism. The literary system, he writes, 'is defined by a play of contradictory temporalities corresponding to automatized and nonautomatized states of language: a play between the more and the less ideological'.[44] Similarly, literary history[45] is the history of a 'general aesthetic imperative which equates artistic value with opposition ... to the norms and values of the hegemonic class' and with opposition to that automatisation of language upon which 'all dominant classes depend ... in order to maintain their hegemony'.[46] It is not at all difficult to recognise here the familiar features of that type of left modernism which Adorno and Horkheimer, Brecht and Benjamin, pioneered both against Lukács and against socialist realism in general. Few today would wish to defend socialist realism, whether in its Zhdanovite or Lukácsian variants. But the socialist realist orthodoxy the Comintern once sought to impose upon the Western left has been superseded by a self-imposed modernist orthodoxy subscribed to by both socialists and feminists alike, which ironically appears all the more automatised the more loudly it proclaims its capacity for defamiliarisation. Thus Frow inherits from French poststructuralism what had become by the 1970s the habitual preference of the radical intelligentsia for the modernist text and for 'the importance of the negative construction of value in the break with systemic norms'.[47]

There is no equivalent in Felperin to Frow's extended theorisation of the dynamics of the literary discursive formation. Indeed Felperin assimilates Foucauldian 'contextualist' poststructuralism to Althusserian Marxism[48] and discards both in favour of a version of 'textualist', that is, deconstructive, poststructuralism. Derridean deconstruction is not quite so textualist as Felperin supposes (nor Foucauldian genealogy quite so contextualist). But Felperin's own deconstructive practice derives its inspiration not so much from Derrida as from the later Barthes and the Yale School. The appeal for Felperin of

---

43 Frow 1986, p. 116.
44 Frow 1986, p. 102.
45 Or, rather, the history of written literatures developed in the period since 1800 (Frow 1986, p. 118).
46 Frow 1986, p. 116.
47 Frow 1986, p. 122.
48 Felperin 1985, pp. 71–2.

deconstruction resides in the promise of an in principle infinite pluralisation of textual meanings and interpretive strategies. It is thus central for Felperin's purposes that deconstruction not become an institutionalised academic orthodoxy. Hence his own project: 'to write *from within theory ... against the institutionization of theory*, including that of deconstructive theory'.[49] For Felperin there can be no theoretical vantage point outside critical practice from which either to describe or to prescribe such practice.[50] What he recommends, then, is the indefinite prolongation of a theoretically reflexive academic pluralism: 'Not a common methodology, ... not a common ideology ... not a meta- or master-discourse either. The most we can expect ... is a new historical dialect ... sufficiently, though still imperfectly, shared to enable the haggle of exchange to go on more or less as usual'.[51] This latter phrase is especially revealing. For, if Felperin is resistant both to 'institutional' analyses of discourse and to the 'institutionisation' of any one literary theory, then this is so only because he wishes to protect and preserve the 'business as usual' of the institution of criticism. Hence his peculiarly poststructuralist defence of the canon:

> the argument for a canon derives ... not from the importance of our reading the *right* texts ... but from the necessity of our reading the *same* texts ... to enable the discourse of the interpretive community to go on. The object of the exercise is not agreement ... but that continuing discussion which enables continuing self-differentiation. In the politics of literary study ... doctrinal consensus or soundness or normalcy is not the aim. Only enough consensus is required to enable us to go on differing.[52]

It is at this point that Felperin's and Frow's respective poststructuralisms reconverge. For just as Frow and Felperin each refuse the appeal to a historical reality located outside discourse, so also they each refuse that to any privileged theoretical position located outside the institution. For Frow a 'Marxist intervention in the discipline of literary studies cannot hope to escape the disciplinary constraints which enable the production of theory';[53] and more pithily: the 'limits of a Marxist intervention in the institution of literature are the limits of the petty-bourgeois intelligentsia'.[54] The purpose of such an intervention can be

---

49   Felperin 1985, p. 145.
50   Felperin 1985, p. 41.
51   Felperin 1985, pp. 222–3.
52   Felperin 1985, p. 47.
53   Frow 1986, p. 3.
54   Frow 1986, p. 122.

neither to produce a 'correct' interpretation of the text nor to redistribute to the working classes the 'cultural capital' it may embody.[55] Its purpose, rather, is to subvert the official cultural value of the text 'by "unframing" it, appropriating it in such a way as to make it subversive of its own legitimacy and so *useful* in the class struggle'.[56] The latter gestural *non sequitur* apart, this is merely the deconstructive programme restated. As Frow himself admits: 'This problematic of limits is characteristically that of Derridean deconstruction'.[57] Frow differs from Felperin, of course, in his insistence that deconstruction be anchored in a Foucauldian account of systems of institutionalised practices and that interpretive interests be focussed on the overdetermination of discourse by power.[58] But for Frow as for Felperin readings are necessarily 'disparate' and interpretations possess only a 'politically and historically relative validity'.[59] The object of such readings for Frow as for Felperin might as well be the literary canon. For although Frow clearly registers the danger of a descriptive history of canon formation, that it might become simply reproductive of the canon itself,[60] he insists also that 'although the process of canon formation is thoroughly political, and although the canon is being constantly challenged, defended, and reconstituted, it is nevertheless a historical given with determinate historical effects'.[61] As a set of empirical statements there can be little doubt as to the accuracy of Frow's and Felperin's shared judgments: literary criticism is now located overwhelmingly (though not exclusively) within the institutions of the academy; the textual meanings and interpretive strategies current within those institutions are indeed (relatively) plural; and they are more often than not, for pragmatic as opposed to principled reasons, directed at the canon. But if this is to add up to a 'politics of reading', as Frow supposes, then it is to a politics which is in no obvious sense specifically Marxist.

That both Frow and Felperin each subscribe to essentially formalist theories of reading should be apparent. This formalism derives centrally from their shared and characteristically poststructuralist over-insistence on the significance of reading itself. For if textual meaning is understood as produced in the moment of its reception, rather than in that of authorial composition (as tra-

---

55   Frow 1986, p. 228.
56   Ibid.
57   Frow 1986, p. 231.
58   Frow 1986, pp. 232–3.
59   Frow 1986, p. 186.
60   Frow 1986, p. 122.
61   Frow 1986, p. 121.

ditional humanisms supposed) or in that of commodification (as I suspect is more normally the case), then contextuality will tend to become attenuated into intertextuality. That such theories of reading are also socially elitist is less apparent, but not the less true. The practice of 'naive' reading is, of course, in principle universalisable and in reality very widespread. But this is not the type of reading which concerns either Frow or Felperin. For Felperin's interpretive community and Frow's literary discursive formation are each constituted in and around the academy. Frow's rhetoric may be that of class struggle, but the practice it seeks to legitimate is recognisably that of the senior common room, in which Professor Felperin and (the recently promoted) Professor Frow regale each other with interesting and provocative textual interpretations for their own mutual edification and delight.

'I do not believe', writes Frow, 'that within current institutional structures, literary study can relate directly to the political needs of the working class or that it can contribute directly to the formation of organic working-class intellectuals'.[62] Within *current* institutions, literary *study* doubtless cannot relate *directly* to the *political* needs of the *working class* (though I suspect it might just contribute to the formation of the occasional organic working class intellectual). But this is a peculiarly stringent set of conditions to impose upon the definition of a radical cultural politics, each of which could quite easily be relaxed without damaging consequences other than to the inviolability of the academic ivory tower. Thus *alternative* institutional structures are not only imaginable but have also actually existed in the not-so-distant historical past: the obvious examples are the Communist inspired cultural initiatives of the 1930s and '40s, the Writers' League, the New Theatre, the Realist Writers Groups and so on. So also a radical cultural politics might better be concerned with literary *production* than with literary study: the central significance for Australian radicalism of Hardy's *Power Without Glory* surely resides not in the relations of non-realist intertextuality that concern Frow, but rather in the way in which its own particular form of oppositional textuality both encoded within itself and practically encouraged alternative relations of literary production that were at once both radical and radicalising.[63] So too the issue of directness merely poses the rhetorical question: how directly is directly? And similarly, how political is political? For it is perfectly possible to imagine even a currently institutionalised form of literary study – say a Council of Adult Education class on Australian radical writers which recruited, as some must do, the occasional militant

---

62 Frow 1986, p. 234.
63 I owe this observation to Paul Adams.

shop steward – which would indeed relate reasonably directly to reasonably working class, reasonably political needs. And in any case why insist exclusively on political needs? Surely working class people as much as the academic intelligentsia have *cultural* needs? And why finally confine one's attentions exclusively to the working class on the one hand, the academy on the other? There are structures of oppression, oppositional social forces, and hence also opportunities for radical cultural intervention other than those located within this exclusive opposition: the obvious instance is that provided by the women's movement. The point of all this is not to recommend, still less to prescribe, such alternative strategies and tactics either for radical criticism or for radical activism. It is, rather, simply to note the extent to which Frow's 'politics of reading' have become predicated upon a deliberate and avoidable refusal of much of what is normally understood by the term politics.

3 Literature and History

Poststructuralism in both its original French and its derivative Australian variants combines an older structuralist insistence on the priority of signification with a more recent relativising insistence on the absolute impossibility of any extra-discursive objectivity. For Frow as for the later Foucault, for Felperin as for Derrida and the later Barthes, a structuralist science of the text remains an impossible project, doomed to failure by that very generalisation of the linguistic model from language in particular to semiosis in general which structuralism itself initiated. A more specifically Marxian science of the text remains similarly impossible, doomed to its own more specific failure by a generalisation of the Althusserian model of ideology to include both science and the discourse of history. There is a strong sense, then, in which poststructuralism merely represents a working out of the immanent logic of structuralism itself, not so much a *post*structuralism as what one Australian commentator has termed an overarching 'superstructuralism'.[64] However judged, whether as its apotheosis or nemesis, poststructuralism inherits from structuralism a radical antipathy to history, whether understood as diachrony or as referent. Indeed the attempt to undermine the epistemological and political status of historical knowledge, which both Frow and Felperin indulge fulsomely, is characteristic of the entire poststructuralist enterprise.

---

64   Harland 1987.

I began with Edward Thompson, both a Marxist and a historian, and it is to this distinction, that between Marxism and history, and to Thompson's defence of each, that I wish now to return. As we have seen, both Frow and Felperin detected in Eagleton an appeal to history as the means to a non-ideological explanation of literature; and both rejected that appeal on the grounds that history too, as discourse, remains irretrievably textual, irretrievably ideological, perhaps even irretrievably literary. As a particular objection to Eagleton's particular uses of history this seems perfectly acceptable. Doubtless Eagleton is indeed on occasion guilty of 'passing off interpretation as explanation, fiction as "reality", marxist ideology as history, and criticism as science'.[65] But this does not imply, as Felperin clearly intended it should, that no distinction can be made between fiction and reality, ideology (Marxist or otherwise) and history. Doubtless Eagleton and Macherey are mistaken to conceive '"science", "literature", and "ideology" ... as fixed and universal forms of cognition'.[66] But this does not imply, as Frow clearly intended it should, that history-writing is a non-referential mode of signification. Despite the suggestion to the contrary in Felperin's distinction between 'marxist ideology' and 'history', what is fundamentally at issue here is not Marxism's particular claim to historical knowledge but rather the very possibility itself of such knowledge. That this is so is evident, for example, from the unselfconscious way in which Frow manages to conflate 'the Real and the Material' during a routinely poststructuralist denunciation of 'Marxism's epistemological certainties'.[67] For, the Reality of the referent is an epistemological postulate that is in no sense distinctively Marxist, but is rather the common intellectual property of almost all empirical history writing.

Relations between the discipline of history on the one hand, and Marxist historical materialism on the other, have been both multiple and variable and have themselves been the object of historical inquiry. Thompson represents, however, a formidable body of professional opinion amongst Anglophone historians when he argues that:

> Historical materialism differs from other interpretive orderings of historical evidence not ... in any epistemological premises, but in its categories, its characteristic hypotheses and attendant procedures ... if Marxist concepts ... differ from other interpretive concepts in historical practice, and

---

65 Felperin 1985, p. 61.
66 Frow 1986, p. 28.
67 Frow 1986, p. 58.

if they are found to be more 'true', or adequate to explanation, than others, this will be because they stand up better to the test of historical logic, and not because they are 'derived from' a true Theory outside this discipline.[68]

Thus the appeal to history need not be, as it undoubtedly was for the Eagleton of *Criticism and Ideology*, an appeal to the Truth of Marxist Theory; it might be, as Thompson supposes it, an appeal to a much more empirical discourse in which 'a dialogue between concept and evidence' is 'conducted by successive hypotheses ... and empirical research'.[69] The real, on this view, is not synonymous with the material, but is rather the touchstone against which particular materialist categories, hypotheses and procedures may be tested. Thompson's *The Poverty of Theory* was, of course, an anti-Althusserian polemic and Eagleton one of its more incidental targets.[70] For Thompson had insisted against Eagleton *and* Frow and Felperin that the real has a reality that is neither, as truth, an effect of theory nor, as illusion, an effect of discourse or ideology.

Thompson's position is neither empiricist nor mechanically materialist, though it certainly is in a sense historicist; moreover, it remains quite independent of any quasi-positivist claims as to the supposed scientificity of the discourse of history. He maintains only that:

> A historian is entitled in his practice to make a provisional assumption of an epistemological character: that the evidence which he handles has a 'real' (determinant) existence independent of its existence within the forms of thought, that this evidence is witness to a real historical process, and that this process (or some approximate understanding of it) is the object of historical knowledge. Without making such assumptions he cannot proceed: he must sit in a waiting-room outside the philosophy department all his life.[71]

Modest though such provisional assumptions might seem to the working historian, they are nonetheless in themselves sufficient to scandalise the proprieties of both Althusserian Marxism and post-Marxist poststructuralism. For it is the real at least as much as the material that is the true – dare I say it the real – cause of much poststructuralist offense. Thompson's remark about the

---

68   Thompson 1978a, p. 236.
69   Thompson 1978a, p. 231.
70   Thompson 1978a, p. 358.
71   Thompson 1978a, p. 220.

philosophy department warrants some further comment, for if Althusserianism (mis)construed as Stalinism provided his text with its political other, then Althusserianism construed as philosophy provided its disciplinary other. Thus Thompson insists that Althusser's own epistemology has no general validity precisely because it derives from academic philosophy:

> The peculiarity of certain branches of philosophy and of mathematics is that these are, to an unusual degree, self-enclosed and self-replicating: logic and quantity examine their own materials, their own procedures ... To confuse these procedures ... with all procedures of knowledge production is the kind of elementary error which (one would suppose) could be committed only by students early in their careers, habituated to attending seminars in textual criticism of this kind ... They have not yet arrived at those other ... procedures of research, experiment, and of intellectual appropriation of the real world, without which the secondary ... critical procedures would have neither meaning nor existence.[72]

The reference to textual criticism might well suggest literary studies itself as a third possible self-enclosed and self-replicating discipline, though Thompson remains determinedly silent on the subject of 'English'. This silence is, as the Althusserians might have said, almost certainly 'symptomatic' of a further set of boundary distinctions and prohibitions, tangential to those between philosophy and history, over which Thompson himself clearly had no particular desire to trespass.

This is not the appropriate place to explore Thompson's theoretical inhibitions *vis à vis* English.[73] It is, however, entirely appropriate to note here both that the philosophical 'theoretical imperialism'[74] Thompson detected in Althusserianism has continued apace throughout the transition from structuralism to poststructuralism; and that its single most important target has almost certainly been literary criticism. The echo of this philosophical imperialism is clearly to be heard in Frow's own concluding invocation of 'a general poetics' in which the 'strategies and interests of literary analysis' would be extended 'to nonaesthetic discursive domains: to legal discourse, scientific discourse, historiography, philosophy; to moral and religious discourse; and to everyday language'.[75] Frow's general poetics, although apparently 'literary' in inspiration

---

72   Thompson 1978a, pp. 202–3.
73   But on the subject of 'English' and the Communist historians, cf. Schwarz 1982.
74   Thompson 1978a, p. 202.
75   Frow 1986, pp. 230–5.

and apparently directed at philosophy itself as one target among many, derive not from any distinctively literary tradition of analysis but from a type of Theory that has been much more typically the prerogative of philosophy. Frow's literary expansionism is thus a peculiarly comprador utopia, an imperialism predicated on the repression of all knowledge of its own dependence. Its obverse is Felperin's self-conscious awareness of the very real threat of a 'proposed merger of deconstructive criticism with philosophy and theory'.[76] Frow's poststructuralist maximum programme is in fact deeply reminiscent of those similar such programmes advanced by the Yale School which cause Felperin such disquiet.[77] Following Rorty, Felperin insists that any such threat to the institution of criticism 'would be at once regressive and counterproductive. It would be like the managing director of a growing company recommending to its shareholders an equal merger with an all but bankrupt competitor, whose imminent collapse will give the company a complete monopoly of the market'.[78] The analogy conveys very precisely Felperin's own 'anxiety of deconstruction', haunted as it is by the 'marginal standing of philosophy as an institution'.[79] For Felperin as for Frow[80] the moment of poststructuralism is also that of the crisis in criticism.

The crisis in English studies has been neither the effect nor the consequence of either structuralism or poststructuralism. It arose rather as a result of the internal history of a distinctive and almost exclusively Anglophone discourse, that of 'English', and of the encounter between that internal history and the external history of the Anglo-American political economies during the postwar period. Historically the discipline of English justified itself to the various political, economic and cultural elites that continued to sustain its institutional existence (and also I suspect to Professor Thompson) essentially on the grounds that literary study, as a study in criticism, could provide a training in discrimination and evaluation which would make of its students better people. This particular liberal humanist rationale for English studies, proclaimed in extreme form and pursued with missionary zeal by the English Leavisites and less extremely and less zealously by the American New Criticism, had its origins more than anywhere in the thought of Matthew Arnold. Its terminus is more difficult to locate with any precision. But at some point during the 1960s the intersection of a complacently privileged academic hierarchy enthralled to a platitudinarious liberalism with an insurrectionary stu-

---

76   Felperin 1985, p. 142.
77   Felperin 1985, pp. 141, 145.
78   Felperin 1985, p. 142.
79   Felperin 1985, p. 136.
80   Frow 1986, p. 2.

dent body mobilised in protest against the Vietnam War precipitated a crisis of values within the institution of criticism such as the discipline had never previously encountered and from which it shows little sign of recovery. Although both diagnose this condition with some accuracy, neither Frow's expansionist fantasies nor Felperin's defensive stratagems seem at all likely to constitute an effective curative strategy. Despite the Marxian rhetoric of Frow's Foucauldianism and despite Felperin's insistence on Foucault's contextualism, each of their respective poststructuralisms remains in effect both fundamentally textualist and fundamentally relativist. They each propose a discipline of 'critical' reading, one generalisable to the whole of the humanities for Frow, one ultimately not even justifiable within the English Department for Felperin, a discipline devoid of any moral or political purpose such as sustained Leavisism, and also of any strongly empirical rationale such as sustains disciplines such as history and geography. Literary criticism thus construed is indeed as Felperin feared it might be the handmaiden of philosophy. As such Frow's aspiration to capture the entire Arts Faculty for criticism (a major conquest, this, in the fleeting moment before the Education Department closes it down) seems a great deal less realistic than Felperin's determination to proceed as if nothing had happened, in the hope that no one will notice. But if ever someone does notice, then it will not only be critical cats that will be let out of the bag.[81]

The alternative to philosophy is, of course, history. I mean by this both a general history, which can indeed be used, despite both Frow and Felperin, to 'explain' literary texts, and also a specifically literary history of the evolution of writing, reading, and their various ancillary social practices. Such histories and the connections between them are realisable only as Thompsonian dialogues between concept and evidence, in which some real existence independent of any place within literary-historical discourse must be attributed to the evidence handled. Whether that evidence concerns initial authorial intentions; or the contemporary and subsequent, necessarily contestable, social organisation of literary production and reproduction; or the contemporary and subsequent, necessarily contestable, socially available forms of reception; or the contemporary and subsequent, necessarily contestable social regulation of intentionality, production, reproduction and reception; or the interconnections between any and each of these and the general histories of the relevant extra-literary social and discursive formations: that evidence would need in each case to be understood as witness to some real historical process. The alternatives to an empirical (but not empiricist) literary history of this type have been either liter-

---

81 The phrase is Paul de Man's, quoted by Felperin (Felperin 1985, p. 141).

ary criticism as an education in moral values (an alternative which is in truth no longer available) or literary criticism as both Frow and Felperin propose it, that is, as a self-enclosed and self-replicating adjunct to philosophy. This is not to suggest that historiography is somehow non-discursive; it is, however, to insist that there is more to discourse than discursivity, that different discourses function differently, and that historiography, unlike either philosophy or literary criticism, whether liberal humanist or deconstructive, entails a real intellectual appropriation of the real world.

4 Culture and Ideology

In Frow and Felperin it did become possible to detect the broader outlines of what might become a new poststructuralist orthodoxy. That orthodoxy is as Docker supposed it might be a formalism embracing both left and right. But the defining feature of this new formalism is not its 'textcentred approach',[82] at least not so long as this is taken to imply some sense of the literary text as possessing determinate properties significantly distinguishable from those of a determinate extra-literary context. For neither Derridean nor Foucauldian poststructuralisms refuse context in quite this fashion. The import of Derrida's famous insistence that 'there is nothing outside the text'[83] is not so much to delimit text from context as to textualise both. And Foucault's genealogy so remorselessly politicises the *episteme* that 'the apparatus in its general form' becomes precisely 'both discursive and non-discursive'.[84] Poststructuralism's defining feature is not so much its textualism as its anti-historicism, and more specifically the peculiarly relativising form taken by that anti-historicism. Structuralism was itself a profoundly anti-historicist doctrine: Althusser's substitution of the category of structural causality for those of both mechanical and expressive causality is thus a characteristically structuralist move.[85] Poststructuralism further radicalises this anti-historicism by deconstructing even the notion of structural causality. In its place we find on the one hand a celebration of the indefinite plurality of textual meaning, on the other a stress on the radical contemporaneity of current constructions of the past. In combination the effect is that of an uninhibited relativism. Doubtless, Williams's own

---

82 Docker 1984, p. 211.
83 Derrida 1976, p. 158.
84 Foucault 1980, p. 197.
85 Althusser and Balibar 1970, pp. 186–7.

recognition that the literary tradition is necessarily a 'selective tradition'[86] can indeed be generalised to include all forms of cultural tradition, including that of historiography. But if pluralism is thus inescapable, relativism most certainly is not. Though there are many truths about any particular text, each such truth is recoverable, if at all, only as a result of systematic empirical investigation. Such investigation requires for its practical efficacy a certain methodological pluralism; but it is predicated as a condition of its very possibility on the epistemological postulate of a past or present reality existing quite independently of any knowledge construction we may place upon it. This is, of course, the central lesson of Thompson's Epistle to the Althusserians, and it is one that might equally be addressed to the Deconstructionists.

Docker quite rightly recognises that 'it is the very strength of an orthodoxy that it can combine difference, variety, even sharp conflict, with an underlying unity of assumptions'.[87] That Frow should espouse – in the name of Marxism, no less – a poststructuralism recognisably akin to that of Felperin suggests very clearly the presence of an emergent literary-critical orthodoxy such as Docker fears. At one point in his crucial third chapter Frow outlines what he takes to be 'the general requirements of a working theory of ideology'.[88] These are:

> First, that it not assert a relationship of truth to falsity (and so its own mastery over error) but concern rather the production and the conditions of production of categories and entities within the field of discourse. Second, that it not deduce the ideological from the structure of economic forces or, directly, from the class positions of real subjects of utterance; that it theorize the category of subject not as the origin of utterance but as its effect. Third, that it not be an ontology of discourse, deriving effects of meaning from formal structure, but rather theorize the multiple and variable limits within which relations of power and knowledge are produced.[89]

Now these are remarkable not only for their negativity, which Frow concedes, but also for the radical incompatibility of all but the third with what I take to be the major requirements of both empirical history writing and Marxian historical materialism. (Frow's third requirement provides a necessary stric-

---

86 Williams 1965, pp. 66–70.
87 Docker 1984, p. 87.
88 Frow 1986, p. 61.
89 Ibid.

ture against both Formalism and formalism, and is as such unobjectionable).[90] Their negative form thus betrays its own truth: these are not at all requirements, but rather prohibitions upon a working theory of culture (or ideology, as Frow prefers).

Let us consider each of these prohibitions in turn and attempt to reformulate them in some more productive fashion. As for the first, whilst an adequate theory of culture is in no sense obligated to assert relationships of truth to falsity inscribed within the textual or other artefacts that it takes as its object, it should not, however, be debarred from the attempt to establish such relationships. That the College of Physicians and the Company of Barber-Surgeons in mid-seventeenth century England were predisposed towards very different theories of medical knowledge, on the one hand Aristotelian and Galenist, on the other Paracelsan, and that neither can be seen as in any sense having mastered error, provides us with an interesting first step in analysis beyond which we may choose not to go. But there is something further to be gained by the further observation that Paracelsan 'empiricism' had some greater purchase on the truth than did Galenism and that this is in some significant sense demonstrable from the superior medical treatment received by the New Model Army during the English Revolution.[91] Frow's self-denying ordinance on truth claims prohibits any such further step and it does so for no very good reason. Furthermore, a theory of culture is obligated to attempt to establish its own credentials as providing more rather than less truthful accounts, if not simply so as to legitimate its own intellectual purpose then at least so as to provide for itself a self-imposed discipline of empirical controls. Such attempts need not, indeed should not, amount to any claim to an absolute mastery over error, but only to an aspiration to produce as truthful accounts as seem possible. Both as regards itself and as regards its objects, cultural theory is indeed required to attend to the production and conditions of production of categories and entities within the field of discourse. But the conditions of production of discursive categories and entities are themselves by no means exclusively discursive and are in fact importantly articulated to such extra-discursive factors as material production and reproduction. Moreover, they can only be known by a theory that claims for itself, no matter how modestly, some modest capacity to know. For Foucault's archaeology as for Althusser's theory of science, different *epistemes* in effect construct their own internal truth criteria and such criteria are neces-

---

90   Its strictures also quite properly operate against that type of formalism which Brecht located at the heart of Lukácsian theories of realism (Brecht 1977, pp. 70–6).
91   Hill 1972, pp. 72, 74–84.

sarily mutually uncomprehending. Here at the heart of structuralism lies the source of much of poststructuralism's relativising logic. It is a logic which must be surmounted for any knowledge of the real, any intellectual appropriation of the world, to become possible. The only available strategy for the supersession of such relativisms, it seems to me, is still that established by Hegel, in which the later *Zeitgeist* is seen as comprehending the earlier by virtue of both its historically subsequent position and its greater capacity for totalisation. If Hegel's own formulations are characteristically absolutist and characteristically theoreticist, both notions are nonetheless recoverable for a much more empirical literary-historical discourse. Neither the idea of intellectual progress *per se* nor the commitment to the 'study of patterns and relationships, in a whole process',[92] to borrow Williams's phrase, need be construed in Hegel's own terms. Each can be formulated much more modestly, much more cautiously, much more provisionally, so as to suggest not the Absolute Idea, but only the possibility of better rather than worse knowledges.

As for Frow's second prohibition, whilst there can be no question of *deducing* the cultural from either the structure of economic forces or the class positions of subjects of utterance, relations between culture, economy and class must nonetheless remain central objects of empirical inquiry for any workable theory of culture. In order so as adequately to theorise such inquiries, it becomes necessary to restore to cultural theory not only the category of structural causality but also the more properly historicist categories of mechanical and expressive causality. As Jameson has argued, each of these can be considered 'as local laws within our historical reality'.[93] Jameson's defence of expressive causality, the object of much structuralist animus, is salutary: 'such allegorical narrative signifieds are a persistent dimension of literary and cultural texts precisely because they reflect a fundamental dimension of our collective thinking and our collective fantasies about history and reality'.[94] Explanation in terms of expressive causality is thus a recurrent requirement within cultural studies and one that can often be attempted only by way of concepts such as Goldmann's 'world vision', Williams' 'structure of feeling' or Jameson's own 'ideologeme',[95] each of which seek to connect class position and culture. Moreover the category of subject, we must insist, remains absolutely central to any theory capable of accounting for cultural creativity and it must on no account be theorised simply as an effect of discourse, ideology, or

---

92 Williams 1965, p. 119.
93 Jameson 1981, p. 34.
94 Ibid.
95 Goldmann 1964, ch. 5; Williams 1965, pp. 64–6; Jameson 1981, p. 87.

any other such structure. Rather, cultural artefacts, practices and institutions must be understood as particular moments in that dialectic of human self-creation by which people make history in circumstances of their own choosing, in which, as Morris wrote, 'men fight and lose the battle, and the thing that they fought for comes about in spite of their defeat, and when it comes turns out not to be what they meant, and other men have to fight for what they meant under another name'.[96] As such these artefacts, practices and institutions are in a significant sense the objects of some anterior human subject, which is itself the referent of the discursive category 'subject'. For certain analytical purposes, as for example in some aspects of the process of interpreting historically recent authorial intentions, the human subject may be theorised individually. But given that individual subjectivity (and with it individual authorship) is a historically variable and historically recent social phenomenon, which is in any case seriously circumscribed by even contemporary socio-cultural structures, it is more commonly necessary to theorise cultural production in terms of some notion or another of a 'transindividual subject'. The term is Goldmann's,[97] of course, but his own remorselessly homogenising and homologising version of the world vision provides a less satisfactory model of analysis than does Williams's more nuanced, because more empirically sensitive, treatment of structures of feeling.[98]

By comparison with Leavisism poststructuralism appears both pedagogically and politically inconsequential. At the furthest extent of its theoretical reach Leavis's Leavisism proposed to construct a discipline that was at once critical, historical and moral. Its text-based pedagogy thus functioned so as to 'ground' simultaneously: a critique of industrial civilisation mounted from the standpoint of 'life'; a historical and historicist account of the emergence and development of that civilisation; and an aesthetico-moral education in right judgement. Of these only the latter remains utterly indefensible, both because literary education is a demonstrable failure in this particular capacity (perhaps poetry can be written after Auschwitz, but criticism of this kind cannot) and because in any case in societies such as ours criteria neither of literary nor of moral worth are actually consensually available for deployment by the education system (what on occasion masquerades as consensus, or worse as literary or moral 'truth', is only ever an instance of hegemony).[99] Criticism, if not as

---

96   Morris 1977, p. 53.
97   Goldmann 1970a, p. 102.
98   Cf. Williams 1974a, pp. 150–6.
99   Eagleton's recognition that this is so leads him to the advocacy of an exlicitly 'political criticism' in which: 'Any method or theory which will contribute to the strategic goal of human

understood by Leavis then as by Said and Horkheimer,[100] and history, as the attempt to know some previously existent past, are each much more readily justified in terms of the limited social consensus actually present in our society: neither the value of freedom nor that of knowledge seem currently open to serious contestation. Perversely and paradoxically the discipline of English, as also Leavis himself, evolved away from both criticism and history and towards an increasingly exclusive preoccupation with the dynamics of aesthetic and moral indoctrination, the ultimate outcome of which has been the contemporary crisis in criticism. To resolve that crisis as poststructuralism proposes, by way of a retreat into an indefinite pluralism which is neither historical nor even necessarily critical (since criticism properly presupposes some real object of criticism external to itself), is simply to relapse into a kind of textual frivolity that is as intellectually self-indulgent as Leavisism was intellectually censorious. The human sciences are threatened politically by the imposition of criteria of value defined almost entirely in terms of economic gain and national interest (or more accurately what businessmen want and what politicians want). But if the best that the academy can manage by way of an alternative to such reductionism is state subsidised *jouissance*,[101] as a minority privilege, then it is one that will neither succeed nor deserve to succeed.

---

      emancipation, the prroduction of "better people" through the socialist transformation of society, is acceptable' (Eagleton 1983, p. 211). This seems to me a hopelessly utopian prescription for teachers working in secondary or higher education (though not, of course, for socialist and feminist activists within what remains of the public sphere). The beleaguerd fates both of British sociology in general and of the Birmingham Centre for Contemporary Cultural Studies in particular under Thatcherism clearly point to the limits of state-tolerated academic dissent. Eagleton's utopianism arises in part from the peculiarities of Oxford University, no doubt, but more importantly from the peculiar license afforded him by poststructuralism. It is because Eagleton cannot conceive of a literary *history* subject to the disciplines of a determinate real object, the findings of which might (but also might not) be of political value to radicalism precisely because they constitute some knowledge of the real, that he is obliged to counter liberal political *criticism* with nothing better than a rival socialist *criticism*. Thus Eagleton: 'It is not a question of debating whether "literature" should be related to "history" or not: it is a question of different readings of history itself' (Eagleton 1983, p. 209). It is curious to note that Eagleton's own distinctly sober and politically judicious rejoinder to *The Poverty of Theory* remains entirely preoccupied with the politics of the encounter (Stalinism/Eurocommunism/Trotskyism) to the exclusion of any discussion whatsoever of the debate over epistemology (Eagleton 1979, pp. 139–44).
100 Said 1984, p. 29; Horkheimer 1972, pp. 245–6.
101 The distinction between *plaisir* and *jouissance* was coined by Barthes in *Le Plaisir du texte* (Barthes 1975, p. 14). Neither Frow nor Felperin fully endorse it, though the latter certainly

The limits and possibilities of an empirical literary history are also the enabling conditions for a radical political intervention within the disciplines of literature. Literary history defined as an attempt to know the past so as better to explain its effects in the present, as also other regional histories (economic, social, political, etc.), can each offer the promise of some real knowledge at least potentially appropriable and usable by subversive, subordinate, or marginalised social groupings. As we have seen, Frow himself conceives of a radical cultural practice almost entirely in terms of politically transgressive readings. 'The task of the reader', he writes:

> cannot be that of a 'correct' interpretation of the text, nor can it simply be the practical one of transferring ... value to those dispossessed of 'legitimate' culture; these two choices entail only a reinvestment or a redistribution of cultural capital, and this leaves the text within the sphere of legitimacy, where it continues to be the property of the dominant class and its administrators ... The interpretive emphasis, then, is thrown onto the use we can make of the text ... The productive role of the reader ... represents a break with a dominant regime of reading and with the institutional context of reading which directly or indirectly sustains this regime.[102]

But if the reader in question is, as Frow most certainly is and as most Marxist intellectuals empirically are, the academic reader reading within the institution of academic criticism, an institution which is itself predicated upon a necessary plurality of readings, then this reading amounts to *no more than* the business as usual of Felperin's haggle of academic exchange. As such it does not so much break with as confirm the institutional context of its own reading. Each of the options he rejects are, in fact, more properly subversive of the social and academic *status quo* than are Frow's politics of reading. To construct a 'correct' interpretation of texts, not in the sense of a politically 'sound' reading but in that of more rather than less truthful accounts of the literary-historical past, is to discover aspects of that past some of which may be of real political value in the present: the recent feminist discoveries of lost, forgotten and repressed instances of women's writing are a case in point. And insofar as literary history is productive of real knowledge rather than simply of cultural capital (through

---

comes close (Felperin 1985, p. 139). But it remains implicated nonetheless in their shared preference for the writerly text.

102 Frow 1986, pp. 228–9.

the use of high literacy as a social status symbol), then to transfer such knowledge to the socially dispossessed may again be of very real political value in the present: the transfer of academic feminist knowledge to newly expanded numbers of women students and to feminist activists located outside the academy altogether is again an obvious case in point.

Frow can reject these options so easily only because he conceives of the past in properly poststructuralist terms as essentially a creation of the present. Hence his insistence that the 'past is an oppression from which we can remove ourselves only by political choices. Marxism is not the predestined heir of history but the possibility of a radical break with its patterns'.[103] There is indeed a sense in which this is so: socialists and feminists do aspire finally to end the exploitation and oppression of the historical past. But this is nonetheless a history that is not yet over, and in that sense there can as yet be no definitive break with its patterns. Moreover for Marxism as a historicism, even if not for feminism, this history of exploitation and oppression has also been that of progress. Frow's failure is not merely theoretical. For it is symptomatic of the practical fate of Western Marxism that the only instances of an alternative cultural politics currently available are provided by contemporary feminism (or, perhaps, environmentalism) rather than by any kind of socialism. For Marxists there has been no recent experience of a counter public sphere situated partly within and partly beyond the academy, such as that which second wave feminism has been able to sustain. The temptation to retreat into a politics of reading is thus understandable, though not thereby forgivable. The intellectual generation which reached young adulthood in the 1960s and early middle age in the 1980s, now lives in the shadow of its own failed revolution. In similar such circumstances Milton wrote *Paradise Regained*, Trotsky founded the Fourth International and Henry Lawson drank himself to death. We, however, have discovered the erotics of the transgressive sign.

---

103   Frow 1986, p. 230.

CHAPTER 13

The Revolutions in Favour of *Capital*

The Eastern European revolutions of 1989 and the subsequent disintegration of the Soviet Union have demonstrated the utter bankruptcy of the Communist project, to the (often evident) satisfaction of the vast majority of their various participants, protagonists and observers. In the currently predominant Western liberal interpretation, they demonstrate also the essential theoretical irrelevancy of any kind of Marxism, most especially that of Marx himself. With the former claim I have little quarrel: Communism is dead and damn near buried and a good thing too. The latter claim, however, strikes me as positively wrongheaded. For what the failure of Communism demonstrated more than anything is the retrospective validity of what we might term 'classical Marxism', that is, the type of Marxism founded by Marx himself, systematised by Engels, and forged into a set of more or less useful guides to political action by the major theoreticians of the Second International, Karl Kautsky, Eduard Bernstein, Rosa Luxemburg, the Austro-Marxists. Much subsequent commentary has concentrated quite understandably on the divisions within classical Marxism, on the revisionist controversy, on Luxemburg's break with Kautsky, and so on. But with the benefit of hindsight we can acknowledge also the surprising extent to which the pre-1914 International constituted a single discursive formation, from Bernstein on the right to Luxemburg on the left, a discursive formation embracing a whole range of shared theoretical assumptions.

Of these three in particular seem to me important. The first is the assumption that Marxism itself is an essentially scientific enterprise, a theoretically guided, but nonetheless empirically testable, attempt to understand, so as to be able to change, a material world possessed of certain determinate and constraining properties, which exists independently of whatever construction theory may place upon it. The second is the shared assumption of the validity of relatively strong versions of what is sometimes termed 'economic determinism', the assumption that economic infrastructures do in some significant sense 'determine' political and ideological 'superstructures'. The third assumption, one in fact shared with nineteenth-century liberalism, is that of progress, the assumption that, whatever 'dialectical' twists it may take in the short term, the long-run general direction of historical process runs from bad to good to better. In Second International Marxism this entailed a conception of socialism as necessarily post-capitalist, as a type of society more democratic, more egalitarian, more affluent and more economically developed than capitalism, a society which would evolve from out of capitalism, and after capitalism, in precisely those places in which capitalism had itself already reached its highest forms of development. In each of these respects, Second International Marxism did little more than echo Marx and Engels themselves. If Kautsky was indeed the movement's Pope, then his claims to orthodoxy were not at all ill-founded.[1]

The Second International fell apart in August 1914, ruined by its own incapacity to resist the various European nationalisms and militarisms, and with it went much of Marx's own intellectual and political legacy. The 'Marxisms' that arose subsequently each owed very much less to Marx than was commonly admitted by their respective champions and detractors. At the risk of oversimplification, it seems possible to identify two major such traditions, Communist Marxism and Western Marxism, and a third relatively minor sub-tradition, that of Trotskyism. Very schematically, we can characterise Communist Marxism in terms of its simultaneous defence of the major theoretical tenets of pre-1914 orthodoxy (Marxism as a science, the base/superstructure model, history as progress) and also of the actually existing 'socialisms' supposedly brought into being initially in the USSR and later elsewhere. This was the kind of Marxism adhered to by the Communist Parties, but also very often by 'left-wing' activists within the social-democratic and labour parties, and later by the Maoist parties and sects which split from the Communist movement during the 1960s. Western Marxism, by contrast, came to combine a strongly 'idealist' version of highly theoreticist Marxism, the key concepts of which (consciousness, will, agency, hegemony, totality) were all essentially anti-materialist, with an increasingly critical political stance *vis à vis* the so-called Communist societies. Despite its original home on the 'infantile' left-wing of organised Communism, Western Marxism survived only by virtue of its eventual institutional location within the Western university system. Finally, we come to Trotskyism, which shared in the general Communist defence of theoretical orthodoxy (although the precise extent of the dogmatism entailed therein proved highly variable), but became increasingly critical of, and hostile towards, the Soviet model. In general, Trotskyism persisted only on the outer margins of Western political life, in the comic opera world of vanguard sectariana, but on occasion its influence became much more far-reaching: the obvious instance here is the post-1968 British New Left.[2]

---

1 Cf. Gay 1962; Nettle 1969; Salvadori 1979.
2 Cf. Marcuse 1971; Hallas 1979; Jacoby 1981.

Each of these traditions seems to me very obviously at an impasse. Indeed, in Australia, where the Communist Party wound itself up in the vague hope that some new New Left Party might somehow take its place, where the leading journal of Western Marxist high theory, *Thesis Eleven*, openly celebrated the triumph of post-Marxism, and where the erstwhile Australian section of the Trotskyist Fourth International announced itself democratic, green, and most certainly not Trotskyist, it becomes difficult to avoid the conclusion that this is not so much an impasse as a terminus.

Despite often loud protestations to the contrary, especially from Communists and Trotskyists, all three traditions were in fact radically 'revisionist' in relation to classical Marxism, in particular over the central strategic questions pertaining to Marxism's own *raison d'être*, that is, the transition from capitalism to socialism. In Marx himself, there are two main elements in the account of the transition: firstly, a general theory of social and historical change; and secondly, a more specific theory of the transition to socialism itself. Marx's general theory is outlined in Part I of *The German Ideology* and, more famously, in the 1859 'Preface' to *A Contribution to the Critique of Political Economy*.[3] We need not read either text in quite so economically determinist a fashion as Kautsky nor so functionalist as G.A. Cohen.[4] But it is clear that Marx does insist: that there *are* relatively close 'fits' between forces of production, relations of production, political superstructures and forms of consciousness, and that the latter two elements are 'conditioned' by the former; that the forces of production *do* tend to develop unless fettered by archaic social relations, and that the point at which such fettering occurs is the point at which an epoch of social revolution begins. This was all well known and happily acceded to by Communists and Trotskyists alike. Less well known, but a necessary corollary of the argument, is Marx's own conclusion that:

> No social order is ever destroyed before all the productive forces for which it is sufficient have been developed, and new superior relations of production never replace older ones before the material conditions for their existence have matured within the framework of the old society.[5]

This theory seems to me perfectly defensible, not as absolute 'truth', but as the better of the currently available theoretical alternatives, in explaining the

---

3   Marx and Engels 1970; Marx 1975a, pp. 424–8.
4   Cohen 1978, chs. 6, 8, 9.
5   Marx 1975a, p. 426.

transition from feudalism to capitalism, for example, or that from antiquity to feudalism.[6] The more specific account of the transition to socialism is also dealt with in *The German Ideology* and the 1859 'Preface'. But it provides a central theme in the rest of Marx's work right through to *Capital*. The novel element here is contained in the thesis that capitalism is the last and highest stage of class society, that capitalist relations of production are or will soon become a fetter on further development, and that the organised working class will overthrow capitalism so as to establish a post-capitalist, classless society. The argument is sustained by a whole complex of subordinate theses. Some of these seem to have been borne out by subsequent events, for example, that capital will become increasingly concentrated, that the class of employees will grow in proportionate strength and the self-employed class decline correspondingly, or indeed the whole range of propositions contained in the theory of alienation. Some have proven false, for example, the pauperization thesis. Some, whilst apparently valid for the late nineteenth century, no longer seem so, for example, the notion of a tendency towards ever greater crises of over-production.[7] That a number of elements in the argument require modification and amendment is barely surprising: these are attempts at scientific prediction rather than prophesy. But, as a general analysis and critique of the developmental tendencies within capitalist civilisation, it remains surprisingly plausible, far more so than either functionalist sociology or neo-classical economics, let alone the textual histrionics of poststructuralism.

Yet it is not poststructuralism, nor neo-classical economics, nor even functionalist sociology, which currently appears bereft of both political and moral purpose: it is Marxism. And this is so because the political linchpin, upon which all else seemed to depend, has apparently failed: the socialist revolution did not in fact develop in the advanced capitalist societies; it did develop on the backward periphery; and its eventual shape, moreover, bore very little resemblance to Marx's own distinctly libertarian vision of a community of equals in which the state, class inequality and even ideological false consciousness would all wither away. The central theoretical problem, in short, is that Soviet and related Communisms defied Marx (and classical Marxism with him) not only at the moment of their dissolution, but also throughout their entire history.

From the standpoint of classical Marxism, the Bolshevik Revolution should simply never have happened. This was the view explicitly argued by Kautsky in 1919:

---

6 Cf. Hilton 1978; Anderson 1974a.
7 Marx 1970a, ch. 25; Marx 1975b, pp. 322–4; Marx 1974, ch. 15.

It is only the old feudal large landed property which exists no longer. Conditions in Russia were ripe for its abolition but they were not ripe for the abolition of capitalism. Capitalism is now once again celebrating a resurrection, but in forms that are more oppressive and harrowing for the proletariat than of old.[8]

But Kautsky did little more than apply in practice Marx's own theoretical observation that:

> development of productive forces ... is an absolutely necessary practical premise [for Communism – A.M.] because without it *want* is merely made general, and with *destitution* the struggle for necessities and all the old filthy business would necessarily be reproduced.[9]

For Marx, as for Kautsky, this leads necessarily to the conclusion that 'communism is only possible as the act of the dominant peoples'.[10] Even the Bolsheviks, whose Marxism had derived from that of the Second International, initially insisted that the Russian Revolution would be bourgeois, rather than socialist, in character: this is a central line of argument in Lenin's *Two Tactics of Social Democracy in the Democratic Revolution*.[11] Soviet Communism was, then, for Marx's Marxism, for Kautsky, even in many respects for Lenin, an impossible object. And yet it moved. How, then, to explain the impossible?

Each of our three Marxisms had its own answer, and each seems in retrospect clearly unsatisfactory. Interestingly, it was the least influential of the three traditions, that is, Trotskyism, which provided the more intellectually powerful attempt to reconcile the fact of the Bolshevik Revolution to the theory of classical Marxism. In Trotsky's account of the 'permanent revolution' an impeccably orthodox theoretical framework was pressed into service as guarantor of the Revolution's legitimacy. Indeed, if there is any one theoretical construct which can reasonably be judged the true contemporary legitimation for the October Revolution, then it is surely this theory of permanent revolution. As we have already noted, Lenin himself, and with him Bolshevik orthodoxy, had argued that the coming Russian revolution would be essentially bourgeois in character. And this remained the Bolshevik position right through until the

---

8   Kautsky 1983, p. 146.
9   Marx and Engels 1970, p. 56.
10 Ibid.
11 Lenin 1975a, p. 503.

dramatic reversal announced in Lenin's *April Theses*, over a month after the February Revolution.[12] Trotsky, however, had long insisted that only the working class would be able to overthrow the Tsarist autocracy, and that it would not and could not content itself with a bourgeois democratic revolution, as the Bolsheviks envisaged; that socialism could nonetheless not be achieved in a backward country in isolation; and that the Russian proletariat would therefore be compelled to internationalise its revolution: 'Thus, permanent revolution will become, for the Russian proletariat, a matter of class self-preservation'.[13]

It is a powerful syllogism, the logically hypothetical character of which is very easily misread as categorical, most especially so in relation to the Russian Revolutions of 1917. Certainly, Trotsky himself chose to regard the theory as decisively vindicated by the Bolshevik Revolution. Moreover, the disastrous failure of Chinese Communist strategy during the period 1925–7 seemed to him to provide, as it were, negative confirmation of the theory's more general applicability beyond the specifics of the Russian case.[14] Subsequent Trotskyist writers advanced even more ambitious claims on its behalf: Ernest Mandel, for many years the chief theoretician of the Western European sections of the Fourth International, proclaimed in 1979 that 'world revolution is a basic reality of our century ... we are living in the age of permanent revolution'.[15]

That there have been a great many revolutions during the twentieth century is impossible to deny. But these have not normally been 'permanently revolutionary' in character, still less have they led to world revolution. There is, in fact, no instance of a working-class movement or party successfully challenging for state power other than that in Russia itself. Elsewhere 'socialism' has been the creation of peasants, intellectuals and military invasion. Nor have these revolutions proven able or even willing to internationalise themselves. Wherever they have possessed any independent vitality, this has invariably been quite fundamentally nationalist in purpose and intent. And even the Russian outcome was ultimately one neither Trotsky himself nor very many Trotskyists were able to admire. The list of revolutionary crises cited by Mandel, from Persia in 1906 to Iran in 1978,[16] far from confirming the theory of permanent revolution, powerfully attests to the monotonous regularity with which the permanent

---

12   Lenin 1975b, pp. 29–33.
13   Trotsky 1972, p. 317.
14   Cf. Trotsky 1969, ch. 7.
15   Mandel 1979, p. 42.
16   Ibid.

revolutionary process failed to take place. Logically, the syllogism cannot but work; empirically, it never did. The theory was, then, substantially falsified by subsequent events.

Exorcised from official Communist Marxism by virtue of its parentage, permanent revolution was unavailable even as a political legitimation within the USSR. It persisted, however, not as the intellectually serious and politically responsible attempt to explain the world intended by Trotsky, but as a theoretical sleight of hand by which later Trotskyists refused any responsibility for the Third World dictatorships with which they chose to fellow travel. In its name, Trotskyists 'critically' applauded Iranian Ayatollahs and Khmer Rouge mass murderers, Libyan fundamentalism and Iraqi expansionism. Trotsky himself remains the single most impressively moral actor in the history of twentieth-century Marxism, Alasdair MacIntyre's man of 'virtue'.[17] It is difficult, however, to accord any analogous respect to the movement he founded, other than by way of comparison with the often positively mendacious theory and practice of Stalinist Communism itself.

For Communist Marxism, formally 'orthodox' yet politically committed to a defence of the Soviet Union, the easiest of all answers to the paradox of the Bolshevik Revolution was, of course, the barefaced lie, by which one of the most economically backward societies in Europe was systematically misrepresented as the embodiment of human progress. Deception and self-deception were perhaps unavoidable accompaniments to a political vision as fundamentally internally contradictory as Stalinist Communist. But no political vision, not even fascism, can sustain itself simply on lies. What, then, was the 'truth' of Soviet Marxism? To pose the question thus is to broach immediately a further question, that of the relation between Leninism and Stalinism. For the Communist movement itself, as also for its libertarian opponents, whether anarchist or liberal, the latter was essentially a continuation of the former. For Trotsky and the Trotskyists, at the other extreme, there was only the discontinuity of a Revolution betrayed, by which the Fourth International rather than the Comintern came to inherit Lenin's political testament. Neither extreme seems ultimately tenable: there *are* discontinuities, marked in blood by the Show Trials and the murder of the Old Bolsheviks; but there are continuities too, for Stalin, unlike Trotsky, was indeed himself an Old Bolshevik.

The nearest approximation to a 'truth' of the matter lies somewhere in that messy middle ground occupied by Victor Serge, an anarchist turned Bolshevik

---

17   MacIntyre 1981, p. 185.

turned near-Trotskyist, whose *The Case of Comrade Tulayev*[18] still provides a far more powerful fictional account of the dynamics of Stalinism than Rybakov's more recently influential *Children of the Arbat*.[19] Reflecting back in 1939, Serge wrote that:

> It is often said that 'the germ of all Stalinism was in Bolshevism at its beginning'. Well, I have no objection. Only, Bolshevism also contained many other germs ... a mass of other germs ...[20]

Serge thus posed what is surely the central question about Bolshevism: not *whether* Leninism led to Stalinism, but *how* and to what extent it did so? In short, and in Serge's own terms, *which* germs led to Stalinism, and which did not?

One influential answer to Serge's question was that provided by Agnes Heller and Ferenc Fehér, by the Budapest School more generally, and in Australia by a number of the writers associated with *Thesis Eleven*, which deemed the Leninist theory of the party to be the ultimate source of Stalinism. Thus Heller: 'In formulating and introducing his party statute, Lenin indeed invented an entirely new and unheard-of pattern: the totalitarian apparatus'.[21] There is no doubt that this account runs roughly parallel to Communist self-perceptions. As Heller rightly observes of Stalin's *History of the Communist (Bolshevik) Party of the Soviet-Union*: 'this account of genesis, regardless of whether historically true or untrue, is essentially correct as self-characterization'.[22] But, whatever the nature of subsequent Stalinist self-characterisations, the small matter of the historical truth or untruth of Stalin's *History* cannot be dispensed with so lightly. Pre-revolutionary Bolshevik practice did indeed often entail something approximating the degree of political centralisation Lenin had advocated in *What Is To Be Done?*, which Heller sees as embryonically Stalinist.

But this centralisation remained tempered: firstly, by the operation of genuinely democratic leadership selection processes within the party, such as Lenin had in fact advocated; secondly, by the fact that the party had no access to state power and so functioned, insofar as it was permitted by the autocracy, as one party alongside others within the institutions of civil society; and thirdly, by the party's ideology which defined its immediate political goals as aiming at a

---

18   Serge 1968.
19   Rybakov 1989.
20   Serge 1967, p. xv.
21   Heller 1990, p. 6.
22   Heller 1990, p. 5.

'democratic, not a socialist dictatorship ... (which) may ... establish consistent and full democracy, including the formation of a republic'.[23] In this context, Bolshevik centralism appears little more than a peculiarly effective organisational response to the problem of operating as a semi-legal, and sometimes illegal, organisation subject to harassment and repression by the Tsarist state.[24] Moreover, whatever later Communists might have made of Leninism, Lenin himself denied 'any intention of elaborating my own formulations, as given in *What Is To Be Done?* to "programmatic" level constituting special principles'. On the contrary, he continued: '*What is to be Done?* is a controversial correction of "economist" distortions and it would be wrong to regard the pamphlet in any other light'.[25]

Neither the principle nor the practice of centralist organisation *per se* contains the original germ of Stalinism. Indeed, there is no single such germ. The totalitarian apparatus, which began to germinate during the 1920s and was brought to maturity only in the 1930s, was the result of a fateful, and entirely contingent, coincidence of centralist organisation, the abolition of inner party democracy, the abolition of the separation between party and state, and finally, and most importantly, a radical transformation in party ideology by which the construction of socialism in Russia came to be defined as a practicable and feasible political objective. Of these, only the first and the last are truly parts of Lenin's legacy. And it is the latter alone, the redefinition of socialism as a project *within backwardness*, which explains the subsequent appeal, such as it was, of those genuinely indigenous Communisms that developed in Yugoslavia, Albania, China, Indochina and Cuba (elsewhere, Communist government was almost always the result of military occupation and very often had no real endogenous origins).

Stalin's doctrine of 'socialism in one country' was thus the central feature of Stalinism as ideology, just as the Trotskyists always maintained. But the germs of this doctrine can in fact be found in Lenin, despite Trotskyist assertions to the contrary. They can be located quite precisely in what Alfred Meyer long ago identified as the apex of Lenin's political thought, that is, the theory of imperialism.[26] It was this notion, as codified and systematised into the so-called 'theory of Marxist-Leninism', which functioned so as to explain to the ruling

---

23   Lenin 1975a, pp. 457–8.
24   Analogous organisational techniques were adopted, for example, by the Resistance movements in German-occupied Europe during the Second World War.
25   Cliff 1975, pp. 175–6.
26   Meyer 1957.

classes and elites within the old Soviet and Soviet-style regimes: how capitalism could perpetuate itself even after socialism had come into being; how it had become possible for socialism to develop in backward countries; and how capitalism and socialism could coexist alongside each other. These were amongst the central organising themes of Soviet Marxism and, although none are actually argued in Lenin himself, they each plausibly derive from a reassessment of classical Marxism in the light of Lenin's theory of imperialism.

As is well known, Lenin had argued that competitive capitalism had been superseded by a higher, indeed the highest, stage of capitalism, that of monopoly capitalism, in which finance capital became increasingly dominant over productive capital; and that this led, by turn, to an increasing substitution of capital exports for commodity exports, and thence to the partition of the world into colonial empires.[27] Further ramifications of the theory included the growing tendency towards inter-imperialist war and the growth of reformism within the 'labour aristocracy' in the advanced capitalist societies.[28] There can be little doubt that the theory did indeed contain important insights at the moment of its original formulation (although it never adequately explained the peculiar case of Latin America where capital flows did not coincide with territorial acquisition). It should be clear, however, that it was of very little continuing relevance to the period after the Second World War, when the extended postwar boom permitted much higher levels of company self-financing, when capital flows increasingly ran between advanced capitalist countries rather than out to the Third World, and when the great powers themselves retreated from empire. Postmodern late capitalism was, very obviously, post-imperialist. As Michael Kidron wryly observed a quarter of a century ago:

> it is difficult to see what value there is in still using the word imperialism to describe the system of big power aggression and coercion of today unless it lies in the reassurance to be derived from familiar sounds. The one feature held in common by all imperialisms to date ... was their direct control of the state in subject territories. Today such control is rapidly becoming vestigial, and the distinction between empire and colony which loomed so large half a century ago increasingly irrelevant, politically and economically.[29]

---

27   Lenin 1969, p. 89.
28   Lenin 1969, pp. 13–14.
29   Kidron 1974, p. 159.

What was rapidly becoming vestigial in 1965 has now long since become so. And yet, both Communist and non-Communist Marxists (for example, the group around *Arena* in Australia) persisted in the attempt to interpret the contemporary world order through this least applicable of theoretical nostrums. The theory of imperialism had little or no explanatory value for most of the postwar period. Its continuing significance derived only from the manner in which it licensed (although not intentionally on Lenin's part) a shift in Marxist sensibilities away from the centre and towards the periphery, away from progress and towards backwardness, away from capitalism and towards precapitalism, away from internationalism and towards nationalism. The Soviet ruling class's own self-perception as a bastion of struggle against imperialism, and the associated and derivative Third Worldist, Maoist and Guevarist currents within international Communism, were of major significance to the political history of the twentieth century. For this was how Communism sought both to explain the paradox of its own existence and to legitimate the perversity of its own barbarism. From the Show Trials to the Killing Fields, it was all done in the name of anti-imperialism. The dissonance between theory and reality was so great as to suggest the presence of a powerfully false consciousness at work. That this should have been so in the Communist states themselves is hardly surprising. What does seem perplexing, and what surely still requires some adequate explanation, is the Western Left's complicity in the entire process. That complicity remains all the more puzzling when one recalls the regular recurrence of properly post-Leninist attempts at theorisation of a third, post-imperialist stage in the history of capitalism. I am familiar with at least three such attempts, namely that by Kidron cited above, E.P. Thompson's famous exterminism essay[30] and Fredric Jameson's magisterial treatment of postmodernism.[31] In each case, no matter what interest might have been stimulated in the more specific debates about nuclear disarmament or postmodern pastiche, the more general import of the argument concerning imperialism was systematically ignored. We appear, then, to be in the presence of a primary taboo, operative at the level of the deep structure of the collective consciousness of the Western radical intelligentsia.

Which brings us to Western Marxism, the third of our theoretical traditions, and by far the most influential amongst the academic intelligentsia itself. The term was originally coined by Maurice Merleau-Ponty to refer to that kind of critical, humanist Marxism which developed in Western Europe by way

---

30   Thompson 1980.
31   Jameson 1984.

of reaction against 'eastern' Communist Marxism.³² The obvious exemplars here include Gramsci, Lukács, Korsch, the Frankfurt School and Sartre, but not in this usage Althusserian theoretical practice. Perry Anderson expanded the term to include the latter, unwisely it seems to me, and added that the tradition shares 'one fundamental emblem: a common and latent *pessimism*'.³³ This was so, he argued, because it was born 'from the failure of proletarian revolutions in the advanced zones of European capitalism after the First World War'.³⁴

Here, Anderson seems to me radically mistaken: to the contrary, Western Marxism was *born* from out of a moment of near-messianic optimism following in the immediate aftermath of the Bolshevik Revolution. Whatever its ultimate focus on the depoliticising consequences of reification, bourgeois hegemony, the culture industries, and so on, the original emphasis in Western Marxism fell on the imminently revolutionary potential of proletarian class consciousness, counter-hegemony and revolutionary will. This is almost self-evidently so in *History and Class Consciousness*, the founding text of the entire tradition, which Lukács himself understood as a theorisation of, rather than a heresy from, Bolshevism. For the young Lukács: 'History is at its least automatic when it is the consciousness of the proletariat that is at issue ... Any transformation can only come about as the product of the – free – action of the proletariat'.³⁵ As the identical subject and object of history, the proletariat was, for Lukács, the bearer of a form of class consciousness that would render the historical process itself, no less, virtually transparent.

Even more startling is Gramsci's much cited, but much less commonly quoted, article on 'the Revolution Against *Capital*', published in *Avanti!* on 24 December 1917, as a salute to the Bolshevik Revolution. 'This is the revolution against Karl Marx's *Capital*', he writes:

> In Russia, Marx's *Capital* was more the book of the bourgeoisie than of the proletariat. It stood as the critical demonstration of how events should follow a predetermined course: how in Russia a bourgeoisie had to develop, and a capitalist era had to open ... The Bolsheviks reject Karl Marx ... These people are not 'Marxists', that is all; they have not used the works of the Master to compile a rigid doctrine ... They live Marxist thought – that thought which is eternal, which represents the continuation of German and Italian idealism, and which in the case of Marx

---

32 Merleau-Ponty 1974.
33 Anderson 1976, p. 88.
34 Anderson 1976, p. 92.
35 Lukács 1971b, pp. 208–9.

was contaminated by positivist and naturalist encrustations. This thought sees as the dominant factor in history, not raw economic facts, but man, men in societies, men in relation to one another, reaching agreements with one another, developing through these contacts ... a collective, social will; men coming to understand economic facts, judging them and adapting them to their will until this becomes the driving force of the economy and moulds objective reality, which lives and moves and comes to resemble a current of volcanic lava that can be channelled wherever and in whatever way men's will determines.[36]

Doubtless, Gramsci was entirely right in this assessment: the Bolshevik Revolution was indeed a revolution against Marx and against classical Marxism. But in retrospect, and with the benefit of much hindsight, it has clearly not been at all successful as such. Hardly anyone in the former Soviet Union, either in the ruling classes or elsewhere, today retains even a residual belief in the old Soviet society's capacity for transformation into a post-capitalist social formation in any way superior to that of capitalism proper. Quite the contrary, both the former USSR and the former Eastern European 'people's democracies' have proceeded as rapidly as possible (which has often been very slowly indeed) towards private capitalism, towards privatisation and liberalisation, towards a market economy and the collective management buy-out. The Western Marxist 'triumph of the will' has thus proven at least as chimerical as Trotsky's theory of permanent revolution or the Marxist-Leninist theory of imperialism.

Western Marxism long since withdrew even critical support for the Soviet Union: Adorno's anti-Stalinist polemics, although extreme, were nonetheless paradigmatic.[37] But this did not entail any retreat from voluntarism, except by way of the detour into Althusserian structuralism, where an idealism of structure came to substitute for an idealism of praxis. The general anti-materialism of the entire tradition persisted, whether or not we redefine its contours so as to include Althusserianism. Hence, the recurrent shift of political allegiances away from the Soviet Union and towards other, even more backward, even more primitive, despotisms: whatever their other differences, both Sartre and Althusser happily flirted with Maoism.

The revolutions against *Capital* are proven failures, their variously Trotskyist, Communist and Western Marxist theorisations dramatically falsified by both the Eastern European revolutions and the disintegration of the Soviet

---

36   Gramsci 1977, pp. 34–5.
37   Adorno 1980.

Union. For these revolutions were, surely, revolutions in favour of *Capital*. They confirmed Marx's own warning that people, even Bolsheviks, make history in circumstances not of their own choosing.[38] They confirmed Kautsky's more immediate insistence that the attempt to build socialism in a backward country would result only in the creation of a kind of state capitalism: 'Industrial capitalism has developed to become state capitalism ... Today the state bureaucracy and the capitalist bureaucracy are merged into one ... that is the upshot of the great socialist revolution brought about by the Bolsheviks'.[39]

If the Soviet Union was not a superior form of post-capitalist society, not even in embryo, as its own leaders would eventually concede, nor was it an entirely new type of society, a dictatorship over needs, for example, as the Budapest School suggested.[40] Quite simply, Soviet Communism proved insufficiently durable to be considered such: it no more represented a distinct social type than did Calvin's dictatorship at Geneva. In retrospect, it becomes clear that the pure form of Soviet-style regime, that is, the endogenously developed variant rather than that imposed from without by military invasion, was indeed a kind of transitional society, as both Stalin and Trotsky maintained, but that it was transitional to capitalism rather than to anything that Marx might have recognised as socialism. As such, Communist society is best understood, it seems to me, in exactly the terms proposed by Kautsky, that is, as a form of state capitalism. This is not state capitalism in the sense coined by Maoism and neo-Maoism, which tended simply to glamourise Stalinism, and which radically overestimated the disjuncture between Stalin and Kruschev. Nor is it quite in the sense coined by neo-Trotskyist writers, such as Tony Cliff and, indeed, Michael Kidron, a sense deriving from Bukharin rather than Trotsky, which mistakenly posited state capitalism as the logically eventual form of fully monopolised private capitalism.[41] State capitalism was rather, just as Kautsky argued, essentially a primitive form of capitalism, which, we can now see, tended over time to develop towards more fully evolved forms of private capitalism.

Had twentieth-century Marxism taken sufficient note of Marx's own criteria for the classification of different kinds of social formation, Soviet Communism's status as a type of capitalism would have become much more readily apparent. The forces of production deployed in the Soviet Union were much the same, although often less well developed, than those characteristic of industrial capitalism: steam technology, electrification, nuclear energy, and so

---

38 Marx 1973, p. 146.
39 Kautsky 1983, p. 146.
40 Fehér, Heller and Markus 1983.
41 Cliff 1988; Kidron 1970; Bukharin 1971; Callinicos 1982, pp. 203–12.

on. The relations of production were, again, either much the same as in capitalism (wage labour) or less developed (peasant agriculture and, during the Stalin period, slavery). The primary form of political superstructure in capitalist societies is the nation state, and, although the Soviet Union like the United Kingdom retained important residues of an older paranational dynastic monarchy, its polity remained nonetheless essentially national in form. The many and varied forms of social consciousness found in Western capitalism, from the realist novel to religious mysticism, from scientific rationalism to market economics, all recurred, albeit in qualitatively distinct complexes, within Soviet-style societies.

Insofar as there were significant patterns of difference between Western and eastern variants, these invariably arose from the systematic backwardness of the latter. The sheer violence of the Communist experience becomes explicable precisely in these terms. For, of course, Western capitalism was itself predicated on an earlier period of primitive accumulation characterised by massive exercises in repression: in Britain, enclosure, the Highland clearances and the slave trade; in North America, the genocidal expropriation of an entire continent, indentured labour and, again, slavery.[42] Western capitalism itself required an initial period of state absolutism by which to effect the administrative and bureaucratic prerequisites for such primitive accumulation.[43] Western capitalism itself required endorsement by a messianically puritan and repressively redemptive ideology, Weber's famous Protestant ethic.[44] Stalinism, it now becomes clear, was Soviet Russia's absolutism, Marxist-Leninism its Calvinism, 'primitive socialist accumulation' simply its primitive capitalist accumulation. And, ghastly though all of this was, it was also historically 'progressive': the present possibilities for both private capitalism and liberal democracy arise precisely from a legacy of successful primitive accumulation in the old USSR.[45]

This reading of the Communist experience is intended as an apologia neither for Western nor eastern capitalisms. That it remains possible to develop a future-oriented critique of capitalism, without denying its continuingly progressive aspects, and without resort to some mythical 'actually existing social-

---

42 As Marx quite rightly insisted, capital comes into the world 'dripping from head to foot, from every pore, with blood and dirt' (Marx 1970a, p. 760).

43 Cf. Anderson 1974b.

44 Weber 1930.

45 This is not to 'excuse' Stalinism, no more than the current state of British, American or French democracy excuses the slave trade, the expropriation of the Amerindian natives or the Terror. It is, however, to point to the *connections* between the inexcusable and the (actually or potentially) desirable.

ism', should be obvious from the example of Marx himself. It was after all Marx, surely the most intellectually distinguished of all capitalism's opponents, who announced that:

> The bourgeoisie, historically, has played a most revolutionary part.
> The bourgeoisie ... has put an end to all feudal, patriarchal, idyllic relations. It has pitilessly torn assunder the motley feudal ties that bound man to his 'natural superiors' ... The bourgeoisie has through its exploitation of the world market given a cosmopolitan character to production and consumption in every country. To the great chagrin of Reactionists, it has drawn from under the feet of industry the national ground on which it stood ... And as in material, so also in intellectual production. The intellectual creations of individual nations become common property. National one-sidedness and narrow-mindedness become more and more impossible ...
> The bourgeoisie, by the rapid improvement of all instruments of production, by the immensely facilitated means of communication, draws all, even the most barbarian, nations into civilization ...
> The bourgeoisie, during its rule of scarce one hundred years, has created more massive and more colossal productive forces than have all preceding generations together.[46]

We have to be quite clear, it seems to me, that capitalism has continued to develop, and still continues to develop, the productive forces, which is to say that it is not yet ready to be destroyed; that the bourgeoisie is still on a world scale a progressive class, as much in South Korea[47] as in Eastern Europe; and that the Western Left's irrelevance to its own society arises, not from the superior stratagems of the bourgeoisie, nor even from the ineffable operations of an

---

46 Marx and Engels 1967, pp. 82–5.
47 Nigel Harris has explicitly argued for the continuingly progressive role of the bourgeoisie in South Korea, in terms which seem to me directly relevant to the Eastern European revolutions of 1989. Thus Harris: 'Can we then identify the long drawn out events in South Korea ..., in Mexico and perhaps other countries, as stages in the process of the "bourgeois revolution"? I think we can. We can also see ... that the development of national capitalism, a system by which accumulation can be sustained, usually requires a preliminary phase of State domination and initiative, whether this is described as economic nationalism or socialism ... What was set up to speed development becomes an inhibition to growth as capital develops ... Thus, the enemy of capitalism as it matures is not feudalism, but the State' (Harris 1988, p. 247).

all-encompassing dominant ideology, but rather, above all from its own self-chosen erstwhile vocation as a cheer squad for backwardness. We need to be clear, finally, that the world has actually changed a lot less since Marx's time than many have imagined, and that it is Marx, rather than Lenin or Trotsky or Gramsci, who provides the better guide to the political economy and practical problems of a capitalism that might well prove a lot less late than has often been assumed.

CHAPTER 14

Cultural Materialism, Culturalism and Post-Culturalism: The Legacy of Raymond Williams*

For much of the twentieth century cultural theory has been polarised between 'idealist' accounts, such as those proposed by traditional literary humanism, and 'materialist' accounts, normally of a specifically 'vulgar' Marxist kind. Comparing such idealisms and materialisms in 1981, Raymond Williams observed that 'the importance of each position ... is that it leads ... to intensive study of the relations between "cultural" activities and other forms of social life ... The sociology of culture, as it entered the second half of the twentieth century, was broadly compounded of work done from these two positions'.[1] During the 1960s and 1970s, however, new theoretical paradigms were brought into play which sought to establish the materiality of culture itself. As Williams continued: 'a new kind of convergence is becoming evident ... it differs in its insistence that "cultural practice" and "cultural production" ... are not simply derived from an otherwise constituted social order but are themselves major elements in its constitution ... it sees culture as the *signifying system* through which necessarily ... a social order is communicated, reproduced, experienced and explored'.[2] Williams himself could write with peculiar authority on this subject quite simply because his own work had come to provide the paradigmatic instance in the English-speaking world at least of precisely that new kind of convergence. The term 'cultural materialism' was one Williams had coined to denote his own break from an older tradition of British Communist Marxism on the one hand, and from that distinctly British version of literary humanism associated above all with the work of the Leavises on the other. But the term can easily be used more generally to describe this emergent body of cultural theory. It is that convergence and more particularly Williams's own contribution therein which provide this paper with its central subject matter.

What exactly are we to understand by the term 'cultural materialism'? Williams himself first used it in a short essay published in the hundredth issue

---

* This chapter has been published previously in *Theory, Culture and Society*, Vol. 11, No. 1, pp. 42–71, 1994.
1 Williams 1981, p. 12.
2 Williams 1981, pp. 12–13.

of the *New Left Review*. Cultural materialism, he explained, 'is a theory of culture as a (social and material) productive process and of specific practices, of "arts", as social uses of material means of production (from language as material "practical consciousness" to the specific technologies of writing and forms of writing, through to mechanical and electronic communications systems)'.[3] The position would be 'spelled out more fully', he added, in *Marxism and Literature* and in the book that would eventually be published as *Culture*.[4] There is an important sense in which these two books do indeed 'spell out' the theory and they will, then, command much of our attention here. But we should note also Williams's own insistence in the 'Introduction' to *Marxism and Literature* that cultural materialism had been 'a position which, as a matter of theory, I have arrived at over the years'.[5] Its pre-history in what I will term Williams's earlier 'left culturalism' thus provides as convenient a starting point as any for a critical appraisal of the later cultural materialism itself.

1   Culturalism and 'Left Culturalism'

Much of the theoretical literature in cultural studies has revolved around a recurrent contrast between 'culturalism' and 'structuralism'[6] in which the former is typically represented by Williams and perhaps by Thompson, the latter by an entire intellectual tradition reaching back from Lévi-Strauss and Barthes to Durkheim and Saussure. If some have more recently sought to 'consign the culturalism-structuralist split to the past',[7] then they have done so nonetheless in terms which radically privilege the latter. By way of correction I wish to stress the presence of a similarly longstanding culturalist tradition, one which in its English variant reaches back at least to Burke and Cobbett and which Williams himself had sought to map out in his *Culture and Society 1780–1950*. I use the term 'culturalism' here to denote a primarily Anglo-German tradition of essentially 'literary' speculation about the relationship between culture and society in which the claims of culture are counterposed, normally antithetically, to those of an industrialised or industrialising, 'mechanical' or materialist civilisation. Culture understood thus, as separate from and yet superior to both economics and politics, is initially the creation of European

---

3 Williams 1980a, p. 243.
4 Ibid.
5 Williams 1977, p. 5.
6 Johnson 1979a; Hall 1980a.
7 Turner 1990, p. 72; Bennett 1986, pp. xii–xvi.

Romanticism. Herder and Coleridge are obviously exemplary instances here.[8] At one level the term clearly denotes the arts and perhaps especially literature: 'Poets are the unacknowledged legislators of the world', wrote Shelley.[9] But the importance of art and the ultimate legislative power of poetry reside in their status as an expression of the distinctive 'spirit' of a people, very often especially the people understood as 'folk'. Which is precisely why art as 'culture' becomes counterposed to the mechanism of industrial 'civilisation'. This 'social' sense of the term is already present in Romanticism and it continues to inform twentieth century literary humanisms: one thinks not only of Leavis's 'organic community',[10] but also of Eliot's definition of culture.[11] It is a sense which is positively foregrounded, moreover, in German sociology. For Weber and Tönnies, for example, the opposition between culture and civilisation runs as that between status and class, *Wertrationalität* and *Zweckrationalität*, *Gemeinschaft* and *Gesellschaft*, feudalism and capitalism.[12] Here as in literary humanism, modern society is understood as distinctively and unusually asocial, its economic and political life characteristically 'rationalised' and 'dehumanised'. In Britain, however, the culturalist tradition had become institutionally organised into the academic discipline of 'English', rather than that of sociology, and in Leavisite literary criticism it attained an unusually extreme formulation.

British cultural studies has its origins in a very specific theoretical 'conjuncture', that of the 1950s, in which cultural debate had appeared deadlocked between the cruder economic determinisms of much Communist Marxism and the seemingly endemic political conservatism and cultural elitism of the Leavisites. The kind of cultural theory which emerged from that deadlock would eventually be represented in poststructuralist retrospect as 'culturalism', but is more accurately described as 'left culturalism'. The founding theoretical moment of such left culturalisms can be located in the early writings of Williams, Thompson and Hoggart. It was Hoggart's achievement to divest Leavisism of something at least of its cultural elitism if not perhaps its nostalgia,[13] Thompson's to divest Marxism of its economic determinism and to make explicit what had previously only ever been an implicit and barely acknowledged Romanticism.[14] But the achievement was in each case both reactive and con-

---

8   Herder 1968; Coleridge 1972.
9   Shelley 1930, p. 109.
10   Leavis and Thompson 1960, pp. 87–91.
11   Eliot 1962, p. 120.
12   Weber 1948, pp. 180–95; Weber 1964, p. 115; Tönnies 1955, pp. 37–9.
13   Hoggart 1958.
14   Thompson 1955.

tained: Hoggart reacted against but nonetheless within Leavisism, Thompson against but nonetheless within the then received version of Marxism. It is only in Williams's *Culture and Society* and in *The Long Revolution*, first published in 1958 and 1961 respectively, that we find something much closer to a proper synthesis between culturalism and materialism, Leavisism and Communist Marxism. Williams inherited from Leavisite literary criticism a commitment to holistic conceptions of culture and methods of analysis, a strong sense of the importance of the particular whether in art or in 'life' and an insistence on the absolute centrality of culture. He rejected its cultural elitism, however, especially as displayed in the 'mass civilization versus minority culture' topos. From Communist Marxism he inherited a radically socialistic critique of the 'materiality' of ruling class political, economic and cultural power, whilst rejecting the barely disguised economic determinism of its preferred base/superstructure model.

The central procedure of *Culture and Society* could not be more Leavisite: to move by way of close readings of a series of particular texts to the account of a distinctively 'English' national 'tradition'. Furthermore, Williams's sense of the intellectual content of this tradition has much in common with that of Leavis or of Eliot. And for Williams as for Leavis the tradition is seen as developing in more or less explicit anatagonism to utilitarianism (though this remains in many respects a surprisingly underdeveloped theme). Williams's strategic purpose was nonetheless radically opposed to the explicit cultural and political conservatism displayed by Eliot and increasingly by the Leavises too. For Williams sought to demonstrate that in its very complexity the 'culture and society' tradition remained not only finally unassimilable to any obvious conservativism, but also often openly amenable to radical, indeed socialistic, interpretation. This is not to suggest that Williams retained anything more than an entirely residual sympathy for Communist Marxism. The particular judgement on Caudwell that 'for the most part his discussion is not even specific enough to be wrong',[15] as also the general conclusion on Marxism that 'even if the economic element is determining, it determines a whole way of life, and it is to this, rather than to the economic system alone, that the literature has to be related',[16] both powerfully attest to the contrary. Quite fundamentally, Williams rejected the Leavisite notion of 'mass civilization', and with it the notion of 'masses': 'There are in fact no masses; there are only ways of seeing people as masses'.[17]

---

15   Williams 1963, p. 268.
16   Williams 1963, p. 272.
17   Williams 1963, p. 289.

He rejected also the Leavisite notion of a distinctively valuable minority culture, but did so nonetheless in distinctly Leavisite terms. A culture, Williams wrote, 'is not only a body of intellectual and imaginative work; it is also and essentially a whole way of life'.[18] In principle this is little different from Leavis's or Eliot's sense of the connectedness of culture as art and culture as way of life. But in the practical application of the principle Williams so expands its range as to include within 'culture' the 'collective democratic institution', by which he means primarily the trade union, the co-operative and the working class political party.[19] As he would later write, 'culture is ordinary'.[20]

Thus redefined, the literary-humanist notion of a single common culture became supplemented and importantly qualified by that of a plurality of class cultures. Yet despite such qualification, the normative ideal of a common culture remained central: 'We need a common culture, not for the sake of an abstraction, but because we shall not survive without it'.[21] A common culture may not yet properly exist, but it nonetheless provided Williams as it had Leavis with the essential theoretical ground from which to mount an organicist critique of utilitarian individualism. A common culture could never be properly such, Williams argued, if established on the basis of the kind of vicarious participation which Leavis and Eliot had sanctioned. 'The distinction of a culture in common', he wrote in the book's closing pages, 'is that ... selection is freely and commonly made and remade. The tending is a common process, based on a common decision'.[22] In a characteristically leftist move, Williams thus relocated the common culture from the idealised historical past it had occupied in Leavis to the not too distant, still to be made, democratically socialist future. And it was in the working class 'idea of solidarity' that Williams found 'potentially the real basis of a society'.[23]

If the common culture is not yet fully common, then it follows that the literary and cultural tradition should be seen not as the objective unfolding of the consciousness of a people, as the Leavisites had argued, but as the outcome in part of a set of interested selections made in the present. A 'tradition is always selective', wrote Williams, 'and ... there will always be a tendency for this process of selection to be related to and even governed by the interests of

---

18   Williams 1963, p. 311.
19   Williams 1963, p. 313.
20   Williams 1958.
21   Williams 1963, p. 304.
22   Williams 1963, p. 322.
23   Williams 1963, p. 318.

the class that is dominant'.[24] Where Leavis had revered a 'great tradition', Williams would thus discover a selective tradition. But even as he insisted on the class determinations of culture, Williams was careful also to note the extent to which such distinctions of class are complicated, especially in the field of intellectual and imaginative work, by 'the common elements resting on a common language'.[25] For Williams any direct reduction of art to class, such as had clearly been canvassed by Communist Marxism, remained entirely unacceptable. 'The area of culture', he observed, 'is usually proportionate to the area of a language rather than to the area of a class'.[26] This argument is repeated and significantly elaborated upon in the opening theoretical chapters of *The Long Revolution*:

> The selective tradition creates, at one level, a general human culture; at another level, the historical record of a particular society; at a third level ... a rejection of considerable areas of what was once a living culture ... selection will be governed by many kinds of special interest, including class interest ... The traditional culture of a society will always tend to correspond to its *contemporary* system of interests and values.[27]

Once again the stress falls on selection according to class-specific criteria, but once again also on the reality of a truly general human culture.

It is here too that Williams proposes an initial theorisation of the concept of 'structure of feeling', a term actually coined in the much earlier *Preface to Film*[28] but not hitherto given any extensive theoretical articulation. 'In one sense', he writes, 'this structure of feeling is the culture of a period: it is the particular living result of all the elements in the general organization'.[29] He continues: 'in this respect ... the arts of a period ... are of major importance ... here ... the actual living sense, the deep community that makes the communication possible, is naturally drawn upon'.[30] A structure of feeling, Williams makes clear, is neither universal nor class specific, though it is 'a very deep and wide possession'.[31] Nor is it formally learned, he speculates, and thence follows its often

---

24 Williams 1963, pp. 307–8.
25 Williams 1963, p. 311.
26 Williams 1963, p. 307.
27 Williams 1965, p. 68.
28 Williams and Orrom 1954.
29 Williams 1965, p. 64.
30 Williams 1965, pp. 64–5.
31 Williams 1965, p. 65.

peculiarly generational character: 'the new generation will have its own structure of feeling, which will not appear to have come "from" anywhere'.[32] This concept of 'structure of feeling' was to prove quite extraordinarily fruitful. In *The English Novel*, for example, Williams would attempt to show how from Dickens to Lawrence the novel became one medium amongst many by which people sought to master and absorb new experience through the articulation of a structure of feeling the key problem of which was that of the 'knowable community'.[33] In *Drama from Ibsen to Brecht* he would produce an account of the development of naturalism and of expressionism in the modern theatre which would be organised around precisely 'the history and significance of the main dramatic forms – the conventions and structures of feeling'.[34] The concept of structure of feeling would also occupy a commanding position in his later cultural materialism.

In *The Long Revolution* Williams sought to chart the long history of the emergence of modernity and of the interrelationships within British society between the democratic revolution, the industrial revolution and the 'cultural revolution' embodied in the extension and democratisation of communications.[35] The central novelty of *The Long Revolution* lies in its form, in its peculiar combination of theoretical discussion, substantive 'sociological' analysis and expressly political argument. There is much that must have been disturbingly innovative in each. The opening theoretical discussions in which the concept of a structure of feeling is elaborated are both dense and original. The book's second part moves to supplement the more conventional procedures of Leavisite textual criticism with a much more sociological account of the historical development of a number of major British cultural institutions: there are pioneering analyses of the education system and the growth of the reading public, the popular press and the development of 'Standard English'; these are followed, in turn, by chapters on the social backgrounds of a selection of canonical English writers and on the social histories of dramatic forms and the contemporary novel. The concluding third part, in effect an exploratory inquiry into the structure of feeling of the early 1960s, critically addresses the politico-cultural problems of the apparent moral decline of the labour movement.[36] The combination of a sharply analytical intelligence and an at times near-utopian

---

32 Ibid.
33 Williams 1974a, pp. 14–15.
34 Williams 1973a, p. 14.
35 Williams 1965, pp. 10–12.
36 Williams 1965, pp. 328–9.

radical vision which informs much of this last essay must have spoken powerfully and provocatively to a society slowly shrugging off the moral and political conservatism of the 1950s.

What holds the book together, however, is its very strong underlying sense of the materiality of culture, at once a restatement and a transcendence of the position originally outlined in *Culture and Society*. 'It was certainly an error', Williams wrote against Leavisite humanism, 'to suppose that values or artworks could be adequately studied without reference to the particular society within which they were expressed'.[37] But, 'it is equally an error', he wrote against Communist Marxism, 'to suppose that the social explanation is determining, or that the values and works are mere by-products'.[38] He moves thence to what might well be the book's central set of propositions:

> If the art is part of the society, there is no solid whole, outside it, to which ... we concede priority. The art is there, as an activity, with the production, the trading, the politics, the raising of families ... It is ... not a question of relating the art to the society, but of studying all the activities and their interrelations, without any concession of priority to any one of them we may choose to abstract ... I would define the theory of culture as the study of relationships between elements in a whole way of life. The analysis of culture is the attempt to discover the nature of the organization which is the complex of these relationships. Analysis of particular works or institutions is, in this context, analysis of their essential kind of organization, the relationships which works or institutions embody as parts of the organization of a whole.[39]

Here, then, was the prospectus for what would become a thoroughgoing cultural materialism.

2 Cultural Materialism

In the interim between the first publication of *The Long Revolution* in 1961 and that of *Marxism and Literature* in 1977, Williams's work proceeded by way of a series of often radically innovative encounters with an extremely diverse set of

---

37 Williams 1965, p. 61.
38 Ibid.
39 Williams 1965, pp. 61–3.

substantive issues, ranging across the whole field of literary and cultural studies: the mass media,[40] the novel,[41] the drama[42] and the pastoral.[43] In the work on theatre and on television a new awareness of the social conventionality of form and of the interrelationship between technology and form is increasingly brought to bear. Williams's coupling of the problem of cultural form to that of cultural technology clearly drew attention in each case to the materiality of what were in orthodoxly Marxist terms 'ideal' superstructures. This led him in turn to a simultaneous rejection both of technological determinism and of the notion of a determined technology, and thence to a much more complex understanding of the notion of determination itself. The chronological overlap between Williams's work in theatre studies and that on the mass media is thus by no means merely 'coincidental'. Disparate though the work might appear, it proceeds along clearly connected lines of inquiry. And these connections are empirical and substantive as well as theoretical and methodological. As Williams had noted in the 'Conclusion' to his *Drama from Ibsen to Brecht*: 'drama is no longer coexistent with theatre ... The largest audience for drama, in our own world, is in the cinema and on television'.[44]

The cumulative effect of these apparently diverse lines of inquiry would finally be registered in *Marxism and Literature*. But that work is nonetheless not the 'extraordinary theoretical "coming out"' in which 'Williams finally admits the usefulness of Marxism'[45] that Turner takes it to be. Much more appropriate is O'Connor's emphasis on 'a *fundamental* theoretical continuity although there were shifts and changes'.[46] In Williams's earlier 'left culturalist' writings the 'deep community' that is culture had been understood as simultaneously transcendent of class and yet irredeemably marked by it. For all the eloquence with which this position had been argued, it remained quite fundamentally incoherent: the competing claims of commonality and difference, culture and class, Leavisism and Marxism, formed a circle which stubbornly refused to be squared. But in the later 'cultural materialist' phase of his work, it finally became possible for Williams to explain to his own satisfaction at least how it could be that structures of feeling are common to different classes and yet nonetheless represent the interests of some particular class. Such explanation

---

40   Williams 1962 and 1974a.
41   Williams 1974a.
42   Williams 1966 and 1973.
43   Williams 1973b.
44   Williams 1973a, p. 399.
45   Turner 1990, p. 65.
46   O'Connor 1989, p. 103.

had been decisively facilitated by Williams's own encounter with the recently translated key texts of the continental European Western Marxist tradition. Initially that encounter had entailed little more than a recognition that not all Marxisms were necessarily economically determinist and a corollary discovery of theoretical preoccupations similar to his own in the work of individual Western Marxist writers. Williams's response to Goldmann, for example, had centred on the recognition that they were 'exploring many of the same areas with many of the same concepts'.[47] The response to Gramsci, however, was of an altogether different order, precipitating a much more positive redefinition of Williams's own theoretical stance. As he would insist in *Marxism and Literature*: 'Gramsci's ... work is one of the major turning-points in Marxist cultural theory'.[48]

Williams was impressed both by Gramsci's work on intellectuals, which seemed to him an 'encouraging' and 'experimental' model for work in the sociology of culture,[49] and by the wider implications of the theory of hegemony. The significance of the latter had registered initially in an essay written for the *New Left Review* in 1973, entitled 'Base and Superstructure in Marxist Cultural Theory'.[50] But in *Marxism and Literature* the argument is elaborated upon at much greater length. The first and last chapters respectively of the book's first part are devoted to two key concepts and two keywords, deriving respectively from Leavisism and Marxism, 'Culture' and 'Ideology'. In a subsequent chapter, Williams argues for the theoretical superiority over each of these of the Gramscian notion of hegemony:

> 'Hegemony' goes beyond 'culture' ... in its insistence on relating the 'whole social process' to specific distributions of power and influence ... Gramsci therefore introduces the necessary recognition of dominance and subordination in what has still, however, to be recognized as a whole process. It is in just this recognition of the *wholeness* of the process that the concept of 'hegemony' goes beyond 'ideology'. What is decisive is not only the conscious system of ideas and beliefs, but the whole lived social process as practically organized by specific and dominant meanings and values.[51]

---

47 Williams 1980b, p. 20.
48 Williams 1977, p. 108.
49 Williams 1977, p. 138.
50 Williams 1980b, p. 37.
51 Williams 1977, pp. 108–9.

For Williams, Gramsci's central achievement consists in the articulation of a culturalist sense of the wholeness of culture with a more typically Marxist sense of the interestedness of ideology. Thus hegemony is 'in the strongest sense a "culture", but a culture which has to be seen as the lived dominance and subordination of particular classes'.[52] Understood thus, culture is no longer either 'superstructural', as the term had normally been defined in the Maxist tradition, or 'ideological', in either the more generally Marxist or the more specifically Althusserian definition. On the contrary, 'cultural tradition and practice ... are among the basic processes', which need to be seen 'as they are ... without the characteristic straining to fit them ... to other and determining ... economic and political relationships'.[53] Whether all of this remains exactly faithful to Gramsci's own intent seems open to some doubt. Gramsci himself repeatedly deployed the distinction between 'structure' and 'superstructure' and, whilst recognising the 'complex, contradictory or discordant' qualities of the latter, nonetheless insisted that the '*ensemble* of the superstructures is the reflection of the *ensemble* of the social relations of production'.[54] But whatever the original authorial intention (and this is by no means at all self-evident), Williams's appropriation of Gramsci finally delivered that resolution of culturalist and Marxist thematics hitherto denied him.

In one respect at least Williams's reading of Gramsci is indeed unusually faithful to its object: for both the Italian revolutionary and his Welsh interpreter it was the counter-hegemonic moment that is especially significant. Hence, Williams's attempt to distinguish between those practices, experiences, meanings and values that are part of the effectively dominant culture and those that are not. The dominant or hegemonic culture, Williams reminds us, 'is always an active process', an organisation of often quite disparate meanings, 'which it specifically incorporates in a significant culture'.[55] Rehearsing an argument first broached in *Culture and Society*, he points once again to the decisive importance of 'selective tradition' in the effective operation of such processes of incorporation: 'tradition is in practice the most evident expression of the dominant and hegemonic pressures and limits. It is always more than an inert historicized segment; indeed it is the most powerful practical means of incorporation'.[56] In *Marxism and Literature*, however, the selective tradition is also seen as necessarily dependent both upon identifiable institutions and upon

52   Williams 1977, p. 110.
53   Williams 1977, p. 111.
54   Gramsci 1971, p. 366.
55   Williams 1977, p. 115.
56   Ibid.

what Williams terms 'formations', that is, intellectual or artistic movements and tendencies.[57] This double stress is explored at greater length in *Culture*, where Williams advances a preliminary historical typology of institutions[58] and formations.[59] For all this attention to the hegemonic, Williams remains insistent that at the level of 'historical' as distinct from 'epochal' analysis, that is, at the level of movement rather than system, there is much in any lived culture that cannot be reduced to the dominant.[60] Here, Williams dissents sharply from the implied consensualism of both Althusserian theories of ideology and the then current sociological versions of 'the dominant ideology thesis': *'no mode and therefore no dominant social order'*, he writes, *'and therefore no dominant culture ever in reality includes or exhausts all human practice, human energy, and human intention'*.[61]

Williams's initial theorisation of the alternatives to hegemony had been broached in the 1973 *New Left Review* essay, where he had sought to distinguish between 'alternative' and 'oppositional', 'residual' and 'emergent' cultural elements.[62] The terminology recurs both in *Marxism and Literature* and in *Culture*. By 'residual' Williams means not so much the simply 'archaic', defined as 'that which is wholly recognized as an element of the past', but rather those cultural elements external to the dominant culture which nonetheless continue to be lived and practised as an active part of the present 'on the basis of the residue ... of some previous social and cultural institution or formation'.[63] Unlike the archaic, the residual may be oppositional or at least alternative in character. Thus Williams distinguishes organised religion and the idea of rural community, which are each predominantly residual, from monarchy, which is merely archaic. But it is the properly 'emergent', that is, those genuinely new meanings and values, practices, relationships and kinds of relationship which are substantially alternative or oppositional to the dominant culture,[64] that most interest Williams. For Williams as for Gramsci, the primary source of an emergent culture is likely to be the formation of a new social class. But there is also a second source of emergence: 'alternative perceptions of others, in immediate relationships; new perceptions and practices of the material

---

57 Williams 1977, pp. 117–20.
58 Williams 1981, pp. 33–56.
59 Williams 1981, pp. 57–86.
60 Williams 1977, p. 121.
61 Williams 1977, p. 125.
62 Williams 1980b, pp. 39–42.
63 Williams 1977, p. 122.
64 Williams 1977, p. 123.

world'.⁶⁵ For Williams as for Gramsci, the exemplary contemporary instance of a new social class is that of the development of the modern working class. At the second level, however, which Williams terms 'the excluded social [human] area',⁶⁶ a level often peculiarly pertinent to the analysis of artistic and intellectual movements, the situation is much less clear. As Williams writes in *Culture*: 'No analysis is more difficult than that which, faced by new forms, has to try to determine whether these are new forms of the dominant or are genuinely emergent'.⁶⁷ This testimony to complexity is no mere rhetorical gesture on Williams's part. Quite the contrary: his work both in drama studies and in media studies had made him all too aware of the difficulties entailed in distinguishing the properly emergent from the merely novel.

Theoretically at least Williams is able in *Marxism and Literature* to offer an unusually interesting formulation of the problem itself, if not necessarily of the ways in which it might be resolved. Here he redeploys and significantly redefines his earlier notion of 'structure of feeling'. An emergent culture, Williams argues, unlike either the dominant or the residual, requires not only distinct kinds of immediate cultural practice but also and crucially 'new forms or adaptations of forms'. Such innovation at the level of form, he continues, 'is in effect a *pre-emergence*, active and pressing but not yet fully articulated, rather than the evident emergence which could be more confidently named'.⁶⁸ And it is precisely at this level of the pre-emergent that the concept of structure of feeling is brought back into play. From *The Long Revolution* onwards Williams had used the term to denote both the immediately experiential and the generationally specific aspects of artistic process. In *Marxism and Literature* both emphases are retained, but are conjoined to a quite new stress on cultural pre-emergence. In this reformulation the experiential remains at odds with official, 'formal' culture precisely insofar as it is indeed genuinely new: 'practical consciousness is what is actually being lived, ... not only what it is thought is being lived'.⁶⁹ And similarly the generationally specific remains different from the experience of previous generations precisely insofar as it too is indeed genuinely new. Structures of feeling, writes Williams, in an unusually arresting formulation, 'can be defined as social experiences *in solution*, as distinct from other social semantic formations which have been *precipitated*

---

65   Williams 1977, p. 126.
66   Ibid.
67   Williams 1981, p. 205.
68   Williams 1977, p. 126.
69   Williams 1977, pp. 130–1.

and are more evidently and more immediately available ... The effective formations of most actual art relate to already manifest social formations, dominant or residual, and it is primarily to emergent formations ... that the structure of feeling, *as solution*, relates'.[70] Structures of feeling are no longer, then, in any sense 'the culture' of a period: they are, rather, precisely those particular elements within the more general culture which most actively anticipate subsequent mutations in the general culture itself; in short, they are quite specifically counter-hegemonic.

At one level this distinctly Gramscian reformulation of the notion of 'structure of feeling' merely recaptures something of what Williams had all along intended: the problem of the knowable community in the English novel and the naturalistic revolution in the modern theatre each delimit a distinct structure of feeling only insofar as they are indeed genuinely innovatory. But in each case these respectively pre-emergent qualities are never fully theorised. It is as if the concept itself is still pre-emergent and requires the encounter with Gramsci for precipitation. Moreover, the substantive question of the precise interplay between the emergent or pre-emergent on the one hand, and novelty within the dominant on the other, in both mass media forms and modernist avant-garde forms, was to become especially pressing for Williams in his later work. The issue is broached very clearly in *Culture*. But it becomes absolutely central to the 1983 reworking of the long revolution analysis *Towards 2000*[71] and to the posthumously published and sadly unfinished *The Politics of Modernism*.[72] Both books attempt to reformulate the earlier aspiration to community and to culture as a whole way of life by way of a critique of 'postmodern' appropriations of both modernism itself and the popular mass media.

In *Towards 2000* Williams shows how postmodernism effectively collapses the distinction between minority and mass arts: 'There are very few absolute contrasts left between a "minority culture" and "mass communications"', he writes, 'many minority institutions and forms have adapted, ... with enthusiasm, to modern corporate capitalist culture'.[73] The older modernisms, which had once threatened to destabilise the certainties of bourgeois life, have been transformed, he argues, into a new '"post-modernist" establishment' which 'takes human inadequacy ... as self-evident'.[74] The deep structures of this now

---

70   Williams 1977, pp. 133–4.
71   Williams 1983.
72   Williams 1989b.
73   Williams 1983, pp. 134, 140.
74   Williams 1983, p. 141.

dominant postmodernism are present, moreover, in effectively popular cultural forms such as film, television and fiction: 'these debased forms of an anguished sense of human debasement ... have become a widely distributed "popular" culture that is meant to confirm both its own and the world's destructive inevitablities'.[75] The 'pseudo-radicalism' of 'the negative structures of post-modernist art'[76] is thus neither pre-emergent nor emergent, but rather a moment of novelty, indeed perhaps the institutionalisation of novelty itself, within the already dominant culture. As Williams would observe in *The Politics of Modernism*, the dominant institutions themselves 'now incorporate or impose' such 'easy labels of radicalism'.[77] But if the dominant culture has indeed so mutated, then Williams is able also to detect a more properly innovatory, pre-emergent 'structure of feeling', though the term itself is not actually used, in the politics of the contemporary new social movements.[78]

Williams's 'Base and Superstructure' essay had signalled not only a new reading of Gramsci, but also a more general attempt to recast the Marxist base/superstructure formula. He had argued for a 'revaluation' of each of the three terms in the formula, 'base', 'superstructure' and 'determination', so that: the first would now denote the primary production of society itself and of people themselves rather than the merely 'economic'; the second, the whole range of cultural practices rather than a merely secondary and dependent 'content'; and the third, the 'setting of limits and exertion of pressures' rather than predetermined causation.[79] The latter proposition is very much the same as that advanced the following year in *Television: Technology and Cultural Form*. In *Marxism and Literature*, however, the argument is taken further, but in a direction that leads perhaps paradoxically very much away from rather than toward the more classically Marxist formulations of the problem. Once again determination is taken to mean the setting of limits and exertion of pressures;[80] once again production is understood as applying to a much wider realm than the merely economic, so that the 'productive forces' are 'all and any activities in the social process as a whole'.[81] But the notions of 'base' and 'superstructure', which had acquired an entirely temporary and very much conditional legitimacy in the 1973 essay, are here consigned to a theoretical

---

75 Williams 1983, pp. 141–2.
76 Williams 1983, p. 145.
77 Williams 1989b, p. 176.
78 Williams 1983, p. 250.
79 Williams 1980b, pp. 34–5.
80 Williams 1977, p. 87.
81 Williams 1977, p. 93.

oblivion much akin to that in *Culture and Society*: 'contrary to the development in Marxism, it is not "the base" and "the superstructure" that need to be studied, but specific and indissoluble real processes'.[82] Ironically, Williams is very much concerned to invoke Marx himself against subsequent Marxism on precisely this point. 'Marx's original criticism', he insists, 'had been mainly directed against the *separation* of "areas" of thought and activity ... The common abstraction of "the base" and "the superstructure" is thus a radical persistence of the modes of thought which he attacked'.[83] It is difficult to avoid the suspicion that here at least Williams protests too much. And yet there is a strong sense in which his position is indeed 'Marxist'. For this is no simple return to the argument of *Culture and Society*, but rather the development of an entirely new argument by which Williams seeks to convict Marxism, in the telling phrase of his 1979 *New Left Review* interlocutors, of 'not so much ... an excess but ... a deficit of materialism'.[84] What the base/superstructure formula fails to acknowledge, he charges, is precisely the materiality of the superstructures themselves. Hence the characteristically ruthless judgement that: 'The concept of "superstructure" was ... not a reduction but an evasion'.[85]

Superstructure, Williams concludes, and other related usages within Marxist discourse such as 'ideology' or 'the realm of art and ideas' each misrepresent what are in fact real and material activities as somehow unreal and immaterial. None of these activities can then be grasped as they are: 'as real practices, elements of a whole material social process; not a realm or a world or a superstructure, but many and variable productive practices, with specific conditions and intentions'.[86] The way forward, he insists, is 'to look at our actual productive activities without assuming in advance that only some of them are material'.[87] If Williams retains a concept of determination, then, as he certainly does, it is nonetheless a concept of multiple determination, much more akin to the culturalist sense of a whole way of life than to the Marxist notion of a determining base and a determined supestructure. But that whole way of life is now both thoroughly material and thoroughly marked by the impress of power and domination, in all its particular aspects. This stress on the materiality of cultural production had been a recurrent theme in Williams's work from *The Long*

---

82 Williams 1977, p. 82.
83 Williams 1977, p. 78.
84 Williams 1979, p. 350.
85 Williams 1977, p. 93.
86 Williams 1977, p. 94.
87 Ibid.

Revolution onwards, most especially so in his writing on drama and on the mass media. But in *Marxism and Literature* it attains a much more explicit formulation than any hitherto.

In *Culture* and in a 1978 essay published by the Yugoslav journal *Prilozi: Drustvenost Komunikacije* the process would be taken even further, as Williams would seek to analyse means of communication as in themselves means of production.[88] In *Marxism and Literature*, however, the argument leads immediately toward what is in effect a 'deconstruction' of probably the most sacred of all Leavisite categories, that of 'Literature' itself. The specialising concept of 'Literature', Williams recognises, is an important instance of 'the aesthetic'[89] and the aesthetic itself a specifically bourgeois evasion by which art and thinking about art 'separate themselves ... from the social processes within which they are ... contained'.[90] To such evasions and to their often transparently elitist ideological functions Williams seeks to counterpose a stress on 'the multiplicity of writing'[91] and on 'the variability, the relativity, and the multiplicity of actual cultural practice'.[92] In the third and final part of *Marxism and Literature* and again in *Culture* this would lead to an extended theorisation of the social processes of art and literature themselves.

This account is premised upon what is clearly the distinguishing proposition of cultural materialism, that of the materiality of cultural production. Drawing extensively on Volosinov,[93] Williams argues for a theory of 'language as activity, as practical consciousness'.[94] Whether spoken or written, language is for Williams not a 'medium', in the sense of an intermediate communicative substance mediating between thought and expression, but rather a constitutive element of material social practice.[95] More particularly: 'Language is in fact a special kind of material practice: that of human socialilty'.[96] Linguistic signification is, then, for Williams as much as for any structuralist, a 'real and demonstrable activity'[97] with its own distinctively material and in a sense 'formal' properties. But signs are not thereby 'arbitary', as structuralism is wont

---

88   Williams 1980c, pp. 50–63; Williams 1981, pp. 87–118.
89   Williams 1977, p. 150.
90   Williams 1977, p. 154.
91   Williams 1977, p. 146.
92   Williams 1977, p. 153.
93   Volosinov 1973.
94   Williams 1977, p. 36.
95   Williams 1977, pp. 158–9, 165.
96   Williams 1977, p. 165.
97   Williams 1977, p. 167.

to claim. Quite the contrary, they function within 'lived and living relationships' and it is these relationships, sociologically determinate rather than arbitrary in character, which in Williams's view '*make all formal meanings significant and substantial*'.[98] Moreover, Williams continues, the structuralist concept of the sign significantly occludes the distinction between speech and writing: 'Spoken words are a process of human activity using only immediate, constitutive, physical resources. Written words ... are a form of material production, adapting non-human resources to a human end'.[99]

Writing, Williams argues, is better understood as 'notation' than as 'sign', since unlike speech it is at once both materially objectified and reproducible and this reproducibility is itself necessarily dependent on the socio-cultural system within which the notation is operative.[100] Such dependence is in fact much more characteristic of writing than of many other cultural techniques such as dance, song and speech. As Williams observes in *Culture*: 'Writing ... is wholly dependent on forms of specialized training, not only ... for producers but also, and crucially, for receivers'.[101] Derrida has charged the Western philosophical tradition with adherence to a falsely 'logocentric' notion of language as 'voice' and of writing as the expression of speech, insisting to the contrary that the true nature of language is more clearly revealed in writing than in speech.[102] Derrida's critique of logocentrism runs interestingly parallel to Williams's own critique of 'expressivism'.[103] But where Derrida, the prophet of *différance*, chooses to privilege writing over speech, it is Williams ironically enough who proves able to register this distinction between speech and writing, word and notation, as quite simply difference. For Williams, moreover, though writing is not speech and notation not expression, expression is nonetheless not thereby excluded from a 'fully social' theory of literature: 'the notations are relationships, expressed, offered, tested, and amended in a whole social process, in which device, expression, and the substance of expression are in the end inseparable'.[104]

Central to Williams's understanding of what any such fully social theory of literature might be is the concept of form. In *Marxism and Literature* Williams argues for the theoretical superiority of notions of form over mere 'genre-

---

98   Williams 1977, p. 168.
99   Williams 1977, p. 169.
100   Williams 1977, pp. 146, 170.
101   Williams 1981, p. 93.
102   Derrida 1973, p. 92; Derrida 1982, p. 316.
103   Williams 1977, p. 165.
104   Williams 1977, p. 172.

classification'.[105] For Williams the problem of form is: firstly, that of the historically variable relations between social modes and individual projects; and secondly, that of the specifiable material practices within which those relations are enacted.[106] Form, then, is not so much a matter of classification as of social relationship: 'it is ... a social process which ... becomes a social product. Forms are ... the common property ... of writers and audiences or readers, before any communicative composition can occur'.[107] Here Williams's argument is primarily theoretical in character. In *Culture*, however, such theorisation is supplemented by a fairly lengthy and nuanced socio-formal analysis of the history of drama and by an attempt to distinguish three different 'levels of form' denoted respectively as 'modes', 'levels' and 'types'. Williams reserves the term 'mode' for those very general conventions at the deepest level of form, for example the dramatic, the lyrical, and the narrative, which, though socially and historically created, nonetheless persist through very different social orders.[108] He rehabilitates the term 'genre' to refer to that level of form which, though certainly enduring, has some definite dependence on epochal change between social orders, for example the genres of tragedy or comedy within the dramatic mode or of epic and romance within the narrative.[109] Finally, he defines as 'types' those effective general forms which in their characteristic distributions of interest are typical only of a particular social order as, for example, in the case of bourgeois drama or the realist novel.[110] At each of these levels form is, of course, by definition reproducible; and for Williams as for Althusser culture is thereby necessarily reproductive.[111] But for Williams culture is also necessarily productive: 'social orders and cultural orders must be seen as being actively made ... unless there is ... production and innovation, most orders are at risk'.[112] And at their furthest reach, as we have seen, such innovations in form will signify what is for Williams perhaps the most important of all cultural possibilities, that of an emergent structure of feeling.

What for Leavis had been a 'Literature', a canon of exemplary creative works expressive of a national tradition, and what for Marxism had been an ideological superstructure of the economic system, becomes in Williams's cultural

---

105   Williams 1977, pp. 185–6.
106   Williams 1977, p. 187.
107   Williams 1977, pp. 187–8.
108   Williams 1977, p. 194.
109   Williams 1977, p. 195.
110   Williams 1977, p. 196.
111   Williams 1977, p. 184.
112   Williams 1977, p. 201.

materialism a distinctive subset of socially specific, materially determinate, forms and practices. It is only a subset because the category 'Literature' denotes for Williams only a particular, socially valorised selection from the whole body of socially available writing, and writing in turn only one amongst many forms of cultural practice. Bereft of canon and national tradition alike, the obvious question arises as to what will become of authorship, in Leavisism the ultimate guarantee in principle at least of the authoritative meaning of the literary work. In its own assault on literary humanism, French structuralism had prosecuted a vigorous campaign against the notion of authorship. Such 'decentring' of the author is very obviously anticipated in Williams's own chapter on 'The Social History of English Writers' in *The Long Revolution*.[113] And in *Marxism and Literature* Williams readily concedes the problematic status of the figure of the author.[114] But for Williams authorship cannot be reduced to an effect either of textuality or of the institutionalised processing of texts. Rather, the central question remains, much as argued by Goldmann, that of the dynamic interrelationship between social formation, individual development and cultural creation: 'Taken together', he concludes, 'these ... allow a fully constitutive definition of authorship'.[115] For Williams, then, the author as writer, though not as authoritative source or origin, remains if not central then at least not yet radically decentred. It is too easy to dismiss this as residual humanism: what matters here is Williams's refusal to reduce the moment of literary production to that of consumption. Where Barthes inaugurates the French section of what would later become, in Terry Eagleton's rather nice joke, the 'Readers' Liberation Movement',[116] Williams continues to hold firmly to the irreducibility of authorship and readership either to each other or to an amorphous 'textuality' and to the necessarily material sociality of each, both in themselves and in relation to each other. 'In this at once social and historical perspective', he writes, 'the abstract figure of "the author" is ... returned to these varying *and in principle variable* situations, relationships, and responses'.[117]

In *Marxism and Literature* Williams had pointed with approval to Marx's own distinction between production in general, that is, the human historical process by which we produce ourselves and our societies; and capitalist

---

113   Williams 1965, pp. 254–70.
114   Williams 1977, p. 192.
115   Williams 1977, p. 197.
116   Eagleton 1986, p. 181.
117   Williams 1977, p. 198.

production, that is, commodity production on the basis of wage labour and capital.[118] It is the social reality of capitalism itself, Williams insists, which progressively reduces production in general to commodity production in particular; the base/superstructure formula in Marxism merely reproduces and replicates that reduction at the level of theory.[119] He repeats this argument in the *Politics and Letters* interviews with *New Left Review*:

> in the 20th century the exponents of capitalism have been the most insistent theorists of the causal primacy of economic production. If you want to be told that our whole existence is governed by the economy, go to the city pages of the bourgeois press – that is really how they see life.[120]

Elsewhere Williams adds a distinctly 'postmodern' inflection to this sense of the specificities of capitalism. For if capitalism begins by extruding cultural production, as also other forms of non-commodity production, from the economic 'base', it eventually proceeds in the late twentieth century to an effective reincorporation of much of our culture back into that 'base', but on terms very much dictated by the economy. This is the commodity culture of postmodernism, of course. And it is a culture which in Williams's view remains radically unamenable to analysis in terms of any base/superstructure metaphor. For Williams cultural materialism is itself at one level a specific theoretical response to the cultural specificities of postmodern, advanced capitalism: 'cultural theory was not reworked as a critique within a theoretical tradition', he writes, 'but as a response to radical changes in the social relations of cultural process'.[121] At a time when broadcasting and publishing, advertising and the press, had already been transformed into major industries, it had simply become impossible, he continues, 'to see cultural questions as practically separable from political and economic questions, or to posit either second-order or dependent relations between them'.[122]

In the *Politics and Letters* interviews Williams credits Lukács as the original proponent of this view that the priority of the economic is not so much a general feature of human social life as a distinguishing peculiarity of capitalism. But there are more obvious sources much closer to hand surely in that very same culturalist tradition which had first inspired *Culture and Society*. When

---

118 Williams 1977, pp. 90–1.
119 Williams 1977, p. 92.
120 Williams 1979, p. 141.
121 Williams 1980a, p. 245.
122 Ibid.

Williams points – rightly in my view – to the complicity between Marxist theoretical reductionism on the one hand, and the real reductions of bourgeois reality on the other, he echoes something of Leavis's own judgement that Communism aims 'at completing the work of capitalism and its products'.[123] And behind Leavis there stands that whole tradition of Romantic and post-Romantic anti-utilitarianism which we have designated as 'culturalism'. This tradition and its legacy in Williams's own early formulations – of 'structure of feeling', of the 'selective tradition', also in truth of the inadequacies of the base/superstructure thesis – remains much more actively present in the later cultural materialism than is often supposed. Indeed, Turner's judgement on *Marxism and Literature* that Williams 'accepted his place within a Marxist tradition only to disappear into it'[124] is in fact perilously close to the exact opposite of the truth. What disappears in Williams's 'Marxism' is precisely the central but false tenet of virtually all hitherto existing Marxist cultural theory, that of a determining base and a determined superstructure; what appears in its place is a radically novel theoretical position, selectively appropriating both Marxist and culturalist traditions so as to theorise not only its own distinctive subject matter, that is, the socio-semiotic systems of late capitalist society, but also the very conditions of its own theoretical novelty. Insofar as Williams became a Marxist, then, it was only ever as a 'heretic in truth' – to borrow Eagleton's borrowing from Milton – whose return to the fold could only ever ensure that 'the fold will never be the same again'.[125] This is not so much a Marxism, then, as a post-Marxism; not so much a culturalism as a post-culturalism.

3   Post-Culturalism, Poststructuralism and Critical Theory

In *Marxism and Literature* Williams describes cultural materialism as 'a theory of the specificities of material cultural and literary production within historical materialism'.[126] This latter term is Marx's and it therefore comes as little surprise that Williams should here view cultural materialism as 'in my view, a Marxist theory, and indeed … in its specific field' as 'part of what I at least see as the central thinking of Marxism'.[127] We are under no obligation, however, to

---

123   Leavis 1933, p. 172.
124   Turner 1990, p. 68.
125   Eagleton 1989, p. 175.
126   Williams 1977, p. 5.
127   Williams 1977, pp. 5–6.

concur in this judgement. Tony Bennett, for example, has recently sought to establish not only that there is nothing especially Marxist about cutural materialism, but also that other intellectual traditions, most notably feminism and Foucauldian poststructuralism, are actually more properly 'historical materialist' than is Marxism itself.[128] The possibility arises, then, that Williams's cultural materialism might be more readily assimilable to French poststructuralism, most plausibly perhaps to the work of Foucault or Bourdieu, than to any kind of Marxism. Certainly, that scepticism *vis à vis* discourse which seeks to identify the possibilities within discourse that discourse itself seeks to repress is as characteristic of Williams as it is of Foucault and Bourdieu, Derrida and Barthes.

Both Foucault and Bourdieu take much more seriously than does its author Derrida's insistence that deconstruction as distinct from critique should interfere 'with solid structures, "material" institutions, and not only with discourses or signifying representations'.[129] For Foucault institutional and discursive practices, powers and knowledges, are inextricably interconnected and in ways that are necessarily internal to each other. Thus, when he rejects the Marxist base/superstructure model, Foucault does so in terms oddly reminiscent of Williams which stress not simply the autonomy of the 'superstructures', but more importantly their materiality.[130] For Bourdieu too the 'symbolic power' of ideology is not some secondary effect of an economy located elsewhere, but is itself fully material. When Bourdieu rejects the 'crude reductionism' of much Marxism, he does so again in terms oddly reminiscent of Williams by emphasising that ideologies 'owe their structure and their most specific functions to the social conditions of their production and circulation – that is to say, to the functions which they fulfil ... for the specialists competing for the monopoly of the established competence in question'.[131] If cultural materialism reduced to essentials holds simply, in Bennett's phrase, 'that cultural practices should be regarded as forms of material production',[132] then clearly there is much both in Foucault and perhaps even more so in Bourdieu that is in this generic sense 'cultural materialist'.

There are nonetheless very significant differences between Williams's cultural materialism and that of both Foucault and Bourdieu. The contrast with

---

128 Bennett 1990, pp. 13–14, 35–6.
129 Derrida 1987, p. 19.
130 Foucault 1980, p. 118.
131 Bourdieu 1977a, p. 116.
132 Bennett 1990, p. 13.

Foucault is particularly striking. Where Williams persists in seeing a history and an evolution, a long revolution that is in some quite fundamental senses progressive, Foucault detects only difference and rupture. *Discipline and Punish*[133] as much as the earlier, more fully structuralist *Madness and Civilisation* and *The Birth of the Clinic*[134] are each built around binary oppositions between the classical *episteme* of the eighteenth century, on the one hand, and our own modern *episteme*, on the other. These discursive regimes are contrasted with each other as equally systemic, equally valid, equally regulative. There is, then, no progress, only difference, and at times Foucault's remorseless demystification of the pretensions to scientificity of modern psychiatry, medicine and penology appears almost to suggest a preference for eighteenth century 'authenticity'. Where Williams persists in seeing the possibilities for a macropolitics that will continue the long revolution and for a kind of intellectual engagement that will be at worst 'organic' to the working class, at best 'universal', Foucault aspires only to a 'specific' micropolitics.[135] Where Williams persists in seeing human society and culture as the products of human agency, albeit an agency that is often alienated from itself, Foucault's position remains resolutely anti-humanist. The strength of the new sciences of psychoanalysis and structural anthropology, he writes in 1966, is in their ability 'to do without the concept of man ... they dissolve man'.[136] This anti-humanism clearly persists from the earlier archaeology into the middle period genealogy: 'genealogy', he insists, requires 'a form of history which can account for the constitution of knowledges ... without having to make reference to a subject'.[137]

Foucault's historical relativism and his modestly libertarian micropolitics remain connected to this anti-humanism by way not so much of a presence as of an absence: that of an ethics. Where Williams's humanist historiography and humanist epistemology both sustain and are sustained by a humanist ethic, there is no such equivalent in Foucault. This is not to suggest that a practical ethics is necessarily logically incompatible with a theoretical anti-humanism, only that Foucault himself is unable to construct one until the later volumes of *The History of Sexuality* and that, when it does appear, it is a poor, pathetic thing, an aestheticist mythologisation of the phallocratic sexual mores of a bunch of Greek slaveowners.[138] Williams's humanism is not, of course, the 'lib-

---

133 Foucault 1977b.
134 Foucault 1965 and 1973a.
135 Foucault 1980, p. 126.
136 Foucault 1973b, p. 379.
137 Foucault 1980, p. 117.
138 Foucault 1985.

eral humanism' so often derided, and rightly so, by both Althusserian Marxists and poststructuralist feminists for its false universalism. It is, rather, a specifically 'materialist' humanism which acknowledges the differences in our present condition precisely so as to distinguish eradicable inequity from desirable plurality and thereby to proceed not to the abstractly universal, but to a concrete commonality. In a world which becomes progressively more totalised by the pressure of global environmental crisis as much as by the drive toward a 'New World Order', Foucault's refusal of a humanist ethics, as also that in poststructuralism generally, seems closer to an ethic of irresponsibility than to one of self-mastery.

Bourdieu's work is much closer to Williams in tone, purpose and subject matter, and clearly excited the latter's positive admiration. In his 1988 obituary, Nicholas Garnham makes something of a virtue out of the necessity that Williams 'was a man who worked, largely alone with the assistance of his wife, outside the institutional bases of communication studies ... He never received foundation or research council funding for communications research'.[139] That this might have been at best a cruel virtue is suggested by the results of such relatively well funded, collaborative research as has been undertaken by Bourdieu. The obvious instance here is *Distinction*.[140] The points of similarity between Bourdieu and Williams are at some levels readily apparent: a shared sense of the continuing importance of social class to the social structures of advanced capitalism; a shared suspicion of the pretensions to exclusive legitimacy of bourgeois 'high culture'; a shared sympathy for popular cultural aspirations; and a shared assessment of the centrality of culture to the social organisation of contemporary capitalism. Bourdieu's pointed contrast between 'the aesthetic disposition' of legitimate taste which 'presupposes the distance from the world ... which is the basis of bourgeois experience'[141] and 'the popular aesthetic' based on 'the affirmation of continuity between art and life' and 'a deep-rooted demand for participation'[142] both echoes and confirms much of what Williams had argued about modernism, postmodernism and popular culture. At a further and perhaps deeper level there is an interesting parallelism between Williams's theory of determination and Bourdieu's theory of practice. Both attempt to theorise human sociality in terms of the strategic action of individuals within a constraining but nonetheless not determining context of values, a

---

139   Garnham 1988, p. 124.
140   Bourdieu 1984.
141   Bourdieu 1984, p. 54.
142   Bourdieu 1984, p. 32.

'structure of feeling' in Williams, the 'habitus' in Bourdieu.[143] These are understood in each case as simultaneously structured and structuring, as materially produced[144] and interestingly as very often generation-specific.[145]

But there are important differences too. Where Williams insists on the concretely experiential quality of such structures, the equivalent in Bourdieu is much more abstract, a system of durable dispositions rather than a pattern of felt experience. Where Williams works with a model of theory as explicitly critical, Bourdieu affects a quasi-positivistic objectivism. Though *Distinction* is indeed 'a social critique of the judgement of taste', it is much less obviously a critique of the aesthetic disposition itself: here the moment of critique remains partly concealed behind a carefully cultivated mask of scientific 'objectivity'. Where Williams conceives of the intellectual function as critical and of intellectuals as significantly productive of emergent sensibility, Bourdieu detects mainly the dominated fraction of the dominant class, the self-interested traders in cultural capital. There is thus a certain cynical quality to Bourdieu's insistence that 'all practices, including those purporting to be disinterested or gratuitous' can be treated as 'economic practices directed towards the maximizing of material or symbolic profit'.[146] That cynicism leads easily to a radical overestimation of the reproductive powers of the social *status quo*. Hence what Garnham and Williams term the 'functionalist/determinist residue'[147] in Bourdieu's concept of reproduction, a residue that might well prove much more than residual. Though Garnham and Williams resist the description, it does seem to me that Bourdieu's work is best understood in its relation to Durkheimian structural anthropology: the positivistic rendering of the empirical as the externally measurable and observable, the sense of the efficacy of collective representations, even the conception of 'sociology' as embracing what the English speakers still distinguish as 'anthropology', all this is characteristically Durkheimian. Indeed, one might venture the suggestion that Bourdieu stands in much the same relation to French anthropology – dissenting, plebeian, but belonging nonetheless – as had the young Williams to English Literature. It matters, then, and more than Garnham and Williams acknowledge, that insofar as they are visible at all Bourdieu's politics appear essentially relativistic. In Bourdieu as in Foucault the structuralist legacy leads to a systematic derogation of the possibilities for progressive social change,

---

143   Bourdieu 1977a, pp. 72–95.
144   Bourdieu 1977a, p. 72.
145   Bourdieu 1977a, p. 78.
146   Bourdieu 1977a, p. 183.
147   Garnham and Williams 1986, p. 129.

collective action and individual politico-ethical commitment. In both it is the initial structuralist insistence on theoretical anti-humanism rather than any particular consequent theoretical or analytical strategy which proves fundamentally disabling. Durkheim and Saussure have a lot to answer for.

Though Bennett does not in fact say as much, Habermas's work too could be represented as in a significant sense cultural materialist. More sympathetic to Marx than either Foucault or Bourdieu, he interprets the base/superstructure model very similarly to Williams as a historical rather than ontological proposition, 'the mark of a seal that must be broken'.[148] His early theorisation of the bourgeois 'public sphere',[149] as also the later borrowing from Weber of the notion of increasingly autonomous and professionalised cultural spheres as constitutive of a distinctive cultural modernity,[150] both suggest the possibilities for an institutional analysis of culture. Habermas's theoretical affiliations have been to Western Marxism, of course, rather than to structuralism: 'I value being considered a Marxist', he declared, significantly at a time when such assertions had long since ceased to be fashionable in the Western European intelligentsia.[151] More specifically Habermas has affirmed his own indebtedness to 'Lukács, Korsch, Gramsci and the Frankfurt School',[152] that is, to the more expressly humanist and culturalist elements within the Western Marxist legacy. This is a Marxism which learnt much from Weber and from German sociology, most importantly that modern capitalism remains subject to a developmental logic of rationalisation. Both Weber's rationalisation thesis and his elaboration of the different types of rational action are central to Habermas. Indeed, the latter's defence of Enlightenment reason against both French poststructuralism and the darkly pessimistic 'dialectic of Enlightenment' of his own former mentors, Adorno and Horkheimer,[153] can be seen as resuming the earlier meliorist expectations not only of Marx but of Weber. There are obvious parallelisms between Williams and Habermas and these have on occasion been remarked upon.[154] Both subscribe to a kind of radical-democratic anti-capitalism which takes its inspiration partly from Marxism, partly from post-Romantic idealism, in Habermas's case that of Weber, in Williams's that of Leavis. Both are as enthusiastically sympathetic to the postmodern 'new social

---

148   Habermas 1990, p. 16.
149   Habermas 1989.
150   Habermas 1985, p. 9.
151   Habermas 1979a, p. 33.
152   Habermas 1979b, p. 83.
153   Habermas 1987a.
154   Eagleton 1990, pp. 404, 409.

movements'[155] as they are suspicious of postmodern theoretical relativism. For Habermas as for Williams the long revolution continues, but it does so in the peculiar guise of a reason immanent within sociality itself. For Habermas as for Williams the theoretical model of an emancipated culture, deriving from the allegedly constitutive properties of actually existing culture, provides the criteria by which both to critique existing social reality and to elaborate the utopian possibilities for real social change. For Williams the model is that of a truly 'common culture', for Habermas that of unimpeded communication: through the structure of language, he writes, 'autonomy and responsibility are posited for us. Our first sentence expresses unequivocally the intention of universal and unconstrained consensus'.[156] The end result is the theory of communicative action itself.[157]

Habermas's departures from Communist Marxism are at least as radical as those of Williams and in one respect very much more so: for Habermas the old class struggle between capital and labour has been rendered archaic by the emergence of the postwar welfare state on the one hand, the struggles of the new social movements on the other.[158] As empirical propositions about the nature of contemporary social reality these seem to me highly implausible, even when applied to the unusually affluent working class and unusually influential Green movement of the *Bundesrepublik*. Williams's sense of the continuing importance of social class seems much more persuasive. Quite apart from this fundamental political difference, there are differences also of intellectual approach which are partly disciplinary and partly national-cultural in origin. For Williams the concretely experiential remains stubbornly relevant, not so much as the antithesis but as the complement to abstract reason. As Eagleton rightly observes: 'Williams's subtle sense of the complex mediations between such necessarily universal formations as social class, and the lived particularities of place, region, Nature, the body, contrasts tellingly with Habermas's universalist rationalism'.[159] I suspect that for Williams class was as much a matter of lived particularity as of universal formation and that it was at this level as much as at any other that he chose to refuse the false opposition between old and new social movements. Be that as it may, it seems difficult to avoid the conclusion that for Habermas as for Bourdieu the disciplinary claims of

---

155 Habermas 1981.
156 Habermas 1971, p. 314.
157 Habermas 1984 and 1987b.
158 Habermas 1981, p. 33.
159 Eagleton 1990, p. 409.

sociology/anthropology appear to pose a recurrent threat to the claims of particularity. That this is as much the case in the German humanistic tradition as in the French structuralist serves to remind us of the ways in which both cultural studies and Williams's cultural materialism emerged from a distinctively British intellectual environment barely touched by sociology. This may not be quite the burden that it once seemed.

Although Williams and Habermas, Foucault and Bourdieu, do indeed share a certain 'cultural materialism', significant divergences nonetheless also arise between their respective positions and these are explicable at least in part as a consequence of 'inherited' differences between British culturalism, French structuralism and German critical theory. In short, Williams stands in an essentially analogous relation to the culturalist tradition as do Foucault and Bourdieu to the structuralist, Habermas to the (Western) Marxist: his cultural materialism is not so much culturalist nor even left-culturalist, as positively *post-culturalist*. This is so in more than the simply chronological sense. In its discovery that all knowledge is social and all meaning plural, poststructuralism discovered the futility of an earlier structuralist aspiration to scientificity. Practically this led to an emergent preoccupation with reader response, the role of the reader and similar related concepts. Before Williams the culturalist tradition had typically subscribed not to a scientism but to a kind of 'objective idealism' by which truth was judged to inhere in the cultural tradition itself. Williams's own deconstruction of this notion through the idea of the selective tradition effects a relativising turn similar to that of poststructuralism in relation to structuralism. It does so, moreover, by virtue of an appeal to the role of the (collective) reader. It more than gestures in the direction of a recognition of the intrication of power within discourse such as is acknowledged by both Foucault and Bourdieu; and a recognition of the materiality, historicity and social arbitrariness of the linguistic sign similar to that in Foucault and Derrida. And all of this remains coupled to a sense of genuinely free communicative action – a truly common culture – as normative, of which even Habermas might have approved. Little wonder, then, that Terry Eagleton would eventually conclude that 'Williams's work has prefigured and pre-empted the development of parallel left positions by, so to speak, apparently standing still'.[160]

---

160 Eagleton 1984, p. 109.

CHAPTER 15

Cultural Studies and Cultural Hegemony: Comparing Britain and Australia*

Cultural Studies suffers from an endemic lack of historical memory, a characteristic it shares with, and perhaps derives from, the two disciplines most commonly recognised as its intellectual predecessors, sociology and semiology. As the study of texts and institutions, but typically *not* histories, Cultural Studies appears notoriously synchronic in theoretical predisposition. John Stratton and Ien Ang have recently observed that the 'mythic history' of British Cultural Studies proceeds by way of three founding fathers, 'Richard Hoggart, Raymond Williams and, though himself young enough to be a son, Stuart Hall'.[1] For Stratton and Ang such histories are suspect as instances of the '(white) Great Man theory of (colonial, patriarchal) history'. But I confess to an enduring susceptibility to histories, even mythic ones, as unpostmodern as they undoubtedly are. My history would be significantly different, however, from the one Stratton and Ang define in order to disown. A more plausible, albeit less economical, genealogy (in the traditional, non-Foucauldian sense of the term) could begin with Queenie Leavis, proceed to Williams and Hoggart, but also to Edward Thompson, and move on to Hall only at the beginning of episode three. Written thus, the history of British Cultural Studies commences, not with Williams, but rather with the Leavises' appalled fascination for 'mass civilisation' and the 'herd instinct', especially as it registered in Q.D. Leavis's *Fiction and the Reading Public*.[2]

1   Comparing Origins: Nation and Class

What eventually became British Cultural Studies began with the Leavises, then, and evolved thereafter, during the late 1950s and early 1960s, primarily by way of an immanent critique of Leavisite English Literature. English Studies had

---

* This chapter has been published previously in *Arena Journal New Series*, No. 9, pp. 133–55, 1997.
1   Stratton and Ang 1996, p. 368.
2   Leavis 1930; Leavis 1979, p. 151.

occupied a very peculiar place in British life, as the primary location of a public intellectual discourse about the prior history, current condition and future prospects for the moral development of English society as a whole. Hence the Leavisite view of their discipline as 'a centre of consciousness (and conscience) for our civilization'.³ For the Leavises, culture was neither literary, in any narrowly technical sense of the term, nor scientific. Rather, it was 'knowledge of basic human need that is transmitted by ... "cultural tradition"'; and such knowledge is the collaborative creation of a whole community, a 'third realm' neither private nor public. Thus understood, culture was necessarily singular: 'We have no other; there is only one, and there can be no substitute. Those who talk of two and of joining them would present us impressively with the sum of two nothings'.⁴ Ironically, it required the creation of an academic discipline specifically devoted to the study of 'culture' to call into question this unitary sense of the term's meaning. For it was precisely this pluralisation of the concept that was effected in Hoggart's *The Uses of Literacy*, Williams's *Culture and Society* and *The Long Revolution*, and Thompson's *The Making of the English Working Class*. For all their many differences, these shared a common recognition of the significance of class cultures, a recognition that led very immediately to a practical 'deconstruction' of the unitary concept of culture deployed by Leavisite English.⁵ Where English Literature had hitherto focussed attention on one particular kind of culture, 'high' literature, and misrepresented it as the inner truth of all culture, Cultural Studies could henceforth be concerned, in principle at least, with all kinds of culture. Borrowing from Giddens, we might say that Hoggart described and endorsed a form of working-class 'identity', Williams a form of working-class 'conflict consciousness', and Thompson 'revolutionary class consciousness' itself.⁶

---

3 Leavis 1962c, p. 30.
4 Leavis 1972a, pp. 92–3.
5 For Hoggart, the values and practices of working-class life had created a 'class culture' much richer than the 'kind of classless culture' marketed by the mass media (Hoggart 1958, p. 343); for Williams, 'working-class culture' was 'a very remarkable creative achievement' (Williams 1963, p. 313); for Thompson, the 'heroic culture' of the early labour movement had been distinguished by its 'intelligence and moral passion' (Thompson 1963, p. 832).
6 Giddens 1981, pp. 111–13. Given their subsequent political and intellectual development, it might seem strange to describe Williams and Thompson thus: by the late 1970s, the terms would need to be reversed. But in the early 1960s it was Thompson who was the revolutionary. This is very clear from Thompson's critique of Williams's *The Long Revolution* (Thompson 1961).

The significance of Stratton and Ang's truncation of this history is twofold. Rhetorically, it (almost) allows them to misrepresent as 'centred' a discourse that was from its inception disproportionately located at the (British) social margins – women (Q.D. Leavis), colonials (Hall), subordinate nationalities (Williams), working-class men (Hoggart), dissenting Protestants (Thompson). Stratton and Ang work in Australia and, as Hall himself has noted, the 'desire to advance ... by way of ... Oedipal revenge ... is very pronounced in Australian cultural studies'.[7] But there is more to this than simply a desire to legitimate 'a more pluralistic de-centred account of the emergence of cultural studies in different parts of the world'.[8] The omission of Q.D. Leavis and E.P. Thompson – and the consequent reading of Williams's legacy as if through Hall, rather than alongside Thompson – has the further effect of a radical dehistoricising of British Cultural Studies. The point, of course, is that Leavis's *Fiction and the Reading Public* and Thompson's *The Making of the English Working Class* were, in the most conventional of senses, *histories*, that is historiographical narratives, as indeed were both *Culture and Society* and *The Long Revolution*. British Cultural Studies in its pre-Birmingham construction was primarily a discourse about class, the masses, and culture and, moreover, primarily a historical discourse at that.

When Cultural Studies first began to be institutionalised in the British academy, it retained much of this initial focus on class and something of the earlier sense of history. The interest in class was particularly evident in the early work of the Birmingham Centre, especially in the first years of Hall's Directorship. If much of this concerned youth cultures, these were nonetheless typically imagined as class-specific rather than cross-class formations. The paradigmatic instance is provided by the essays collected in *Resistance Through Rituals*.[9] The interest in history persisted in the work of Richard Johnson, but only at the price of a progressive alienation between history as done by Cultural Studies and the more properly Thompsonian history pursued by *History Workshop*.[10] Moreover, both class and history would soon become progressively 'decentred': substantively, by an increasing preoccupation with the effects of other kinds of cultural difference – gender, race, ethnicity, sexuality; theoretically, by the growing influence of poststructuralism and postmodernism. The substantive issue was itself the highly politicised effect of highly political movements, the

---

7   Hall and Chen 1996, p. 398.
8   Stratton and Ang 1996, p. 368.
9   Clarke et al. 1976.
10   Johnson 1979b and 1980.

'new social movements' as Touraine dubbed them.[11] Unlike the labour movement, the 'old' social movement as it was increasingly depicted, these new movements were each explicitly organised around a social category other than class, typically one or another instance of what Weber had meant by 'status', that is, 'every typical component of ... life fate ... determined by a specific, positive or negative, social estimation of *honour*'.[12] A self-consciously politicised discipline, Cultural Studies would always have been predisposed to engage with the new politics of a new movement. But the questions these movements sought to address were also concerned precisely with differences in cultural identity ('honour'), such as seemed peculiarly appropriate to Cultural Studies. Here, then, was a new research agenda for the new discipline, holding out the prospect of almost indefinite extension. The initial response was to 'add on' these differences – of gender and race in particular – to the existing discourse about class. With hindsight, however, this moment of simultaneous engagement with class and gender, class and race, appears both brief in duration and transitional in character. The political demise of British Labour after 1979 seemed to attest to the need for both a cultural theory and a practical politics that would go beyond class. And so British Cultural Studies embraced the new postmodern pluralism, with its characteristic play of differences, thereby opening up the theoretical space within which some at least of the culturally marginalised could assert their own cultural specificities.[13]

Where British Cultural Studies suffers from a certain lack of historical memory, Australian Cultural Studies is positively amnesiac. In Australia, as in England, the prototypical forms of what would eventually become Cultural Studies developed by way of an immanent critique of English Literature. In Australia, as in England, English Studies had justified itself as a discipline primarily in terms of its contribution to the maintenance of a unitary (Greater British imperial) culture. In Australia, however, the initial pluralisation of the concept of culture was effected by way of an appeal to nation rather than class. From at

---

11   Touraine 1981.
12   Weber 1948, p. 187.
13   The results have become familiar, in Cultural Studies and in many of the more traditional humanities disciplines: radical feminism, queer theory, postcolonial theory, black studies, and so on. But in theory, as in practice, some differences are more equal than others. As Stefan Collini has noted, in a discussion directly aimed at Cultural Studies: 'In the frequently incanted quartet of race, class, gender and sexual orientation, there is no doubt that class has been the least fashionable in recent years ... despite the fact that all the evidence suggests that class remains the single most powerful determinant of life-chances' (Collini 1994, p. 3).

least as early as the 1890s, Australian radical nationalisms had sought to relocate the national community and a putative national literary canon away from the past and toward a liberal-democratic or even socialistic future, away from England and toward Australia. Despite the eventual attenuation of the *Bulletin*'s more generalised republican political nationalism, a structural opposition clearly persisted thereafter between the more Anglophile forms of academic literary criticism, on the one hand, and radical nationalist non-academic criticism, on the other.[14] In the 1940s and 1950s, that opposition crystallised around *Meanjin* and around the work of Vance Palmer, Brian Fitzpatrick, Russel Ward and Arthur Phillips.[15] Significantly, none of these were employed then or later as academic teachers of English Literature, although Fitzpatrick and Ward – and later Serle, to continue the genealogy[16] – were in fact historians. Insofar as there was ever a 'totalising discourse' in Australian intellectual life, its site was certainly not literary criticism, as Perry Anderson once argued Leavisite English was for England,[17] but rather the discipline of history. This first approximation to an Australian Cultural Studies was, then, very often the work of historians. And it continued thus with the post-1956 'New Left' – Ian Turner, Stephen Murray-Smith and *Overland*.[18] From anything but the most historically blind of perspectives, it should be apparent that Australian Cultural Studies actually began here, in the columns of *Meanjin* and *Overland*.

But this is not at all what Stratton and Ang have in mind for inclusion in their decentred history of Cultural Studies: for all the commitment to 'questioning Britishness', they are more knowledgeable about Birmingham than about *Meanjin*.[19] As in Australian Cultural Studies more generally – witness the essays collected by Frow and Morris under that title[20] – Stratton and Ang often seem to prefer no history at all to the possible dangers of mythic history. History of this kind – 'real' and mythic alike – is available in Australia, but as 'Australian studies' rather than Australian Cultural Studies. For, just as in

---

14 Hence, the famous exchange during the 1930s between G.H. Cowling, Professor of English at Melbourne, and P.R. Stephensen, a non-academic journalist and critic, over the possibilities for an Australian national culture (Stephensen 1986).
15 Palmer 1963; Fitzpatrick 1956; Ward 1966; Phillips 1950; Phillips 1958.
16 Serle 1973.
17 Anderson 1970, pp. 268–76.
18 Turner 1968; Murray-Smith 1982.
19 For example, Stratton and Ang appear to believe that Phillips coined the phrase 'cultural cringe' eight years later than in fact and somewhere other than in *Meanjin* (Stratton and Ang 1996, p. 390n).
20 Frow and Morris 1993.

Britain Williams's intellectual legacy devolved primarily upon literary 'cultural materialism', Thompson's on 'history from below', so in Australia the equivalent genealogy runs from Turner and Phillips to John McLaren and Chris Wallace-Crabbe. Graeme Turner summarises the difference thus: 'What cultural studies had that Australian studies lacked was theory'.[21] What he means by theory is, of course, 'structuralist and poststructuralist theory',[22] that is, ahistorical, synchronic theory, in either the sociological or semiological mode, but especially the latter. Theory of this kind gained currency in Australia during the mid-1970s. Its subsequent influence can be charted very sketchily by way of a series of institutional landmarks: the 'Foreign Bodies Conference' organised early in 1981; the *Australian Journal of Cultural Studies*, launched in 1983; the second national semiotics conference held in 1984; the inaugural conference of the Cultural Studies Association of Australia at the University of Western Sydney in 1990. There are clearly significant differences between 'semiological' Cultural Studies as it is practised in Britain and in Australia: the more obvious include the extended reliance on 'post-Marxist' thematics at Birmingham; and the project to develop a specifically Foucauldian form of cultural policy studies at Griffith. But what seems more surprising in retrospect is the extent to which British and Australian Cultural Studies proved equally able to consign history and class, humanism and Marxism (and even literature) into the discard tray marked 'modernity'.

'Class' but not 'nation', we should add, for whilst British Cultural Studies seemed ready to move beyond class, its Australian counterpart betrayed very little enthusiasm for the corollary move beyond nation. Quite the contrary, what was on offer in Australia was increasingly a 'peculiarly Australian' semiotics.[23] More explicitly than most writers in Australian Cultural Studies, Graeme Turner has summarised the case for what might well be termed 'semio-nationalism':

> it seems unwise to abandon ... the category of the national as if it were irredeemably tainted ... nationalism is immensely flexible. The terms in which it is currently constructed in Australia may well be established ... but they are not fixed. While nationalism has proved to be a problem ... we don't resolve this by dispensing with the category altogether; nor should we, while we can still contest it and its constitutive discourses.[24]

---

21 Turner 1996, p. 12.
22 Turner 1996, p. 10.
23 Threadgold et al. 1986, p. 11.
24 Turner 1993, p. 154.

In Australia, at least, the nation was still up for grabs. So what had begun as a theoretical argument against humanism, and with it a cosmopolitan argument against the older styles of cultural nationalism, progressively acquired nationalist inflections of its own. But this was an oddly *empty* nationalism, one which affirmed and asserted its Australianness, not out of any loyalty to the particularities and peculiarities of a distinctly Australian national culture, but rather as a means to secure a place of its own, a niche market in fact, in the increasingly globalised business of Anglo-American higher learning. Witness the 'new Australian feminism',[25] for example, a marketing tag that would work much better with overseas than with Australian audiences. This is perhaps at its clearest in the case of Australian 'postcolonial theory', which often seems little more than a fashionable, that is, internationally saleable, theoretical refurbishment of older themes drawn from radical nationalist cultural criticism on the one hand, 'Commonwealth literature' on the other. The theoretical cachet and radical political glamour, which attaches to such 'Third World' theorists as Edward Said, Gayatri Spivak and Homi Bhabha, is thus mobilised, by way of Routledge's international marketing strategies, for no better purpose than to sell Australian criticism of Australian literature to Anglo-American audiences.[26]

2   British Cultural Studies: Appropriating Gramsci

In Britain, the shift toward poststructuralism proceeded briefly by way of Althusserianism, much more extensively by way of a series of very peculiar appropriations of Gramsci. The earlier Althusserian moment requires little by way of explication: few would disagree with Easthope's judgement that British poststructuralism was heavily indebted to Althusserian Marxism.[27] But we should also note the particular significance attached by British Cultural Studies to Althusser's distinction between the economic, the political and the ideological, especially as subsequently inflected in Poulantzas's theory of class. The first step toward what would eventually become a more or less complete unravelling of the notions of class and culture is that taken by Poulantzas, when he insists that 'class determination involves economic, political and ideological class struggle',[28] thereby drawing attention to the political and ideological

---

25   Barrett 1988, p. xxix.
26   Ashcroft et al. 1989; Ashcroft et al. 1995.
27   Easthope 1988, pp. 21–2, 161–4.
28   Poulantzas 1975, p. 16.

constitution of class itself. In 1977 Laclau would draw the plausible inference from Althusserianism that ideological 'elements' can have no necessary class connotation and that, at the concrete level of the social formation, the dominant contradiction is that between the 'people' and the 'power-bloc' rather than between classes.[29] In their later collaborations, Laclau and Mouffe would go further: to argue that, insofar as there is any determinate relation between social position and cultural identity, this can only ever be the effect of the struggle for hegemony itself. 'The logic of hegemony', they conclude, is 'a logic of articulation and contingency', which 'has come to determine the very identity of the hegemonic subjects'.[30] Whilst conceding the 'seminal' character of Laclau and Mouffe's work, Hall also clearly identified its central weakness: for Laclau, 'there is no reason why anything is or isn't potentially articulable with anything ... critique of reductionism has apparently resulted in the notion of society as a totally open discursive field'.[31] Whatever Hall's reservations in this interview – which dates originally from 1986 – his remark seems to describe with uncanny precision more or less exactly the direction subsequently taken by Cultural Studies, both in Britain and in Australia.

What Bennett described as the 'turn to Gramsci'[32] requires slightly more by way of elucidation. Gramsci's *Quaderni del carcere* were written between 1929 and 1935, from a Fascist prison in the most difficult of circumstances, and first appeared in English translation in a very limited selection in 1957, in a much more extensive collection in 1971. The *Quaderni* eventually inspired almost universal admiration on the Western Left: as the editor of the British *New Left Review* observed in 1977, 'no Marxist thinker after the classical epoch is so ... respected in the West'.[33] Nowhere was this admiration more widespread nor more enthusiastic than in British Cultural Studies: Gramsci's concept of hegemony seemed to Williams 'one of the major turning points' in cultural theory;[34] for Hall, it 'played a seminal role in Cultural Studies'.[35] There was always a certain improbability in this choice of the martyred Italian Communist as a source of theoretical inspiration for a mainly Anglophone academic proto-discipline. It is difficult to avoid the suspicion that some of the enthusiasm derived from the notorious opacity of the *Quaderni*, occasioned in the

---

29 Laclau 1977, pp. 99, 108.
30 Laclau and Mouffe 1985, p. 85.
31 Grossberg 1996, pp. 146–7.
32 Bennett 1986.
33 Anderson 1977, p. 5.
34 Williams 1977, p. 108.
35 Hall 1980b, p. 35.

first instance by the necessity to evade the Fascist censorship. As Hall candidly observed of the *Prison Notebooks*: 'What was undoubtedly a limitation from a textual point of view – namely, the fragmentary nature of his writings – was ... a positive advantage'[36] for subsequent theory. That said, Gramsci's work really did seem to suggest the possibility of a mid-way position, somewhere between the 'culturalist' stress on agency and experience, and the structuralist on determination and ideology, where working-class consciousness could be analysed as neither necessarily virtuously heroic nor necessarily hopelessly duped.

Initially, the British reception of Gramsci was refracted through Althusserianism, so that the distinction between civil and political society appeared little more than a prototypical formulation of that between ideological and repressive state apparatuses. But where Althusser theorised his ISAs as structural determinants of the subordinate subject's subordinacy, Gramsci had viewed the creation and maintenance of hegemony as crucially a matter of practical 'intellectual and moral leadership'.[37] As Williams recognised, this was very different from Althusserianism: hegemony, in Gramsci's sense of the term, is 'ideological' in neither the more generally Marxist nor the more specifically Althusserian definition; but rather 'cultural', in 'the strongest sense' of this term, albeit as applying to a culture 'which has to be seen as the lived dominance and subordination of particular classes'.[38] For Gramsci, hegemony was materially produced by the practice of conscious agents and so might be countered by alternative, counter-hegemonic, practices: where ideology as structure is essentially a matter for textual decoding or 'symptomatic reading', hegemony as culture is a matter for political and moral contestation. Hegemony is thus never in principle either uncontested or absolute, but is only ever an unstable equilibrium, ultimately open to challenge by alternative social forces. For Gramsci himself the central problem had been that of the creation of a layer of organic working-class intellectuals capable of leading their class in the battle for counter-hegemony. As he had written in the closing pages of *The Modern Prince*: 'one has to ... stimulate the formation of homogeneous, compact social blocs, which will give birth to their own intellectuals, ... their own vanguard – who in turn will react upon those blocs in order to develop them'.[39] This is a recognisably pseudo-Leninist formulation, but with two characteristically

---

36   Hall 1991, p. 8.
37   Gramsci 1971, p. 57.
38   Williams 1977, p. 110.
39   Gramsci 1971, p. 205.

Gramscian inflections: firstly, the stress on pedagogy as distinct from organisation ('to develop them'); and secondly, the much more 'organic' conception of the relationship between party and class (the vanguard is 'their own').

The latter question bears directly on the matter of Gramsci's subsequent impact both on British Cultural Studies and on the British Left. For, insofar as the relationship between intellectuals and the social movements for which they claim to speak is indeed organic, then it becomes possible to imagine that relationship as requiring no party-political mediation of the kind prescribed by both Lenin and Gramsci. Stripped of its close identification with expressly Communist organisational forms, this was a model which could speak powerfully to left-wing intellectuals, especially to those working in Cultural Studies, whose business was in any case the academic study of 'hegemony'. As Hall later recalled of the Birmingham Centre during the 1970s: 'we were trying to find an institutional practice that might produce an organic intellectual ... We were organic intellectuals without any organic point of reference ... with a nostalgia or will or hope ... that at some point we would be prepared in intellectual work for that kind of relationship, if such a conjuncture ever appeared'.[40] There is a certain disingenuousness to this formulation, nonetheless, for whatever else Hall's Centre had aspired to, it was certainly not to an institutionally organic relationship with either the existing working class or the existing labour movement[41] (ironically, this remains a much more accurate description of the early Frankfurt School). In a strange caricature of the vanguardist pretensions of would-be Leninists, the would-be Gramscians were ready to 'organise and lead' only the ideal proletariat that never was, in Hall's phrase 'the emerging historical movement' that couldn't be found.[42] And even if Hall himself might have been prepared to 'simulate such a relationship in its absence', the more general tendency was to give up on the working class altogether. If the Centre's graduates were to become organic intellectuals, then it would only ever be as organic to one or another of the 'new social movements': Marxist-feminists applied Gramsci to gender relations; Hall argued for Gramsci's relevance to the study of race and ethnicity.[43] For such purposes, only a radically rewritten Gramscianism could suffice, such as neither Gramsci himself nor even Williams would

---

40 Hall 1992, p. 281.
41 At the height of the 1984–5 miners' strike, when substantial sections of the existing working class were locked in bitter dispute with the Tory Government, Hall seriously argued that the Greater London Council had 'become the most important front in the struggle against Thatcherism' (Hall 1984, p. 37).
42 Hall 1992, p. 281.
43 Hall 1986.

have been able to recognise as such. Hence, Hall's eventual view of Gramsci as anticipating 'many of the actual advances in theorizing' brought about by 'structuralism, discourse and linguistic theory or psychoanalysis'.[44]

3 Comparing Hegemonies: Thatcherism and Laborism

The socio-political context in which British Cultural Studies turned to Gramsci was, of course, that of 'Thatcherism'. During the 1980s and 1990s, the Conservative Party won four successive general elections and presided over a substantial restructuring, both of the British economy toward privatisation and away from socialisation, and of the British state toward neo-liberalism and away from social-democratic corporatism. For much of this period, Hall himself and many of his colleagues were radically preoccupied with the problems of how to analyse the particularities and peculiarities of Thatcherism. In 1978, the Birmingham Centre had attempted a Cultural Studies account of 'mugging' and related phenomena conventionally deemed political, sociological or criminological.[45] From 1979 on, this was extended into a much more theoretically ambitious analysis of the more general and more expressly political phenomenon of Thatcherite Toryism. The issues at stake were claimed for Cultural Studies insofar as they pertained to the social construction of consent: 'What is particularly significant for our purposes', wrote Hall, 'is Thatcherism's capacity to become popular, especially among those sectors of society whose interests it cannot possibly be said to represent in any conventional sense of the term'.[46] The analysis commenced from the assumption that Thatcherism was substantially different from earlier forms of Conservatism and that this difference centred on the particular ways in which hegemony was established and maintained. The matter at issue, Hall explained, is the 'move toward "authoritarian populism" – an exceptional form of the capitalist state which ... has been able to construct around itself an active popular consent'.[47] The approach was strongly influenced by Laclau and Mouffe: hence, Hall's central contention that such popular consent had been secured by the effective 'articulation' of Thatcherism with certain key elements in traditional working-class culture. Thatcherite discourse operated directly, he wrote, 'on popular elements in the traditional philosophies and practical ideologies of the *dominated* classes'. This

---

44   Hall 1988, p. 56.
45   Hall et al. 1978.
46   Hall 1988, p. 41.
47   Hall 1983, pp. 22–3.

was possible, he explained, because such elements 'have no intrinsic, necessary or fixed class meaning', and could therefore be recomposed in new ways, so as 'to construct the people into a populist political subject: *with*, not against, the power bloc'.[48]

In subsequent reformulations, the account was modified and augmented by a theory of postmodernism redefined, in peculiarly British terms, as 'New Times'. Here Hall sought to 'disarticulate' the politics of the Anglo-American New Right, on the one hand, economic and cultural postmodernity on the other. 'These changes ... form the necessary shaping context, the material and cultural conditions of existence, for *any* political strategy ...', he wrote:

> Thatcherism represents ... an attempt ... to harness and bend to its political project circumstances ... not of its making, which have a much longer history and trajectory, and which do not necessarily have a 'New Right' political agenda inscribed in them.[49]

In the abstract, there is little to disagree with in any of this. Hall was absolutely right to insist that the British Left could neither revive nor survive if 'wholly cut off from the landscapes of popular pleasures, however contradictory and "commodified"'.[50] But some critical distance, some continuing sense of the 'classed' nature of (even postmodern late) capitalism – such as one clearly does find in Jameson – is surely necessary if the Left is to go on being left. Ultimately, this was what was missing from Australian Laborism, what is missing from Tony Blair's New Labour, and what often seems almost entirely absent from Cultural Studies, in both its British and Australian variants. That said, it is difficult to discount the 'New Times' thesis in its entirety. Whatever the merits of Hall's particular argument – and the analysis was often hotly contested, not least, in its early stages, by the grand old man of Cultural Studies, Raymond Williams himself[51] – it does seem reasonable to suppose that an extended period

---

48   Hall 1983, p. 30.
49   Hall 1989, pp. 116–17.
50   Hall 1989, pp. 128–9.
51   The scale of Conservative electoral victory seemed to Williams much more readily explicable in terms of the peculiar, 'first-past-the-post', British electoral system, than of any successfully Thatcherite ideological mobilisation (Williams 1989a, p. 163). Moreover, he also showed very clearly that pro-Labour loyalties persisted amongst union members, the unemployed, and manual workers and argued that the fall in the Labour vote was as much a consequence of the splits in the Party as of any direct transfer to the Conservatives (Williams 1983, pp. 155–7). However, Williams's objections to the kind of analysis developed by

of political dominance, such as that enjoyed by the British Tories from 1979 to 1997, probably bespeaks something more properly social (and cultural) than the mere accident of electoral good fortune.

The political conjuncture Hall and his co-workers chose to understand as 'New Times' was by no means peculiar to Britain. To the contrary, the 1980s and 1990s witnessed the peculiar combination of a progressively weakening labour movement with progressively strengthening new social movements right across the western world. The novelty of this conjuncture warrants re-emphasis: a quarter of a century ago, the coincidence of a legal and successful Sydney Gay and Lesbian Mardi Gras and a President Mandela in South Africa with apparently ever-widening income differentials throughout the OECD would have seemed inconceivable. This is a pattern that is even more pronounced in Australia than in Britain. British media commentators often tended to characterise the Australian Labor governments of 1983–96 as 'Thatcherite'. In strictly economic-policy terms, there was some substance to this: the Hawke-Keating governments were indeed committed to economic deregulation, privatisation and the supposed virtues of the market more generally. But nonetheless, and all of that not withstanding, the ALP federal governments were very different from the Thatcher-Major administrations. This difference may not have been about economics, but it was certainly about politics nonetheless.

The cement that held the Hawke-Keating project together was Australian nationalism. Much radical commentary on the ALP still often treats it as essentially a failed socialist party, like the German SPD or the British Labour Party. But the ALP has been both more and less than this: a 'post-colonial' nationalist party, its central political project, not the socialisation of the economy, but rather the creation of a unitary, independent Australian nation-state. This project has remained oppositional insofar as – and only insofar as – significant sections of the Australian political and cultural elites retained their own residual attachments to such legacies of Empire as the British monarchy and English Literature. Australian Labor was thus residually oppositional precisely to the extent that its conservative opponents were still residually Anglophile. By the early 1990s, the chickens were beginning to come home to roost: the Liberal premier of Victoria deemed the republic a matter for discussion, whilst erstwhile Shakespeare scholars discussed the semiotics of *Crocodile*

Hall were fundamentally neither empirical nor empiricist: it was simply unthinkable that the working class should prove as susceptible to bourgeois hegemony as Hall appeared to believe.

Dundee. But the eggs were still to be hatched: neither the Windsors nor *The Merry Wives of Windsor* were done for quite yet. The new Labor republicanism, like the new cultural theory, professed an amost entirely *empty* nationalism, much flag-waving but no real 'independence', the political corollary of the ill-starred 'Melba margarine' advertising campaign (which assured Melburnians they were big enough to have their own margarine). This was semio-nationalism, of course, the sign of a nation, unaccompanied by any national referent. Australia had long-since been politically independent from Britain and no constitutional change could make a fully independent state any more independent than it already was. The hopes for an economically independent Australia, which had inspired the ALP throughout much of its earlier history, were quite decisively repudiated by the Hawke-Keating governments in their general enthusiasm for the unfettered workings of the world market. The republic and its prospective new flag (which – appropriately enough – remained undesigned) were to be the signs of a national independence, the reality of which actually became diminished by the day. Indeed, this republic had almost no connection at all with any positive sense of any distinctly Australian nationhood. One of the main pro-republican arguments actually canvassed by the Labor governments was that of the need to 'sell' Australia more effectively in the Asia-Pacific region, as a properly post-colonial, non-European, trading partner. Like Australia's academic cultural theorists, the Labor governments were in search of a niche market.

Australian Cultural Studies has advanced no claim for the relevance of its own distinctive modes of analysis to the explanation of the years of Labor dominance between 1983 to 1996.[52] On first consideration this seems surprising, given that the ALP's success was at least as remarkable as that of the British Tories. During this period, the Labor Party won five successive federal elections and presided over a substantial restructuring of the Australian economy toward deregulation and privatisation, and of the Australian state toward a peculiar combination of nationalist republicanism and the articulation into the political system of new social movement interests such as feminism, environmentalism, gay rights and multiculturalism. If the Menzies years had represented the practical functioning of one particular pattern of hegemony – welfarist, monarchist, racist, patriarchal and homophobic – then the new Labor hegemony, inaugurated in 1972 but only fully functional from 1983, represented as dramatic

---

52   There is a large and growing literature on the ALP in government, but hardly any of it from a Cultural Studies perspective (cf. Beilharz 1994; Frankel 1997; Jaensch 1989; Johnson 1989; Maddox 1989).

a reorganisation of the hegemonic value system as any attempted by the British Thatcherites. Like Thatcherism, Australian Laborism sought to reorder the pattern of cultural hegemony – toward corporatist nationalism rather than authoritarian populism – by constructing the people, as the multicultural nation, into a nationalist political subject, with, not against, the logics of multinational corporate capitalism. And, like Thatcherism, it was remarkably successful. So much so that the Howard Government still finds itself obliged to govern within this new hegemony, rather than against it: witness the ways in which both the Liberal and National political leaderships strove to distance themselves from the overt racism of Pauline Hanson.[53] If Australian Labor and British Tory governments were almost equally 'Thatcherite' in their economic policies, they differed very markedly in the ways in which they sought to articulate the new social movements into this economic rationalism.

In Australia, the Hawke and Keating governments attempted to combine new social movement radicalism and market deregulation through a rhetoric of rationalising efficiency and an expanding institutional network of political incorporation and articulation. To take the paradigmatic instance, equal opportunity legislation almost certainly achieved very little for the majority of working-class women. But it provided real equalities of opportunity for a significant layer of middle-class career women, whilst simultaneously creating a salaried profession of Equal Opportunity officers disproportionately recruited from amongst former feminist activists. The Labor governments of the 1980s and 1990s brought with them very few class-based social reforms of the kind traditionally associated with Laborism. Quite the contrary, their main reforming impetus was inspired by and directed towards the new social movement reformers, and invariably on terms strikingly consonant with the rationality of the market. Frankel's description of Australian Laborism as 'a new blend

---

53   This remains true despite the Coalition government's post-Wik reversal of the ALP's post-Mabo policy. The point, of course, is that the Aboriginal movement is not a new social movement, but rather the latest stage in a protracted struggle as old as the European conquest of Australia. Its central dynamic, to slow down or even reverse the effects of that conquest, is much less obviously compatible with the logics of capitalism than are those of the new social movements. Native title is in some respects analogous to the kind of common law rights once enjoyed by the European peasantry, but later extinguished by bourgeois property. The Liberal Premier of South Australia went so far as to declare that: 'What Pauline Hanson stands for is against the Australian ethos' (*The Australian*, 16 October 1996, p. 3). If this is so, then it is an ethos dating from no earlier than the Whitlam Government's breach with the White Australia policy, and running in flat contradiction to much of the racist commonsense of the Menzies era.

of economic liberalism mixed with conspicuous "yuppie" consumption and cultural liberalism' is very telling, but underestimates the extent to which this cultural 'liberalism' was in fact cultural *radicalism* of a distinctively 'new social movement' variety – which is why it so 'shocked ... the old Rotarian middle class, embattled workers and the traditional Left'.[54] In Britain, by comparison, Thatcherism often managed to combine an apparently 'postmodern' economic rationalism with a distinctly pre-modern antipathy to status-egalitarianisms of the kind advocated by the new social movements. Thus the characteristic 'internal contradiction' of British Toryism, that between the claims of moral conservatism and the demands of the market, its characteristic political vice, that of hypocrisy, and its characteristic political form, that of the sex scandal, were each readily resolvable in Australian Laborism through the resort to multicultural moral relativism.[55] But Australian Labor was unable to resolve its own equally characteristic internal contradiction, that between the solidaristic claims of the union movement and the compulsions of market efficiency. Its characteristic political vice was thus that of obfuscation, its characteristic political form the 'summit' which solved nothing.

Had Australian Cultural Studies been as essentially 'right-wing' a discourse as, say, Leavisite English or neo-classical econonomics, then this Labor hegemony might well have prompted an analysis of 'authoritarian corporatism' akin to Hall's account of authoritarian populism. But these successive Australian Labor victories were as unproblematic for Australian Cultural Studies as their equivalent in Britain would have been for British Cultural Studies. Insofar as Australian Cultural Studies registered the new Labor hegemony, it did so primarily by way of the resort to cultural policy studies, that is, in terms of a willingness to be of service to the new Laborism. Organised institutionally around

---

54   Frankel 1997, p. 18. It also explains the failure of the various attempts to establish a 'left-wing' alternative to the ALP, for example the Rainbow Alliance. Frankel sees this as a consequence of a 'growing depoliticization' (Frankel 1997, p. 30) he leaves largely unexplained. More plausibly, that failure derives from the ALP's real success in articulating the needs and desires of precisely the social class the Alliance sought to mobilise. When defeat finally came for Labor, the intelligentsia, at least, remained loyal.

55   Interestingly, this internal contradiction appears to run *between generations* within the British Conservative Party. A recent survey of 300 young Tory activists and 300 senior members of Tory constituency associations found a very clear 'generation gap': whereas some 60% of the younger Tories favoured legalising prostitution, 48% legalising cannabis, 74% privatising the BBC and 29% privatising the monarchy, the figures for the older respondents were respectively 26%, 10%, 29% and 1% (*The Guardian*, 30 August 1996, p. 6). Presumably, these younger Conservatives would find much less than their older counterparts to object to in contemporary Australian Laborism.

the Institute for Cultural Policy Studies at Griffith, underpinned theoretically by a complex and sophisticated neo-Foucauldianism developed primarily by Ian Hunter and Tony Bennett,[56] cultural policy studies stands in much the same relation to Australian Cultural Studies as Fabian social engineering once did to British empirical sociology. Both make sense only in relation to the prospects for a would-be reforming Labo(u)r Government. As Bennett has it, Cultural Studies should aim to examine 'the truth/power symbiosis which characterises particular regions of social management – with a view not only to undoing that symbiosis but also ... installing a new one in its place'.[57] The enthusiasm with which Bennett, Hunter and their co-workers, notably Stuart Cunningham, prosecuted the 'policy debate' at the founding CSAA conference and immediately thereafter prompted much disquiet, for example from no less a luminary than Meaghan Morris. The 'policy *debate* seems to me to be not a "debate" at all', she complained, 'but a one-sided head-kicking exercise that polarizes its rather small audience ... by violent polemic'.[58] But for all these quasi-aesthetic reservations, Morris herself clearly shared in this more general aspiration to be useful.[59]

4   The Intellectuals, Class Analysis and the New Social Movements

I have argued that the central difference between Australian Laborism and British Thatcherism devolved upon their differential responses to the new social movements. From popular feminist movies to successful gay newspapers, there is no doubting the very real achievements of the new social movements, certainly in the United States and in Australia, but even to some extent in Britain. They have effected a quite unprecedented 'decentring' of traditional (white, straight, male, middle-class) cultural authority. In practice, however, this has been the direct effect of a combination of the hopes and aspirations of the more financially 'empowered' segments of the new social movements with the logics of the market and the commodity aesthetics they enjoin. The new sub-cultures of difference were typically initiated by political movements of an often quasi-socialistic character, but they were sustained only by an effective monetary

---

56   Hunter 1988; Hunter et al. 1991; Bennett 1989; Bennett 1990; Bennett 1992.
57   Bennett 1990, p. 270.
58   Morris 1992, p. 546.
59   Hence, the approving citation of Sneja Gunew as 'an academic who produces specialized cultural criticism for an international audience, engages locally in public debate, and works for national policy outcomes in the field of multiculturalism' (Morris 1992, p. 548).

demand for commodifiable counter-cultural texts. It seems likely, then, that identity politics will eventually be better understood as an effect of, rather than an alternative to, postmodern late capitalism. The resultant redistributions of cultural advantage have unsurprisingly turned out to be a less than equitable process: in the market for gay lifestyles, black consciousness or sisterhood, as in other markets, one only gets what one pays for. In the words of a prominent British gay activist: 'Consumerism is the new gay zeitgeist ... Too bad if you're poor. If you haven't got the lifestyle, you aren't a proper gay ... The gay community is being hijacked by the gay market'.[60] There is no gainsaying either the general accuracy of this observation nor the justifiable sense of outrage it seeks to express. But hijacking cannot be the right word for a process that has been almost entirely endogenous to the new social movements themselves. For most of their short histories, these movements have contained an overwhelming preponderance of intellectually-trained personnel amongst their activists. Typically, they have been organised and led, not by some random sample of those whom they claim to represent, but by professional intellectuals the class position of which has in fact been systematically unrepresentative. These are 'middle-class' movements, as I will provisionally but clumsily designate them. It is barely surprising, then, that they should have become increasingly attracted to individualist and consumerist solutions to discrimination, as distinct from more structural changes.[61]

'Middle-class' is far too a vague a term, however: intellectuals, it seems to me, can plausibly be understood as constituting something like a relatively distinct social class in their own right. Most Marxists have proven stubbornly resistant to this contention, since intellectuals – defined as specialised and professionalised cultural workers employed in the culture industries – clearly share no common relation to any means of production, neither to land nor to capital nor to labour power. Only if knowledge itself has become a means of production in contemporary 'late capitalism', does it then become possible to treat the intelligentsia as something Marx would have recognised as a class, by virtue of their common relation to knowledge. This is Frow's position, as I understand it, in his recent *Cultural Studies and Cultural Value*. He argues that the intelligentsia is not, as Bourdieu had concluded, a dominated part of the bourgeoisie, but rather a new 'knowledge class' dealing in education-generated information.[62] It is 'a more or less coherent class in some respects, but not in others', he insists, a

---

60 Tatchell 1996, p. 13.
61 This argument concerning the radical intelligentsia and the new social movements in Australia is developed in greater detail elsewhere (Burgmann and Milner 1996).
62 Frow 1995, pp. 39–46, 121.

'weakly formed' class because formed around claims to knowledge rather than property, but with a common class interest, nonetheless, in the 'institutions of cultural capital'.[63] This argument seems to me instructive but ultimately unpersuasive, if only because the 'liberal' intelligentsia are much better characterised by an expertise in legitimation than by possession of economically 'productive' knowledge.

I suspect that if we are adequately to theorise the class position of the intelligentsia, we might well have to abandon Marxism altogether and turn to the obviously available alternative, that of Weberian sociology. Weber's account of the social class structure of contemporary capitalism runs closely parallel to Marx's: there are four major classes, Weber observes, the working class, the petty bourgeoisie, the privileged class, and the intelligentsia.[64] Only the latter directly contradicts more conventionally Marxian accounts of advanced capitalism. By the term 'social class', Weber meant a 'plurality of class statuses between which an interchange of individuals on a personal basis or in the course of generations is *readily possible* and typically observable'.[65] If we superimpose Marx's and Weber's respective versions of the social class structure the nett effect appears thus: on the one hand, there are classes such as the bourgeoisie and the proletariat which share both a common relation to the means of production and a regular interchange of individuals between market positions and which thereby constitute, as it were, classes both in themselves and for themselves;[66] on the other, there are classes such as the intelligentsia which share no common relation to the means of production but which nonetheless experience a regular interchange of individuals between market situations, and which thereby constitute classes for themselves, but not, paradoxically, classes in themselves. The intelligentsia thus occupies a position something like the obverse of that Marx attributed to the French peasantry. If this formulation appears clumsy, it succeeds nonetheless in identifying in the intelligentsia a group possessed of a very real sense of collective identity, an identity founded moreover on common material interests, but on material interests that are not those of a shared relation to the means of production. These material interests have been variously theorised: by Parkin, for example, as the outcome of a shared monopoly over the means of certification;[67] by Bourdieu as a function of the rate of exchange between economic and cultural capital within the

---

63   Frow 1995, pp. 121, 125, 130.
64   Weber 1964, p. 427.
65   Weber 1964, p. 424.
66   Marx 1973, p. 239.
67   Parkin 1979, pp. 47–8.

dominant class itself.[68] But, however theorised, the system of higher education seems central to the social functioning of a relatively autonomous, secular intelligentsia: its common class interests and its internal bonds of affiliation each derive from possession of and continuing access to academically legitimated 'culture'.

How do we explain the social role of the intelligentsia and the new social movements in relation to the new patterns of hegemony formed in Britain and Australia? In the first place, we need to acknowledge the quintessentially *postmodern* character of the new social movements. Perhaps the most fundamental of all Jameson's insights is his recognition that postmodernism is in no sense post-capitalist. Quite the contrary:

> late ... capitalism ... constitutes ... the purest form of capital yet to have emerged, a prodigious expansion of capital into hitherto uncommodified areas. This purer capitalism of our own time thus eliminates the enclaves of precapitalist organization it had hitherto tolerated and exploited in a tributary way.[69]

If we understand postmodern late capitalism thus, then we can begin to understand the peculiar place occupied within it by both the intelligentsia and the new social movements: they have each drawn attention to and challenged types of social inequality that, in their most inflexible forms, had become unnecessary and even dysfunctional to contemporary capitalism. As late as the early 1960s, class-based relations of exploitation coexisted alongside apparently equally permanent patterns of essentially *pre-capitalist* social inequality: super-exploitative but inefficient race-based relations of production, in South Africa and elsewhere; near-universal gender relations that systematically under-utilised female paid labour; widespread taboos on homosexuality that imposed severe restrictions on the prospects for its commodification; patterns of generational hierarchy that acted as a persistent depressant on the commercial viability of youth subcultures. In retrospect, we can see that each of these 'enclaves' had already ceased to be functional to the system. Non-market forms of social hierarchy have declined markedly in significance over the past thirty years, thereby opening up the opportunities precisely for 'a prodigious expansion of capital into hitherto uncommodified areas'.

---

68 Bourdieu 1977b, pp. 183–97.
69 Jameson 1991, p. 36.

To borrow a much-quoted phrase from Marx and Engels, much that was once solid – patriarchy, compulsory heterosexuality, 'White Australian' immigration policies – has indeed begun to melt into air.[70] In Britain, the process was effected through civil society itself, with little or no help from the Thatcherite state; in Australia, by contrast, the Labor Party clearly facilitated the articulation of status equality with economic rationality. Hence the different vantage points provided by British and Australian Cultural Studies. Although non-market forms of oppression persist in both countries, contemporary social relations are now in each case much more consistently *capitalistic* than thirty years ago. Thus rationalised, the social order is also very probably more resilient than in the 1960s, and this regenerative process has been significantly facilitated by the politico-cultural interventions of the radical intelligentsia and the new social movements. As Frow and Morris note, in the 'Introduction' to their Australian Cultural Studies *Reader*, Rupert Murdoch's demand that we 'change the culture' is in fact 'strikingly close to one dimension of the way the word is used in contemporary Australian cultural studies'.[71] This coincidence and convergence of interests between the commanders of the commanding heights of the global political economy and the erstwhile critical intelligentsia has become increasingly characteristic of late-capitalist culture. It is surely a less than happy prospect.

70   Marx and Engels 1967, p. 83.
71   Frow and Morris 1993, pp. vii–viii.

CHAPTER 16

Class and Cultural Production: The Intelligentsia as a Social Class*

Bennett, Emmison and Frow's recently published *Accounting for Tastes* might well mark a theoretical turning point in Australian Cultural Studies. Despite its mid-century origins as a discourse overwhelmingly preoccupied with class, the masses and culture, late twentieth-century Cultural Studies became progressively uninterested in the cultural politics of class. This was in part, no doubt, an effect of poststructuralism and postmodernism, in part of empirical concerns with other kinds of cultural difference. But, for whatever reason, social class had become by the last decade of the century 'the least fashionable' of cultural differences, in Collini's phrase, even though still 'the single most powerful determinant of life-chances'.[1] *Accounting for Tastes* threatens to reverse this trend, firstly, by virtue of its theoretical indebtedness to the work of Pierre Bourdieu, secondly by that of its substantive attention to class as one culturally important variable amongst others (those analysed include gender, age and education, but not sexuality). Bourdieu's *Distinction* was an immensely ambitious exercise in theoretically informed empirical social research, combining ethnographic analysis with detailed sociological surveys of the cultural preferences of over 1200 people from three French urban areas.[2] *Accounting for Tastes* is less original theoretically and less rich ethnographically than the French prototype its authors cite as their 'main source of inspiration'.[3] But it is an impressive achievement, nonetheless, almost certainly the most important work of scholarship in Australian Cultural Studies to date. Based on a national survey of the cultural practices and preferences of over 2,750 Australian adults conducted during 1994–5, and on follow-up interviews with 34 respondents during 1996–7, it sets out to provide a 'social cartography', no less, of everything that 'counts' as 'culture': 'home-based leisure activities, fashion, the ownership of cars and electronic equipment, eating habits, friendships, holidays, outdoor activities, gambling, sport, reading, artistic pursuits, watching

---

* This chapter has been published previously in *Arena Journal New Series*, No. 15, pp. 117–37, 2000.
1 Collini 1994, p. 3.
2 Bourdieu 1984, p. 503.
3 Bennett, Emmison and Frow 1999, p. 3.

television, cinema-going, ... the use of libraries, museums and art galleries'.[4] It is, in short, a study of what Bennett, Emmison and Frow term the 'regimes of value' that organise cultural consumption.[5]

Their findings leave us in little doubt that social class matters, even in as self-proclaimedly 'classless' a society as Australia: perhaps not so much as the 'founding fathers' of Cultural Studies, Williams, Thompson and Hoggart, once imagined; but a great deal more, nonetheless, than Lyotard, Baudrillard and postmodernism have tended to allow.[6] In Cultural Studies, as in sociology, many of the more enthusiastically theoreticist critics of 'class analysis' have been disillusioned erstwhile New Leftists, whose engagement in the debates over class was often entangled with other largely political debates about Soviet Communism. Bennett, Emmison and Frow nicely sidestep such diversion by deriving their models eclectically and pragmatically from what they identify as the three main theoretical sources currently available: Bourdieu himself; the American neo-Marxist, Erik Olin Wright; and the British neo-Weberian sociologist, John H. Goldthorpe.[7] Bourdieu's work has been widely influential in Anglophone Cultural Studies,[8] precisely because of its commitment to specifically cultural levels of analysis.[9] But it has also retained a distinctive analytical focus on social class, even when engaged with issues such as ethnicity and gender.[10] Wright and Goldthorpe have been less influential on Cultural Studies, but more so in sociology. Wright developed an early theory of 'contradictory class locations', which identified six main classes, and a later theory of exploitation, which identifies twelve.[11] Goldthorpe designed the so-called 'Hope-Goldthorpe occupational scale' and later still the 'Goldthorpe class schema', the first version of which identified seven main social classes, the latest eleven.[12] Both make use of elaborate statistical techniques to analyse very expensively collected and

---

4   Bennett, Emmison and Frow 1999, pp. 1–2.
5   Bennett, Emmison and Frow 1999, pp. 103–4.
6   So Bennett, Emmison and Frow replicate the findings of much mainstream empirical sociology: 'an overwhelming majority of our sample (89%) agreed that there was a class structure in Australia. Sixty-eight percent were able to place themselves in a class without hesitation, and of the remaining 32 per cent, a further 29 per cent were able to do so when prompted' (Bennett, Emmison and Frow 1999, p. 22).
7   Bennett, Emmison and Frow 1999, pp. 17–18.
8   Cf. Garnham and Williams 1986; Frow 1987; Frow 1995.
9   As Klaus Eder has observed, Bourdieu can best be understood as pushing class analysis 'beyond Marx and Weber' by giving it 'a genuine *culturalist twist*' (Eder 1993, p. 63).
10 Cf. Bourdieu 1993 and 1998.
11 Wright 1979, pp. 55, 84; Wright 1985, p. 195.
12 Goldthorpe and Hope 1974; Goldthorpe 1980, p. 39; Erikson and Goldthorpe 1992, pp. 38–9.

collated, large-scale quantitative data and both have been widely applied internationally. Wright's twenty-year long 'Comparative Class Analysis Project' has involved closely replicated social surveys in fifteen countries.[13] Goldthorpe's schema has been described as 'the most influential measure of social class in use among European sociologists ... developed over a long period of research into class structure and social mobility in Britain and comparatively ... devised, defended and applied with considerable sophistication'.[14]

From Bourdieu, Bennett, Emmison and Frow take the view of culture as constitutive of class position; from Wright, the stress on relationship to the means of production; from Goldthorpe, the significance of status differentials between blue-collar and white-collar and supervisory and non-supervisory occupational roles. The result is a seven-class model comprising respectively: employers, the self-employed, managers, professionals, 'para-professionals', supervisors, sales and clerical workers and manual workers.[15] This model structures and frames the analysis that follows. So, for example, they find the strongest class preference for poetry amongst employers, for crime and mystery amongst managers, for science fiction, supervisors.[16] I have no quarrel with their eclecticism nor with their choice of theoretical resources. I merely note that their class model is much better suited to cultural consumption than it would be to cultural production. Cultural producers, in the sense of the stratum of intellectuals that produces the texts and artefacts which provide Cultural Studies with its subject matter, are dispersed across at least four of Bennett, Emmison and Frow's classes (employers, self-employed, managers and professionals) and possibly a fifth (para-professionals). Clearly, most contemporary intellectuals are indeed 'professionals', in the sense used by *Accounting for Tastes*, that is, as describing a certain type of employee. This is rather different, however, from the everyday sense, which refers to an occupational task – that of the doctor or dentist, for example – rather than to the relations of production it is entailed in. So in everyday usage all medical doctors, whether employers, self-employed, managers or employees, are professionals.

The growth and development of a substantial stratum of white-collar, 'middle-class' employees has indeed been one of the central dynamics in the occupational structure of advanced capitalist societies, its theorisation one of the central theoretical conundrums both for Marxism and for sociology. Cultural producers are increasingly and disproportionately located in this class

---

13   Wright 1994, p. 11.
14   Evans 1996, p. 209.
15   Bennett, Emmison and Frow 1999, pp. 17–20.
16   Bennett, Emmison and Frow 1999, p. 165.

position: in Williams's terms, the dominant relations of cultural production have moved progressively from 'market professional' to 'corporate professional'.[17] If there is an 'intelligentsia' in contemporary society, in the sense of a social class or at least a definable collectivity of 'intellectuals', then it is disproportionately a grouping of this kind. But it is by no means exclusively so. For intellectuals in general, as for medical practitioners in particular, class identity often derives as much from occupational task as from relationship to the means of production. The question I pose here, then, is that of how to theorise the class position of intellectuals. Like Bennett, Emmison and Frow, I will attempt to use Bourdieu, Wright and Goldthorpe, testing each of their models for its respective adequacy to explain the social composition and dynamics of the intelligentsia, considered as a putative class or class fraction.

1   Culturalism: Bourdieu

For Bourdieu, the 'symbolic power' of culture is not some secondary effect of an economy located elsewhere, but is itself fully material. When he rejects the 'crude reductionism' of much Marxism, he does so by emphasising that ideologies 'owe their structure and their most specific functions to the social conditions of their production and circulation – that is to say, to the functions which they fulfil ... for the specialists competing for the monopoly of the established competence in question'.[18] This sense of culture as itself material, and of its practitioners as themselves materialists, finds many an echo in contemporary cultural theory, but for Bourdieu an important source of inspiration is clearly Weber, whom he describes as having opened the way to a 'radical materialism' that will seek out 'the economic determinants' even 'in areas where the ideology of "disinterestedness" prevails', for example art and religion.[19] This is a kind of class analysis that seeks to overcome what Bourdieu perceives to be the 'false opposition' between 'objectivism' and 'subjectivism': in his account, social actors 'are both classified and classifiers, but they classify according to (or depending upon) their position within classifications'.[20] This means that class is neither simply an 'analytical construct' nor simply a 'folk category'. Rather, it exists only to the extent that 'historical agents' are able to trans-

---

17   Williams 1981, pp. 47–54.
18   Bourdieu 1977a, p. 116.
19   Bourdieu 1993a, p. 12.
20   Bourdieu 1987, p. 2.

form the latter into the former 'by the magic of social belief'.²¹ The existence or non-existence of classes is thus itself a major stake in the political struggle: 'through this endless work of representation', he concludes, '... social agents try to impose their vision of the world ... and to define their social identity'.²² As is well known, Bourdieu's key sociological concept is that of 'the habitus', a constraining, but not determining, value context, in relation to which individuals act meaningfully and strategically.²³ The habitus, he explains, is 'an acquired system of generative schemes objectively adjusted to the particular conditions in which it is constituted'.²⁴ For Bourdieu, the dominant and dominated classes are distinguishable from each other, not simply as a matter of economics, but also and primarily as a matter of habitus: 'social class, understood as a system of objective determinations', he insists, 'must be brought into relation ... with the class habitus, the system of dispositions (partially) common to all products of the same structures'.²⁵ If his understanding of class is substantially 'encultured', then the obverse is also true: his understanding of culture is similarly 'enclassed'. 'Position in the classification struggle', he concludes, 'depends on position in the class structure'.²⁶

Even though Bourdieu is insistent on the central importance of social class, he remains relatively uninterested in detailed class maps of the kind developed by Wright and Goldthorpe. If class remains primarily a matter of cultural classification, the value of such 'objectivist' class schema will appear strictly limited. Hence, his amused contempt for a study designed to 'count ... how many *petits bourgeois* there are in France ... to the nearest digit, without even rounding the figures up!'.²⁷ This is not to suggest that he is insensitive to the claims of quantitative analysis. Quite the contrary, the analytical logic of *Distinction* is quite fundamentally empirical in character, designed 'not to propound a theory of social classes', as he would later explain, 'but rather ... to uncover principles of differentiation capable of accounting ... for the largest possible number of observed differences'.²⁸ For Bourdieu, the major social classes are distinguishable according to their 'overall volume of capital' that is, their 'set of actually

---

21   Bourdieu 1987, p. 9.
22   Bourdieu 1987, pp. 10–11.
23   Bourdieu 1977a, pp. 72–95.
24   Bourdieu 1977a, p. 95.
25   Bourdieu 1977a, p. 85.
26   Bourdieu 1984, p. 484.
27   Bourdieu 1990a, p. 50.
28   Bourdieu 1990b, p. 117.

usable resources and powers – economic capital, cultural capital and ... social capital'. Within each of these classes, different class fractions can be identified according to the 'different distributions of their total capital among the different kinds of capital'.[29] The classes thus constructed are 'classes on paper' or 'theoretical classes', he reminds us, rather than 'groups which would exist as such in reality'.

In practice, however, they turn out to be aggregates of occupations: in the extended version, 24 'class fractions' combined into four classes; in the more condensed, 16 fractions combined into three classes.[30] Analysing his sample data by way of the latter version, Bourdieu identified three main 'zones of taste', 'legitimate' 'middle-brow' and 'popular', which correlate respectively with the cultural preferences of the dominant class, the middle classes (les classes moyennes) and the working classes (les classes populaires).[31] Defining the dominant class as that possessed of a high overall volume of capital, whatever its source – whether economic, 'social' or cultural – Bourdieu locates the intellectuals in the dominant class by virtue of their access to the latter. A comparison of the degree of 'closure', or social immobility, displayed by each of the different fractions in the dominant class then leads him to identify three higher-ranking fractions – industrial employers, commercial employers and the professions – and three lower-ranking – engineers, public-sector executives and teachers in higher and secondary education.[32] The dominant class thus includes a dominant fraction, the bourgeoisie proper, which disproportionately controls 'economic capital', and a dominated fraction, the intelligentsia, which disproportionately controls 'cultural capital'.

In his more recent work, Bourdieu has specifically acknowledged the development of a new kind of intelligentsia, a new dominated fraction of '*Bourgeois employees*', a group 'whose development goes hand in hand with the spread of corporate bureaucratization'.[33] Moreover, he specifically argues that this new salaried intelligentsia has been much more effectively integrated into, but also subordinated to, the bourgeoisie than had previous intellectual formations. The dominant class can thus be characterised by a form of 'organic solidarity', he concludes, where the networks of institutions and agents that compose, respectively, the academic, bureaucratic, economic and political fields, together 'protect the interests of the dominants while officially rejecting ...

---

29   Bourdieu 1984, p. 114.
30   Bourdieu 1984, pp. 504, 16–17.
31   Bourdieu 1984, pp. 16–17.
32   Bourdieu 1984, p. 120.
33   Bourdieu 1996a, p. 336.

forms of hereditary transfer'.³⁴ This is a single dominant class, then, united in solidarity by the very fact of its internal divisions. The notion of organic solidarity derives from Durkheim and denotes a complex form of mutual interdependence that 'presumes ... difference'.³⁵ But even if internal differences do indeed make for social solidarity, as Durkheim had argued, they remain differences nonetheless. And when Bourdieu turns to their substance, his dominated fraction becomes increasingly reminiscent of what Wright would term a contradictory class location. 'This is what distinguishes ... engineers, researchers, teachers, etc. ... from members of the professions', Bourdieu writes:

> bourgeois employees, and more generally, those known as *cadres*, are doomed by the ambiguity of their position to a profound ambiguity in their stances. The advantage they enjoy as holders of cultural capital ... moves them closer to the dominant pole of the field of power, ... while the subordinate position of this kind of capital distances them from those who ... have control over the use of their capital.³⁶

The patterns of interdependence between bourgeoisie and intelligentsia betray a similarly contradictory character: on the one hand, the bourgeoisie has become increasingly reliant on academic credentialism as a source of legitimation; on the other, and as its necessary corollary, as its obverse in fact, the bourgeoisie makes increasingly successful attempts to extend its control over the field of cultural production. For Bourdieu, then, the intelligentsia has become at once both more essential and more directly subordinated. Both qualities find expression in the shift from independent self-employment to dependent employment. So Bourdieu reads the changing structure of intellectual establishments and the growing complexity of technology as together propelling the contemporary equivalents of erstwhile independent cultural producers into a salaried dependency that progressively deprives intellectual work of its 'charismatic aura'.³⁷

In an earlier work, John Frow has taken great exception to this conflation of the bourgeoisie and the intelligentsia. In an argument directed at Bourdieu, he insists that professional intellectuals are a separate 'new middle class', a 'knowledge class' dealing in education-generated information, albeit only 'weakly

---

34 Bourdieu 1996a, p. 386.
35 Durkheim 1964, p. 131.
36 Bourdieu 1996a, p. 336.
37 Bourdieu 1996a, pp. 336–7.

formed as a class', because formed around claims to knowledge rather than property.[38] Frow dissents from Bourdieu's account at a peculiarly significant juncture in the latter's more general theory of culture, given the intelligentsia's central role within the processes of cultural production and reproduction. In Frow's own account, both the intellectuals themselves and their characteristically intellectual virtues enjoy a much greater autonomy from the bourgeoisie (and from other classes) than Bourdieu will allow. Indeed, Frow's analytical focus falls increasingly on 'the knowledge class's own interests' and on the need to represent their 'cultural politics ... openly and without embarrassment ... as their politics, not someone else's'.[39] As Frow notes, even Bourdieu is by no means entirely immune to such arguments.[40] To some extent, the disagreement is merely one of terminology: where Frow sees a different class, Bourdieu detects a different fraction of the same class, but both acknowledge the fact of difference. The disagreement becomes one of substance, however, over the question as to whether the bourgeoisie and the intelligentsia share any necessarily common interests. For Bourdieu, the two fractions are bound together by their common and mutually antagonistic rights to capital of one kind or another, and by their common and mutually supportive claims to 'distinction'. Frow takes issue on both counts: economic and cultural capital are neither truly equivalent, he insists, nor reciprocally convertible; intellectual culture is not only a matter of distinction, he argues, but can be both genuinely critical and economically productive as knowledge.[41] Bourdieu therefore conflates what are in fact quite different positions in the relations of production, so that an abstract concept of 'privilege' comes to substitute 'for any more rigorous conception of class'.[42]

It is difficult to dissent from the gist of Frow's critique. Clearly, Bourdieu's account of the class structure of late-capitalist society is far too internally undifferentiated to accommodate adequately the data yielded by his own research. Indeed, his two class (dominated and dominant) and three class (popular, middle and dominant) models are each analytically less complex than those used by Marx and Weber themselves. The attempt to produce a culturalist theory of class remains in itself entirely commendable: the social functions of culture are indeed in part as Bourdieu reads them. But the models he deploys

---

38 Frow 1995, pp. 121, 125.
39 Frow 1995, pp. 165, 169.
40 Frow 1995, pp. 166–7; cf. Bourdieu 1989.
41 Frow 1995, pp. 40, 38, 91–6.
42 Frow 1995, p. 43.

are inadequate to the task he asks them to perform. For a more sophisticated account of the class structure itself, we need to turn to the kinds of class analysis developed by Wright and Goldthorpe.

2 Marxism: Wright

As in most Marxism, Wright understands social classes as groups that share a particular relation to the means of production. His own work was formed in the shadow of Althusserian structuralism and so exhibited a distinctly theoreticist inflection in its initial formulations. Thereafter, however, it has increasingly fallen under the influence of Cohen and Roemer's 'Analytical Marxism'.[43] His sympathies for this self-described 'Non-Bullshit Marxism' date from at least the mid-1980s[44] and have been restated with some force only recently. As he explains, this 'school' is committed to *'conventional scientific norms* in the elaboration of theory and the conduct of research'.[45] For a professional philosopher like Cohen, this might mean little more than a subscription to analytical philosophy *per se*, but for a theorist who defines Marxism as 'the social science of class analysis',[46] these conventional norms are unavoidably close to those of the discipline of sociology. As with Poulantzas, Carchedi and a whole range of post-Althusserian theorists, Wright set out to refurbish the more traditional Marxist class categories so as to account for changes in the class structure, especially as they pertain to the employed middle classes. Despite their relatively unambiguous status as employees, Poulantzas had chosen to define this layer, not as part of the working class, but as a 'new petty bourgeoisie', that is, the twentieth-century equivalent of Marx's self-employed petty bourgeoisie. This was so for reasons that were at once economic, political and ideological: economically, Poulantzas insisted somewhat implausibly that this stratum doesn't actually produce surplus value; politically, that it exercises a supervisory role in relation to the working class (which is sometimes true empirically and sometimes not); and ideologically, that it is separated from the working class by virtue of the distinction between mental and manual labour.[47] As Wright himself noted, the full effect of Poulantzas's insistently Althusserian rigour would be to consign something like 70% of the American workforce to the ranks of

---

43 Cohen 1978; Roemer 1986.
44 Wright 1985, p. 2.
45 Wright 1994, p. 181.
46 Wright 1994, p. 210.
47 Poulantzas 1975, pp. 222–3, 228–9, 233–5.

the petty bourgeoisie.[48] Hence, a whole range of attempts by various post-Poulantzan class theorists to secure a more restricted definition of the new middle class.

These ranged from Carchedi's relatively tight definition of the new middle class as those who perform the global function of capital, without owning the means of production (essentially managers and supervisors); through the Ehrenreichs' 'Professional-Managerial Class'; to Wright's own understanding of the new middle class as a compound of two 'contradictory class locations', occupied by managers and supervisors on the one hand, semi-autonomous credentialled employees on the other.[49] The empirical problem of the new middle class of semi-autonomous employees, the 'embarrassment' of the middle class[50] as he would later term it, was central to Wright's work from its inception. So the theory of contradictory class locations was formulated precisely so as to explain the supposedly anomalous status of 'intermediate strata' other than the classic petty bourgeoisie. Where Poulantzas had redefined class as constituted as much in ideology and politics as in economics, whilst simultaneously insisting on a very tight definition of the working class as the class that produces surplus value, Wright sought both to retain a more conventionally politico-economic definition of class and to sidestep the distinction between productive and unproductive labour. For Wright, class in the sense of a relationship to the means of production could be analysed into three relatively distinct aspects: control, respectively, over the physical means of production, over the labour power of others, and over investment and resource allocation.[51] Whereas the latter is a relation of 'economic ownership' in the full legal sense of the term, the first and second are 'relations of possession', that is, relations of domination, which may or may not be accompanied by formal rights of ownership. Marx's bourgeoisie possessed all three, Wright concluded, the proletariat none, and the classic self-employed petty bourgeoisie the first and third but not the second.[52] In addition, however, a further series of intermediate strata each occupied '*objectively contradictory locations*' between the three main classes.[53] In this initial version, the three major contradictory locations were inhabited by small employers, managers and supervisors, and 'semi-autonomous employ-

---

48 Wright 1979, p. 55.
49 Carchedi 1977, p. 89; Ehrenreich and Enrenreich 1979, p. 12; Wright 1979, p. 63.
50 Wright 1989, p. 3.
51 Wright 1979, p. 73.
52 Wright 1979, pp. 73–4.
53 Wright 1979, p. 61.

ees'.⁵⁴ The latter are located between the petty bourgeoisie and the proletariat, he argued, because: like the proletariat and unlike the petty bourgeoisie, they exercise no real control over the physical means of production or investment and resource allocation; but like the petty bourgeoisie and unlike the proletariat, they exercise control over their own immediate labour-process and not over the labour-power of others.⁵⁵ For Wright, the secret of their contradictory class location thus resided in these relatively autonomous work practices. This is a strange notion for a self-proclaimed Marxist, however, if only because workplace autonomy has been a recurrent feature of skilled working-class occupations and very often a close corollary of successful socialist and trade-union organisation.

Later versions of the theory were reformulated in terms of exploitation rather than domination, but retained the same empirical focus nonetheless. Wright now distinguished three main forms of exploitation, based respectively on ownership of capital assets, control of organizational assets, and possession of skill or credential assets. This led to a twelve class model comprising: three capital-owning classes, the bourgeoisie, small employers and the petty bourgeoisie; three managerial classes, expert managers, semi-credentialled managers and uncredentialled managers; three supervisory classes, expert supervisors, semi-credentialled supervisors and uncredentialled supervisors; and three classes of non-managing employees, expert non-managers, semi-credentialled workers and proletarians.⁵⁶ In all its essential features, this is the model Wright continues to use in his most recent work.⁵⁷ I have grouped the non-owning classes here according to their capacity to exploit organisational assets, but for Wright they can just as easily be represented according to the capacity to exploit skill or credential assets, which would give us three expert classes, three semi-credentialled classes and three uncredentialled classes. On this model, the occupants of middle class contradictory class locations become *'simultaneously* exploiters and exploited'.⁵⁸ Determined to avoid any 'economistic' reading of the salaried intelligentsia as part of the working class, Wright now defined the new middle class as beneficiaries of either 'skill exploitation' or 'organization exploitation'.⁵⁹ Again, the solution seems strangely inappropri-

---

54 Wright 1979, p. 63.
55 Wright 1979, pp. 80–2, 84.
56 Wright 1985, p. 195.
57 Wright 1997, p. 25.
58 Wright 1985, p. 285.
59 Wright 1985, pp. 56–7, 64–98.

ate for a Marxist, the entire procedure resting on the notion of 'rent',[60] surely as 'bourgeois' an ideological construct as ever they come, expressly designed to delegitimise landowning as against capitalist profit-taking, and of little apparent use for much else.

Whatever the merits of Wright's more general theory, his specific handling of the problem of the new middle class seems open to serious question. Indeed, he has himself expressed clear reservations as to the full extent to which experts constitute a separate class in relation to non-experts.[61] More recently, he has also argued that the analysis needs to be supplemented by an account of how class locations are mediated through extra-occupational social relations, such as those of family, and also embedded temporally in different career trajectories.[62] These revisions produce only a marginal amendment to the earlier treatment of managers and supervisors, but a fairly substantial modification to that of professionals and experts. In short, Wright now suggests that the middle-class character of the latter arises, not from any property of the expert job itself, but from the way professional careers develop over time. This has three distinct aspects: a growing capacity to convert increasingly high incomes through savings into capitalist property; a career trajectory that tends towards management; and the increasing availability of opportunities for petty bourgeois self-employment.[63] These arguments have been repeated and rehearsed elsewhere.[64] Yet, for all the apparent rigour, Wright's own doubts as to their adequacy are betrayed by his appeal to the 'standard intuition' that professional employment is nonproletarian. Such intuition is based on the 'lived experience' of inequality, he explains, in which working-class people are 'bossed around' and subjected to 'basic powerlessness'.[65] By comparison, professionals and experts are 'less alienated ... and in this sense ... "middle class"'.[66] Once again, the appeal to experience seems strangely at odds with the general tenor of Wright's own approach and, in any case, it tends to exaggerate the subjective experience of 'alienation', at least as it is lived in sections of the skilled manual working class.

The latest version of Wright's Comparative Class Analysis Project is organised around the exploitation-centred concept of class, modified so as to ac-

---

60   Wright 1985, p. 70.
61   Wright 1985, p. 95.
62   Wright 1989a, pp. 325–31.
63   Wright 1989a, pp. 332–4.
64   Wright 1994, pp. 251–2.
65   Wright 1989a, p. 337.
66   Ibid.

count for temporal and mediated class locations. Marxist though the approach still remains, he now admits the theoretical possibility that 'an eclectic hybrid between Marxist and Weberian class analysis' could see 'exploitation as defining the central cleavages within a class structure and differential market capacities as defining salient *strata within classes*'. One important practical effect of any such synthesis, he speculates, would be to represent the middle class as 'privileged strata within the working class'.[67] Returning to this question in his own concluding remarks, Wright concedes that the general conceptual framework 'does not achieve the level of comprehensive coherence, either theoretically or empirically, which I had hoped for'.[68] Quite specifically, he identifies two especially anomalous findings in his own data: the fact that authority boundaries appeared persistently more permeable than skill boundaries, despite authority being more fundamental to the capital-labour relation; and the muting of ideological differences in Japan along lines of authority rather than skill. He notes that both could be accounted for by treating authority and skill, not as aspects of class, but as 'the bases for gradational strata within the class of employees'.[69] Although Wright declines to pursue this line of inquiry, it clearly remains available to us as one possible way into the sociology of the intelligentsia. In my view, more plausible solutions to Wright's problem with the class of employed professionals seem likely to arise from a Marxian-Weberian synthesis of exactly this kind.

3   Sociology: Goldthorpe

Goldthorpe happily acknowledges a debt both to Marx and to Weber,[70] but the latter is clearly the more significant. Weber had used the term 'class' to denote a group sharing common life chances which arise from its position 'under the conditions of the commodity or labor markets';[71] and 'social class' to denote an aggregate of immediately contiguous such market positions 'between which an interchange of individuals on a personal basis or in the course of generations is readily possible and typically observable'.[72] For Goldthorpe, class means in the first instance an aggregation of occupational categories, the members of which

---

67   Wright 1997, p. 36.
68   Wright 1997, p. 528.
69   Ibid.
70   Erikson and Goldthorpe 1992, p. 37.
71   Weber 1948, p. 181.
72   Weber 1964, p. 424.

occupy 'typically comparable' market situations (income, economic security, chances for advancement) on the one hand, work situations (place in the system of authority, degree of autonomy in the performance of work-tasks) on the other.[73] The debt to Weber should be obvious. Goldthorpe's original seven-class model comprised: Class I, the higher 'service' class (higher-grade professionals, managers of large businesses, large proprietors); Class II, the 'subaltern' service class (lower-grade professionals, managers of small businesses, supervisors of non-manual employees); Class III, the 'white-collar labour force' (routine non-manual employees); Class IV, the 'petty bourgeoisie' (the self-employed); Class V, the 'aristocracy of labour or "blue-collar" élite' (lower-grade technicians, supervisors of manual workers); Class VI, the skilled manual working class; and Class, VII, the semi- and unskilled manual working class.[74] Later variants distinguished between routine non-manual employees in administration and commerce (IIIa) and personal service workers (IIIb); between small proprietors with employees (IVa), small proprietors without employees (IVb) and farmers, smallholders and fishermen (IVc); and between non-agricultural (VIIa) and agricultural manual workers (VIIb).[75]

These are clearly 'dimensional' categories, with which to locate the position of individuals in relation to a class 'map'. But the purpose of the analysis is by no means merely classificatory. To the contrary, Goldthorpe is insistent that 'social classes' can have a real existence quite apart from their construction within sociological discourse; that these occupational aggregates can in fact acquire both 'demographic' and 'socio-cultural' identity.[76] This is why he defines class, much to the annoyance of many feminist sociologists, not simply as an aggregate of individuals, but as an aggregate of families, the 'heads' of which work in particular occupations.[77] The primary focus for much of his work has been the empirical study of comparative social mobility rates, both over time and internationally. He and his various co-workers regard social mobility as of central sociological importance, both in itself as a measure of liberal 'openness' and by virtue of its substantial 'implications for class formation and class action'.[78] For Goldthorpe, classes are thus at once both analytical categories and social collectivities. As collectivities, they consist in aggregates of individuals and families, who are to varying degrees exposed to the competing claims of class

---

73   Goldthorpe 1980, p. 39.
74   Goldthorpe 1980, pp. 39–42.
75   Goldthorpe 1987, pp. 280, 305.
76   Goldthorpe 1982, pp. 171–2.
77   Goldthorpe 1983, p. 468.
78   Goldthorpe 1987, p. 28.

identity and social mobility: other things being equal, the higher the social mobility rate, the more open the social structure, and hence the more attenuated the forms of class identity. Again, the debt to Weber should be obvious.

By comparison with either Bourdieu or Wright, the problem of the intelligentsia is relatively unimportant for Goldthorpe: merely one class amongst many, he needs it only to fill in the gaps in the overall class map. The treatment accorded intellectuals remains interesting, nonetheless, deriving as it does from Renner's notion of the *Dienstklasse*, or 'service class',[79] as subsequently redeployed by Dahrendorf. The latter had suggested that, from the standpoint of authority and power relations, the middle class is best seen as comprising 'free-floating intellectuals', on the one hand, and a 'service class' of 'those who assist the ruling groups ... a bridge between rulers and ruled', on the other.[80] This service class is employed primarily in bureaucratic hierarchies, he continued, and is thus a stratum preoccupied with its own individual prospects for competitive promotion, rather than with any sense of collective class identity.[81] He added that the older free-floating intelligentsia had increasingly been reorganised into a service class and that there is a sense in which the social system as a whole can be seen as evolving toward a 'service class society'.[82] Whatever the merits of Dahrendorf's general understanding of class as an authority relation, this account of the middle classes seems far too undifferentiated. Moreover, the stress on bureaucratic hierarchy is clearly exaggerated, given that so many of the new professionals work in relatively unhierarchical structures. In retrospect, his expectations as to the emergence of a 'post-capitalist' society dominated by 'bureaucratic conservatism' are also belied by the recommodification of social life, we might almost say 'recapitalisation', that has occurred in the last two decades of the century. Stripped of its more grandiose applications, however, *Dienstklasse* might still serve as the description for a particular type of middle class, one amongst others. This is the sense of the concept developed in Goldthorpe.

Goldthorpe concludes that the persistence of class structure as closure makes for a corresponding persistence in patterns of class formation and identity. He argues that it is possible to detect, at the demographic level, at least two clear instances of class formation in modern Britain, respectively the service class and the working class, and a possible third, the petty bourgeoisie.[83]

---

79 Renner 1953; Renner 1978.
80 Dahrendorf 1964, pp. 225, 248–9.
81 Dahrendorf 1964, pp. 251–2.
82 Dahrendorf 1964, pp. 260–3.
83 Goldthorpe 1987, p. 338.

The service class provides a relatively clear instance of demographic class formation, he insists: despite relatively heterogeneous social origins, it displays 'a high degree of ... intergenerational stability and work-life continuity'.[84] At the socio-cultural level, he concludes that both the service class and the working class display evidence of a strengthening cultural identity, partially offset during the 1980s only by the emergence, from within the working class, of a new underclass of the long-term unemployed and their families.[85] In Goldthorpe's account, then, the 'service class' is one of the more established and stable social collectivities within the wider social structure. Like Dahrendorf, Goldthorpe had borrowed the term from Renner to denote the entire 'class of professional, administrative and managerial employees', thus stipulating a 'basic commonality' of employed-professional and managerial work situations.[86] He argued that managers and experts both require considerable autonomy for the effective exercise of their work roles and that the resultant 'service relationship' is necessarily invested with 'an important measure of *trust*', in return for which these employees are rewarded with a range of privileged employment conditions, notably job security and promotion prospects.[87] This is, in effect, a clear rejection of any analytical distinction between managers and experts, such as that proposed by Wright, even in the original six-class model. When Goldthorpe does distinguish different middle classes, the boundary runs between 'higher' professionals and managers on the one hand, and 'subaltern' professionals and managers on the other.[88] But in Goldthorpe's view there is clear evidence of a developing sense of socio-cultural class identity in the service class.[89] This will not be the 'new radicalism' eagerly anticipated by sixties Marxism, he suggests, nor that feared by conservative 'new class' theorists. Quite the contrary, even middle-class 'trade unionism' seems likely to become 'an attempt to prevent proletarianisation and ... maintain class differentials'.[90] As the service class develops into 'an increasingly important basis of collective action', he predicts, 'it will be seen to constitute a primarily conservative force within modern society, so far at least as the prevailing structure of class inequality is concerned'.[91] The latter qualification seems especially pertinent: if Goldthorpe is right, then

---

84   Goldthorpe 1987, p. 333.
85   Goldthorpe 1987, pp. 341, 344–5.
86   Goldthorpe 1982, pp. 162, 170.
87   Goldthorpe 1982, pp. 167–9.
88   Goldthorpe 1980, pp. 39–40.
89   Goldthorpe 1982, pp. 178–9.
90   Goldthorpe 1982, p. 181.
91   Goldthorpe 1987, p. 341.

there are good reasons to suppose that middle-class radicalism is in principle likely to be directed at almost anything and everything other than class inequality itself.

Interestingly, Goldthorpe firmly rejected Anthony Giddens's attempt at a neo-Weberian rewriting of Poulantzas's theory of the new petty bourgeoisie. Giddens had argued that the 'new middle class' comprised 'workers whose tasks are not primarily "manual", but who are not so clearly involved in any ... identifiable hierarchy, and who, while they may often be connected with the professions, are not of them'.[92] The middle classes were best understood as internally differentiated along two major axes, he obseved, market capacity on the one hand, the division of labour on the other: in relation to the former, the new middle class, like self-employed professionals, possess 'the capacity to offer marketable technical knowledge, recognised and specialised symbolic skills', as distinct from the merely 'general symbolic competence' characteristic of clerical workers;[93] in relation to the latter, they are outside the hierarchy of management, much like skilled manual workers.[94] For Goldthorpe, this stress on the distinction between management and expertise is unimportant, registering merely '*situs* divisions ... *within* the service class'.[95] No doubt, there is good reason to question Giddens's emphasis on scientific and technical knowledge, as distinct from cultural capital more generally, as the key to an account of the new middle class. But the differences between managers and experts in their respective relations to manual labour surely cannot be dismissed so lightly. More seriously, Goldthorpe himself fails to provide any real evidence of convergence between management and experts at that level of social interaction to which a self-proclaimed Weberian might be expected to pay particularly close attention. As Scott points out, Goldthorpe makes no explicit use of mobility data in the construction of his social classes, preferring to rely on 'professional judgement' to identify their boundaries.[96] Now it may well be that there are good technical reasons for this strategy, just as Scott suggests, at least at the level of the overall class structure. In the specific instance of managers and experts, however, it appears peculiarly suspect, if only because of the lack of any external evidence for such interchange.

---

92   Giddens 1981, p. 187.
93   Giddens 1981, p. 186.
94   Giddens 1981, p. 188.
95   Goldthorpe 1982, p. 170.
96   Scott 1994, p. 937.

4 Conclusion

We have surveyed three different accounts of the class position of the intelligentsia, as deployed respectively by Bourdieu, Wright and Goldthorpe. We have seen how Bourdieu's culturalist reading of the intellectuals, as the dominated fraction of a dominant class, assumes a commonality of interests between bourgeoisie and intelligentsia which it singularly fails to demonstrate; and how this arises from a prior insistence on an over-simplified model of class structure. We have seen how Wright's theory of the new petty bourgeoisie of salaried employees, as occupying a contradictory class location between classic petty bourgeoisie and proletariat, succesfully isolates the distinction between management and expertise; but then flounders through a whole series of unsatisfactory revisions, occasioned by a presumed need to reconcile fidelity to Marx, which would ordinarily suggest that non-managerial employees are proletarians, with an intuitive sense that this cannot and must not be so. Finally, we have seen how Goldthorpe's notion of the service class brackets together managers and experts, in a way that belies the general theoretical sophistication of his overall class schema and, like Bourdieu, in effect assumes what actually has to be demonstrated, that is, the commonality of class identity and interests between intelligentsia and management. Strangely enough, Wright insists on a distinction between intellectuals and workers that might be better sustained in a Weberian analytical framework than in a Marxist, Goldthorpe on an identity between managers and experts clearly belied by Weber's own understandings of 'social class' as kind of status group. Conversely, however, there is much to be said for Bourdieu's notion that cultural capital provides the basis for whatever social power intellectuals may possess; much too for the Weberian stress on the importance of social interaction between those with immediately cognate market capacities; much for the Marxist sense of the crucial significance of relations of economic production (which are also necessarily authority relations, as Wright rightly recognised).

How do we begin to reconcile these competing accounts of the class position of cultural producers? We could commence from a recognition that Marx and Marxism, Weber and sociology, each identified real processes at work in class formation, not all of which operate on all social classes. It thus becomes possible to distinguish classes like the bourgeoisie and the proletariat, which share both a common relation to the means of production and a regular interchange of individuals between market positions; and classes like the intelligentsia, which share no common relation to the means of production, but nonetheless experience a regular interchange of individuals between a cluster of cognate market situations. The intelligentsia is indeed a weakly formed class, as Frow has it, but this is so primarily because it shares no common relation to any means of production, not even to knowledge itself as capital. Clearly, all intellectuals possess a common interest in the general market value of cultural capital, as evident most obviously in their collective commitment to the status of academic titles, degrees and diplomas. So radical literary critics and insurgent sociologists are as committed to 'academic standards' as conservative economists, lawyers, doctors and dentists. No matter how sisterly the feminism, how brotherly the black activism, how egalitarian the socialism, credentialled radicals almost invariably insist on the use of their titles, 'Professor', 'Doctor', and so on. This is a tradition that dates back at least to the good Dr Marx. But these degrees and the knowledges and distinction they signify are mobilised in different ways, for different purposes, by different fractions of the intellectual class. Some intellectuals are self-employed petty bourgeois, who will use their credentials to legitimise the services offered for sale by their independent small businesses; others are wage or salary earning proletarians, who will use theirs in the collective bargaining process, as a basis for claims to superior conditions of employment and higher wages; others are managers, that is, occupants of a contradictory class location between capital and labour, who will use their credentials to justify claims to authority over intellectual labour, and hence to managerial salaries; some intellectuals are even able to transform their cultural capital into economic capital to the extent that they become capitalists, credentialled employers of credentialled employees. Elsewhere, I have described the intelligentsia as a class for itself, but not in itself.[97] The formulation is clumsy, no doubt, but sensitises us to the fact that intellectuals possess a real sense of collective identity, founded on common material interests, which are nonetheless not those of a shared relation to the means of production.

These interests have been theorised by Bourdieu as a function of the rate of exchange between economic and cultural capitals within a single dominant class.[98] Frow too stresses the central importance of definable class interests in the 'institutions of cultural capital'.[99] But whereas, for Bourdieu, cultural capital had been almost entirely a matter of distinction and of the 'symbolic domination exerted by or in the name of culture',[100] for Frow, it becomes primarily a matter of knowledge 'as a central productive force'.[101] This latter move seems

---

97 Milner 1996, p. 185.
98 Bourdieu 1977a, pp. 183–97.
99 Frow 1995, p. 130.
100 Bourdieu 1984, p. 511.
101 Frow 1995, p. 91.

slightly suspect, if only because the surplus-generating qualities of deconstruction are by no means apparent, not even to the initiate. It is clear that certain knowledges are indeed economically productive, in much the fashion Frow suggests, but that others are not. Later, however, he concedes that what is really at issue is 'the *claim* to knowledge rather than its actual possession'.[102] This suggests a more interesting line of inquiry, which Frow registered but declined to pursue, that of the significance of credentialism. Bourdieu has argued that such 'state magic'[103] is becoming increasingly important to the mechanisms by which the entire bourgeoisie, not only the intelligentsia, legitimates itself. Indeed, he very nearly suggests that credentialism has superseded the more 'effortless' forms of distinction which once legitimated bourgeois dominance. Doubtless, there is some substance to this argument, especially as applied to the French bourgeoisie, perhaps also the American, but it seems less applicable elsewhere. By contrast, it is clear that the intellectual class, as distinct from the bourgeoisie proper, is almost invariably credentialled, so that credentialism *per se* can more plausibly be read as a specific attribute of modern (and postmodern) intelligentsias than of bourgeois distinction in general.

I would guess that the social power of the intelligentsia is more obviously grounded in credentialism than in either cultural distinction or economic productivity. But however we theorise cultural capital – whether as distinction, knowledge or accreditation – it is clear that the universities have been of fundamental importance to the establishment and maintenance of a relatively autonomous intelligentsia: its common class interests and internal bonds of affiliation each derive from possession of and continuing access to academically legitimated 'culture'. This is true even of intellectual professions possessed of no formal educational prerequisites, writers for example. The emergence of a distinct intellectual class, we may then hypothesise, remains crucially dependent on the prior expansion of higher education. It follows that in Marx's time the intelligentsia almost certainly did not constitute a separate social class, not even as defined by Weber. And it was only in the twentieth century that the central processes of class formation finally occurred, and then mainly in the advanced capitalist societies. As the class has formed and developed, it has progressively acquired common class interests, not only in the legitimacy of credentialism itself, but also in the struggle to delegitimise alternative claims to authority running directly contrary to its own. Typically these have proven to be, not those of property, as many conservatives had once feared, but

---

102   Frow 1995, p. 117.
103   Bourdieu 1996a, p. 376.

rather those of (white) race, (dominant) ethnicity, (male) gender and (hetero) sexuality. Whilst inequality in the distribution of property appears compatible with credentialism, which itself denotes a kind of intellectual property, the logic of intellectual class interest tends to require that equivalent certificates be accorded equal treatment, whether these are obtained by black people or Jews, women or homosexuals. As Frow observes, the intelligentsia has 'real, though ambivalent, class interests in the implementation of modernity'.[104] In practice, moreover, those interests have been commonly associated with what Frow terms the intelligentsia's capacity to speak (uneasily) 'for' others.[105] It is this very specifically conditioned 'progressive potential', we may conclude, which both informs and inhibits the kinds of radicalism normally available to the intelligentsia.

---

104 Frow 1995, p. 165.
105 Frow 1995, p. 164.

CHAPTER 17

Left Out? Marxism, the New Left and Cultural Studies*

The spectre that haunted Europe in 1848 seems to have been exorcised, at least for the moment, at least from the eastern half of the continent. But its theoretical counterpart – Marxism as distinct from communism – still haunts the crossroads of international Cultural Studies, a ghostly Laius to the latter's Oedipus. Thirty years ago it would have been merely truistic to call attention to the Marxian origins of the new proto-discipline. But those origins have been progressively occluded in most subsequent histories, especially those centred on categories like 'culturalism', 'structuralism' and 'poststructuralism', which powerfully inform both the collective wisdom and the pedagogical strategies of the (proto-) discipline. To speak of Cultural Studies, as I have, as a 'proto-discipline' or 'discipline', is to beg the question, however, as to what exactly we mean by Cultural Studies. Let us begin at the end, then, with the third term in my title, with Oedipus rather than Laius, that is, with a preliminary account of the various self-definitions encoded in the recent history of Cultural Studies.

1   Oedipus: Four Versions of Cultural Studies

Cultural Studies is, of course, an unusually polysemic sign. Its various senses tend to cluster, nonetheless, around four main meanings: as an interdiscipline; as a political intervention into the existing disciplines; as an entirely new discipline, defined in terms of an entirely new subject matter; or finally as a new discipline, defined in terms of a new theoretical paradigm. No doubt, other available definitions remain in play, but these four seem especially prominent. The first was clearly that intended by Hoggart in the initial proposal to establish a Centre for Contemporary Cultural Studies at Birmingham. Here Cultural Studies was understood as an interdisciplinary postgraduate research field, which would recruit from amongst people already trained in 'the social

---

* This chapter has been published previously in *Arena Journal New Series*, No. 19, pp. 85–98, 2002.

sciences, history, psychology, anthropology, literary study'.[1] For Hoggart, then, Cultural Studies was – and still should be – a 'field of study', rather than a discipline: 'the student should have an initial discipline outside Cultural Studies', he has written, 'an academic and intellectual training, and a severe one'.[2] There is a clear echo here of F.R. Leavis's earlier conception of an English School requiring its students 'to come to fairly close terms ... with ... other disciplines'.[3] For Hoggart, the enterprise was to be much more fully interdisciplinary than for Leavis, although literature would still be its single 'most important' element.[4] The second conception, that of Cultural Studies as a kind of political intervention, is more readily associated with Hall, Hoggart's immediate successor as Director of the Birmingham Centre. For Hall, the 'seriousness' of Cultural Studies was inscribed in its 'political' aspect: 'there is something *at stake* in cultural studies', he has insisted, 'in a way that ... is not exactly true of many other ... intellectual ... practices'.[5] Similarly 'political' conceptions recur throughout the Cultural Studies literature, even in the 'Introduction' to Simon During's widely used textbook reader, where 'engaged forms of analysis' are described as one of the discipline's two distinguishing features.[6]

A third conception of Cultural Studies sees the subject as a new discipline defined in terms of a new subject matter, that is, as the study of popular culture. Shorn of pretension to both interdisciplinarity and political relevance, this is perhaps the most 'modest' of the four meanings and the most readily compatible with existing disciplinary structures. There can be no doubt that Cultural Studies emerged in part by way of a quasi-populist reaction against the cultural elitism of older forms of literary study: all three of the discipline's widely acknowledged 'founding fathers', Hoggart, Thompson and Williams, were committed to the study of popular or working-class culture. However, none of these had imagined Cultural Studies as coextensive with the study of the 'popular arts'. But in the subsequent history of the Birmingham Centre itself and of Cultural Studies more generally, it has often appeared as such. Hence the growing sense of Cultural Studies as a sociology or ethnography of mass media consumption, nicely symbolised in Hall's appointment to the chair in sociology at the Open University and his subsequent election as President of the British Sociological Association. The development of such sub-specialisms as Commu-

---

1 Hoggart 1995, p. 173.
2 Ibid.
3 Leavis 1948, p. 57.
4 Hoggart 1970, p. 255.
5 Hall 1992, p. 278.
6 During 1999, p. 2.

nication and Media Studies is thus an important legacy of this kind of Cultural Studies. We should add, however, that there is an 'immodest Cultural Studies' too, a fourth option defined in terms of a new paradigm, connecting the study of the popular to the study of the 'literary'.[7] In this definition, Cultural Studies represents a shift not so much in empirical subject matter as in theoretical paradigm. This conception was important for Hoggart, but even more especially so for Williams, whose 'empirical' work quite systematically transgressed the boundaries between elite and popular cultures: he was as interested in canonical literature and drama as in television and the press. Hence his insistence that, as concepts, both 'literature' and 'criticism' were 'forms of a class specialization and control of a general social practice, and of a class limitation of the questions ... it might raise'.[8]

This sense of the 'literary' as one element amongst others within the more general processes of 'writing' and 'communication' became characteristic of Williams's later work. But it is present elsewhere too. It informs Easthope's understanding, for example, of the 'double movement' by which 'literary study becomes increasingly indistinguishable from cultural studies' and 'cultural studies makes incursions into the traditionally literary terrain of textuality'.[9] It is present in Bennett's sense of Cultural Studies as fundamentally concerned with 'the relations of culture and power'.[10] If this description is overly Foucauldian (and designed with intention to divert Cultural Studies towards policy studies moreover), it clearly gestures in the same direction as Williams and Easthope, towards what might be termed a 'social-scientific' study of all culture, whether elite or popular, in both its textual and extra-textual aspects. No doubt, there is something to be said for each of these four senses of the term 'Cultural Studies': they each register important aspects of different phases in its theoretical and practical development. But there is a cumulative logic to this development, nonetheless, which suggests that the greater promise lies with the fourth conception: not in the discovery of a new empirical subject matter, but in the deconstruction of the theoretical boundaries that demarcated literature from fiction, art from culture, the elite from the popular; and in the development of new methods for the analysis of both.

Definition is a dangerous business, I know, so let me settle for pastiche. Borrowing from the textbook procedures of the dismal science, let me suggest that we might productively define Cultural Studies as *the social science of the study*

---

7   Milner 1996, pp. 18–26.
8   Williams 1977, p. 49.
9   Easthope 1991, p. 65.
10 Bennett 1998, p. 53.

of the production, distribution, exchange and reception of textualised meaning. I use the term 'social science' here, not in any strongly positivist sense, such as one finds in high structuralist semiology or functionalist sociology, but in the much looser sense of a discipline the primary purposes of which are description and explanation rather than judgement and canonisation. The term 'textualised meaning' denotes a concern with signifying practices in general rather than literature or art or the mass media in particular. Finally, 'production, distribution, exchange and reception' are intended to denote an interest in how texts are produced and received, how they are productive, and with the practices that articulate them and that they articulate, as well as with texts 'in their own right'. Such concerns are necessarily political, of course, since all texts are always produced and received in contexts significantly affected by the structures of social power.

2 Laius: Marxism and Cultural Studies

If this is indeed what we mean by Cultural Studies, then its theoretical novelty, in relation both to humanist literary criticism and to positivist social science, should be apparent. But what were the sources of this novelty? Where exactly did the paradigm shift 'come from'? The name, of course, came from Hoggart, but the more general intellectual framework can plausibly be read as deriving from, or at least significantly anticipated by, three relatively distinct primary sources – respectively, Frankfurt School Critical Theory, Cambridge English, and the French 'structuralist' reworking of Saussurean linguistics into a general semiology – and one important secondary source, through which each of these were refracted, the 'sixties' (which in practice meant seventies) 'New Left', especially as constructed at Birmingham. I want to call attention here to the distinctly (Western) Marxist character of each of the three primary sources. We turn, then, from the substance to the spectre, from Oedipus to Laius.

That the Frankfurt School were broadly 'Marxist' is almost self-evident. For all their undoubted elitism and for all their political antipathy to the German SDS, the School's general theoretical outlook was very obviously Marxist. Adorno might have called in the police to evict the student radicals from his Institut and Habermas did indeed describe them as 'red fascists'.[11] But it is impossible to read *Dialectic of Enlightenment* except in relation to the Marxist tradition. And even Habermas, a much less obviously Marxian thinker than

---

11   Leslie 1999, p. 120; Adorno and Marcuse 1999, p. 128.

Adorno, could still declare as late as 1979 that he valued 'being considered a Marxist'.[12] In any case, it was Marcuse, rather than Adorno, who bore primary responsibility for transmitting the Frankfurt School legacy into the English-speaking world, where what we now know as Cultural Studies first became established. *Dialectic of Enlightenment* remained unavailable in English translation until 1972, whilst *One-Dimensional Man* had become part of the intellectual furniture of the radical sixties.[13] The Marcusean argument was thus simultaneously both more clearly Marxist than that in Adorno and Horkheimer and also much more influential in New Left debates.

Cambridge English in its specifically Leavisite formation is as near to a German or French intellectual 'school' as anything in twentieth-century British intellectual history. In retrospect, it might even warrant acknowledgement as a distinctive 'Cambridge School'. Clearly, neither of the Leavises was in any sense a Marxist, though their anti-utilitarianism ran strangely parallel to certain Marxisms, most obviously that of the Frankfurt School itself. But if we extend the sense of a 'Cambridge School' to include both Williams and the young Eagleton, then the lineage acquires a more properly Marxist character. This extension seems warranted, if only because there is no doubting Williams's debt to Leavis: 'The immense attraction of Leavis lay in his cultural radicalism ...', Williams would explain: 'It was the range of Leavis's attacks on academicism, on Bloomsbury, on metropolitan literary culture, on the commercial press, on advertising, that first took me'.[14] And even Eagleton shared in this. As he explained in a 1985 interview, Cambridge in his undergraduate days 'was ... buzzing with the Leavis argument ... There was a sense in which, by a kind of negative identification, if one was a working-class student reading English one might easily become a Leavisite. The Leavisites were seen both as a victimised minority and as attempting ... to speak in broader critical terms ... during the 1960s, Cambridge remained in many ways the centre ...'.[15] The Cambridge 'tradition' can plausibly be read, then, as leading from the Leavises to Williams and Eagleton, rather than to Hoggart, that is, as progressively acquiring a distinctly Marxist inflection.

A similar inflection informs general semiology. The key figure here was neither Saussure nor Durkheim, neither Lévi-Strauss nor Althusser, but rather Barthes. It was Barthes who initiated the post-Second World War revival of Saussurean semiology with *Mythologies*, which was first published in French

---

12   Habermas 1979a, p. 33.
13   Adorno and Horkheimer 1972; Marcuse 1964.
14   Williams 1979, pp. 65–6.
15   Eagleton 1985, p. 131.

in 1957, though not in English translation until 1973. Barthes was *the* 'French structuralist' of the 1960s, *Mythologies* an enormously influential text on Anglophone Cultural Studies. It was also a much more 'Marxist' text than we typically tend to allow. Its central theoretical argument, that in bourgeois society myth is 'depoliticized speech',[16] clearly rehearses obviously Marxian thematics already available in Sartre and Brecht. Jameson has described *Mythologies* as part of a 'universal crystallization of Marxism among French intellectuals', occasioned in part by the influence of Brecht's 1954 and 1955 *Théâtre des nations* visits to Paris, which included productions of *Mother Courage* and the *Caucasian Chalk Circle* respectively. Jameson's conclusion warrants repetition:

> Barthes's dealings with 'nature' ... represent a creative and explosive wiring together of the Sartrean philosophical polemics and the Brechtian practical and aesthetic estrangements of the same illusion of stasis and the eternal. The Brechtian origin of some of these themes and positions might help us to recover some of their original political content as well.[17]

So Adorno and Habermas, Williams and Eagleton, even the young Barthes, can be read as 'Marxists'. But why should this matter? Let me be clear that I'm not really concerned to demonstrate that 'we' Marxists were 'correct'; nor to complain that 'we' have been given insufficient credit (though I am inclined to think that both statements are more or less true). What interest me, rather, are the ways in which Western Marxism came to constitute something like a 'condition of possibility' for the emergence of Cultural Studies. To put the case as succinctly as possible: in order to be able to imagine a social science of the study of both elite and popular cultures, it was necessary to become relatively 'distanced' from both. And Western Marxists were so distanced, simultaneously opposed both to the elitist complacencies of establishment 'high culture' and to the commercialism of capitalist 'popular culture'. Most conservative, liberal and social-democratic intellectuals were far too closely implicated in the former, many (mostly American) liberals and some (mostly European) social democrats too closely in the latter, to be able to establish the required critical distance. The Leavises shared this dual antipathy, but, as Eagleton hinted, they were unusual in this respect: theirs was a peculiarly eccentric biographical trajectory, unlikely to be replicated elsewhere in the intellectual culture.

---

16   Barthes 1973, p. 142.
17   Jameson 1998, p. 172.

Critical Theory, left Leavisism and general semiology each rehearse all four of our versions of Cultural Studies and they do so, moreover, in much the same cumulative fashion. So Critical Theory defined itself in 'totalistic' opposition to the discrete disciplines of 'traditional theory',[18] but also as a kind of political intervention into the discipline of sociology, in short a 'critical sociology'.[19] Likewise, it defined the 'culture industries' as a crucial part of its subject matter, but also insisted that they be understood only in relation to high culture. Much the same can be said of Barthes and Williams, with linguistics and English Literature respectively substituted for sociology. From the specific standpoint of Cultural Studies, however, Williams's achievement is the greater, for he was able to define more explicitly than either Adorno or Barthes our fourth sense of the project, that of a non-canonising, social-scientific, study of all aspects of the production and reception of all texts, whether elite or popular. By comparison with Hoggart, Williams uses the term Cultural Studies only sparingly, although it is certainly there in his last unfinished book.[20] During the late seventies and early eighties he even seemed to prefer the idea of a 'cultural sociology': at one point he chooses to describe Cultural Studies as 'a branch of general sociology'.[21] But, whatever the term, the project is recognisably that of a Cultural Studies as first mapped out in *The Long Revolution*.

3   Jocasta: The New Left

If Cultural Studies stands in an analogously patricidal relation to Marxism as Oedipus to Laius, then the seventies New Left clearly performs the part of Jocasta: lover by turn to each, haunted by the repressed memory of the earlier, but unable and unwilling to admit either to the incest or to the murder. In the standard histories of the discipline, this repression is commonly effected through the tale of how French 'structuralism' superseded British 'culturalism'.[22] No doubt, there is much truth in all this and it certainly provides teachers in higher and further education with a suitably convenient pedagogical device. Most of these culturalists and structuralists had, however, tended to think of themselves as Marxists, a slight detail almost invariably occluded in accounts centred on categories like 'culturalism' and 'structuralism'. The most famous of

---

18   Horkheimer 1972.
19   Adorno 1976.
20   Williams 1989b, pp. 151–62.
21   Williams 1981, p. 14.
22   Johnson 1979a; Turner 1996.

these is still Hall's 'Cultural Studies: Two Paradigms', first published in *Media, Culture and Society* in 1980 and subsequently much republished elsewhere. His representative culturalists were Hoggart, Williams and Thompson; his structuralists Althusser and Lévi-Strauss. Hall's determination to compound Williams and Thompson, both self-declared 'Marxists', with Hoggart, who clearly was not, is one example amongst many of what Paul Jones, after Williams himself, nicely terms 'the myth of "Raymond Hoggart".[23] We should note, however, that Hall worked almost as hard to bracket together Althusser and Lévi-Strauss. This isn't quite 'the myth of Claude Althusser', since Althusser was clearly more of a structuralist than Williams had ever been a culturalist. But the conflation was intended, nonetheless, to remind Hall's readers of Althusserian Marxism's 'immense theoretical debt' to non-Marxist structuralism.[24]

None of this mattered very much until the postmodern eighties, when Marxism went from being *de rigueur* to *passé* in what seemed like the blink of an eye (though we were busy having children at the time and it is possible that I missed something). The earlier Marxist interest in class was suddenly 'decentred' by an increasing preoccupation with the cultural effects of other kinds of cultural difference – gender, race, ethnicity, sexuality; and by the growing influence of poststructuralism and postmodernism. It then became possible for Cultural Studies to rewrite its history as if there were only ever culturalists, structuralists and postmodernists, never any Marxists at all. Possible and perhaps even necessary for former Marxists busily covering their tracks, the cynic in me is tempted to add. In short, the Left was suddenly left out of the history of what had been its 'own' discipline. I am inclined to think, then, that it matters now. So let me repeat: Western Marxism was almost certainly the single most important condition of possibility for the emergence of Cultural Studies.

4   History and Cultural Studies

Those of us who still choose to think of ourselves as 'Marxists' – as distinct from culturalists, structuralists, poststructuralists – are thus confronted with the problem of how to relate to a Cultural Studies that is quite clearly not Marxist. There is a precedent for this situation, not in Cultural Studies itself, but in history, which seems to have been the preferred discipline for Communist Party academics both in Britain and Australia (I cannot speak for the United

23   Jones 1994.
24   Hall 1980a, p. 64.

States). In the story of Cultural Studies, E.P. Thompson normally rates a bit-part as one of the early 'founding fathers', but then tends to leave the stage much earlier than either Williams or Hoggart. As indeed he did. Thompson's 1978 *The Poverty of Theory* was intended as a wholesale attack on much that Cultural Studies then most admired: on Althusser in particular, but also on 'Theory' and 'structuralism' more generally. It was also – and quite deliberately – a performative act of identification with the discipline of history, as distinct from Cultural Studies, sociology, or English (like Hall, Thompson had been trained in the latter).

Here Thompson directly addressed the relationship between history as a discipline and historical materialism as a particular argument in relation to it. He was insistent on two points: that historical evidence has a determinate objectivity, an independent existence quite apart from any significance the historian may accord it;[25] and that there is a common 'historical logic', defined in terms of both theoretical and evidential procedures, to which both Marxist and non-Marxist history must submit. If Marxist concepts are 'found to be more "true", or adequate to explanation, than others', he explained:

> this will be because they stand up better to the test of historical logic, and not because they are 'derived from' a true Theory outside this discipline ... I refuse ... to escape from criticism by leaping from the court of appeal. For historical knowledge, this court lies within the discipline of history and nowhere else ... Appeal may take two forms ... evidential ... and ... theoretical ... But both forms of appeal may be conducted only within the vocabulary of historical logic. The court has been sitting in judgement upon historical materialism for one hundred years, and it is continually being adjourned.[26]

Let me note in passing the interesting homology between how Thompson conceived of his own interventions into the discipline of history and how Popular Front Communism, of which he had once been part, had conceived of its into the labour movement and the peace movement. In both cases, the intervention is judged by how well it stands up to the demands of the discipline/movement.

Whatever his sources, however, Thompson was surely right, at least in principle, and Althusserian theoreticism surely equally mistaken. Which poses the

---

25   Thompson 1978a, pp. 231–5.
26   Thompson 1978a, pp. 236–7.

interesting question as to why the Thompsonian option wasn't available to Williams, in many respects the more politically 'moderate' figure. At one level the answer is obvious: Cultural Studies wasn't yet a discipline. The only equivalent to Thompson's history would thus have been 'English Literature', an essentially hostile formation, which could only ever have been a kangaroo court. As Williams himself explained:

> The reason my attack was ... so radical was that I had decided, from within the tradition of literary criticism itself, that its categories of literature and of criticism were so deeply compromised that they had to be challenged *in toto*.[27]

But that was then and this is now; and in the interim Cultural Studies has indeed finally begun to emerge as something approximating a conventional academic discipline.

5   Cultural Materialism

If Williams had helped to create Cultural Studies – and he more or less defined the field, just as it says in the standard accounts – then he had also begun to define a particular position roughly analogous to Thompson's historical materialism, one position amongst others within Cultural Studies, for which he coined the term 'cultural materialism'. Williams had first used the phrase in a short essay published in the hundredth issue of the *New Left Review*, where he explained that cultural materialism:

> is a theory of culture as a (social and material) productive process and of specific practices, of 'arts', as social uses of material means of production (from language as material 'practical consciousness' to the specific technologies of writing and forms of writing, through to mechanical and electronic communications systems).[28]

As he had promised in this essay, the position was 'spelled out more fully' in *Marxism and Literature* and in the book eventually published as *Culture*.

---

27   Williams 1979, p. 326.
28   Williams 1980a, p. 243.

Moreover, cultural-materialist thematics continued to inform his work right through until the last sadly unfinished book, the posthumously published *The Politics of Modernism*.

Cultural materialism has subsequently become very fashionable, especially in literary studies. Scott Wilson even claims that 'cultural materialism in Britain and New Historicism in America ... now constitute the new academic order, particularly in Renaissance studies'.[29] This is a very large claim indeed, especially when linked to Wilson's later description of the New Historicism as 'American cultural materialism'.[30] But this 'cultural materialism' derives not so much from Williams as from Jonathan Dollimore and Alan Sinfield. Dollimore readily admits to borrowing the term from Williams, but nonetheless describes his own cultural materialism as growing 'from an eclectic body of work ... which can be broadly characterised as cultural analysis'. He adds that this work includes:

> the considerable output of Williams himself, and, more generally, the convergence of history, sociology and English in cultural studies, some of the major developments in feminism, as well as continental Marxist-structuralist and poststructuralist theory, especially that of Althusser, Macherey, Gramsci and Foucault.[31]

But this surely isn't cultural materialism: rather, it is Cultural Studies itself, in the sense that we have been using the term here. And if cultural materialism is simply reduced to Cultural Studies in this fashion, then the effect is very different from that intended by either Dollimore or Sinfield: in short, the Left is left out once again, this time from the history of its own interventions.

John Higgins has taken understandable exception to Dollimore and Sinfield's apparent failure to register the specificity of Williams's position. 'At least as far as Williams was concerned', he writes:

> the 'term' cultural materialism was intended to have a clearly defined conceptual content ... which would put it at odds with ... 'Marxist-structural and poststructuralist theory' ...[32]

---

29   Wilson 1995, p. viii.
30   Wilson 1995, p. 53.
31   Dollimore 1994, pp. 2–3.
32   Higgins 1999, p. 172.

Higgins is surely right to insist on this difference, no matter how much one might sympathise with Dollimore and Sinfield, or with Greenblatt in the United States, in their increasingly successful attempts to recast literary studies as a sub-branch of Cultural Studies. Williams's cultural materialism was never intended as coextensive with Cultural Studies, but rather as a particular argument within and against it. What, then, are its the distinctive features? Higgins identifies four: a rejection of the opposition between high and low culture; a rejection of the aesthetic/evaluative function of literary study and the shift towards a new model of textual, historical and theoretical analysis; a stress on the active role of human agency; and a stress on the active self or subject.[33] This is a perfectly adequate summary insofar as it goes, although one might also wish to call attention to the more expressly 'materialist' aspects of Williams's position. That said, Higgins very successfully registers the distinctive combination in Williams of post-Leavisite and post-Marxist thematics, which is neither 'Marxist-structural' nor 'poststructuralist' in character, but rather quite specifically 'post-culturalist'.

6   Cultural Politics and the Politics of Culture

In *The Idea of Culture*, Eagleton distinguishes between 'cultural politics' on the one hand, in the sense of a politics internal to culture, and 'the politics of culture' on the other, in the sense of culture's extra-cultural political preconditions. He stresses that, whilst postmodern identity politics has mainly been about the former, Williams was much more interested in the latter.[34] So, for example, Williams was concerned with the problem of how to establish democratic socialism as the political condition for a common culture, rather than with the attempt to identify the specific content of such a culture. This distinction of Eagleton's – which is in some ways analogous to that in Benjamin between politicised aesthetics and aestheticised politics[35] – seems useful both in itself and as a way into what most clearly distinguishes Williams from the postmodern left.

Williams's cultural materialism had clear political consequences: the simultaneous stress on conscious creativity on the one hand, material determination on the other, is much more amenable to alignment with emancipat-

---

33   Higgins 1999, pp. 173–4.
34   Eagleton 2000, p. 122.
35   Benjamin 1973, pp. 243–4.

ory than exploitative or oppressive politics. For Williams himself this meant a commitment to the radical libertarian and socialist currents within the labour movement and a developing sympathy for Welsh nationalism. His socialism has often been criticised as insufficiently 'postmodern'. But there is evidence, nonetheless, of a real attempt at solidarity with the postmodern 'new social movements' in his later work: in *Towards 2000* he famously identified these – the peace movement, the ecology movement, the feminist movement, and the movement of 'oppositional culture' – as major 'resources for a journey of hope' beyond capitalism.[36] If it is true that he seemed unable to theorise questions of sexual politics with real adequacy, his commitment to the ecology movement seems much more substantial. There are real continuities between the ecological arguments in *Towards 2000* and older themes aired in *The Country and the City*, for example. As with Adorno, Williams's Marxism significantly anticipates contemporary ecocriticism and has on occasion been quite specifically recognised as such.[37]

So where do we go from here? Now that we have finally erected the tribunal of Cultural Studies before which to plead, now surely is the time to begin pleading: for cultural materialism certainly and perhaps even for Marxism too. In short, it is time for Laius. It is also time to recognise Williams's work as the resource of hope it is, not least for the significance it attached to the idea of a common culture. This is a distinctly unfashionable notion, except perhaps amongst American conservatives. Even Williams's admirers have often been ill at ease with it: for Jardine and Swindells, it was a 'minefield';[38] for Brenkman, multiculturalism sounded its 'death knell'.[39] Eagleton, however, has few such doubts. 'The paradox of Williams's position', he writes, is that the conditions for a truly common culture:

> can be laid only by politically securing ..., in effect, socialist institutions. And this ... involves common belief, commitment and practice. Only through a fully participatory democracy, including one which regulated material production, could the channels of access be fully opened to give vent to ... cultural diversity. To establish genuine cultural pluralism ... requires concerted socialist action. It is precisely this that contemporary pluralism fails to see. Williams's position would no doubt

---

36 Williams 1983, pp. 249–50.
37 Head 1998, p. 37.
38 Jardine and Swindells 1989, p. 115.
39 Brenkman 1995, p. 253.

seem to it quaintly residual, not to say positively archaic; the problem in fact is that we have yet to catch up with it.[40]

I have little to add to this, except that Eagleton is more or less exactly right. But let me conclude by drawing attention to what seem to be the three main senses of the concept of a common culture (or some close synonym) at work in Williams. At times, it functions theoretically, as an equivalent to the concept of totality in Lukács, totalisation in Sartre, or cognitive mapping in Jameson, that is, as an injunction to see the whole, to find the connections. At others, it functions practically, as an equivalent to the notion of solidarity in labour and socialist practice. At yet others, it functions as a normative political ideal, an equivalent to the idea of socialism itself, in the sense of Eagleton's 'participatory democracy, regulating material production'. We live in dangerously interesting times, where a rampantly hegemonic corporate capitalism increasingly threatens to empty the 'social' of virtually all content and meaning. In such times, I fail to see how we can begin to cope, let alone hope, without resort to all three of these.

---

40 Eagleton 2000, p. 122.

CHAPTER 18

From Media Imperialism to Semioterrorism

We are concerned here with the ethical consequences of 11 September 2001, the al-Qaida attack on New York, as distinct from 11 September 1973, the CIA-engineered overthrow of the democratically elected government of Chile. It is a mistake ever to suggest to ethicists that any ethical problem is essentially simple, but nonetheless this one seems so. I am an unreconstructed Kantian, I'm afraid, and so far as I can see there is no plausible reading of the categorical imperative to universalisability which could render it ethical:

a) *either* for any group of private citizens, no matter what their political or religious motives, to fly an aircraft full of captive civilian passengers into a public building occupied by thousands of other civilians going about their lawful business;
b) *or* for any government, no matter what its motives, to launch a campaign of air strikes – that is, bombing raids – against towns and cities, inhabited by large numbers of civilians, in any country, no matter what political or religious organisations might also have taken shelter in those towns and cities;
c) *or* for any political party, no matter what its aims and objectives, to attempt to exploit public outrage and horror at either or both of the above class of actions, in such a way as to incite collective antipathy towards an individual or group of individuals in no way implicated in either, merely for the purposes of short-term electoral advantage.

The behaviour of al-Qaida, the American and British governments, the Australian Liberal-National and Labor Parties, over these past 12 months, is thus incontrovertibly unethical in these particular respects. We live in a fallen world, in short, and political actors can generally be counted upon to do the right thing having exhausted all other possibilities.

Neither Australian political party is guilty of terrorism, of course, merely of bad faith (although some would argue there is nothing 'mere' about *mauvaise foi*). But both al-Qaida and the US and UK governments are so guilty. You will remember that, in the immediate aftermath of 9/11, when President Bush announced his 'war on terrorism', there was much public comment on the difficulty of defining terrorism, given that one person's terrorist is another's freedom fighter. But I have a definition to offer and it runs thus: an action may be considered terrorist insofar as it involves the relatively indiscriminate use of violence against civilians for political purposes. It is irrelevant whether the act is committed by governments or by private individuals: the first 'terrorists' were agents of the French Revolutionary Government in 1793–4; and subsequent history is replete with Red, White and Black governmental terror. It is irrelevant whether or not one agrees with the terrorists' motives: I happen to sympathise with Jacobin notions of republican virtue, but doubt they could ever be established by terrorist means. It does matter that the victims are civilians because a soldier wills himself into a position where he might be killed in battle and so violence directed against him is therefore compatible with the categorical imperative. It does matter that the violence is relatively indiscriminate because one cannot escape from indiscriminate violence, no matter what one chooses to do, and such violence is therefore incompatible with the categorical imperative.

An obvious implication of this argument is that all bombing campaigns directed against civilian populations, including the Allied bomber offensive against Nazi Germany, are essentially terrorist in character. The Nazis described the bomber crews as *Terrorflieger*, or 'terror-flyers', and in my view they were right to do so. I don't say this lightly: my own father flew with RAF Bomber Command during the Second World War. But he was so appalled by the ruins of both Frankfurt an der Oder and Berlin, which he witnessed respectively before and after his time in the Stalag Luft, that he has been a pacifist ever since. He is also a resolute anti-Nazi, which makes for intellectual and moral difficulties, as you might well imagine. I am not a pacifist, however: it seems to me that there are just wars and that the war against Hitler was indeed such. But I do believe that just wars should not be fought by unjust means, such as the bombing of civilians (collaterally or otherwise). Both the al-Qaida attack, which appeared to them as a counter-attack against American violence in the Middle East, and the Anglo-American counter-attack against Afghanistan, which country they held responsible for harbouring al-Qaida, were in effect bombing raids and both were essentially terrorist, irrespective of motive. These are such cheap and easy conclusions, however, that I remain suspicious of them, even as I articulate them. It is not so much that they are mistaken, as that ethical judgement – practical reason – might not be the key issue here. It seems more important to understand and explain what happened – *rerum cognoscere causas*, in the motto of my alma mater – than to rush to judge it.

My own immediate reaction to the attack on New York on 11 September itself was visceral: I still had vivid memories of ten years previously taking my sons David (then seven) and James (then two) up the World Trade Center and therefore had no difficulty in imagining the terror and panic. We watched it all on television in a blur of identification, empathy, sympathy and outrage, although as it turned out, the viewing platforms were not yet open at the time of the attack. But the lack of reflexivity in subsequent official rhetoric began to worry me. These people weren't cowards, as President Bush had insisted, but by their own standards heroes and martryrs, and the US surely had to ask what it was about its own behaviour that made it so hated by such people. Yes, it was partly a matter of religion and religious fundamentalism (although there is plenty of both in America as well as in Afghanistan and Saudi Arabia). But it was also something to do with the position of the American Presidency as a de facto World Government elected only by Americans and, in Bush's case, by less than half of those who voted. There is an emerging problem of international legitimacy here, legitimacy in the sense of a right not to be bombed as well as the more classically Weberian sense of a right to be obeyed. For so long as the US has the power to govern the world and a policy of simply looking out for itself, which in Bush's case reached extreme form over Kyoto, it will remain an illegitimate world government. And the effects of that illegitimacy will run from grumbling in official Europe, through street protests by the Greens, to dreadful acts of terrorism by Islamic fundamentalists.

Ethically, a dead Afghan killed in the American bombing counts for neither more nor less than a dead American. But I doubt that most Australians or Britons felt that way. I've explained my own sense of identification with the New York victims, as distinct from the Afghan, as a consequence of my having been there as a tourist. But this can't be true of the many millions of other Australians and Britons who also seem to have reacted as if 'we' had been attacked. This is not literally true, of course: we aren't Americans, we certainly aren't New Yorkers, we haven't been attacked, we actually live thousands of miles away from both (all?) sides in this conflict. Reluctant though I am to say so, I think this amounts to a process of collective over-identification. I am reluctant because, like any good Kantian, I'm obliged to agree with Donne that:

> any man's *death* diminishes *me*, because I am involved in *Mankind*; And therefore never send to know for whom the *bell* tolls; It tolls for *thee* ...

But Afghan or Iraqi deaths diminish us too. And there is something radically disproportionate about our collective identification with New York and our corollary indifference to Kabul.

How do we explain this over-identification? A clue comes from Tony Blair, the British Prime Minister, who insisted shortly after '9/11', that America had stood by Britain when Britain itself stood alone during the 'Blitz'. As a matter of historical record, this isn't actually true: Australia and New Zealand – and Canada and the Free French and the Polish Government in exile – all stood by

Britain. But the United States remained neutral throughout the Blitz, that is, the German air campaign against London and other British cities, which lasted from September 1940 to May 1941. The US actually entered the War as an act of self-defence when attacked by Japan at Pearl Harbor on 7 December 1941, that is, over six months later. But it seems true, nonetheless, to most Britons with no real memory of the war because, by and large, this is how the war is represented filmically and televisually. Blair wasn't referring to the real Blitz, but to its subsequent 'simulacric' representation in the mass media.

Let me explain what I mean by simulacric. Here, I turn from Kant to the unlikely figure of Jean Baudrillard, one of the key theorists of 'the postmodern' and famously the author of *Simulacra and Simulation*, the book within which Neo hides his money at the beginning of the Wachowski brothers' *The Matrix*, thus signifying both how cleverly 'postmodern' the film is and also what its key theme will be.[1] For Baudrillard, postmodernity is characterised by 'the disappearance of history and the real in the televisual'.[2] He uses the term simulacrum to mean a sign without a referent, that is, without a real object to which it refers. A simulacrum is thus 'never exchanged for the real, but exchanged for itself'.[3] By simulation he means the processual aspects of simulacra, or the non-referential equivalent of representation, that is, the representation of simulacra, as distinct from the representation of the real. Baudrillard argues that there has been a succession of three orders of simulacra since the Renaissance, which he calls, respectively, the natural, the productive, and 'the simulacra of simulation'. This third order is founded on information and characterised by hyperreality.[4] In this new world: 'Simulation is ... the generation by models of a real without origin or reality: a hyperreal'.[5]

Let me be clear that I'm by no means a loyal Baudrillardian: at full tilt, much of what he writes seems quite mad. And I'm inclined to agree with Bauman's comment on Baudrillard that 'there is life after and beyond television' and that for many of us 'reality remains what it always used to be: tough, solid, resistant and harsh'.[6] But I cannot see how else to explain this over-identification with New York except as simulacral: it is not the real attack that moves us, but rather its simulation in the media. The attack on the Twin Towers was so obviously scripted by the terrorists for consumption by the international mass media, and

---

1 Wachowski and Wachowski 1999.
2 Baudrillard 1988, p. 101.
3 Baudrillard 1994, p. 6.
4 Baudrillard 1994, p. 121.
5 Baudrillard 1994, p. 1.
6 Bauman 1992, p. 155.

the script so obviously borrowed from Hollywood, that it invites Baudrillardian analysis as a kind of semiotic terrorism, or what I will term 'semioterrorism'. These deaths were real, of course, and tragically so. But politically they seem to have been incidental to the destruction of the buildings as signifiers.

Compare this with my father's war. When Nazi Germany bombed Britain during the Second World War, and when the Western Allies in turn bombed Germany, the resulting civilian casualties were clearly a central object of the exercise. The intention was to destroy cities and to kill civilians up to and until the point of surrender. This logic became self-evident at Hiroshima and Nagasaki in August 1945, but was already apparent in 'Bomber' Harris's earlier accounts of the bomber offensive against Germany. The logic in New York and Washington was quite different: to damage or destroy the symbols of American power. And the Anglo-American attack on Afghanistan had an analogous character. So, although this third Gulf War did actually take place, it too was largely simulacral. Why should any of this matter? Because it suggests that al-Qaida also over-identifies with New York. We all – all of us, Bin Laden included – know far too much about New York, not in the way that a New Yorker does, that is, as a concrete referent, but in the way Tony Blair knows about the Blitz, that is, as a simulacral media construct. And this is so primarily because American media products, especially film and television, dominate the world market in what some have described as 'media imperialism'. In short, we all know about New York because we've all seen *Ghostbusters* and we've all watched *Seinfeld*, so much so that, when you visit New York for the first time, you experience *déjà vu*. We all similarly 'know' George Bush, the Pentagon and the White House, but not Kabul or Baghdad.

The attacks on New York, the Pentagon and the White House (if this was indeed the intended target for the plane that came down in Pennsylvania), the Anglo-American air strikes against Afghanistan, the attack on Iraq currently being scripted in the Pentagon, these are all incidents in a developing encounter between media imperialism, on the one hand, and semioterrorism, on the other. But where does that leave us in terms of political and moral action? Here, Baudrillard doesn't help, although Bauman – and Kant – still might. Having begun to understand the causes of things, we need now to return to practical reason. And here the problem seems to be essentially threefold: to see around the media, deconstruct the simulacra and the simulations, so as to recover the real insofar as we can; to attempt to understand the real pain and suffering in New York a year ago, in Kabul shortly thereafter, in Baghdad very soon I fear; and to judge the morality or otherwise of these actions as Kant would have, according to the universalisabilty of the moral maxims upon which they are predicated.

PART 3

Science Fiction

∴

CHAPTER 19

Utopia and Science Fiction in Raymond Williams*

Raymond Williams was a significant figure in late twentieth-century intellectual life, a pioneer in the early history of what we now known as Cultural Studies and also a central inspiration for the early British New Left. He was variously – and inaccurately – likened to a British Lukács,[1] a British Bloch[2] and even, according to *The Times*, 'the British Sartre'. Habermas's initial theorisation of the public sphere derived something from Williams's *Culture and Society*;[3] Stuart Hall, the Jamaican cultural theorist, cited Williams as 'a major influence' on his 'intellectual and political formation';[4] Edward Said claimed to have 'learned so much' from Williams;[5] Stephen Greenblatt, the guru of the New Historicism, recalled with enthusiasm the 'critical subtlety and theoretical intelligence' of Williams's lectures at Cambridge;[6] Cornel West, the most prominent contemporary exponent of Black Cultural Studies, described Williams as 'the last of the great European male revolutionary socialist intellectuals'.[7] There are Williamsites in Italy,[8] in Brazil,[9] in Australia.[10] None seem to have made anything of Williams's enduring interest in science fiction, however, an oversight this essay will attempt to rectify.

I have argued elsewhere that there are three main 'phases' in Williams's thought, each explicable in terms of its own differentially negotiated settlement between the kind of literary humanism associated with the English literary critic, F.R. Leavis, and some version or another of Marxism; and each characterisable in relation to a relatively distinct, consecutive moment in the history of the British New Left.[11] The first and second sphases are associated

---

* This chapter has been published previously in *Science Fiction Studies*, No. 90 (Vol. 30, Part 2), pp. 199–216, 2003.
1 Eagleton 1976, p. 36.
2 Pinkney 1989, pp. 28–31.
3 Habermas 1989, p. 37.
4 Hall 1993, p. 349.
5 Williams and Said 1989, pp. 181, 192.
6 Greenblatt 1990, p. 2.
7 West 1995, p. ix.
8 Ferrara 1989.
9 Cevasco 2000.
10 Lawson 2002, pp. 33–65.
11 Milner 2002.

with the moments of '1956' and '1968', that is, to borrow Peter Sedgwick's terms, the 'Old New Left' and the 'New New Left'. Where the Old New Left had been formed from out of the double political crisis of 1956, that occasioned by the suppression of the Hungarian Revolution, on the one hand, and the Anglo-French invasion of Egypt, on the other, the New New Left was inspired by the May '68 Events in Paris, the Vietnam Solidarity Campaign, the Prague Spring and the revolt on the campuses.[12] Where the Old New Left had attempted to preserve the particularities of the British national experience from Stalinist internationalism, the New New Left spurned nationalism in general, and the peculiarities of the English especially, in favour of an uncompromising internationalism and active political solidarity with the Vietnamese Revolution. Where the Old New Left had situated itself somewhere in the political space between the left-wing of the Labour Party and the liberalising wing of the Communist Party, the New New Left rejected both Labourism and Communism in favour of various 'ultraleftisms', Guevarism, Maoism, Trotskyism, and so on. Where the Old New Left had sought to counterpose 'experience' and 'culture' to Communist dogmatism, the New New Left discovered in various continental European 'Western Marxisms' a type of 'Theory' which could be counterposed to the empiricism of English bourgeois culture and the pragmatism of the British Labour Party.

To this typology we can now add a third phase, roughly that from the 1980s to the present, in which a 'Postmodern New Left' confronted the developing globalisation of corporate capitalism, the emergence of a postmodern radicalism centred on the new social movements and of a new theoretical relativism associated with 'difference' theory. Each of these three phases registers in a corollary phase in Williams's own thought, respectively, his 'left culturalism', his 'cultural materialism' and what we might describe, a little improbably, as his 'postmodernism'. Each also gave rise to a relatively distinct understanding on Williams's part of the relationship between science fiction (henceforth SF), utopia and dystopia. It will be my task here to track Williams's changing sense of this latter complex in relation to his more general theoretical interests.

More than twenty years ago, Darko Suvin's *Metamorphoses of Science Fiction* established itself as the classic text of academic SF criticism. As one authoritative commentary has it: 'More than any other study, Suvin's *Metamorphoses* is *the* significant forerunner of all the major examinations of the genre'.[13] Suvin had argued that SF was best understood as an 'estranged' genre, distin-

---

12 Sedgwick 1976.
13 Hollinger 1999, p. 233.

guished by the narrative dominance of a fictional 'novum' validated 'by cognitive logic';[14] and utopia as *'the socio-political subgenre of science fiction',*[15] that is, as social-science-fiction. For Suvin, a fictive utopia was thus an *'imaginary community ... in which human relations are organized more perfectly than in the author's community'.*[16] This insistence on the comparative – 'more perfectly', rather than 'perfect' – allowed him to accommodate Saint-Simon, Wells and Morris as well as Bacon and Fénelon. There are indeed 'perfect' utopias, he acknowledged, but these are only a limit case, a sub-class of the much wider species of merely more perfect worlds. Moreover, as we move from utopia to anti-utopia, or dystopia, it becomes clear that there are only ever comparatives, since absolute imperfection appears to beggar both description and articulation.

No doubt, there are aspects of Suvin's work – perhaps especially his insistence on the cognitive purpose of SF and the ferocity of his attendant opposition between the latter and fantasy – which do not quite stand the test of time. As Parrinder recently observed: 'Suvin's poetics has ... outlived its moment ... "Cognitive estrangement" may be taken to be a fact about the 1970s, just as T.S. Eliot's "dissociation of sensibility" was a fact about the 1920s'.[17] Indeed, Suvin himself has conceded that: 'Novum is as novum does: it does not supply justification, it demands justification. Where is the progress progressing to?'.[18] This said, Suvin's definitions of SF, utopia and the novum still seem to me defensible, at least if the focus falls on knowledge as enlightenment in general, rather than science in particular, and if augmented by some expanded sense of the critical potential within dystopia. This, then, is the sense in which I will use these terms in the argument that follows.

1 Science Fiction and Left Culturalism

In the first of our three phases, that from the mid-1950s to the mid-1960s, Williams addressed himself very directly to the definition of a third position between Leavisism and Marxism, a peculiarly British 'left culturalism' combining Leavisite aesthetics with socialist politics. His key texts from this period were *Culture and Society 1780–1950* and *The Long Revolution.* Though not his first

---

14 Suvin 1979, p. 63.
15 Suvin 1979, p. 61.
16 Suvin 1979, p. 45.
17 Parrinder 2000, p. 10.
18 Suvin 2000, p. 1.

book, Williams's intellectual and political reputation was established by *Culture and Society*. As his biographer, Fred Inglis, observes, it was one of the two 'sacred texts of this ... new political movement'.[19] Utopia and dystopia figured prominently in the preoccupations of the first British New Left. For the ex-Communist intellectuals associated with *The New Reasoner*, the key theoretical problem was the legacy of Stalinist Marxism, one possible solution a recovery of older utopian socialist traditions. For E.P. Thompson, the historian whose first major work had been a biography of Morris, this meant a return to Romanticism, to poetry and to *News from Nowhere*.[20] For many of the younger radicals intrigued by the new popular culture and appalled by Cold War and the threat of nuclear warfare, both Orwell and his great dystopian novel, *Nineteen Eighty-Four*, seemed to offer a more directly contemporary alternative to Stalinism. As Williams would later recall: the 'New Left respected Orwell directly, especially in its early years'.[21]

One might expect *Culture and Society* to echo something of this interest in Morris or in Orwell. And, to some extent, it did. The book is organised into two main parts, dealing respectively with the years 1790 to 1870 and 1914 to 1950, linked by a less substantial treatment of a turn-of-the-century 'Interregnum' which clearly failed to engage Williams.[22] Each of the main parts concluded with a discussion of political writing, the first with Morris, the second with Orwell. But neither *News from Nowhere* nor *Nineteen Eighty-Four* appeared to excite Williams's interest or sympathy. He saw Morris's significance in the attempt to attach the general values of the 'culture and society' tradition to 'an actual and growing social force: that of the organized working class'.[23] But this is more apparent in the expressly political essays, he argued, such as *How we Live, and How we might Live* or *A Factory as it might be*, than in the utopian novel, where the weaknesses 'are active and disabling'.[24] As for Orwell, if the man had been 'brave, generous, frank, and good',[25] his dystopia nonetheless fully replicated that very minority culture/mass civilisation topos which had propelled Williams away from T.S. Eliot and Leavis. 'Orwell puts the case in these terms', Williams concluded, 'because this is how he really saw present society, and *Nineteen Eighty-Four* is desperate because Orwell recognized that

---

19 Inglis 1995, p. 157.
20 Thompson 1955.
21 Williams 1971, p. 87.
22 Williams 1963, p. 165.
23 Williams 1963, p. 153.
24 Williams 1963, p. 159.
25 Williams 1963, p. 284.

on such a construction the exile could not win, and then there was no hope at all'.[26] Hence, the paradox of 'a humane man who communicated an extreme of inhuman terror; a man committed to decency who actualized a distinctive squalor'.[27]

This lack of sympathy for Morris's more explicitly utopian writings and for Orwell's more explicitly dystopian had been prefigured in a little-known essay Williams published two years previously in *The Highway*, the journal of the British Workers' Educational Association. The occasion was a critical review of recent SF, entitled simply 'Science Fiction', which has been republished only once, in *Science Fiction Studies* shortly after Williams's death. As Patrick Parrinder explained in his introduction to this 1988 republication, the essay combined 'an ideological critique of the genre with some pithily individual observations and an avid curiosity about SF'.[28] Williams had argued that stories of 'a secular paradise of the future' had 'reached their peak' in Morris and that thereafter they were 'almost entirely converted into their opposites: the stories of a future secular hell'.[29] The 'ideological critique' was directed, in particular, at the recent corruption – literally, the putrefaction – of Morris's utopianism. Its immediate target is presented by three 'putropian' novels: *Nineteen Eighty-Four*, Huxley's *Brave New World* and Bradbury's *Fahrenheit 451*. Here Williams distinguished three main types of contemporary literary SF, which he termed respectively 'Putropia, Doomsday, and Space Anthropology'.[30] By the first, he meant dystopian SF of the kind exemplified by Huxley, Orwell, Bradbury and Zamyatin; by the second, the kind of fictional catastrophe in which human life itself is extinguished, as in van Vogt's *Dormant*, Latham's *The Xi Effect*, Christopher's *The New Wine* and almost, but not quite, Wyndham's *The Day of the Triffids*; by the third, 'stories ... which consciously use the SF formula to find what are essentially new tribes, and new patterns of living'.[31]

While cheerfully confessing to an intense dislike of 'most of the examples' of the first two, Williams added that even these were interesting 'because they belong, directly, to a contemporary structure of feeling'.[32] We should note this early use – though not quite the first – of a concept, or at least its term, that would be distinctive to Williams and which would be theorised at length in

---

26 Williams 1963, p. 283.
27 Williams 1963, p. 277.
28 Williams 1988, p. 356.
29 Williams 1988, p. 357.
30 Ibid.
31 Williams 1988, p. 359.
32 Williams 1988, p. 357.

The Long Revolution and in *Marxism and Literature*. The particular structure of feeling that concerned him here, which underlay both putropian and doomsday fictions, was 'that of the isolated intellectual, and of the "masses" who are at best brutish, at worst brutal', in short, the myth of the defence of minority culture against barbarism. The reference to Eliot is made quite explicitly at one point, that to Leavis clearly implied. These dystopian fictions are often defended as cautionary tales, Williams concedes, but 'they are less warnings about the future ... than about the adequacy of certain types of contemporary feeling'. 'I believe, for my own part', he declared, 'that to think, feel, or even speak of people in terms of "masses" is to make the burning of the books and the destroying of the cities just that much more possible'.[33] As he would soon write in the 'personal conclusion' to *Culture and Society*: 'There are in fact no masses; there are only ways of seeing people as masses'.[34]

If Suvin is right that utopia and dystopia are indeed the socio-political subgenres of SF, then Williams seemed to have come dangerously close to rejecting this genre in which he had nonetheless shown an avid interest. Except that there is still the third SF mode, which had inspired his admiration precisely for its capacity to move beyond the then dominant forms of English *Kulturpessimismus*. So he found in James Blish's *A Case of Conscience* – a later version of which would win the 1959 Hugo Award – with its 'beautifully imagined tribe' of eight-foot tall, reptilian Lithians, 'a work of genuine imagination, and real intelligence'.[35] Such preferences as this – for Blish, as against Huxley and Orwell – might seem uncontroversial in contemporary cultural studies, but were clearly eccentric to the academic literary criticism of the 1950s. Moreover, Williams's preference was for Blish, not only against Orwell, but also against Morris. For if dystopianism as putropia constituted an important part of the problem, utopianism was not thereby part of the solution. It is precisely the less than utopian plausibility of Blish's 'human voice, ... far away, among the galaxies'[36] that Williams finds interesting. For the young Williams, utopia was indeed about perfection, dystopia about radical imperfection – secular heavens and secular hells – and neither allowed for the distinctively 'human' voice present in the best of space anthropology.

It is tempting to read this general aversion to utopia and dystopia as a displaced objection to the content of these particular utopias and dystopias. Certainly, Orwell had commanded both his attention and his disagreement. 'I

---

33   Williams 1988, p. 358.
34   Williams 1963, p. 289.
35   Williams 1988, p. 360.
36   Ibid.

would certainly insist that his conclusions have no general validity', Williams wrote in *Culture and Society*.[37] But the argument seems to proceed at a more general level too, where the extremism of the form itself is read as unrealistically anti-human. This is certainly the shape of the argument as it appears in *The Long Revolution*, where SF is again represented by Huxley, Orwell and Bradbury, but here augmented by Golding's *Lord of the Flies* and *The Inheritors*, and used as a key element in one of Williams's exercises in literary typology. There have been two main types of realist novel in the twentieth century, he argues, the 'social novel' and the 'personal novel', each of which has 'documentary' and 'formula' sub-types.[38] The 'social formula novel' in Williams's schema works by way of the abstraction of a particular pattern from the sum of social experience, accentuating it so as to create a fictional society. The best example of this kind of novel, he observes, is the 'future-story', which is virtually coextensive with 'serious "science fiction"'.[39] This kind of SF is 'lively' because 'about lively social feelings', but lacks both a 'substantial society' and 'substantial persons': 'For the common life is an abstraction, and the personal lives are defined by their function in the formula'.[40] Neither the social nor the personal novel, neither the documentary nor the formula, are at all adequate, Williams concluded. The problem is one of 'balance', he wrote, in terms clearly reminiscent of Leavis – even at one point invoking the 'great tradition'[41] – and the effort to create such balance is necessary 'if we are to remain creative'.[42]

An obvious objection to this conclusion is that it illegitimately judges SF according to criteria more appropriate to the realistic 'literary' novel and thus ignores the formal conventions of the genre. In the 1965 edition of *The Long Revolution*, Williams addressed this argument, insisting to the contrary that: 'the form itself, and what "by definition" it "cannot do", must submit to be criticized from a general position in experience'.[43] The implication is striking: that, if only it would try, SF could indeed create both a substantial society and substantial persons. Which returns us, by implication if not expressly, to space anthropology and Blish's Lithians. He would revisit this notion on more than one occasion: in a 1971 column for the BBC's *The Listener*, for example, where he insisted that, for all the patent inadequacies of television SF, the genre

---

37 Williams 1963, p. 284.
38 Williams 1965, pp. 306, 308.
39 Williams 1965, p. 307.
40 Williams 1965, pp. 307–8.
41 Williams 1965, p. 314.
42 Williams 1965, p. 316.
43 Williams 1965, p. 387.

had peculiar 'advantages' for the exploration of themes such as 'identity and culture-contact';[44] and more extensively in the various discussions from the late 1970s of the work of Ursula Le Guin.

2   Science Fiction and Cultural Materialism

The second phase of Williams's work, that of the moment of '1968' and the emergence of a second New Left, was characterised above all by his development of a full-blown theory of 'cultural materialism'. By this, he meant 'a theory of culture as a (social and material) productive process and of specific practices, of "arts", as social uses of material means of production'.[45] Here, Williams's engagement with a series of continental European Western Marxisms (Lukács, Goldmann, Althusser, Gramsci) and with various forms of Third Worldist political radicalism, clearly ran parallel to that of the younger generation of radical intellectuals associated with the *New Left Review* under the editorship of Perry Anderson. For Williams, the import was a strange double movement by which, on the one hand, his declared politics acquired a more explicitly 'leftist' – and presumably 'unrealistic' – character; but, on the other, they also became more analytically distinct from his scholarly work, which was itself increasingly understood as 'social-scientific' rather than 'literary-critical' in character. Williams sought to substitute a loosely Gramscian theory of 'hegemony' for both Leavisite notions of 'culture' and more orthodoxly Marxist notions of 'ideology'. More generally, he also sought to substitute description and explanation for judgement and canonisation, as the central purposes of analysis. This is what we have come to call 'Cultural Studies' and it is important to note that this move from literary into cultural studies had been occasioned, in part, by an aversion to prescriptive criticism of the Leavisite variety. Hence, his insistence that 'we need not criticism but analysis ... the complex seeing of analysis rather than ... the abstractions of critical classification'.[46]

The key texts from this period were *The Country and the City* and *Marxism and Literature*, though for our purposes we might add *George Orwell*. *Marxism and Literature* was 'almost wholly theoretical' in form, to borrow Williams's own description and, as such, had nothing to say about SF nor about any other substantive area of inquiry. But, as he himself insisted, 'every position in it

---

44   Williams 1989c, p. 144.
45   Williams 1980a, p. 243.
46   Williams 1989d, p. 239.

was developed from the detailed practical work that I have previously undertaken, and from the consequent interaction with other ... modes of theoretical assumption and argument'.[47] And some of this detailed practical work had indeed been concerned with SF. In *The Country and the City*, Williams's primary concern was with the pastoral and the counter-pastoral, but he found examples of each in the future cities of SF. In *George Orwell* – which Williams doesn't actually cite as relevant to *Marxism and Literature* – he had, however, worried away yet again at the precise significance of dystopianism in *Nineteen Eighty-Four*.

The essential novelty of Williams's procedure in *The Country and the City* was to compare literary representations with 'questions of historical fact',[48] so as to test his texts for the extent to which they misrepresented their contexts. In his treatment of SF, Williams stressed the importance of the city as a site of utopian and dystopian imaginings, emphasising the historical recency of the social experience of the megalopolis. The science-fictional 'experience of the future' came out of an 'experience of the cities', he wrote:

> At a crisis of metropolitan experience, stories of the future went through a qualitative change ... traditional models ... were eventually transformed. Man did not go to his destiny, or discover his fortunate place; he saw, in pride or error, his own capacity for collective transformation of himself and his world.[49]

Williams traced this 'deep transformation' in the first instance to late nineteenth-century London, citing as key examples Morris's *News from Nowhere* and Wells's *A Story of the Days to Come*. But he is clear that the central dynamic extended into the twentieth century, into cities elsewhere and into film as well as the novel, tracing a line of descent from Wells to Lang's *Metropolis*.[50] Williams follows the history of the SF city through Huxley and Orwell, James Thomson, Aldiss and Clarke, Ballard and Miller, Don A. Stuart, Henry Ruttner, E.M. Forster, Robert Abertheney and, once again, James Blish.[51] And he still seemed to prefer Blish to Orwell, specifically the flying cities of *Earthman, Come Home* to the 'shabby, ugly, exposed and lonely city' of *Nineteen Eighty-Four*.[52] The comparison is much less pointed, however, than in the earlier formula-

---

47   Williams 1977, p. 6.
48   Williams 1973b, p. 12.
49   Williams 1973b, p. 272.
50   Williams 1973b, pp. 273–4.
51   Williams 1973b, pp. 274–7.
52   Williams 1973b, pp. 277, 275.

tions. For the intent of the analysis is now not so much to take sides – or at least not immediately so – as to chart and explain the more general movement. 'In a sense', Williams concluded:

> everything about the city – from the magnificent to the apocalyptic – can be believed at once. One source of this unevenness is the complexity of the pressures and problems. But another ... is the abstraction of the city, as a huge isolated problem, and the traditional images have done much to support this.[53]

A roughly analogous procedure informs the treatment of *Nineteen Eighty-Four* in *George Orwell*. Here, he developed what appears to be a more evenhanded account, weighing the novel's strengths against its weaknesses, rather than the author against his text. For Williams, the convincing elements were twofold: the treatment of language on the one hand, and of international power politics on the other.[54] Against this, the identification of totalitarianism with socialism and the pessimism about human capacity, evident in Winston's loveless relationship with Julia and in the reduction of the people to passive 'proles', amount to a failure of experience. Here, as in *Culture and Society*, Williams concluded that 'the question about *Nineteen Eighty-Four*' is why Orwell should have 'created situations and people that, in comparison with his own written observations, are one-dimensional and determined'.[55] But here the answer is essentially sociological in character:

> The central significance is not in the personal contradictions but in the much deeper structures of a society and its literature. In making his projections, Orwell expressed much more than himself.[56]

Hence, the book's final conclusion that the only 'useful' thing, now, 'is to understand how it happened'.[57]

The aspiration to understand is betrayed, nonetheless, by Williams's aversion to Orwell's 'anti-socialism', which falls far short of the 'complex seeing of analysis'. At one point, Williams chides Orwell thus:

---

53 Williams 1973b, p. 278.
54 Williams 1971, pp. 75–6.
55 Williams 1971, p. 82.
56 Williams 1971, p. 83.
57 Williams 1971, p. 97.

he had the best of reasons ... to know that political police ... were not a socialist or communist invention ... By assigning all modern forms of repression and authoritarian control to a single political tendency, he not only misrepresented it but cut short the kind of analysis that would recognize these inhuman and destructive forces wherever they appeared ...[58]

Now the strange thing about this is that, in the immediately preceding paragraph, Williams had quoted from Orwell's letter of 16 June 1949 to the United Auto Workers Union, to the effect that *Nineteen Eighty-Four* was intended 'NOT ... as an attack on Socialism ... but as a show-up of ... perversions ... partly realised in Communism and Fascism'.[59]

That is, Orwell had intended neither to represent political police as a 'socialist invention' nor to assign authoritarian control to a 'single political tendency', but rather had assigned it quite expressly to both Communism *and* Fascism, totalitarianisms respectively of the Left and the Right. Williams quotes from the letter with scrupulous accuracy, but nonetheless appears not to hear what it says. And this is so, I suspect, because his private judgements were far more hostile to Orwell and to *Nineteen Eighty-Four* than those actually published in the book. As he would explain to the editors of the *New Left Review* in an interview conducted in 1977: 'I cannot bear much of it now ... its projections of ugliness and hatred ... onto the difficulties of revolution or political change, seem to introduce a period of really decadent bourgeois writing in which the whole status of human beings is reduced ... I am bound to say, I cannot read him now'.[60] For my part, I am bound to say that this really is left-Leavisite critical frothing at the mouth. But, as we shall see, this would not be Williams's last word on the subject.

For the moment, let us turn from the dystopian pole to the utopian, so as to consider Williams's developing response to *News from Nowhere*. Both in *The Highway* and in *Culture and Society*, he had found Morris's utopia almost as unsatisfactory as Orwell's dystopia. He would repeat something of this criticism in the interviews with *New Left Review*, where he described Morris's treatment of the 'discontinuity' between the real world and his fictional utopia as generating an 'untenable' notion of 'social simplicity'.[61] In the same interview, however, Williams also announced his intention to look again at representations of utopian discontinuity in Morris, Wells and in 'subsequent attempts in

---

58   Williams 1971, pp. 77–8.
59   Williams 1971, p. 77; Orwell 1970d, p. 564.
60   Williams 1979, pp. 391–2.
61   Williams 1979, pp. 128–9.

science fiction'. The tone was less than optimistic: 'I would hope to be able to find, but ... rather expect I shall not find, that I could revise my judgement' on utopianism.[62] The result of this inquiry – announced in two essays which date from the year immediately following the publication of *Marxism and Literature* – would prove less predictable than Williams had anticipated.

3   Science Fiction and Postmodernism: From Le Guin to *The Volunteers*

The third and final phase of Williams's work, that produced mainly during the 1980s, is best characterised by his developing engagement with the globalisation of corporate capitalism and with the promise of a postmodern radicalism centred around the new social movements. The key text here is the 1983 reworking of the long revolution analysis, *Towards 2000*, not by any standards a work of SF, but nonetheless, as it title suggests, an exercise in futurology. Here, Williams coined the term 'Plan X' to describe the 'new politics of strategic advantage' characteristic of the late-capitalist political-economy. This is what we have since learned to name as 'globalisation', the politics of the World Trade Organisation and the International Monetary Fund, the World Bank and the World Economic Forum. Williams's own description of such 'X Planning' remains startlingly prescient:

> their real politics and planning are ... centred on ... an acceptance of the indefinite continuation of extreme crisis and extreme danger ... there will be a long series of harshly administered checks; of deliberately organised reductions of conditions and chances; of intensively prepared emergencies of war and disorder ...[63]

Against this, he pitted the labour movements, but no longer the labour parties, which merely 'reproduce the existing definitions of issues and interests';[64] and also the new social movements – the peace movement, the ecology movement, the feminist movement, and the movement of 'oppositional culture' – his additional 'resources for a journey of hope' beyond capitalism.[65] Two decades later, the analysis stands up remarkably well, though the X Planners have proven

---

62   Williams 1979, p. 128.
63   Williams 1983, pp. 244, 268.
64   Williams 1983, p. 250.
65   Williams 1983, pp. 249–50.

stronger, and the opposition weaker, than Williams had hoped. But, as Francis Mulhern observes, *Towards 2000* is still 'actual and exemplary' in its 'commitment to the renewal of rational historical imagination'.[66]

Such questions of rational futurological imagination had been broached previously, however, in his two 1978 discussions of SF: 'Utopia and Science Fiction', first published in *Science Fiction Studies*; and 'The Tenses of Imagination', originally presented as lectures at the University of Wales, Aberystwyth; and in his only SF novel, *The Volunteers*, which dates from the same year. The first of the essays is clearly Williams's major theoretical statement on SF. Here, he expanded on the notion, originally broached in *The Country and the City*, that SF represents a distinctly modern form of utopia and dystopia. There are four characteristic types of each, he argued: the paradise or hell, the positively or negatively externally-altered world, the positive or negative willed transformation and the positive or negative technological transformation. The latter two are the more characteristically utopian/dystopian modes, he concluded, especially in SF, because transformation is normally more important than mere otherness.[67] Moreover, he was now clear that utopia and dystopia were comparative rather than absolute categories, dealing respectively with 'a happier life' and 'a more wretched kind of life'.[68]

Borrowing Abensour's distinction between 'systematic' and 'heuristic' utopias, that is, those focussed respectively on alternative organisational models and on alternative values,[69] Williams cast new light on the old controversy between Bellamy and Morris. If Bellamy's *Looking Backward* had been an essentially systematic utopia, Williams observed, *News from Nowhere* is a 'generous but sentimental heuristic transformation'.[70] Thus far, the argument runs much as in *Culture and Society*. The difference, however, is in the insistence on what is properly 'emergent' in Morris: 'the crucial insertion of the *transition* to utopia' as something 'fought for'.[71] At this point, the heuristic becomes distinctly unsentimental. Much the same occurs in Wells, moreover, and it is in relation to these willed transformations to utopia, Williams continued, that the dystopias of Zamyatin, Huxley and Orwell need be situated. Orwell's *1984* is neither more nor less plausible than Morris's 2003, he argued, but the latter's fictional revolution of 1952 is more plausible than either: 'because its energy flows both

---

66 Mulhern 1998, p. 115.
67 Williams 1980c, pp. 196–9.
68 Williams 1980c, p. 196.
69 Abensour 1973.
70 Williams 1980c, pp. 202–4.
71 Williams 1980c, p. 204.

ways, forward and back, ... its issue ... can go either way'. For Williams, this kind of openness – when the 'subjunctive is a true subjunctive, rather than a displaced indicative' – powerfully calls into question 'the now dominant mode of dystopia' represented paradigmatically in *Nineteen Eighty-Four*.[72]

But this re-evaluation of Morris is not quite Williams's last word on utopianism, for he also points to a parallel openness at work in a more immediately contemporary novel, Le Guin's *The Dispossessed*, which had won the 1975 Hugo Award. Her anarcho-feminist Anarres is a getaway, rather than a transformation, he observed, but 'an open utopia', nonetheless, 'shifted, deliberately, from its achieved harmonious condition', thereby 'depriving utopia of its classical end of struggle, its image of perpetual harmony and rest'.[73] And in its very realism this openness represented a 'strengthening' of the utopian impulse, he continued, which 'now warily, self-questioningly, and setting its own limits, renews itself'.[74] He makes an analogous point in the second essay. At an important stage in certain kinds of future story, he observed, 'a writer sits and *thinks*; assembles and deploys variables ... when even the factors are only partly known ... and when their interaction ... is quite radically uncertain'. Such is the case with *The Dispossessed*, for here 'there is evidence ... of deliberate and sustained thought about possible futures'.[75] His point is that Le Guin's thinking is deliberate and sustained, rather than 'sentimental'; and directed toward the possible, rather than the 'untenable'. What had been a moment only in Morris – essentially chapters XVII and XVIII of *News from Nowhere* – thus informs the whole life of Le Guin's 'Odonian' utopia.

Williams's interest in Le Guin warrants three further observations. First, it should be apparent that this enthusiasm for 'realistic' utopias and utopian 'realism' clearly rehearses his earlier sympathy for space anthropology. In 1956, he had conceived the latter as quite distinct from utopia and dystopia. By 1978, however, he had come to realise that utopian plausibility required something very much like it. It is a truism, but nonetheless true, that Le Guin's Hainish novels exhibit an extraordinary richness of precisely such 'anthropological' detail, in their treatment of myth and language, kinship, child-rearing, and so on. If that is perhaps less true of *The Dispossessed* than of *The Left Hand of Darkness*, *The Word for World is Forest* or *The Telling*, it is still clearly this very quality which makes Anarres so believable. Second, Williams's sense of what was dif-

---

72   Williams 1980c, p. 208.
73   Williams 1980c, pp. 211–12.
74   Williams 1980c, p. 212.
75   Williams 1980c, p. 266.

ferent about *The Dispossessed* – and what would be different about his own *The Volunteers* – interestingly prefigures what Sargent, Baccolini, Moylan and others would later write about the 'critical dystopias' of late twentieth-century SF.[76] What Moylan says of critical dystopia in general is clearly true of Williams's reading of Le Guin and of *The Volunteers* itself:

> They burrow within the dystopian tradition in order to bring utopian and dystopian tendencies to bear on their exposé of the present moment and their explorations of new forms of oppositional agency ... Albeit generally, and stubbornly, utopian, they do not go easily toward that better world. Rather, they linger in the terrors of the present even as they exemplify what is needed to transform it.[77]

Third, we should note that, unlike *News from Nowhere* or *A Story of the Days to Come* – or indeed Gethen in *The Left Hand of Darkness* – Anarres is unambiguously feminist, if not unambiguously utopian. This not to suggest that its textual politics are somehow either 'ideal' or 'correct'. No doubt, there are good arguments to be made against the specific content of its anarcho-feminism. Hence, Delany's conclusion that its excitement lay in 'the book's ambition more than its precise accomplishments',[78] a view much echoed elsewhere, for example, in Moylan, who judged it 'an important, if flawed, critical utopia'.[79] My point, however, is not that *The Dispossessed* was some kind of perfectly realised feminist novel – whatever that might be – but only the much more obvious one that its politics were indeed expressly and explicitly feminist in a way that had not been true of *The Left Hand of Darkness*. This matters if only because Williams's own sexual politics had been anything but feminist. As one of his former students, Morag Shiach, wryly observed: 'Feminists can find much of use to them in the work of Raymond Williams; they cannot, however, find many women'.[80] In his later years, however, Williams had at least begun to make more sympathetic noises: in *Politics and Letters*, for example, he conceded that it had been both a political weakness and an intellectual failing 'not to confront the problem' of gender;[81] and in *Towards 2000*, he would include feminism amongst his resources of hope. No doubt, the wider feminist movement had itself com-

---

76   Sargent 1994; Baccolini 2000; Moylan 2000.
77   Moylan 2000, pp. 198–9.
78   Delany 1977, p. 308.
79   Moylan 1986, p. 120.
80   Shiach 1995, p. 51.
81   Williams 1979, p. 150.

pelled some of this belated attention. It is possible, however, that Odonian Anarres also played some small part of its own.

If Anarres is distinctly 'postmodern' in its 'realism' and in its anarcho-feminist politics, then Le Guin's Urras possesses a correspondingly 'late capitalist' character: not so much dystopian as 'non-utopian', in Williams's phrase, 'sensually overwhelming' in its 'abundance, ... affluence, ... vitality', but with an 'underside' of the 'repressed and rejected'.[82] Anarres and Urras thus represent what Ann Kaplan would later term the 'twin faces of postmodernism', respectively, the 'utopian' and the 'commercial'.[83] Interestingly, these same twin faces also structure both the futurology in *Towards 2000* and the fictional world of *The Volunteers*. Williams's eventual reputation will no doubt depend on his academic and scholarly work, perhaps even his political involvement, rather than on his novels or television plays. This does not seem to have been his own view, however, and, whatever we might make of his Welsh trilogy or *Loyalties*, *The Volunteers* still seems an interesting novel.

He thought of it as a 'political thriller', rather than SF, and even insisted he had 'no direct experience' of writing the latter.[84] Yet his recollection of wanting 'to write a political novel set in the 1980s',[85] that is, in what was then the near-future, marks it out as the kind of future story he had closely associated with SF in *The Long Revolution*. According to Suvin's definitions, at any rate, it is very obviously SF and, ironically enough, SF written precisely in the dystopian mode. For it is organised around the sociopolitical novum of a complete ideological and organisational collapse of the British Labour Party into X Planning and coalition government with the Conservatives. This is, of course, more or less exactly what Tony Blair's New Labour would eventually achieve in historical reality, but in 1978 it remained a dystopian fictional novum. This novum is set within a changed technological landscape: a jet from London to Cardiff, an 'air-taxi' to St Fagans, coin-operated 'seat-screens' in railway station waiting-rooms.[86] As Tony Pinkney observes, *The Volunteers* is 'packed with gadgetry' and SF is the genre 'that in its heart of hearts it truly aspired to'.[87] But, as with Orwell's telescreens or Huxley's feelies, these technological devices remain narratively subordinate to the hegemonic sociopolitical novum.

---

82   Williams 1980c, p. 210.
83   Kaplan 1988, p. 4.
84   Williams 1984a, p. 265.
85   Williams 1979, p. 296.
86   Williams 1978, pp. 9, 10, 188.
87   Pinkney 1991, p. 93.

The novel begins *in media res*, on 9 July 1987 – *Nineteen Eighty-Four* had begun on 4 April 1984 – with news of an attempted assassination of Edmund Buxton, Secretary of State for Wales, '*shot as a murderer and as an enemy of the people*' by the Volunteer, 'Marcus'.[88] Lewis Redfern, the novel's narrator and central protagonist; Marcus and his comrades; Mark Evans, the onetime Labour junior minister turned NGO organiser; the secret Volunteers with whom he is involved: all share connections with seventies 'utopian' activism. But, by virtue of these very connections, Redfern has now become a 'consultant analyst' for 'Insatel', a global satellite TV station, specialising in spectacle and news, 'tin gods of the open sky', as a critic describes it.[89] Geo-spatially, the novel is structured around this opposition between hi-tech, global capitalism and its ruined and impoverished localities, from Wales to East Africa. In Williams's 1987, Wales enjoys pseudo self-government through a Welsh Senate, but its finances are firmly controlled by the 'Financial Commission', represented by Buxton, also a former Labour minister, but now in the service of the coalition. 'So it is not his inherited class', Redfern tells us, 'that has produced his undoubted authoritarian character. He is that now more dangerous kind of man, whose authority and whose ruthlessness derive from his absolute belief in his models'.[90] In short, he is an X Planner. He is also widely suspected of having ordered in the strike-breaking troops who shot and killed Gareth Powell, a picketing loader, at Pontyrhiw Power Depot. Hence, the 'murderer' charge.

Redfern's assignment is Buxton's shooting, but the investigation leads back to Powell's, to Evans and to the Volunteers. The cynical journalist as hardboiled detective, Redfern makes use of his own radical connections to unravel what is, at one level, a mystery story. But it is also at least as good an attempt at postmodern 'cognitive mapping' as that Jameson found in Gibson's *Neuromancer*.[91] Provided with proof that Buxton was indeed personally responsible for ordering in the Army, and that Evans is indeed a Volunteer, Redfern is forced to choose between his profession and his erstwhile political allegiances. He resigns, goes into hiding and finally gives evidence against Buxton at the Pontyrhiw Inquiry. As Pinkney notes, there are interesting parallels between Williams's Lewis Redfern and Ridley Scott's Rick Deckard in *Blade Runner*: both are eventually turned into that which they hunt.[92] Though Pinkney fails to notice this, both also provide their respective texts with the occasion for an

---

88   Williams 1978, pp. 104, 5, 32.
89   Williams 1978, pp. 6, 154.
90   Williams 1978, p. 12.
91   Jameson 1991, pp. 54, 38.
92   Pinkney 1991, pp. 104–5.

ambiguously optimistic resolution. For though Redfern testifies to the Inquiry, he neither joins the underground, nor comes to identify with his ancestral Welshness, nor even accepts the lift to the station offered by Powell's brother-in-law, Bob James. 'No thanks, Bob', Redfern replies in the novel's closing line, 'I'll find my own way back'.[93]

4   Science Fiction and Postmodernism: 1987 in *Nineteen Eighty-Four*

This qualified hope, this realism of purpose, even in a darkening future – and Williams was clear that the future imagined in his novel 'is not a desirable one, but it is … perfectly possible'[94] – provided the dystopian counterpart to what he had found in Le Guin's ambiguous utopia. It would also provide a benchmark by which to measure *Nineteen Eighty-Four* in his third and last approach, published in 1984 itself as an afterword to the second edition of *Orwell*. Here, Williams began by observing that the novel had three distinct layers: an 'infrastructure', where the hero-victim moves through a degraded world in search of a better life; a 'structure of argument' concerning the nature of the fictional society; and a 'superstructure' of fantasy, satire and parody which renders this society ludicrous and absurd.[95] Williams's main interest was in the second layer, which he saw as comprising three main themes: the division of the world into super-states; their internal organisation along totalitarian lines; and the crucial significance to the latter of media manipulation through 'thought control'.[96] He is clear, as he had not been in the first edition, that these societies have 'developed beyond both capitalism and socialism' and that the novel is not therefore 'anti-socialist'. Indeed, he requotes exactly the same passage from the Auto Workers Union letter, so as to insist that:

> what is being described … is not only a universal danger but a universal process … He saw the super-states, the spy states, and the majority populations controlled by induced ideas as the way *the world* was going … This is a much harder position than any simple anti-socialism or anti-communism.[97]

---

93   Williams 1978, p. 208.
94   Williams 1979, p. 301.
95   Williams 1991, pp. 95–6.
96   Williams 1991, p. 99.
97   Williams 1991, p. 101.

Indeed it is and Williams was right to recognise it as such, as he had failed to do in previous accounts.

Which is not to suggest that Williams is here uncritical of *Nineteen Eighty-Four*. Rather, he subjected it to much the same mode of analysis as that deployed in *The Country and the City*, comparing Orwell's projections, as developed both in the novel and in political essays, with the real world that eventuated in the post-Second World War period. Unitary super-states did not emerge, Williams points out, only superpowers and their attendant military alliances; the arms race between these superpowers generated affluence and technological innovation, rather than the stagnation and poverty envisaged by Orwell; and the superpowers were often resisted, both by local tradition in the metropolitan heartlands and by national-liberation movements in the former colonial periphery.[98] More fundamentally, what Orwell had most failed to anticipate was the 'spectacular capitalist boom', which falsified 'virtually every element of the specific prediction'.[99] Here, Williams revisited his own earlier charge that Orwell had 'specialised' the argument about totalitarianism to the socialist tradition. Here, however, he adds the important and paradoxical parenthesis: 'by his own choice, though he protested against it'.[100] If this still seems not quite right – where exactly was the choice? – it does suggest a more developed sense of Orwell's political vision.

Williams quotes extensively from Orwell's 1946 essay on James Burnham – which he had ignored in the first edition of *Orwell* – so as to situate the novel in a very precise politico-intellectual context. Like Burnham, Orwell had believed capitalism finished, unlike Burnham he hoped to see it replaced by democratic socialism, but like Burnham he also acknowledged the strong possibility that quasi-socialist rhetoric would be used to legitimise 'managerial revolution' and bureaucratic dictatorship. Burnham anticipated this prospect with some relish, Orwell with much fear. Hence, the latter's insistence, both with and against Burnham, that: 'the question is whether capitalism, now obviously doomed, is to give way to oligarchy or to true democracy'.[101] This, then, was for Williams Orwell's crucial mistake: to have imagined capitalism already beaten and, hence, the central issue as that between different 'socialisms'. As it turned out, the real 'question' would be that of a resurgent capitalism, re-legitimised by postwar affluence and radically oligarchic in its own later responses to the renewed depression and unemployment of the last quarter of the century.

---

98   Williams 1991, pp. 106–10.
99   Williams 1991, p. 117.
100 Williams 1991, p. 119.
101 Orwell 1970d, p. 198.

What really survives, Williams concluded, was 'Orwell's understanding of propaganda and thought control',[102] even though the thought-controllers would be press lords and film magnates rather than totalitarian ideologues.

In effect, Williams had pitted his own futurology against Orwell's, *Towards 2000* against *Nineteen Eighty-Four*:

> The national and international monetary institutions, with their counterparts in the giant paranational corporations, ... established a ... practical and ideological dominance which so far from being shaken by the first decade of depression ... was actually reinforced by it ... Internally and externally they had all the features of a true oligarchy ... 'centralisation' is not just an old socialist nostrum but ... a practical process of ever-larger and more concentrated capitalist corporations and money markets.[103]

This seems exactly right, not only as an account of how late capitalism actually works, but also as a way into understanding why *Nineteen Eighty-Four* seems so dated by comparison with Huxley's *Brave New World*, for example. From *Alien* and *Blade Runner*, through cyberpunk, to Kim Stanley Robinson and David Cronenberg, the most persuasive near-future SF of the late twentieth and early twenty-first centuries has taken, as its central thematic, precisely that collusion between state power and transnational corporate-media capital, which Williams himself had targetted fictionally in *The Volunteers* and politically in *Towards 2000*.

Williams also turned the essay on Burnham against the novel in what would turn out to be his own last word on dystopia. He repeats the earlier argument that, in its very hopelessness, *Nineteen Eighty-Four* had killed hope; that its warnings against totalitarianism were themselves so totalitarian that, 'in the very absoluteness of the fiction', it became 'an imaginative submission to its inevitability'.[104] But here he adds that Orwell himself rejected precisely this kind of submission before power in Burnham. 'Burnham never stops to ask *why* people want power', Orwell had written: 'He seems to assume that power hunger ... is a natural instinct that does not have to be explained'.[105] This is exactly O'Brien's answer to Winston in Room 101, Williams comments, the only answer available anywhere in the novel:

---

102 Williams 1991, p. 120.
103 Williams 1991, p. 117.
104 Williams 1991, pp. 125–6.
105 Orwell 1970d, p. 211.

This is the terrifying irrationalism of the climax of *Nineteen Eighty-Four*, and it is not easy, within the pity and the terror, to persist with the real and Orwell's own question.[106]

'There *are* reasons', Williams continues, 'as outside the fiction Orwell well knew',[107] and these reasons must be sought for and distinguished, the good from the bad, the better from the worse, so as to avert the brute cynicism of Burnham's attempt 'to discredit all actual political beliefs and aspirations'.[108]

Williams's last reading of *Nineteen Eighty-Four* is clearly richer than its predecessors: it combined a developed understanding of the novel's workings as a text with an expanded sense of its socio-political and intertextual contexts. In thirty years of occasional writing about SF, Williams had learnt to substitute the complex seeing of analysis for moralistic criticism; and to situate texts in their material and intellectual contexts. He had come to understand the kind of honourable personal motives and socially effective structures of feeling that underpinned both utopian and dystopian forms. He had come to realise that neither was inherently antithetical to the space anthropology he had admired in Blish and, more importantly, in Le Guin. But his suspicion of radical dystopia remained essentially unchanged: without resistance, without 'realism', without the 'true subjunctive', dystopia will still kill hope, as surely as the unrealistic utopia will fail to inspire it. Two decades further into the gathering gloom of neo-liberalism, in a world desperately in need of 'realistic' resources of hope, who are we to disagree with him?

106   Williams 1991, p. 124.
107   Williams 1991, p. 125.
108   Williams 1991, p. 124.

CHAPTER 20

Darker Cities: Urban Dystopia and Science Fiction Cinema*

Critical theory has transformed science fiction studies from a 'fan' enthusiasm into a scholarly sub-discipline in the years since 1979, when Darko Suvin first published his *Metamorphoses of Science Fiction*. As one observer recently commented: 'More than any other study, ... *Metamorphoses* is *the* significant forerunner of all the major examinations of the genre'.[1] Its approach was Western-Marxist in theoretical inspiration (especially Bloch), its disciplinary orientation primarily towards comparative literature. Suvin famously argued that science fiction (henceforth SF) was best understood as a '*literature of cognitive estrangement*', a genre distinguished by '*the narrative dominance or hegemony of a fictional "novum" ... validated by cognitive logic*'.[2] There was clear prescriptive intent here: to exclude myth, folktale and fantasy.[3] This insistence on the cognitive functions of SF and the ferocity of the attendant opposition to fantasy have been called into question on more than one occasion. Thus Parrinder: 'Suvin's poetics has ... outlived its moment ... "Cognitive estrangement" may be taken to be a fact about the 1970s, just as T.S. Eliot's "dissociation of sensibility" was a fact about the 1920s'.[4] Even Suvin now concedes that: 'Novum is as novum does: it does not supply justification, it demands justification. Where is the progress progressing to?'.[5] Nevertheless, the Suvinian definition of SF in relation to the novum seems defensible, at least insofar as the focus falls on knowledge as enlightenment in general, rather than on science in particular. This is the sense in which I will use the term here.

As Suvin's subtitle made clear, his interests were with the poetics of a 'literary' genre. But there was always a certain inherent improbability to this resolutely anti-populist intent. The term 'science fiction' and its associated generic self-consciousness had derived, after all, not from literature, in any sense that

---

* This chapter has been published previously in *International Journal of Cultural Studies*, Vol. 7, No. 3, pp. 259–79, 2004.
1 Hollinger 1991, p. 233.
2 Suvin 1979, pp. 4, 63.
3 Suvin 1979, pp. 20, 68–9.
4 Parrinder 2000, p. 10.
5 Suvin 2000, p. 1.

a literary critic would recognise, but from the 'pulp fiction' magazines of the inter-war United States. Hugo Gernsback (after whom the annual 'Hugo awards' are named) had coined the word 'scientification' in 1926 in the first issue of *Amazing Stories*; 'science fiction' became common only after 1938, when John W. Campbell Jr changed the name of a rival 'pulp' from *Astounding Stories* to *Astounding Science-Fiction*.[6] This was a 'low' genre, then, lower than literature, lower than film, perhaps even lower than television. Yet, there is more to a genre than its name. There was indeed, as Suvin recognised, and as even Gernsback had acknowledged, an older tradition of literary and quasi-literary writing about 'science'. Gernsback himself traced the genre's origins to Verne, Wells and Poe;[7] the most influential history of the genre, written by one of its leading contemporary practitioners, to Shelley's *Frankenstein*.[8] Despite the absence of the term from the earlier writing, this seems right: there is a real, if retrospective, commonality.

The effects of this commonality are contradictory: on the one hand, it threatens to undermine Suvin's fidelity to the distinction between SF as 'literature' and as mere 'fiction'; but on the other, it acknowledges that the genre has a properly 'literary' history, just as Suvin suggests. The value of *Metamorphoses* is thus as a specifically literary history of an only partly literary genre. Its lack of interest in popular fiction pales into insignificance, moreover, when set against its radical indifference to cinema. This is clearly problematic, if only because SF has a long history in film, not merely as a matter of contingent empirical fact, but for reasons that are, in important respects, intrinsic to the nature of the genre. By most accounts, the first SF movie is Georges Méliès's *Le Voyage dans la lune*, produced in 1902, that is, less than seven years after the Lumières organised their first film projections for a paying audience. For Méliès, as for most subsequent SF film directors and their audiences, the genre's appeal consisted precisely in the use of special effects to render an SF novum visually. No doubt, this is not what Suvin had in mind in his famous definition. Like most fan devotees of literary SF, post-Suvinian literary criticism has tended to assume that special effects preclude SF film from doing what the written form does best: that is, experiment with ideas. Clearly, they each have a point. Film theorists have often taken understandable exception to Adorno and Horkheimer's thesis that:

---

6   Clute and Nicholls 1993, pp. 25, 64.
7   Clute and Nicholls 1993, p. 311.
8   Aldiss 1986, p. 7.

The development of the culture industry has led to the predominance of the effect, the obvious touch, and the technical detail over the work itself – which once expressed an idea, but was liquidated together with the idea.[9]

If this is clearly overstatement as a comment on film in general, it might nonetheless retain a peculiar pertinence to SF cinema in particular. For in this genre, where the literary novum is indeed typically an 'idea' and the central cinematic device typically an 'effect', there is likely to be a very real tension between the novum and its representation as spectacle. Insofar as this is so, then it will only ever be as a 'law of tendency', towards the conceptualisation of the novum as idea in the written medium, towards its specularisation as effect in the cinematic, but understood as points on a continuum, nevertheless, rather than as permanent structural properties of the respective media.

1 Theories, Methods and Texts

I want to approach SF cinema in ways that circumvent both the Adornian high/low binary and the SF community's own literature/film binary. Hence, my resort to what Raymond Williams termed 'cultural materialism'. By this he meant 'a theory of culture as a (social and material) productive process and of specific practices, of "arts", as social uses of material means of production'.[10] If Williams has become a distinctly unfashionable figure in popular culture studies, he is almost entirely invisible in SF studies. The critical revolution inaugurated by Suvin has inspired Marxist, feminist, queer and Foucauldian approaches to the genre, but nothing at all equivalent, for example, to the cultural materialism of Dollimore and Sinfield in Renaissance literary studies.[11] This last has become the 'the new academic order' according to one observer,[12] 'the effective horizon of advanced ... study' according to another.[13] The discrepancy is doubly ironic given Williams's own comparative indifference to Shakespeare studies and his enduring interest in SF: he served on the editorial board of *Science Fiction Studies*, wrote one SF novel[14] and an extensive body of SF criticism.

---

9   Adorno and Horkheimer 1979, p. 125.
10 Williams 1980a, p. 243.
11 Dollimore and Sinfield 1994.
12 Wilson 1995, p. viii.
13 Ryan 1996, p. ix.
14 Williams 1978.

Williams developed his cultural materialism through an engagement with continental European Western Marxism, which led him increasingly to recast his work as 'social-scientific' rather than 'literary-critical' in character. As is well-known, he substituted a Gramscian theory of hegemony for both literary-humanist notions of culture and orthodoxly Marxist notions of ideology. More generally, however, he also sought to substitute description and explanation for judgement and canonisation, as the central purposes of analysis. This is precisely what we have come to call 'cultural studies'. And it is important to note that Williams's move from literary into cultural studies was occasioned, in part, by an aversion to prescriptive criticism of the literary-humanist variety. Hence, his insistence that 'we need not criticism but analysis ... the complex seeing of analysis rather than ... the abstractions of critical classification'.[15] The general argument for cultural materialism is elaborated in *Marxism and Literature*, a book Williams described as 'almost wholly theoretical' in form, with nothing to say about SF nor anything very much about any other substantive areas of inquiry. But, as he also insisted, 'every position in it was developed from ... detailed practical work ... I have previously undertaken, and from the consequent interaction with other ... modes of theoretical assumption and argument'.[16] Some of this detailed practical work had in fact been concerned with SF.

I have argued elsewhere that there are three main 'phases' in Williams's thought, which I term respectively 'left culturalist', 'cultural materialist' and 'postmodernist', in each of which he had formulated a relatively distinct understanding of the relationship between SF, utopia and dystopia. The first was characterised by a polemical rejection of utopianism and dystopianism, represented paradigmatically by Morris's *News from Nowhere* and Orwell's *Nineteen Eighty-Four*, in favour of the kind of 'space anthropology' which uses 'the SF formula' to find 'what are essentially new tribes, and new patterns of living' (Williams, 1988: 359). The second is best represented by *The Country and the City*, where Williams traced the history of the SF city from Huxley and Orwell through to Abertheney and Blish.[17] Here, the intent of the analysis was not so much to take sides – or at least not immediately so – as to chart and explain the more general movement. The third and final phase entailed a positive re-evaluation of utopianism, especially of Le Guin's *The Dispossessed*, and also eventually a more developed reading of Orwell's dystopia. In thirty years of

---

15   Williams 1989d, p. 239.
16   Williams 1977, p. 6.
17   Williams 1973b, pp. 274–7.

writing about SF, Williams thus slowly learnt to substitute his own 'complex seeing' for moralistic criticism; and to situate texts in their material and intellectual contexts. This led to an understanding of the kind of honourable personal motives and socially effective 'structures of feeling' that underpinned the utopian and dystopian forms he had initially disliked. In the process, he also came to realise that neither was inherently antithetical to the space anthropology he admired in writers like Blish and Le Guin.

Williams's major theoretical statement on SF, first published in 1978 in *Science Fiction Studies*, was concerned above all with the relationship between utopia and SF. Here, he expanded on a notion originally broached in *The Country and the City* that SF represents a distinctly modern form of utopia and dystopia. There are four characteristic types of each, he argued: the paradise or hell, the positively or negatively externally-altered world, the positive or negative willed transformation and the positive or negative technological transformation. The latter two are the more characteristically utopian/dystopian modes, he concluded, especially in SF, because transformation is normally more important than mere otherness.[18] This emphasis on the connection between SF and utopia is by no means exclusive to Williams. It was shared with Suvin, who in *Metamorphoses* defined utopia as '*the socio-political subgenre of science fiction*', that is, as social-science-fiction.[19] Neither Williams nor Suvin accepted the equation of utopia with radical perfection. For the latter, a fictive utopia was an '*imaginary community ... in which human relations are organized more perfectly than in the author's community*'.[20] For Williams, utopia and dystopia dealt respectively with 'a happier life' and 'a more wretched kind of life'.[21] This insistence on the comparative – 'more perfectly' or 'happier', rather than 'perfect' – allowed Suvin to accommodate Saint-Simon, Wells and Morris as well as Bacon and Fénelon; and Williams to find in Le Guin a utopian 'realism' which strengthened and renewed an older utopian impulse.[22] Perfect utopias are thus only a limit case, a sub-class of the much wider species of merely more perfect worlds. Moreover, as we move from utopia to dystopia, there are only ever comparatives, since absolute imperfection beggars both description and articulation.

We should also note the special significance for Williams of the city in dystopian SF. If *The Country and the City* is concerned primarily with the pastoral

---

18   Williams 1980c, pp. 196–9.
19   Suvin 1979, p. 61.
20   Suvin 1979, p. 45.
21   Williams 1980c, p. 196.
22   Williams 1980c, p. 212.

and the counter-pastoral, Williams found examples of each in SF's future cities. The central novelty of his procedure here was to compare literary representations with 'questions of historical fact',[23] so as to test his texts for the extent to which they misrepresented their contexts. In the treatment of SF, he stressed the importance of the city as a site of utopian and dystopian imaginings, emphasising both the historical recency and the historical reality of the social experience of the megalopolis. The science-fictional 'experience of the future' came out of an 'experience of the cities', he wrote:

> At a crisis of metropolitan experience, stories of the future went through a qualitative change ... traditional models ... were eventually transformed. Man did not go to his destiny, or discover his fortunate place; he saw, in pride or error, his own capacity for collective transformation of himself and his world.[24]

Williams traced this 'deep transformation' in the first instance to late nineteenth-century London, citing as key examples *News from Nowhere* and Wells's *A Story of the Days to Come*. But he is clear that the argument applies to film as well as to the novel – indeed he traces a line of descent from Wells to Fritz Lang's *Metropolis*.[25] This, then, will be my own understanding of the connections between utopia, dystopia and the city as we proceed to a preliminary sketch of some of the key differences between modern and postmodern urban dystopias.

2 From the Modern to the Postmodern: Class and Gender in Three Dark Cities

Whatever else it might be, *The Country and the City* is in no sense 'postmodern': both its SF and its cities are clearly modern. But the hyperurban experience that so interested Williams has in fact become characteristic of postmodern hyperreality, as understood by writers like Jameson and Baudrillard, both of whom have also written interestingly on SF. In my view, modernism and postmodernism are best analysed as examples of what Williams meant by a 'structure of feeling', that is 'a particular community of experience hardly needing expres-

---

23 Williams 1973b, p. 12.
24 Williams 1973b, p. 272.
25 Williams 1973b, p. 274.

sion, through which the characteristics of our way of life ... are in some way passed, giving them a particular and characteristic colour'.[26] Structure of feeling is 'as firm and definite as "structure" suggests', he continued, 'yet it operates in the most delicate and least tangible parts of our activity'.[27] 'In one sense', he wrote:

> structure of feeling is the culture of a period: it is the particular living result of all the elements in the general organization. And it is in this respect that the arts ... are of major importance. For here, if anywhere, this characteristic is likely to be expressed; often not consciously, but by the fact that here ... the actual living sense, the deep community that makes the communication possible, is naturally drawn upon.[28]

Jameson has toyed with the notion that postmodernism might be a structure of feeling, only to reject it finally as 'very odd'.[29] Here, he seems to me mistaken, not least because of his own subsequent insistence – deliberately echoing Williams – that the postmodern is 'the force field in which very different kinds of cultural impulses – ... "residual" and "emergent" forms of cultural production – must make their way'.[30] This is a minor methodological point, however, which need not detract from the power of Jameson's substantive analyses.

Let me gesture here towards a few key ideas in Jameson and in Baudrillard: that in the late twentieth-century western culture and society entered into a third 'post-industrial' or 'multinational' stage, founded on electronics rather than electricity, information and 'hyperreality' rather than production and productivism;[31] that these transformations were themselves the effect of mutations in the nature of capital;[32] that this 'late capitalism' is increasingly mass-mediated, asocial and transnational rather than national in scope;[33] that postmodern media culture becomes so 'imprinted on human subjectivity and existential experience'[34] that identity itself is increasingly understood as constructed and hence indeterminate; that referentiality becomes so atten-

---

26 Williams 1965, pp. 63–4.
27 Williams 1965, p. 64.
28 Williams 1965, pp. 64–5.
29 Jameson 1991, pp. xiv, xix.
30 Jameson 1991, p. 6.
31 Jameson 1991, p. 35; Baudrillard 1994, p. 121.
32 Jameson 1991, pp. 35–6; Baudrillard 1993, p. 8.
33 Jameson 1991, p. 49; Baudrillard 1983, p. 19.
34 Jameson 1992, p. 131.

uated that the 'signifier becomes its own referent', the 'sign no longer designates anything at all', the real is superseded by the hyperreal, and intertextuality *per se* becomes the characteristically postmodern aesthetic effect.[35] To this we should add the further proposition, central to neither Jameson nor Baudrillard, but much canvassed elsewhere, from Haraway to Hayles to Fukuyama, that the posthuman as against the human has become a characteristically postmodern thematic.[36] I want to use this set of propositions as a way into a cultural-materialist reading of three dystopian SF films, a reading intended both to chart the shift from a modern to a postmodern structure of feeling and that from modern to postmodern systems of cultural production. I have selected two quasi-'canonical' films for analysis and a third that might reasonably be expected to become so: *Metropolis*, *Blade Runner* and *Dark City*.

Metropolis was nearly two years in the making, had its first theatre release in January 1927, and is still, by some counts, one of the most expensive films ever made in Germany. It was directed by the Austrian film-maker Fritz Lang, who had earlier made *Dr Mabuse, Der Spieler* (1922), a quasi-SF film about an evil criminal genius, which triggered a series of sequels and the six-hour fantasy *Die Niebelungen* (1923–4). *Metropolis* featured Bridgette Helm as Maria, a kind of childcare worker for working-class children and would-be social reformer and 'moderate' agitator to their parents. Alfred Abel played Joh Fredersen, the tyrannical master of Metropolis, Gustav Froelich his son, Freder, who falls in love with Maria. Rudolph Klein-Rogge played Rotwang, the mad scientist/sorcerer, who designs and builds the first ever screen robot and, on Fredersen's instructions, turns it into a duplicate Maria.[37] This was a black and white silent film, a mechanically reproducible marketable commodity, sold to distributors to be consumed collectively and, in Walter Benjamin's phrase 'in a state of distraction', in the darkness of the cinema theatre.[38] Like much filmically

---

35   Baudrillard 1975, pp. 127–8; Baudrillard 1993, p. 3; Jameson 1991, p. 20.
36   Haraway 1991; Hayles 1999; Fukuyama 2002.
37   Interestingly, Lang uses 'Mensch-Maschine' or, in the plural, 'Maschinen-Menschen', rather than 'robot', even though the latter had already been coined – from the Czech 'robotá' – by Josef Čapek for his brother Karel's 1920 play *R.U.R.*, itself available in both German and English translations at the time *Metropolis* was in production.
38   Benjamin 1973, p. 242. Film theorists often rightly insist that cinema is consumed much less 'distractedly' than television. Benjamin's implicit comparison is with the printed book, however, rather than either television, with which he was unfamiliar, or radio. And here Benjamin is surely right: film's mode of reception is much less distracted than that of radio or television, but nonetheless much more so than that of the book.

ambitious SF, it was prohibitively expensive, costing some DM 5 million, which nearly bankrupted the state-sponsored Universum Film Aktiengesellschaft. It was very obviously the product of a still recognisably national German cinema, but acquired speedy distribution in Britain, the US and Australia (the Australian premiere was in Melbourne in April 1928), in part thanks to the absence of sound, since the translation of intertitles was a much cheaper process than either subtitling or dubbing. The initial three-hour version no longer exists: it was cut to 128 minutes for the 1927 UK print, 75 minutes for the 1927 US print and 90 minutes for the 1928 German re-release. A near-complete restoration, including a soundtrack based on the score for the 1927 Berlin premiere, was released by the Murnau Foundation in 2002, however, and this is the version I have used here.

Blade Runner was first released in 1982, a second *Director's Cut* in 1992. It was directed by the English film-maker, Ridley Scott, who had earlier made *Alien* (1979), and was loosely based on Philip K. Dick's 1968 novel *Do Androids Dream of Electric Sheep?* It starred Harrison Ford as Rick Deckard, the 'blade runner' of the title, whose job is to 'retire' escaped 'replicants' or androids. Rutger Hauer played Roy Batty, the leader of a group of fugitive replicants, Sean Young played Rachael, the replicant with whom Deckard eventually falls in love, and Joe Turkell, Eldon Tyrell, the head of the Tyrell Corporation which manufactures the replicants. By comparison with *Metropolis*, *Blade Runner* is the product of much more highly developed corporate relations of production: it is a full-colour, sound film; a marketable commodity to be consumed initially in the cinema theatre, but subsequently recycled as TV and (in the case of the *Director's Cut*) as video, its music by Vangelis on tape and later CD. The film was produced for Warner Brothers by the 'Blade Runner Partnership' at a reported cost of $US 27 million. For all its cult reputation, Scott had clearly aimed at commercial as much as critical success. Initially, however, it achieved only the latter: it won two 1982 Academy Awards, but turned out to be a box office disaster, losing $US 12 million. Despite its English director, the film is recognisably American: set in an American future, starring American actors, addressed primarily to an American audience, and based on an American novel.

Dark City was first released in 1998. It was directed by the Australian Alex Proyas, who had earlier made *Spirits of the Air, Gremlins of the Clouds* (1988) and *The Crow* (1994). It featured Rufus Sewell as John Murdoch, the amnesiac protagonist, who may or may not be a serial killer. Kiefer Sutherland played Dr Schreber, the only human who actively collaborates with the alien 'Strangers' running the 'dark city' as an experiment to discover how the human 'soul' works. Jennifer Connelly played Murdoch's apparent 'wife', Emma, who eventually becomes Anna; William Hurt, Detective Bumstead, who is leading an investigation into the serial murders; Ian Richardson, Mr Book, the chief Stranger; and Richard O'Brien, his assistant, Mr Hand. Like *Blade Runner*, *Dark City* is a product of highly developed corporate relations of production, a marketable commodity to be consumed in the cinema theatre and subsequently recycled as video and CD (the music is by Trevor Jones). Unlike *Blade Runner*, it was launched with its own website: www.darkcity.com. It was produced by 'Mystery Clock Cinema' for New Line Cinema, part of what had now become Time-Warner, the old Warner Brothers expanded into a multi-media conglomerate through a merger with Time-Life Publishing (merger with AOL would come later). Unlike *Blade Runner*, it is clearly the product of a transnational rather than national industry: largely financed in the United States, its key 'stars' were American and British, but it was made at Fox's Sydney Showground studios, with mainly Australian labour, including virtually all the actors playing minor roles.

In all three films, the architecture of the dystopian cityscape functions as a synecdoche for the wider catastrope that has overcome their respective populations. In all three, the city *is* the dystopian novum, the shape of the prior catastrophe encoded deep within its social and architectural forms. In all three, this catastrophe is refracted through social relations of class and gender. Lang's Metropolis is clearly an extrapolation from the early twentieth-century German city, transformed both for the better and the worse, through both will and technology, into the city of 2026, a modern urban dystopia very much in the pattern described by Williams. Although not explicitly identified with Berlin or any other particular place, it is clearly organised around much the same conflict between capital and labour that had dominated the German cities of the 1920s. This is a class-divided city, vertically stratified between the darkest proletarian depths where the workers live, the intermediary levels where they work in conditions of extreme alienation – illustrated at length in one of the film's best-known sequences – and the high city of light inhabited by the privileged classes. Gesturing towards the sunlit heights of this proto-modernist cityscape, Freder demands of his father:

und wo sind die Menschen ... deren Hände Deine Stadt erbauten –?

[and where are the people ... whose hands built your city –?]

The camera cuts to a shot of the next shift descending by lift to the subterranean factories, as Fredersen retorts:

> Wo sie hingehören ... in die Tiefe
>
> [Where they belong ... in the depths].

Interestingly, this vertical social stratification – which would become a standard trope in SF cinema – has no real equivalent in reality, where cities still tend to be stratifed horizontally. The film's strikes, crowds, riots and even the false Maria as female agitator all clearly echo something of the reality of the German Revolution of 1918, in which Rosa Luxemburg had played such a key role. Importantly, there is still hope in this city, both the false hope of revolution, as Lang saw it, and the real hope of social reconciliation, finally attained in its closing scenes. The extraordinarily ambitious architecture of the high city, which much preoccupied Lang in its making, signifies this hope at least as much as it does Fredersen's hubris.

Blade Runner is set in a post-catastrophic dystopia, the Los Angeles of November 2019, a city soaked in acid rain and choking on pollution, where most healthy humans have already moved 'off-world'. Scott's 'retrofitted' city has often been cited as the quintessentially postmodern urban landscape: for Giuliana Bruno, its postmodernity consisted in a combination of 'postindustrial decay' with 'hybrid architectural design';[39] for David Harvey, in that of 'deindustrialisation' and, again, 'post-industrial decay'.[40] Like Lang's *Metropolis*, it is a city transformed by will and technology, but overwhelmingly for the worse: there is little hope here, other than that of escape. The cityscape itself is dominated by the Tyrell Corporation building, a gleaming glass and concrete pyramid reaching so far above street level as to be lit by natural sunlight: everything and everywhere else is dark and wet. Tyrell, Batty ironically observes, is 'the God of bio-mechanics' and bio-mechanics is the city's ruling technology. Scott's Los Angeles is thus vertically stratified along analogous lines to those in *Metropolis*, between high and low, light and dark (and here also dry and wet). But unlike in *Metropolis*, we see nothing of the production process, not even the process of producing replicants, apart from a brief glimpse of the outsourced eye manufacture conducted by Chew. Here class differences are both ethnicised – as between Caucasians, like Tyrell and Bryant, and Asiatics or Latinos, like Chew and Gaff – and also essentially matters of consumption rather than of production. In short, the city is a recognisable extrapolation from late twentieth-century consumer capitalism and the great corporate towers that

---

39   Bruno 1990, p. 186.
40   Harvey 1990, p. 310.

cluster at the heart of its metropoles. And its purpose is the same. As Tyrell explains to Deckard:

> Commerce is our goal here at Tyrell. More human than human is our motto.

The giant electronic advertisements for Coca-Cola, which Deckard and Gaff pass en route to and from the Tyrell building, serve to reinforce this motif: commerce is everbody's goal here in Los Angeles. This is what has brought the city to its present impasse, in which both humans and replicants are already less human than human. As Deckard's voice-over tells us in the theatre release version:

> I'd quit because I'd had a belly full of killing. But then I'd rather be a killer than a victim. And that's exactly what Bryant's threat about little people meant.

In *Blade Runner*, as in *Alien*, the will to dystopia is thus overwhelmingly the effect of corporate power and its extension into policing, but not, as in Zamatyin or Orwell, that of the totalitarian state per se.

Dark City is a very different matter, the product neither of willed nor of technological transformation, but rather, as it first appears, an externally-altered world – through the intervention of the Strangers; and, as we later learn, a hell existing elsewhere altogether – since we aren't actually on Earth at all. 'First came the Strangers ...', announces Schreber's prologue:

> They were a race as old as time itself. They had mastered the ultimate technology, the ability to alter physical reality by will alone. They called this ability 'tuning' ... Their endless journey brought them to a small blue world at the farthest corner of the galaxy. Our world.

But if the Strangers have manufactured the city, then how has this been done? Mr Hand explains to Murdoch:

> The city is ours, we made it ... We fashioned this city on stolen memories: different eras, different pasts, all rolled into one. Each night we revise it, refine it ...

The film's own city had been made in much the same way, as a series of stolen memories, borrowings from other films, especially from 1940s Hollywood detective movies, but also, of course, from *Blade Runner*. If it looks quite literally fantastic, then this is because that is what it is: a fantasm, an impossible city made from different pasts rolled into one, including even a small slice of Sydney beachfront. The city has a human class structure – witness the transformation of the sleeping couple from poverty to riches – but this is both radically arbitrary (it can be changed overnight) and immaterial. Its real rulers are the Strangers, hidden deep within, rather than elevated high above, the cityscape. This city has no fixity, but rather changes shape, grows and shrinks like an organic lifeform, thanks to computer graphics simply unavailable to Scott, let alone Lang.

All three cities exhibit an essentially masculinist view of gender, in which the 'otherness of woman' is represented, to borrow Huyssen's description of *Metropolis*, by 'two traditional images of femininity – the virgin and the vamp, ... both focused on sexuality'.[41] In Lang, these roles are played, respectively, by the human Maria and the robot Maria; in Scott, by Rachael and Zhora or Pris; in Proyas by Anna and Emma. All three cities use the nightclub, the female performer and the prostitute as signifiers of urban life. The false Maria in *Metropolis*, Zhora in *Blade Runner*, Emma in *Dark City*, all perform simultaneously before their respective nightclub audiences and for the voyeurism of what Laura Mulvey termed the 'cinematic gaze'. Mulvey, it will be recalled, insisted that the general structure of conventional narrative cinema positions the male as active, the female as passive, quite apart from the particular contents of particular films. As she summarised her case: 'WOMAN AS IMAGE, MAN AS BEARER OF THE LOOK'.[42] The spectator position itself is thus masculinised, she argued, the patterns of pleasure and identification encoded within narrative cinema in effect prescribing a masculine point of view for the audience. So the film-goer comes to occupy a position of voyeuristic dominance over woman as the sexualised object of the cinematic gaze. This has become a distinctly unfashionable view in cinema studies and one Mulvey herself had occasion to question.[43] But all three of these films function exactly as her account suggests. Interestingly, *Metropolis* self-reflexively draws attention to the process – by placing a montage of gazing male eyes into the frame – and thereby undermines it. As Huyssen observed: 'by thematizing male gaze and vision ... the film lays open a fundamental filmic convention usually covered up by narrative cinema'.[44]

---

41 Huyssen 1986, p. 72.
42 Mulvey 1989, p. 19.
43 Mulvey 1989, pp. 29–37.
44 Huyssen 1986, p. 75.

Nonetheless, all three films proceed to punish their respective 'women' for inviting this gaze. In *Metropolis* the false Maria, a flesh-covered robot found raucously celebrating amidst the bourgeois revellers at Yoshiwara's nightclub, is seized by the angry working-class insurrectionists, here led by Grot, Fredersen's foreman and also on occasion his company spy. Played by Heinrich George, Grot urges the mob on to vengeance against 'die Hexe', the ubiquitous 'witch' of misogynist fantasy:

> Verbrennt die Hexe. – Auf den Scheiterhaufen mit ihr!!!
>
> [Burn the witch. – To the stake with her!!!]

And this, indeed, will be her fate, even if the sudden exposure of a metallic body beneath her burning flesh somehow absolves all concerned – Freder included – of the medieval barbarism entailed in this summary justice. In *Blade Runner* Zhora is a replicant – as are all the other female characters – and, like Batty's lover, Pris, she is shot to death by Deckard. Zhora has disguised herself as Madame Salome, a stripper/exotic dancer (the equivalent character in the novel is Luba Luft, an opera singer); Pris is a 'foreskin job', a 'standard pleasure model', according to Bryant. In *Dark City* Emma survives, but only after she has lost all memory of her nightclub singing days and become Anna; and, if she is spared, the hooker we meet shortly after her performance, and six others before, have all been brutally murdered and mutilated. Do male film directors dream of electric women, Marleen Barr asked of Scott.[45] Apparently they do, and almost as much in German Expressionist or transnational 'Australian' cinema as in Hollywood itself. This reproduction of stereotypically patriarchal gender relations stands in interesting contrast to the written form's comparative openness to feminism during the last three decades of the twentieth century.[46] Here, as elsewhere, the cinematic medium accords a priority to (sexualised) effect over idea.

3   Text and Intertext, Human and Posthuman

No doubt art has always made extensive use of intertextuality. For Jameson, however, this has become peculiarly characteristic of postmodernism: 'we are

---

45   Barr 1991.
46   Cf. Le Guin 1969; Piercy 1976; Russ 1985; Atwood 1986; Merrick and Williams 1999.

now ... in "intertextuality"', he writes, 'as a deliberate, built-in feature of the aesthetic effect'.[47] In this respect, *Metropolis* is clearly modern rather than postmodern, original in precisely an older modernist avant-garde sense. The Expressionist sets, by Otto Hunte, Eric Kettelhut and Karl Vollbrecht, bespeak the style of a very particular time and place. Whilst the film has functioned as an intertext for much subsequent SF cinema, its own central effect is nonetheless that of novelty, rather than of intertextuality. In *Blade Runner*, by contrast, the deliberate intertextuality is characteristically postmodern: the references to *Metropolis* – high/low, light/dark, the cityscape itself, even the closing curtains in Tyrrell's office, as compared to those in Fredersen's – are clearly deliberate; those to the 1940s detective movie – the clothes, the voice-over, the liquor and the tobacco – constitute a crucial component in its cinematic pleasure. The *Director's Cut* even ends, in the characteristically postmodern move of intertextuality for its own sake, with a knowing gesture toward film noir. *Dark City* borrows from a very similar range of intertextual reference, much of it refracted through *Blade Runner*. The obvious addition is Tim Burton's Gotham City in *Batman* and *Batman Returns*, a dark city if ever there was one.

If intertextuality is the characteristically postmodern aesthetic effect, then the posthuman is arguably its characteristic thematic. It has, of course, become a commonplace that late twentieth and early twenty-first century postmoderns have become in some significant sense 'posthuman'. Where for classical humanism, the self had been a fixed centre of conscious meaning, in much late twentieth-century thought – structuralism, psychoanalysis, poststructuralism – it came to be understood as decentred and multiple. Moreover, the decentred self of poststructuralist theory tends to replicate the multiple postmodern self of late-capitalist consumer society. In this respect too, *Metropolis* is clearly a modern rather than postmodern text. For there is little uncertainty here as to the nature of individual identity. True, the film invokes the threat of the robot Maria as a man-made substitute for woman, but we are never in doubt that Freder will be able to distinguish the true from the false. Almost at a glance, he sees that:

Du bist nicht Maria –!!!

[You are not Maria –!!!]

The line is repeated:

---

47   Jameson 1991, p. 20.

DU BIST NICHT MARIA –! Maria redet zum Friden, nicht zum Mord –! Das ist nicht Maria –!!

[YOU ARE NOT MARIA –! Maria speaks of peace, not killing –! This is not Maria –!].

'Du bist nicht Maria', Freder insists, and he is right. But this is precisely what is thrown into doubt in *Blade Runner* and even more radically so in *Dark City*. In Scott's film, we know only that replicants have implanted memories and humans don't; what we don't know, however, is who is and who isn't human. Crucially, we don't even know whether Deckard himself is a replicant: his memories are supported only by photographs, the same kind of flimsy material evidence provided the replicants; in *The Director's Cut*, he dreams of a unicorn, Gaff's symbol for the replicant. 'Are you for real?', Zhora asks Deckard. In truth, neither he nor we can be sure of the answer. Scott himself thought that 'having Deckard be a replicant is the *only* reasonable solution'.[48] In *Dark City* the argument is moved a step further, so that no-one possesses both memory and individual identity: the Strangers share memory and a group mind, devoid of individual identity; the humans exist as individuals, but with false memories changed nightly at midnight. So Murdoch is and is not a murderer, he has and has not been married to Emma, and so on. Here, identity is constructed and multiple in the strongest of senses.

If the 'human' is becoming progressively 'decentred', then this is an effect not only of poststructuralist and postmodern theory, but also of such new technologies for re-embodiment and dis-embodiment as genetic engineering and prosthetics, artificial intelligence and virtual reality. If the 'human' is by 'nature' not genetically-engineered, not augmented by prosthetics, not extended either by AI or into VR, then the obvious question arises as to what exactly we are becoming or going to be replaced by. This is an old question in SF, at least as old as *Frankenstein*, but it acquired a new urgency in the last decades of the twentieth century. All three films acknowledged the prospect, *Metropolis* in distinctly modern fashion, however, *Blade Runner* and *Dark City* in distinctly postmodern, a difference most apparent in their respective resolutions. *Metropolis* recognises the danger of the robot Maria as man-made substitute for woman, especially in the 'Hel' narrative omitted from many later versions. However, the robot's destruction by fire provides a classically humanist resolution to the problem of the posthuman, reminiscent of that in *Frankenstein* itself. The true

---

48   Kolb 1991b, p. 177n.

Maria then inspires Freder to unite capital and labour, Fredersen and Grot, in a movement that simultaneously endorses the division of labour both by class and by gender, assuring him that:

> Hirn und Hände wollen zusammenkommen
>
> [Head and hands want to join together].

As the film concludes, Maria continues:

> aber es fehlt ihnen das Herz dazu ... Mittler Du, zeige ihnen, den Weg zueinander ... MITTLER ZWISCHEN HIRN UND HÄNDEN MUSS DAS HERZ SEIN!
>
> [but they don't have the heart to do it ... Oh mediator, show them the way to each other ... THE MEDIATOR BETWEEN HEAD AND HANDS MUST BE THE HEART!]

Apparently, a good man needs a good supportive woman at his side, rather than a spitefully subversive 'Mensch-Maschine'. This denouement, argues Huyssen, is 'but a lingering residue of expressionism, ... which covers up the persisting domination of labor by capital and high technology, the persisting domination of woman by the male gaze and the reestablished repression of ... sexuality'.[49] It can be read as either nicely social-democratic or horribly fascist, and is quite possibly both, not simply because all signs are polysemic, but also because the screenplay was co-written by Lang and his then wife, Thea von Harbou. She joined the Nazi Party in 1932, he fled into exile in the USA. In 1926, the contradiction between readings hadn't yet become so apparent.

Blade Runner is very different, if only because all of Tyrell's creations are more impressive than their creator, a thematic signalled in the film's prologue:

> The NEXUS 6 *Replicants* were superior in strength and agility, and at least equal in intelligence, to the genetic engineers who created them.

They are also morally superior, we eventually realise, since Batty will show mercy to Deckard, the blade runner who has shown none to the other escaped replicants. The film's conclusion, explicit in the theatre release, implied in the

---

49 Huyssen 1986, p. 81.

Director's Cut, where Deckard and Rachael escape from Los Angeles, decisively relocates audience sympathy from the human to the replicant. In both versions, Gaff tells Deckard, 'It's too bad she won't live. But then again, who does?' In both, the line is later repeated. In both, Deckard asks for and receives from Rachael the promise of love and of trust. A good male replicant apparently needs a supportive female replicant to trust him. In both, Deckard and Rachael discover an origami unicorn and thus realise that Gaff has previously found but nonetheless not killed her. The *Director's Cut* ends with a lift door closing on the ambiguous possibility of their escape from Los Angeles. The theatre release version is much more explicit, concluding with a subsequent sequence of their flight over an improbably pastoral countryside, as Deckard's voice-over explains, not only that Gaff has let Rachael go, but also that:

> Tyrell had told me Rachael was special: no termination date. I didn't know how long we'd have together. Who does?

Scott disliked this ending and deleted it from the *Director's Cut*. But Leonard Heldreth has argued that, although it 'may seem intellectually contrived and out of tone with the rest of the film, ... it's the emotional ending we want'.[50] In the most literal of senses, he is surely right: the studio chose this ending precisely because it was preferred by their pre-release sample audiences. But Heldreth himself prefers it for reasons that are quite explicitly humanist in ideology: 'At the end of the film', he writes, 'Deckard [is] ... no longer trying to remain a human being while he kills the very emotional responses that define his humanity ... Deckard, i.e., man, is presented as a human being who makes his escape into the new Eden with a new Eve'. There is indeed a sense in which Deckard and Rachael can be read as a new Adam and Eve escaping into a new Eden. But Rachael is certainly not a woman and, if Scott is to be believed, nor is Deckard a man: these are replicants. If that is the ending postmodern humans want, then this is so for reasons precisely the obverse of Heldreth's, not only because we like our men to be men, and our women women, but because we're also no longer very concerned whether either is still actually human, no longer entirely persuaded of our evolutionary superiority as a species. As Boozer says of *Blade Runner*: 'This near-future tech *noir* edition of ... the postmodern city ... is ... in an advanced state of decay. Rather than reharmonizing itself with nature through knowledge, the world of Tyrell is further removed than ever'.[51] This

---

50   Heldreth 1991, p. 51.
51   Boozer 1991, p. 219.

is surely how 'we' have increasingly come to see 'our' cities, as the mounting wreckage of a civilisation nearly beyond repair. In 1982 *Blade Runner*'s solution seemed quite staggeringly audacious: to give up on humanity in a wager on the prospects for a posthuman future. The *Director's Cut* spells out this replicant solution much more explicitly in almost every respect except its ending, the closing gesture toward film noir thus detracting from the originality of its posthuman narrative resolution.

In *Dark City* the equivalent anxieties revolve around the alien abduction of an entire city and invasive alien scientific experimentation on its citizens, a theme curiously reminiscent of *The X-Files*, the most popular 1990s SF television series in the United States. Superficially, the film can be read as providing an essentially humanist narrative solution, when Murdoch finally defeats Mr Book in mind-to-mind combat. 'You wanted to know what it was about us that made us human. Well you're not going to find it in here …', he tells the Stranger, pointing towards his own forehead: 'You went looking in the wrong place'. We are thus prepared for a traditional appeal to the heart, much like that at the end of *Metropolis*. But this isn't what happens: rather, Murdoch turns away, he sighs, his eyes light up in conventional signification of the alien, as he begins to re-tune the city into light. He can do this only because he too has mastered the ultimate technology, the ability to alter physical reality by will alone, in short, because he has already mutated into something posthuman. By conventionally humanist standards, this makes him a deeply dangerous man. And yet we are reassured that he is a good (post-human) man, with a nicely supportive good woman, Anna, waiting for him at the end of the pier, with a good view of Shell Beach. In this respect, *Dark City* is a more dangerous film than *The Matrix* trilogy, made at the same studios, reworking the same Sydney cityscape into similarly fantastic form (though as a city of light rather than of darkness), premised on similarly posthuman possibilities, and drawing on a similarly postmodern range of intertextual effect (including the famously knowing reference to *Simulacra and Simulation*). But where *The Matrix* would opt for a conventionally humanist narrative in which Neo, as Christ-like human, strives to save humanity from its own posthuman progeny, *Dark City* pursued the more disturbing hypothesis that it might be possible to save the species only by its mutating into the posthuman.

To say that the film is more dangerous and more disturbing is not, of course, to say that it is 'right'. It is better to think with, that is all, better to disagree with, as we try to find ways from the dominant to the emergent, from the postmodern to whatever better possibilities it still precludes and prevents. For what *Dark City* represents, even more powerfully than *Blade Runner*, is a near-complete retreat from the possibility of humanly-willed transformation, whether for better or for worse. In this respect, it bespeaks the truth of a wider culture, in which, as Jameson has it, time can be imagined only as 'an eternal present and, much further away, an inevitable catastrophe'.[52] Revisiting his earlier accounts of Morris and Orwell in 1978, Williams borrowed from Abensour the distinction between 'systematic' and 'heuristic' utopias, meaning those focussed respectively on organisational models and on values.[53] *News from Nowhere*, he concluded, was a 'generous but sentimental heuristic transformation'. Morris's heuristic had become distinctly unsentimental at one point, however, through 'the crucial insertion of the *transition* to utopia' as something to be 'fought for'.[54] Orwell's 1984 is neither more nor less plausible than Morris's 2003, Williams observed, but the latter's fictional revolution of 1952 is more plausible than either 'because its energy flows both ways, forward and back, ... its issue ... can go either way'. For Williams, this kind of openness – when the 'subjunctive is a true subjunctive, rather than a displaced indicative' – powerfully called into question the then still dominant mode of dystopia represented paradigmatically by *Nineteen Eighty-Four*.[55] Moreover, he found a parallel openness at work in Le Guin's *The Dispossessed*.[56] At an important stage in certain kinds of future story, Williams wrote, 'a writer sits and *thinks*; assembles and deploys variables ... when even the factors are only partly known ... and when their interaction ... is quite radically uncertain'. *The Dispossessed*, he continued, is characterised by 'deliberate and sustained thought about possible futures'.[57] In short, Le Guin's thinking is deliberate and sustained, rather than 'sentimental', and thus directed toward the possible rather than the ideal. This kind of openness, when the subjunctive is a true subjunctive, is surely missing from both Scott's Los Angeles and Proyas's dark city.

In *The County and the City*, Williams had observed of written SF dystopias that:

> everything about the city – from the magnificent to the apocalyptic – can be believed at once. One source of this unevenness is the complexity of the pressures and problems. But another ... is the abstraction of the city, as a huge isolated problem ...[58]

---

52 Jameson 1994, p. 70.
53 Abensour 1973.
54 Williams 1980c, p. 204.
55 Williams 1980c, p. 208.
56 Williams 1980c, p. 212.
57 Williams 1984a, p. 266.
58 Williams 1973b, p. 278.

Part of what it might mean to move beyond the postmodern would surely be to move beyond the apocalyptic (and the magnificent), to apprehend the city both in itself and in its relations with the country as real, active and concrete. To judge by SF cinema, we still have a long way to go.

CHAPTER 21

Postmodern Gothic: *Buffy*, *The X-Files* and the Clinton Presidency*

Mary Shelley's 1817 novel, *Frankenstein, or The Modern Prometheus*, is now widely regarded as one of the founding texts of the science fiction and horror genres. The modern myth it established has been enormously influential across a whole range of media and forms. Here, I want to examine how its story was retold in two of the most successful American television series of the last decade of the twentieth century and the first of the twenty-first: *The X-Files*, which ran from 1993 until 2002; and *Buffy the Vampire Slayer*, which ran from 1997 until 2003. I will focus on particular episodes from each series: 'The Postmodern Prometheus', which first went to air in November 1997, as part of the fifth season of *The X-Files*; and the 'Adam' sequence from *Buffy*'s fourth season, a set of four linked episodes, comprising 'The I in Team', 'Goodbye Iowa', 'The Yoko Factor' and 'Primeval', first broadcast during 2000, on 8 and 15 February, 9 and 16 May respectively. First, however, I want to say something about the more general characteristics of the two series.

1 A Tale of Two Television Series

The X-Files was produced by Chris Carter for the American Fox Network, a subsidiary of Rupert Murdoch's News Corporation; *Buffy* by Joss Whedon's own production company, Mutant Enemy, and broadcast on the Warner and Paramount networks, though its wider distribution was also handled by Fox. By televisual standards, both were subject to and acknowledge unusually strong claims to authorship. The credits for *The X-Files* described it as 'created' by Carter, he was its executive producer, he wrote the scripts for the first two episodes (and for 9 out of 24 in the first season, two as co-author) and directed many of the key episodes. Whedon was listed as 'creator' and 'executive producer' for *Buffy* and, during the first five seasons, directed 16 episodes and wrote 22. Both

---

* This chapter has been published previously in *Continuum: Journal of Media and Cultural Studies*, Vol. 19, No. 1, pp. 103–16, 2005, http://www.tandfonline.com/doi/full/10.1080/10304310520000336324

series were immensely successful. In February 1995, during its second season, the *X-Files* episode entitled 'Fresh Bones' reached some 10.8 million American homes.[1] This success was repeated elsewhere, in Britain for example, both on the BBC and News Corporation's Sky TV, and in Australia on Channel 10 and Murdoch's Foxtel. *Buffy* had a similar impact, again not only in the US, but also in Britain, again on the BBC, and in Australia, on Channel 7 and again on Foxtel. Both generated a considerable secondary spin-off industry of 'collectible' toys, comics and books (often published by News's HarperCollins), for *The X-Files* a film, and for *Buffy* the *Angel* television series.

The 'X-Files' provided Carter's programme with its title and central organising motif: each individual episode was supposed to be a file from the American Federal Bureau of Investigation's inquiries into the paranormal. For most of the series, the investigators were Agent Fox Mulder, played by David Duchovny, and Agent Dana Scully, played by Gillian Anderson. In the penultimate series Duchovny was for the main part replaced by Robert Patrick, in the role of Agent John Doggett. The episode that concerns us is taken from the main body, however, featuring Duchovny and Anderson. As the title made clear, it was a self-consciously postmodern retelling of Shelley's *Frankenstein*. Carter had never been entirely happy with the notion that *The X-Files* was science fiction: in a 1995 online interview, he insisted he 'never was a science fiction fan'.[2] But for the main part, *The X-Files* meets even Darko Suvin's fairly restrictive definition of the genre as one distinguished by '*the narrative dominance or hegemony of a fictional "novum" ... validated by cognitive logic*'.[3] Its long-run story arc was provided by a threatened alien invasion and collaboration by sections of the American elite, both entirely compatible with 'cognitive logic'. And, even where the paranormal became less obviously rational in content, Scully would seek to explain it through the cognitive logic of medical science. We should qualify these observations, by adding that this was a distinctly 'postmodern' science fiction, nonetheless, not only in the obvious sense that both Jameson and Baudrillard see science fiction and television as characteristically postmodern cultural phenomena, but also because the programme displayed postmodern characteristics of its own, which we will explore below.[4]

Buffy the Vampire Slayer was not science fiction as Suvin understood it, but rather Gothic horror fantasy, descended from Shelley by way of a rather different genealogy. The Southern Californian town of Sunnydale, where the series

---

1 Lowry 1995, p. 247.
2 Badley 1996, p. 150n.
3 Suvin 1979, p. 63.
4 Jameson 1991, pp. 38, 76; Baudrillard 1994, pp. 121–7.

is set, is a 'Hellmouth', the entrance to a world of ancient books and archaic weapons, bibles and wooden stakes, vampires, demons and magic. This Hellmouth is a Suvinian novum, but of the distinctly non-cognitive variety. The central protagonist, Buffy Summers, is a Vampire Slayer by nature and destiny, but a thoroughly contemporary Californian young woman by upbringing and preference. The conflict between nature and nurture had generated much of the narrative drive and comic effect in the 1992 film that inspired the series. Directed by Fran Rubel Kuzui for 20th Century Fox, with Whedon as its scriptwriter, it was set in 'Southern California: the Lite Ages', as opposed to the Dark Ages, and was overwhelmingly comic in register. In the television series, this conflict between nature and nurture is significantly occluded through the naturalisation of the fantastic as an everyday feature of Southern Californian life. Television's Buffy, played by Sarah Michelle Gellar, graduated year by year, season by season, through Sunnydale High School and the University of California, Sunnydale, as one fresh-faced middle-class youngster amongst others, situated within and contextualised by an ensemble of friends (the 'Scooby Gang') and lovers.

The friends included Nicholas Brendon as Xander, Alyson Hannigan as Willow and Charisma Carpenter as Cordelia; the lovers, David Boreanaz as Angel, the vampire with a soul, Marc Blucas as Riley, of whom more later, and James Marsters as Spike, the vampire eventually deprived of his capacity to kill humans. The programme's central adult authority figure was Buffy's 'watcher', Giles, played by Anthony Stewart Head, here nicely naturalised as the High School librarian. This naturalisation of the supernatural suggests how closely science fiction and fantasy had come to overlap in 'New Age' late twentieth- and early twenty-first century America. The *Buffy* episodes that will concern us here are unusually close to science fiction, nonetheless. In these and the immediately contiguous episodes, the programme's monsters and vampires were both rationalised and naturalised as 'HSTs', or Hostile Sub Terrestrials, pursued and hunted down by the ultra-scientific 'Initiative', which planned to use their body parts to create a cyborg, the demonoid, 'Adam'. Here, as in 'The Postmodern Prometheus', the linking theme is a postmodern retelling of the *Frankenstein* story.

Although the special effects were technically proficient in both series, ideas were clearly more important, not in the sense that they were necessarily 'serious', but rather that they made the shows 'work'. Their sheer range was crucial to the distinctive appeal of *The X-Files* and *Buffy*: in both, the viewer could never be quite certain what would happen next. By the standards of American television, this is a strong claim to make. The tension between idea and effect, which Adorno and Horkheimer famously identified in their critique of Hollywood cinema,[5] seems to be resolved differently in television, primarily because of the low-budget nature of the medium. At one level, financial constraints clearly militate against both idea and effect, which is why so much television is interesting as neither. But ideas can come more cheaply than their specularisation, which leads to the possibility that television might sometimes reverse the cinematic prioritisation of effect over idea. This may well be the case here. At the very least, we need to note that these were unusually adventurous and interesting programmes.

Their novelty functioned at the level of form, moreover, as well as content. Raymond Williams identified three main forms in television drama: the series, the serial and the single television play, the latter often part of an anthology.[6] All three have been used in science fiction and fantasy, though the third seems to have become less common over time, probably because its use of different combinations of production and performance personnel for each episode makes it relatively high-cost. Formally, *The X-Files* and *Buffy* were neither pure series nor serial nor anthology, but, rather, examples of what Reeves, Rodgers and Epstein described as 'episodic/serial straddle', that is, 'a sort of mini-serial within the series'.[7] There were discrete episodes, but also multi-part episodes (such as 'Duane Barry' and 'Ascension' in *The X-Files* or the Adam sequence in *Buffy*). More importantly, a range of developing story lines continued from episode to episode: in *The X-Files*, Mulder and his sister's abduction, Scully and her father, the Cancer Man (William B. Davis) and the conspiracy in high places; in *Buffy*, the mother/daughter relationship between Joyce Summers (Kristine Sutherland) and Buffy, the romances with Angel, Riley and Spike, Willow's lesbian relationship with Tara (Amber Benson), the Scooby Gang's steady progress through high school and university. Such long-term story arcs allowed for a cumulative character development unavailable to the conventional series.

The X-Files and *Buffy* were examples of late-capitalist relations of cultural production in two interesting aspects: both were the product, simultaneously, of transnational capitalism and niche marketing. The transnational character of *The X-Files* is perhaps most readily apparent: Fox Broadcasting, which produced, broadcast, syndicated and marketed the programme, was a subsidiary of what was still then an Australian-based media conglomerate; the key 'stars' were American; but all except the last series were made in Canada, with mainly Canadian labour, including the actors playing the minor roles; and its audience was near-global. *Buffy* was less obviously transnational in production, but

---

5   Adorno and Horkheimer 1979, p. 125.
6   Williams 1974, pp. 57–61.
7   Reeves, Rodgers and Epstein 1996, pp. 33–4.

nonetheless had a distinctly transatlantic accent: Buffy, Willow and Xander – and Sunnydale – were firmly Californian; but Giles, Spike and Buffy's second Watcher, Wesley (Alexis Denisof), were played as English. Like *The X-Files*, *Buffy* also acquired a global market. That *The X-Files* belonged to Fox was more than merely coincidental: it also explains something of its success. Reeves, Rodgers and Epstein distinguish between what they term 'TVI', which lasted from the 1950s to the 1970s, and 'TVII', which dated from the 1980s and 1990s.[8] In the former, American television was dominated by three major 'free-to-air' networks, ABC, NBC and CBS, each producing programmes for very large 'mass' audiences. To survive in this market, a programme had to command something like a third of the American television audience. Children's television aside, science fiction and fantasy could rarely manage this: even *Star Trek* lasted for only two seasons. TVII was characterised by the development of alternative outlets, such as satellite TV, cable TV and home videorecording. During this period, the audience share commanded by the big three networks fell from 90% to 60%, creating the space, not only for science fiction, but also for News Corporation's fourth network.[9] Murdoch's company used *The X-Files* as a flagship for the Fox Network and as a key resource for its other satellite and cable interests, such as Sky in Britain and Foxtel in Australia. Similarly, *Buffy* was broadcast on the minor Warner network, which was itself part of a larger international media-conglomerate, Time-Warner.

Both series were spectacular cult – that is, niche market – successes. Both were aimed at a target demographic of late teenagers and young adults, rather than 'mature' adults or children: in the United States, the peak audience for *Buffy* was in the 18–34 range, the average age 29.[10] Both seemed to be pitched at a disproportionately female market. Both also inspired unusually strong loyalties amongst relatively clearly defined and demarcated 'fan' audiences. The first convention of 'X-Philes' was held in San Diego in June 1995, some 2,500 people attending, with twenty conventions in total scheduled for the same year across the USA. Both series generated a proliferation of collectibles and other spin-offs, and an extraordinarily well developed on-line fandom, devoted to 'The Truth' or the 'Buffyverse'. In 1995, something like 25,000 people per month logged on to *X-Files* sites.[11]

---

8   Reeves, Rodgers and Epstein 1996, 24–5, 29.
9   Reeves, Rodgers and Epstein 1996, p. 30.
10 Ono 2000, p. 165.
11 Lowry 1995, pp. 239–40.

2   Postmodern Gothic

Both series exhibited at least three characteristically postmodern tropes: 'politically correct' identity politics; intertextual aesthetics; and the posthuman as thematic. As to the first, Scully and Buffy were instances of the late twentieth-century fashion in American television for 'powerful women'. In *The X-Files*, Scully was the more rational, scientific and sceptical, Mulder the more prone to 'believe'. This was 'gender-bending' of a kind, except insofar as the narrative tended to support his credulity as much as her scepticism. But the play with gender was real, nonetheless, and it was thus unsurprising that the show should have had a very large female audience. Shots of Mulder sometimes invited a female gaze as surely as anything in Hollywood narrative cinema invites the male.[12] Moreover, as Wilcox and Williams approvingly observe, for the lead characters themselves: 'Their looks acknowledge each other as subjects rather than fetishizing or denying the other person'.[13] *Buffy* was similarly non-homophobic and unsexist: witness the sympathetic treatment of the Willow/Tara relationship; or Buffy's capacity to take the initiative, not only in encounters with vampires and demons, but also in her relations with Riley and Angel. So it was Buffy, rather than Riley, who initiated their mutual seduction in 'The I in Team'. Shots of Riley during their subsequent lovemaking not only invite a female gaze, but also actually acquired one from within the televisual frame, when the camera panned away from a screen-within-the-screen, to reveal Professor Maggie Walsh as the female voyeur. No doubt, sections of the male audience would gaze along with her, but at Buffy rather than Riley. The more general success of these powerful women had arisen, however, precisely from their capacity to function simultaneously as male sex objects and positive female role models.

If intertextuality is indeed the central postmodern aesthetic effect, then it is as evident in these shows as anywhere. In *The X-Files*, Mulder and Scully clearly refer to Woodward and Bernstein in *All the President's Men*, just as their initial insider contact with a penchant for meetings in car parks refers to the original 'Deep Throat'. But Mulder also borrows from Dale Cooper, the FBI agent in *Twin Peaks*, and Scully from Agent Starling in *The Silence of the Lambs*.[14] *Buffy* rifles through the horror and teen-movie genres, borrowing everything from werewolves to graduation days, so that in the television series, as in the earlier film, much of the humour derives from running the two genres against each other.

---

12   Mulvey 1989, p. 19.
13   Wilcox and Williams 1996, p. 120.
14   Lowry 1995, pp. 14–50.

In both programmes, intertextual aesthetics are often combined with a posthuman thematic. In *The X-Files*, these anxieties typically revolved around themes of alien abduction and/or invasive scientific experimentation on the human body. Buffy is actually a super-human, but supposedly stands in a long line of Slayers, each human, rather than posthuman. Riley and Adam, however, are more properly posthuman and, as we shall see, in these episodes the anxieties over posthumanism centre on the linked themes of monstrous rebellion and irresponsible scientific experimentation.

3   The Postmodern Prometheus

The core narrative in 'The Postmodern Prometheus' tells of how Mulder and Scully are summoned by Shaineh Berkowicz, a plump, mid-Western fan of *The Jerry Springer Show*, played by Pattie Tierce, to investigate claims that she has suffered two completely unwanted pregnancies, one contemporary, the other eighteen years previously. In both, she fears she might have been drugged and impregnated by some kind of monster, apparently to the accompaniment of music by Cher Bono. The FBI agents proceed to consider claims that the town has indeed been the unwitting home to a resident monster, the Great Mutato, played by Chris Owens; and thence, to investigate the genetic researches of a prominent local scientist, Professor Polidori, played by John O'Hurley. Represented by herself and by Polidori as a 'scientist', Scully's response is to insist that this is merely a populist hoax:

> Isn't it obvious? I think what we're seeing here is an example of the culture for whom daytime talkshows and tabloid headlines have become a reality against which they measure their lives, a culture so obsessed by the media and a chance for self-dramatisation that they'll do anything in order to gain a spotlight.

Mulder is less sure:

> I'm alarmed that you would reduce these people to a cultural stereotype. Not everybody's dream is to get on *Jerry Springer*.

Even setting aside its title, the programme is characteristically postmodern, both in the thematic concern for the posthuman and a strong sense of intertextuality as fun. The referent, the real to which the sign refers, was pretty well suppressed in most *X-Files* episodes, but here the focus fell even more than usual on the interplay of signifiers. This is apparent, for example, from the way the episode deliberately signals its own fictionality. It was the only X-File to be filmed in black and white, rather than in colour, a device to alert the audience to its cinematically fictional aspects. It had a well-defined frame narrative, another obviously fictional device, not simply Carter's own, but the frame-within-a-frame provided by *The Great Mutato* comic book, written by Shaineh's son, Izzy, performed by Stewart Gale. It played with the problem of how fiction constructs endings by allowing Mulder to object to a likely unhappy ending, then contriving the happy ending he asked for. More fundamentally, the entire narrative is structured around the opposition between high and popular culture, here represented through different forms of textuality, the one as literature (Shelley's *Frankenstein*) and science (Polidori's research), the other as comic book (*The Great Mutato*), television (*The Jerry Springer Show*) and recorded music (Cher).

Moreover, the programme comprises a tissue of intertextual references to Shelley's novel, to the occasion of its composition and to subsequent film adaptations, especially James Whale's 1931 movie, *Frankenstein*. The name of the Frankenstein figure in Carter's retelling, Polidori, refers, of course, to Byron's physician and secretary. The first meeting between this Polidori, Scully and Mulder is introduced by a headline from the university newspaper: 'PROFESSOR CREATES OWN MONSTERS'. The meeting is shot, not simply in black and white, but to the accompaniment of thunder and lightning flashes, which quote directly from Whale. When the professor brings the interview to a close, he explains he will be travelling that night to the University of Ingolstadt to give an international address. There is no university at Ingolstadt, nor has there been since 1800, but it was nonetheless there that Shelley's Frankenstein had been educated.[15] Polidori's wife, we later learn, is an Elizabeth, just as Frankenstein's would be. By no means all viewers spot the intertextual references. But for those who don't, Mulder, representing literature as against science, spells them out to Scully:

> When Victor Frankenstein asks himself 'Whence did the principle of life proceed?' and then, as the gratifying summit to his toils, creates a hideous phantasm of a man, he prefigures the postmodern Prometheus, the genetic engineer, whose power to reanimate matter – genes – into life – us – is only as limited as his imagination is.

---

15   Shelley 1980, pp. 42, 235n.

It remains for Scully to spell out the joke:

> Mulder, I'm alarmed that you would reduce this man to a literary stereotype.

The references to Whale are also important. So, when Mulder discovers the family album of Mutato photographs and exclaims 'It's Alive!', he quotes from the movie, rather than the novel, where this line never actually appears. The town mob's pursuit of the monster, in an angry torch-burning procession, with Polidori at their head, is yet another quotation from Whale. Modern film and postmodern television programme end differently, however, the first in a serious endorsement of small-town mob violence, the second in a comic resolve to live and let live with the monstrously posthuman. Whale's monster had been killed in a windmill set alight by the vigilantes' torches, burnt to death in scenes that invited audience complicity with sadistic violence. But Carter's escapes the burning barn and is rescued from mob vengeance by his own eloquent plea in self-defence:

> What we did was wrong, but in our trespasses we gave you a loving son. And in your homes I went places I'd never dreamed of. With your books and your records and your home media centres I learned of the world and of a mother's love that I'll never know.

Izzy then speaks for his wronged mother and the entire town, Polidori excepted, when he responds: 'Hey, he's no monster'. He speaks also for ordinariness, Cher and Jerry Springer, as against science and literature. The mother love Mutato invokes here is no mere abstraction, moreover, but rather a specific reference to Bogdanovich's 1985 movie, *Mask*, where Cher had played the part of Rusty Denis, the biker mother of a radically deformed teenage boy. Hence, the alternative ending nominated by Mulder, in which he and Scully take Mutato to a Cher concert, where the singer, played by Tracey Bell, performs 'Walking in Memphis'. There are at least three good jokes in this closing sequence. First, if this monster was a product of late twentieth-century science, then according to much contemporary popular wisdom, Cher too is a substantial tribute to the art of the plastic surgeon. Second, whilst Bell performs Cher performing, the camera cuts to a fictional episode of *The Jerry Springer Show*, where Springer, playing himself, interviews Elizabeth Polidori and Shaineh Berkowicz about their monstrous infants, leading the latter to exclaim: 'What's not to love?' Finally, Mulder and Scully are moved to dance to Cher's music, thus edging towards what could have been their then much-anticipated first screen kiss, only for it to be rendered instantly fictive in the closing frame, as a panel from one of Izzy's comic books.

4 The Biomechanical Demonoid

Whilst Carter directed and wrote 'The Postmodern Prometheus', none of the four episodes in *Buffy*'s Adam sequence were written or directed by Whedon. James A. Contner directed 'The I in Team' and 'Primeval', David Grossman 'The Yoko Factor' and David Solomon 'Goodbye Iowa'; David Fury wrote 'The I in Team' and 'Primeval', Marti Noxon 'Goodbye Iowa' and Douglas Petrie 'The Yoko Factor'. Where Carter's monster had been a genetically-engineered 'mistake', in Polidori's phrase, *Buffy*'s 'Adam', played by George Hertzberg, is a deliberately-designed cyborg warrior, a demon-human-machine hybrid. The Frankenstein/God figure here was Buffy's psychology lecturer, Professor Walsh, played by Lindsay Crouse, who is also employed, we later learn, by a top-secret Government research facility located beneath the University, the so-called Initiative, where she is working on Project 314, the making of the 'biomechanical demonoid'. That this particular Frankenstein should be female is an instance of the feminisation of erstwhile masculine authority in postmodern genderbending. Her authority is exercised over male figures, moreover, notably her assistant, Dr Angleman, played by Jack Stehlin, and Riley, Buffy's soon-to-be lover, introduced into the show in the first episode of this same season. Riley had first appeared as Walsh's teaching assistant at the University, but he too is employed by the Initiative, as a peculiar kind of commando, subject to full military discipline. Both the commandos and the research are designed to defeat and take advantage of the demon threat to humanity.

The Adam sequence shares with 'The Postmodern Prometheus' both an intertextual aesthetic and a posthuman thematic. References to both *Frankenstein* and *Genesis* recur throughout. Whilst the monster's name obviously points to the second, Spike equally obviously gestures towards the first, describing the demonoid as 'big, scary, Frankenstein-looking'. In the 'Goodbye Iowa' episode, the scene where Adam murders the little boy also refers very directly to the killing of the little girl in Whale's *Frankenstein*. The two sequences are almost exactly homologous in narrative structure. In each, a smiling child innocently enters into conversation with the monster; the scene is structured around the physical contrast between their respective heights; the monster then becomes curious to see how the child 'works'; the camera cuts away prior to the killing, in a moment of 'tact' signalling its imminence and its horror; and the cut is to a public arena, the town square in 1931, the television news in 2000, where the death is then announced. The posthuman thematic in the Adam sequence centres on Walsh's various experiments to improve on human life, 'for the greater good', as she says towards the end of 'The I in Team'. Her motives are thus close to Frankenstein's, not so much evil as hubristic, both by her own account and in Riley's. Despite her choice for his name, Adam is actually a closer counterpart to the monster in *Frankenstein*, that is, the posthuman creation who turns on its human creator. Planning to rid herself of Buffy and so re-establish Riley's loyalties, Walsh is suddenly and fatally stabbed from behind by the newly conscious Adam. The Biblical figure of Adam is rehearsed more fully, however, in the character of Riley. He too is a significantly augmented, 'posthuman' creation, but one we can identify as still recognisably 'human'; he too disobeys Walsh and the Initiative, but for reasons close to those that prompted Adam to disobedience, his love for Buffy, the programme's unlikely Eve.

The first encounter between Adam and Riley in 'Goodbye Iowa' is a key exchange for the entire four-episode sequence and can usefully be compared to the confrontation between Shelley's Frankenstein and the monster on Mont Blanc.[16] In the *Buffy* episode, the creator is already dead, but, by accessing her software, Adam is able to speak on her behalf. This, in turn, enables him to position Riley, not as Walsh's co-creator, but as his own co-creature. Adam begins by defining himself as a 'kinematically redundant, biomechanical demonoid designed by Maggie Walsh', adding that she 'called me Adam and I called her Mother'. When Buffy observes that he must therefore be made 'from parts of other demons', he agrees, but continues:

> And man. And machine. Which tells me what I am, but not who I am. Mother wrote things down, hard data but also her feelings. That's how I learned that I have a job here and that she loved me.

Riley objects forcefully to this notion that Adam is a mother's son, rather than a scientist's experiment, prompting the demonoid to retort: 'Mother created you too'. The monster then explains just exactly how Walsh had created Riley, most of which is meant to come as a surprise, not only to Buffy, but also to the audience:

> she ... shaped your basic operating system. She taught you how to think, how to feel, she fed you chemicals to make you stronger, your mind and

---

16   Shelley 1980, p. 100.

body. She said that you and I were her favourite children, her art. That makes us brothers, family.

Riley angrily denies the connection, only to be confounded, yet again, by Adam's astute speculation that such discomfiture can have only two possible causes:

Because your feeding schedule – the chemicals – have been interrupted? Or do you miss her?

The most striking aspect of this exchange, as in its prototype on Mont Blanc, is that the monster has almost all the interesting lines and asks almost all the interesting questions. For Adam is more concerned than Riley to discover the true nature of their respective identities, to search for the meanings the latter prefers to avoid. Riley's resort to violence, when he brings the dialogue to a close by drawing his gun, underlines his own lack of intellectual curiosity and emotional honesty.

Adam cannot be allowed to excite our sympathies, however, not even to the extent of the monsters in *Frankenstein* or 'The Postmodern Prometheus'. For in *Buffy*, the demonic is almost invariably an irreconcilable threat, the solution to which is equally invariably violent extinction. Adam had spoken to Riley of Walsh's 'plan', which gave him his 'job', the details of which remained unclear. But in 'Primeval' we learn that Adam had killed Walsh, and later Angleman and others, as part of his own scheme – which had been hers – to use their bodies to create a species of human-demon hybrids, in short, Frankenstein's 'race of devils'.[17] How, then, does the denouement proceed? Unable to defeat Adam from within her own resources, the Vampire Slayer destroys him through magic, a powerful 'enjoining spell', combining her strengths with those of Willow, Xander and Giles, the friends Spike contrived to turn against each other in the immediately preceding episode. This is the problem with fantasy, as against science fiction: even the most intractable of situations can be readily resolved by means near to, or even identical with, wish fulfilment. Conveniently enough, the Initiative is also destroyed in a mighty battle between soldiers and demons, UC Sunnydale's local version of the *Götterdämmerung*. This resolution is both far too easily bought and fundamentally conservative, closer to Mary Shelley than to Chris Carter. But its conservatism consists, not only in a determination to extinguish the posthuman, but also in the programme's refusal to acknowledge either its own or its audience's deeper fears.

---

17   Shelley, 1980, p. 165.

5   Policing Difference

We noted the presence of 'politically correct' identity politics in *The X-Files* and *Buffy the Vampire Slayer*. Such notions were characteristic features of what Touraine dubbed the 'new social movements' of the late twentieth century.[18] Unlike the old social movement, the labour movement, these movements were not in principle anti-capitalist. And it is an important insight in Jameson that postmodernism is not at all post-capitalist, but rather the product of the 'purer capitalism of our own time', which 'eliminates the enclaves of precapitalist organization it ... hitherto tolerated and exploited in a tributary way'.[19] Understanding postmodernism thus, we can begin to explain the peculiar place occupied within it by these unprecedented attempts to 'decentre' white, straight, male, cultural authority. In a culture so commodified, so subject to the logics of the simulacrum, the widening rift between sign and referent produced formidable structural inhibitors to the type of class consciousness which informed the labour movement. As Jameson writes: 'For a society that wants to forget about class ... reification ... is very functional indeed'.[20] But this forgetfulness is itself a peculiar kind of class consciousness, he suggests, deriving from the particular new class fraction 'variously ... labeled ... new petit bourgeoisie, ... professional-managerial class, or more succinctly "the yuppies"'.[21] During the late twentieth century, radical politics mutated into identity politics, the preserve of these new movements, whose characteristic narratives typically lacked 'the allegorical capacity to map or model the system'.[22] Partly as a result, non-market forms of hierarchy declined markedly in significance, thus opening up the opportunities for what Jameson describes as a 'prodigious' expansion of capitalism into 'hitherto uncommodified areas'.[23]

Neither Buffy, Mulder nor Scully are exactly new social movement activists, though the latter has been involved in antinuclear protests. But both they and their friends clearly provide idealised fictional representations of the late twentieth century American yuppie. Physically attractive and well dressed, mobile phones invariably at the ready, Scully and Mulder might almost be considered archetypically yuppie heroes. Both are highly educated: he is a former Rhodes

---

18   Touraine 1981, pp. 9–10.
19   Jameson 1991, p. 36.
20   Jameson 1991, p. 315.
21   Jameson 1991, p. 407.
22   Jameson 1991, p. 349.
23   Jameson 1991, p. 36.

Scholar, an Oxford BA in Psychology, with academic publications to his credit; she is a medical doctor, with a degree in Physics from the University of Maryland and a thesis on Einstein.[24] Significantly younger, Buffy and friends are aspirant, rather than realised yuppies, physically attractive, but not yet educated, well dressed, but not yet employed. Xander aside, however, they are students at the fictional Sunnydale campus of the real University of California, the more prestigious of the state's public universities. Indeed, Willow has even been offered places at Eastcoast private universities, but turned them down to attend Sunnydale. Both the Sunnydale setting and the major positive characters, Giles apart, are representative of comfortably middle-class, liberal America. Both series also position themselves against what might be the most obvious 'Others' of yuppieness: redneck hillbillies, on the one hand; Big Government, Big Science and Big Business, on the other. In *The X-Files*, threat tends to come from either or both directions, albeit mainly the latter: one of the key themes is hidden Government, extending to the possibility of complicity in alien abduction. *Buffy* is similarly positioned socio-discursively, especially in the Adam sequence, where Big Government and Big Science are cosignified by the Initiative, the lower classes by lowlife 'monsters'.

Noting how difference and identity substitute for each other in the political rhetoric of the new social movements – as simultaneously the 'politics of difference' and 'identity politics' – Jameson concluded that such difference was possible only through the prior consolidation of something like universal identity. Postmodern politics entailed a 'ceaseless alternation' between identity and difference, he concluded, a kind of cultural 'blockage' obstructing any further development through interaction.[25] Hence, the inability to imagine the future, except as 'an eternal present and, much further away, an inevitable catastrophe'.[26] Jameson had in mind here the politics of real catastrophe, as in environmental or military disaster, but it is worth noting how *The X-Files* and *Buffy* construct their fictional worlds precisely thus, alternating between an eternal present which is ever American and the ultimate catastrophe of alien or demonic invasion. The universalism Jameson detects is, in part, that of the 'empowered', middle-class consumer at play in the marketplace. For, as Žižek insists, the 'dispersed, plural, constructed subject' of postmodernism is the *'form of subjectivity that corresponds to late capitalism'*. Capital itself, he continues, is 'the ultimate power' that undermines the 'traditional fixity of ideological

---

24 Lowry 1995, pp. 261, 264.
25 Jameson 1994, pp. 65–6, 70.
26 Jameson 1994, p. 70.

positions (patriarchy, fixed sexual roles, etc.)', in order to eliminate the remaining barriers to the 'unbridled commodification of everyday life'.[27]

This peculiar combination of transnational corporate commodification and postmodern cultural politics was powerfully resonant in the last decades of the twentieth century and the first of the twenty-first. Politically, its most significant expression was in the US Democratic Party, especially during the Presidency of another Rhodes scholar, Bill Clinton, which ran from 1993 to 2000. It is always risky to postulate close correlations between politics and culture, but I want to argue that this particular political moment was refracted fairly precisely in *The X-Files*, which went to air during the first year of the first Clinton administration, and *Buffy*, which followed in the first of the second. Chronologically, this is a less than exact fit, but sufficiently close to be suggestive. We have observed the post-feminist 'political correctness' of both series. But now we need note how much this was always a matter of gender and sexuality, rather than class or race-as-class. As Helford observed of the entire cohort of television 'fantasy girls':

> Though we now have female warriors, ship's captains, witches, aliens, and superheroes, they remain overwhelmingly white ..., heterosexual, and silent on such issues as class disenfranchisement.[28]

American television's female heroes were never quite so uniformly and explicitly heterosexual as this implies: witness, Willow and Tara. But in general Helford gets it right. Indeed, we might go further: not just white, but blonde or redhead, that is, not darkhaired; not just white, but North European in appearance, that is, not Latino; not merely silent on issues of class, but often positively and aggressively middle-class. Helford sees this kind of post-feminism as symptomatic of the Clinton years, when the dominant political culture combined a nominally left-wing 'social' liberalism with right-wing economic liberalism. She describes the politics of the period, a little cynically, as 'sameness reconstructed to appear as progressive shift'.[29] This is echoed in Kent Ono's argument, elsewhere in the same volume, that, for all its apparent feminism, *Buffy*'s central fear was of difference:

> Normalcy not only regulates Buffy's personal desire to be a normal *human* ..., but ... also serves as a regulating feature to demarcate appropriate

---

27   Žižek 1993, p. 216.
28   Helford 2000, p. 5.
29   Helford, 2000, p. 6.

behaviors and privileges affecting all characters ... Because vampires and *other others* are defined as abnormal by the show, it is easy to see them in general through a racial metaphor ...[30]

Much the same point might be applied to *The X-Files*, though less obviously to 'The Postmodern Prometheus' than to many other episodes. But Helford and Ono both misrecognise the phenomenon, in part, I suspect, due to their complicity with the culture they describe. For there was progress as well as sameness under Clinton; and tolerance, rather than fear, for certain kinds of difference, such as lesbianism and strong women more generally, in *Buffy* and *The X-Files*. Like the postmodern culture which hosted them, these programmes feared some differences, but not others. If *Buffy* can be read through a racial metaphor, then this is 'race' only in the very specific sense of race-as-class. For these vampires, demons and others are coded as neither black nor native American: relocated to Los Angeles, *Buffy*'s Angel would acquire a black sidekick, Charles Gunn, played by J. August Richards, as keen to hunt demons as anyone in the Buffyverse; confronted by an apparently advanced alien civilisation, Mulder and Scully would repeatedly resort to Navajo traditional wisdom as a key weapon in their armoury. The key sociodiscursive function of both series, as of Clintonesque politics more generally, was surely to *police* difference. And the difference that cannot be resolved through commodification, and which therefore requires indefinite policing, is that of class. In the second episode of the first season of *The X-Files*, Deep Throat had warned Mulder that: 'They have been here for a very, very long time'. Throughout the history of all hitherto existing societies, Marx insisted in *The Communist Manifesto*; only all recorded history, Engels added cautiously; and all telerecorded history too, we might well now add.

---

30   Ono, 2000, p. 172

CHAPTER 22

Framing Catastrophe: The Problem of Ending in Dystopian Fiction*

Orwell's *Nineteen Eighty-Four* is the most famous of all English-language dystopias. And we all know how it ends: 'But it was all right, everything was all right, the struggle was finished. He had won the victory over himself. He loved Big Brother'. Reminding us exactly where we have arrived at, the novel then reads, in most subsequent editions, as in the first: 'THE END'.[1] Little wonder that Williams should have read it as 'desperate because … on such a construction the exile could not win, and … there was no hope at all'; and its author as 'a man committed to decency who actualized a distinctive squalor'.[2] It was a judgement he would amend, but never revise. So the last of his many readings continued to deplore 'the terrifying irrationalism of the climax of *Nineteen Eighty-Four*'.[3] Jameson's work on science fiction and utopia shares a similarly longstanding animus towards both novel and author. So he writes that:

> the force of the text … springs from a conviction about human nature itself, whose corruptions and lust for power are inevitable, and not to be remedied by new social measures or programs, nor by heightened consciousness of impending dangers.[4]

Both Williams and Jameson had grasped the central political dilemma of dystopian fiction: if its serious purpose is in its warning, then the more grimly inexorable the fictive world becomes, the less effective it will be as a call to resistance. As Douglas Adams's Vogons were inclined to repeat: 'Resistance is

---

* This chapter has been published previously in *Arena Journal New Series*, No. 25/26, pp. 333–54, 2006.
  My thanks to Roland Boer, David Jack, Brian Nelson, Kate Rigby, Robert Savage and Millicent Vladiv-Glover for helpful comments, ideas, suggestions, which contributed to this paper. Thanks too to Richard Overell and the staff in the Rare Book Library at Monash University.
1 Orwell 1981, p. 311; Orwell 1949, p. 298.
2 Williams 1963, pp. 283, 277.
3 Williams 1991, p. 124.
4 Jameson 2005, p. 198.

useless!'.[5] Or as Engels had it: 'Freedom is the recognition of necessity'.[6] In short, there is no point in resisting the inevitable. Hence, Williams's judgement that 'in the very absoluteness of the fiction', it becomes 'an imaginative submission to ... inevitability';[7] or Jameson's that *Nineteen Eighty-Four* is not so much a critical dystopia as an 'anti-Utopia ... informed by a central passion to denounce and to warn against Utopian programs in the political realm'.[8]

There is no doubting that Orwell's later writings had express political purposes, but these are hardly as Jameson has them. 'Every line of serious work that I have written since 1936', Orwell insisted in 1946, 'has been written, directly or indirectly, *against* totalitarianism and *for* democratic Socialism'.[9] Jameson sidesteps the question of Orwell's peculiar politics – his combination of anti-fascism, neo-Trotskyism and libertarian socialism – by dismissing all reference to the '"if this goes on" principle' in *Nineteen Eighty-Four* as 'mere biographical affirmation'.[10] But when Orwell invited his American trade-union readers to read the novel in precisely these terms, he surely provided a gloss, not simply to his own beliefs, but to the text's intended political effects. 'I do not believe that the kind of society I describe necessarily *will* arrive', he had explained to the United Auto Workers, 'but ... that ... it *could* arrive ... totalitarianism, *if not fought against*, could triumph'.[11] *Nineteen Eighty-Four* was written, at least in part, as exactly that inspiration to political resistance Williams and Jameson insist it cannot be. Their judgement is sustained, moreover, by a surprising lack of interest in the novel's more formally literary properties. Williams writes as if it were written wholly within the conventions of literary realism, which it most definitely is not: witness the lengthy extracts from Goldstein's *Theory and Practice of Oligarchical Collectivism*.[12] Worse still, Jameson virtually reduces it to its American reception as the paradigmatic 'Cold War dystopia', uncritically repeating the dominant American reading of both author and text as 'at one

---

5   Adams 1979, p. 57.
6   In truth, Engels wrote 'die Einsicht in die Notwendigkeit' (Engels 1962, p. 106), which is more accurately translated by Burns as 'the insight into necessity' (Engels 1987, p. 105). But 'recognition' remains the best known English translation and better suits my (apparently illegitimate) purposes here.
7   Williams 1991, pp. 125–6.
8   Jameson 2005, pp. 198–9.
9   Orwell 1970a, p. 28.
10 Jameson 2005, p. 198.
11 Orwell 1970d, p. 564.
12 Orwell 1989, pp. 191–208, 209, 210–26.

with contemporary ... anti-socialisms'.¹³ More importantly for my purposes, however, neither seems to register that the novel doesn't end at 'THE END', but continues, in my edition for over fourteen more pages, in the first for over thirteen.¹⁴

Nineteen Eighty-Four actually ends at the conclusion to the *Appendix* on Newspeak, with: 'It was chiefly in order to allow time for the preliminary work of translation that the final adoption of Newspeak had been fixed for so late a date as 2050'.¹⁵ In content, these lines add little, but their form is redolent with meaning. For, as Margaret Atwood observes of the whole *Appendix*, it:

> is written in standard English, in the third person, and in the past tense, which can only mean that the regime has fallen, and that language and individuality have survived. For whoever has written the essay on Newspeak, the world of *1984* is over.¹⁶

This must be right: the *Appendix* is internal to the novel, neither an author's nor a scholarly editor's account of how the fiction works, but rather a part of the fiction, a fictional commentary on fictional events. And, although Atwood fails to notice this, it is anticipated within the main body of the text, by a footnote in the first chapter, which assures us, again in standard English, in the third person, in the past tense, that: 'Newspeak was the official language of Oceania'.¹⁷ Atwood uses a similar device in *The Handmaid's Tale*, the first of her two dystopian science fiction novels, which concludes with an extract from the proceedings of a 'Symposium on Gileadean Studies', written in some utopian future set long after the collapse of the Republic of Gilead.¹⁸ Moreover, she readily admits that *Nineteen Eighty-Four* provided her with a 'direct model' for this.¹⁹ If she is to be believed, then both Orwell's *Appendix* and her 'Historical Notes' work as framing devices, by which to blunt the force of dystopian inevitability.

---

13   Jameson 2005, pp. 200, 199.
14   Orwell 1989, pp. 312–26; Orwell 1949, pp. 299–312.
15   Orwell 1989, p. 326; Orwell 1949, p. 312.
16   Atwood 2005, p. 337.
17   Orwell 1989, p. 5n; Orwell 1949, p. 7n.
18   Atwood 1987, pp. 311–24.
19   Atwood 2005, p. 337.

1 Science Fiction as a Generic Context for *Nineteen Eighty-Four*

There are good reasons to take Atwood seriously, not least her science fiction (henceforth SF) novels, though the later *Oryx and Crake*[20] clearly owes less to Orwell in particular than to mainstream SF in general. But it might be more productive to pursue, not so much the matter of her critical credentials as that of Orwell's intellectual contexts. Let me begin by noting how SF, or at least something very close to it, provided him with a generic context and related set of intertexts. Literary criticism tends to resist such identification between Orwell and SF: he is a 'great writer', after all, not some second-rate Trekkie. In 1943, however, when he began work on what was still entitled *The Last Man in Europe*, he hadn't known he was a great writer: none of his books had sold particularly well nor received much in the way of critical acclaim. But he had known about SF, not the term perhaps, still rarely used outside the United States, but certainly 'that kind of book', as he had written to Struve of Zamyatin's *Mi*.[21]

The authors of that kind of book included, for Orwell, not only Zamyatin, but also Wells, Huxley and Čapek. Add in Mary Shelley and Verne and one would have something close to a canon of European, as distinct from American, SF writing. Canons aside, however, we may still ask what exactly were Orwell's interests in this European tradition of utopian and dystopian future fictions. Zamyatin is by common consent one of the most important figures in early twentieth-century Russian SF: Suvin describes him as, along with Čapek, 'the most significant world SF writer between the World Wars'.[22] He was certainly not appreciated as such, however, in Orwell's England. Zamyatin's dystopian novel *Mi* had been written in Russia and in Russian in 1920–1. But it wasn't published in the original language until 1952, and then only in the United States: first publication in Russia came as late as 1988. The book had become available in English, however, in an American – but not British – translation, as

---

20 Atwood 2003.
21 Orwell 1970c, p. 118. In the United States, Hugo Gernsback had coined the word 'scientification' in 1926 for the first issue of his pulp magazine *Amazing Stories*. But 'science fiction' became common only after 1938, when John W. Campbell Jr changed the name of a rival 'pulp' from *Astounding Stories* to *Astounding Science-Fiction* (Clute and Nicholls 1993, pp. 25, 64). By 1939, Orwell was already familiar with Gernsback's term, the paternity of which he traced to Wells (Orwell 1970a, p. 521), but not with Campbell's more recent coinage.
22 Suvin 1979, p. 280.

We, in 1924, and in French translation, as *Nous autres*, in 1929.[23] Orwell had 'not heard of' it until 1944, when he first read Struve's *25 Years of Soviet Russian Literature*.[24] Unable to obtain the American translation, then still unavailable in England, Orwell acquired a copy of *Nous autres* 'several' years later, which he promptly reviewed for *Tribune*, advising its readers that: 'This is a book to look out for when an English version appears'.[25] In 1946, he wrote approvingly of the novel in his famous essay on Burnham; in 1948, he offered to review a proposed English translation, which unfortunately failed to eventuate, for the *Times Literary Supplement*; and in 1949, he urged it on Fred Warburg, who had published *Animal Farm* in 1945 and would shortly publish *Nineteen Eighty-Four* itself.[26]

If Zamyatin was effectively unknown in England, Wells, by contrast, was clearly the leading English SF writer of the day, although, like Orwell, he remained unfamiliar with the term: as with Verne in English translation, Wells's novels were marketed as 'scientific romance'.[27] His utopian fictions included *A Modern Utopia, The Dream, Men Like Gods* and *The Shape of Things to Come*.[28] This last, which predicted and argued for the creation of a technocratic 'World State', became the best-known English literary utopia of the 1930s. The 1936 film version, *Things to Come*, directed by W. Cameron Menzies with a screenplay co-authored by Wells, occupied an equally prominent position in British SF cinema. Orwell could be fulsome in retrospective praise for Wells:

> The minds of all of us, and therefore the physical world, would be perceptibly different if Wells had never existed ... Back in the nineteen-hundreds it was a wonderful experience ... to discover H.G. Wells ... here was this wonderful man who ... knew that the future was not going to be what respectable people imagined.[29]

But his work had become increasingly irrelevant to the twentieth century, Orwell continued: 'A crude book like *The Iron Heel* ... is a truer prophecy ... than ... *The Shape of Things to Come*'.[30] Orwell particularly disliked Wells's uto-

---

23 Zamiatin 1952; Zamiatine 1929; Zamyatin 1952.
24 Orwell 1970c, p. 118.
25 Orwell 1970d, pp. 95, 99.
26 Orwell 1970d, p. 195; Orwell 1970d, p. 473; Orwell 1970d, pp. 546–7.
27 James 1994, p. 9.
28 Wells 2005; Wells 1923; Wells 1924; Wells 1993.
29 Orwell 1970b, p. 171.
30 Orwell 1970b, p. 172; cf. London 1958.

pianism: as early as 1935, he had described these 'Utopiae infested by nude school-marms' as a 'kind of optimistic lie'; in 1941, he objected to the sheer uselessness of 'rigmarole about a World State'; and as late as 1946, he repeated his 'low opinion' of Wells's writing after 1920.[31] Unsurprisingly, the great man had not taken kindly to such criticism, famously dismissing Orwell as a 'Trotskyist with big feet'.[32]

For Orwell, Huxley clearly represented a more formidable figure than the later Wells. Orwell made a point of insisting that *Brave New World* had been 'plagiarized' from Zamyatin's *We*, a calumny later redirected at *Nineteen Eighty-Four* itself.[33] Unlike Orwell, always essentially a literary outsider, Huxley came from one of the leading intellectual families in England, descended on his father's side from T.H. Huxley and on his mother's from Matthew Arnold. When *Brave New World* was published in 1932, its author was already a well-established writer, with *Crome Yellow*, *Point Counter Point* and *Do What You Will* to his credit.[34] He had been a friend of D.H. Lawrence, whose letters he was then editing for publication, and of writers like Virginia Woolf and E.M. Forster.[35] Orwell, by contrast, was out of work, impoverished and staying with his elder sister in Leeds, where he borrowed Huxley's novel from the local public library.[36] Orwell would in retrospect treat Huxley, along with Joyce, Eliot and Lawrence, as part of 'the movement' of the 'middle and late twenties'.[37] And, despite mixed initial responses,[38] *Brave New World* had indeed become one of the intellectual landmarks in what we might now think of as the long twenties.

Orwell is at his most enthusiastic about Huxley in *The Road to Wigan Pier*, which denounces Wells at some length,[39] citing *Brave New World* with approval for its caricature of Wellsian utopianism as a 'paradise of little fat men'.[40] Huxley had indeed intended to expose 'the horror of the Wellsian Utopia'.[41] But in

---

31   Orwell 1970a, p. 179; Orwell 1970b, p. 167; Orwell 1970d, p. 293.
32   Crick 1980, p. 294.
33   Orwell 1970d, p. 96; Orwell 1970d, p. 547.
34   Huxley 1921; Huxley 1928; Huxley 1929.
35   Huxley 1932.
36   Crick 1980, p. 137.
37   Orwell 1970a, p. 554.
38   The book was much more successful in Britain, where it sold 13,000 copies in 1932 and 10,000 in 1933, than in the United States (Bedford 1973, p. 251).
39   Orwell 1962, pp. 169–72, 177–8.
40   Orwell 1962, p. 169.
41   Huxley 1969, p. 348.

writing *Brave New World*, he acquired a series of other targets – American capitalism and Soviet Communism; state planning and eugenics; sexual, pharmacological and mass media induced hedonism; Keynesian economics and Lawrentian primitivism – many of which he would elsewhere explore more positively. Part of the novel's peculiar character, at once both strength and weakness, is its capacity to represent sympathetically many different sides of many different questions. But this was hardly an Orwellian virtue. By 1940, Orwell would dimiss Huxley's dystopia as having no bearing on the actual future; the following year, he judged its failure reminiscent of Wells.[42]

Orwell's primary objection to *Brave New World* was to its anti-political pessimism. So he found Huxley guilty of a:

> refusal to believe that human society can be fundamentally improved. Man is non-perfectible, merely political changes can effect nothing, progress is an illusion.

'The connection between this belief and political reaction', he continued, 'is ... obvious. Other worldliness is the best alibi a rich man can have'.[43] Here, the argument is specifically directed at Huxley's pacifism, rather than at his dystopian novel. But in the review of *Nous autres* for *Tribune*, where the charge of plagiarism is first aired, Orwell was explicit that what distinguished Huxley from Zamyatin was the latter's 'political point'. The irony should be obvious: these were exactly the charges – that he plagiarised Zamyatin; that he was pessimistic about the possibilities for political change; that there was no practicable political point to his argument – which would be directed at *Nineteen Eighty-Four* by later leftist critics.

But Orwell continues:

> In Huxley's book ... no clear reason is given why society should be stratified in the elaborate way ... described. The aim is not economic exploitation, but the desire to bully and dominate does not seem to be a motive either. There is no power hunger, no sadism, no hardness of any kind.[44]

By contrast:

---

42   Orwell 1970b, p. 33; Orwell 1970b, p. 46; Orwell 1970b, p. 172.
43   Orwell 1970c, p. 82.
44   Orwell 1970d, p. 97.

> It is [the] ... intuitive grasp of the irrational side of totalitarianism – human sacrifice, cruelty as an end in itself, the worship of a Leader ... – that makes Zamyatin's book superior to Huxley's.[45]

The political point of Orwell's own dystopia was already becoming apparent. His book would need to be unremittingly horrible so as to expose the sheer ghastliness of totalitarianism. But it would therefore need something external to itself to inspire belief in the possibility of resistance. Which is why 'THE END' could not actually be the end.

Karel Čapek interested Orwell less than either Wells, Zamyatin or Huxley.[46] He and his brother, Josef, were nonetheless amongst the best-known figures in inter-war Czech literary life. Moreover, Karel's play *R.U.R. Rossum's Universal Robots* – the title is in English even in the Czech original – had proven an extraordinary international success. The first Czech production was early in 1921. An American English-language version was performed in 1922 by the New York Theatre Guild, a British version by the Reandean Company at St Martin's Theatre in London in 1923. Distinct British and American translations followed in book form later that year. A Japanese translation appeared in 1923, French and Russian in 1924, Rumanian and Turkish in 1927, Italian in 1929, Bulgarian in 1931, Swedish in 1934.[47] Orwell could not have attended the London production, since he was serving in Burma at the time, but he might well have noticed the reviews. He seems not to have owned a television set, so nor is he likely to have seen the BBC's 1938 35-minute adaptation, the first ever televised SF programme.[48] But he certainly knew of the play's existence and seemed familiar with its themes. In *The Road to Wigan Pier*, he cites Čapek approvingly as a critic of mechanical progress for its own sake. '[T]he unfortunate thing', Orwell writes:

---

45   Orwell 1970c, p. 98.
46   Presumably this is so, in part, because *R.U.R.* is unconcerned with the issue of totalitarianism. Orwell seems to have been unfamiliar with Čapek's 1937 SF play, *Bílá nemoc*, which addressed the question very directly and was very promptly translated into English (Čapek 1937; Čapek 1938).
47   Čapek 1966, pp. 117, 204–5.
48   The television adaptation, broadcast on 11 February 1938, was by Nigel Playfair, the production by Jan Bussell. At the time, the Orwells were living in Wallington, Hertfordshire, and might conceivably have known someone with access to a set. Playfair and Bussell later worked together on a 90-minute television version, again for the BBC, broadcast on 4 March 1948. By this time, the first draft of *Nineteen Eighty-Four* was already completed and Orwell himself was in a sanatorium near Glasgow, where the facilities would not have extended to television.

> is that Socialism, as usually presented, is bound up with the idea of mechanical progress ... as an end in itself, almost as a kind of religion ... Karel Čapek hits it off well enough in the horrible ending of R.U.R., when the Robots, having slaughtered the last human being, announce their intention to 'build many houses' (just for the sake of building houses, you see).[49]

This is interesting for two reasons: because it directly addresses our own question of horrible endings; and because the (slight mis-)quotation suggests direct familiarity with the play, at least in book form. For this is indeed what their leader, Radius, demands of the robots, production for production's sake:

> The Robots will build much. They will build new houses for new Robots.[50]

The sentiment is repeated in the Epilogue:

> Sir, have pity. Terror is coming upon us. We have intensified our labour. We have obtained a million million tons of coal from the earth. Nine million spindles are running by day and night. There is no more room to store what we have made. Houses are being built throughout the world.[51]

But, as we shall see, Orwell was mistaken to describe the play as ending thus.

2   Three Intertexts: *Nous autres, Brave New World* and R.U.R.

We have traced Orwell's responses to Wellsian utopia and to the dystopias of Zamyatin, Huxley and Čapek. The problem of ending remains to be examined, however, at least for the dystopias – since here the formal issues confronting, respectively, utopian and dystopian writers become very different. Let us elab-

---

49 Orwell 1962, pp. 165–6.
50 Čapek 1961, p. 89. The Czech is more or less identical: 'Roboti budou mnoho stavět. Budou stavět nové domy pro nové Roboty' (Čapek 1966, p. 85).
51 Čapek 1961, p. 93. This speech by Radius in Selver's translation is actually a composite and elaboration of two different speeches in the Czech original:
    2. ROBOT/ Pane, měj slitování. Padá na nás hrůza. Všechno napravíme, co jsme učinili.
    3. ROBOT/ Znásobili jsme práci. Není už kam dát, co jsme vyrobili. (Čapek 1966, p. 89).
   There is no reference here to coal, spindles or houses. But this is immaterial to our analysis, since Orwell was familiar only with the Selver translation.

orate a little. Jameson has observed that the citizens of what he terms 'political' utopias are normally 'grasped as a statistical population', that is, that 'there are no individuals any longer, let alone any existential "lived experience"'. Hence the 'boredom or dryness' often attributed to the form. This is not a weakness, he continues, but rather a 'central strength' of the form, insofar as it reinforces 'plebeianisation', that is, our 'desubjection in the utopian political process'.[52] There is a certain perversity to this observation, which makes sense only given Jameson's subsequent insistence that:

> utopias are non-fictional, even though they are non-existent. Utopias in fact come to us as barely audible messages from a future that may never come into being.[53]

But the instance he cites, from Marge Piercy's *Woman on the Edge of Time*, runs directly contrary to the gist of his argument. For it is precisely insofar as some utopian texts work as novels, that is, as fictions – as Piercy's clearly does – that these attempt the kind of existential plausibility Jameson discounts. This is true, not only of Morris (as distinct from Bellamy), as Jameson half concedes,[54] but also of Piercy, Le Guin and virtually all other 'utopian' SF novelists, albeit not of More, who provides the template both for the form itself and for Jameson's reading. The sheer persistence of utopian strategies for discounting such boredom and dryness suggests how mistaken Jameson might be. Obviously relevant topoi include: the sexual romance within utopia (Morris successfully, Bellamy unsuccessfully, and almost everyone else to some extent); the distant view of utopia from its extremities (a recurring motif in Le Guin's Hainish and Banks's 'The Culture' novels, but also, for example, in *Star Trek*); the external threat to utopia (Banks again, but also Piercy and Kim Stanley Robinson); and so on.

If utopias are communities imagined as more perfect, as both Suvin and Williams argued,[55] then their political purposes will tend to range from negative critique of the real through to positive inspiration to the better-than-real. The nearer any particular utopian fiction – novel or film – approximates to the latter, the greater will be its attempt at existential plausibility, since such plausibility tends to render the fiction, and hence the utopia itself, credible.

---

52 Jameson 2004, pp. 39–40.
53 Jameson 2004, p. 54.
54 Jameson 2004, pp. 39–40.
55 Suvin 1979, p. 45; Williams 1980c, p. 196.

This is not to discount Suvin's insight that utopia is an estranged rather than naturalistic form,[56] but merely to insist that novels and films work in a very different register from the truly non-fictional utopias of political philosophy proper, that they must work as art or entertainment and are therefore more directly implicated in the conventions of literary and cinematic naturalism than Suvin allows. The worse worlds of dystopian fiction are similarly implicated, but here the relevant political purpose is not the inspiration, but the warning. As Huxley observed of *Brave New World*: 'This ... was the message of the book – *This is possible: for heaven's sake be careful*'.[57] Dystopias are rarely charged with either boredom or dryness, since their stock in trade of human beastliness remains captivating to conventional post-lapsarian sensibilities. The equivalent problem remains, however, that of how to represent a naturalistically plausible danger sufficiently terrible to be threatening, but insufficiently so as to be demoralising. Hence, what we have termed the problem of ending in dystopia. How, then, is it resolved in Orwell's three dystopian intertexts?

Zamyatin's *Nous autres* had much in common with *Nineteen Eighty-Four*, but was far more directly a critique of scientific positivism. So its 'l'Etat Unique' (the Sole State or the One State) is ruled by mathematics and science as much as by the dictatorial 'Bienfaiteur' (Benefactor): like all its members, the novel's central protagonist, D-503, the builder of the *Intégral* space probe, is merely a 'numéro'; like all these numbers, his daily routine is ordered with arithmetical precision by 'les Tables des Heures'; and the novel itself famously comprises a series of his laboratory 'Notes'.[58] D-503 is seduced into the cause of rebellion, both sexually and politically, by I-330. At one level, she provides the model for Orwell's Julia, a sexually proactive woman whose affections serve to promote the male protagonist's resistance to the state, but who he will therefore eventually be forced to betray. D-503's final Note, reporting his subjection to the Benefactor's lobotomy-like 'Grande Opération' to eliminate the imagination, and his subsequent impassive witness to I-330's torture under 'la Cloche' (the Bell), is thus a moment of simultaneous defeat and betrayal, a model for the moment in *Nineteen Eighty-Four* when '*I sold you and you sold me*'.[59]

There are obvious differences, however. Where Orwell's tripartite structure of rival totalitarianisms, Oceania, Eurasia and Eastasia, is a self-sealing, fully enclosed system of domination, Zamyatin's Sole State remains encircled by the wild country outside 'le Mur Vert' (the Green Wall) and threatened from

---

56   Suvin 1979, p. 18.
57   Bedford 1973, p. 245.
58   Zamiatine 1929, pp. 7–8, 16.
59   Zamiatine 1929, pp. 233–4; Orwell 1989, p. 307.

within and without by the 'Méphi' underground. Moreover, I-330 is a much stronger character than Julia, not only a leader in the Méphi, but also the novel's chief intellectual anatagonist to official positivism: her insistence that there can be no final number, and therefore no final revolution, radically undermines D-503's faith in the mathematical foundations of the social order.[60] If there is some homology between the destruction of Julia and Winston in *Nineteen Eighty-Four* and that of I-330 and D-503 in *Nous autres*, there is, nonetheless, no equivalent to the latter's illicit child by O-90, who will be born and brought up beyond the Green Wall. If the Benefactor still rules the Sole State at Zamyatin's conclusion, his rule has been challenged more effectively in the course of the narrative by the unsuccessful Méphi revolution, than is Big Brother's by either the illusory promise of the Brotherhood or Winston's vague hope in the proles.

The contrast between the novels is perhaps at its keenest in their respective accounts of the mathematics of totalitarianism. For where Orwell's O'Brien can make Winston see five fingers, I-330's insistence that there is no final number will haunt D-503 through to this novel's 'La Fin' in Note 39:

> Ecoutez, je vous dis! Répondez-moi: de l'autre côté de la limite de votre univers fini, qu'y a-t-il?[61]

> [Listen, I'm talking to you! Answer me this: beyond the limit of your finite universe, what's there?][62]

This isn't quite the end, of course, since Note 40 is still to come. But even there, in the novel's closing paragraphs, Zamyatin reminds us that the Green Wall has been successfully breached from the outside, that the Sole State is actually already in retreat:

> à l'ouest, des régions où règnent le chaos et les bêtes sauvages et qui, malheureusement, renferment une grande quantité de numéros ayant trahi la raison.
> Nous avons cependant réussi à établir, dans la 40° avenue, un mur provisoire d'ondes à haute tension.[63]

---

60 Zamiatine 1929, p. 179.
61 Zamiatine 1927, p. 232.
62 Zamyatin 1972, p. 202.
63 Zamiatine 1927, p. 234.

[to the west, some regions are ruled by chaos and savage beasts and, unfortunately, contain many numbers who have betrayed reason.

We have nevertheless succeeded in establishing, along the 40th avenue, a temporary high-voltage wall.][64]

The particular defeats of D-503 and I-330 are thus contextualised and mitigated against by the overarching promise of infinite revolution. As Suvin comments:

> the protagonist's defeat is of the day but not necessarily of the epoch. The defeat in the novel ... is not the defeat of the novel itself, but an exasperated shocking of the reader into thought and action.[65]

Like *Nous autres*, *Brave New World* is set in the twenty-sixth century. Like *Nous autres*, its target is an affluent, technologically sophisticated dystopia. But where Zamyatin's Sole State anticipated Oceanian sexual puritanism, Huxley explored the dystopian potential of the mass commodification of sexual, pharmacological and mass media pleasures. As Orwell observed, it was directed at 'the hedonistic principle', at a world 'turned into a Riviera hotel' and was thus a 'brilliant caricature' of the 'present of 1930', that is, the 1920s. From a twenty-first-century vantage point, we might want to add the present of 1960, 1970, 1980, 1990 and perhaps even 2000, but for Orwell, writing in 1940, it seemed to cast 'no light on the future'.[66] Like *Nous autres*, *Brave New World* famously ends with a death, but a media-saturated suicide rather than a political execution:

> 'Mr Savage!'
> Slowly, very slowly, like two unhurried compass needles, the feet turned towards the right; north, north-east, east, south-east, south, south-south-west; then paused, and after a few seconds, turned as unhurriedly back towards the left. South-south-west, south, south-east, east, ...[67]

If John, the Savage, were the novel's hero and his resistance to the pseudo-Wellsian World State heroic, then this ending would be tragic. But it is closer to bathetic comedy. For he is clearly neither hero nor protagonist: he doesn't actually appear until Chapter Seven; his rebellion is comically excessive; his

---

64 Zamyatin 1972, p. 204.
65 Suvin 1979, p. 259.
66 Orwell 1970b, p. 46.
67 Huxley 1955, p. 237.

public self-flagellation in the closing chapter is near-ludicrous; and the Savage Reservation that nurtured him is as drug-obsessed and socially conformist as the civilization he pits it against. If the novel had a central protagonist, it would probably be the intelligent but self-important and self-pitying Bernard Marx. But he is too obviously yet another butt for the novel's humour to be its hero.[68] And this, surely, is the point: *Brave New World* is above all a comic novel, a scattershot satire of Huxley's contemporary intellectual landscape, from Hollywood hedonism to Pavlovian psychology, Freudianism to Fordism (both in the sense used in the novel and that of more recent sociology and economics). As Huxley explained in a letter to his father, it is 'a comic, or at least satirical, novel about the Future'.[69] In this respect, it remains very different from our other three dystopias: the first act of *R.U.R.* is comic and, indeed, vaguely reminiscent of Shaw, but thereafter the dominant register becomes closer to Chekhov or Ibsen; there are comic moments in *Nous autres*, as for example when D-503 imagines I-330 as one of the Valkyries,[70] but these are comparatively few; and there is virtually no comedy to speak of in *Nineteen Eighty-Four*.

The one character exempt from such satire in *Brave New World* is Mustapha Mond, the World Controller for Western Europe. Significantly, it is only in the debate with him, in Chapters Sixteen and Seventeen, that the Savage becomes a truly serious figure. This is the philosophical core of the novel, where Mond speaks for Enlightenment *civilisation* and the utilitarian felicific calculus, the Savage for Romantic *Kultur*, but also for primitivist barbarism. The first of these chapters ends with Bernard Marx's and Helmholtz Watson's banishment to an island reserved for those 'too self-consciously individual to fit into community-life'.[71] This is handled with explicit comic effect for Bernard, less so for Helmholtz, but in neither case is there much suggestion that the outcome is especially intolerable. The World State inspires satirical amusement rather than terrified dread. The second ends with the interestingly ambivalent philosophical conclusion to the entire novel. 'What you need', the Savage argues, 'is something *with* tears for a change. Nothing costs enough here'. 'We prefer to do things comfortably', Mond retorts a little later. 'But I don't want comfort', the Savage replies:

---

68 Donald Watt's careful examination of the novel's manuscript revisions leads him to conclude that: 'Huxley at first thought of Bernard as the novel's hero, then switched to John as more fitting for the hero's role, and finally decided that Helmholtz, if anyone, should be the book's only authentically uplifting character' (Watt 1996, p. 80).
69 Huxley 1969, p. 351.
70 Zamiatine 1929, p. 204.
71 Huxley 1955, p. 178.

'I want God, I want poetry, I want real danger, I want freedom, I want goodness. I want sin.'

'In fact,' said Mustapha Mond, 'you're claiming the right to be unhappy.'

'Not to mention the right to grow old and ugly and impotent; the right to have syphilis and cancer; the right to have too little to eat; the right to be lousy; the right to live in constant apprehension of what may happen tomorrow; the right to catch typhoid; the right to be tortured by unspeakable pains of every kind.'

There was a long silence.

'I claim them all,' said the Savage at last.

Mustapha Mond shrugged his shoulders. 'You're welcome,' he said.[72]

Chapter Eighteen, narrating the Savage's self-exile, self-mutilation and self-destruction, remains to come, but the philosophical argument ends here, with an unresolved choice between what Huxley would later describe as 'an insane life in Utopia, or the life of a primitive in an Indian village, ... in some respects ... hardly less queer and abnormal'.[73] In short, Huxley's ending surrounds a philosophical impasse with a set of highly elaborate comic and satiric trappings.

We noted Orwell's description of Čapek's R.U.R. as ending with the Robots producing for production's sake, after their slaughter of the human race. But this isn't how the play ends in either the Czech original or its British translation. The original was organised into a comic prologue and three acts, with the speech to which Orwell refers coming at the end of the second act. Paul Selver's translation, as adapted for the London stage by Nigel Playfair, had three acts and an epilogue, with the speech coming at the end of the third act.[74] But in both one human remains alive, R.U.R.'s head of construction, Stavitel Alquist, and in both his function is to provide the play with a less horrible ending than Orwell recalled. Alquist has been retained by the Robots in an apparently futile effort to find ways to reproduce themselves in the absence of humans, who alone knew the secret of their creation. In R.U.R. humankind is led to extinction, through a combination of technological excess and unbridled capitalism; the Robots to a parallel near-extinction, through their cruelty in disposing of their onetime human masters. The play's logic thus tends remorselessly toward the self-destruction of both, just as Orwell remembered. Indeed, the play might

---

72   Huxley 1955, pp. 186–7.
73   Huxley 1955a, p. 7.
74   Compare Čapek, R.U.R. Rossum's Universal Robots. Kolektivní Drama o Vstupní Komedii a Trech Dejstvích (literally, a collective drama in a comic prologue and three acts) with Čapek R.U.R. (Rossum's Universal Robots). A Play in Three Acts and an Epilogue.

plausibly have ended there, with the theatrical equivalent of what Marx and Engels had called 'the common ruin of the contending classes'.[75]

Its actual conclusion, however, is that life will continue even though humanity may not, which is more optimistic, but nonetheless distinctly improbable because belied by almost everything that precedes it. Where no politics will work, the alternative turns out to be unconditional romantic love. In ways both unexplained and inexplicable, the play insists that self-sacrificial heterosexual love between the Robot, Primus, and the Robotess, Helena, will yield the promise of new life. Alquist is thus given the play's last speech, in which to pronounce them the new Adam and Eve. Opening the *Bible*, he quotes directly from *Genesis* and then concludes by citing the song of Simeon from the Gospel according to St Luke. This is rendered slightly misleadingly in Selver's British translation, but with more dramatic effect for an English audience, as a direct quotation from the 'Nunc Dimittis', in the form given by the Anglican *Book of Common Prayer*, then still recited daily in the Church of England's 'Order for Evening Prayer':

> Now, Lord, lettest Thou Thy servant depart in peace, according to Thy will, for mine eyes have seen Thy salvation.[76]

Čapek's conclusion is clear: no matter what the sterilities of human (capitalist) robotics and inhuman (communist) Robots, love and life will finally survive. Christian rhetoric thus serves to underwrite an essentially pantheist solution: that life will out, no matter what the actions of humans and their robotic creations. In some ways, this anticipates more recent deep-ecological speculation about the planet's capacity to survive the depredations of our species. But for Čapek it was, rather, the way to square a circle, to produce an optimistic resolution where none was available. Certainly, it seems to have been insufficiently persuasive for Orwell to remember its details.

---

75   Marx and Engels 1967, p. 79.
76   Čapek 1961, p. 104; cf. St. Luke 11: 29–30. In the Czech original, the reference is an allusion rather than a quotation: 'Nyní propustíš, Pane, služebníka svého v pokoji; nebot uzřely oči mé – uzřely – spasení tvé skrze lásku, a život nezahyne! ... Nezahyne! ... Nezahyne!' (Čapek 1966, p. 102).

TABLE 3   *An ideal typology of possible solutions to the problem of ending*

		Form (continuity with the main narrative)	
		Internal	External
Content (continuity with the imaginary world represented in the fiction)	Internal	*Nous autres*	*Nineteen Eighty-Four*
	External	*Brave New World*	*R.U.R.*

3   Dystopian Endings: An Ideal Typology and Some Hypotheses

To summarise: Zamyatin's *Nous autres* resolves the problem of dystopian ending by framing the particular catastrophes that overcome D-503 and I-330 in relation to a surrounding context of infinite – or at least continuing – revolution; Huxley's *Brave New World* by framing its philosophical impasse comically and satirically; and Čapek's *R.U.R.* by the contrivance of an optimistic outcome, in many respects at odds with the main narrative. The first seems to me the most persuasive, the last the least. But, however effective, they together provide three out of the four instances of a possible ideal typology, arranged around measures of internality and externality applied, respectively, to the formal question of narrative structure and to the dystopian content of the imaginary worlds represented in the fiction. So the solution in *Nous autres* is both internal to the text's main narrative and to the fictional history of the world it describes. That in *Brave New World* is also internal to the main narrative, but external to the fictional history of A.F. 632, insofar as satire necessarily implies a position outside the reality it satirises. That in *R.U.R.* is both external to the main narrative in form – the English translation is right to represent the fourth act as an epilogue – and also in content, insofar as the closing transcendental religiosity occupies a quite different conceptual space from that postulated in the first three acts. This ideal typology is represented diagrammatically in Table 3 above.

The fourth possibility, that of narrative externality in form, but historical internality in fictional content, is what we find in Orwell's *Appendix*. Given that we know he was familiar with each of the other texts, we may plausibly infer that this device was in fact a deliberate invention, an experiment in relation to 'that kind of book', that is, in relation to the genre of SF. Interestingly, there is no trace of the *Appendix* on Newspeak in what remains of Orwell's own manuscript.[77] Given its dilapidated state – there is much missing – this in itself proves very little. But it is suggestive of the possibility that the *Appendix* really was written last, as the real 'END' to the novel, the solution to a problem that had become apparent only once the main text was more or less complete. These inferences are strongly supportive of Atwood's reading of both the novel itself and its more general significance. We may reasonably conclude, then, that readings of *Nineteen Eighty-Four*, which remain premised on the assumption that the novel ends at 'THE END', are radically misconceived.

Comparing *Nineteen Eighty-Four* unfavourably with *News from Nowhere*, Williams argued that the difference lay in the greater plausibility of the latter's fictional 1952 revolution: 'because its energy flows both ways, forward and back, ... its issue ... can go either way'. He judged this kind of openness, where the 'subjunctive is a true subjunctive, rather than a displaced indicative', absent from the 'dominant mode of dystopia', as represented paradigmatically by Orwell.[78] Williams was right to draw our attention to what he elsewhere termed 'the tenses of the imagination'.[79] But he was mistaken, nonetheless, in his understanding of *Nineteen Eighty-Four*. For this true subjunctive is precisely what occupies the space between 'THE END' of the novel and the *Appendix* on 'THE PRINCIPLES OF NEWSPEAK'. Moreover, the subjunctive takes a particularly interesting form within the actual text of the *Appendix*, that of the subjunctive future perfect.

Citing Freud's notion of 'working through' and Paul Cohen on mathematical 'forcing', Badiou has observed that:

> Forcing is the point at which a truth ... authorizes anticipations of knowledge concerning not what is but *what will have been if truth attains completion*.

'This anticipatory dimension', he continues, 'requires that truth judgements be formulated in the future perfect'.[80] To be able to say something about a truth means, then, that at some future moment this truth will have been realised, that it will have been true. 'A forcing', Badiou writes elsewhere, 'is the powerful fiction of a *completed* truth'.[81] Effective political and religious myths are therefore,

---

77   Orwell 1984.
78   Williams 1980c, p. 208.
79   Williams 1984a.
80   Badiou 2004, p. 127.
81   Badiou 2003, p. 65.

for Roland Boer, precisely instances of such forcings: they construct or postulate worlds the truth of which will have been upon their completion.[82] To be more precise, however, the tense to which Badiou and Boer both refer is the indicative future perfect. And, as such, it is the informing tense of all positively utopian myth, as in Boer's own example of Exodus.

This has an interesting theoretical corollary: that the equivalent tense of dystopian prevention, of that we seek to avoid by negative example, will be the subjunctive future perfect. We began with Atwood's observation that Orwell's *Appendix* had been written in the past tense. We should now add that there are other tenses at work there, notably the subjunctive future perfect. So that, in the sentences which provide its chronological frame, Orwell writes:

> It was expected that Newspeak would have finally superseded Oldspeak ... by about the year 2050 ...

and:

> within a couple of generations even the possibility of such a lapse would have vanished ... When Oldspeak had been once and for all superseded, the last link would have been severed.[83]

Orwell's use of the subjunctive functions here almost exactly as Williams observed it in Morris: to mean that these events will not necessarily have eventuated. The subjunctive future perfect is by no means always empirically present in dystopian SF: its use in Atwood's 'Historical Notes', for example, is merely trivial. But, even when this is so, even where the tense fails to appear altogether, it remains nonetheless the logically informing tense of dystopia. For this is what dystopian future fictions recount: what *would have happened* if their empirical and implied readerships had not been moved to prevent it. Orwell knew this and that may well be an important part of his lasting significance.

The End.

---

82   Boer 2006.
83   Orwell 1989, pp. 312, 324.

CHAPTER 23

Archaeologies of the Future: Jameson's Utopia or Orwell's Dystopia?*

Terry Eagleton has described Fredric Jameson as 'one of the world's most eminent cultural theorists' and 'a peerless literary critic in the classical sense of the term'.[1] Jameson himself once characterised his work more modestly as a 'vocation to explain and to popularize the Marxist intellectual tradition'.[2] But his Marxism owes far more to Adorno and the young Lukács than to Engels and one of its distinctive features has been an enduring fascination with utopia. Indeed, the category of the utopian is fundamental to Jameson's own method. In *The Political Unconscious*, the most influential of his works of literary criticism and also, perhaps, the most theoretically original, he developed a systematic outline of a neo-Lukácsian 'totalising' critical method capable of subsuming other apparently incompatible critical methods, by 'at once canceling and preserving them'.[3] Against more conventionally Marxian understandings of art as ideology, Jameson argued for a 'double hermeneutic', which would simultaneously embrace both the negative hermeneutic of ideology-critique and the positive of a utopian 'non-instrumental conception of culture'. For Jameson, all art, indeed all class consciousness, can be understood as at once both ideological and utopian: 'the ideological would be grasped as somehow at one with the Utopian', he wrote, 'and the Utopian at one with the ideological'.[4] The category reappears at another level, moreover, in his work on utopia as a specific literary and philosophical genre. In a 1982 essay written for the journal *Science Fiction Studies*, he famously defined the problem of 'Progress v. Utopia' through the question 'Can We Imagine the Future?'.[5] Jameson has worried away at this and related matters for more than thirty years and the long anticipated end result is his *Archaeologies of the Future: The Desire Called Utopia and Other Science Fictions*.

---

* This chapter has been published previously in *Historical Materialism*, Vol. 17, No. 4, pp. 101–19, 2009.
1 Eagleton 2006, p. 26.
2 Jameson 1988b, p. xxvi.
3 Jameson 1981, p. 10.
4 Jameson 1981, p. 286.
5 Jameson 1982. The essay is reprinted in Jameson 2005, pp. 281–95.

1   From Metamorphosis to Archaeology

Jameson's *Archaeologies* is the most important theoretical contribution to utopian and science fiction studies since 1979, when Darko Suvin's *Metamorphoses of Science Fiction* transformed the latter from a 'fan' enthusiasm into a scholarly sub-discipline.[6] It is dedicated to Suvin amongst others of Jameson's 'comrades in the party of Utopia'.[7] Like Suvin's *Metamorphoses*, its approach is Western-Marxist, more specifically Blochian, in theoretical inspiration, its disciplinary orientation primarily towards comparative literature and what we might term critical cultural studies. Like Suvin's *Metamorphoses*, it treats utopia as science fiction (henceforth SF). Indeed, Jameson cites with approval Suvin's still controversial description of utopia as 'the socio-political sub-genre of Science Fiction' on no fewer than five occasions.[8] Like Suvin's *Metamorphoses*, it is also a defence of the continuing political relevance of utopia and SF. Indeed, Jameson's derivation of 'anti-anti-Utopianism' from Sartrean 'anti-anti-communism' will no doubt provide the party of utopia with as good a slogan as it will find for the foreseeable future. The terms of this derivation are interesting, nonetheless: Sartre, Jameson recalls, had invented this 'ingenious political slogan' so as 'to find his way between a flawed communism and an even more unacceptable anti-communism'.[9] The inference is clear: utopia may be flawed, but anti-utopianism is even more unacceptable.

Moreover, the reference is to communism and anti-communism, utopianism and anti-utopianism, movements rather than texts. For, where Suvin's *Metamorphoses* was essentially a post-Formalist analysis of the poetics of a literary genre, Jameson's *Archaeologies* attempts to situate this level of analysis in relation to what he terms, after Bloch, the wider 'Utopian impulse'.[10] *Archaeologies* comprises two relatively discrete parts: the second entitled 'As Far as Thought Can Reach', containing twelve separate essays, all but one of which have been previously published, the oldest as early as 1973, the latest as recent

---

6   'More than any other study, ... *Metamorphoses* is *the* significant forerunner of all the major examinations of the genre' (Hollinger 1999, p. 233).
7   Jameson 2005, p. vi.
8   Suvin 1979, p. 61; Jameson 2005, pp. xiv, 57, 393, 410, 414–15.
9   Jameson 2005, p. xvi.
10 Jameson 2005, pp. 2–3. Jameson and others (cf. Fitting 2006, p. 42) attribute a much more formal status to the distinction between 'Program' and 'Impulse' than I can find in Bloch. Nonetheless, it is clear from the overall structure of the whole argument that Bloch is at least as interested in utopian impulses as in utopian texts (cf. Bloch 1995).

as 2003;[11] and the first a more or less continuous, more or less previously unpublished, thirteen-chapter argument entitled 'The Desire Called Utopia'.[12] There is much to admire in the reprinted essays on (mainly) American SF, especially those on Ursula Le Guin, Philip K. Dick, whom Jameson famously dubbed the 'Shakespeare of Science Fiction',[13] William Gibson and Kim Stanley Robinson, whose thesis on Dick Jameson famously supervised.[14] But the new material is in the book's first part and it is this that most clearly commands our attention. Eagleton once described Jameson's Hegelian Marxism a little uncharitably as part 'Californian supermarket of the mind', part 'unrepentant *bricoleur*, reaching for a Machereyan spanner here or a Greimasian screwdriver there'.[15] For better and for worse, the same method and style informs *Archaeologies*. It exhibits the same strenuous '*mastering*' Eagleton once judged 'too eirenic, easygoing and all-encompassing' for Jameson's 'own political good'.[16] There is the same commitment to *Aufhebung*, the same scholarly erudition, the same elaboration and resolution through incorporation of formalist taxonomic binaries, even the same repeated invocation of Greimas's semiotic rectangle (though Macherey is much less in evidence).

The taxonomy proceeds by way of double focus on the utopian form and the utopian wish,[17] to the slightly different distinction between the utopian programme, which is 'systemic', and the utopian impulse, 'obscure yet omnipresent', which surfaces across a wide range of human activities.[18] This is, at one level, simply a reworking of Bloch. In Jameson's hands, however, it generates a distinctly odd classification of the utopian text alongside the intentional community, revolutionary practice, space and the city as 'program', but the texts of political and social theory alongside political reformism, the individual building, the body, time and the collectivity as 'impulse'.[19] The implication seems to be that More's *Utopia* is programmatic, but Bernstein's *Die Voraussetzungen des Sozialismus und die Aufgaben der Sozialdemokratrie* mere impulse, an improb-

---

11   Jameson 2005, pp. 237–416; cf. Jameson 1973 and Jameson 2003a. The new essay is 'History and Salvation in P.K. Dick' (Jameson 2005, pp. 363–83).
12   Jameson 2005, pp. 1–233. An earlier version of the third chapter was published as Jameson 2003b.
13   Jameson 2005, p. 345.
14   Robinson 1984.
15   Eagleton 1986, pp. 70–1.
16   Eagleton 1986, p. 71.
17   Jameson 2005, p. 1.
18   Jameson 2005, p. 3.
19   Jameson 2005, p. 4.

ably over-politicised distinction if ever there was one.[20] Thereafter, we proceed through a classification of utopian enclaves, a reading of *Utopia* itself in relation to the genres of travel narrative and satire, and a more than passing nod to Marx in the chapter on 'utopian science' and 'utopian ideology'. Chapter Five, on 'The Great Schism' between SF and fantasy, rehearses the Suvinian aversion to the latter. Suvin now apparently has doubts on this score himself,[21] but Jameson at least still keeps the cognitive-rationalist faith: 'the invocation of magic by modern fantasy ...', he writes, 'is condemned by its form to retrace the history of magic's decay and fall, its disappearance from ... the disenchanted world of prose, of capitalism and modern times'.[22] The implication seems to be that only a Tolkienesque reactionary could have written *Perdido Street Station*, *The Scar* and *Iron Council*, an improbably under-politicised observation if ever there was one.[23]

One could easily continue with similar such criticisms, indeed one could even elaborate them into a critique of what Jameson ironically describes as his 'perversely formalist approach'.[24] And yet, whenever he turns his attention to writers he admires – Le Guin, Dick, Stapledon (an interestingly unfashionable choice, this), Lem, even Asimov – we can see how right Hayden White was to describe Jameson as 'the best socially-oriented critic of our time'.[25] Who but Jameson could describe Stapledon as 'the Fourier of SF just as he is the Dante Alighieri of Utopias'?; or describe the conclusion to Asimov's *Nightfall* as having 'the literal force of the word *aesthetic* – in Greek designating perception as such'?[26] Quite apart from these particular judgements, however, the book's more general thesis advances a powerfully political case for the continuing importance of SF and utopia. The argument is broached in the 'Introduction', where Jameson insists that:

> What is crippling is ... the universal belief ... that the historic alternatives to capitalism have been proven unviable and impossible, and that no other socio-economic system is conceivable, let alone practically available.

---

20   More 2001; Bernstein 1961.
21   Suvin 2000.
22   Jameson 2005, p. 71.
23   Their author, China Miéville, is of course a member of the Socialist Workers Party and co-editor of *Historical Materialism*.
24   Jameson 2005, p. 85.
25   Or so it says on the back cover of my copy of *The Political Unconscious*.
26   Jameson 2005, pp. 124, 94.

The value of the utopian form, he continues, thus consists precisely in its capacity as 'a representational meditation on radical difference, radical otherness, and ... the systematic nature of the social totality'.[27] This is a wonderfully precise thesis, which tells us most of what we need to know about the politics of the genre. Systematically followed through, it would surely also have led Jameson to more positive readings of (at least some) fantasy and, as we shall see, (at least some) dystopia, than those on offer in *Archaeologies*.

The argument is resumed in the superb last chapter of the book's first part, where Jameson writes that utopia as a form provides 'the answer to the universal ideological conviction that no alternative is possible'. It does so, he elaborates, 'by forcing us to think the break itself ... not by offering a more traditional picture of what things would be like after the break'. Hence, the memorable conclusion that utopia is 'a meditation on the impossible, on the unrealizable in its own right'.[28] Here, however, the argument is linked to a distinctly non-Marxist, but nonetheless not thereby mistaken, argument for the peculiar contemporary relevance of utopia. Ever since Marx and Engels, scientific socialism has asserted its superiority over utopian socialism on the grounds that it knows, scientifically and theoretically, how to achieve what utopians can only imagine in fantasy. Jameson, however, picks up on an observation of the ageing Lukács that, by the 1960s, this had already ceased to be so. The erstwhile weaknesses of utopianism, its inability to provide an adequate account of either agency or transition, thus 'becomes a strength', Jameson writes, 'in a situation in which neither ... seems currently to offer candidates for solution'. In the early twenty-first century, then, and for much the same reasons as before 1848, utopia 'better expresses our relationship to a genuinely political future than any current program of action'.[29] Surveying the scattered rubble of the second, third and fourth Internationals, it is difficult to disagree. Which is why 'anti-utopianism' thus becomes the other of Jameson's text, 'anti-anti-utopianism' its slogan.

2   Historicising Science Fiction: America and Its Others

At the pretextual level, Jameson is surely right to define himself against anti-utopianism: confronted by a capitalism as hubristic as at any time in history, we do surely 'need to develop an anxiety about losing the future ... analog-

---

27   Jameson 2005, p. xii.
28   Jameson 2005, p. 232.
29   Ibid.

ous to Orwell's anxiety about the loss of the past'. The book's first part finally closes with a moving invocation of Marge Piercy's Mattapoisett utopians travelling back in time 'to enlist the present in their struggle to exist'.[30] Elsewhere, Jameson has used Piercy's time travellers to even greater rhetorical effect, writing that: 'utopias are non-fictional, even though they are non-existent. Utopias in fact come to us as barely audible messages from a future that may never come into being'.[31] It is as good a line as any in *Archaeologies* and somehow seems to belong there. But Jameson's juxtaposition of Orwell and Piercy also serves to remind us that his anti-anti-utopianism is textual as well as pretextual and that it is both informed by and in turn informs a clear preference for the utopian SF of his own time and place – American since the 'New Wave' – as against the tradition of early to mid-twentieth-century European dystopian writing. The vantage point from which Jameson writes is unavoidably that of an American 'sixties' radical set adrift in postmodern late capitalism. And this inner sympathy with Piercy and Le Guin, Robinson and Dick, provides the book with some of its real strength. But, to reverse Jameson's own reversal of Benjamin, the effectively utopian is also, at the same time, necessarily ideological[32] and this is as likely to be true of anti-anti-utopianism as of utopianism itself.

There are two issues here: first, Jameson's overwhelming concentration on American SF, which seems strangely parochial in such a distinguished comparatist; and second, his aversion to dystopia, which sets him at odds with what many would regard as a tradition of central significance to SF. The American-centredness is apparent in much of Jameson's detail. So feminist SF is represented by Le Guin, Russ and Piercy, but not the equally distinguished Canadian, Margaret Atwood; fantasy and magic by Le Guin, but not the English China Miéville, whose New Crobuzon novels represent a serious theoretical challenge to Jameson; cyberpunk by Gibson and Sterling, but not the Australian Greg Egan; contemporary utopianism by Kim Stanley Robinson's Mars trilogy, but not its Scottish equivalent, Iain M. Banks's Culture novels; there is no mention at all of Karel Čapek, the greatest of Czech SF writers; nor of Fritz Lang, the Austrian film director, whose *Metropolis* effectively founded SF cinema; nor Michel Houellebecq, the leading contemporary French exponent of dystopian SF; whilst Dick warrants three chapters, his equally prolific and equally influential English counterpart, J.G. Ballard, rates merely a few pages. It is also true, however, of the schematic history of SF underpinning these details, which

---

30   Jameson 2005, p. 233; cf. Piercy 1976, pp. 197–8.
31   Jameson 2004, p. 54.
32   Jameson 1981, p. 286.

proceeds through six 'stages' (space opera, science, sociology, subjectivity, speculative fiction and cyberpunk), the first represented paradigmatically by Jules Verne, the others by Americans (Gernsbach [sic], Pohl and Kornbluth, Dick, Delany and, finally, Gibson).[33] This does real injustice to Verne, whose work was far more seriously 'scientific' than Jameson suggests – as Gernsback himself famously acknowledged.[34] That aside, it also seems an oddly old-fashioned way of thinking about the genre.

Borrowing from Franco Moretti's 'world-systems' approach to comparative literature,[35] we might tell this story much more productively as one in which: a genre is conceived in England and France at the very core of the nineteenth-century world literary system (Shelley initially, but above all Verne and Wells); it continues in both literary economies throughout the twentieth and into the twenty-first century (through Huxley, Orwell, Lewis, Wyndham, Hoyle, Clarke, Moorcock, Ballard, Banks, Macleod and Miéville in Britain, Rosny, Anatole France, Renard, Spitz, Boulle, Merle, Walther, Brussolo, Arnaud, Dantec and Houellebecq in France); its frontiers expand to include the Weimar Republic (Gail, von Harbou and Lang, von Hanstein), early Soviet Russia (Belyaev, Bogdanov, Bulgakov, Mayakovsky, Platonov, Alexei Tolstoy, Zamyatin) and inter-war Czechoslovakia (Karel Čapek, Troska); exported to Japan in the post-Second World War period (Abe, Hoshi, Komatsu, Murakami), it also flourished in Communist Poland (Fialkowski, Lem, Wisniewski-Snerg) and more significantly in late-Communist Russia (Altov, Bilenkin, Bulychev, Emtsev and Parnov, the Strugatsky brothers, Tarkovsky). There is an American story, of course, but this comes later and only becomes central and eventually near-hegemonic, from the inter-war period (Gernsback, Campbell, Asimov, Heinlein and 'the pulps') through the New Wave (Delany, Dick, Ellison, Spinrad, Tiptree, Zelazny) and on to the present (Gibson, Sterling and post-cyberpunk; Le Guin, Russ, Piercy and feminism; Kim Stanley Robinson and the new humanism). Moreover, this eventual American hegemony extends from print to film (Whale, Kubrick, Lucas, Spielberg, Scott, Cameron, Burton and Verhoeven) and television (Roddenberry, Straczynski, Carter and Whedon).

The late nineteenth- and early twentieth-century pattern more or less exactly replicates the general Anglo-French literary hegemony Moretti sketched in his *Atlas of the European Novel*. Just as the earlier decades had been dominated, both in terms of sales and translations, by the historical novels of Scott

---

33 Jameson 2005, p. 93.
34 Clute and Nicholls 1993, p. 311.
35 Moretti 1998 and 2005.

and Dumas, so were the later by Verne's *voyages extraordinaires* and Wells's 'scientific romances'. The later geographical trajectory is less predictable. Csicsery-Ronay has argued it is best understood as a correlate of imperialism.[36] But Moretti's own approach suggests a more plausible explanation, that 'peripheral' literatures can in fact be 'sustained' by 'historical backwardness', that new geographical spaces can produce new fictional spaces.[37] Thus, what each of the non-Anglo-French SF 'nations' have in common, Poland and Czechoslovakia as much as the USSR and the Weimar Republic, is their semiperipheral status in relation to the cultural core of the world system. And this is also true of the United States: American 'backwardness' eventually produced a paradigm shift in this marginal sub-form, which later generalised itself across the entire field of popular culture, from novel to film to television, so as to become the nearest we now have to a 'postmodern epic'.

3 Anti-Utopia and Dystopia

At the specifically textual level, Jameson's anti-anti-utopianism requires him to counterpose 'anti-Utopia' to 'Utopia', rather than – as has become increasingly common in utopian and SF studies – 'dystopia' to 'eutopia'.[38] So Jameson argues that there are two main kinds of loosely 'dystopian' text: the 'critical dystopia', which functions by way of a warning, through an 'if this goes on' principle; and the anti-Utopia proper, which springs from a quite different conviction that human nature is so inherently corrupt it could never be salvaged by any 'heightened consciousness of the impending dangers'.[39] Jameson borrows the term 'critical dystopia' from Tom Moylan[40] and, like Moylan, he argues that this form is essentially utopian in intent and import and thus a kind of 'negative cousin' of utopia.[41] Only the second variant, the anti-Utopia, is a true antonym

---

36 Csicsery-Ronay 2003.
37 Moretti 1998, pp. 195–7.
38 Lyman Tower Sargent famously defined the 'utopia (eutopia, dystopia, or utopian satire)' as 'a species of prose fiction that describes in some detail a non-existent society located in time and space' (Sargent, 1976: 275). Whilst the terminology is slightly different – utopia for Sargent's eutopia – it is clear that Raymond Williams also insisted on the formal symmetry between 'utopia' and 'dystopia', as on that between other cognate forms, such as the paradise and the hell (Williams, 1980: 196–9).
39 Jameson 2005, p. 198.
40 Moylan 2000, pp. 198–9.
41 Jameson 2005, p. 198.

of Utopia, a systemic and textual equivalent to the anti-utopian impulse in politics, 'informed by a central passion to denounce and to warn against Utopian programs'.[42] There are other examples of what Jameson terms the 'classic Cold War dystopia', from 'horror films to respectable literary and philosophical achievements', but the key instance, he argues, which establishes several of the form's 'symptomatic and paradoxical features', is Orwell's *Nineteen Eighty-Four*.[43]

Jameson has some interesting observations on 'the elegiac sense of the loss of the past' and 'the uncertainty of memory' in Orwell's dystopia. He is less convincing on the supposed inconsistency between Oceania's advanced surveillance technologies and the novel's insistence that science cannot function under totalitarianism: as Jameson must know, science is by no means coextensive with technology. And he is surely mistaken to read Orwell's 'linguistic anxieties' as a 'critique of the dialectic' – Derridean deconstruction would have far more plausible, if anachronistic, pretensions to be 'the original doublespeak, in which any utterance can have two diametrically opposed meanings' – but right to describe these as evidence of 'a convergence theory in which Stalinism and Anglosaxon commercialism and empiricism are sent off back to back'.[44] He is right, too, to insist that the novel should not 'be reduced – via pop-psychological notions of sublimation – to the mere disguised expression of other impulses such as those of sexuality (or even personal frustration)'.[45]

But these are essentially secondary matters, tangential to Jameson's central analysis, which proceeds by distinguishing three levels at work in Orwell: an 'articulation of the history of Stalinism', which the novelist had 'observed and experienced empirically'; a supposed 'historical universalization' of this experience into a vision of human nature as 'an insatiable and lucid hunger for power'; and the conversion of this 'conjuncture' into 'a life-passion'. This passion, Jameson insists, has 'become the face of anti-Utopianism in our own time'.[46] Comparing Orwell's 'Cold War public' to that for 18th century 'gothic nightmares of imprisonment and ... evil monks or nuns', Jameson concludes that these two 'dystopian awakenings' can each be considered 'collective responses of the bourgeoisie':

---

42 Jameson 2005, p. 199.
43 Jameson 2005, p. 200.
44 Ibid.
45 Jameson 2005, p. 201.
46 Jameson 2005, p. 200.

the first in its struggle against feudal absolutism and arbitrary tyranny, the second in its reaction to the possibility of a workers' state. This terror clearly overrides that other collective impulse which is the Utopian one, which, however, as irrepressible as the libido, continues to find its secret investments in what seems most fundamentally to rebuke and deny it: thus the projected oppressors, whether of clerical or party-bureaucratic nature, are fantasized as collectivities which distantly reproduce a Utopian structure, the difference being that I am included in the latter but excluded from the former. But at this point, the dynamic has become that of group behavior, with its cultural envy and its accompanying identity politics and racisms.[47]

What are we to make of this latter sentence? The conjuncture of identity politics and racism is hardly self-evident; in any case, they are each almost entirely absent from *Nineteen Eighty-Four*; and Orwell himself was famously hostile to both. Jameson must have a point, but it's not clear what exactly it might be. The import of the preceding sentences is brutally apparent, however: Orwell's anti-Stalinism is essentially 'bourgeois' in character and prompted by hostility to the very idea of a workers' state. It may best be understood, Jameson continues, as 'a dispirited reaction to postwar Labor Britain' or 'a depressive symptom of revolutionary discouragement'.[48] Later still, he extrapolates from Orwell in particular to the generalising conclusion that:

> there is a systemic perspective for which it is obvious that whatever threatens the system as such must be excluded: this is indeed the basic premise of all modern anti-Utopias from Dostoyevsky to Orwell and beyond, namely that the system develops its own instinct for self-preservation and learns ruthlessly to eliminate anything menacing its continuing existence without regard for individual life.[49]

The objection is immediate: surely, Jameson can't mean *all* modern anti-Utopias? Zamyatin's *We*? Čapek's *R.U.R.*? Huxley's *Brave New World*? As we have noted he ignores Čapek, but Jameson has the other bases covered: in Zamyatin, 'it is not the personal and the political that are confused but rather aesthetics and bureaucracy'; and if the novel is an anti-Utopia, it is one 'in which the

---

47   Jameson 2005, pp. 201–2.
48   Jameson 2005, p. 202.
49   Jameson 2005, p. 205.

Utopian impulse is still at work, with whatever ambivalence'; in Huxley, we find 'an aristocratic critique of the media and mass culture, rather than of any Orwellian "totalitarianism" '.[50] It follows, then, that neither is an anti-Utopia in Jameson's sense.

The danger should be obvious: that the category of anti-Utopian text becomes virtually coextensive with *Nineteen Eighty-Four*. At one point Jameson asks: 'Can we separate anti-Utopianism in Orwell from anti-communism?'.[51] We might equally ask: can we separate anti-anti-Utopianism in Jameson from anti-anti-communism? The answer seems in the negative, which is doubly unfortunate if only because, as Jameson himself notes, 'the history of the communist adventure is not co-terminous with the history of socialism as such'.[52] Orwell's place in this latter history deserves far greater respect than Jameson accords it. 'Every line of serious work that I have written since 1936', Orwell insisted in 1946, when he was already actively engaged in writing *Nineteen Eighty-Four*, 'has been written, directly or indirectly, *against* totalitarianism and *for* democratic Socialism'.[53] This question of Orwell's peculiar politics, a combination of anti-fascism, neo-Trotskyism and libertarian socialism, cannot legitimately be dismissed, after Jameson's fashion, as 'mere biographical affirmation'.[54] It might be excusable to argue thus if the politics were merely personal or found no expression in the novel. But neither is true: Orwell belonged to an important and continuing tradition of anti-Stalinist leftism; and those politics clearly inform the text of *Nineteen Eighty-Four*. The problem arises essentially because Jameson treats both the politics and the novel as products of the Cold War 1950s, an oddly perverse move in a theorist renowned for the injunction to 'Always historicize!'.[55] *Nineteen Eighty-Four* was published in June 1949 and its author was already dead by the end of January 1950: both were necessarily products of the two decades that preceded the Cold War, but not of the latter itself.

---

50 Jameson 2005, p. 202.
51 Jameson 2005, p. 201.
52 Jameson 2005, p. 21.
53 Orwell 1970a, p. 28.
54 Jameson 2005, p. 198.
55 Jameson 1981, p. 9.

4   Orwell and the Left

Jameson's misreading of Orwell and *Nineteen Eighty-Four* is no minor matter: it is, in fact, the central point of weakness in *Archaeologies*, from which we are able to trace out and untangle the thread of most that is wrong with the book. To justify this assertion will require me briefly to elaborate, firstly, on Orwell's politics and, secondly, on his novel. Whatever we make of the particular details, it is clear that Eric Blair the man and George Orwell the author were moved to anti-imperialism by the experience of British rule in Burma, to populist sympathy for the poor through living rough in Paris and London, positive identification with the working-class Left through reportage in the industrial North of England, and support for revolutionary socialism by fighting on the Republican side in the Spanish Civil War. This is well-known biographical material, easily garnished from the obvious Orwell texts, *Burmese Days*, *Down and Out in Paris and London*, *The Road to Wigan Pier*, *Homage to Catalonia*. No doubt, it has a strongly autobiographical element, but this is more than mere biographical affirmation, for these are also what Jameson would easily recognise elsewhere as intertexts. Indeed, the main source for Orwell biographies – Bernard Crick's for example – is in the writings, in the texts. And it is the writing, whether considered biographical datum or intertextual referent, that renders Jameson's reading radically suspect.

There is no doubting Orwell's anti-Stalinism, nor its origins in the experience of the Spanish Revolution, but there is no evidence at all to suggest that it was ever universalised into either a blanket pessimism about human nature or a life-passion. Reflecting on his Spanish experiences from wartime Britain, Orwell concluded that:

> one sees only the struggle of the gradually awakening common people against the lords of property and their hired liars and bumsuckers. The question is very simple ... Shall the common man be pushed back into the mud, or shall he not? I myself believe ... that the common man will win his fight sooner or later, but I want it to be sooner and not later ... That was the real issue of the Spanish war, and of the last war, and perhaps of other wars yet to come.[56]

There is no universalised pessimism here, rather the very opposite, a belief that, no matter how dire the current circumstances, the working-class cause

---

56   Orwell 1966, p. 245.

will eventually triumph. Yet this essay was written in 1943, when Orwell was already at work on *Animal Farm*. Jameson himself suggests in parentheses that the narrative force of Orwell's fable springs from the same conviction about the inevitably corrupting effects of power on human nature which later inspired *Nineteen Eighty-Four*.[57] This is simply incompatible with the text of *Animal Farm* itself – there is nothing corrupt about Boxer, surely? – and with what we actually know to have been Orwell's self-declared beliefs at the time of its composition. If universalised pessimism ever became a life passion for Orwell, then it was only very briefly so, no more than in the last three years before he died. And even that seems distinctly improbable, as we shall see when we turn to *Nineteen Eighty-Four*.

In Spain, Orwell had fought for the Partido Obrero de Unificación Marxista (POUM), the United Marxist Workers' Party, rather than the Communist-led International Brigades. As the name suggests, it was an independent – that is, non-Communist – Marxist organisation. It was also the Spanish sister party of the Independent Labour Party (ILP) in Britain, which had split from the Labour Party in 1931. Throughout the 1930s, the ILP managed to combine a significant parliamentary representation, always substantially larger than the Communists, a national organisation and membership and a policy of 'revolutionary' socialism, suspicious of and increasingly hostile to both the USSR and the local Communist Party. The ILP was effectively swept aside by the Labour landslide in 1945, but it remained an important precursor for the British New Left of the 1950s. In the concluding chapter to *The Road to Wigan Pier*, Orwell insists on the urgent necessity to:

> bring an effective Socialist party into existence. It will have to be a party with genuinely revolutionary intentions, and it will have to be numerically strong enough to act.[58]

Clearly, such an effective socialist party would be neither the Labour nor Communist Party, dismissed in the same pages as respectively 'backstairs-crawlers' and a 'stupid cult of Russia',[59] but rather an expanded version of the political party he would eventually join in June 1938, the ILP.

Which explains why he fought for the POUM: he had 'slight connexions, mainly personal'[60] with the ILP and was broadly sympathetic even before going

---

57 Jameson 2005, p. 198.
58 Orwell 1962, p. 202.
59 Orwell 1962, p. 190.
60 Orwell 1970b, p. 352.

to Spain. By contrast, the vast majority of Communist and Labour Party volunteers fought in the International Brigades. This broad sympathy grew into close agreement, as he would later elaborate:

> I was with the I.L.P. contingent in Spain. I never pretended, then or since, to agree in every detail with the policy the P.O.U.M. put forward and the I.L.P. supported, but the general course of events has borne it out. The things I saw in Spain brought home to me the fatal danger of mere negative 'anti-Fascism'. Once I had grasped the essentials of the situation in Spain I realized that the I.L.P. was the only British party I felt like joining – and also the only party I could join with at least the certainty that I would never be led up the garden path in the name of capitalist democracy.[61]

Orwell's objections to Stalinism were clearly neither bourgeois nor predicated on hostility to the idea of a workers' state. Rather, he had been inspired to join the ILP by the lived experience of working-class power in Catalonia: 'It was the first time I had ever been in a town where the working class was in the saddle', he wrote of his arrival in Barcelona:

> Practically every building of any size had been seized by the workers ... Practically everyone wore rough working-class clothes ... There was much in it that I did not understand ... but I recognized it immediately as a state of affairs worth fighting for.[62]

For Orwell to choose the POUM and Barcelona, as against the OGPU and Moscow, was to opt for a workers' state that might still have a future, as against the counter-revolutionary terror that had already destroyed a previous one.

5 *Nineteen Eighty-Four*

What, finally, of *Nineteen Eighty-Four* itself? Clearly, it is not a dispirited reaction to postwar Labour Britain: the very suggestion – Clement Attlee as Big Brother – would be risible were it not seriously entertained in the United States. Hence, Orwell's own explanation to the American United Auto Workers Union, written six months before his death, that his novel:

---

61 Orwell 1970c, pp. 374–5.
62 Orwell 1966a, pp. 8–9.

is NOT intended as an attack on Socialism or on the British Labour Party (of which I am a supporter) but as a show-up of the perversions to which a centralised economy is liable and which have been partly realised in Communism and Fascism.[63]

The reference to Fascism here is important: Ingsoc was designed to signify not so much British Labourism as National Socialism, that is Fascism (and also, as it happens, Stalinist Communism).

To read the novel as a symptom of revolutionary discouragement might remains plausible, however, especially given the Spanish Fascist victory in 1939, not reversed in 1945, even more especially so if we assume, as Jameson does, that *Nineteen Eighty-Four* ends with:

> But it was all right, everything was all right, the struggle was finished. He had won the victory over himself. He loved Big Brother.

immediately followed by:

> THE END.[64]

But the novel actually continues, in my edition for over fourteen more pages, until the conclusion to the *Appendix* on Newspeak: 'It was chiefly in order to allow time for the preliminary work of translation that the final adoption of Newspeak had been fixed for so late a date as 2050'.[65] In content, these lines add little, but their form is redolent with meaning. For, as Margaret Atwood observes of the whole *Appendix*, it:

> is written in standard English, in the third person, and in the past tense, which can only mean that the regime has fallen, and that language and individuality have survived. For whoever has written the essay on Newspeak, the world of *1984* is over.[66]

This must be right: the *Appendix* is internal to the novel, neither an author's nor a scholarly editor's account of how the fiction works, but rather a part of the fiction, a fictional commentary on fictional events. And, although Atwood

---

63   Orwell 1970d, p. 564.
64   Orwell 1989, p. 311.
65   Orwell 1989, p. 326.
66   Atwood 2005, p. 337.

fails to notice this, it is anticipated within the main body of the text, by a footnote in the first chapter, which assures us, again in standard English, in the third person, in the past tense, that: 'Newspeak was the official language of Oceania'.[67] Atwood uses a similar device in *The Handmaid's Tale*, the first of her own dystopian SF novels, which concludes with an extract from the proceedings of a 'Symposium on Gileadean Studies', written in some utopian future set long after the collapse of the Republic of Gilead.[68] Moreover, she readily admits that *Nineteen Eighty-Four* provided her with a 'direct model' for this.[69] If she is to be believed, then both Orwell's *Appendix* and her 'Historical Notes' work as framing devices, by which to blunt the force of dystopian inevitability so as to establish what Jameson would understand precisely as a 'critical dystopia'.

There are good reasons to take Atwood seriously, not least her own SF novels. But I myself have pursued this matter further, by way of an analysis of the 'problem of ending' in four intertexts to *Nineteen Eighty-Four*, with all of which Orwell was himself familiar: Zamyatin's *We*, in Cauvet-Duhamel's French translation as *Nous autres*; Huxley's *Brave New World*; and Selver's British translation of Čapek's *R.U.R.*[70] Insofar as dystopian fictions do share a utopian intent, then they typically confront the problem of how to represent a naturalistically plausible danger sufficiently terrible to be threatening, but insufficiently so as to be demoralising. And this is precisely the problem faced by Orwell in *Nineteen Eighty-Four*. We know he was much impressed by *Nous autres*: in 1946, he wrote approvingly of it in his famous essay on Burnham; in 1948, he offered to review a proposed English translation, which failed to eventuate, for the *Times Literary Supplement*; in 1949, he urged it on Fred Warburg, who had published *Animal Farm* and would shortly publish *Nineteen Eighty-Four*. And we know *Nous autres* is organised into forty chapters, or 'Notes', the penultimate of which is entitled 'LA FIN'. But it actually continues for a further six pages after LA FIN,[71] just as the first edition of *Nineteen Eighty-Four* continues for a further fourteen after THE END.[72] Given Orwell's familiarity with the other texts, especially *Nous autres*, it seems very plausible that the *Appendix* on Newspeak was in fact a deliberate invention, an experiment in relation to the genre of SF, designed to achieve the effect Atwood describes in her own work.[73]

---

67 Orwell 1989, p. 5n.
68 Atwood 1987, pp. 311–24.
69 Atwood 2005, p. 337.
70 Milner 2006.
71 Zamiatine 1929, pp. 227–32.
72 Orwell 1949, pp. 299–312.
73 Interestingly, there is no trace of the *Appendix* in what remains of Orwell's manuscript.

These are formal solutions to formal problems of a kind critical theorists such as Jameson are peculiarly well-equipped to understand. Why, then, should his analysis prove so thoroughly misconceived? Why should such a distinguished literary critic ignore the entirety of the last fourteen pages of a text? The answer must be, in part, because Jameson is located in the United States, rather than Western Europe, and his reading is therefore perhaps unavoidably overdetermined by the novel's American Cold War reception. But it is also, I fear, because – like the *New Left Review* in Britain, which often publishes his essays – Jameson inherits from the Trotskyist Fourth International a peculiar loyalty to the legacy of Trotsky's murderers. To cite the obvious example, his reference to Stalinist Russia as a 'workers' state' repeats a long-standing Trotskyist formulation, which seems utterly perverse: Stalin's Russia was in no sense a workers' state, but rather a primitive form of monopoly state capitalism, not so much 'socialism' as 'barbarism', to rework Luxemburg's famous formulation.[74] To cite another, Jameson's single most influential work, *Postmodernism, or The Cultural Logic of Late Capitalism*, is famously underwritten by the analysis of 'late capitalism' developed in the first instance by Ernest Mandel, the most distinguished of Trotskyist intellectuals after Trotsky himself.[75]

This is not to suggest that Orwell's life, his politics and his dystopia remain immune to criticism. But Raymond Williams showed far more insight than Jameson, when he sought to situate *Nineteen Eighty-Four* in relation to Orwell's 1946 essay on James Burnham. Like Burnham, Orwell had believed capitalism finished, unlike Burnham he hoped to see it replaced by democratic socialism, but like Burnham he acknowledged the strong possibility that a quasi-socialist rhetoric would be used to legitimate 'managerial revolution' and bureaucratic dictatorship. Burnham anticipated this prospect with some relish – witness his involvement with the CIA – Orwell with much fear. Hence, the latter's insistence that 'the question is whether capitalism, now obviously doomed, is to give way to oligarchy or to true democracy'.[76] This was, for Williams, Orwell's crucial mistake: to have imagined capitalism already beaten and, hence, the central issue as that between different 'socialisms'. As it turned out, what Orwell most failed to anticipate, Williams concludes, is the 'spectacular capitalist boom',

---

Given its dilapidated state, this proves little. But it is suggestive of the possibility that the *Appendix* was written last, as the real 'END' to the novel, the solution to a problem that had become apparent only when the main text was more or less complete.

74 Luxemburg 1970, p. 327.
75 Jameson 1991, pp. 35–6; Mandel 1975.
76 Orwell 1970d, p. 198.

which falsified 'virtually every element of the specific prediction'.[77] There is much truth in this judgement. But we all misread the future, utopians as much as anyone. For *Nineteen Eighty-Four*, as for any other SF novel, the key question remains that identified by Jameson, not 'did it get the future right?', but rather 'did it sufficiently shock its own present as to force a meditation on the impossible?'. What Jameson misses is that the process works for dystopia as well as eutopia, for barbarism as well as socialism. So this is more than a passing mistake about either Orwell or *Nineteen Eighty-Four*: it is, rather, a crucial failure to theorise adequately one of the central forms of contemporary science fiction.

77   Williams 1991, p. 117.

CHAPTER 24

Time Travelling: Or, How (Not) to Periodise a Genre*

In 2011 the British Library held a major public exhibition on science fiction under the rubric *Out of This World: Science Fiction But Not as You Know It*. Both the exhibition itself and the companion book by Mike Ashley were insistent that the genre had an ancient pedigree, 'dating back … at least as far as the ancient Greeks'.[1] Both placed particular emphasis on Lucian of Samosata's *Alēthēs Historia* (*The True History*), which dates from the second century AD. So, too, do a range of well-known academic texts, from Darko Suvin's *Metamorphoses of Science Fiction*, still commonly regarded as the foundational text for academic science fiction studies, through to David Seed's recent *Very Short Introduction* to the genre.[2] Yet the vast majority of science fiction (henceforth SF) readers have nonetheless almost certainly never heard of Lucian. There seems to be a certain disjuncture between institutional and lay perceptions of the genre.

1   Long Histories of Science Fiction: Suvin and Roberts

Suvin is best known for his influential definitions of SF as a literary genre 'whose *necessary and sufficient conditions are the presence and interaction of estrangement and cognition*', and which is distinguished by '*the narrative dominance or hegemony of a fictional 'novum'* (novelty, innovation) *validated by cognitive logic*'.[3] An important effect of these definitions was to expand the genre so as to incorporate into it a substantial part of the western literary and philosophical canon. There were thus, according to Suvin, six main instances of SF in the 'Euro-Mediterranean tradition': the Hellenic, the Hellenic-cum-Roman, the Renaissance-Baroque, the democratic revolution, the fin-de-siècle, and the

---

*   This chapter has been published previously in *Foundation: The International Review of Science Fiction*, Vol. 43, No. 117, pp. 70–9, 2014.
1   Ashley 2011, p. 7.
2   Suvin 1979, pp. 54, 97–8; Seed 2011, pp. 2–3.
3   Suvin 1979, pp. 7–8, 63.

modern.⁴ Adam Roberts's *The History of Science Fiction* takes a similarly long view, tracing the genre back, first, to the ancient Greek novel and, second, to Reformation Protestantism, the two beginnings separated by an 'interlude' between AD 400 and 1600, during which fantasy prevailed over SF.⁵ Unlike Suvin, Roberts insisted on the specifically religious context of the genre's seventeenth century re-emergence, through what he termed 'a cultural dialectic between "Protestant" rationalist post-Copernican science on the one hand, and "Catholic" theology, magic and mysticism, on the other'.⁶

For Suvin the science in SF was essentially a matter of cognitive rationality. It follows, then, that the genre has no necessary connection with any specifically modern understandings of science and technology. Indeed, he was at pains to insist that SF embraces a whole range of subgenres 'from Greek and earlier times ... the Islands of the Blessed, utopias, fabulous voyages, planetary novels, *Staatsromane*, anticipations, and dystopias'.⁷ The core of the genre, however, lies in its connection with utopia. Hence, his stress on Thomas More and H.G. Wells. 'More's *Utopia*', he wrote, 'subsumes all the SF forms of its epoch'.⁸ A very similar claim is made for Wells: 'He collected ... all the main influences of earlier writers ... and transformed them in his own image, whence they entered the treasury of subsequent SF'.⁹ Roberts's notion of science is similarly disconnected from contemporary understandings of the relation between science and technology. SF is not so much about science, he argued, as about *technē*, in the Heideggerian sense, not as an instrument, but as a way of knowing the world by 'enframing' it.¹⁰ This is a 'fundamentally philosophical outlook', he added, closer to soft than hard SF, which suggests a version of the genre 'many readers of SF will not recognise'.¹¹ Roberts's overall sense of the genre is thus similar to Suvin's in outline, except that *voyages extraordinaires* displace utopia at its centre: 'Travels "upwards" through space, or sometimes "downwards" ... are the trunk ... from which the various other modes of SF branch off'.¹² Utopias do figure in this account – just as voyages had in Suvin's – but only insofar

---

4   Suvin 1979, pp. 87, 205.
5   Roberts 2005, pp. ix, 32–5.
6   Roberts 2005, p. 3.
7   Suvin 1979, pp. 12.
8   Suvin 1979, p. 92.
9   Suvin 1979, pp. 219–20.
10   Roberts 2005, pp. 11–12.
11   Roberts 2005, p. 18.
12   Roberts 2005, p. vii.

as they deal with 'lands that might actually be reached by a voyager, strange but *material* new forms of human life and society'.[13]

Despite the different theorisations, these two long histories are devoted to a similar range of pre-modern subgenres. Both also see SF as fundamentally incompatible with totalising versions of religious idealism.[14] Both even cite the burning at the stake of Giordano Bruno the Nolan by the Inquisition in 1600 as a crucial turning point in the development of the genre.[15] Despite differences in emphasis, both are also directed at a similar range of pre-modern writers: Aristophanes, Antonius Diogenes, Lucian, More, Bacon, Campanella, Cyrano, Swift. Interestingly, both draw attention to Lucian as, respectively, providing the 'paradigm for the whole "prehistory" of SF'[16] and the 'father of science fiction'.[17] There is no doubting the connections Suvin and Roberts establish between particular classical texts and their seventeenth or twentieth century counterparts: Aristophanes' *Ornithes*, Campanella's *La città del Sole* and Ursula K. Le Guin's *The Dispossessed* are indeed all utopias; just as Lucian's *Alēthēs Historia*, Cyrano's *L'Autre Monde ou les États et Empires de la lune* and 'the voyages of the starship *Enterprise*' are all *voyages extraordinaires*. It remains open to doubt, however, whether either or both lineages yield any adequate sense of the early twenty-first century functioning of the SF 'selective tradition', to borrow a term from Raymond Williams.[18]

2   Science and Science Fiction: Lucian or Shelley?

When Suvin treats science as cognition and Roberts as philosophical outlook both overlook the fundamental historical difference between contemporary understandings of science and those of antiquity and early modernity: that the Industrial Revolution decisively and definitively redefined science into an intensely practical activity inextricably productive of new technologies, in the everyday rather than the Heideggerian sense. This is clearly how SF continues to understand science: Le Guin's Hainish Ekumen is made possible by the ansible eventually produced from Shevek's science; Gene Roddenberry's United Federation of Planets by the science that produced Star Fleet's warp drive; nothing

---

13   Roberts 2005, p. 54.
14   Suvin 1979, pp. 7, 26–7; Roberts 2005, p. xiii.
15   Suvin 1979, p. 98; Roberts 2005, p. 36.
16   Suvin 1979, p. 98.
17   Roberts 2005, p. 27.
18   Williams 1977, p. 115.

even vaguely similar exists in Aristophanes or Lucian, Campanella or Cyrano. Samuel R. Delany famously described 'genealogies, with Mary Shelley for our grandmother or Lucian of Samosata as our great-great grandfather' as 'preposterous and historically insensitive'.[19] He was quite right about the second, but nonetheless mistaken about the first.

For the novelty of Shelley's *Frankenstein* was precisely that it imagined biological science as practically applicable to medical technology. As the 1818 Preface to the first edition insists: 'The event on which this fiction is founded has been supposed, by Dr. Darwin, and some of the physiological writers of Germany, as not of impossible occurrence'.[20] Which is why Brian Aldiss was quite right to trace the 'origins of the species' to Shelley.[21] It is also why *Frankenstein*, like Wells's *The Time Machine* and Verne's *Vingt mille lieues sous les mers*, remains actively present in contemporary SF, continuously available as an intertextual reference point in SF literature, film, radio and television. To take only one recent example, William Gibson's *Zero History* can have its Hollis Henry refer to her boyfriend Garreth's seriously damaged and reconstructed leg as 'Frank'[22] only because it knows that SF readers always-already know about Frankensteinian science, in a way they simply do not about Lucian's King Endymion.

Lucian's *Alēthēs Historia* is claimed for SF primarily as an early example of a *voyage extraordinaire* to the moon. The narrator tells of how, sailing west from the Pillars of Hercules, his ship and crew were swept into the sky by a waterspout, which carried them, after a week, to an island in the air we soon learn to be the moon:

Περὶ μεσημβρίαν δὲ οὐκέτι τῆς νήσου φαινομένης ἄφνω τυφὼν ἐπιγενόμενος καὶ περιδινήσας τὴν ναῦν καὶ μετεωρίσας ὅσον ἐπὶ σταδίους τριακοσίους οὐκέτι καθῆκεν εἰς τὸ πέλαγος, ἀλλ' ἄνω μετέωρον ἐξηρτημένην ἄνεμος ἐμπεσὼν τοῖς ἱστίοις ἔφερεν κολπώσας τὴν ὀθόνην

[But about midday, when we were out of sight of the island, a waterspout suddenly came upon us, which swept the ship round and up to a height of some three hundred and fifty miles above the earth. She did not fall back into the sea, but was suspended aloft, and at the same time carried along by a wind which struck and filled the sails][23]

---

19 Delany 1994, p. 26.
20 Shelley 1980, p. 13.
21 Aldiss 1986, pp. 25–52.
22 Gibson 2011, p. 300.
23 Lucian 1972, I, 9, pp. 6–10; Lucian 1905, p. 139.

They are taken prisoner by Endymion, the Selenite king, whose side they join in war against Phaethon, the king of the Sun. The Solites are victorious, however, after which articles of peace are concluded and the voyagers left free to explore the Moon: "Ἃ δὲ ἐν τῶι μεταξὺ διατρίβων ἐν τῆι σελήνηι κατενόησα καινὰ καὶ παράδοξα, ταῦτα βούλομαι εἰπεῖν [I am now to put on record the novelties and singularities which attracted my notice during our stay on the Moon]'.[24]

These novelties include a universal diet of the fumes from roast flying frogs, mucus made of honey and sweat made of milk, glass clothing for the rich and brass for the poor, removable eyes and a capacity to overhear and see everything on Earth.[25] The voyagers take their leave of Endymion and journey on through the skies, to Lucifer the Morning Star, the Zodiac and the Sun, swept along by the wind:

ἐν δὲ τῶι παράπλωι πολλὰς μὲν καὶ ἄλλας χώρας παρημείψαμεν, προσέσχομεν δὲ καὶ τῶι Ἑωσφόρωι ἄρτι συνοικιζομένωι, καὶ ἀποβάντες ὑδρευσάμεθα. ἐμβάντες δὲ εἰς τὸν ζωιδιακὸν ἐν ἀριστερᾶι παρήιειμεν τὸν ἥλιον, ἐν χρῶι τὴν γῆν παραπλέοντες· οὐ γὰρ ἀπέβημεν καίτοι πολλὰ τῶν ἑταίρων ἐπιθυμούντων, ἀλλ' ὁ ἄνεμος οὐκ ἐφῆκεν. ἐθεώμεθα μέντοι τὴν χώραν εὐθαλῆ τε καὶ πίονα καὶ εὔυδρον καὶ πολλῶν ἀγαθῶν μεστήν

[We passed on our way many countries, and actually landed on Lucifer, now in process of settlement, to water. We then entered the Zodiac and passed the Sun on the left, coasting close by it. My crew were very desirous of landing, but the wind would not allow of this. We had a good view of the country, however, and found it covered with vegetation, rich, well-watered, and full of all good things].[26]

They sail to Lamp town, which is inhabited entirely by lamps, and then to Aristophanes' Cloud-cuckoo-land, where they are prevented from landing by the direction of the wind. Eventually, however, the wind drops and their vessel is returned to the ocean from which it had been plucked.[27] All this occurs in the first 29 of 42 sections in Book I, with a further 47 to follow in Book II. In the remainder, there are a series of subsequent Terrestrial adventures, which include being swallowed by a 200 mile long whale and living inside it for many

---

24   Lucian 1972, I, 22, pp. 7–8; Lucian 1905, p. 145.
25   Lucian 1972, I, pp. 23–6.
26   Lucian 1972, I, 28, pp. 25–30; Lucian 1905, p. 147.
27   Lucian 2011, I, p. 29.

months,[28] a visit to the Island of the Blessed, the home of the dead heroes,[29] and to the Isle of Dreams, the inhabitants of which are, quite literally, dreams and nightmares.[30]

All this is good fun, to be sure, and Suvin quite right to describe it as 'a string of model parodies', but less obviously so to add that each parody translates 'a whole literary form into a critical, that is, cognitive, context'.[31] That parody is critical is indisputable; that it is cognitive seems open to question if cognition is non-identical with ethical or aesthetic judgement; that it is scientific, as the use of the term cognitive seems to connote, seems simply wrong. Roberts is similarly effusive about *Alēthēs Historia*: 'outrageous, inventive, bizarre and very funny ... The ironic title indicates the way in which the book explores the playful exuberance of lies and lying'.[32] This, too, seems fair comment. Nonetheless, it is not at all obvious that these particular qualities have any necessary connection with anything we today regard as SF. Lucian's adventures in the skies are essentially of a piece with those on the Earth and both are part of the wider world of classical myth.

Antiquity made extraordinary scientific advances, especially in mathematics, but there is little or no trace of any of these in Lucian. Still less is there any evidence of our modern sense of science as technology: he is simply uninterested in how a ship designed to sail the seas might be adapted to sail the skies; rather, it is all left to a waterspout and the winds. Roberts eventually has the good grace to admit that 'Lucian's sympathy is ... with the mythic, not the scientific, mode' and that the work is 'anti-SF rather than proto-SF', but spoils the effect by adding that 'anti-SF nevertheless involves an engagement in the terms of SF'.[33] Not necessarily, especially not if the terms of SF were defined in the nineteenth and twentieth centuries, rather than in the second and seventeenth. Neither Lucian nor any other classical author would have imagined science as productive of technologies. Their societies were slave economies, in which labour was both debased and cheapened, and labour-saving therefore a matter of indifference. As Perry Anderson observed of what he called 'slave relations of production', 'no major cluster of inventions ever occurred to propel the Ancient economy forward ... Nothing is more striking ... than

---

28   Lucian 2011, I, pp. 30–42; Lucian 2011, II, pp. 1–2.
29   Lucian 2011, II, pp. 6–29.
30   Lucian 2011, II, pp. 32–5.
31   Suvin 1979, p. 97.
32   Roberts 2005, p. 28.
33   Roberts 2005, p. 29.

the overall technological stagnation of Antiquity'.[34] Imperial Rome, the society for which Lucian wrote, 'possessed very little objective impetus for technological advance', Anderson concludes. Hence, its inability to apply and develop the two most important inventions actually made within its boundaries during the 1st century AD, the water-mill and the reaping machine.[35] The sixteenth and seventeenth centuries are a different matter, but remained so distracted by the ideological warfare between Protestantism and Catholicism that science figured primarily as worldview, rather than potentially productive technique.

3 Reformation or Enlightenment?

Periodisation is a notoriously tricky business, as much for literary history as for historiography more generally. But I take my cue here from Kim Stanley Robinson, who observes that:

> there do seem to be differences in human life between, for instance, the Middle Ages and the Renaissance, or the Enlightenment and the Postmodern; and whether these differences were caused by changes in modes of production, structures of feeling, scientific paradigms, dynastic succession, technological progress, or cultural metamorphosis, it almost doesn't matter. The shapes invoked make a pattern, they tell a story that people can follow.[36]

Antiquity is one such term, the Reformation another, the Enlightenment yet another. When Adam Roberts writes that SF 'still bears the imprint of the cultural crisis that gave it birth',[37] he is absolutely right, but when he adds that the crisis 'happened to be a European religious one', he misrecognises the relevant cultural crisis. For, in the sense that we now understand the terms, both science and SF emerge, not from the culture wars of the sixteenth and seventeenth centuries, but from those of the eighteenth and nineteenth. The genre's foundational dialectic is therefore not that between Catholicism and Protestantism, but that between Enlightenment and Romanticism.[38] Both native Londoners

---

34 Anderson 1974a, pp. 25–6.
35 Anderson 1974a, pp. 79–80.
36 Robinson 2012, p. 244.
37 Roberts 2005, p. 3.
38 For the idea of cultural modernity as a stalled dialectic between Enlightenment and

and tourists are often familiar with the Latin inscription, describing the course of the Great Fire of London of 1666, on the North face of Christopher Wren and Robert Hooke's Monument. Few, however, recall the line, blaming the Fire on Popish frenzy, added to the Monument in 1681 but removed in 1830. The addition marks the dialectic between Protestantism and Catholicism, the removal that between Enlightenment and Romanticism.

The novelty of the Enlightenment's version of science was, in Adorno and Horkheimer's phrase, that it 'behaves toward things as a dictator toward men. He knows them in so far as he can manipulate them'.[39] This kind of science had, of course, been anticipated in Bacon and Newton, but was only made practicable by the key developments of the Industrial Revolution: Edmund Cartwright's invention of the power operated loom in 1785, James Watt's of the rotary steam engine in 1782, the construction of a national canal network across Britain between 1790 and 1794. All this, in turn, gave force to the Romantic counter-critique:

> For was it meant
> That we should pore, and dwindle as we pore,
> For ever dimly pore on things minute,
> On solitary objects, still beheld
> In disconnection dead and spiritless,
> And still dividing and dividing still,
> Break down all grandeur ...[40]

As Kate Rigby observes, Wordsworth here represents the objects of scientific study as doubly dead, literally because killed and metaphorically because isolated 'in disconnection'.[41] The monster forged by Shelley's Victor Frankenstein from the disconnected parts of dead bodies would be the fictional product of exactly this kind of alienated science, applied as medical technology.

From the late eighteenth century, the experience of industrialisation progressively displaced the dialectic between Catholicism and Protestantism with that between Enlightenment and Romanticism. This displacement is registered in the emergence of what Williams called a new 'structure of feeling'.[42] And a

---

Romanticism, I am indebted to Roberts and Murphy's *Dialectic of Romanticism: A Critique of Modernism* (Roberts and Murphy 2004).
39   Adorno and Horkheimer 1979, p. 9.
40   Wordsworth 1949, p. 402.
41   Rigby 2004, p. 18.
42   Williams 1965, pp. 64–5.

crucial element in the emergent structure of feeling of the nineteenth century was, as Williams himself observed, the new industrial science and its new technologies. 'Again and again', Williams wrote:

> even by critics of the society, the excitement of this extraordinary release of man's powers was acknowledged and shared ... 'These are our poems', Carlyle said in 1842, looking at one of the new locomotives, and this element ... is central to the whole culture.[43]

This is the element that most clearly distinguishes the new worlds of SF from the alternative islands of older utopian fictions. The nineteenth-century SF novel was, then, a literary form radically different from those that preceded it. What is more, insofar as it was an adaptation of any pre-existing form, this might well be, not so much the utopia – or, indeed, the fantasy – as the historical novel.

4 Science Fiction and the Historical Novel

Fredric Jameson's 2005 *Archaeologies of the Future* was without doubt the most important critical intervention into SF studies since Suvin's *Metamorphoses*. It was avowedly Suvinian in its declared focus on the connections between utopia and SF: hence the subtitle. Nonetheless, Jameson traces the genre's history back only so far as More and devotes most of his analysis to the nineteenth and twentieth centuries. Moreover, he also toys with an alternative understanding of SF as a development from the historical novel rather than the utopia. So he stresses that the historical novel ceased to be 'functional' roughly contemporaneously with the beginnings of SF, in the simultaneous historical moment of Gustave Flaubert's *Salammbô*, first published in 1862, and Jules Verne's *Cinq Semaines en ballon*, first published in 1863.[44] This is empirically astute, for, just as French publishing in the early decades of the nineteenth century had been dominated, in terms of both sales and translations, by the historical novels of Alexandre Dumas, so in the later decades it would be by Verne's *voyages extraordinaires* (we might add that Verne was a protégé of Dumas).

The 'new genre', Jameson writes, is 'a form which ... registers some nascent sense of the future ... in the space on which a sense of the past had once

---

43 Williams 1965, p. 88.
44 Jameson 2005, p. 285.

been inscribed'.⁴⁵ The connection between SF and the historical novel arises, he argues, because each is 'the symptom of a mutation in our relationship to historical time'.⁴⁶ Both the emergence of SF and the decline of the historical novel into 'archaeology' are functions of a growing collective inability to understand the present as history. The new genre's sense of the future cannot therefore entail the imaginary representation of any real future, but must rather work primarily 'to defamiliarize and restructure our experience of our own *present*'.⁴⁷ And it does so, furthermore, primarily by 'transforming our own present into the determinate past of something yet to come'. SF thereby 'enacts and enables a structurally unique "method" for apprehending the present as history', a method which operates irrespectively 'of the "pessimism" or "optimism" of the imaginary future world which is the pretext for that defamiliarization'.⁴⁸

Jameson repeats this argument in *The Antinomies of Realism*, but with a slightly revised periodisation. The 'invention of Science Fiction', he writes, 'was … a modification of our historicity to which a genuine historical cause can be assigned with some precision: the emergence of imperialism on a world scale in the Berlin conference of 1885'.⁴⁹ So the key foundational SF writer becomes H.G. Wells rather than Jules Verne, the key text *The War of the Worlds*, which, Jameson notes, deliberately 'evokes the extermination of the Tasmanians as his inspiration'. Indeed, it does.⁵⁰ But it isn't clear what exactly connects the Berlin conference either to Wells's novel, which wasn't published until 1898, or to Governor Arthur's genocidal 'Black War' of 1828–32. Jameson's more general thesis is, however, more persuasive than the periodisation itself. The 'historical novel of the future', he concludes, '… will necessarily be Science-Fictional inasmuch as it will have to include questions about the fate of our social system'. And, he continues, 'we are fortunate to have at least one recent novel which … gives us an idea of what that might look like'.⁵¹ Interestingly, the novel in question is David Mitchell's 2004 *Cloud Atlas*,⁵² the pessimism of which might well be read as antithetical to Jameson's larger utopian concerns.

---

45   Jameson 2005, p. 286.
46   Jameson 2005, p. 284.
47   Jameson 2005, p. 286.
48   Jameson 2005, p. 288.
49   Jameson 2013, p. 298.
50   Wells 2005, p. 9.
51   Jameson 2013, p. 298.
52   Mitchell 2004.

For Jameson, however, 'the most valuable works are those that make their points by way of form rather than content'[53] and, in these terms, he judges both the novel and the 2012 film adaptation by Lana Wachowski, Tom Tykwer and Andy Wachowski to be successes.[54] There are problems with Jameson's attempts at periodisation, not least their internal inconsistency. But the notion that SF and the historical novel are cognate genres, insofar as, at the most fundamental of levels, both take human historicity as their central subject matter, seems a more productive starting point than the post-Suvinian preoccupation with utopia which directs much of *Archaeologies*. For, the typical subject matter of SF is future history, euchronia and dyschronia rather than eutopia and dystopia, its precursors therefore more plausibly Scott and Dumas than More and Bacon.

The Antinomies of Realism is dedicated to Kim Stanley Robinson, whose PhD thesis, on Philip K. Dick, Jameson supervised.[55] The dedication is entirely warranted, for the book's conclusions clearly echo Robinson's own. In a 1987 essay he specifically argued that SF 'is an historical literature', in which there is always 'an explicit or implicit fictional history that connects the period depicted to our present moment'. 'The two genres are not the same', he continued, but 'more alike ... than either is like the literary mainstream'. 'They share some methods and concerns', he concluded:

> in that both must describe cultures that cannot be physically visited by the reader; thus both are concerned with alien cultures, and with estrangement. And both genres share a view of history which says that times not our own are yet vitally important to us.[56]

There is much truth in this. And yet, SF is no more necessarily co-extensive with future history than with utopia. Shelley's *Frankenstein* was set in her historical past rather than the future (the Walton frame narrative clearly locates the story in the eighteenth century); Verne's *voyages extraordinaires* mainly in his present (the only future history, *Paris au XXe siècle*, was left unpublished until 1994); even some of Wells – *The Island of Doctor Moreau*, for example – is set in his present.

---

53 Jameson 2013, p. 311.
54 Jameson 2013, pp. 310–13.
55 Robinson 1984.
56 Robinson 1987, pp. 54–5.

5   Conclusion

We can take the connection between SF and the historical novel to be established at least tentatively, far more so than that between SF and utopia. This conclusion needs, however, to be reconciled with an understanding of SF as the product of the dialectic of Enlightenment and Romanticism, that is, as a genre focussed above all on the practical capacity of sciences to become technologies. If the historical novel is, as Lukács argued, a product of the mass experience of the present as history occasioned by the French Revolution,[57] then the SF novel is, in the first instance, a product of the related but different experience of the present as history occasioned by the Industrial Revolution. If SF displaces the historical novel later in the nineteenth century, as Jameson argues, then it does so by fusing the fading cultural memory of these two experiences. This is, at one level, merely to repeat the truism that the European variant of capitalist modernity is at its core a combined effect of French political revolution and British economic revolution, the twin faces of the Enlightenment; and to add that SF is the literature *par excellence* of this modernity. No doubt, there are newer SFs, some of which we might wish to call 'postmodern', in which Shelley's monster is progressively reworked as robot and android, cyborg and simulacrum, artificial intelligence and clone warrior. But they all remain irretrievably bound to the quintessentially modern founding assumption that their fictional sciences can and will produce technologies sufficiently effective as to shape human being itself. And there is nothing at all like it in Lucian.

---

57   Lukács 1969, p. 20.

CHAPTER 25

The Sea and Eternal Summer: An Australian Apocalypse*

Despite the international success of individual writers like Greg Egan and of individual novels like Nevil Shute's *On the Beach*,[1] Australian science fiction (henceforth SF) remains essentially peripheral to the wider contours of the genre. Yet, there is a long history of what Adam Roberts describes as 'works that located utopias and satirical dystopias on the opposite side of the globe',[2] that is, in Australia. The earliest example he gives is Joseph Hall's 1605 *Mundus alter et idem sive Terra Australis ante hac semper incognita lustrata* (*A World Other and the Same, or the Land of Australia until now unknown*), the latest Nicolas Edme Restif de la Bretonne's 1781 *La Decouverte Australe par une homme-volant* (*The Discovery of Australia by a Flying Man*).[3] Lyman Tower Sargent's bibliography begins slightly later, with Peter Heglin's 1667 *An Appendix To the Former Work, Endeavouring a Discovery of the Unknown Parts of the World. Especially of Terra Australis Incognita, or the Southern Continent*, and proceeds to list something like 300 'Australian' print utopias and dystopias published during the period 1667–1999.[4]

There are yet others overlooked by even Sargent and Roberts: neither mention Denis Veiras's *L'histoire des Sévarambes*, for example, first published in part in English in 1675, in whole in French in 1679.[5] European writers made very extensive use of Australia as a site for utopian imaginings well before the continent's conquest, exploration and colonisation; even Marx's *Capital* ends its first volume with an unexpected vision of Australia as an open frontier yet beyond capital's grasp.[6] There are two reasons for this, the one obvious, the

---

* This chapter has been published previously in Gerry Canavan and Kim Stanley Robinson (eds.), *Green Planets: Ecology and Science Fiction* (Middletown: Wesleyan University Press, 2014), pp. 115–26.
1 Shute 1957.
2 Roberts 2005, p. 56.
3 Roberts 2005, pp. 56–7, 85–6.
4 Sargent 1999, pp. 138–73.
5 Veiras 2001 and 2006.
6 Marx 1970a, p. 768.

other less so. First, Australia remained one of very few real-world *terrae incognitae* available for appropriation by European fantasy as late as the mid- to late nineteenth century. And second, although Australia is often described as a continent, it is also in fact an island,[7] possessed of all the properties of self-containment and isolation that have proven so helpful to authors of utopias ever since Thomas More.

Most of the earlier Australian utopian fictions took the form of an imaginary voyage narrated by travellers on their return home. Such imaginings became increasingly implausible as European explorers brought back increasingly detailed accounts of Australia's climate, topography and people. The utopias were therefore progressively relocated further into the interior, until the realities of inland exploration eventually proved equally disappointing. Thereafter, in Australia as elsewhere, utopias were increasingly superseded by future-fictional 'uchronias'. Robyn Walton cites Robert Ellis Dudgeon's *Colymbia*, published in 1873, as the first Australian SF utopia,[8] although Joseph Fraser's *Melbourne and Mars* is probably better known.[9] In Australia, again as elsewhere, as the twentieth century proceeded, utopias were also increasingly displaced by dystopias. The best-known Australian examples are almost certainly Shute's *On the Beach*, a nuclear doomsday novel, and George Turner's *The Sea and Summer*, one of the first novels to explore the fictional possibilities of the effects of global warming. Both make powerful, albeit often scientifically implausible, use of Australia's self-contained isolation.

Much SF has been both deliberately intended by its authors and deliberately received by its readers as value-relevant. Some, but not all, SF consists in future stories; and some, but not all, is concerned either to advocate what its authors and readers see as desirable possible futures or to urge against what they see as undesirable possible futures. In short, the future story can be used as a kind of futurology. SF of this kind is intended to be politically or morally effective, that is, to be socially useful. '*We badly need a literature of considered ideas*', Turner himself argued in 1990: '*Science fiction could be a useful tool for serious consideration, on the level of the non-specialist reader, of a future rushing on us at unstoppable speed*'.[10] Three years earlier, in the 'Postscript' to *The Sea and Summer*, he had written that: 'We *talk* of leaving a better world to our children,

---

7   Which is not true for either North America or South America or Europe or Asia or Africa. Of the six commonly recognised inhabited continents, only Australia is an island.
8   Walton 2003, p. 7.
9   Fraser 1889.
10 Turner 1990, p. 209.

but in fact do little more than rub along with day-to-day problems and hope that the long-range catastrophes will never happen'. This novel, he explained, 'is about the possible cost of complacency'.[11]

Much radical SF scholarship exhibits a certain antipathy to dystopia, essentially on the grounds that it tends, in Fredric Jameson's phrase, 'to denounce and ... warn against Utopian programs'.[12] But many dystopias, including some of those most disliked by Jameson, actually function as implicitly utopian warnings, rather than as 'anti-utopias' in the strict sense of the term. This is true, I would argue, for *On the Beach* and *The Sea and Summer*. Writing in the Australian newspaper, *The Age*, in January 2008, Peter Christoff, the then Vice President of the Australian Conservation Foundation, observed that *On the Beach* had 'helped catalyse the 1960s anti-nuclear movement'. Comparing the threat of nuclear war in the 1950s with that of global warming in the early twenty-first century, he warned that: 'we are ... suffering from a radical failure of imagination'. When Christoff connected *On the Beach* to climate change, he did so precisely to urge the need for a parallel contemporary effort to imagine the unimaginable. 'These are distressing, some will argue apocalyptic, imaginings', he admits: 'But without them, we cannot undertake the very substantial efforts required to minimise the chances of their being realised'.[13] *The Sea and Summer*, it seems to me, had attempted more or less exactly this two decades previously.

1   The Novel within the Novel

Turner was born in Melbourne in 1916, published the first of five non-SF novels in 1959, began reviewing genre fiction for *The Age* during the 1970s, produced his first SF novel *Beloved Son* in 1978, followed by sequels in 1981 and 1983,[14] and by the time of his death in 1997 had become in effect the genre's Australian elder statesman. He published four further SF novels between 1987 and 1994, a collection of SF short stories in 1990, and two posthumous works, an unfinished novella *And Now Time Doth Waste Me* in 1998, and the novel *Down There in Darkness* in 1999.[15] All were essentially exercises in futurology, all preoccupied with the ethics of socio-political action, all distinctively Australian

---

11   Turner 1987a, p. 318.
12   Jameson 2005, p. 199.
13   Christoff 2008, p. 13.
14   Turner 1978, 1981 and 1983.
15   Turner 1987a, 1991, 1993, 1994, 1990, 1998 and 1999.

in tenor. By far the most critically successful was *The Sea and Summer*, which in 1988 won both the Commonwealth Writers' Prize Best Book Award, for the South East Asia and South Pacific Region, and the Arthur C. Clarke Award for best SF novel published in Britain (the previous year's Clarke Award had gone to Margaret Atwood for *The Handmaid's Tale*). In 1985 Turner had published a short story, 'The Fittest', in which he began to explore the fictional possibilities of the effects of global warming on his home city.[16] He quickly expanded this story into the full-length novel, published in 1987 as *The Sea and Summer* in Britain, and as *Drowning Towers* in the United States.[17] Global warming recurs as a theme thereafter both in his 1994 novel *Genetic Soldier* and in his last, unfinished novella.

Like *On the Beach*, *The Sea and Summer* is set mainly in and around Melbourne, a vividly described, particular place, terrifyingly transformed into the utterly unfamiliar. The novel is organised into a core narrative comprising two parts set in the mid-twenty-first century, and a frame narrative comprising three shorter parts set a thousand years later, amongst 'the Autumn People' of the 'New City', located in what are today the Dandenong Ranges to the east of Melbourne.[18] The core narrative deals with the immediate future of our 'Greenhouse Culture', the frame narrative with the retrospective reactions to it of a slowly cooling world. The latter depicts a utopian future society, which uses submarine archaeology to explore the drowned remains of the 'Old City'; but which is also simultaneously aware of the imminence of a 'Long Winter' that might well last a hundred thousand years. The novel opens by introducing the frame narrative's three main characters: Marin, a part-time student and enthusiastic Christian, who pilots the powercraft used to explore the drowned city; his great-aunt, Professor Lenna Wilson, an expert on the collapse of the Greenhouse Culture in Australia, who teaches history at the University; and Andra Andrasson, a visiting actor-playwright from Sydney, researching the twenty-first century as possible material for a play.[19] Together they explore the remains of the substantially submerged 'Tower Twenty-three',[20] investigate the ruins of the only Swill 'Enclave' never to have flooded[21] and debate their meaning both on-site and at the University.

---

16   Turner 1985.
17   Turner 1987b.
18   Turner 1987a, pp. 3–16, 87–100, 315–16.
19   Turner 1987a, pp. 3–6.
20   Turner 1987a, pp. 6–11.
21   Turner 1987a, pp. 93–6.

The core narrative takes the form of a novel within the novel, also entitled *The Sea and Summer*, written by Lenna as an 'Historical Reconstruction' of the thirty-first century's real past.[22] In form it is polyphonic, tracing the development of the Greenhouse Culture through a set of memoirs and diary extracts written during the years 2044–61 by six main protagonists: Alison Conway, Francis Conway, Teddy Conway, Nola Parkes, Captain Nikopoulos and Arthur Derrick. The only silent voice is that of the Tower Boss, Billy Kovacs, the remains of whose flat Lenna and Andra eventually explore,[23] the novel's central character and also, perhaps, its central enigma. This core narrative is counter-chronological, beginning and ending in 2061, but moving through the 2040s and '50s as it proceeds. The sections set in 2061 might themselves be considered a frame within the frame. In the first of these, Alison recalls her own childish delight in play on the beach at Elwood, from the vantage point of what we will later learn to be the last year of her life. She wistfully concludes: 'The ageing woman has what the child desired – the sea and eternal summer'.[24] In the second, her son Francis records his intermittent diary entries from the period February 2056 to March 2061, concluding with that for 20th March:

> Mum is dead ... Once, she said very forcefully, 'I've had a *good* life, Francis. So full.' Full, I thought, of what would have been avoided in a saner world ... Billy came in later, but by then she was rambling about the past, about summertime and the glistening sea.[25]

Professor Wilson's historical reconstruction depicts the twenty-first century as a world of mass unemployment and social polarisation, where rising sea levels have resulted in the inundation of the city's bayside suburbs. As it opens, the poor 'Swill' already live in high-rise tower blocks, the lower floors of which are progressively submerged; the wealthier 'Sweet' in suburbia on higher ground; the 'Fringe' in the zones in between. In 2033 a third of Australia has been set aside for Asian population relocation, by 2041 the global population has reached ten billion and the cost of iceberg tows and desalinisation projects has brought the economy close to bankruptcy.[26] On his sixth birthday in 2041, Francis and his nine-year-old brother, Teddy, are taken by their parents, Fred and Alison, to see the sea. What they find is a concrete wall 'stretching out of sight

---

22   Turner 1987a, p. 15.
23   Turner 1987a, p. 9.
24   Turner 1987a, p. 20.
25   Turner 1987a, p. 311.
26   Turner 1987a, pp. 29, 21, 30.

in both directions'. Francis's mother surprises him, however, by explaining that: 'This is Elwood and there was a beach here once. I used to paddle here. Then the water came up and there were the storm years and the pollution, and the water became too filthy'. 'It must be terrible over there in Newport when the river floods', she continues: 'A high tide covers the ground levels of the tenements'.[27] In 2044 Fred is laid off and commits suicide, leaving Allie and the boys to move to Newport.[28] There they meet Billy, the local Tower Boss, who becomes Alison's lover, Francis's mentor and the reader's guide to the social geography of an Australian dystopia.

In adolescence both Teddy and Francis abandon their mother in pursuit of upward social mobility, although both will eventually be returned 'home'. For Teddy, mobility comes through formal education, leading to Police Intelligence Recruit School[29] and thence to a career as a Police Intelligence Officer. For Francis, it comes by way of an unusual aptitude for mental arithmetic, leading to a career as a 'cally that spouts answers without using a key or chip',[30] for illicit business deals. Each acquires an appropriate sponsor: for Teddy, 'Nick' Nikopoulos, a Captain in Police Intelligence;[31] for Francis, Mrs Nola Parkes, the owner of a small import-export firm, who, after the collapse of the money economy, directs the State sub-department performing essentially the same function.[32] Alison and the boys tell their own stories, Nikopoulos and Parkes retell the boys' stories from different vantage points; eventually, these are all contextualised by Derrick, a senior State official with a quite literal power of life or death over the other characters.[33] 'Why don't you all go home?', he tells them, 'We're finished here'.[34]

The novel is at its most compelling in its representations of the everyday horror of life in the drowning towers, and of the sheer ferocity of status consciousness within a class structure mutating into a caste system. Both are recurrent motifs in both the frame and core narratives, although in the latter they invariably prove more telling because more experientially-grounded. There is a terrible poignancy, for example, to Francis's diary entries for 11 February 2056:

---

27   Turner 1987a, pp. 23–4.
28   Turner 1987a, pp. 30–4.
29   Turner 1987a, pp. 48–9.
30   Turner 1987a, p. 57.
31   Turner 1987a, p. 113.
32   Turner 1987a, p. 72.
33   Turner 1987a, p. 291.
34   Turner 1987a, p. 301.

> Five years back in the Fringe and resigned to it. Not reconciled, never that. What a hopeless, helpless lot the Swill are.[35]

And 22 March 2057:

> Three times this month the water has raced through the house. Sea water, salt and cold. We pay now for our great-grandparents' refusal to admit that tomorrow would eventually come.[36]

In the novel's final sub-plot, Captain Nikopoulos, Billy Kovacs and Teddy discover that Mrs Parkes and Francis are unwittingly involved in a State-sponsored conspiracy to 'cull' the Swill, by means of a highly addictive 'chewey' designed to produce infertility. 'A State that strikes its own', Nola Parkes observes, 'at random, for experiment, is past hope'.[37] Arthur Derrick's response is directed at Turner's twentieth century readers as much as at Parkes herself:

> Nola, idealism was for the last century, when there was still time ... we're down to more primitive needs. The sea will rise, the cities will grind to a halt and the people will desert them ... the State has no time to concern itself with moral quibbles ...[38]

2 The Future and the Futurology

The debates in the frame narrative amongst the Autumn People are clearly designed to make meaningful sense of the Greenhouse Culture. For Marin, its meaning is straightforward and simple: 'They were wicked – they ... ruined the world for all who came after ... they *denied* history'.[39] Lenna, however, conceives of their distant ancestors more sympathetically, as victims of the unintended consequences of their own collective action. 'In the twentieth and twenty-first centuries', she tells Andra, 'the entire planet stood with its fingers plugging dykes of its own creation until the sea washed over their muddled status quo. Literally'.[40] Andra's own underlying response is incomprehension. Attempting

---

35   Turner 1987a, p. 306.
36   Turner 1987a, pp. 306–7.
37   Turner 1987a, p. 303.
38   Turner 1987a, p. 304.
39   Turner 1987a, p. 6.
40   Turner 1987a, p. 13.

to grapple with the social inequalities of the Greenhouse era, he can only ask: *'How did this division arise? Why no revolution?'*.[41] Lenna suggests the answer might lie in the 'rise of the Tower Bosses' to run 'small states within the State'. This allowed the poor 'a measure of contentment', she explains, 'by letting them run their own affairs'. Moreover, she continues, the Political Security executive was also able 'to convince the Tower Bosses that only a condition of status quo could preserve a collapsing civilization'.[42] Ultimately, however, Andra remains as uncomprehending as ever and, after 'three years and a dozen attempts', abandons his play.[43]

A primary effect of this frame narrative is to blunt the force of dystopian inevitability driving the core narrative. 'We're very well equipped to endure a million years of cold', Lenna tells Andra, '... We have knowledge and we have the Forward Planning Centres. We'll make the change smoothly'.[44] A secondary effect, however, is to suggest how little control humanity actually exercises over its destiny. 'It is history that makes *us* ...' Andra observes in his letter to Lenna: 'The Greenhouse years should have shown that plainly; the Long Winter will render it inescapable'.[45] Much the same is true of the frame within the frame when it moves forward into the late 2050s. For here we learn how Teddy, Nikopoulos and Kovacs, and eventually even Francis and Derrick, become involved in an attempt by the 'New Men' to organise the Swill in preparation 'for the dark years coming'.[46] The crisis will not be averted, we know from the thirty-first century, but 'little human glimpses *do* help', Lenna will conclude, 'if only in confirming our confidence in steadfast courage'.[47]

The least persuasive aspect of the novel is surely its understanding of how the crisis developed. In the 'Postscript' Turner identifies six 'major matters' of futurological concern: population growth, food shortage, mass unemployment, financial collapse, nuclear war and the Greenhouse effect, only one of which – nuclear war – fails to feature in the novel, because it seemed to him increasingly unlikely in any foreseeable future.[48] Empirically, Turner's predictions have often proven surprisingly close to the mark. In the novel, world

---

41 Turner 1987a, p. 16.
42 Turner 1987a, p. 93.
43 Turner 1987a, p. 315.
44 Turner 1987a, pp. 12–13.
45 Turner 1987a, p. 315.
46 Turner 1987a, p. 310.
47 Turner 1987a, p. 316.
48 Turner 1987a, pp. 98, 317–18.

population reaches ten billion during the early 2040s;[49] according to the 2010 biennial revision of the United Nations *World Population Prospects*, it will reach between 8 billion (low projection) and 10.5 billion (high projection) by 2050.[50] In the novel, 'two-thirds of the world starves' by 2045.[51] This might have seemed hopelessly pessimistic during the 1980s and 1990s, when world hunger rates were persistently trending downwards. But the numbers of hungry people have increased from 825 million people in 1995–7, to 857 million in 2000–2, 873 million in 2004–6, and were projected to reach a historic high of 1,020 million, or a sixth of the world's population, in 2009.[52]

In the novel, the Australian and world unemployment rate has reached 90% by 2041.[53] Again, this must have seemed an extraordinarily gloomy prognosis on the book's first publication, as indeed it still is for Australia, where the unemployment rate was as low as 4.9% early in 2012. But the situation is very different across much of the European Union, where Spain has an unemployment rate of 23.6%, Greece 21%, Portugal 15%, Ireland 14.7% and France 10%.[54] Moreover, youth unemployment rates are higher still: in the fourth quarter of 2011, the figure was 49.3% for Greece, 48.9% for Spain, 34.1% for Portugal, 30.5% for both Ireland and Italy, 22.7% for France and 22% for the United Kingdom.[55] In the novel, the financial crisis that bespeaks the collapse of the international monetary system comes in the 2040s; in reality, something like it almost certainly began during the 'Global Financial Crisis' of 2007–12. In the novel, there have been no nuclear wars, but the 'armaments factories' nonetheless continue 'belching out weapons … for a war nobody dared start … and an industry nobody dared stop';[56] in reality, we have indeed been spared nuclear war, but nonetheless, as at January 2011, eight states possessed between them about 20,530 nuclear warheads, 5,000 ready for use and 2,000 on high operational alert.[57] In the novel, average temperatures have risen by 4½ degrees and sea levels by 30 centimeters between 1990 and 2041;[58] the current projections of the Intergovernmental Panel on Climate Change are less dramatic, pointing

---

49   Turner 1987a, p. 21.
50   United Nations, Department of Economic and Social Affairs, 2010.
51   Turner 1987a, p. 158.
52   Food and Agricultural Organization of the United Nations 2008, p. 1.
53   Turner 1987, p. 25.
54   Wikipedia 2012.
55   European Commission 2012.
56   Turner 1987a, p. 71.
57   SIPRI 2011, pp. 319–20.
58   Turner 1987a, pp. 74–5.

to temperature increases of between 1.1 and 6.4 degrees between 1980–99 and 2090–9 and rises in sea level of between 18 and 59 centimeters.[59]

But neither Turner nor his characters have any sense of which, if any, of these processes is the driver of the catastrophic crisis that overcame the Greenhouse Culture. One suspects his own answer might well have been essentially Malthusian. Mine, by contrast, would be Marxian, that is, that all six – including the nuclear arms race, if not nuclear war itself – are likely outcomes, within a world of finite resources, of any system of unregulated competitive capital accumulation akin to that sketched in *The Communist Manifesto* and analysed in detail in *Capital*.[60] No doubt, the days are long gone when one could take a creative writer to task simply for being insufficiently Marxist. One might, however, still object to the implausibility of a thousand years of hindsight failing to provide the history profession with any generally accepted account of so significant an event as the collapse of an entire social order.

This isn't entirely fair: Professor Wilson has, in fact, written a 5,000-page *Preliminary Survey of Factors Affecting the Collapse of the Greenhouse Culture in Australia*.[61] But she decides to offer Andra her fictionalised account instead, since he would need 'a general historical and technical grounding' to get much from the *Survey*.[62] Three years later he still appears not to have read it. So we do not know what, ultimately, drove the system into crisis. We do, however, know how Turner thought it could best be avoided, that is, by rational planning based on scientific advice. The epigraph to the novel, repeated in the 'Postscript', is taken from Sir Macfarlane Burnet, the Australian virologist, immunologist and public policy activist, who won the Nobel Prize for Medicine in 1960: 'We must plan for five years ahead and twenty years and a hundred years'.[63] Lenna Wilson gives Andra Andrasson essentially cognate advice:

> Keep up as well as you can with the scientific information and you could be able to think usefully if the time for action should arrive. Otherwise, live as suits you. Be like the Swill, aware but unworried.[64]

The obvious question to ask is why, when faced with the incontrovertible evidence of impending catastrophe, not only the Swill, but also the Sweet, the

---

59   Solomon et al. 2007, p. 13.
60   Marx and Engels 1967, pp. 80–90; Marx 1970a, pp. 612–48; Marx 1972, pp. 211–31.
61   Turner 1987a, p. 13.
62   Turner 1987a, p. 14.
63   Turner 1987a, p. 317.
64   Turner 1987a, p. 99.

Fringers and the State, should have failed to plan adequately. The novel is clear that science had indeed sounded warnings. 'As I understand it', Andra observes to Lenna, '... *they* knew what was coming ... Yet they did nothing about it'. 'They fell into destruction', she replies, 'because they *could* do nothing about it; they had started a sequence which had to run its course in unbalancing the climate'.[65] What neither she nor Turner adequately explain, however, is *why* they were unable to do anything about it, why they had started this sequence, and why it had to run its course. Logically, the answer can only be that some social power prevented them from acting on scientific advice.

Yet, Turner is at pains to insist that his fictional Australian elites were essentially well-motivated. As Marin tells Andra:

> The idea was not oppression but preservation. The Sweet, educated and by and large the most competent sector of the population ... were necessary to administer the State. With the collapse of trade and ... industry the Swill became a burden on the economy, easier and cheaper to support if ... concentrated into small areas.[66]

When Derrick, the most senior representative of Turner's Australian State, defends the cull to Nola, he does so in similarly benevolent terms:

> If there has to be a cull – and you know damned well that sooner or later there has to be – let's at leasy learn to do it with a minimum of suffering for the culled.[67]

How could an elite so well educated, so competent, so concerned to minimise suffering – in short, so much like the one Macfarlane Burnet had hoped for – have failed to prevent such preventable catastrophe? The answer must be that it, in turn, had been confronted by social powers more powerful and also less rational than itself. No doubt, there are a range of possible candidates available in the real world, but none within the novel. The competition between global capitalist corporations fits the bill rather nicely, however, as explanation for this peculiar combination of historically unprecedented power with historically unprecedented irrationality.

---

65   Turner 1987a, p. 13.
66   Turner 1987a, p. 91.
67   Turner 1987a, p. 297.

Which leads me, finally, to the linked questions of Turner's representations of the State and of Australian insularity. The novel is clear that, when the world financial system collapses, the nation state takes over the administration of the economy. So Francis Conway recalls that:

> I was fifteen when the money system collapsed worldwide. That, in a single sentence, records the passing of ... private-sector capitalism ... The commercial Sweet had spent months preparing for the changeover ... With forgetful speed it became *convenient* to present an allocation card at a State Distribution Store ...[68]

This is also the moment at which Mrs Parkes's import-export company becomes a Government sub-department. At one level, Turner is very astute here, recognising the way conventional left versus right disputes over public versus private ownership actually obscure the more fundamental continuities in management and structure that persisted, in both western and eastern Europe, through both the socialisations of the 1940s and '50s and the privatisations of the 1980s and '90s. But, at another, he ignores the likelihood that truly global corporations might not be as readily devolved into state subsidiaries as are national firms. No matter how convenient the fictional device of insularity might be to utopian writers, one is left wondering what had happened to the international parent companies, to the World Bank, the International Monetary Fund, the General Agreement on Tariffs and Trade, the United States Federal Reserve Bank, the European Central Bank, the People's Bank of China, and so on. Did the economy simply wither away, much as Engels had imagined the state might?[69] It seems unlikely.

Turner's *The Sea and Summer* is clearly not the game-changing climate dystopia for which Christoff might have hoped. It has been out of print for over a decade and, unlike *On the Beach*, has never been adapted for film, television or radio. As Verity Burgmann and Hans Baer recently observed: '*The Sea and Summer* is an extraordinarily well-crafted and gripping novel that received international awards and critical acclaim but has not received the popular attention it deserves'.[70] Its reissue early in 2013, as the first Australian title to be included in Gollancz's list of 'SF Masterworks', is thus especially to be welcomed. It has its flaws, no doubt, not least an underlying failure to acknowledge the deep

---

68 Turner 1987a, p. 71.
69 Engels 1959, p. 387.
70 Burgmann and Baer 2012, p. 37.

contradictions between the emancipatory potential of scientific research and the political economy of late capitalism. Nonetheless, Turner's novel is long overdue for a positive critical re-evaluation and, hopefully, this essay will make some small contribution to that effect. I for one have very selfish reasons to hope so, for I live in Elwood, only a few minutes walk from the beach where Alison Conway used to play as a little girl.

CHAPTER 26

Ice, Fire and Flood: Science Fiction and the Anthropocene*

Co-authored with J.R. Burgmann, Rjurik Davidson and Susan Cousin

Despite the occasional upsurge of climate change scepticism amongst conservative politicians and journalists, there is still a near-consensus amongst climate scientists that current levels of atmospheric greenhouse gas are sufficient to alter global weather patterns to possibly disastrous effect. Current projections of the Intergovernmental Panel on Climate Change (IPCC) point to global surface temperature increases of between 0.3 and 4.8 degrees between 1986–2005 and 2081–2100 and global rises in sea level of between 26 and 82 centimeters.[1] There is also evidence that recent increases in heat waves and flooding are related to climate change; and that these indicate 'significant vulnerability' to climate variability on the part of both ecosystems and human systems.[2]

Climate change, like other forms of ecological change, is situated 'across the nature/culture binary'.[3] Like the hole in the ozone layer described by Bruno Latour, global warming is a 'hybrid' natural-social discursive phenomenon.[4] And science fiction (henceforth SF) seems increasingly to occupy a critical location within this nature/culture nexus. The late George Turner, a distinguished Australian SF author and critic, famously argued that: *'We badly need a literature of considered ideas. Humanity is on a collision course with over-population, ecological disaster and meteorological catastrophe on the grand scale ... Science fiction could be a useful tool for serious consideration, on the level of the non-specialist reader, of a future rushing on us at unstoppable speed ...'*.[5] On this view, SF would ideally function as an adjunct to 'futurology'. There are other very different versions of the genre's vocation – almost as many, in fact, as there are of its definition – and we have no desire to privilege Turner's over, say, Mar-

---
* This chapter has been published previously in *Thesis Eleven*, No. 131, pp. 12–27, 2015.
1 Stocker et al. 2013, p. 23.
2 Bindoff and Stott et al. 2013, p. 871; Field et al. 2014, p. 6.
3 Rose 2001, p. 35.
4 Latour 1997, p. 1.
5 Turner 2009, p. 209.

garet Atwood's or China Miéville's.[6] But it does seem to us that, insofar as SF defines itself in relation to science, then it finds itself obliged to produce fictional responses to problems actually generated by contemporary scientific research. As Paolo Bacigalupi, co-winner with Miéville of the 2010 Hugo Award for best SF novel, explained in interview: 'Environmental science is telling us a lot about our future ... The surfeit of bad trends pushes me to set my stories in worlds which are often diminished versions of our own present'.[7] Moreover, insofar as SF is indeed written in response to genuinely scientific concerns, then it will not normally be 'apocalyptic' in the strict sense of deriving from the Christian *Book of Revelation*, or *Apokalypsis*. Those who stress the continuity between religious (specifically, Christo-Islamic) and secular 'apocalypticisms', tend thereby to downplay the historical novelty of modern SF as a genre defined primarily in relation to modern science and technology. No doubt, SF makes use of tropes and topoi borrowed from other genres – not only the apocalypse, but also eutopia, dystopia, fabulous voyages, and so on – but it does so in ways distinctively compatible with modern scientific rationalism. The fact that real science can provide detailed and realistic models of the likely effects of nuclear war or anthropogenic climate change makes their treatment by SF amenable to analysis in such rationalist, and distinctly non-mystical, terms. Our paper will aim to test the extent to which SF has in practice been able to live up to Turner's hopes and expectations, with special reference to this problem of 'ecological disaster and meteorological catastrophe'.

The paper is, in part, the product of an Australian Research Council funded project, which aimed, first, to explore the possibilities for a new paradigm for SF studies loosely based on Raymond Williams's 'cultural materialism'; second, to produce a case study of SF's practical capacity to represent three main kinds of possible catastrophic future development, plague, nuclear war, and extreme climate change. The project reached five main conclusions: first, that Williams's cultural materialism can indeed generate a theoretical framework more adequate to its object of study than those currently available in SF studies, but only if supplemented by concepts drawn from Pierre Bourdieu's sociology of culture and Franco Moretti's notion of 'distant reading'; second, that 'plague fictions' have typically been exercises in metaphor rather than in futurology; third, that 'nuclear fictions', especially those produced during the Cold War period, were by comparison much more properly futurological and thereby correspondingly unamenable to the kinds of 'apocalyptic' analysis to which

---

6   Atwood 2011; Miéville 2009b.
7   Bacigalupi 2009a.

they are often subject; fourth, that, although meteorological catastrophes such as flooding have been common in SF, especially in Britain,[8] historically these were only loosely related to real-world concerns over climate change; and fifth, that the period since the 1970s has, however, witnessed a sharp increase in the volume of futurologically-inspired climate fictions (our data base currently lists 101 novels, 39 short stories, 7 graphic novels, 12 films and 6 manga/anime, in ten main languages).

There is a very substantial body of critical work on nuclear war SF, most recently, for example, Paul Williams's *Race, Ethnicity and Nuclear War*[9] and David Seed's *Under the Shadow: The Atomic Bomb and Cold War Narratives*.[10] The last five to ten years have also witnessed the emergence of a body of ecocritical writing on literature and climate change ably summarised by Kate Rigby.[11] But both nuclear criticism and ecocriticism are predicated upon versions of traditional literary-critical 'close reading'. Whilst our substantive interests clearly overlap with those of ecocriticism, Moretti's distant reading nonetheless seems to us theoretically and methodologically more adequate to a subject matter as quantitatively extensive as that which Daniel Bloom dubs 'cli-fi'.[12]

1   Close Reading and Distant Reading

We have described our conceptual framework as a combination of ideas deriving from Williams, Bourdieu and Moretti. From Williams, we take the general notion of 'cultural materialism', by which he meant 'a theory of culture as a (social and material) productive process and of specific practices, of "arts", as social uses of material means of production'.[13] On this view, the arts are a distinctive subset of socially specific, materially determinate, forms and practices. SF can thus be seen as a particular cultural form established in nineteenth-century Europe by way of a radical redistribution of interests towards science and technology within the novel and the short story. During the twentieth century, this same concentration of interests extended into various theatrical, film, radio and television forms. And during the last half century, a distinctive concentration on extreme climate change has given rise to the sub-genre

---

8   Wyndham 1953; Ballard 1962.
9   Williams 2011.
10   Seed 2012.
11   Rigby 2014.
12   Merchant 2013.
13   Williams 1980a, p. 243.

we can now designate as climate fiction, Bloom's 'cli-fi'. From Williams, we also take two more specific notions, 'structure of feeling' and 'selective tradition'. The first denotes the patterned articulation of different texts and sign-systems. It provided him with a way to theorise the 'historical formation' of a 'structure of meanings' as 'a wide and general movement in thought and feeling'.[14] Moreover, he was particularly insistent that the new industrial science and its technologies were a crucial element in the emergent structure of feeling of mid-nineteenth century Britain. The 'excitement of this extraordinary release of man's powers', he observed, became 'central to the whole culture'.[15] It is precisely this element that most clearly distinguishes the new worlds of SF from the alternative islands of older eutopian fiction. The second notion denotes the way cultural tradition necessarily entails 'a continual selection and re-selection of ancestors'.[16] For Williams himself, this argument was directed at the high literary canon, but it can also be seen to apply to what Darko Suvin calls the 'SF tradition'.[17] This too is necessarily a retrospectively selective attempt to establish and maintain types of predisposed continuity.

Williams was well aware of the institutional grounding of both structures of feeling and selective traditions. Nonetheless, these are almost certainly better theorised through Bourdieu's notion of the 'cultural field'. For Bourdieu, even disinterested and gratuitous practices can be treated as directed towards the maximisation of some kind of profit. Applied to the arts, this approach produced a model of 'the field of cultural production' as structured externally in relation to the 'field of power' and internally in relation to two 'principles of hierarchization', or ways of allocating value.[18] The modern literary and artistic field is thus for Bourdieu a site of contestation between the 'heteronomous' principle, which subordinates art to economy, and the 'autonomous', which resists such subordination in the name of 'art for art's sake'.[19] In Bourdieu's map of the late nineteenth-century French literary field, the principle of autonomy governs the left of the field, that of heteronomy the right, so that the most autonomous of genres, that is, the least economically profitable, are to the left, whilst the most heteronomous, or the most economically profitable, are to the right. Each genre is also characterised by an internal hierarchy, corresponding to the social hierarchy of its audiences, so that high social status audiences gov-

---

14   Williams 1963, p. 17.
15   Williams 1965, p. 88.
16   Williams 1965, p. 69.
17   Suvin 1979, p. 220.
18   Bourdieu 1993b, pp. 37–8, 40–1.
19   Bourdieu 1993b, p. 40.

ern the upper end of the field, low status audiences the lower.[20] Conventional wisdom often tends to treat SF as a necessarily heteronomous and low status genre. But if we factor in such variants as academic SF criticism, the 'literary' SF novel, the various SF 'new waves', 'art house' and 'underground' SF cinema – as Milner has done[21] – then it becomes clear that the SF subfield is actually structurally homologous to the whole of the general cultural field rather than to any particular part therein. It also becomes clear that one of the subfield's central social functions is to produce and reproduce the SF selective tradition.

Our cultural materialism differs crucially from Williams's own in respect, not so much of our debt to Bourdieu as to Moretti's appropriation of world systems theory. The latter is an approach to modern economic history developed by Immanuel Wallerstein, the enduring concern of which has been with how modern capitalism functions as a world system, comprising a 'core', 'periphery' and 'semi-periphery', defined in relation to three main variables, the degree of profitability, the degree of monopolisation and the degree of state patronage. Core-like processes tend to constitute the bulk of production in comparatively few states, peripheral in a much larger number, semi-peripheral in an intermediate zone containing a near-even mix of core-like and peripheral production.[22] This is the model Moretti applies to Comparative Literature and which Milner has, in turn, applied to SF.[23]

Moretti argues that the study of what Goethe termed *Weltliteratur* can no longer be conceived simply as national literature writ large, 'literature, bigger', but should be reorganised around entirely different categories and conceptual problems. It 'is not an object', he continues, '... it's a *problem*, and a problem that asks for a new critical method'. The model he proposes, directly adapted from Wallerstein, is that of a world literary system, simultaneously '*one*, and *unequal*: with a core, and a periphery ... bound together in a relationship of growing inequality'.[24] If this is how the system functions, then the appropriate mode of analysis becomes 'distant reading', where distance '*is a condition of knowledge*', permitting the analyst 'to focus on units ... much smaller or much larger than the text: devices, themes, tropes – or genres and systems'.[25] The result is a history of the modern novel understood as a 'system *of variations*', in which during the nineteenth and early twentieth century pressure from the

---

20 Bourdieu 1992, p. 176.
21 Milner 2012, p. 45.
22 Wallerstein 2004, p. 28.
23 Moretti 2013; Milner 2014.
24 Moretti 2013, p. 46.
25 Moretti 2013, pp. 48–9.

Anglo-French core tended towards uniformity, while variable local realities in the periphery and semi-periphery tended towards difference. Tendency and counter-tendency thus produced a series of localised structural 'compromises', between foreign plot, local characters and local narrative voice, in which the 'one-and-unequal literary system' became embedded in the form itself.[26]

In *Distant Reading*, Moretti doesn't so much apply world systems theory as invoke it. For there is no equivalent there to Wallerstein's own detailed account of the interconnections between profitabilty, monopolisation and patronage, only the borrowed vocabulary of core, semi-periphery and periphery. The nearest Moretti came to such detail was in the earlier *Atlas of the European Novel 1800–1900*, where he used the number of titles published and the volume of translations recorded in national bibliographies as key empirical indicators. There he shows how more than half of all nineteenth-century European novels were originally published in either London or Paris. French novelists were more successful in translation in the Catholic South and British in the Protestant North, but the whole continent nonetheless read Walter Scott, Edward Bulwer-Lytton, Charles Dickens, Alexandre Dumas, Eugene Sue and Victor Hugo.[27] The number of titles and volume of translations need not necessarily correlate with profitability, monopolisation and state patronage, but in the long run they are very likely to do so, and in the case of British and French publishing almost certainly did.

Our method here is much the same as Moretti's, not so much an application of Wallerstein as an invocation, centred on the core-periphery model. However, the methodological problems entailed by an attempt to identify specifically science-fictional sub-sets of Moretti's aggregate figures are considerable, not least those posed by changes over time in definition and nomenclature, and by the institutionalised effects of policing the boundaries between 'genre fiction' and the 'literary canon'. We therefore intend to take our base data from: first, a combination of aggregate book publishing and translation data, drawn from UNESCO's annual *Statistical Yearbook* and *Index Translationum*; and second, a distant reading of the history of the genre, derived in part from earlier close readings, in part from secondary accounts, especially those provided in the on-line third edition of *The Encyclopedia of Science Fiction*.[28] The latter is, as Fredric Jameson observed of the hardcopy second edition, a 'superb' resource.[29] Measured in these terms, we can identify an initial Anglo-French core, which is

---

26   Moretti 2013, pp. 57–9.
27   Moretti 1998, pp. 186, 178–9.
28   Clute et al. 2011.
29   Jameson 2005, p. 1n.

later supplemented by new American and Japanese cores, whilst Russia, Germany, Poland and Czechoslovakia function as longstanding semi-peripheries. We might well hypothesise that Latin America also constitutes a newly emergent semi-periphery.[30]

2   Ice, Fire and Flood

Climate is an important aspect of fictional scene setting, whether it be geographical – are we in the desert or in the tropics? – or seasonal – is it winter or is it summer? And SF seems particularly predisposed to use climate as explanatory shorthand. So, to take an obvious example, in George Lucas's first *Star Wars* trilogy, Tatooine is rapidly established as a desert planet, Hoth an ice planet, Endor a temperate forest moon. Treatments of catastrophic climate change in both print and audio-visual media have tended to be organised around three main tropes: the new ice age, the burning world and the drowned world; or, more succinctly, ice, fire and flood.

Of these only the last has a deep history in the Western mythos, dating back to the story of Noah in *Bereshith/Genesis* VI–VIII and, beyond it, to the story of Utnapishtim in the *Sha naqba īmuru/Epic of Gilgamesh* Tablet XI. Early modern SF continued this particular preoccupation: witness the flood sequences in Mary Shelley's *The Last Man*[31] and Richard Jefferies's *After London*.[32] Cooling and warming are much more recent preoccupations, dating essentially from the widespread acceptance of ice age theory, following the publication of James Croll's *Climate and Time, in Their Geological Relations* in 1875, and of greenhouse theory, following that of Svante Arrhenius's *On the Influence of Carbonic Acid in the Air upon the Temperature of the Ground* in 1896. For most of the twentieth century both science and SF were more interested in cooling than in warming. In geological terms, the period we inhabit, the 'Holocene' as it is termed, is an 'interglacial', that is, a comparatively warm period within the longer, colder 'ice age' defined by the 'Quaternary period'. When located in relation to the so-called 'Malenkovitch cycles', which measure the effects of orbital variation on the Earth's climate, we can be seen to live in a time of cooling that has lasted for some 6,000 years. So the most likely future climate change was widely anticipated to be a return to the ice age. This motif recurs throughout the SF of

---

30   Bell and Molina-Cavilán 2003.
31   Shelley 1998, pp. 438–40.
32   Jefferies 2007, pp. 26–30.

the period, from John Christopher's *The World in Winter* (1962) and Robert Silverberg's *Time of the Great Freeze* (1964) through Michael Moorcock's *The Ice Schooner* (1966) and John Gribbin and Daniel Orgill's *The Sixth Winter* (1979) to Doris Lessing's *Mara and Dann* (1999).

The earliest exception to this observation is Kōbō Abe's *Daiyon Kanpyoki*, often claimed as the foundational text of postwar Japanese SF, which as early as 1959 foresaw global warming leading to the melting of the polar ice caps and rising sea levels. But widespread concern that anthropogenic warming might more than offset longer-term cooling dates primarily from the 1970s. In 1979, both the US National Research Council and the World Meteorological Organization published predictions that then current levels of CO_2 emission would result in increases in average global temperature. In the early 1980s, Eugene F. Stoermer coined the term 'Anthropocene' to describe the two centuries since the beginning of the Industrial Revolution and in 2000 he and Paul Crutzen formally proposed it to the International Geosphere-Biosphere Programme;[33] in 1988, the World Meteorological Organisation and the United Nations Environmental Programme combined to establish the IPCC; and in 1990 it completed its *First Assessment Report*. This concluded that emissions from human activities had substantially enhanced the natural greenhouse effect; that CO_2 emissions were responsible for more than half the enhanced greenhouse effect; and that, if emissions proceeded on a 'business as usual' basis, this would result in levels of global warming during the 21st century greater than those seen in the previous 10,000 years.[34] Where science and Kōbō Abe led, global SF followed. Arthur Herzog's *Heat* explored the fictional possibilities of a runaway greenhouse effect as early as 1977. George Turner's own most acclaimed SF novel, *The Sea and Summer*, appeared in 1987. Set mainly in Melbourne, it depicted a world of mass unemployment and social polarisation, in which global warming had produced rising sea levels and consequent inundation of the city's Bayside suburbs.

The range of imaginative responses to global warming appears to run from the gloomiest dystopia to the brightest eutopia by way of many kinds of intervening ambiguity. We use eutopia here as the antonym of dystopia, since, as Thomas More's original usage makes clear, utopia is strictly speaking neither a better nor worse place, but rather a no place.[35] These fictional responses run roughly parallel to the options available in real-world discourse. Contempor-

---

33   Crutzen and Stoermer 2000.
34   Houghton et al. 1990, p. xi.
35   More 1995, pp. 18–19.

ary climate policy distinguishes between mitigation and adaptation strategies and between positive and negative variants of adaptation, the former seeking possible advantages to be seized upon, the latter disadvantages to be minimised. To these we can add as a fourth option various forms of climate change denial; and, as a fifth, the kind of deep ecological anti-humanism sometimes associated with James Lovelock's 'Gaia hypothesis'.[36] Instances of all five kinds of response – denial, mitigation, positive adaptation, negative adaptation, deep ecology – can be observed in climate fiction. Good examples of denial include Michael Crichton's *State of Fear* (2004) and Nele Neuhaus's *Wer Wind sät* (2011); of the special kind of denial that calls into question the scientists rather than the science, Ian McEwan's *Solar* (2010) and Sven Böttcher's *Prophezeiung* (2011); of mitigation, Herzog's *Heat* (1977) and Kim Stanley Robinson's *2312* (2012); of positive adaptation, Bernard Besson's *Groenland* (2011); of negative adaptation Turner's *The Sea and Summer* (1987), Robinson's *Science in the Capital* trilogy (2004–7), Bacigalupi's *The Windup Girl* (2009a), Dirk C. Fleck's *Das Tahiti-Project* (2008) and *MAEVA!* (2011); of fictional deep ecology Brian Aldiss's *Helliconia* trilogy (1982–5) and Frank Schätzing's *Der Schwarm* (2004).

Our preliminary research has concentrated on novels and short stories, but it is clear that other media have also engaged in fictional and non-fictional representations of various kinds of extreme climate change. Examples of graphic novels and comics include: Jacques Lob and Jean-Marc Rochette's *Le Transperceneige* (1982); Hayao Miyazaki's *Kaze no Tani no Naushika* (1982–94); Josh Neufeld's *A.D.: New Orleans after the Deluge* (2010); Grant Calof and Eric Eisner's *H2O* (2011); John Hicklenton's *100 Months* (2012); and Brian Wood's *The Massive* (2012–14). Examples from film and animation include: Miyazaki's adaptation of *Kaze no Tani no Naushika* for anime (1984); Kevin Reynolds's *Waterworld* (1995); Steven Spielberg's *A.I. Artificial Intelligence* (2001); Roland Emmerich's *The Day After Tomorrow* (2004); Andrew Stanton's *Wall-E* (2008); Ivan Engler and Ralph Etter's *Cargo* (2009); Neill Blomkamp's *Elysium* (2013); Bong Joon-Ho's *Seolgungnyeolcha* (2013); Darren Aronofsky's *Noah* (2014) and Christopher Nolan's *Interstellar* (2014). There is also a large and growing body of young adult fiction, most recently, for example, J.L. Morin's *Nature's Confession* (2015).

---

36   Lovelock 1979.

3 Narrative Strategies and Tactics

An important issue relevant across media is that of how central a position climate change actually occupies within any particular narrative. Suvin famously described SF as a genre '*distinguished by the narrative dominance or hegemony of a fictional "novum" (novelty, innovation) validated by cognitive logic*'.[37] In some SF, climate change functions essentially only as a setting for another more central novum, whereas in others it is itself the novum. In addition, we might note the presence of 'hybrid' texts, where climate change is the primary science-fictional novum, but where a non-SF component, such as romance or crime, is nonetheless actually dominant. Texts where climate change functions primarily as 'mise en scène', to borrow a term from theatre and film studies, include: Margaret Atwood's *MaddAddam* trilogy (2003–13), where genetic engineering is the primary novum; Michel Houellebecq's *La Possibilité d'une île* (2005), where it is cloning; Wolfgang Jeschke's *Das Cusanus Spiel* (2005), where it is time travel; Chang-Rae Lee's *On Such a Full Sea* (2014), where it is future agriculture and pharmaceuticals; and David Mitchell's *The Bone Clocks* (2014), where it is the struggle for immortality. Texts where anthropogenic climate change provides the primary novum clearly include: Herzog's *Heat*, Turner's *The Sea and Summer*, Maggie Gee's *The Ice People* (1998) and *The Flood* (2004), T.C. Boyle's *A Friend of the Earth* (2000), Robinson's *Science in the Capital* trilogy, Schätzing's *Der Schwarm*, Jean-Marc Ligny's *Aqua*™ (2006) and *Exodes* (2012), Jeanette Winterson's *The Stone Gods* (2007), Ilija Torjanow's *Eis Tau* (2011), Barbara Kingsolver's *Flight Behavior* (2012), Nathaniel Rich's *Odds Against Tomorrow* (2013) and Alexis Wright's *The Swan Book* (2013). Examples of 'hybrid' texts would include Homero Aridjis's *¿En quién piensas haces el amor?* (1996), which is primarily a love story, Jordi de Manuel's *L'olor de la pluja* (2006) and Antti Tuomainen's *Parantaja* (2010), both of which are primarily crime novels. The key issue here is not so much classification per se, but rather that of rhetorical efficacy. Our research suggests that all three strategies can work well, but that the second is likely to be the more rhetorically persuasive.

A second issue relevant across media is that of the relative efficacy of different cultural forms. The panel on 'Climate Change Narratives' held at the 2014 72nd World Science Fiction Convention debated the difficulties of telling human stories concerning 'the distinctly larger-than-human problem of climate change'.[38] This doesn't seem to us as serious a problem as it might at

---

37   Suvin 1979, p. 63.
38   Sieber et al. 2014.

first appear. All realist fiction tended to set human stories in larger-than-human contexts and there is no obvious reason why SF shouldn't have the capacity to do the same. If there is a problem it is that, by comparison with plague or nuclear war, climate change is a relatively slow process. But so too was the decline of Scottish clan society depicted in Scott's Waverley novels, or the rise of bourgeois Paris depicted in Balzac's *La Comédie humaine*.

There might be a specific problem for SF cinema, however, insofar as it finds itself obliged to work within much shorter time frames than those available to either the novel or the TV mini-series. This could explain why Emmerich's *The Day After Tomorrow*, for example, was so obviously scientifically implausible: climate change just won't happen quite that quickly. One alternative approach would be to set the film well after the catastrophe, as in the 2009 Swiss SF film *Cargo* or the 2013 South African film *Elysium*. Jameson identifies a second alternative, however, in Christopher Nolan's *Inception* (2010), David Mitchell's novel *Cloud Atlas* (2004), and its 2012 film adaptation by Lana Wachowski, Tom Tykwer and Andy Wachowski. In these texts, Jameson argues, the artwork functions as 'an immense elevator that moves us up and down in time'; and it does so precisely because 'historicity today ... demands a temporal span far exceeding that of the biological limits of the individual human organism'.[39] Interestingly, this is exactly the strategy subsequently adopted by Mitchell himself in his 2014 climate change novel *The Bone Clocks* and by Nolan in his *Interstellar*.

This leads us into yet another cross-media issue, that of whether art can ever expect to change reality. Creative artists and humanities academics are no doubt inclined to overestimate the likely effects of the arts, corporate CEOs and economists to underestimate them. The issue was canvassed directly in respect of climate change in a *New York Times* opinion piece in July 2014. J.P. Telotte, Professor of Film and Media Studies at the Georgia Institute of Technology, argued that SF represents pressing cultural anxieties rather than real problems; George Marshall, founder of the Climate Outreach Information Network, that it merely reinforces people's existing prejudices; Sheree Renée Thomas, editor of the *Dark Matter* anthology series, that what is imagined can sometimes come true; and Daniel Bloom, predictably enough, that '"Cli-fi" movies and novels have the power to change minds. That's their mission'.[40] If this opinion piece is any guide, the issue clearly remains an open question.

---

39   Jameson 2013, p. 302.
40   *New York Times* 2014.

4 Learning from *On the Beach*

One of the members of the 2014 'Climate Change Narratives' panel, Euan G. Nisbet, Professor of Earth Sciences at Royal Holloway, University of London, volunteered the opinion that what climate science now most needs from SF is a contemporary equivalent to Nevil Shute's nuclear doomsday novel *On the Beach* (1957). Much the same view has been expressed previously.[41] A novel from Australia, in the outer periphery of the world literary system, might seem an unlikely candidate as the template for contemporary climate fiction. And yet, as Moretti himself observed, peripheral literatures can in fact be sustained by historical backwardness.[42] Shute's novel was published in hardback in Australia, Britain and the U.S.A., went through several reprintings, became a critical and commercial success, was very quickly republished in paperback, translated into at least twenty-five other languages, adapted for film by Stanley Kramer in 1959, later still for television and radio, and, last but not least, almost certainly changed the realities of the nuclear arms race of the 1950s and 60s. The great and not-so-great powers retained their nuclear weapons, of course, but Shute's novel and Kramer's film exercised an enormous influence, not only on the early mass campaigns for nuclear disarmament, but also on elite opinion in America, Russia and Britain; so much so as to contribute significantly to the climate of opinion that enabled the 1963 Test Ban Treaty between the USA, the USSR and the UK.[43] Obviously, we cannot predict the nature of the novel, film or other artwork likely to have similar such effect on climate politics. But we can use *On the Beach* as a template by which to assess likely candidates. In this concluding section we will briefly examine the strengths and weaknesses of three such candidates, one each taken from the Australian periphery of the world cultural system, the German semi-periphery, and the North American core: respectively, Turner's *The Sea and Summer*, Schätzing's *Der Schwarm* and Robinson's *Science in the Capital* trilogy.

The Sea and Summer is a comparatively early example of climate fiction, published in the UK by Faber and in the US by Arbor (under the title *Drowning Towers*), in both instances to considerable critical acclaim. In 1988 it won the Commonwealth Writers' Prize Best Book Award, for the South East Asia and South Pacific Region, and the Arthur C. Clarke Award for best SF novel published in Britain, and was shortlisted for the Nebula Award for best SF novel

---

41 Christoff 2008.
42 Moretti 1998, pp. 195–7.
43 Baker 2012, pp. 158–9.

published in the US. It is today still the only Australian title in Gollancz's series of 'SF Masterworks'.[44] The novel mounts a stunningly powerful indictment of our 21st century 'Greenhouse Culture'.[45] And it has an interestingly complex structure, which moves between a frame narrative of three parts set in the 31st century[46] and a longer core narrative of two parts, beginning and ending in the year 2061,[47] but moving through the 2040s and 50s as it proceeds. This means, in short, that it is an interestingly early example of Jameson's future-historical novel as elevator. But this very complexity, and its marketing as a 'literary' novel by Faber, the largest British 'independent' publisher, also help to explain why it was a less than spectacular commercial success and, perhaps, why it has never been adapted for film or television. Moreover, its peripheral status decisively tells against it in some significant aspects, which might explain why it has only ever been translated into Danish and Spanish. Like *On the Beach*, *The Sea and Summer* is set mainly in Melbourne. But whereas in Shute's novel there are good global reasons for this exclusive focus – much of what is left of the human race, including the crew of a surviving American nuclear submarine, converge on the city after the northern hemisphere has destroyed itself in nuclear war – there are no correspondingly plausible reasons in Turner. In his novel, the state takes over the administration of the Australian economy when the world financial system collapses during the 2040s.[48] At this point, even Australian readers are left wondering what exactly has happened to the international parent companies of Australian subsidiaries, to the World Bank, the International Monetary Fund, the General Agreement on Tariffs and Trade, the United States Federal Reserve Bank, the European Central Bank, the People's Bank of China, and so on. And for non-Australian readers, the question becomes more pressing and more general: what exactly has happened to the rest of the world?

We have said that climate change is the primary novum in Schätzing's *Der Schwarm*, but this is not self-evidently so. An alternative candidate would be the eponymous Schwarm, 'die Yrr', 'Der sich seiner selbst bewusst gewordene Ozean [the ocean become conscious of itself]'.[49] But the Yrr play an essentially reactive role in the novel, merely responding to the anthropogenic environmental crisis which actually drives the narrative. The primary novum is thus 'der globalen Klimaerwärmung [global warming]', compounded by 'Ströme von

---

44 Turner 2013.
45 Turner 1987a, p. 4.
46 Turner 1987a, pp. 3–16, 87–100, 315–16.
47 Turner 1987a, pp. 19–20, 306–11.
48 Turner 1987a, p. 71.
49 Schätzing 2005, p. 965.

Schadstoffen, Überfischung, die rücksichtslose Erschließung der Küsten [pollution, overfishing, reckless coastal development]' and other human offences against the integrity of the seas.[50] Moreover, the ultimate source of this crisis, it is clear, is the 'Mineralölkonzerne [oil industry]' with its 'Interessengeflecht' [web of interests] that has 'den Planeten überzog [overwhelmed the planet]'.[51] Hence, the most spectacular of the Yrr's counter-attacks: a Tsunami that destroys the North Sea oil wells.[52]

By contrast with *The Sea and Summer*, *Der Schwarm* was a very considerable commercial success, both domestically and internationally. First published in hardback in Germany and Austria, it was the bestselling German novel for eight successive months during 2004, was adapted for Hörspiel, or audio-play, in the same year, republished in paperback in 2005, and subsequently translated into at least twenty other languages. It was also critically well received, not least for the quality of its background scientific research, and in 2005 won both the Bauer Group's Goldene Feder media award and the Deutscher Science Fiction Preis for best novel. A German-Italian film adaptation was announced in 2007, although this has still to appear, and was presumably delayed by the death of Dino De Laurentis in 2010. The novel's success in Germany can be explained in part as the obverse of Turner's in the Anglosphere, that is, by the fact that it was marketed as 'Roman' rather than 'Science Fiction'. German literary culture, from the book trade through to the academy, tends to make sharp distinctions between 'Literatur' and 'Trivialliteratur', firmly consigning to the latter 'Science Fiction', written thus in English. That *Der Schwarm* was a novel, rather than mere SF, thus almost certainly enhanced its sales. Moreover, its status as an an ecofiction must have had special appeal to the sizable part of the German electorate that votes Green: die Grünen were the world's first organised Green Party and are still amongst the most electorally successful, holding 63 seats in the present Bundestag. The novel's ecopolitics are almost Lovelockian in character, insofar as the Yrr are in effect Gaia surrogates. *Der Schwarm* is a very long novel, 987 pages in all, but has a comparatively simple narrative structure, moving chronologically forward from 14th January to 15th August of a year in the near future, followed by a very brief 'Epilog' set exactly one year later. This too may have enhanced its commercial appeal.

Der Schwarm has an interestingly ambivalent attitude towards the United States. At one level, it is structured around a binary political opposition be-

---

50   Schätzing 2005, p. 234.
51   Schätzing 2005, p. 366.
52   Schätzing 2005, pp. 402–4.

tween European and Canadian scientists on the one hand, and the American political, military and intelligence elite on the other. But at another, it remains deeply indebted to American SF film and TV: Schätzing's scientists don't themselves appear to read many novels, but they do repeatedly draw deliberate analogies between their own actions and those of characters from Hollywood cinema. Moreover, some of the novel's central sequences are clearly very well suited to American 'blockbuster' treatment, for example, that where Sigur Johanson, the urbane Norwegian marine biologist, arrives by helicopter at the Shetland Islands in the nick of time to rescue Karen Weaver, a British scientific journalist, from the imminent impact of the North Sea Tsunami.[53] But Schätzing's treatment of the main US characters nonetheless sometimes borders on quite explicit anti-Americanism. So, for example, the US President is represented as a Christian fundamentalist believer in the literal truth of *Genesis*, in effect a kind of dumbed down George W. Bush.[54] Worse still, Judith Li, the commander of the *USS Independence*, a state-of-the-art helicopter carrier used to transport the international scientific taskforce to the Greenland Sea, turns out to be a murderous psychopath, who would rather kill the scientists than treat with the Yrr. This anti-Americanism might well have strengthened the novel's appeal in Europe, but it could also explain why the English translation underperformed in the US. And the United States is still at the core, not only of the world economy, but also of the world literary system.

Which takes us, finally, to North America itself. Robinson was already a successful, well-established SF writer when he wrote the *Science in the Capital* novels. He had won the John W. Campbell Memorial Award for Best SF Novel for *Pacific Edge* in 1991, Hugo Awards for *Green Mars* and *Blue Mars* in 1994 and 1997 respectively, and a Nebula Award for *Red Mars* in 1993. His work thus enjoyed professional, fan and academic legitimacy: the Nebula Awards are made by a professional writers association, the Science Fiction and Fantasy Writers of America; the Hugo Awards by a fan organisation, the World Science Fiction Society; and the Campbell Memorial Award by a panel of experts appointed by the Center for the Study of Science Fiction at the University of Kansas. Interestingly, Fredric Jameson, the doyen of American academic SF critics, has dedicated two books to Robinson.[55] In 2008 Robinson was even named a 'Hero of the Environment' by *Time* magazine.[56] His work has also been translated into at least 23 other languages, although the complete *Science in the Capital* trilogy

---

53 Schätzing 2005, pp. 410–17.
54 Schätzing 2005, p. 591.
55 Jameson 2005, p. v; Jameson 2013, p. v.
56 Walsh et al. 2008.

only into French and Dutch. Nonetheless, and perhaps surprisingly, none of Robinson's work has ever been adapted into other media. For these particular novels, this might be in part an effect of their sheer length, 1,632 pages in total in the first edition. But there are reasons pertaining to content as well as to form.

Robinson's work is often described as 'hard SF' and justly famous for the quality of its scientific research. But in *The Science in the Capital* trilogy, where the subject matter appears closest to its author's deepest concerns, the reader is almost overwhelmed by the details, not only of the science, but also of the internal mechanisms of scientific policy-making. Indeed, remarkably little actually happens in the first volume, *Forty Signs of Rain*, until the spectacular flooding of Washington DC at its conclusion.[57] *Fifty Degrees Below*, which deals with the stalling of the Gulf Steam, and *Sixty Days and Counting*, which recounts the opening stages of the Presidency of the environmentally activist, former Californian Senator, Phil Chase, are more fast-moving, but still often overburdened with scientific and technical detail. Moreover, the whole trilogy suffers from a preoccupation with American internal politics that might not excite much international interest, even were the US still the only global superpower. The trilogy's central protagonist, Frank Vanderwal, is a Californian biomathematician and rock climber, whose initial cynicism about science policy is eventually superseded by active enthusiasm for a Chase administration. Chase himself, a character Robinson takes over from an earlier novel,[58] is the radical obverse of Schätzing's President, an idealised amalgam of an Al Gore who managed to get elected and a Barack Obama who managed to get things done. It's not difficult to see why American readers might find the character both plausible and attractive, but Europeans neither. This is surmise, of course, but nonetheless only the first volume has as yet been translated into Spanish, none into German, Italian, Czech, Polish or Russian (or, for that matter, Japanese or Chinese).

All three of these texts have distinctive weaknesses and strengths that acquire their character in part from their distinctive geographical locations within the world cultural system. That none quite reaches the benchmark set by the *On the Beach* template no doubt tells us something of the scale of Shute's often under-rated achievement. But it also suggests the scale of what might still need to be done.

---

57   Robinson 2004, pp. 326–56.
58   Robinson 1997.

Conclusion: Towards 2050
Andrew Milner and J.R. Burgmann: A Dialogue

JRB: In our opening conversation we mainly looked backwards. But one of Williams's most famous books was the essentially forward-looking *Towards 2000*, which you updated to 'Towards 2050' as the title of the last chapter in your *Re-Imagining Cultural Studies*. So let's ask the question again: where do we go – in the sociology of literature, in cultural materialism, in science fiction [henceforth SF] studies – between now and 2050?

AM: Can we take those one at a time?

JRB: Sure.

AM: Let's begin by noting that prophecy is a notoriously unreliable business. Nobody really has the faintest idea what will be happening in 2050. But with that cautionary rider in mind, I'm prepared to have a go. As far as the sociology of literature is concerned, I haven't changed my views since the *'Conscience Collective'* essay. I cannot see how sociology, as an institutionalised discipline, will ever provide a welcoming home for anything other than the most routinised kind of sociology of literature. Sociology and literary studies are simply too far apart for that to happen. I hope there will be more landmarks, of course, but the sad truth is that the average Anglophone sociology department couldn't accommodate a Bourdieu, let alone a Williams. The most likely occasional home for the sociology of literature will therefore probably be in literary studies, as one approach amongst many to the study of the same common object. The problem there is that literary studies – whether English Literature or Comparative Literature – is increasingly threatened by institutional rivalry from Cultural Studies, media studies, film studies, television studies and the rest. I had hoped that an immodest Cultural Studies could head off the threat, but that now seems increasingly unlikely. Oh dear, I've begun to sound like Harold Bloom.

JRB: And, then, what about cultural materialism?

AM: Cultural materialism almost certainly has a much more hopeful future. It's by the far the most persuasive theoretical approach, not only to literary studies, but also to those other fields – film and media studies and so on. Even when the term itself isn't used, and when Williams himself isn't directly cited, you can see people using those sorts of methods. Of course, Williams thought cultural materialism was a specifically Marxist theory and he tied it to a specifically socialist politics. I really don't know how viable a future Marxism has. It certainly fell into disrepute during the 1990s, but has made something of a comeback since the Global Financial Crisis of 2007–8. And where Marxism goes, so too goes socialism.

JRB: Do you agree with Williams that cultural materialism was a specifically Marxist theory?

AM: I once did, but now I'm not so sure. There is, after all, a sense in which Bourdieu, Foucault and Habermas, not to mention Max Weber, can each be considered cultural materialists. And, as for Williams himself, the more he developed his cultural materialism, the further he moved from a strictly Marxist base/superstructure model. Marx's legacy is still vitally important, but it needs to be supplemented by later theoretical developments. It might follow, then, that there is also nothing specifically socialist about cultural materialism. Nevertheless, I continue to be a socialist and I'm greatly heartened by the revival of socialist politics in Europe – I'm thinking of Syriza in Greece, Podemos in Spain, Die Linke in Germany and even, to some extent, the English Corbynistas.[1] Here in Australia, however, we will have to settle for the ecosocialist wing of the Greens.

JRB: Is there a specifically ecosocialist wing of the Greens?

AM: Not in the sense of a formally organised faction, no. But Adam Bandt is clearly a socialist, so too is Scott Ludlum. And, in England, so too is Caroline Lucas.[2]

JRB: It's interesting to me that cultural materialism in its original conception was so inextricably bound to a politics. SF studies, however, need not always be so, although in your case it normally is.

---

[1] In 2015 the rank and file membership of the British Labour Party elected the left-wing Jeremy Corbyn as Party leader despite determined opposition from the overwhelming majority of the Parliamentary Labour Party.

[2] Adam Bandt, Green MP for Melbourne since 2010; Scott Ludlum, Green Senator for Western Australia 2008–2017. Caroline Lucas, Green MP for Brighton Pavilion since 2010.

CONCLUSION: TOWARDS 2050

AM: Not only me. That's also true for Darko Suvin, Fred Jameson, Tom Moylan and many others. And there is a reason for this: insofar as SF is about possible futures, whether dystopian or utopian, then it necessarily becomes political.

JRB: Yes, in theory that's perfectly true. However, it does seem as if contemporary written SF is constantly torn between *ideas* and cinema-like *spectacle*. The two need not be opposed, but the latter can often occlude the former. Would you agree?

AM: Yes, I would. Which is not to say that *Star Wars: The Force Awakens* wasn't a whole lot of fun. I've theorised this issue as a tension between ideas and effects. Clearly, the novel has effects and cinema has ideas, but the latter is always especially tempted by the lure of the spectacle.

JRB: It occurs to me that this particular tension might be comparable to that identified by Leavis, Bloom and other cultural conservatives between the literary canon and genre fiction.

AM: Well, yes, of course. And to some extent they were right, popular fiction can indeed sometimes be about action rather than intellect. But it's a mistake to assume in advance that all genre fiction is necessarily spectacular rather than intellectual. And, to be fair, Bloom doesn't actually make that assumption. What most interests me about SF is precisely its capacity to handle truly remarkable ideas and not only the more expressly political ones. The genre's capacity to deal with fascinating science – quantum physics, genetics, climate change, artificial intelligence – this is surely its great strength. The ray guns and rocket ships are just a hook.

JRB: Let's try for another dangerous vision. What do you think the future of SF will look like?

AM: I'd very much like to know your own views on that. Personally, I'd point to three likely future trends. First, I think Chinese SF is going to become much more important globally. If I could rewrite the 'World Systems' essay – and it's only two years old – it would be to discuss the wider significance of Liu Cixin's *The Three-Body Problem*,[3] which won this year's Hugo Award for best novel,

---

3 刘慈欣 2008, 三体, Chongqing: Chongqing Publishing Group; Liu Cixin 2014, *The Three-Body Problem*, trans. Ken Liu, New York: Tor Books.

and of *Science Fiction World*,⁴ the Chinese SF magazine in which it was first published. The latter has a circulation of about 300,000, which is only a small proportion of the total Chinese population, I know, but an awful lot of SF fans by any measure. Second, I think we will see a great many more 'Cli-Fi' novels: as the world heats up so too will the writing. And third, I think the genre boundaries between SF and literary fiction, SF and fantasy, SF and crime, and so on, will continue to crumble. So now it's my turn: what do you think the future of SF will look like?

JRB: The point you make about the growth of Chinese SF hadn't occurred to me, but the more general development of an increasingly globalised SF seems highly likely to continue. As for the nascent sub-genre of climate fiction, yes, again you're right. However, I would add that Australia is uniquely placed to make significant contributions to this area, perhaps because its geographical position is so precarious: we are regularly subject to flood and fire, and it's not likely to get much better in the foreseeable future. Quite apart from George Turner, whom you've already written about, I'd name James Bradley's *Clade*, Alexis Wright's *The Swan Book*, Ellen van Neerven's *Heat and Light* and Alice Robinson's *Anchor Point*.⁵ I wholeheartedly accept your third observation about the disintegration of genre boundaries. As to the reasons for it, I'd hypothesise that it has something to do with the way the millennial generation – my generation – has developed a propensity for the omnivorous consumption of media. Our capacity to access stories is far greater than ever before: HBO shows, Amazon and e-books, downloaded movies, archival quantities of music, we consume these effortlessly, and so see no need to differentiate between genres in traditional fashion. Perhaps the book is dying, but stories aren't.

AM: That's interesting. And I certainly agree about *Clade*. It's a remarkable novel, better than *The Sea and Summer*, and deserving of a much wider audience than that provided by Penguin Australia.

JRB: You can always order it from Amazon as an e-book, wherever you happen to live.

---

4   刘慈欣 2006, 三体科幻世界/*Science Fiction World*, Chengdu.
5   James Bradley 2015, *Clade*, Ringwood: Penguin; Alexis Wright 2013, *The Swan Book*, Artarmon: Giramondo; Ellen van Neerven 2014, *Heat and Light*, St Lucia: University of Queensland Press; Alice Robinson 2015, *Anchor Point*, South Melbourne: Affirm Press.

AM: Point taken.

JRB: What's also apparent to me, in reading climate fiction, is that this genre-blurring occurs in two ways, either as the mainstreaming of science-fictional ideas or as the creation of properly hybrid texts. By the latter I mean works that, although they contain a science-fictional novum – in this case climate change – they actually read as something else, a detective or romance novel for example.

AM: You're absolutely right about mainstreaming. Excellent examples include Margaret Atwood in Canada, Michel Houllebecq in France, David Mitchell in England and Vladimir Sorokin in Russia. I'm not so sure about hybridity. There is a long history of SF texts that include elements of the detective or the romance. Think of Isaac Asimov's Elijah Baley robot detective stories.[6] And some of those more recent hybrids actually turn out to be much more science-fictional than they first appear. Think of Antti Tuomainen's *The Healer*, which was marketed as a crime novel and won the 2011 prize for best Finnish crime novel. But climate change isn't merely a setting for this novel; rather, it eventually turns out to be the motive behind the crime. The eponymous Healer, Pasi Tarkiainen, is in fact an ecoterrorist, determined to ensure that those who have made the catastrophe should be punished for it.[7]

JRB: Yes, I take your point. In fact, that is *exactly* what appears to be happening in this sub-genre: climate novels seem to be very contextually marketed, that is, depending on style, language and nationality, their publishers either downplay or play up the science-fictional aspects.

AM: It's certainly true that in Australia and Germany, for example, Cli-Fi novels seem to sell much better if they're marketed as something other than SF. But is this merely a matter of marketing? Or, are we talking about real differences in the kinds of text? In short, is Dan Bloom right to think of Cli-Fi as a new genre?

JRB: I'd like to think it is some new miraculous genre that will save the world; but the truth is that it isn't. If you read the genre carefully and thoroughly it becomes apparent that its authors are writing within pre-existing generic conventions, with climate change inserted in the place of older plot devices:

---

6   Isaac Asimov 1954, *The Caves of Steel*, New York: Doubleday; Isaac Asiov 1957, *The Naked Sun* New York: Doubleday; Isaac Asimov 1983, *The Robots of Dawn*, New York: Doubleday.

7   Antti Tuomainen 2010, *Parantaja*, Helsinki: Helsinki-Kirirat; Antti Tuomainen 2013, *The Healer*, trans. Lola Rogers, New York: Henry Holt and Company.

nuclear war and plague at one extreme, the quotidian conditions of modernity at the other. This is not to suggest that there is no potential for future innovations. In fact, the way these writers – Bradley, Mitchell, Robinson and Atwood to name a few – have renovated the narrative uses of time, place and climate is truly remarkable.

AM: I've long since stopped believing in miracles. But I do think that literature and the other arts have a significant capacity to change the world. That's the point I've made before about Shute's *On the Beach*. And I'm hoping for a Cli-Fi novel that will have a similar impact.

JRB: I think it will happen, but perhaps as the cumulative achievement of the writerly community rather than as a single novel. But now we're once again getting into prophecy and speculation.

AM: Which is, of course, what SF routinely does.

JRB: We've been talking about SF, but what about SF studies? What is its likely trajectory?

AM: I'm not sure. Obviously, it will become more concerned with film, television and digital media, less with literature and theatre. Obviously, it will pay more attention to climate fictions in all media. Hopefully, it will become more cultural-materialist in its approach. But a lot depends on what happens in the wider world, both to the politics and to the climate.

JRB: From a Cultural Studies point of view, the primacy of the screen might not be such a problem. However, literature has been far more active in addressing climate change than either film or television. Neither *The Day After Tomorrow* nor *2012* have anything much to do with the realities of climate change; they have more to do with explosions. And it does seem that, for the foreseeable future, literature will be at the forefront of addressing these questions. Which is fine, so long as adequate screen adaptations are produced – which unfortunately has not really been the case.

AM: HBO are currently working on a televisual adaptation of Atwood's *MaddAddam* trilogy.[8] Hopefully, it will be the first of many.

---

8 Margaret Atwood 2003, *Oryx and Crake*, London: Bloomsbury; Margaret Atwood 2009, *The*

JRB: Well, that's very good news because, although I can recall a large number of Cli-Fi novels, and a significant number of Cli-Fi films, I cannot think of a single television show. And we're supposedly in 'the golden age' of television.

AM: Yes, it's strange, not least because TV is in principle much better able to respond to long run historical processes than cinema: the TV series simply lasts so much longer.

JRB: We've used the word 'hopefully' rather a lot. Yet a lot of your work is focussed on dystopias that might arguably be seen to kill hope. When Tom Moylan turned his attentions to dystopia, he stressed that what he calls 'critical dystopias' necessarily contain some element of hope. Do you think he was right about that?

AM: Tom actually coined the term 'critical dystopia' and, since all definitions are true by definition, he must be right. But, if you're asking the more general question as to whether a dystopia intended as warning must contain that kind of positive element, then I'm not so sure. I have, of course, argued that the *Appendix* on Newspeak in *Nineteen Eighty-Four* functions so as to introduce such an element of hope – and thus in effect turns it into a critical dystopia. But many editions of the novel omitted the *Appendix* and many readers didn't read it anyway. Did that make it any the less effective as warning? Perhaps, perhaps not. Conversely, however – and there is always a conversely, isn't there? – it does seem to me that practically realisable hope tends to strengthen both utopias and dystopias. Think about Jean-Marc Ligny's climate change trilogy.[9] The first novel, *Aqua*™, is by far the best precisely because it contains hope, hope both for Burkina Faso and for the main character, Laurie Prigent. It's a splendid example of Cyberpunk Cli-Fi, better even than Sterling's *The Caryatids*.[10] There are also some very good things about *Exodes*: I particularly like the idea that the elites will lock themselves away under a three kilometer long dome covering Davos of all places, that is, precisely where the World Economic Forum already holds its annual winter junkets. But the novel's ending is so bleak that the only remaining hope seems to lie with the ants. *Semences*, the final volume, is clearly meant to reintroduce hope, but not for anything remotely

---

Year of the Flood, London: Bloomsbury; Margaret Atwood 2013, *MaddAddam*, London: Bloomsbury.

9 Jean-Marc Ligny 2006, *Aqua*™, Nantes: L'Atalante; Jean-Marc Ligny 2012, *Exodes*, Nantes: L'Atalante; Jean-Marc Ligny 2015, *Semences*, Nantes: L'Atalante.
10 Bruce Sterling 2009, *The Caryatids*, New York: Ballantine Books.

resembling our civilisation. There are still humans, of course, but the main evolutionary step forward has nonetheless been taken by the ants – 'les fourmis' – who have mutated into near-telepathic 'les fourmites'. It's all strangely unsatisfactory. That said, the whole trilogy – and especially *Aqua*™ – is long overdue an English translation. The same goes for Dirk C. Fleck's *Maeva* trilogy by the way.[11]

JRB: I suppose what we've been talking about here – and in the essays too – is hope.

AM: Yes, of course, it is. The origins of socialism are in Fourier, Saint-Simon and Robert Owen, well before Marx and Engels; and the origins of SF are in H.G. Wells, if not in Thomas More, well before Hugo Gernsback. As for cultural materialism, Williams was an inveterate optimist, continually fighting for Manod. You just used the term 'novum', a concept you borrowed from Suvin, as everyone else does in SF studies. But Suvin himself borrowed it from Ernst Bloch's *The Principle of Hope*. What connects socialism to SF and both to cultural materialism is a shared sense of what Bloch himself termed '*Ungleichzeitigkeit des Gleichzeitigen*' – Mark Ritter translates this as 'nonsynchronous synchronicity' – which becomes, when future-oriented, the 'not-yet in the now'.[12] Bloch's work is a significant absence from the essay collection, although not from my writing more generally. So this is an appropriate point to register its continuing significance for socialism, for utopianism, and for utopian studies.

JRB: But wasn't Bloch very dismissive about Wells in particular and SF in general?

AM: Yes, he was. Like many other anti-Nazi exiles – Adorno, Horkheimer, Brecht – he hated both America and American popular culture, SF included. I can understand this: at times, I've felt something similar about Australia. But it was a failure of imagination on their part, nonetheless: all across Europe, American boys were fighting and dying to make Germany safe for the return of the exiles; those boys deserved, in return, much better than that kind of cultural condescension. And I'm very glad to say that academic SF studies – Tom Moylan, for example – has gone some way towards righting this wrong.

---

11   Dirk C. Fleck 2008, *Das Tahiti-Projekt*, München: Pendo Verlag; Dirk C. Fleck 2011, *MAEVA!* Rudolstadt & Berlin: Greifenverlag; Dirk C. Fleck 2015, *Feuer am Fuss*, Murnau: p.machinery Verlag.

12   Ernst Bloch 1977, 'Nonsynchronism and the Obligation to its Dialectics', trans. Mark Ritter, *New German Critique*, 11: 22–38.

JRB: Would you like to end there?

AM: Not quite. I'd like to add that the alternative to hope isn't so much despair, as capitulation – to commodification, to the competitive accumulation of capital, to the possibility, perhaps probability, that corporate capitalism will simply ruin the world. It's becoming an ecosocialist cliché, I know, but I'd like to conclude by misquoting Rosa Luxemburg's quotation from Engels in her *Junius Pamphlet*: 'Capitalist society faces a dilemma, either an advance to ecosocialism or a reversion to barbarism'.[13]

JRB: Yes, that seems as good a place to end as any.

---

13   In the original, 'ecosocialism' reads as 'socialism' – Rosa Luxemburg 1970, 'The Junius Pamphlet: The Crisis in the German Social Democracy', in *Rosa Luxemburg Speaks*, ed. M.-A. Waters, New York: Pathfinder Press, p. 269.

Bibliography

1 Film and Television

Aronofsky, D. (dir.) 2014. *Noah*, Paramount: 138 mins.
Blomkamp, N. (dir.) 2013. *Elysium*, TriStar: 109 mins.
Bong, J.-H. (dir.) 2013. *Seolgungnyeolcha*, Moho Films: 126 mins.
Carter, C. (dir.) 1997. 'The postmodern prometheus', *The X-Files*, Twentieth Century Fox Television: 44 mins.
Contner, J.A. (dir.) 2000. 'The I in team', *Buffy the Vampire Slayer*, Mutant Enemy Inc/Twentieth Century Fox Television: 44 mins.
Contner, J.A. (dir.) 2000. 'Primeval', *Buffy the Vampire Slayer*, Mutant Enemy Inc/Twentieth Century Fox Television: 44 mins.
Emmerich, R. (dir.) 2004. *The Day After Tomorrow*, 20th Century Fox: 124 mins.
Engler, I. and R. Etter (dir.) 2009. *Cargo*, Atlantis: 120 mins.
Grossman, D. (dir.) 2000. 'The Yoko factor', *Buffy the Vampire Slayer*, Mutant Enemy Inc/Twentieth Century Fox Television: 44 mins.
Kramer, S. (dir.) 1959. *On the Beach*, United Artists: 134 mins.
Kuzui, F.R. (dir.) 1992. *Buffy the Vampire Slayer*, Twentieth Century Fox: 81 mins.
Miyazaki, H. (dir.) 1984. *Kaze no Tani no Naushika*, Toei: 117 mins.
Nolan, C. (dir.) 2010. *Inception*, Warner Brothers: 148 mins.
Nolan, C. (dir.) 2014. *Interstellar*, Paramount/Warner Brothers: 169 mins.
Reynolds, K. (dir.) 1995. *Waterworld*, Universal: 135 mins.
Sackheim, D. (dir.) 1993. 'Deep throat', *The X-Files*, Twentieth Century Fox Television: 44 mins.
Solomon, D. (dir.) 2000. 'Goodbye Iowa', *Buffy the Vampire Slayer*, Mutant Enemy Inc/Twentieth Century Fox Television: 44 mins.
Spielberg, S. (dir.) 2001. *A.I. Artificial Intelligence*, Warner Brothers: 146 mins.
Stanton, A. (dir.) 2008. *Wall-E*, Walt Disney: 98 mins.
Wachowski, L., T. Twyker and A. Wachowski (dir.) 2012. *Cloud Atlas*, Studio Babelsberg: 172 mins.
Whale, J. (dir.) 1931. *Frankenstein*, Universal Studios: 71 mins.

2 Books and Articles

Abe, K. 1964. *Daiyon Kanpyoki*, Tokyo: Hayakawa Shobo [1959].
Abensour, M. 1973. *Les Formes de l'utopie socialistes-communiste*, Paris: thèse pour le Doctorat d'État en science politique.

Adam, I. and Tiffin, H. (eds) 1991. *Past the Last Post: Theorizing Post-Colonialism and Post-Modernism*, London: Harvester Wheatsheaf.
Adams, D. 1979. *The Hitch Hiker's Guide to the Galaxy*, London: Pan Books.
Adorno, T.W. 1949. *Philosophie der neuen Musik*, Tübingen: J.C.B. Mohr.
Adorno, T. 1976. 'Sociology and Empirical Research', trans. G. Bartram, in P. Connerton (ed.) *Critical Sociology*, Harmondsworth: Penguin.
Adorno, T.W. 1980, 'Reconciliation Under Duress', trans. R. Livingston, in New Left Review (ed.) *Aesthetics and Politics*, London: Verso.
Adorno, T.W. and Horkheimer, M. 1947, *Dialektik der Aufklärung*, Amsterdam: Querido Verlag.
Adorno, T.W. and M. Horkheimer 1979, *Dialectic of Enlightenment*, trans. J. Cumming, London: Verso.
Adorno, T. and H. Marcuse 1999, 'Correspondence on the German Student Movement', trans. E. Leslie *New Left Review* 233.
Agamben, G. 2003, (*Homo Sacer III*) *Stato di eccezione*, Torino: Bollati Boringhieri.
Aldiss, B.W. 1982, *Helliconia Spring*, London: Triad Granada.
Aldiss, B.W. 1983, *Helliconia Summer*, London: Triad Granada.
Aldiss, B.W. 1985, *Helliconia Winter*, London: Triad Granada.
Aldiss, B. with D. Wingrove 1986, *Trillion Year Spree: The History of Science Fiction*, London: Victor Gollancz.
Althusser, L. and É. Balibar 1970, *Reading Capital*, trans. B. Brewster, London: New Left Books.
Anderson, B. 1983, *Imagined Communities: Reflections on the Origins and Spread of Nationalism*, London: Verso.
Anderson, P. 1964, 'Origins of the Present Crisis', *New Left Review* 23.
Anderson, P. 1970, 'Components of the National Culture', in A. Cockburn and R. Blackburn (eds) *Student Power*, Harmondsworth: Penguin.
Anderson, P. 1974a, *Passages from Antiquity to Feudalism*, London: New Left Books.
Anderson, P. 1974b, *Lineages of the Absolutist State*, London: New Left Books.
Anderson, P. 1976, *Considerations on Western Marxism*, London: New Left Books.
Anderson, P. 1977, 'The Antinomies of Antonio Gramsci', *New Left Review* 100.
Anderson, P. 1980, *Arguments Within English Marxism*, London: New Left Books.
Anderson, P. 1988, 'Modernity and Revolution', in C. Nelson and L. Grossberg (eds) *Marxism and the Interpretation of Culture*, London: Macmillan.
Anon. 1960, *The Bible*, Authorized Version, Oxford: Oxford University Press.
Aridjis, H. 1996, *¿En quién piensas cuando haces el amor?*, México: Santillana.
Arnold, M. 1980, 'The Function of Criticism at the Present Time', in L. Trilling (ed.) *The Portable Matthew Arnold*, Harmondsworth: Penguin.
Arrhenius, S. 1896, 'On the Influence of Carbonic Acid in the Air upon the Temperature of the Ground', *Philosophical Magazine and Journal of Science*, Fifth Series, 41.

Ashcroft, B. et al. 1989, *The Empire Writes Back: Theory and Practice in Post-Colonial Literatures*, London: Routledge.
Ashcroft, B. et al. (eds) 1995, *The Post-Colonial Studies Reader*, London: Routledge.
Ashley, M. 2000, *The Time Machines: The Story of the Science-Fiction Pulp Magazines from the beginning to 1950*, Liverpool: Liverpool University Press.
Ashley, D. 2011, *Out of This World: Science Fiction But Not as You Know It*, London: The British Library.
Asimov, I. 1954, *The Caves of Steel*, New York: Doubleday.
Asimov, I. 1957, *The Naked Sun*, New York: Doubleday.
Asimov, I. 1983, *The Robots of Dawn*, New York: Doubleday.
Atwood, M. 1986, *The Handmaid's Tale*, Boston: Houghton Mifflin.
Atwood, M. 1987, *The Handmaid's Tale*, London: Virago.
Atwood, M. 2003, *Oryx and Crake*, London: Bloomsbury.
Atwood, M. 2005, 'George Orwell: Some Personal Connections', in *Curious Pursuits: Occasional Writing 1970–2005*, London: Virago, 2005 [2003].
Atwood, M. 2009, *The Year of the Flood*, London: Bloomsbury.
Atwood, M. 2011, 'Dire Cartographies: The Roads to Ustopia', in *In Other Worlds: Science Fiction and the Human Imagination*, London: Virago.
Atwood, M. 2013, *MaddAddam*, London: Bloomsbury.
Baccolini, R. 2000, 'Gender and Genre in the Feminist Critical Dystopias of Katherine Burdekin, Margaret Atwood, and Octavia Butler', in M. Barr (ed.) *Future Females, the Next Generation: New Voices and Velocities in Feminist Science Fiction*, Boston: Rowman and Littlefield.
Bacigalupi, P. 2009a, 'Interview', *SF Signal*, 14 September http://www.sfsignal.com/archives/2009/09/interview-paolo-bacigalupi/.
Bacigalupi, P. 2009b, *The Windup Girl*, San Francisco: Night Shade Books.
Badiou, A. 1998, *Abrégé de métapolitique*, Paris: Seuil.
Badiou, A. 2003, *Infinite Thought: Truth and the Return to Philosophy*, trans. and ed. O. Feltham and J. Clemens, London: Continuum.
Badiou, A. 2004, 'Truth: Forcing and the Unnameable', in *Theoretical Writings*, ed. and trans. R. Brassier and A. Toscano, London: Continuum.
Badley, L. 1996, 'The rebirth of the clinic: the body as alien in The X-Files', in *Deny All Knowledge: Reading the X-Files*, David Lavery, Angela Hague and Maria Cartwright (eds), London: Faber.
Baker, B. 2012, '*On the Beach*: British Nuclear Fiction and the Spaces of Empire's End', in D. Seed (ed.) *Future Wars: The Anticipations and the Fears*, Liverpool: Liverpool University Press.
Baldick, C. 1983, *The Social Mission of English Criticism 1848–1932*, Oxford: Oxford University Press.
Ballard, J.G. 1962, *The Drowned World*, New York: Berkley Books.

Barnes, J. (ed.) 1969, *The Writer in Australia 1856–1964*, Melbourne: Oxford University Press.

Barr, M. 1991, 'Metahuman "Kipple" or, Do Male Movie Makers Dream of Electric Women?: Speciesism and Sexism in *Blade Runner*', in J.B. Kerman (ed.) *Retrofitting Blade Runner: Issues in Ridley Scott's Blade Runner and Philip K. Dick's Do Androids Dream of Electric Sheep?*, Bowling Green: Bowling Green State University Popular Press.

Barrett, M. 1988, *Women's Oppression Today: The Marxist/Feminist Encounter*, London: Verso.

Barthes, R. 1957, *Mythologies*, Paris: Seuil.

Barthes, R. 1973, *Mythologies*, trans. A. Lavers, St Albans: Paladin.

Barthes, R. 1966, *Critique et vérité*, Paris: Éditions du Seuil.

Barthes, R. 1975, *The Pleasure of the Text*, trans. R. Miller, New York: Hill and Wang.

Barthes, R. 1977, *Image-Music-Text*, trans. S. Heath, New York: Hill and Wang.

Baudrillard, J. 1975, *The Mirror of Production*, trans. M. Poster, St Louis: Telos Press.

Baudrillard, J. 1983, *In the Shadow of the Silent Majorities, or, The End of the Social and Other Essays*, trans. P. Foss, J. Johnston and P. Patton, New York: Semiotexte.

Baudrillard, J. 1988, *America*, trans. C. Turner, London: Verso.

Baudrillard, J. 1993, *Symbolic Exchange and Death*, trans. I.H. Grant, London: Sage.

Baudrillard, J. 1994, *Simulacra and Simulation*, trans. S.F. Glaser, Ann Arbor: University of Michigan Press.

Bauman, Z. 1992, *Intimations of Postmodernity*, London: Routledge.

Bedford, S. 1973, *Aldous Huxley: A Biography, Vol. One: 1894–1939*, London: Chatto and Windus in association with William Collins.

Beilharz, P. 1994, *Transforming Labor: Labour Tradition and the Labor Decade in Australia*, Melbourne: Cambridge University Press.

Bell, A.L. and Y. Molina-Cavilán (eds) 2003, *Cosmos Latinos: An Anthology of Science Fiction from Latin America and Spain*, Middletown: Wesleyan University Press.

Bell, D. 1973, *The Coming of Post-Industrial Society*, New York: Basic Books.

Bell, D. 1976, *The Cultural Contradictions of Capitalism*, London: Heinemann.

Bell, D. 1977, 'Beyond Modernism, Beyond Self', in Q. Anderson, S. Donadio and S. Marcus (ed.) *Art, Politics and Will: Essays in Honor of Lionel Trilling*, New York: Basic Books.

Belsey, C. 1988, *John Milton: Language, Gender Power*, Oxford: Blackwell.

Benjamin, W. 1928, *Ursprung des deutschen Trauerspiels*, Berlin: Rowohlt.

Benjamin, W. 1969, *Charles Baudelaire, Ein Lyriker im Zeitalter des Hochkapitalismus*, ed. R. Tiedemann, Frankfurt am Main: Suhrkamp Verlag [written 1938–39].

Benjamin, W. 1973, *Illuminations*, trans. H. Zohn, Glasgow: Fontana.

Bennett, T. 1985, 'Really Useless "Knowledge": A Political Critique of Aesthetics', *Thesis Eleven* 12.

Bennett, T. 1986, 'Introduction: Popular Culture and "the Turn to Gramsci"', in T. Bennett et al. (eds) *Popular Culture and Social Relations*, Milton Keynes: Open University Press.
Bennett, T. 1989, 'Culture: Theory and Policy', *Culture and Policy* 1, 1.
Bennett, T. 1990, *Outside Literature*, London: Routledge.
Bennett, T. 1992, 'Useful Culture', *Cultural Studies* 6, 3.
Bennett, T. 1998, *Culture: A Reformer's Science*, Sydney: Allen and Unwin.
Bennett, T., M. Emmison and J. Frow 1999, *Accounting for Tastes: Australian Everyday Cultures*, Cambridge: Cambridge University Press.
Bernstein, E. 1961, *Evolutionary Socialism: A Criticism and Affirmation*, trans. E.C. Harvey, New York: Schocken Books [1899].
Besson, B. 2011, *Groenland*, Paris: Odile Jacob.
Bindoff, N.L. and P.A. Stott, with K.M. AchuraRao, M. Allen, N. Gillett, D. Gutzler, K. Hansingo, G. Hegerl, Y. Hu, S. Jain, I. Mokhov, J. Overland, J. Perlwitz, R. Sebbari and X. Zhang 2013, 'Detection and Attribution of Climate Change: from Global to Regional', *Climate Change 2013: The Physical Science Basis. Working Group 1 Contribution to the Fifth Assessment Report of the Intergovernmental Panel on Climate Change*, Cambridge: Cambridge University Press.
Blainey, G. 1957, *A Centenary History of the University of Melbourne*, Melbourne: Melbourne University Press.
Bloch, E. 1977, 'Nonsynchronism and the Obligation to its Dialectics', trans. Mark Ritter *New German Critique* 11.
Bloch, E. 1995, *The Principle of Hope*, 3 vols, trans. N. Plaice, S. Plaice and P. Knight, Cambridge MA: MIT Press [1959].
Bloom, H. 1994, *The Western Canon: The Books and School of the Ages*, New York: Harcourt Brace & Co.
Boer, R. 2006, 'Political Myth: Fable, Politics and the Bible', *International Journal of the Humanities* 2, 2.
Boozer, J. Jr. 1991, 'Crashing the Gates of Insight: *Blade Runner*', in J.B. Kerman (ed.) *Retrofitting Blade Runner: Issues in Ridley Scott's Blade Runner and Philip K. Dick's Do Androids Dream of Electric Sheep?*, Bowling Green: Bowling Green State University Popular Press.
Böttcher, S. 2011, *Prophezeiung*, Köln: Kiepenheuer & Witsch.
Bould, M. 2009, 'Rough Guide to a Lonely Planet, from Nemo to Neo', in M. Bould and C. Miéville (eds) *Red Planets: Marxism and Science Fiction*, London: Pluto Press.
Bourdieu, P. 1974, 'The School as a Conservative Force: Scholastic and Natural Inequalities', in J. Eggleston (ed.) *Contemporary Research in the Sociology of Education*, London: Methuen.
Bourdieu, P. 1977a, 'Symbolic Power', trans. C. Wringe, in D. Gleeson (ed.) *Identity and Structure: Issues in the Sociology of Education*, Driffield: Nafferton Books.

Bourdieu, P. 1977b, *Outline of a Theory of Practice*, trans. R. Nice, Cambridge: Cambridge University Press.

Bourdieu, P. 1979, *La Distinction: critique sociale du jugement*, Paris: Éditions de Minuit.

Bourdieu, P. 1984, *Distinction: a Social Critique of the Judgement of Taste*, trans. R. Nice, London: Routledge and Kegan Paul.

Bourdieu, P. 1987, 'What Makes a Social Class? On the Theoretical and Practical Existence of Groups', trans. L.J.D. Wacquant and D. Young *Berkeley Journal of Sociology* 32.

Bourdieu, P. 1988, *Homo Academicus*, trans. P. Collier, Cambridge: Polity Press.

Bourdieu, P. 1989, 'The Corporatism of the Universal: the Role of Intellectuals in the Modern World', trans. C. Betensky *Telos* 81.

Bourdieu, P. 1990a, 'Landmarks', trans. M. Adamson, in *In Other Words: Essays Towards a Reflexive Sociology*, Cambridge: Polity Press.

Bourdieu, P. 1990b, 'A Reply to Some Objections', trans. L.J.D. Wacquant, in *In Other Words: Essays Towards a Reflexive Sociology*, Cambridge: Polity Press.

Bourdieu, P. 1992, *Les Règles de l'art: genèse et structure du champ littéraire*, Paris: Éditions du Seuil.

Bourdieu, P. 1993a, *Sociology in Question*, trans. R. Nice, London: Sage.

Bourdieu, P. 1993b, *The Field of Cultural Production: Essays on Art and Literature*, ed. R. Johnson, Cambridge: Polity Press.

Bourdieu, P. 1993c, *La Misère du monde*, Paris: Seuil.

Bourdieu, P. 1996a, *The State Nobility: Elite Schools in the Field of Power*, trans. L.C. Clough, Cambridge: Polity Press.

Bourdieu, P. 1996b, *The Rules of Art: Genesis and Structure of the Literary Field*, trans. S. Emanuel, Cambridge: Polity Press.

Bourdieu, P. 1998a, *Acts of Resistance: Against the New Myths of Our Time*, trans. R. Nice, Cambridge: Polity Press.

Bourdieu, P. 1998b, 'Pour une gauche de gauche', *Le Monde* 8 April.

Bourdieu, P. 1998c, 'Rethinking the State: Genesis and Structure of the Bureaucratic Field', trans. L. Wacquant and S. Farage, in *Practical Reason: On the Theory of Action*, Cambridge: Polity Press.

Bourdieu, P. 1998d, *La Domination masculine*, Paris: Seuil.

Bourdieu, P. et al. 1999, *The Weight of the World: Social Suffering in Contemporary Society*, trans. P.P. Ferguson et al., Cambridge: Polity Press.

Boyle, T.C. 2000, *A Friend of the Earth*, New York: Viking.

Bradbury, M. 1976, 'The Cities of Modernism', in M. Bradbury and J. McFarlane (eds) *Modernism 1890–1930*, Harmondsworth: Penguin.

Bradbury, M. and McFarlane, J. (eds) 1976, *Modernism 1890–1930*, Harmondsworth: Penguin.

Bradley, J. 2015, *Clade*, Ringwood: Penguin.

Brailsford, H.N. 1961, *The Levellers and the English Revolution*, London: Cresset Press.
Brecht, B. 1977, 'Against Georg Lukács', in E. Bloch et al. *Aesthetics and Politics*, London: New Left Books.
Brenac, P. and Stevens, A. 1978, *The Reading and Buying of Books in Australia*, Sydney: Philip Shrapnel.
Brenkman, J. 1995, 'Raymond Williams and Marxism', in C. Prendergast (ed.) *Cultural Materialism: On Raymond Williams*, Minneapolis: University of Minnesota Press.
Bruno, G. 1990, 'Ramble City: Postmodernism and *Blade Runner*', in A. Kuhn (ed.) *Alien Zone: Cultural Theory and Contemporary Science Fiction Cinema*, London: Verso.
Bukharin, N. 1971, *The Economics of the Transformation Period*, New York: Bergmann.
Bürger, P. 1974, *Theorie der Avantgarde*, Frankfurt am Main: Suhrkamp Verlag.
Burgmann, V. 1980, *Revolutionaries and Racists: Australian Socialism and the Problem of Race 1887–1917*, Ph.D. Thesis, Canberra: Australian National University.
Burgmann, V. and H.A. Baer 2012, *Climate Politics and the Climate Movement in Australia*, Melbourne: Melbourne University Press.
Burgmann, V. and A. Milner 1996, 'Intellectuals and the New Social Movements', in R. Kuhn and T. O'Lincoln (eds) *Class and Class Conflict in Australia*, Melbourne: Longman.
Burianyk, M., S. Krawczyk, I. Raseta, I. Shmilev and I. Belogrîs 2014, 'The World at Worldcon: Eastern European and Baltic SF/F', *Loncon 3. The 72nd World Science Fiction Convention*, London: World Science Fiction Society.
Calof, G. and E. Eisner 2011, *H20*, Mt. Laurel, NJ: Dynamite Comics.
Callinicos, A. 1982, *Is There a Future for Marxism?*, London: Macmillan.
Callinicos, A. 1989, *Against Postmodernism: A Marxist Critique*, Oxford: Polity Press.
Cantrell, L. (ed.) 1978, *A.G. Stephens: Selected Writings*, Sydney: Angus and Robertson.
Čapek, K. 1922, *W.U.R. Werstands Universal Robots*, trans. O. Pick, Prague: Lipsko, Orbis.
Čapek, K. 1928, *Power and Glory*, trans. P. Selver and R. Neale, London: Allen and Unwin.
Čapek, K. 1937, *Bílá nemoc*, Prague: Fr. Borovny.
Čapek, K. 1961, *R.U.R. (Rossum's Universal Robots). A Play in Three Acts and an Epilogue*, trans. P. Selver, in The Brothers Čapek *R.U.R. and The Insect Play*, Oxford: Oxford University Press.
Čapek, K. 1966, *R.U.R. Rossum's Universal Robots. Kolektívní Drama o Vstupní Komedii a Trench Dejstvích*, Prague: Ceskoslovensky Spisovatel [1921].
Carchedi, G. 1977, *On the Economic Identification of Social Classes*, London: Routledge and Kegan Paul.
Casanova, P. 1999, *La République mondiale des lettres*, Paris: Éditions du Seuil.
Casanova, P. 2005, *The World Republic of Letters*, trans. M.B. Debevois, Cambridge, Mass.: Harvard University Press.
Cevasco, M.E. 2000, 'Whatever Happened to Cultural Studies: Notes from the Periphery', *Textual Practice* 14, 3.

Christoff, P. 2008, 'The End of the World as We Know It', *The Age*, January 15.
Christopher, J. 1962, *The World in Winter*, London: Eyre and Spottiswoode.
Cixous, H. 1981, 'The Laugh of the Medusa', trans. K. Cohen and P. Cohen, in E. Marks and I. de Courtivron (eds) *New French Feminisms: An Anthology*, Brighton: Harvester.
Clarke, J. et al. 1976, 'Subcultures, Cultures and Class: A Theoretical Overview', in S. Hall and T. Jefferson (eds) *Resistance Through Rituals: Youth Sub-Cultures in Post-War Britain*, London: Hutchinson.
Cliff, T. 1975, *Lenin*, Vol. 1, London: Pluto Press.
Cliff, T. 1988, *State Capitalism in Russia*, London: Bookmarks.
Clute, J. and P. Nicholls (eds) 1993, *The Encyclopedia of Science Fiction*, London: Orbit.
Clute, J.D. Langford, P. Nicholls and G. Sleight (eds) 2011–14, *The Encyclopedia of Science Fiction*, third edition, London: Victor Gollancz. http://sf-encyclopedia.com.
Cockrell, R. 2005, 'Future Perfect: H.G. Wells and Bolshevik Russia, 1917–32', in P. Parrinder and J.S. Partington (eds) *The Reception of H.G. Wells in Europe*, London: Continuum.
Cohen, G.A. 1978, *Karl Marx's Theory of History: A Defence*, Oxford, Oxford University Press.
Coleridge, S.T. 1972, *On the Constitution of the Church and State*, London: J.M. Dent.
Collier, T. 1965, 'A Discovery of the New Creation', in A.S.P. Woodhouse (ed.) *Puritanism and Liberty*, London: Dent.
Collini, S. 1994, 'Escape from DWEMsville', *Times Literary Supplement*, May 27.
Cook, J.R. and P. Wright 2006, '"Futures Past": An Introduction to and Brief Survey of British Science Fiction Television', in J.R. Cook and P. Wright (eds) *British Science Fiction Television: A Hitchhiker's Guide*, London: I.B. Tauris.
Comte, A. 1855, *The Positive Philosophy*, trans. H. Martineau, New York: Calvin Blanchard.
Cornea, C. 2007, *Science Fiction Cinema: Between Fantasy and Reality*, Edinburgh: Edinburgh University Press.
Coser, L.A., Charles Kadushin and Walter W. Powell 1985, *Books: The Culture and Commerce of Publishing*, Chicago: University of Chicago Press.
Crichton, M. 2004, *State of Fear*, London: HarperCollins.
Crick, B. 1980, *George Orwell: A Life*, London: Secker and Warburg.
Croll, J. 1875, *Climate and Time, in Their Geological Relations*, London: Daldy, Tsbister and Co.
Crutzen, P.J. and E.F. Stoermer 2000, 'The "Anthropocene"', *Global Change Newsletter* 41.
Csicsery-Ronay Jr., I. 2003, 'Science Fiction and Empire', *Science Fiction Studies* 30, 2.
Culler, J. 1975, *Structuralist Poetics: Structuralism, Linguistics and the Study of Literature*, London: Routledge and Kegan Paul.
Dahrendorf, R. 1964, 'Recent Changes in the Class Structure of the European Societies', *Daedalus* 93.

De Burgh, H. 2000, 'Investigating Corporate Corruption: An Example from the BBC's *File on Four*', in H. de Burgh (ed.) *Investigative Journalism: Context and Practice*, London and New York: Routledge.

De Certeau, M. 1984, *The Practice of Everyday Life*, trans. S. Rendall, Berkeley: University of California Press.

Delany, S.R. 1977, *The Jewel-Hinged Jaw: Notes on the Language of Science Fiction*, Elizabethtown: Dragon Press.

Delany, S.R. 1994, 'The Semiology of Silence: The *Science Fiction Studies* Interview', in *Silent Interviews: On Language, Race, Sex, Science Fiction, and Some Comics: A Collection of Written Interviews*, Hanover: Wesleyan University Press, 1994 [1987].

Derrida, J. 1970, 'Structure, Sign and Play in the Discourse of the Human Sciences', trans. R. Macksey, in *The Languages of Criticism and the Sciences of Man*, ed. R. Macksey and E. Donato, Baltimore: Johns Hopkins University Press.

Derrida, J. 1973, *Speech and Phenomena and Other Essays on Husserl's Theory of Signs*, trans. D.B. Allison, Evanston: Northwestern University Press.

Derrida, J. 1976, *Of Grammatology*, trans. G.C. Spivak, Baltimore: Johns Hopkins University Press.

Derrida, J. 1978, *Writing and Difference*, trans. A. Bass, Chicago: University of Chicago Press.

Derrida, J. 1982, *Margins of Philosophy*, trans. A. Bass, Chicago: University of Chicago Press.

Derrida, J. 1987, *The Truth in Painting*, trans. G. Bennington and I. McLeod, Chicago: University of Chicago Press.

Desser, D. 1991, 'The New Eve: The Influence of *Paradise Lost* and *Frankenstein* on *Blade Runner*', in J.B. Kerman (ed.) *Retrofitting Blade Runner: Issues in Ridley Scott's Blade Runner and Philip K. Dick's Do Androids Dream of Electric Sheep?*, Bowling Green: Bowling Green State University Popular Press.

Dick, P.K. 1968, *Do Androids Dream of Electric Sheep?*, Garden City, NY: Doubleday.

Docker, J. 1974, *Australian Cultural Elites: Intellectual Traditions in Sydney and Melbourne*, Sydney: Angus and Robertson.

Docker, J. 1981, 'How I Became a Teenage Leavisite and Lived to Tell the Tale', *Meanjin* 40, 4.

Docker, J. 1984, *In a Critical Condition: Reading Australian Literature*, Melbourne: Penguin.

Dollimore, J. 1994, 'Introduction: Shakespeare, Cultural Materialism and New Historicism', in J. Dollimore and A. Sinfield (eds) 1994, *Political Shakespeare: Essays in Cultural Materialism*, Manchester: Manchester University Press.

Doyle, B. 1982, 'The Hidden History of English Studies', in P. Widdowson (ed.) *Re-Reading English*, London: Methuen.

Duncan, W.G.K. and Leonard, R.A. 1973, *The University of Adelaide 1875–1974*, Adelaide: Rigby.

During, S. 1990, 'Postmodernism or Post-Colonialism Today?', in A. Milner et al. (eds) *Postmodern Conditions*, Oxford: Berg.

During, S. (ed.) 1999, *The Cultural Studies Reader*, second edition, London: Routledge.

Durkheim, E. 1960, *Les Formes élémentaires de la vie religieuse: le système totémique en Australie*, Paris: Presses Universitaires de France [first published 1912].

Durkheim, E. 1964, *The Division of Labor in Society*, trans. G. Simpson, New York: Free Press.

Durkheim, E. 1976, *The Elementary Forms of the Religious Life*, trans. J.W. Swain, London: George Allen and Unwin [first published 1915].

Dussel. E. 1998, 'Beyond Eurocentrism: The World System and the Limits of Modernity', in F. Jameson and M. Miyoshi (eds) *The Cultures of Globalization*, Durham, NC: Duke University Press.

Eagleton, T. 1976, *Criticism and Ideology: A Study in Marxist Literary Theory*, London: New Left Books.

Eagleton, T. 1979, 'The Poetry of E.P. Thompson', *Literature and History* 5, 2.

Eagleton, T. 1981, *Walter Benjamin or Towards a Revolutionary Criticism*, London: Verso.

Eagleton, T. 1983, *Literary Theory: An Introduction*, Oxford: Basil Blackwell.

Eagleton, T. 1984, *The Function of Criticism*, London: Verso.

Eagleton, T. 1985, 'Criticism and Ideology: An Interview', *Thesis Eleven* 12.

Eagleton, T. 1986, *Against the Grain: Essays 1975–1985*, London: Verso.

Eagleton, T. 1989, 'Base and Superstructure in Raymond Williams', in T. Eagleton (ed.) *Raymond Williams: Critical Perspectives*, Cambridge: Polity Press.

Eagleton, T. 1990, *The Ideology of the Aesthetic*, Oxford: Basil Blackwell.

Eagleton, T. 2000 *The Idea of Culture*, Oxford: Blackwell.

Eagleton, T. 2006, 'Making a Break', *London Review of Books* 28, 5.

Easthope, A. 1988, *British Post-Structuralism Since 1968*, London: Routledge.

Easthope, A. 1991, *Literary Into Cultural Studies*, London: Routledge.

Eder, K. 1993, *The New Politics of Class: Social Movements and Cultural Dynamimcs in Advanced Societies*, London: Sage.

Ehrenreich, B. and J. Ehrenreich 1979, 'The Professional-Managerial Class', in P. Walker (ed.) *Between Labour and Capital*, Hassocks: Harvester Press.

Eliot, T.S. 1962, *Notes Towards the Definition of Culture*, London: Faber.

Eliot, T.S. 1968, *Milton: Two Studies*, London: Faber.

Ellis, K. 2010, 'Update', *Das Tahiti-Virus* 19 June 2010. (http://tahiti-virus.blogspot.co.uk/2010/06/update.html). Accessed 3 September 2014.

Ellison, H. 2002, '1967: Introduction Thirty-Two Soothsayers', in H. Ellison (ed.) *Dangerous Visions: 35th Anniversary Edition*, New York: Edgeworks Abbey/ibooks.

Engels, F. 1959, *Anti-Dühring: Herr Eugen Dühring's Revolution in Science*, Moscow: Foreign Languages Publishing House [1878].

Engels, F. 1962, 'Herrn Eugen Dührings Umwälzung der Wissenschaft (Anti-Dühring)', in K. Marx und F. Engels *Werke*, Band 20, Berlin: Dietz Verlag.

Engels, F. 1970, 'Introduction' to *Socialism: Utopian and Scientific*, trans. E. Aveling, in K. Marx and F. Engels *Selected Works*, Moscow: Progress Publishers.

Engels, F. 1987, 'Anti-Dühring: Herr Eugen Dühring's Revolution in Science', trans. E. Burns, in K. Marx and F. Engels *Collected Works*, Vol. 25, London: Lawrence and Wishart.

Erikson, R. and J.H. Goldthorpe 1992, *The Constant Flux: A Study of Class Mobility in Industrial Societies*, Oxford: Oxford University Press.

European Commission 2012, *Eurostat*, (une_rt_q,lfsi_act_a). http://epp.eurostat.ec.europa.eu/statistics_explained/index.php/Unemployment_statistics. Last accessed 31 May 2012.

Evans, G. 1996, 'Putting Men and Women into Classes: An Assessment of the Cross-sex Validity of the Goldthorpe Class Schema', *Sociology* 30, 2.

Evans, R. 1988, 'Keeping Australia Clean White', in V. Burgmann and J. Lee (eds) *A Most Valuable Acquisition*, Melbourne: Penguin.

Escarpit, R. 1958, *Sociologie de la littérature*, Paris: Presses Universitaires de France.

Escarpit, R. 1965, *La Révolution du livre*, Paris: UNESCO/Presses Universitaires de France.

Fehér, F. 1990, 'The Pyrrhic Victory of Art in its War of Liberation: Remarks on the Postmodernist Intermezzo', in A. Milner et al. (eds) *Postmodern Conditions*, Oxford: Berg.

Fehér, F., A. Heller and G. Markus 1983, *Dictatorship Over Needs*, Oxford: Basil Blackwell.

Felperin, H. 1985, *Beyond Deconstruction: The Uses and Abuses of Literary Theory*, Oxford: Oxford University Press.

Ferrara, F. 1989, 'Raymond Williams and the Italian Left', in T. Eagleton (ed.) *Raymond Williams: Critical Perspectives*, Cambridge: Polity Press.

Field, C.R., V.R. Barros, D.J. Dokken, K.J. Mack, M.D. Mastrandrea, T.E. Bilir, M. Chatterjee, K.L. Ebi, Y.O. Estrada, R.C. Genova, B. Girma, E.S. Kissel, A.N. Levy, S. MacCracken, P.R. Mastrandrea and L.L. White (eds) 2014, 'Summary for Policymakers', *Climate Change 2014: Impacts, Adaptation and Vulnerability. Contribution of Working Group II to the Fifth Assessment report of the Intergovernmental Panel on Climate Change*, Cambridge: Cambridge University Press.

Fitting, P. 2006, 'Fredric Jameson and Anti-Anti-Utopianism', *Arena Journal* 11, 25/26.

Fitzgerald, S.W. 2012, *Corporations and Cultural Industries: Time Warner, Bertelsmann, and News Corporation*, Lanham, MD: Lexington Books.

Fitzhardinge, L.F. 1979, *The Little Digger 1914–1952*, Sydney: Angus and Robertson.

Fitzpatrick, B. 1956, *The Australian Commonwealth*, Melbourne: Cheshire.

Fleck, D.C. 2008, *Das Tahiti-Projekt*, München: Pendo Verlag.

Fleck, D.C. 2011, *MAEVA!*, Rudolstadt & Berlin: Greifenverlag.

Fleck, D.C. 2015, *Feur am Fuss*, Murnau: p.machinery Verlag.
Food and Agricultural Organization of the United Nations 2008, *More People Than Ever are Victims of Hunger*, Press Release (Rome: FAO Media Centre, 2008).
Forry, S.E. 1990, *Hideous Progenies: Dramatizations of Frankenstein from Mary Shelley to the Present*, Philadelphia: University of Pennsylvania Press.
Foucault, M. 1965, *Madness and Civilisation: A History of Insanity in the Age of Reason*, trans. R. Howard, New York: Vintage Books.
Foucault, M. 1973a, *The Birth of the Clinic*, trans. A.M. Sheridan, London: Tavistock.
Foucault, M. 1973b, *The Order of Things: An Archaeology of the Human Sciences*, New York: Vintage Books.
Foucault, M. 1977a, *Language, Counter-Memory, Practice*, ed. D.F. Bouchard, trans. D.F. Bouchard and S. Simon, Ithaca: Cornell University Press.
Foucault, M. 1977b, *Discipline and Punish: The Birth of the Prison*, trans. A.M. Sheridan, Harmondsworth: Allen Lane.
Foucault, M. 1980, *Power/Knowledge: Selected Interviews and Other Writings, 1972–1977*, ed. C. Gordon, Brighton: Harvester.
Foucault, M. 1985, *The Use of Pleasure*, trans. R. Hurley, New York: Pantheon Books.
Frankel, B. 1997, 'Beyond Labourism and Socialism: How the Australian Labor Party Developed the Model of "New Labour"', *New Left Review* 221.
Frankel, B. and A. Roberts 1983, 'Open Letter to the French Left', *Arena* 65.
Fraser, J. 1889, *Melbourne and Mars: My Mysterious Life on Two Planets. Extracts from the Diary of a Melbourne Merchant*, Melbourne: E.W. Cole.
Fraser, N. 1984, 'The French Derrideans: Politicizing Deconstruction or Deconstructing the Political?', *New German Critique* 33.
Freedman, C. 2000, *Critical Theory and Science Fiction*, Hanover: Wesleyan University Press.
Frow, J. 1986, *Marxism and Literary History*, Oxford: Basil Blackwell.
Frow, J. 1987, 'Accounting for Tastes: Some Problems in Bourdieu's Sociology of Culture', *Cultural Studies* 1, 1.
Frow, J. 1995, *Cultural Studies and Cultural Value*, Oxford: Oxford University Press.
Frow, J. and M. Morris (eds) 1993, *Australian Cultural Studies: A Reader*, Sydney: Allen and Unwin.
Fukuyama, F. 2002, *Our Posthuman Future: Consequences of the Biotechnology Revolution*, New York: Farrar, Straus & Giroux.
Garnham, N. 1988, 'Raymond Williams, 1921–1988: A Cultural Analyst, A Distinctive Tradition', *Journal of Communication* 38, 4.
Garnham, N. and Williams, R. 1980, 'Pierre Bourdieu and the Sociology of Culture', *Media, Culture and Society* 2, 3.
Garnham, N. and Williams, R. 1986, 'Pierre Bourdieu and the Sociology of Culture', in R. Collins et al. *Media, Culture and Society: A Critical Reader*, London: Sage.

Gay, P. 1962, *The Dilemma of a Democratic Socialism*, New York: Collier.
Gee, M. 1998, *The Ice People*, London: Telegram.
Gee, M. 2004, *The Flood*, London: Saqi.
Gellner, E. 1959, *Words and Things*, London: Victor Gollancz.
Gellner, E. 1964, *Thought and Change*, London: Weidenfeld and Nicolson.
Gellner, E. 1983, *Nations and Nationalism*, Oxford: Basil Blackwell.
Gellner, E. 1997, *Nationalism*, London: Weidenfeld and Nicolson.
Gernsback, H. 1926, 'A New Sort of Magazine', *Amazing Stories: The Magazine of Scientifiction* 1.
Gibson, W. 2011, *Zero History*, London: Penguin [2010].
Giddens, A. 1981, *The Class Structure of the Advanced Societies*, second edition, London: Hutchinson.
Giddens, A. 1994, *Beyond Left and Right: The Future of Radical Politics*, Cambridge: Polity Press.
Giddens, A. 1998, *The Third Way: The Renewal of Social Democracy*, Cambridge: Polity Press.
Gilbert, S.M. and Gubar, S. 1984, *The Madwoman in the Attic: The Woman Writer and the Nineteenth-Century Literary Imagination*, New Haven: Yale University Press.
Goethe, J.W. 1950, 'Bezüge nach außen', *Gedenkausgabe der Werke, Briefe und Gespräche*, Band 14, Zürich: Artemis-Verlag.
Goldmann, L. 1955, *Le Dieu caché: étude sur la vision tragique dans les Pensées de Pascal et dans le théâtre de Racine*, Paris: Éditions Gallimard.
Goldmann, L. 1964, *The Hidden God*, trans. P. Thody, London: Routledge and Kegan Paul.
Goldmann, L. 1967, 'The Sociology of Literature: Status and Problems of Method', *International Social Science Journal* 19, 4.
Goldmann, L. 1970a, 'Structure: Human Reality and Methodological Concept', trans. R. Macksey and E. Donato, in R. Macksey and E. Donato (eds) *The Languages of Criticism and the Sciences of Man*, Baltimore: Johns Hopkins University Press.
Goldmann, L. 1970b, *The Human Sciences and Philosophy*, trans. H.V. White and R. Anchor, London: Jonathan Cape.
Goldmann, L. 1971, *Immanuel Kant*, trans. R. Black, London: New Left Books.
Goldmann, L. 1972, 'Is There a Marxist Sociology?', trans. I.H. Birchall, *International Socialism*, first series, 34.
Goldthorpe, J.H. 1980, *Social Mobility and Class Structure in Modern Britain*, with C. Llewellyn and C. Payne, Oxford: Oxford University Press.
Goldthorpe, J.H. 1982, 'On the Service Class, its Formation and Future', in A. Giddens and G. Mackenzie (eds) *Social Class and the Division of Labour: Essays in Honour of Ilya Neustadt*, Cambridge: Cambridge University Press.
Goldthorpe, J.H. 1983, 'Women and Class Analysis: in Defence of the Conventional View', *Sociology* 17, 4.

Goldthorpe, J.H. 1987, *Social Mobility and Class Structure in Modern Britain*, with C. Llewellyn and C. Payne, second edition, Oxford: Oxford University Press.

Goldthorpe, J.H. and K. Hope 1974, *The Social Grading of Occupations: A New Approach and Scale*, Oxford: Oxford University Press.

Gollan, R.A. 1975, *Revolutionaries and Reformists: Communism and the Australian Labour Movement 1920–1955*, Canberra: ANU Press.

Gordon, J. 2003, 'Reveling in Genre: An Interview with China Miéville', *Sscience Fiction Studies* 30, 3.

Gouldner, A. 1971, *The Coming Crisis of Western Sociology*, London: Heinemann.

Gramsci, A. 1971, *Selections from Prison Notebooks*, trans. Q. Hoare and G. Nowell Smith, London: Lawrence and Wishart.

Gramsci, A. 1977, 'The Revolution Against *Capital*', in *Selections from Political Writings 1910–1920*, trans. J. Mathews, London: Lawrence and Wishart.

Grass, G. and Bourdieu, P. 2002, 'The "Progressive" Restoration', *New Left Review*, (II) 14.

Green, M. 1959, 'British Decency', *Kenyon Review* 21, 4.

Greenblatt, S. 1990, *Learning to Curse: Essays in Early Modern Culture*, London: Routledge.

Greenland, C. 1983, *The Entropy Exhibition: Michael Moorcock and the British 'New Wave' in SF*, London: Routledge and Kegan Paul.

Gribbin, J. and D. Orgill 1979, *The Sixth Winter*, London: Bodley Head.

Grossberg, L. 1996, 'On Postmodernism and Articulation: An Interview with Stuart Hall', in D. Morley and K.-H. Chen (eds) *Stuart Hall: Critical Dialogues*, London: Routledge.

Habermas, J. 1971, *Knowledge and Human Interest*, trans. J.J. Shapiro, Boston: Beacon Press.

Habermas, J. 1979a, 'Interview with Jürgen Habermas', trans. R. Smith *New German Critique* 18.

Habermas, J. 1979b, 'Conservatism and Capitalist Crisis', *New Left Review* 115.

Habermas, J. 1981, 'New Social Movements', *Telos* 49.

Habermas, J. 1984, *The Theory of Communicative Action*, vol. I, *Reason and the Rationalisation of Society*, trans. T. McCarthy, Boston: Beacon Press.

Habermas, J. 1985, 'Modernity – An Incomplete Project', in H. Foster (ed.) *Postmodern Culture*, London: Pluto Press.

Habermas, J. 1987a, *The Philosophical Discourse of Modernity*, trans. F. Lawrence, Cambridge: Polity Press.

Habermas, J. 1987b, *The Theory of Communicative Action*, vol. II, *Lifeworld and System: A Critique of Functionalist Reason*, trans. T. McCarthy, Cambridge: Polity Press.

Habermas, J. 1989, *The Structural Transformation of the Public Sphere: An Inquiry into a Category of Bourgeois Society*, trans. T. Burger, Cambridge: Polity Press.

Habermas, J. 1990, 'What Does Socialism Mean Today? The Rectifying Revolution and the Need for New Thinking on the Left', trans. B. Morgan *New Left Review* 183.

Hall, S. 1980a, 'Cultural Studies: Two Paradigms', *Media, Culture and Society* 2, 1.

Hall, S. 1980b, 'Cultural Studies and the Centre: Some Problematics and Problems', in S. Hall et al. (eds) *Culture, Media, Language*, London: Hutchinson.

Hall, S. 1983, 'The Great Moving Right Show', in S. Hall and M. Jacques (eds) *The Politics of Thatcherism*, London: Lawrence and Wishart.

Hall, S. 1984, 'Face the Future', *New Socialist*, September.

Hall, S. 1986, 'Gramsci's Relevance for the Study of Race and Ethnicity', *Journal of Communication Inquiry* 10.

Hall, S. 1988, 'The Toad in the Garden: Thatcherism among the Theorists', in C. Nelson and L. Grossberg (eds) *Marxism and the Interpretation of Culture*, London: Macmillan.

Hall, S. 1989, 'The Meaning of New Times', in S. Hall and M. Jacques (eds) *New Times: The Changing Face of Politics in the 1990s*, London: Lawrence and Wishart.

Hall, S. 1991, 'Introduction', in R. Simon *Gramsci's Political Thought*, second edition, London: Lawrence and Wishart.

Hall, S. 1992, 'Cultural Studies and its Theoretical Legacies', in L. Grossberg, C. Nelson and P. Treichler (eds) *Cultural Studies*, London: Routledge.

Hall, S. 1993, 'Culture, Community, Nation', *Cultural Studies* 7, 3.

Hall, S. et al. 1978, *Policing the Crisis: Mugging, the State, and Law and Order*, London: Macmillan.

Hall, S. and K.-H. Chen 1996, 'The Formation of a Diasporic Intellectual: An Interview with Stuart Hall by Kuan-Hsing Chen', in D. Morley and K.-H. Chen (eds) *Stuart Hall: Critical Dialogues in Cultural Studies*, London: Routledge.

Hallas, D. 1979, *Trotsky's Marxism*, London: Pluto Press.

Hand, R.J. 2006, *Terror on the Air!: Horror Radio in America 1931–1952*, Jefferson: McFarland.

Haraway, D.J. 1991, *Simians, Cyborgs and Women: The Reinvention of Nature*, London: Routledge.

Harding, D.W. 1957, 'The Character of Literature from Blake to Byron', in B. Ford (ed.) *The Pelican Guide to English Literature. Vol. 5: From Blake to Byron*, Harmondsworth: Penguin.

Harland, R. 1987, *Superstructuralism: The Philosophy of Structuralism and Post-Structuralism*, London: Methuen.

Harris, N. 1988, 'New Bourgeoisies?', *Journal of Development Studies* 24, 2.

Hartman, G. (ed.) 1979, *Deconstruction and Criticism*, New York: Seabury Press.

Hartman, G. 1997, *The Fateful Question of Culture*, New York: Columbia University Press.

Harvey, D. 1990, *The Condition of Postmodernity: An Enquiry into the Origins of Cultural Change*, Oxford: Blackwell.

Harvey, D. 2000, *Spaces of Hope*, Berkeley: University of California Press.

Harvey, D. 2001, *Spaces of Capital: Towards a Critical Geography*, New York: Routledge.

Hayles, N.K. 1999, *How We Became Posthuman: Virtual Bodies in Cybernetics, Literature and Informatics*, Chicago: University of Chicago Press.

Head, D. 1998, 'The (Im)possibility of Ecocriticism', in R. Kerridge and N. Sammells (eds.) *Writing the Environment: Ecocriticism and Literature*, London: Zed Books.

Heldreth, L.G. 1991, 'The Cutting Edges of *Blade Runner*', in J.B. Kerman (ed.) *Retrofitting Blade Runner: Issues in Ridley Scott's Blade Runner and Philip K. Dick's Do Androids Dream of Electric Sheep?*, Bowling Green: Bowling Green State University Popular Press.

Helford, E.R. 2000, 'Introduction', in Elyce Rae Helford (ed.) *Fantasy Girls: Gender in the New Universe of Science Fiction and Fantasy Television*, Lanham: Rowman and Littlefield.

Heller, A. 1990, 'The End of Communism', *Thesis Eleven* 27.

Heller, A. 2005, *Immortal Comedy: The Comic Phenomenon in Art, Literature and Life*, Boston: Rowman and Littlefield.

Herder, J.G. 1968, *Reflections on the Philosophy of the History of Mankind*, trans. T.O. Churchill, Chicago: University of Chicago Press.

Herzog, A. 1977, *Heat*, New York: Signet.

Heseltine, H.P. 1979, 'John le Gay Brereton', in B. Nairn and G. Serle (eds) *Australian Dictionary of Biography*, Vol. 7, Melbourne: Melbourne University Press.

Hicklenton, J. 2012, *100 Months*, London: Cutting Edge Press.

Higgins, J. 1999, *Raymond Williams: Literature, Marxism and Cultural Materialism*, London: Routledge.

Hill, C. 1972, *Intellectual Origins of the English Revolution*, London: Panther.

Hill, C. 1977, *Milton and the English Revolution*, London: Faber.

Hill, C. 1985, *The Experience of Defeat: Milton and Some Contemporaries*, Harmondsworth: Penguin.

Hilton, R. (ed.) 1978, *The Transition from Feudalism to Capitalism*, London: New Left Books.

Hoggart, R. 1957, *The Uses of Literacy*, London: Chatto and Windus.

Hoggart, R. 1958, *The Uses of Literacy*, Harmondsworth: Penguin.

Hoggart, R. 1970, *Speaking To Each Other: Vol. 2 About Literature*, Harmondsworth: Penguin.

Hoggart, R. 1995, *The Way We Live Now*, London: Chatto annd Windus.

Hohendahl, P.U. 1982, *The Institution of Criticism*, Ithaca: Cornell University Press.

Hollinger, V. 1999, 'Contemporary Trends in Science Fiction Criticism, 1980–1999', *Science Fiction Studies* 26, 2.

Horkheimer, M. 1972, *Critical Theory: Selected Essays*, trans. M.J.O. O'Connell, New York: Seabury Press.

Houellebecq, M. 1991, *Contre le monde, contre la vie, essai sur Lovecraft*, Paris: Éditions du Rocher.

Houellebecq, M. 2005, *La Possibilité d'une île*, Paris: Fayard.
Houghton, J.T., G.J. Jenkins and J.J. Ephraums (eds) 1990, 'Policy Makers Summary', *Climate Change: The IPCC Scientific Assessment. A Report Prepared for the IPCC by Working Group 1*, Cambridge: Cambridge University Press.
Hunter, I. 1988, *Culture and Government: The Emergence of Literary Education*, London: Macmillan.
Hunter, I. et al. 1991, *Accounting for the Humanities: The Language of Culture and the Logic of Government*, Brisbane: Institute for Cultural Policy Studies.
Huxley, A. 1921, *Crome Yellow*, London: Chatto and Windus.
Huxley, A. 1928, *Point Counter Point: A Novel*, London: Chatto and Windus.
Huxley, A. 1929, *Do What You Will: Essays*, London: Chatto and Windus.
Huxley, A. 1932, *The Letters of D.H. Lawrence*, New York: Viking Press.
Huxley, A. 1955, *Brave New World*, Harmondsworth: Penguin [1932].
Huxley, A. 1969, *Letters of Aldous Huxley*, ed. G. Smith, London: Chatto and Windus.
Huyssen, A. 1988, *After the Great Divide: Modernism, Mass Culture and Postmodernism*, London: Macmillan.
Inglis, F. 1995, *Raymond Williams*, London: Routledge.
Jacoby, R. 1981, *Dialectic of Defeat: Contours of Western Marxism*, Cambridge: Cambridge University Press.
Jaensch, D. 1989, *The Hawke-Keating Hijack: the ALP in Transition*, Sydney: Allen and Unwin.
James, E. 1994, *Science Fiction in the Twentieth Century*, Oxford: Oxford University Press.
James, H. 1879, *Hawthorne*, London: Macmillan.
Jameson, F. 1971, *Marxism and Form*, Princeton: Princeton University Press.
Jameson, F. 1973, 'Generic Discontinuities in Science Fiction: Brian Aldiss' Starship', *Science Fiction Studies* 1, 2.
Jameson, F. 1981, *The Political Unconscious: Narrative as a Socially Symbolic Act*, London: Methuen.
Jameson, F. 1982, 'Progress v. Utopia; or, Can We Imagine the Future?', *Science Fiction Studies* 9, 2.
Jameson, F. 1984, 'Postmodernism, or the Cultural Logic of Late Capitalism', *New Left Review* 146.
Jameson, F. 1988a, 'Discussion', in C. Nelson and L. Grossberg (eds) *Marxism and the Interpretation of Culture*, London: Macmillan.
Jameson, F. 1988b, 'Introduction', in *The Ideologies of Theory: Essays 1971–1986; Volume 1: Situations of Theory*, London: Routledge.
Jameson, F. 1991, *Postmodernism, or, the Cultural Logic of Late Capitalism*, London: Verso.
Jameson, F. 1992, *The Geopolitical Aesthetic: Cinema and Space in the World System*, Bloomington: Indiana University Press.
Jameson, F. 1994, *The Seeds of Time*, New York: Columbia University Press.

Jameson, F. 1998, *Brecht and Method*, London: Verso.
Jameson, F. 2003a, 'Fear and Loathing in Globalization', *New Left Review*, II, 23.
Jameson, F. 2003b, 'Morus: The Generic Window', *New Literary History* 34, 3.
Jameson, F. 2004, 'The Politics of Utopia', *New Left Review*, (II) 25.
Jameson, F. 2005, *Archaeologies of the Future: The Desire Called Utopia and Other Science Fictions*, London: Verso.
Jameson, F. 2013, *The Antinomies of Reason*, London: Verso.
Jardine, L. and J. Swindells 1989, 'Homage to Orwell: The Dream of a Common Culture and Other Minefields', in T. Eagleton (ed.), *Raymond Williams: Critical Perspectives*, Cambridge: Polity Press.
Jefferies, R. 2007, *After London or Wild England*, Cirencester: The Echo Library [1895].
Jenkins, H. 1992, *Textual Poachers: Television Fans and Participant Culture*, New York: Routledge.
Jeschke, W. 2005, *Das Cusanus-Spiel*, München: Droemer Knaur.
Johnson, C. 1989, *The Labor Legacy: Curtin, Chifley, Whitlam, Hawke*, Sydney: Allen and Unwin.
Johnson, R. 1979a, 'Histories of Culture/Theories of Ideology: Notes on an Impasse', in M. Barrett et al. (eds) *Ideology and Cultural Production*, London: Croom Helm.
Johnson, R. 1979b, 'Culture and the Historians', in J. Clarke et al. (eds) *Working Class Culture: Studies in History and Theory*, London: Hutchinson.
Johnson, R. 1980, 'Barrington Moore, Perry Anderson and English Social Development', in S. Hall et al. (eds) *Culture, Media, Language*, London: Hutchinson.
Jones, P. 1994, 'The Myth of "Raymond Hogart": on "Founding Fathers" and Cultural Policy', *Cultural Studies* 8, 3.
Jones, P. 1999, '"The Problem is Always One of Method ...": Cultural Materialism, Political Economy and Cultural Studies', *Key Words* 2.
Juszczyk, A. 2005, 'H.G. Wells's Polish Reception', in P. Parrinder and J.S. Partington (eds) *The Reception of H.G. Wells in Europe*, London: Continuum.
Kaplan, E.A. 1988, 'Introduction', in E.A. Kaplan (ed.) *Postmodernism and Its Discontents: Theories, Practices*, London: Verso.
Kautsky, K. 1983, 'Terrorism and Communism', in *Karl Kautsky: Selected Political Writings*, ed. and trans. P. Goode, London: Macmillan.
Kedourie, E. 1960, *Nationalism*, London: Hutchinson.
Kidron, M. 1970, *Western Capitalism Since the War*, Harmondsworth: Penguin.
Kidron, M. 1974, *Capitalism and Theory*, London: Pluto Press.
Kingsolver, B. 2012, *Flight Behavior*, New York: HarperCollins.
Kirmess, C.H. 1909, *The Australian Crisis*, London: Walter Scott Publishing Co.
Klein, N. 2001, 'Reclaiming the Commons', *New Left Review* (II) 9.
Kolb, W.M. 1991a, 'Script to Screen: *Blade Runner* in Perspective', in J.B. Kerman (ed.) *Retrofitting Blade Runner: Issues in Ridley Scott's Blade Runner and Philip K. Dick's Do*

Androids Dream of Electric Sheep?, Bowling Green: Bowling Green State University Popular Press.

Kolb, W.M. 1991b, '*Blade Runner* Film Notes', in J.B. Kerman (ed.) *Retrofitting Blade Runner: Issues in Ridley Scott's Blade Runner and Philip K. Dick's Do Androids Dream of Electric Sheep?*, Bowling Green: Bowling Green State University Popular Press.

Kristal, E. 2002, '"Considering Coldly" ... A Response to Franco Moretti', *New Left Review* (11) 15.

Kristeva, J. et al. 1977, 'Pourquoi les États-Unis?', *Tel Quel* 71–73.

Laclau, E. 1977, *Politics and Ideology in Marxist Theory: Capitalism, Fascism, Populism*, London: New Left Books.

Laclau, E. and C. Mouffe 1985, *Hegemony and Socialist Strategy: Towards a Radical Democratic Politics*, trans. W. Moore and P. Cammack, London: Verso.

Lang, F. (dir.) 1927, *Metropolis*, Universum Film Aktiengesellschaft.

Lang, F. (dir.) 2002, *Metropolis*, Transit Film/Friedrich Wilhelm Murnau Stiftung.

Lash, S. 1990, *Sociology of Postmodernism*, London: Routledge.

Latour, B. 1997, *Nous n'avons jamais été modernes: Essai d'anthropologie symétrique*, Paris: La Découverte/Poche.

Laurenson, D.T. and A. Swingewood 1972, *The Sociology of Literature*, London: MacGibbon and Kee.

Lawson, S. 2002, 'How Raymond Williams Died in Australia', in *How Simone de Beauvoir Died in Australia*, Sydney: University of New South Wales Press.

Layh, S. 2014, 'Ecotopia's Dystopian Turn', *Utopia and Nonviolence. 15th International Conference of the Utopian Studies Society*, Prague: Charles University.

Leavis, F.R. 1930, *Mass Civilization and Minority Culture*, Cambridge: Minority Press.

Leavis, F.R. 1933, *For Continuity*, Cambridge: Minority Press.

Leavis, F.R. 1938, *New Bearings in English Poetry*, London: Chatto and Windus.

Leavis, F.R. 1948, *Education and the University: A Sketch for an 'English School'*, London: Chatto and Windus.

Leavis, F.R. 1962a, *The Great Tradition*, Harmondsworth: Penguin.

Leavis, F.R. 1962b, *The Common Pursuit*, Harmondsworth: Penguin.

Leavis, F.R. 1962c, *Two Cultures?*, London: Chatto and Windus.

Leavis, F.R. 1972a, *Nor Shall My Sword: Discourses on Pluralism, Compassion and Social Hope*, London: Chatto and Windus.

Leavis, F.R. 1972b, *Revaluation*, Harmondsworth: Penguin.

Leavis, F.R. and Thompson, D. 1960, *Culture and Environment*, London: Chatto and Windus.

Leavis, Q.D. 1979, *Fiction and the Reading Public*, Harmondsworth: Penguin.

Lee, C.-R. 2014, *On Such a Full Sea*, New York: Riverhead.

Lee, S.E. 1976, '*The Bulletin* – J.F. Archibald and A.G. Stephens', in G. Dutton (ed.) *The Literature of Australia*, Melbourne: Penguin.

Le Guin, U.K. 1969, *The Left Hand of Darkness*, New York: Ace Books.
Le Guin, U.K. 1974, *The Dispossessed: An Ambiguous Utopia*, New York: Harper and Row.
Lenin, V.I. 1969, *Imperialism: The Highest Stage of Capitalism*, New York: International Publishers.
Lenin, V.I. 1975a, 'Two Tactics of Social-Democracy in the Democratic Revolution', in *Selected Works*, Vol. 1, Moscow: Progress Publishers.
Lenin, V.I. 1975b, 'The Tasks of the Proletariat in the Present Revolution', in *Selected Works*, Vol. 2, Moscow: Progress Publishers.
Lentricchia, F. 1980, *After the New Criticism*, Chicago: University of Chicago Press.
Leslie, E. 1999, 'Introduction to Adorno/Marcuse Correspondence on the German Student Movement', *New Left Review* 233.
Lessing, D. 1999, *Mara and Dann*, London: Flamingo.
Ligny, J.-M. 2006, *Aqua™* Nantes: L'Atalante.
Ligny, J.-M. 2012, *Exodes*, Nantes: L'Atalante.
Ligny, J.-M. 2015, *Semences*, Nantes: L'Atalante.
Lilburne, J. 1965, 'Legal Fundamental Liberties', in A.S.P. Woodhouse (ed.) *Puritanism and Liberty*, London: Dent.
Liu, C. 2006, 三体 Chengdu: 科幻世界 Kehuan Shijie.
Liu, C. 2008, 三体 Chonging: Chonging Publishing Group.
Liu, C. 2014, *The Three-Body Problem*, trans. Ken Liu New York: Tor Books.
Lob, J. and J.-M. Rochette 1982, *Le Transperceneige*, Tournai: Casterman.
Lofficier, J.-M. and R. Lofficer 2000, *French Science Fiction, Fantasy, Horror and Pulp Fiction: A Guide to Cinema, Television, Radio, Animation, Comic Books and Literature*, Jefferson: McFarland.
London, J. 1958, *The Iron Heel*, New York: Macmillan [1908].
Lovelock, J. 1979, *Gaia: A New Look at Life on Earth*, Oxford: Oxford University Press.
Lowry, B. 1995, *The Truth is Out There: The Official Guide to 'The X-Files'*, London: Harper Collins.
Lucian of Samosata 1905, 'The True History', in *The Works of Lucian of Samosata: Volume II*, trans. H.W. Fowler and F.G. Fowler, Vol. II, Oxford: Oxford University Press.
Lucian of Samosata 2011, *Alēthēs Historia*, on-line version of the full Greek text at http://www.hs-augsburg.de/~harsch/graeca/Chronologia/S_post02/Lukianos/luk_vero.html.
Luckhurst, R. 2005, *Science Fiction*, Cambridge: Polity Press.
Lukács, G. 1963, *Die Theorie des Romans: Ein geschichtsphilosophischer Versuch Über die Formen der grossen Epik*, Neuwied am Rhein: Luchterhand [first published 1916].
Lukács, G. 1955, *Der historische Roman*, Berlin: Aufbau-Verlag [first published 1947 as *A történelmi regény*].
Lukács, G. 1969, *The Historical Novel*, trans. H. and S. Mitchell, Harmondsworth: Penguin.

Lukács, G. 1971a, *The Theory of the Novel*, trans. A. Bostock, London: Merlin Press.
Lukács, G. 1971b, *History and Class Consciousness*, trans. R. Livingstone, London: Merlin Press.
Luxemburg, R. 1970, 'The Junius Pamphlet: The Crisis in the German Social Democracy', in *Rosa Luxemburg Speaks*, ed. M.-A. Waters, New York: Pathfinder Press [1916].
Lyotard, J.-F. 1979, *La Condition postmoderne: rapport sur le savoir*, Paris: Minuit.
Lyotard, J.-F. 1984, *The Postmodern Condition: A Report on Knowledge*, trans. G. Bennington and B. Massumi, Minneapolis: University of Minnesota Press.
MacCabe, C. 1985, *Theoretical Essays: Film, Linguistics, Literature*, Manchester: Manchester University Press.
MacDermott, K. 1983, 'The Discourse of Assessment: English Studies at Melbourne University', *Melbourne Working Papers 4, 1982/83*, Melbourne: Melbourne University Department of Education.
Macdonnell. D. 1986, *Theories of Discourse*, Oxford: Basil Blackwell.
Macherey, P. 1966, *Pour une théorie de la production littéraire*, Paris: François Maspero.
Macintyre, A. 1981, *After Virtue: A Study in Moral Theory*, London: Duckworth.
Maddox, G. 1989, *The Hawke Government and Labor Tradition*, Ringwood: Penguin, 1989.
Mandel, E. 1979, *Trotsky: A Study in the Dynamic of His Thought*, London: New Left Books.
Mandel, E. 1975, *Late Capitalism*, trans. J. De Bres, London: New Left Books [1972].
Manuel, J. de 2006, *L'olor de la pluja*, Barcelona: RBA/La Magrana.
Marcuse, H. 1964, *One-Dimensional Man: Studies in the Ideology of Advanced Industrial Society*, Boston: Beacon Press.
Marcuse, H. 1971, *Soviet Marxism: A Critical Analysis*, Harmondsworth: Penguin.
Margot, J.-M. 2005, 'Jules Verne, Playwright', *Science Fiction Studies* 32, 1.
Markus, A. 1988, 'Everybody Become a Job: Twentieth Century Immigrants', in V. Burgmann and J. Lee (eds) *A Most Valuable Acquisition*, Melbourne: Penguin.
Marx, K. 1970a, *Capital*, Vol. I, trans. S. Moore and E. Aveling, London: Lawrence and Wishart.
Marx, K. 1970b, 'The Eighteenth Brumaire of Louis Bonaparte', in K. Marx and F. Engels *Selected Works*, Moscow: Progress Publishers.
Marx, K. 1972, *Capital: A Critique of Political Economy*, Vol. III, ed. F. Engels, London: Lawrence and Wishart [1894].
Marx, K. 1973, 'The Eighteenth Brumaire of Louis Bonaparte', trans. B. Fowkes, in D. Fernbach (ed.) *Surveys From Exile*, Harmondsworth: Penguin.
Marx, K. 1974, *Capital*, Vol. III, London: Lawrence and Wishart.
Marx, K. 1975a, 'Preface' to *A Contribution to the Critique of Political Economy*, in *Early Writings*, Harmondsworth: Penguin.
Marx, K. 1975b, 'Economic and Philosophical Manuscripts', trans. G. Benton, in *Early Writings*, Harmondworth: Penguin.

Marx, K. and F. Engels 1967, *The Communist Manifesto*, trans. S. Moore, Harmondsworth: Penguin.
Marx, K. and F. Engels 1970, *The German Ideology*, Part One, trans. W. Lough, C. Dutt and C.P. Magill, ed. C.J. Arthur, London: Lawrence and Wishart.
Marxism Today 1988, Special Issue on 'New Times', October.
McEwan, I. 2010, *Solar*, London: Jonathan Cape.
McQueen, H. 1977, 'National Independence and Socialism', *Melbourne Journal of Politics* 9.
Méliès, G. (dir.) 1902, *Le Voyage dans la lune*, Star Films.
Merchant, B. 2013, 'Behold the Rise of Dystopian "Cli-Fi"', *Vice: Motherboard* 1 June 2013. (http://motherboard.vice.com/blog/behold-the-rise-of-cli-fi). Accessed August 8 2014.
Merleau-Ponty, M. 1974, *Adventures of the Dialectic*, trans. J. Bien, London: Heinemann.
Merrick, H. and T. Williams (eds) 1999, *Women of Other Worlds: Excursions Through Science Fiction and Feminism*, Nedlands: University of Western Australia Press.
Merrington, J. 1968, 'Theory and Practice in Gramsci's Marxism', in R. Miliband and J. Saville (eds) *The Socialist Register 1968*, London: Merlin Press.
Meyer, A.G. 1957, *Leninism*, Cambridge, Mass.: Harvard University Press.
Miéville, C. 2009a, 'Weird Fiction', in M. Bould, A.M. Butler, A. Roberts and S. Vint (eds) *The Routledge Companion to Science Fiction*, London and New York: Routledge.
Miéville, C. 2009b, 'Cognition as Ideology: A Dialectic of SF Theory', in M. Bould and C. Miéville (eds) *Red Planets: Marxism and Science Fiction*, Middletown: Wesleyan University Press.
Miéville, C. and M. Bould (eds) 2002, 'Symposium: Marxism and Fantasy', *Historical Materialism: Research in Critical Marxist Theory* 10, 4.
Milgate, W. 1952, 'The Language and Literature Tradition', in University of Sydney *One Hundred Years of the Faculty of Arts*, Sydney: Angus and Robertson.
Mills, C.W. 1970, *The Sociological Imagination*, Harmondsworth: Penguin.
Milner, A. 1981, *John Milton and the English Revolution: A Study in the Sociology of Literature*, London: Macmillan.
Milner, A. 1996, *Literature, Culture and Society*, Sydney: Allen and Unwin.
Milner, A. 2002, *Re-Imagining Cultural Studies: The Promise of Cultural Materialism*, London: Sage.
Milner, A. 2006, 'Framing Catastrophe: The Problem of Ending in Dystopian Fiction', *Arena Journal* 11, 25/26.
Milner, A. 2012, *Locating Science Fiction*, Liverpool: Liverpool University Press.
Milner, A. 2014, 'World Systems and World Science Fiction', *Paradoxa* 26.
Milner, A. and R. Savage 2008, 'Pulped Dreams: Utopia and American "Golden Age" Science Fiction', *Science Fiction Studies* 25, 1.

Milton, J. 1848, *Prose Works*, four vols., London: Bohn's Standard Library.
Milton, J. 1966, *Poetical Works*, ed. D. Bush, London: Oxford University Press.
Mitchell, A.G. 1983, 'Ernest Rudolph Holme', in B. Nairn and G. Serle (eds) *Australian Dictionary of Biography*, Vol. 9, Melbourne: Melbourne University Press.
Mitchell, D. 2004, *Cloud Atlas*, London: Hodder and Stoughton.
Mitchell, D. 2014, *The Bone Clocks*, London: Sceptre.
Miyazaki, H. 1982–94, *Kaze no Tani no Naushika*, Tokyo: Tokuma Shoten.
Monash University Department of English 1986, *Why Study English Literature?*, Melbourne: Monash University.
Moorcock, M. 1964, 'A New Literature for the Space Age', *New Worlds* 48, 142.
Moorcock, M. 1966, 'Ballard: The Voice', *New Worlds* 50, 167.
Moorcock, M. 1993, 'The Ice Schooner', in *Sailing to Utopia*, London: Millenium [1966].
More, T. 1995, *Utopia: Latin Text and English Translation*, ed. G.M. Logan, R.M. Adams and C.H. Miller, Cambridge: Cambridge University Press [1516].
More, T. 2001, *Utopia*, trans. C. Miller, New Haven: Yale University Press [1516].
Moretti, F. 1983, *Signs Taken for Wonders*, trans. S. Fischer, D. Forgacs and D. Miller, London: Verso.
Moretti, F. 1986, *Il romanzo di formazione*, Milano: Garzanti.
Moretti, F. 1987a, *Segni e stili del moderno*, Torino: Giulio Einaudi.
Moretti, F. 1987b, *The Way of the World: The Bildungsroman in European Culture*, trans. A.J. Sbragia, London: Verso.
Moretti, F. 1988, *Signs Taken For Wonders: Essays in the Sociology of Literary Forms*, trans. S. Fischer, D. Forgacs and D. Miller, London: Verso.
Moretti, F. 1994, *Opere mondo: Saggio sulla forma epica dal Faust a Cent'anni di solitudine*, Torino: Giulio Einaudi.
Moretti, F. 1996, *Modern Epic: The World System from Goethe to García Márquez*, trans. Q. Hoare, London: Verso.
Moretti, F. 1997, *Atlante del romanzo europeo 1800–1900*, Torino: Giulio Einaudi.
Moretti, F. 1998, *Atlas of the European Novel 1800–1900*, London: Verso.
Moretti, F. 2000, 'Conjectures on World Literature', *New Left Review* (11) 1.
Moretti, F. 2003, 'More Conjectures', *New Left Review* (11) 20.
Moretti, F. 2005, *Graphs, Maps, Trees: Abstract Models for a Liteary History*, London: Verso.
Moretti, F. 2013, *Distant Reading*, London: Verso, 2013.
Morin, J.L. 2015, *Nature's Confession*, New York: Harvard Square.
Morris, M. 1988, *The Pirate's Fiancée: Feminism, Reading, Postmodernism*, London: Verso.
Morris, M. 1992, 'A Gadfly Bites Back', *Meanjin* 51, 3.
Morris, W. 1977, *Three Works by William Morris*, London: Lawrence and Wishart.
Moylan, T. 2000, *Scraps of the Untainted Sky: Science Fiction, Utopia, Dystopia*, Boulder, Co: Westview Press.

Mulhern, F. 1981, *The Moment of 'Scrutiny'*, London: Verso.
Mulhern, F. 1998, *The Present Lasts a Long Time: Essays in Cultural Politics*, Cork: Cork University Press.
Mulhern, F. 2000, *Culture/Metaculture*, London: Routledge.
y, L. 1989, *Visual and Other Pleasures*, London: Macmillan.
Murray-Smith, S. 1982, 'Foreword', in I. Turner *Room for Manoeuvre*, Melbourne: Drummond.
Nairn, T. 1964a, 'The British Political Elite', *New Left Review* 23.
Nairn, T. 1964b, 'The English Working Class', *New Left Review* 24.
Nairn, T. 1964c, 'The Anatomy of the Labour Party', *New Left Review* 27–28.
Nairn, T. 1977, *The Break-Up of Britain*, London: New Left Books.
Nettle, P. 1969, *Rosa Luxemburg*, Oxford: Oxford University Press.
Neufeld, J. 2010, *A.D.: New Orleans after the Deluge*, New York: Pantheon Graphic Novels.
Neuhaus, N. 2011, *Wer Wind sät*, Berlin: Ullstein.
nytimes 2014, http://www.ntimes.com/roomfordebate/2014/07/29/will-fiction-influence-how-we-react-to-climate-change.
O'Connor, A. 1989, *Raymond Williams: Writing, Culture, Politics*, Oxford: Basil Blackwell.
O'Flinn, P. 1986, 'Production and Reproduction: The Case of *Frankenstein*', in P. Humm et al. (eds) *Popular Fictions: Essays in Literature and History*, London: Methuen.
Ong, W.J. 1982, *Orality and Literacy: The Technologizing of the Word*, London: Methuen.
Ono, K.A. 2000, 'To be a vampire on *Buffy the Vampire Slayer*: race and ('Other') socialy marginalizing positions on horror TV', in Elyce Rae Helford (ed.) *Fantasy Girls: Gender in the New Universe of Science Fiction and Fantasy Television*, Lanham: Rowman and Littlefield.
Orwell, G. 1949, *Nineteen Eighty-Four: A Novel*, London: Secker and Warburg.
Orwell, G. 1962, *The Road to Wigan Pier*, Harmondsworth: Penguin [1937].
Orwell, G. 1966, *Homage to Catalonia and Looking Back on the Spanish War*, Harmondsworth: Penguin.
Orwell, G. 1970a, *Collected Essays, Journalism and Letters of George Orwell, Vol. 1: An Age Like This*, ed. S. Orwell and I. Angus, Harmondsworth: Penguin.
Orwell, G. 1970b, *Collected Essays, Journalism and Letters: Vol. 2 My Country Right or Left*, ed. S. Orwell and I. Angus, Harmondsworth: Penguin.
Orwell, G. 1970c, *Collected Essays, Journalism and Letters: Vol. 3 As I Please*, ed. S. Orwell and I. Angus, Harmondsworth: Penguin.
Orwell, G. 1970d, *Collected Essays, Journalism and Letters of George Orwell, Vol. 4: In Front of Your Nose*, ed. S. Orwell and I. Angus, Harmondsworth: Penguin.
Orwell, G. 1984, *Nineteen Eighty-Four: The Facsimile of the Extant Manuscript*, ed. P. Davison, London: Secker and Warburg.
Orwell, G. 1989, *Nineteen Eighty-Four*, Harmondsworth: Penguin [1949].
Ozolis, U. 1981, 'Victorian HSC Examiners' Reports: A Study of Cultural Capital', *Mel-

bourne Working Papers 1981, Melbourne: University of Melbourne Department of Education.
Palmer, D.J. 1965, *The Rise of English Studies*, Oxford: Oxford University Press.
Palmer, V. 1963, *The Legend of the Nineties*, Melbourne: Melbourne University Press.
Parkin, F. 1979, *Marxism and Class Theory: A Bourgeois Critique*, London: Tavistock.
Parrinder, P. 2000, 'Introduction: Learning from Other Worlds', in P. Parrinder (ed.) *Learning from Other Worlds: Estrangement, Cognition and the Politics of Science Fiction and Utopia*, Liverpool: Liverpool University Press.
Parrinder, P. 2005, 'Introduction: An Outline of Wells's Reception in Europe', in P. Parrinder and J.S. Partington (eds) *The Reception of H.G. Wells in Europe*, London: Continuum.
Parrinder, P. and P. Barnaby 2005, 'Timeline: European Reception of H.G. Wells', in P. Parrinder and J.S. Partington (eds) *The Reception of H.G. Wells in Europe*, London: Continuum.
Penley, C. 1997, NASA/TREK: *Popular Science and Sex in America*, London: Verso.
Peter, J. 1960, *A Critique of Paradise Lost*, London: Longman.
Phillips, A.A. 1950, 'The Cultural Cringe', *Meanjin* 9, 4.
Phillips, A.A. 1958, *The Australian Tradition*, Melbourne: Cheshire.
Pickering, M. 1997, *History, Experience and Cultural Studies*, London: Macmillan.
Piercy, M. 1976, *Woman on the Edge of Time*, New York: Kopf.
Pinkney, T. 1989, 'Williams and the "Two Faces of Modernism"', in T. Eagleton (ed.) *Raymond Williams: Critical Perspectives*, Cambridge: Polity Press.
Pinkney, T. 1991, *Raymond Williams*, Bridgend: Seren Books.
Poggioli, R. 1968, *The Theory of the Avant-Garde*, trans. G. Fitzgerald, Cambridge, Mass.: Harvard University Press.
Poovey, M. 1984, *The Proper Lady and the Woman Writer: Ideology as Style in the Works of Mary Wollstonecrafft, Mary Shelley, and Jane Austen*, Chicago: Chicago University Press.
Posnett, H.M. 1973, 'The Science of Comparative Literature', (first published in 1901) in H.-J. Schulz and P.H. Rhein (eds) *Comparative Literature: The Early Years, An Anthology of Essays*, Chapel Hill: University of North Carolina Press.
Poulantzas, N. 1975, *Classes in Contemporary Capitalism*, trans. D. Fernbach, London: Verso.
Proyas, A. (dir.) 1998, *Dark City*, Mystery Clock Cinema/New Line Cinema.
Prynne, W. 1965, 'Anti-Arminianism', in A.S.P. Woodhouse (ed.) *Puritanism and Liberty*, London: Dent.
Raleigh, W. 1913, *Milton*, London: Arnold.
Reeves, J.L., M.C. Rodgers and M. Epstein 1996, 'Rewriting Popularity: the Cult Files', in D. Lavery, A. Hague and M. Cartwright (eds) *Deny All Knowledge: Reading the X-Files*, London: Faber.

Remak, H. 1961, 'Comparative Literature, Its Definition and Function', in N. Stallknecht and H. Frenz (eds) *Comparative Literature: Method and Perspective*, Carbondale: Southern Illinois University Press.

Renner, K. 1953, *Wandlungen der modernen Gesellschaft: Zwei Abhandlungen Über die Probleme der Nachkriegzeit*, Vienna, Verlag der Wiener Volksbuchhandlung.

Renner, K. 1978, 'The Service Class', trans. T. Bottomore and P. Goode, in T. Bottomore and P. Goode (eds) *Austro-Marxism*, Oxford: Oxford University Press.

Rich, N. 2013, *Odds Against Tomorrow*, New York: Farrar, Straus and Giroux.

Rigby, K. 2004, *Topographies of the Sacred: The Poetics of Place in European Romanticism*, Charlottesville: University of Virginia Press.

Rigby, K. 2014, 'Confronting Catastrophe: Ecocriticism in a Warming World', in L. Westlin (ed.) *The Cambridge Companion to Literature and Environment*, Cambridge: Cambridge University Press.

Roberts, A. 2005, *The History of Science Fiction*, Basingstoke: Palgrave Macmillan.

Robinson, A. 2015, *Anchor Point*, South Melbourne: Affirm Press.

Robinson, K.S. 1984, *The Novels of Philip K. Dick*, Ann Arbor: University of Michigan Research Press [1982].

Robinson, K.S. 1987, 'Notes for an Essay on Cecilia Holland', *Foundation: The Review of Science Fiction* 40.

Robinson, K.S. 1997, *Antarctica*, London: HarperCollins.

Robinson, K.S. 2004, *Forty Signs of Rain*, London: HarperCollins.

Robinson, K.S. 2005, *Fifty Degrees Below*, London: HarperCollins.

Robinson, K.S. 2007, *Sixty Days and Counting*, London: HarperCollins.

Robinson, K.S. 2012, *2312: A Novel*, London: Orbit.

Roemer, J. (ed.) 1986, *Analytical Marxism*, Cambridge: Cambridge University Press.

Rolfe, P. 1979, *The Journalistic Javelin*, Sydney: Wildcat Press.

Rose, D.B. 2001, 'Connecting with Ecological Futures', in M. Gillies (ed.) *Position Papers: The National Humanities and Social Sciences Summit*, Canberra: Australian Academy of the Humanities and Academy of the Social Sciences in Australia.

Rose, L. 2005, 'Hollywood's Most Expensive Movies', *Forbes* 12.

Ross, L. 1935, *William Lane and the Australian Labour Movement*, Sydney: Forward Press.

Royal Commission on the University of Melbourne 1904, *Final Report*, Melbourne: Government of Victoria.

Russ, J. 1985, *The Female Man*, London: Women's Press.

Ryan, K. 1996, 'Introduction', in *New Historicism and Cultural Materialism: A Reader*, London: Arnold.

Ryan, M. 1982, *Marxism and Deconstruction: A Critical Articulation*, Baltimore: Johns Hopkins University Press.

Rybakov, A. 1989, *Children of the Arbat*, trans. H. Shukman, London: Arrow Books.

Said, E.W. 1984, *The World, the Text, and the Critic*, London: Faber.
Said, E.W. 1993, *Culture and Imperialism*, London: Chatto and Windus.
Salvadori, M. 1979, *Karl Kautsky and the Socialist Revolution 1880–1938*, trans. J. Rothschild, London: New Left Books.
Samuel, R. 1980, 'British Marxist Historians 1880–1980: Part One', *New Left Review* 120.
Sargent, L.T. 1976, 'Themes in Utopian Fiction in English Before Wells', *Science Fiction Studies* 3, 3.
Sargent, L.T. 1994, 'The Three Faces of Utopianism Revisited', *Utopian Studies* 5, 1.
Sargent, L.T. 1999, 'Australian Utopian Literature: An Annotated, Chronological Bibliography 1667–1999', *Utopian Studies* 10, 2.
Sartre, J.-P. 1976, *Critique of Dialectical Reason*, trans. A. Sheridan-Smith, London: New Left Books.
Saunders, S. 1973–74, 'Towards a Social Theory of Literature', *Telos* 18.
Saurat, D. 1924, *Milton: Man and Thinker*, London: Cape.
Schätzing, F. 2005, *Der Schwarm*, Frankfurt am Main: S. Fischer Verlag [2004].
Schenkel, E. 2005, 'White Elephants and Black Machines: H.G. Wells and German Culture, 1920–45', in P. Parrinder and J.S. Partington (eds) *The Reception of H.G. Wells in Europe*, London: Continuum.
Schwarz, B. 1982, '"The People" in History: The Communist Party Historians' Group, 1946–56', in R. Johnson et al. *Making Histories: Studies in History-Writing and Politics*, London: Hutchinson.
Scott, E. 1936, *A History of the University of Melbourne*, Melbourne: Melbourne University Press.
Scott, J. 1984, 'Class Analysis: Back to the Future', *Sociology* 28, 4.
Scott, R. (dir.) 1982, *Blade Runner*, the Blade Runner Partnership/Warner Brothers.
Scott, R. (dir.) 1992, *Blade Runner: The Director's Cut*, Blade Runner Partnership/Warner Brothers.
Sedgwick, P. 1976, 'The Two New Lefts', in D. Widgery (ed.) *The Left in Britain 1956–1968*, Harmondsworth: Penguin.
Seed, D. 2011, *Science Fiction: A Very Short Introduction*, Oxford: Oxford University Press.
Seed, D. 2012, *Under the Shadow: The Atomic Bomb and Cold War Narratives*, Kent, OH: Kent State University Press.
Serge, V. 1967, *Memoirs of a Revolutionary 1901–1941*, trans. P. Sedgwick, Oxford: Oxford University Press.
Serge, V. 1968, *The Case of Comrade Tulayev*, trans. W.R. Trask, Harmondsworth: Penguin.
Serle, G. 1973, *From Deserts the Prophets Come*, Melbourne: Heinemann.
Serle, P. 1949, *Dictionary of Australian Biography*, Vol. 2, Sydney: Angus and Robertson.
Shelley, M. 1980, *Frankenstein, or The Modern Prometheus*, M.K. Joseph (ed), Oxford: Oxford University Press.

Shelley, M. 1998, *The Last Man*, ed. M.D. Paley, Oxford: Oxford University Press [1826].
Shelley, P.B. 1931, *A Defence of Poetry* (with Sidney, P. *An Apology for Poetry*), ed. H.A. Needham, London: Ginn and Co.
Shiach, M. 1995, 'A Gendered History of Cultural Categories', in C. Prendergast (ed.) *Cultural Materialism: On Raymond Williams*, Minneapolis: University of Minnesota Press.
Shiner, L. 1992, 'Inside the Movement: Past, Present, and Future', in G. Slusser and T. Shippey (eds) *Fiction 2000: Cyberpunk and the Future of Narrative*, Athens: University of Georgia Press.
Shklovsky, V. 1965, 'Art as Technique', trans. L. Lemon and M. Reis, in L. Lemon and M. Reid (eds) *Russian Formalist Criticism: Four Essays*, Lincoln: University of Nebraska Press.
Shute, N. 1950, *A Town Like Alice*, London: Heinemann.
Shute, N. 1957, *On the Beach*, Melbourne: Heinemann.
Shute, N. 1984, *On the Beach*, Guilford: Ulverscroft.
Shute, N. 1990, *On the Beach*, London: Mandarin.
Shuttleworth, A. 1980, 'Two Working Papers in Cultural Studies', in P. Davison et al. (eds) *Literary Taste, Culture and Mass Communication: Vol. 14: The Cultural Debate Part II*, Cambridge: Chadwyck-Healey.
Sieber, R., K.S. Robinson, E.G. Nisbet, S. Dillon and A. Milner 2014, 'Climate Change Narratives', *Loncon 3. The 72nd World Science Fiction Convention*, London: World Science Fiction Society.
Silverberg, R. 1964, *Time of the Great Freeze*, San Diego, CA: Holt, Rinehart and Winston.
SIPRI (Stockholm Institute for Peace Research) 2011, *SIPRI Yearbook 2011: Armaments, Disarmaments and International Security*, Oxford: Oxford University Press.
Slusser, G. 1989, 'Science Fiction in France: An Introduction', *Science Fiction Studies* 16, 3.
Slusser, G. 1992, 'The Frankenstein Barrier', in G. Slusser and T. Shippey (eds) *Fiction 2000: Cyberpunk and the Future of Narrative*, Athens: University of Georgia Press.
Smith, J. 1976, *Nevil Shute*, Boston: Twayne Publishers.
Smith, V. 1981, 'Poetry', in L. Kramer (ed.) *The Oxford History of Australian Literature*, Melbourne: Oxford University Press.
Solomon, S. et al. 2007, 'Summary for Policymakers', in *Climate Change 2007: The Physical Science Basis. Contribution of Working Group I to the Fourth Assessment Report of the Intergovernmental Panel on Climate Change*, Cambridge: Cambridge University Press.
Spivak, G.C. 1987, *In Other Worlds: Essays in Cultural Politics*, New York: Methuen.
Spivak, G.C. 2003, *Death of a Discipline*, New York: Columbia University Press.
Steiner, G. 1998, *No Passion Spent: Essays 1978–1995*, London: Faber.
Stephensen, P.R. 1986, *The Foundations of Culture in Australia*, Sydney: Allen and Unwin.

Sterling, B. 1986, 'Preface', in B. Sterling (ed.) *Mirrorshades: The Cyberpunk Anthology*, New York: Arbor House.

Sterling, B. 2009, *The Caryatids*, New York: Ballantine Books.

Stocker, T.F., D. Qin, G.-K. Plattner, M. Tignor, S.K. Allen, J. Boschung, A. Nauels, Y. Xia, V. Bex and P.M. Midgley (eds) 2013, 'Summary for Policymakers', *Climate Change 2013: The Physical Science Basis. Contribution of Working Group I to the Fifth Assessment Report of the Intergovernmental Panel on Climate Change*, Cambridge: Cambridge University Press.

Stratton, J. and I. Ang 1996, 'On the Impossibility of a Global Cultural Studies: "British" Cutural Studies in an "International" Frame', in D. Morley and K.-H. Chen (eds) *Stuart Hall: Critical Dialogues in Cultural Studies*, London: Routledge.

Stricker, M., J. Honisch, O. Plaschka, V. Tanger and S. Zurek 2014, 'The World at Worldcon: German-language SF/F', *Loncon 3. The 72nd World Science Fiction Convention*, London: World Science Fiction Society.

Suvin, D. 1979, *Metamorphoses of Science Fiction: on the Poetics and History of a Literary Genre*, New Haven: Yale University Press.

Suvin, D. 2000, 'Novum Is as Novum Does', in K. Sayer and J. Moore (eds) *Science Fiction, Critical Frontiers*, Basingstoke: Macmillan.

Tatchell, P. 1996, 'Cashing in, Coming out', *The Guardian*, supplement, August 29.

Thompson, E.P. 1955, *William Morris: Romantic to Revolutionary*, London: Lawrence and Wishart.

Thompson, E.P. 1961, 'The Long Revolution', *New Left Review* 9 and 10.

Thompson, E.P. 1963, *The Making of the English Working Class*, London: Victor Gollancz.

Thompson, E.P. 1965, 'The Peculiarities of the English', in R. Miliband and J. Saville (eds) *The Socialist Register 1965*, London: Merlin Press.

Thompson, E.P. 1977, *William Morris*, second edition, London: Merlin Press.

Thompson, E.P. 1978a, *The Poverty of Theory and Other Essays*, London: Merlin Press.

Thompson, E.P. 1978b, 'Eighteenth Century English Society: Class Struggle without Classes?', *Social History* 3, 2.

Thompson, E.P. 1980, 'Notes on Exterminism, the Last Stage of Civilization', *New Left Review* 121.

Threadgold, T. et al. 1986, 'Preface' to *Semiotics – Ideology – Language*, Sydney: Sydney Association for Studies in Society and Culture.

Todorov, T. 1973, 'The Structural Analysis of Literature: The Tales of Henry James', in D. Robey (ed.) *Structuralism: An Introduction*, Oxford: Oxford University Press.

Tönnies, F. 1955, *Community and Association*, trans. C.P. Loomis, London: Routledge and Kegan Paul.

Torjanow, I. 2011, *Eis Tau*, München: Carl Hanser Verlag.

Toronto *Telos* Group 1976, 'Short Journal Reviews', *Telos* 27.

Touraine, A. 1981, *The Voice and the Eye: An Analysis of Social Movements*, trans. A. Duff, Cambridge: Cambridge University Press.
Trilling, L. 1967, *Beyond Culture*, Harmondsworth: Penguin.
Trotsky, L. 1960, *Literature and Revolution*, trans. R. Strunsky, Ann Arbor: University of Michigan Press.
Trotsky, L. 1969, 'The Permanent Revolution', in *The Permanent Revolution and Results and Prospects*, New York: Pathfinder Press.
Trotsky, L. 1972, 'Our Differences', in *1905*, New York: Vintage Books.
Trotsky, L. 1973a, *The Transitional Programme for Socialist Revolution*, New York: Pathfinder Press.
Trotsky, L. 1973b, *On Britain*, New York: Pathfinder Press.
Tulloch, J. and H. Jenkins 1995, *Science Fiction Audiences: Watching Dr Who and Star Trek*, London: Routledge.
Tuomainen, A. 2010, *Parantaja*, Helsinki: Helsinki-kirjat.
Tuomainen, A. 2013, *The Healer*, trans. Lola Rogers, New York: Henry Holt and Company.
Turner, G. [George] 1978, *Beloved Son*, London: Faber and Faber.
Turner, G. 1981, *Vaneglory*, London: Faber and Faber.
Turner, G. 1983, *Yesterday's Men*, London: Faber and Faber.
Turner, G. 1985, 'The Fittest', in D. King and R. Blackford (eds) *Urban Fantasies*, Melbourne: Ebony Books.
Turner, G. 1987a, *The Sea and Summer*, London: Faber and Faber.
Turner, G. 1987b, *Drowning Towers*, New York: Arbor House.
Turner, G. 1990, *A Pursuit of Miracles: Eight Stories*, Adelaide: Aphelion Publications.
Turner, G. 1991, *Brainchild*, New York: William Morrow.
Turner, G. 1993, *The Destiny Makers*, New York: William Morrow.
Turner, G. 1994, *Genetic Soldier*, New York: William Morrow.
Turner, G. 1998, 'And Now Time Doth Waste Me', in J. Dann and J. Webb (eds) *Dreaming Down-Under*, Sydney: Voyager.
Turner, G. 1999, *Down There in Darkness*, New York: Tor Books.
Turner, G. 2013, *The Sea and Summer*, London: Gollancz.
Turner, G. [Graeme] 1990, *British Cultural Studies: An Introduction*, London: Unwin Hyman.
Turner, G. 1993, *National Fictions: Literature, Film and the Construction of Australian Narrative*, Sydney: Allen and Unwin.
Turner, G. 1996, 'Discipline Wars: Australian Studies, Cultural Studies and the Analysis of National Culture', *Journal of Australian Studies* 50/51.
Turner, I. 1968, *The Australian Dream*, Melbourne: Sun Books.
UNESCO 1963–99, *Statistical Yearbook*, Paris: UNESCO.
UNESCO 1978, *Statistical Yearbook*, 1977 Paris: UNESCO.

UNESCO 1990, *UNESCO Statistical Yearbook*, Paris: UNESCO.
UNESCO 1999, *UNESCO Statistical Yearbook*, Paris: UNESCO.
UNESCO 2013, *Index Translationum*, Paris: UNESCO. http://www.unesco.org/xtrans/bsstatexp.aspx?crit1L=5&nTyp=min&topN=50. Accessed August 8 2014.
United Nations, Department of Economic and Social Affairs 2010, *World Population Prospects, the 2010 Revision*, New York: United Nations. http://esa.un.org/wpp/Other-Information/faq.htm#q3. Last accessed 31 May 2012.
Vallorani, N. 2005, '"The Invisible Wells" in European Cinema and Television', in P. Parrinder and J.S. Partington (eds) *The Reception of H.G. Wells in Europe*, London: Continuum.
VanderMeer, A. and J. 2008, *The New Weird*, San Francisco: Tachyon Publications.
Van Hise, J. 1982, 'Interview with Philip K. Dick', *Starlog*, February.
Van Neerven, E. 2014, *Heat and Light*, St Lucia: University of Queesland Press.
Van Vogt, A.E. 1975, *Reflections of A.E. van Vogt: The Autobiography of a Science Fiction Giant*, Lakemont: Fictioneer Books.
Veblen, T. 1912, *Theory of the Leisure Class: An Economic Study of Institutions*, New York: Macmillan [first published 1899].
Veiras, D. 2001, *L'Histoire des Sévarambes*, ed. A. Rosenberg, Paris: Champion [1679].
Veiras, D. 2006, *The History of the Sevarambians: A Utopian Novel*, ed. J.C. Laursen and C. Masroori, New York: State University of New York Press [1675–1679].
Volosinov, V.N. 1973, *Marxism and the Philosophy of Language*, trans. L. Matejka and I.R. Titunik, New York: Seminar Press.
Wachowski, A. and L. Wachowski (dir.) 1999, *The Matrix*, Groucho II Film Partnership/Village Roadshow Pictures/Warner Brothers.
Waldock, A.J.A. 1951, *Sophocles the Dramatist*, Cambridge: Cambridge University Press.
Waldock, A.J.A. 1961, *Paradise Lost and Its Critics*, Cambridge: Cambridge University Press.
Walker, J. (ed.) 1991, *Halliwell's Film Guide*, 8th ed., London: Harper Collins.
Wallerstein, I. 2000, 'World-Systems Analysis', in *The Essential Wallerstein*, New York: The New Press.
Wallerstein, I. 2004, *World-Systems Analysis: An Introduction*, Durham: Duke University Press.
Walsh, B., M. Elliott, J.E. Stiglitz, M. Grunwald, L. Blue, J. Stein, O. Morton, A. Baker, T. Padgett, P. Gumbel, L. Cendrowicz, F. Krupp, A. Smith, B. Powell, T. McGirk, B. Schwan, A. Ramzy, A.L. Butters, H. Beech, M. Singh, A. Perry, S. Faris, K. Mahr and W. Boston 2008, 'Heroes of the Environment 2008: A Special Report on the Eco-Pioneers Fighting for a Cleaner, Greener Future', *Time*, September 24.
Walton, R. 2003, 'Utopian and Dystopian Impulses in Australia', *Overland* 173.
Ward, R. 1966, *The Australian Legend*, Melbourne: Oxford University Press.

Watson, G. 1977, *The Leavises, the 'Social' and the Left*, Swansea: Brynmill.

Watt, D. 1996, 'The Manuscript Revisions of *Brave New World*', in J. Mecker (ed.), *Critical Essays on Aldous Huxley*, New York: G.K. Hall & Co.

Webb, S. and Webb, B. 1937, *Soviet Communism: A New Civilization*, London: Victor Gollancz.

Weber, M. 1921, *Die rationalen und soziologischen Grundlagen der Musik*, Tübingen: J.C.B. Mohr.

Weber, M. 1930, *The Protestant Ethic and the Spirit of Capitalism*, trans. T. Parsons, London: Unwin.

Weber, M. 1948, *From Max Weber: Essays in Sociology*, ed. H.H. Gerth and C.W. Mills, London: Routledge and Kegan Paul.

Weber, M. 1952, *Ancient Judaism*, trans. H.H. Gerth and D. Martindale, New York: Free Press.

Weber, M. 1964, *The Theory of Social and Economic Organization*, trans. A.M. Henderson and T. Parsons, New York: Free Press.

Wellek, R. and Warren, A. 1976, *Theory of Literature*, Harmondsworth: Penguin.

Wells, H.G. 2005, *A Modern Utopia*, ed. G. Glaeys and P. Parrinder, London: Penguin [1905].

Wells, H.G. 1923, *Men Like Gods*, London: Cassell.

Wells, H.G. 1924, *The Dream*, London: Jonathan Cape.

Wells, H.G. 1993, *The Shape of Things to Come: The Ultimate Revolution*, ed. J. Hammond, London: Everyman [1933].

Wells, H.G. 2005, *The War of the Worlds*, ed. P. Parrinder, London: Penguin [1898].

West, C. 1995, 'In Memoriam: The Legacy of Raymond Williams', in C. Prendergast (ed.) *Cultural Materialism: On Raymond Williams*, Minneapolis: University of Minnesota Press.

Widdowson, P. 1982, 'The Crisis in English Studies', in P. Widdowson (ed.) *Re-Reading English*, London: Methuen.

Wikipedia 2012, 'List of countries by unemployment rate', *Wikipedia, the free encyclopedia*. http://en.wikipedia.org/wiki/List_of_countries_by_unemployment_rate. Last accessed 31 May 2012.

Wilcox, R. and J.P. Williams 1996, '"What do you think?": *The X-Files*, liminality and gender pleasure', in David Lavery, Angela Hague and Maria Cartwright (eds) *Deny All Knowledge: Reading the X-Files*, London: Faber.

Wilde, W.H. et al. (eds) 1985, *The Oxford Companion to Australian Literature*, Melbourne: Oxford University Press.

Willey, B. 1972, *The Seventeenth Century Background*, Harmondsworth: Penguin.

Williams, P. 2011, *Race, Ethnicity and Nuclear War*, Liverpool: Liverpool University Press.

Williams, R. 1958, 'Culture is Ordinary', in N. Mackenzie (ed) *Conviction*, London: MacGibbon and Kee.

Williams, R. 1962, *Communications*, Harmondsworth: Penguin.

Williams, R. 1963, *Culture and Society 1780–1950*, Harmondsworth: Penguin (first published London, Chatto and Windus, 1958).

Williams, R. 1965, *The Long Revolution*, Harmondsworth: Penguin (first published London, Chatto and Windus, 1961).

Williams, R. 1966, *Modern Tragedy*, London: Chatto and Windus.

Williams, R. 1971, *George Orwell*, New York: Viking Press.

Williams, R. 1973a, *Drama from Ibsen to Brecht*, Harmondsworth: Penguin (first published London, Chatto and Windus, 1968).

Williams, R. 1973b, *The Country and the City*, New York: Oxford University Press.

Williams, R. 1974a, *The English Novel: From Dickens to Lawrence*, St Albans: Paladin (first published London, Chatto and Windus, 1970).

Williams, R. 1974b, *Television: Technology and Cultural Form*, Glasgow: Fontana.

Williams, R. 1976a, *Communications*, third edition, Harmondsworth: Penguin.

Williams, R. 1976b, *Keywords: A Vocabulary of Culture and Society*, Glasgow: Fontana.

Williams, R. 1977, *Marxism and Literature*, Oxford: Oxford University Press.

Williams, R. 1978, *The Volunteers*, London: Eyre Methuen.

Williams, R. 1979, *Politics and Letters: Interviews with New Left Review*, London: New Left Books.

Williams, R. 1980a, 'Notes on Marxism in Britain since 1945', in *Problems in Materialism and Culture: Selected Essays*, London: Verso.

Williams, R. 1980b, 'Base and Superstructure in Marxist Cultural Theory', in *Problems in Materialism and Culture*, London: New Left Books.

Williams, R. 1980c, 'Utopia and Science Fiction', in *Problems in Materialism and Culture*, London: New Left Books [first published in *Science Fiction Studies* 5, 3 (1978)].

Williams, R. 1981, *Culture*, Glasgow: Fontana.

Williams, R. 1983, *Towards 2000*, London: Chatto and Windus.

Williams, R. 1984a, *Writing in Society*, London: Verso.

Williams, R. 1984b, 'Seeing a Man Running', in D. Thompson (ed.) *The Leavises: Recollections and Impressions*, Cambridge: Cambridge University Press.

Williams, R. 1988, 'Science Fiction', *Science Fiction Studies* 15, 3 [first published in *The Highway* 48 (1956)].

Williams, R. 1989a, *Resources of Hope: Culture, Democracy, Socialism*, ed. R. Gable, London: Verso.

Williams, R. 1989b, *The Politics of Modernism: Against the New Conformists*, ed. T. Pinkney, London: Verso.

Williams, R. 1989c, 'Terror', in *Raymond Williams on Television: Selected Writings*, ed. A. O'Connor, London: Routledge [first published in *The Listener* 3 June (1971)].

Williams, R. 1989d, 'A Defence of Realism', in *What I Came To Say*, ed. N. Belton, F. Mulhern and J. Taylor, London: Hutchinson Radius.

Williams, R. 1991, 'Nineteen Eighty-Four in 1984', in *Orwell*, third edition, London: Fontana.
Williams, R. and Orrom, M. 1954, *Preface to Film*, London: Film Drama.
Williams, R. and E.W. Said 1989, 'Appendix: Media, Margins and Modernity', in R. Williams *The Politics of Modernism: Against the New Conformists*, ed. T. Pinkney, London: Verso.
Wilson, S. 1995, *Cultural Materialism: Theory and Practice*, Oxford: Blackwell.
Winterson, J. 2007, *The Stone Gods*, London: Hamish Hamilton.
Wittgenstein, L. 1958, *Philosophische Untersuchungen, Philosophical Investigations*, trans. G.E.M. Anscombe, Oxford: Basil Blackwell [first published 1953].
Wolff, J. 1983, *Aesthetics and the Sociology of Art*, London: George Allen and Unwin.
Wood, B., K. Donaldson, G. Brown, G. Erskine, D. Shalvey, D. Zezelj, J.P. Leon, D. Stewart and J. Bellaire 2012–14, *The Massive*, Milwaukee: Dark Horse Comics.
Woodhouse, A.S.P. 1965, *Puritanism and Liberty*, London: Dent.
Woolf, V. 1966, 'Mr Bennett and Mrs Brown', *Collected Essays* I, London: Hogarth Press.
Wordsworth, W. 1949, 'The Ruined Cottage, Addendum to MS, 58–64', in *Poetical Works*, ed. E. de Selincourt and H. Darbishire, Oxford: Oxford University Press [1798].
Wright, A. 2013, *The Swan Book*, Sydney: Giramondo.
Wright, E.O. 1979, *Class, Crisis, and the State*, London: Verso.
Wright, E.O. 1985, *Classes*, London: Verso.
Wright, E.O. 1989, 'A General Framework for the Analysis of Class Structure', in E.O. Wright (ed.) *The Debate on Classes*, London: Verso.
Wright, E.O. 1989a, 'Rethinking, Once Again, the Concept of Class Structure', in E.O. Wright (ed.) *The Debate on Classes*, London: Verso.
Wright, E.O. 1994, *Interrogating Inequality: Essays on Class Analysis, Socialism and Marxism*, London: Verso.
Wright, E.O. 1997, *Class Counts: Comparative Studies in Class Analysis*, Cambridge: Cambridge University Press.
Wykes, O. 1974, 'Edward Ellis Morris', in D. Pike (ed.) *Australian Dictionary of Biography*, Vol. 5, Melbourne: Melbourne University Press.
Wyndham, J. 1953, *The Kraken Wakes*, London: Michael Joseph.
Yule, G. 1958, *The Independents in the English Civil War*, Cambridge: Cambridge University Press.
Zamiatine, E. 1929, *Nous autres*, trad. B. Cauvet-Duhamel, Paris: Gallimard.
Zamyatin, Y. 1952, *Mi*, New York: Chekhov Publishing House.
Zamyatin, Y. 1972, *We*, trans. M. Ginsburg, New York: Viking Press.
Zamyatin, E. 1997, 'Wells's Revolutionary Fairy-Tales', trans. L. Milne, in P. Parrinder (ed.) *H.G. Wells: The Critical Heritage*, London: Routledge.
Žižek, Slavoj 1993, *Tarrying with the Negative*, Durham: Duke University Press.

Index

Abbott, Tony   7
Abe, Kōbō   178, 444, 488
Abel, Alfred   389
Abensour, Miguel   373, 401
Abertheney, Robert   369, 385
Adam, Ian   84
Adams, Douglas   419, 420
Adams, Paul   237
Addison, Joseph   24
Adler, Max   200
Adorno, Theodor W.   6, 94, 126, 127, 138, 144, 145, 148, 156, 205, 229, 234, 264, 295, 343, 344, 345, 346, 352, 383, 384, 405, 406, 438, 463, 504
Agamben, Giorgio   135
Aldiss, Brian W.   161, 369, 383, 459, 489
Allende, Salvador   198, 210
Althusser, Louis   3, 120, 188, 189, 190, 191, 196, 198, 199, 201, 203, 205, 206, 207, 208, 211, 212, 213, 214, 218, 222, 223, 230, 241, 244, 246, 264, 287, 304, 306, 344, 347, 348, 350, 368
Altov, Genrikh   174, 444
Anderson, Benedict   30, 31, 32
Anderson, Gillian   404
Anderson, Perry   22, 23, 24, 26, 27, 29, 41, 49, 82, 187, 188, 194, 196, 198, 204, 205, 206, 207, 208, 209, 210, 211, 212, 213, 214, 215, 216, 217, 218, 219, 220, 221, 226, 232, 255, 263, 266, 302, 305, 368, 461, 462
Andrevon, Jean-Pierre   159
Ang, Ien   298, 300, 302
Anno, Hideaki   179
Archibald, J.F.   32, 36, 130
Aridjis, Homero   490
Aristophanes,   458, 459, 460
Aristotle,   119
Arnaud, G.-J.   173, 444
Arnold, Matthew   122, 123, 132, 242, 424
Aronofsky, Darren   489
Arrhenius, Svante   487
Ashcroft, Bill   84, 134, 304
Ashley, Mike   165, 456
Asimov, Isaac   163, 177, 178, 441, 444, 501
Astaire, Fred   78
Attlee, Clement   451

Atwood, Margaret   166, 395, 421, 422, 436, 437, 443, 452, 453, 471, 482, 490, 501, 502
Auerbach, Erich   95
Austen, Jane   11
Austin, J.L.   140
Ayer, A.J.   140

Baccolini, Rafaella   375
Bacigalupi, Paolo   178, 181, 482, 489
Bacon, Francis   363, 386, 458, 463, 466
Badiou, Alain   135, 436, 437
Badley, Linda   404
Baer, Hans   479
Baker, Brian   492
Bakhtin, Mikhail   231
Baldick, Chris   15, 21, 22, 25, 26
Balibar, Étienne   3, 244
Ballard, J.G.   1, 163, 165, 169, 173, 369, 443, 444, 483
Balzac, Honoré de   491
Bandt, Adam   498
Banks, Iain M   173, 428, 443, 444
Barnaby, Paul   173
Barnes, John   30
Barr, Robert   158
Barr, Marleen   395
Barrett, Michèle   146, 304
Barthes, Roland   6, 44, 45, 94, 119, 127, 223, 230, 234, 238, 249, 270, 288, 291, 344, 345, 346
Baudrillard, Jean   86, 147, 320, 357, 358, 387, 388, 389, 404
Bauman, Zygmunt   87, 147, 357, 358
Bazin, André   168
Bedford, Sybille   424, 429
Beilharz, Peter   311
Bell, Andrea L.   487
Bell, Daniel   83, 84, 86
Bell, Tracey   411
Bellamy, Edward   173, 178, 373, 428
Belsey, Catherine   101
Belyaev, Alexander Romanovitch   174, 444
Benjamin, Walter   144, 145, 155, 231, 234, 351, 389, 443
Bennett, Tony   18, 94, 95, 109, 110, 146, 270, 291, 295, 305, 314, 319, 320, 321, 322, 342

Benson, Amber   406
Berkeley, George, Bishop of Cloyne   49
Bernstein, Basil   233
Bernstein, Carl   408
Bernstein, Eduard   252, 440, 441
Besson, Luc   175, 489
Bhabha, Homi K.   304
Bilenkin, Dimitri Aleksandrovich   174, 444
Bin Laden, Osama   358
Bindoff, N.L.   481
Blainey, Geoffrey   30, 41
Blair, Tony   2, 114, 309, 356, 357, 358, 376
Blish, James   163, 366, 367, 369, 381, 385, 386
Bloch, Ernst   361, 382, 439, 440, 504
Blomkamp, Neill   489
Bloom, Harold   93, 94, 95, 98, 102, 105, 109, 111, 130, 131, 135, 168, 169, 181, 483, 484, 491, 497, 499, 501
Blucas, Marc   405
Boer, Roland   419, 437
Bogdanov, Alexander   174, 444
Bogdanovich, Peter   411
Bois, Guy   212
Bong, Joon-Ho   489
Bono, Cher   409, 410, 411
Boozer, Jack (Jr)   399
Boreanaz, David   405
Borges, Jorge Luis   174
Böttcher, Sven   181, 489
Bould, Mark   167, 168
Boulle, Pierre   173, 444
Bourdieu, Pierre   3, 17, 86, 112, 113, 114, 115, 116, 117, 118, 119, 120, 121, 122, 123, 124, 125, 142, 143, 145, 148, 149, 150, 151, 152, 153, 160, 161, 174, 224, 233, 291, 293, 294, 295, 296, 297, 315, 316, 317, 319, 320, 321, 322, 323, 324, 325, 326, 333, 336, 337, 338, 482, 483, 484, 485, 497, 498
Boyle, T.C.   490
Bradbury, Malcolm   81, 85
Bradbury, Ray   365, 367
Bradley, James   500, 502
Brailsford, H.N.   52
Brecht, Bertolt   234, 246, 345, 504
Brenac, P.   15, 16
Brendon, Nicholas   405
Brenkman, John   352
Brereton, John le Gay   34
Bruno, Giordano   458

Bruno, Giuliana   392
Brussolo, Serge   173, 444
Buckley, Vincent   37, 39, 40
Bukharin, Nikolai   265
Bulgakov, Mikhail   174, 176, 444
Bulwer-Lytton, Edward G.E., 1st Baron Lytton   171, 486
Bulychev, Kirill   174, 444
Bunyan, John   55
Bürger, Peter   6, 85, 86, 145, 164
Burgmann, Verity   197, 315, 479
Burianyk, M.   179
Burke, Edmund   126, 270
Burnet, Sir Macfarlane   477, 478
Burnham, James   379, 380, 381, 423, 453, 454
Burns, Emile   420
Burton, Tim   178, 396, 444
Bush, George W.   354, 356, 358, 495
Bussell, Jan   158, 426
Butler, Octavia   166, 178
Byron, George Gordon, 6th Baron   410

Callinicos, Alex   3, 82, 265
Calof, Grant   489
Calvin, John   47, 51, 265
Calvino, Italo   174
Cameron, James   155, 156, 178, 444
Campanella, Tommaso   458, 459
Campbell, J.W.   161, 164, 167, 178, 383, 422, 444
Cantrell, Leon   30
Čapek, Josef   426
Čapek, Karel   6, 153, 154, 155, 158, 160, 168, 174, 176, 389, 422, 426, 427, 433, 434, 435, 443, 444, 447, 453
Carchedi, Guglielmo   327, 328
Carlyle, Thomas   11, 12, 464
Carpenter, Charisma   405
Carter, Chris   158, 160, 178, 403, 404, 410, 411, 412, 414, 444
Cartwright, Edmund   463
Casanova, Pascale   145, 152
Caudwell, Christopher   272
Cauvet-Duhamel, B.   453
Cevasco, Maria Elisa   361
Chaucer, Geoffrey   94, 131
Chekhov, Anton   432
Chifley, Ben   37
Childe, Vere Gordon   41
Christoff, Peter   471, 480, 492

INDEX

Christopher, John   365, 488
Cixous, Hélène   47
Clark, Manning   41
Clarke, Arthur C.   158, 173, 178, 300, 369, 444
Cliff, Tony   260, 265
Clinton, Bill   143, 417, 418
Clute, John   157, 163, 168, 169, 383, 422, 444, 486
Cobbett, William   270
Cockrell, Roger   176
Cohen, G.A.   254, 327, 436
Coleridge, Samuel Taylor   271
Colletti, Lucio   205
Collier, Thomas   53, 54
Collini, Stefan   301, 319
Comte, Auguste   144, 146
Connelly, Jennifer   390
Conrad, Joseph   11
Contner, James A.   412
Cook, John R.   158
Cornea, Christine   156
Coser, Lewis A.   146
Cousin, Susan   7
Cowling, G.H.   36, 37, 129, 302
Crichton, Michael   181, 489
Crick, Bernard   424, 449
Croll, James   487
Cromwell, Oliver   4, 48, 50, 54, 55, 64, 98
Cronenberg, David   168, 380
Crouse, Lindsay   412
Crutzen, Paul   488
Csicsery-Ronay, Istvan (Jr)   445
Culler, Jonathan   224
Cunningham, Stuart   314
Curtin, John   36
Curtius, Ernest Robert   95
Cyrano de Bergerac, Hercule-Savinien   458, 459

Dahrendorf, Ralf   333, 334
Dante, Alighieri   65, 66, 441
Dantec, Maurice G.   163, 173, 444
Darwin, Erasmus   459
Davies, Russell T.   160
Davidson, Rjurik,   7
Davis, William B.   406
De Burgh, Hugo   158
De Certeau, Michel   167
D'Ennery, Adolphe   151, 154

De la Bretonne,   468
De Laurentis, Dino   494
De Man, Paul   243
De Manuel, Jordi   490
Debray, Régis   225
Defoe, Daniel   24
Delany, Samuel R.   166, 178, 375, 444, 459
Della Volpe, Galvano   205
Denisof, Alexis   407
Derrida, Jacques   46, 142, 223, 224, 226, 227, 234, 238, 244, 286, 291, 297
Descartes, René   49, 52
Desser, David   107, 109
Deutscher, Isaac   180, 181, 182, 216
Dick, Philip K.   105, 106, 107, 108, 163, 164, 169, 178, 390, 440, 441, 443, 444, 466
Dickens, Charles   93, 118, 172, 275, 486
Diogenes,   458
Disch, Thomas M.   165
Docker, John   37, 38, 39, 40, 42, 43, 227, 228, 229, 244, 245
Dollimore, Jonathan   350, 351, 384
Donne, John   356
Dostoyevsky, Fyodor   447
Doyle, Brian   25
Duchovny, David   404
Dudgeon, Robert Ellis   469
Dumas, Alexandre   172, 445, 464, 466, 486
Duncan, W.G.K.   36, 129
During, Simon   84, 131, 341
Durkheim, Émile   4, 119, 143, 144, 145, 270, 295, 325, 344
Dürrenmatt, Friedrich   6, 158
Dussel, Enrique   182

Eagleton, Terry   13, 18, 19, 24, 25, 29, 30, 31, 32, 35, 38, 42, 43, 223, 224, 226, 229, 230, 231, 239, 240, 248, 288, 290, 295, 296, 297, 344, 345, 351, 352, 353, 361, 438, 440
Easthope, Anthony   304, 342
Eco, Umberto   94
Eder, Klaus   320
Egan, Greg   443, 468
Ehrenreich, Barbara   328
Ehrenreich, John   328
Eisner, Eric   489
Eliot, George   11
Eliot, T.S.   11, 48, 65, 95, 98, 132, 271, 272, 273, 363, 364, 366, 382, 424

Ellis, Kimberley 182
Ellison, Harlan 1, 162, 163, 165, 178, 444
Emmerich, Roland 489, 491
Emmison, Michael 319, 320, 321, 322
Emtsev, Mikhail Tikhonovich 174, 444
Engels, Friedrich 50, 60, 61, 170, 193, 209, 210, 211, 252, 253, 254, 256, 267, 318, 418, 420, 434, 438, 442, 477, 479, 504, 505
Engler, Ivan 489
Epstein, Michael 160, 406, 407
Erikson, Robert 320, 331
Ermshwiller, Carol 166
Escarpit, Robert 6, 146
Etter, Ralph 489
Evans, Raymond 92, 321

Fancher, Hampton 106
Farmer, Philip Hosé 165
Fehér, Ferenc 80, 259, 265
Felperin, Howard 39, 228, 229, 230, 231, 234, 235, 236, 237, 238, 239, 240, 242, 243, 244, 245, 249, 250
Fénelon, François 363, 386
Ferrara, Fernando 361
Fialkowski, Konrad 174, 444
Field, C.R. 481
Fitzgerald, Scott W. 181
Fitzhardinge, L.F. 92
Fitzpatrick, Brian 302
Flaubert, Gustave 149, 464
Fleck, Dirk C. 182, 489, 504
Flew, Anthony 140
Ford, Harrison 105, 390
Forry, Steven Earl 152
Forster, E.M. 163, 369, 424
Foucault, Michel 44, 88, 119, 120, 225, 227, 231, 232, 233, 238, 243, 244, 246, 291, 292, 293, 294, 295, 297, 350, 498
Fourier, Charles 441, 504
Fowles, John 14
Fox, George 72
France, Anatole 168, 173, 444
Frankel, Boris 225, 311, 312, 313
Fraser, Nancy 227
Fraser, Joseph 469
Freedman, Carl 154
Freeman, E.A. 16, 18
Freud, Sigmund 436
Froelich, Gustav 389

Frow, John 228, 229, 230, 231, 232, 233, 234, 235, 236, 237, 238, 239, 240, 241, 242, 243, 244, 245, 246, 247, 249, 250, 251, 302, 315, 316, 318, 319, 320, 321, 322, 325, 326, 337, 338, 339
Fryer, Peter 199
Fukuyama, Francis 389
Fury, David 412

Gail, Otto Willi 174, 444
Gale, Stewart 410
Galeen, Henry 155
García Márquez, Gabriel 170
Gardner, Ava 78, 80
Garnham, Nicholas 115, 123, 125, 293, 294, 320
Gay, Peter 253
Gee, Maggie 490
Gellar, Sarah Michelle 405
Gellner, Ernest 30, 140, 141, 142, 143, 145, 147
George, Heinrich 395
Gernsback, Hugo 161, 162, 167, 174, 177, 178, 383, 422, 444, 504
Gibbons, Dave 163
Gibson, William 163, 178, 377, 440, 443, 444, 459
Giddens, Anthony 114, 299, 335
Gilbert, Sandra M. 101
Glucksmann, André 225
Glukhovsky, Dimitri 180, 182
Godard, Jean-Luc 168
Goethe, Johann Wolfgang von 103, 136, 170, 485
Goldberg, S.L. 37, 38, 39, 40, 41
Golding, William 367
Goldmann, Lucien 1, 2, 3, 44, 45, 46, 47, 48, 49, 50, 77, 115, 144, 145, 148, 192, 205, 223, 229, 247, 248, 278, 288, 368
Goldthorpe, John H. 320, 321, 322, 323, 327, 331, 332, 333, 334, 335, 336
Gollan, Robin 197
Gordon, Joan 166
Gore, Al 496
Gouldner, Alvin 22, 146
Arthur, George, Lieutenant-Governor 465
Gramsci, Antonio 8, 87, 88, 121, 195, 197, 200, 202, 205, 215, 216, 219, 263, 264, 268, 278, 279, 280, 281, 282, 283, 295, 304, 305, 306, 307, 308, 350, 368

INDEX

Grass, Günter   124
Green, Martin   29
Greenblatt, Stephen   133, 351, 361
Greenland, Colin   165
Greimas, Algirdas Julien   440
Gribbin, John   488
Grossberg, Lawrence   131, 305
Grossman, David   412
Grousset, Paschal   151
Gubar, Susan   101
Gunew, Sneja   314

Habermas, Jürgen   24, 31, 82, 226, 295, 296, 297, 343, 344, 345, 361, 498
Hall, Joseph   468
Hall, Stuart   127, 131, 270, 298, 300, 305, 306, 307, 308, 309, 310, 313, 341, 347, 348, 361
Hallas, Duncan   253
Halliday, M.A.K.   231
Hand, Richard J.   157
Hannigan, Alyson   405
Hanson, Pauline   312
Haraway, Donna   389
Harding, D.W.   102
Hardy, Frank   13, 237
Harland, Richard   238
Harris, Sir Arthur, 1st Baronet   358
Harris, Max   91
Harris, Nigel   3, 267
Harrison, Thomas   54
Hart, Kevin   6
Hartman, Geoffrey   132, 226
Harvey, David   135, 392
Hashimoto, Kohji   178
Hauer, Rutger   105, 390
Hawke, Bob   310, 311, 312
Hayles, N. Katherine   389
Head, Anthony Stewart   405
Head, Dominic   352
Hegel, Georg Wilhelm Friedrich   84, 195, 247
Heglin, Peter   468
Heidegger, Martin   141
Heinlein, Robert A.   163, 178, 444
Heldreth, Leonard G.   108, 399
Helford, Elyce Rae   417, 418
Heller, Agnes   145, 259, 265
Helm, Bridgette   389

Herbert, Edward, 1st Baron Herbert of Cherbury   52
Herder, Johann Gotfried   271
Hertzberg, George   412
Herzog, Arthur   488, 489, 490
Heseltine, H.P.   30, 39
Hexter, J.H.   193, 207
Hicklenton, John   489
Higgins, John   350, 351
Hill, Christopher   13, 99, 246
Hilton, Rodney   255
Hindess, Barry   226
Hirst, Paul Q.   226
Hitchens, Christopher   3, 5
Hitler, Adolf   84, 355
Ho, Chi Minh   219
Hoggart, Richard   6, 93, 94, 114, 124, 127, 131, 271, 272, 298, 299, 300, 320, 340, 341, 342, 343, 344, 346, 347, 348
Hohendahl, Peter   24, 38
Hollinger, Veronica   362, 382, 439
Holme, E.R.   34
Homer,   66
Honda, Ishirō   178
Hooke, Robert   463
Hope, Keith   320
Horkheimer, Max   6, 94, 126, 127, 145, 156, 229, 234, 249, 295, 344, 346, 383, 384, 405, 406, 463, 504
Horne, C.J.   36
Hoshi, Shinichi   178, 444
Houellebecq, Michel   6, 166, 168, 169, 173, 443, 444, 490, 501
Houghton, J.T.   488
Hoyle, Fred   173, 444
Hughes, Billy   92
Hugo, Victor   172, 486
Hume, David   49
Hunte, Otto   396
Hunter, Ian   314
Hurt, William   391
Huxley, Aldous   168, 173, 176, 365, 366, 367, 369, 373, 376, 380, 385, 422, 424, 425, 426, 427, 429, 431, 432, 433, 435, 444, 447, 448, 453
Huxley, T.H.   424
Huyssen, Andreas   86, 394, 398
Hyde, Edward, 1st Earl of Clarendon   73

Ibsen, Henrik   275, 277, 432
Inglis, Fred   364
Ireton, Henry   54

Jack, David   419
Jacobson, Howard   40
Jacoby, Russell   253
Jaensch, Dean   311
James, Edward   423
James, Henry   23, 44,
Jameson, Fredric   19, 46, 47, 77, 81, 82, 86, 88, 89, 90, 137, 145, 147, 149, 154, 164, 173, 224, 227, 230, 231, 247, 262, 309, 317, 345, 353, 377, 387, 388, 389, 395, 396, 401, 404, 415, 416, 419, 420, 421, 428, 438, 439, 440, 441, 442, 443, 444, 445, 446, 447, 448, 449, 450, 452, 453, 454, 455, 464, 465, 466, 467, 470, 486, 491, 493, 495, 499
Jardine, Lisa   352
Jefferies, Richard   487
Jenkins, Henry   167
Jeschke, Wolfgang   180, 181, 182, 490
Johnson, Richard   270, 300, 311, 346
Johnson, Samuel   75
Jones, Paul   123, 137, 138, 347
Jones, Trevor   391
Joyce, James   40, 424
Juszczyk, Andrzej   175

Kafka, Franz   128
Kant, Immanuel   44, 126, 357, 358
Kaplan, Ann E.   376
Kautsky, Karl   195, 252, 253, 254, 255, 256, 265
Keating, Paul   310, 311, 312
Keats, John   13
Kedourie, Elie   30, 141
Kermode, Frank   225
Kettelhut, Eric   396
Kidron, Michael   3, 217, 221, 261, 262, 265
Kingsolver, Barbara   490
Kirmess, C.H.   92
Klein, Naomi   113
Klein-Rogge, Rudolph   389
Kneale, Nigel   158
Knight, Damon   162
Knopfelmacher, Andrew   141
Knopfelmacher, Frank   141
Knox, John   51

Kolb, William M.   105, 106, 397
Komatsu, Sakyo   178, 444
Kornbluth, Cyril M.   444
Korsch, Karl   195, 200, 202, 205, 263, 295
Kramer, Leonie   39
Kramer, Stanley   78, 492
Kristal, Efrain   182
Kristeva, Julia   225
Krupskaya, Nadezhda Konstantinovna   42
Kruschev, Nikita Sergeyevich   265
Kubrick, Stanley   178, 444
Kuzui, Fran Rubel   405

Laclau, Ernesto   226, 305, 308
Lakatos, Imre   207
Lane, William   32
Lang, Fritz   155, 174, 175, 179, 369, 387, 389, 391, 392, 394, 398, 443, 444
Lash, Scott   86
Latham, Philip   365
Latour, Bruno   481
Laurenson, Diana T.   172
Lawrence, D.H.   40, 275, 424
Lawson, Henry   32, 34, 251
Lawson, Sylvia   361
Layh, Susanna   179
Le Guin, Ursula K.   158, 166, 178, 368, 372, 374, 375, 376, 378, 381, 385, 386, 395, 401, 428, 440, 441, 443, 444, 458
Leavis, F.R.   17, 18, 20, 21, 22, 27, 28, 29, 39, 40, 41, 48, 86, 98, 102, 117, 127, 128, 132, 248, 249, 271, 272, 273, 274, 287, 290, 295, 298, 299, 341, 344, 361, 364, 366, 367, 499
Leavis, Q.D.   102, 298, 300
Lee, Chang-Rae   490
Lee, S.E.   30, 32, 36
Leibniz, Gottfried Wilhelm   49
Lem, Stanisław   6, 168, 174, 176, 177, 441, 444
Lenin, Vladimir Ilyich   42, 198, 200, 202, 215, 216, 219, 256, 257, 258, 259, 260, 261, 262, 268, 307
Lentricchia, Frank   226, 227
Leonard, R.A.   36, 129
Leslie, Esther   343
Lessing, Doris   488
Levi, Primo   174
Lévi-Strauss, Claude   44, 120, 270, 344, 347
Lewis, C.S.   173, 444
Ligny, Jean-Marc   173, 490, 503

INDEX

Lilburne, John 53
Lindsay, Jack 41
Liska, General Alois 140
Liu, Cixin 499
Lob, Jacques 489
Locke, John 49, 58
Lofficier, Marc 168
Lofficier, Randy 168
Lovecraft, H.P. 163, 166
Lovell, Terry 232
Lovelock, James 489
Lowry, Brian 404, 407, 408, 416
Lucas, George 178, 444, 487, 489
Lucian of Samosata, 456, 458, 459, 460, 461, 462, 467
Luckhurst, Roger 165
Ludlum, Scott 498
Lukács, Georg 2, 28, 65, 66, 73, 144, 148, 192, 195, 200, 202, 205, 216, 224, 229, 234, 263, 289, 295, 353, 361, 368, 438, 442, 467
Luke, Saint 71, 434
Lumière, Auguste 155
Lumière, Louis 155
Lunacharsky, Anatoly Vasilyevich 42
Luther, Martin 51
Luxemburg, Rosa 200, 202, 215, 216, 252, 392, 454, 505
Lyotard, Jean-François 82, 83, 84, 85, 86, 147, 320

MacCabe, Colin 222, 225
MacCallum, Sir Mungo 30, 31, 33, 34, 129
MacDermott, Kathy 17, 19
Macdonnell, Diane 226
Macherey, Pierre 223, 229, 239, 350, 440
MacIntyre, Alasdair 258
Maclean, Marie 6
Macleod, Ken 173, 444
Maddox, Graham 311
Major, John 310
Mandel, Ernest 221, 257, 454
Mandela, Nelson 310
Mao, Zedong 219
Marcuse, Herbert 138, 253, 343, 344
Margot, Jean-Michel 151, 152
Markus, Andrew 92
Markus, Gyorgy 265
Marshall, George 491

Marsters, James 405
Marx, Karl 4, 5, 84, 118, 123, 144, 170, 193, 194, 195, 203, 208, 211, 223, 252, 253, 254, 255, 256, 263, 264, 265, 266, 267, 268, 284, 288, 290, 295, 315, 316, 318, 320, 326, 327, 328, 331, 336, 337, 338, 418, 434, 441, 442, 469, 478, 499, 505
Mauss, Marcel 119
Mayakovsky, Vladimir 167, 174, 444
McAuley, James 37, 39, 91
McEwan, Ian 181, 489
McFarlane, James 85
McLaren, Johh 303
McQueen, Humphrey 33
Méliès, Georges 155, 383
Mellor, Adrian 146
Menzies, Sir Robert 311, 312
Menzies, William Cameron 175, 423
Merchant, Brian 181, 483
Merle, Robert 173, 444
Merleau-Ponty, Maurice 262, 263
Merrick, Helen 395
Merril, Judith 163
Merrington, John 219
Meyer, A.G. 260
Miéville, China 163, 166, 167, 173, 441, 443, 444, 482
Milgate, W. 30, 31, 35, 129
Miliband, Ralph 141
Miller, Walter M. 369
Mills, C. Wright 21
Milner, Andrew 133, 138, 144, 164, 172, 179, 315, 337, 342, 361, 453, 485
Milner, David 355
Milner, James 355
Milton, John 2, 4, 5, 6, 12, 13, 29, 34, 47, 48, 50, 53, 54, 55, 56, 57, 58, 59, 60, 61, 62, 63, 64, 65, 66, 67, 68, 69, 70, 71, 72, 73, 74, 75, 76, 77, 94, 98, 99, 100, 101, 102, 103, 106, 110, 131, 251, 290
Mitchell, A.G. 30
Mitchell, David 465, 490, 491, 501, 502
Miyazaki, Hayao 489
Molina-Gavilán, Yolanda 487
Moorcock, Michael 1, 163, 165, 173, 444, 488
Moore, G.E. 140
Moore, Alan 163
More, Sir Thomas 428, 440, 441, 457, 458, 464, 466, 469, 488, 504

Moretti, Franco   6, 14, 128, 129, 135, 136, 137, 138, 144, 145, 148, 170, 171, 172, 174, 177, 180, 182, 183, 444, 445, 482, 483, 485, 486, 492
Morin, J.L.   489
Morris, E.E.   30, 35, 129
Morris, Meaghan   80, 81, 302, 314, 318
Morris, William   173, 215, 248, 363, 364, 365, 366, 369, 371, 373, 374, 385, 386, 401, 428, 437
Mosley, Walter   166
Mouffe, Chantal   226, 305, 308
Moylan, Tom   375, 446, 499, 503, 504
Mulhern, Francis   27, 28, 132, 373
Mulvey, Laura   394, 408
Murakami, Haruki   178, 444
Murdoch, Rupert   130, 318, 403, 407
Murphy, Peter   463
Murray-Smith, Stephen   130, 302

Nairn, Tom   30, 204, 205, 218
Nelson, Brian   419
Nettle, J.P.   253
Neufeld, Josh   489
Neuhaus, Nele   181, 489
Newbolt, Sir Henry   26, 34, 129
Newton, Sir Isaac   463
Nicholls, Peter   157, 163, 168, 169, 383, 422, 444
Nisbet, Euan G.   492
Nolan, Christopher   489, 491
Noxon, Marti   412

O'Bannon, Rockne S.   160
O'Brien, Richard   391
O'Connor, Alan   277
O'Flinn, Paul   103
Oates, Titus   76
Obama, Barack   496
O'Hurley, John   409
Ong, Walter J.   97
Ono, Kent   407, 417, 418
Orgill, Daniel   488
Orrom, Michael   274
Orwell, George   5, 6, 126, 158, 168, 173, 176, 201, 202, 364, 365, 366, 367, 369, 370, 371, 373, 376, 379, 380, 381, 385, 393, 401, 419, 420, 421, 422, 423, 424, 425, 426, 427, 429, 430, 431, 433, 434, 435, 436, 437, 438, 443, 444, 446, 447, 448, 449, 450, 451, 452, 453, 454, 455
Oshii, Mamoru   163, 179
Oshikawa, Shunrō   174
Otomo, Katsuhiro   179
Overell, Richard   419
Owen, Robert   504
Owens, Chris   409
Ozolis, Uldiz   17

Palmer, D.J.   16
Palmer, Nettie   33, 39
Palmer, Vance   30, 33, 39, 302
Parkin, Frank   316
Parnov, Eremei Iudovich   174, 444
Parrinder, Patrick   173, 363, 365, 382
Parsons, Talcott   190
Pascal, Blaise   44
Patrick, Robert   404
Pêcheux, Michel   231
Peck, Gregory   78
Penley, Constance   167, 168
Peoples, David   106
Perceval, Lieutenant-General Arthur Ernest   36
Peter, John   69
Petrie, Douglas   412
Phillips, A.A.   302, 303
Pickering, Michael   120
Piercy, Marge   166, 178, 395, 428, 443, 444
Pinkney, Tony   361, 376, 377
Platonov, Andrey Platonovich   174, 444
Playfair, Nigel   158, 426, 433
Plekhanov, Georgi   229
Plutarch,   103
Poe, Edgar Allan   173, 177, 178, 383
Poggioli, Renato   164
Pohl, Frederick   444
Poovey, Mary   103
Popper, Karl   141, 190, 207
Posnett, H.M.   126
Pot, Pol   219
Potter, Dennis   160
Poulantzas, Nicos   205, 304, 327, 328, 335
Proudhon, Pierre-Joseph   118
Proust, Marcel   128
Proyas, Alex   175, 390, 394, 401
Prynne, William   59

INDEX 549

Quiller-Couch, Sir Arthur 26

Racine, Jean 44
Raleigh, Sir Walter 26, 48
Rancière, Jacques 135
Reed, John 91
Reeves, Jimmie L. 160, 406, 407
Reith, John, 1st Baron Reith 158
Remak, Henry 126
Renard, Maurice 158, 173, 444
Renner, Karl 333, 334
Reynolds, Kevin 489
Rich, Nathaniel 490
Richards, J. August 418
Richardson, Ian 391
Rigby, Kate 6, 419, 463, 483
Ritter, Mark 504
Roberts, Adam 456, 457, 458, 461, 462, 468
Roberts, Alan 225
Roberts, David 6, 463
Robinson, Kim Stanley 7, 178, 181, 380, 428, 440, 443, 444, 462, 466, 489, 490, 492, 495, 496, 502
Robinson, Alice 500
Rochette, Jean-Marc 489
Roddenberry, Gene 153, 178, 444, 458
Rodgers, Mark C. 160, 406, 407
Roemer, John 327
Rolfe, Patricia 30, 31
Rolland, Romain 8
Rorty, Richard 242
Rose, Deborah Bird 481
Rose, Lacey 156
Rosny, J.H. 173, 444
Ross, Lloyd 30
Ruskin, John 11
Russ, Joanna 166, 178, 395, 443, 444
Russell, Bertrand 140
Ruttner, Henry 369
Ryan, Kiernan 384
Ryan, Michael 227
Rybakov, Anatoly Naumovich 259
Ryle, Gilbert 140

Said, Edward W. 130, 134, 135, 227, 249, 304, 361
Saint-Simon, Henri de 146, 363, 386, 504
Salmasius, 13
Salvadori, Massimo 253

Samuel, Raphael 201
Sargent, Lyman Tower 375, 445, 468
Sartre, Jean-Paul 3, 48, 114, 126, 141, 202, 205, 220, 221, 223, 229, 263, 264, 345, 353, 361, 439
Saunders, Scott 39
Saurat, Denis 69, 70
Saussure, Ferdinand de 270, 295, 344
Savage, Robert 164, 419
Schätzing, Frank 6, 7, 181, 182, 489, 490, 492, 493, 494, 495, 496
Schenkel, Elmar 175
Schwarz, Bill 241
Scott, Sir Ernest 30
Scott, John 335
Scott, Ridley 105, 106, 107, 108, 175, 178, 377, 390, 392, 394, 395, 397, 399, 401, 444
Scott, Sir Walter 171, 444, 466, 486, 491
Sedgwick, Peter 3, 5, 187, 362
Seed, David 456, 483
Selver, Paul 427, 433, 434, 453
Serge, Victor 173, 258, 259
Geoffrey Serle, 30, 33, 39, 302
Sewell, Rufus 390
Shakespeare, William 4, 11, 66, 94, 131, 136, 164, 310, 384, 440
Shapiro, Stephen 171
Shaw, George Bernard 11, 432
Shelley, Mary 102, 103, 104, 105, 106, 152, 173, 383, 403, 404, 410, 413, 414, 422, 444, 458, 459, 463, 466, 467, 487
Shelley, Percy Bysshe 16, 18, 271
Shiach, Morag 375
Shiner, Lewis 166
Shklovsky, Victor 47
Shuster, Joe 161
Shute, Nevil 5, 6, 78, 79, 80, 81, 92, 468, 469, 492, 493, 496, 502
Shuttleworth, Alan 22
Sieber, Renee 490
Siegel Jerry 161
Silverberg, Robert 488
Simmel, Georg 144
Sinfield, Alan 350, 351, 384
Skinner, Cyriack 12
Słonimski, Antoni 175
Slusser, George 105, 162
Smith, D.N. 36
Smith, E.E. 'Doc' 11, 12, 154

Smith, Julian 78, 79
Smith, Vivian 91
Solomon, David 412
Solomon, S. 477
Sophocles, 34
Sorokin, Vladimir 180, 182, 501
Spielberg, Stephen 178, 444, 489
Spinoza, Baruch 212
Spinrad, Norman 163, 165, 178, 444
Spitz, Jacques 173, 444
Spivak, Gayatri Chakravorty 126, 130, 134, 137, 182, 227, 304
Springer, Jerry 409, 411
Stalin, Josef 84, 218, 258, 259, 260, 265, 266, 454
Stanton, Andrew 489
Stapledon, Olaf 441
Steele, Sir Richard 24
Stehlin, Jack 412
Steiner, George 93
Stephens, A.G. 30, 32, 40
Stephensen, P.R. 36, 129, 130, 133, 302
Sterling, Bruce 163, 166, 178, 443, 444, 503
Stevens, A. 15, 16
Stevens, Wallace 94, 131
Stewart, Harold 91
Stocker, T.F. 481
Stoermer, Eugene F. 488
Stott, P.A. 481
Straczynski, J. Michael 158, 160, 178, 444
Stratton, Jon 298, 300, 302
Stricker, Martin 179
Strong, Sir Archibald 35, 36, 129
Strugatsky, Arkady 6, 168, 174, 177, 444
Strugatsky, Boris 6, 168, 174, 177, 444
Struve, Gleb 422, 423
Stuart, Charles, King of England, Scotland and Ireland 53, 62
Stuart, Don A. 369
Sue, Eugène 172, 486
Sutherland, Kiefer 390
Sutherland, Kristine 406
Suvin, Darko 153, 154, 155, 164, 362, 363, 366, 376, 382, 383, 384, 386, 404, 422, 428, 429, 431, 439, 441, 456, 457, 458, 461, 464, 484, 490, 499, 504
Swift, Jonathan 458
Swindells, Julia 352
Swingewood, Alan 172

Tarkovsky, Andrei 168, 174, 444
Tatchell, Peter 315
Telotte, J.P. 491
Tezuka, Osamu 159, 179
Thatcher, Margaret 2, 310
Thomas, Dylan 11
Thomas, Sheree Renée 491
Thompson, E.P. 3, 6, 28, 114, 187, 188, 189, 190, 191, 192, 193, 194, 195, 196, 197, 198, 199, 200, 201, 202, 203, 204, 205, 206, 207, 208, 209, 210, 211, 212, 213, 214, 215, 216, 217, 218, 220, 221, 222, 229, 230, 239, 240, 241, 242, 245, 262, 270, 271, 272, 298, 299, 300, 303, 320, 341, 347, 348, 349, 364
Thomson, James 369
Thomson, Philip 6
Threadgold, Terry 133, 303
Tierce, Pattie 409
Tiffin, Helen 84
Timpanaro, Sebastiano 205
Tiptree, James (Jr) 178, 444
Todorov, Tzvetan 44
Tolstoy, Alexei 174, 176, 444
Tönnies, Ferdinand 271
Torjanow, Ilija 181, 490
Touraine, Alain 301, 415
Trevelyn, G.M. 20
Trilling, Lionel 83
Troska, J.M. 174, 444
Trotsky, Leon 42, 64, 198, 199, 200, 202, 213, 214, 215, 216, 219, 220, 229, 251, 256, 257, 258, 264, 265, 268, 454
Truffaut, François 168
Tulloch, John 146, 167
Tuomainen, Antti 490, 501
Turkell, Joe 105, 390
Turner, George 7, 469, 470, 471, 472, 473, 474, 475, 476, 477, 478, 479, 480, 481, 482, 488, 489, 490, 492, 493, 494, 500
Turner, Graeme 133, 270, 277, 290, 303, 346
Turner, Ian 33, 39, 302
Tykwer, Tom 466, 491

Vallorani, Nicoletta 156
Van Hise, James 106
Van Neerven, Ellen 500
Van Vogt, A.E. 163, 365
VanderMeer, Ann 167
VanderMeer, Jeff 167

INDEX

Vane, Sir Henry   54
Vangelis,   390
Veblen, Thorstein   142
Veiras, Denis   468
Veit, Walter   6
Verall, A.W.   26
Verhoeven, Paul   178, 444
Verne, Jules   149, 151, 152, 154, 155, 159, 161, 163, 173, 174, 176, 177, 178, 383, 422, 423, 444, 445, 459, 464, 465, 466
Vladiv-Glover, Millicent   419
Vollbrecht, Karl   396
Volosinov, Valentin   285
Von Hanstein, Otfrid   174, 444
Von Harbou, Thea   174, 175, 398, 444
Vorländer, Karl   200

Wachowski, Andy   357, 466, 491
Wachowski, Lana   466, 491
Wachowski, Larry   357
Waldock, A.J.A.   34, 35, 36, 37
Walker, John   78
Wallace, R.S.   35, 36, 129
Wallace-Crabbe, Chris   303
Wallerstein, Immanuel   136, 170, 171, 173, 174, 182, 485, 486
Walsh, Bryan   495
Walther, Daniel   173, 444
Walton, Robyn   469
Walwyn, William   54
Warburg, Fred   423, 453
Ward, Russell   30, 33, 39, 302
Warnock, Geoffrey   140
Warren, Austin   19
Watson, Garry   28
Watt, James   463
Webb, Beatrice   216
Webb, Sidney   216
Weber, Max   3, 4, 21, 50, 60, 97, 98, 118, 120, 123, 144, 266, 271, 295, 301, 316, 320, 322, 326, 331, 332, 333, 336, 338, 498
Wellek, René   17, 19, 127
Welles, Orson   157
Wells, H.G.   155, 158, 161, 163, 173, 174, 175, 176, 177, 178, 363, 369, 371, 373, 383, 386, 387, 422, 423, 424, 425, 426, 444, 445, 457, 459, 465, 466, 504
Wentworth, W.C.   134
West, Cornel   361

Westergaard, J.H.   141
Whale, James   178, 410, 411, 412, 444
Whedon, Joss   178, 403, 405, 412, 444
White, Hayden   441
Widdowson, Peter   127
Widgery, David   3
Wilcox, Rhonda   408
Wilde,   91
Wilkes,   37, 39
Willey,   52
Williams, J.P.   408
Williams, Paul.   483
Williams, Raymond   3, 6, 7, 11, 12, 27, 82, 86, 94, 97, 110, 111, 112, 113, 114, 115, 116, 117, 118, 119, 120, 121, 122, 123, 124, 125, 126, 127, 128, 131, 132, 137, 138, 144, 148, 152, 160, 174, 223, 225, 229, 244, 245, 247, 248, 269, 270, 271, 272, 273, 274, 275, 276, 277, 278, 279, 280, 281, 282, 283, 284, 285, 286, 287, 288, 289, 290, 291, 292, 293, 294, 295, 296, 297, 298, 299, 300, 303, 305, 306, 307, 309, 320, 322, 341, 342, 344, 345, 346, 347, 348, 349, 350, 351, 352, 353, 361, 362, 363, 364, 365, 366, 367, 368, 369, 370, 371, 372, 373, 374, 375, 376, 377, 378, 379, 380, 381, 384, 385, 386, 387, 388, 391, 401, 406, 419, 420, 428, 436, 437, 445, 454, 455, 458, 463, 464, 482, 483, 484, 485, 497, 498, 504
Williams, Tess   395
Wilson, Harold   2
Wilson, Scott   350, 384
Winawer, Bruno   175
Winterson, Jeanette   490
Wisniewski-Snerg, Adam   174, 444
Wittgenstein, Ludwig   140, 141
Wolff, Janet   19
Wollheim, Donald A.   165
Wood, Brian   489
Woodhouse, A.S.P.   51, 52
Woodward, Bob   408
Woolf, Virginia   85, 424
Wordsworth, William   94, 131, 463
Wren, Sir Christopher   463
Wright, Judith   320, 321, 322, 323, 325, 327, 328, 329, 330, 331, 333, 334, 336, 490, 500
Wright, Peter   158
Wykes, Olive   30
Wyndham, John   2, 158, 163, 173, 365, 444, 483

Young, Sean   105, 390
Yule, George   61

Zamyatin, Yevgeny   6, 168, 174, 176, 365, 373, 393, 422, 423, 424, 425, 426, 427, 429, 430, 431, 435, 444, 447, 453

Zeh, Juli   181
Zelazny, Roger   178, 444
Žižek, Slavoj   416, 417
Zoline, Pamela   165
Żulawski, Jerzy   175

www.ingramcontent.com/pod-product-compliance
Lightning Source LLC
Chambersburg PA
CBHW071144070526
44584CB00019B/2646